N. Gregory Mankiw   Mark P. Taylor

Macroeconomics

Australia • Brazil • Japan • Korea • Mexico • Singapore • Spain • United Kingdom • United States

Macroeconomics, 3rd Edition
N. Gregory Mankiw and Mark P. Taylor

Commissioning Editor: Annabel Ainscow

Senior Production Editor: Alison Burt

Senior Manufacturing Buyer: Eyvett Davis

Typesetter: diacriTech

Cover design: Adam Renvoize

Text design: Design Deluxe

For product information and technology assistance, contact **emea.info@cengage.com**

For permission to use material from this text or product, and for permission queries, email **emea.permissions@cengage.com.**

British Library Cataloguing-in-Publication Data
A catalogue record for this book is available from the British Library.

ISBN: 978-1-4080-8197-6

Cengage Learning EMEA
Cheriton House, North Way, Andover, Hampshire SP10 5BE
United Kingdom

Cengage Learning products are represented in Canada by Nelson Education Ltd.

For your lifelong learning solutions, visit
www.cengage.co.uk

Purchase your next print book, e-book or e-chapter at
www.cengagebrain.com

Printed in China by RR Donnelley
1 2 3 4 5 6 7 8 9 10 – 16 15 14

BRIEF CONTENTS

CONTENTS

ABOUT THE AUTHORS

AUTHORS

N. GREGORY MANKIW is Professor of Economics at Harvard University. As a student, he studied economics at Princeton University and the Massachusetts Institute of Technology (MIT). As a teacher he has taught macroeconomics, microeconomics, statistics and principles of economics. Professor Mankiw is a prolific writer and a regular participant in academic and policy debates. In addition to his teaching, research and writing, Professor Mankiw has been a research associate of the National Bureau of Economic Research, an advisor to the Federal Reserve Bank of Boston and the Congressional Budget Office. From 2003 to 2005, he served as chairman of the US President's Council of Economic Advisors and was an advisor to Presidential candidate Mitt Romney during the 2012 US presidential election. Professor Mankiw lives in Wellesley, Massachusetts, with his wife Deborah, their three children and their border terrier Tobin.

MARK P. TAYLOR is Dean of Warwick Business School at the University of Warwick and Professor of International Finance. He obtained his first degree in philosophy, politics and economics from Oxford University and his Master's degree in economics from London University, from where he also holds a doctorate in economics and international finance. Professor Taylor has taught economics and finance at various universities (including Oxford, Warwick and New York) and at various levels (including principles courses, advanced undergraduate and advanced postgraduate courses). He has also worked as a senior economist at the International Monetary Fund and at the Bank of England and, before becoming Dean of Warwick Business School, was a managing director at BlackRock, the world's largest financial asset manager, where he worked on international asset allocation based on macroeconomic analysis. His research has been extensively published in scholarly journals and he is today one of the most highly cited economists in the world. Professor Taylor lives with his family in a 15th-century farmhouse near Stratford upon Avon, Warwickshire, where he collects clocks and keeps bees.

CONTRIBUTING AUTHOR

ANDREW ASHWIN has over 20 years experience as a teacher of economics. He has an MBA and is currently researching for a PhD investigating assessment and the notion of threshold concepts in economics. Andrew is an experienced author, writing a number of texts for students at different levels and journal publications related to his PhD research, and learning materials for the website Biz/ed, which was based at the University of Bristol. Andrew was Chair of Examiners for a major awarding body for business and economics in England and is a consultant for the UK regulator, Ofqual. Andrew has a keen interest in assessment and learning in economics and has received accreditation as a Chartered Assessor with the Chartered Institute of Educational Assessors. He is also Editor of the Economics, Business and Enterprise Association (EBEA) journal. Andrew lives in Rutland with his wife Sue and their twin sons Alex and Johnny.

PREFACE

The third edition of *Macroeconomics* has a different look to the previous two editions. Feedback from users, both students and instructors, has resulted in some reorganization of the material and some new sections covering more depth in both micro- and macroeconomic issues. Readers should note that this edition adapts Greg Mankiw's best-selling US undergraduate *Macroeconomics* text to reflect the needs of students and instructors in the UK and European market. As each new edition is written, the adaptation evolves and develops an identity distinct from the original US edition on which it is based.

We have tried to retain the lively, engaging writing style and to continue to have the novice economics student in mind. Economics touches every aspect of our lives and the fundamental concepts which are introduced can be applied across a whole range of life experiences. 'Economics is a study of mankind in the ordinary business of life.' So wrote Alfred Marshall, the great 19th-century British economist, in his textbook, *Principles of Economics*. As you work through the contents of this book you would be well advised to remember this.

Whilst the news might focus on the world of banking and finance, tax and government policy, economics provides much more than a window on these worlds. It provides an understanding of decision making and the process of decision making across so many different aspects of life. You may be considering travelling abroad, for example, and are shocked at the price you have to pay for injections against tropical diseases. Should you decide to try and do without the injections? Whilst the amount of money you are expected to give up seems high, it is a small price to pay when you consider the trade-off – the potential cost to you and your family of contracting a serious disease. This is as much economics as monetary policy decisions about interest rates and firm's decisions on investment.

Welcome to the wonderful world of economics – learn to think like an economist and a whole new world will open up to you.

ACKNOWLEDGEMENTS

Michael Barrow, *University of Sussex, UK*
Brian Bell, *London School of Economics, UK*
Thomas Braeuninger, *University of Mannheim, Germany*
Eleanor Denny, *Trinity College Dublin, UK*
Gaia Garino, *University of Leicester, UK*
Chris Grammenos, *American College of Thessaloniki, Greece*
Getinet Haile, *University of Nottingham, UK*
Luc Hens, *Vrije Uni, Belgium*
William Jackson, *University of York, UK*
Colin Jennings, *King's College London, UK*
Sarah Louise Jewell, *University of Reading, UK*
Arie Kroon, *Utrecht Hogeschool, The Netherlands*

Jassodra Maharaj, *University of East London, UK*
Paul Melessen, *Hogeschool van Amsterdam, The Netherlands*
Jørn Rattsø, *Norwegian University of Science & Technology, Norway*
Frédéric Robert-Nicoud, *University of Geneva, Switzerland*
Jack Rogers, *University of Exeter, UK*
Erich Ruppert, *Hochschule Aschaffenburg, Germany*
Noel Russell, *University of Manchester, UK*
Munacinga Simatele, *University of Hertfordshire, UK*
Robert Simmons, *University of Lancaster, UK*
Alison Sinclair, *University of Nottingham, UK*

PART 1
INTRODUCTION TO ECONOMICS

1 TEN PRINCIPLES OF ECONOMICS

WHAT IS ECONOMICS?

The word *economy* comes from the Greek word *oikonomos,* which means 'one who manages a household'. At first, this origin might seem peculiar. But, in fact, households and economies have much in common.

A household faces many decisions. It must decide which members of the household do which tasks and what each member gets in return: Who cooks dinner? Who does the laundry? Who gets the extra slice of cake at tea time? Who chooses what TV programme to watch? In short, the household must allocate its scarce resources among its various members, taking into account each member's abilities, efforts and desires.

Like a household, a society faces many decisions. A society must decide what jobs will be done and who will do them. It needs some people to grow food, other people to make clothing and still others to design computer software. Once society has allocated people (as well as land, buildings and machines) to various jobs, it must also allocate the output of goods and services that they produce. It must decide who will eat caviar and who will eat potatoes. It must decide who will drive a Mercedes and who will take the bus.

The Economic Problem

These decisions can be summarized as representing the economic problem. There are three questions that any society has to face:

● What goods and services should be produced?
● How should these goods and services be produced?
● Who should get the goods and services that have been produced?

The answer to these questions would be simple if resources were so plentiful that society could produce everything any of its citizens could ever want, but this is not the case. Society will never have enough resources to produce the goods and services which will satisfy the wants and needs of its citizens. These resources can be broadly classified into three categories:

- **Land** – all the natural resources of the earth. This includes things like mineral deposits such as iron ore, gold and copper, fish in the sea, coal and all the food products that land yields. David Ricardo (1817) in his book *On the Principles of Political Economy and Taxation* referred to land as the 'original and indestructible powers of the soil'.
- **Labour** – the human effort both mental and physical that goes in to production. A worker in a factory producing precision tools, an investment banker, a road sweeper, a teacher – these are all forms of labour.
- **Capital** – the equipment and structures used to produce goods and services. Capital goods include machinery in factories, buildings, tractors, computers, cooking ovens – anything where the good is not used for its own sake but for the contribution it makes to production.

> **land** all the natural resources of the earth
> **labour** the human effort both mental and physical that goes in to production
> **capital** the equipment and structures used to produce goods and services

Scarcity and Choice

What resources society does have need to be managed. The management of society's resources is important because resources are scarce. **Scarcity** means that society has limited resources and therefore cannot produce all the goods and services people wish to have. Just as a household cannot give every member everything he or she wants, a society cannot give every individual the highest standard of living to which he or she might aspire.

Economics is the study of how society manages its scarce resources and attempts to answer the three key questions we noted above. In most societies, resources are allocated through the combined actions of millions of households and firms through a system of markets. Economists:

- Study how people make decisions: how much they work, what they buy, how much they save and how they invest their savings.
- Study how people interact with one another. For instance, they examine how the multitude of buyers and sellers of a good together determine the price at which the good is sold and the quantity that is sold.
- Analyse forces and trends that affect the economy as a whole, including the growth in average income, the fraction of the population that cannot find work and the rate at which prices are rising.

> **scarcity** the limited nature of society's resources
> **economics** the study of how society manages its scarce resources

Although the study of economics has many facets, the field is unified by several central ideas. In the rest of this chapter we look at the *Ten Principles of Economics*. Don't worry if you don't understand them all at first, or if you don't find them completely convincing. In the coming chapters we will explore these ideas more fully. The ten principles are introduced here just to give you an overview of what economics is all about. You can think of this chapter as a 'preview of coming attractions'.

HOW PEOPLE MAKE DECISIONS

There is no mystery to what an 'economy' is. Whether we are talking about the economy of a group of countries such as the European Union (EU), or the economy of one particular country, such as India, or of the whole world, an economy is just a group of people interacting with one another as they go about their lives. **The economy** refers to all the production and exchange activities that take place every day – all the buying and selling. The level of **economic activity** is how much buying and selling goes on in the economy over a period of time.

> **the economy** all the production and exchange activities that take place every day
> **economic activity** how much buying and selling goes on in the economy over a period of time

Because the behaviour of an economy reflects the behaviour of the individuals who make up the economy, we start our study of economics with four principles of individual decision making.

Principle 1: People Face Trade-offs

The first lesson about making decisions is summarized in an adage popular with economists: 'There is no such thing as a free lunch.' To get one thing that we like, we usually have to give up another thing that we also like. Making decisions requires trading off the benefits of one goal against those of another.

Consider a student who must decide how to allocate her most valuable resource – her time. She can spend all of her time studying economics which will bring benefits such as a better class of degree; she can spend all her time enjoying leisure activities which yield different benefits; or she can divide her time between the two. For every hour she studies, she gives up an hour she could have devoted to spending time in the gym, riding a bicycle, watching TV, napping or working at her part-time job for some extra spending money.

Consider parents deciding how to spend their family income. They can buy food, clothing or a family holiday. Or they can save some of the family income for retirement or perhaps to help the children buy a house or a flat when they are grown up. When they choose to spend an extra euro on one of these goods, they have one less euro to spend on some other good.

When people are grouped into societies, they face different kinds of trade-offs. The classic trade-off is between spending on defence and spending on food. The more we spend on national defence to protect our country from foreign aggressors, the less we can spend on consumer goods to raise our standard of living at home. Also important in modern society is the trade-off between a clean environment and a high level of income. Laws that require firms to reduce pollution raise the cost of producing goods and services. Because of the higher costs, these firms end up earning smaller profits, paying lower wages, charging higher prices, or some combination of these three. Thus, while pollution regulations give us the benefit of a cleaner environment and the improved levels of health that come with it, they have the cost of reducing the incomes of the firms' owners, workers and customers.

Another trade-off society faces is between efficiency and equity. Efficiency means that society is getting the most it can (depending how this is defined) from its scarce resources. **Equity** means that the benefits of those resources are distributed fairly among society's members. In other words, efficiency refers to the size of the economic cake, and equity refers to how the cake is divided. Often, when government policies are being designed, these two goals conflict.

> **equity** – the property of distributing economic prosperity fairly among the members of society

Consider, for instance, policies aimed at achieving a more equal distribution of economic well-being. Some of these policies, such as the social security system or unemployment insurance, try to help those members of society who are most in need. Others, such as income tax, ask the financially successful to contribute more than others to support government spending. Although these policies have the benefit of achieving greater equity, they have a cost in terms of reduced efficiency. When the government redistributes income from the rich to the poor, it reduces the reward for working hard; as a result, people work less and produce fewer goods and services. In other words, when the government tries to cut the economic cake into more equal slices, the cake gets smaller.

Recognizing that people face trade-offs does not by itself tell us what decisions they will or should make. A student should not abandon the study of economics just because doing so would increase the time available for leisure. Society should not stop protecting the environment just because environmental regulations reduce our material standard of living. The poor should not be ignored just because helping them distorts work incentives. Nevertheless, acknowledging life's trade-offs is important because people are likely to make good decisions only if they understand the options that they have available.

A typical supermarket shelf offering a variety of cereals. What are the trade-offs an individual faces in this situation?

SELF TEST Does the adage 'there is no such thing as a free lunch' simply refer to the fact that someone has to have paid for the lunch to be provided and served? Or does the recipient of the 'free lunch' also incur a cost?

Principle 2: The Cost of Something is What You Give Up to Get It

Because people face trade-offs, making decisions requires comparing the costs and benefits of alternative courses of action. In many cases, however, the cost of some action is not as obvious as it might first appear.

Consider, for example, the decision whether to go to university. The benefit is intellectual enrichment and a lifetime of better job opportunities. But what is the cost? To answer this question, you might be tempted to add up the money you spend on tuition fees, books, room and board. Yet this total does not truly represent what you give up to spend a year at university.

The first problem with this answer is that it includes some things that are not really costs of going to university. Even if you decided to leave full-time education, you would still need a place to sleep and food to eat. Room and board are part of the costs of higher education only to the extent that they might be more expensive at university than elsewhere. Indeed, the cost of room and board at your university might be less than the rent and food expenses that you would pay living on your own. In this case, the savings on room and board are actually a benefit of going to university.

The second problem with this calculation of costs is that it ignores the largest cost of a university education – your time. When you spend a year listening to lectures, reading textbooks and writing essays, you cannot spend that time working at a job. For most students, the wages given up to attend university are the largest single cost of their higher education.

The **opportunity cost** of an item is what you give up to get that item. When making any decision, such as whether to go to university, decision makers should be aware of the opportunity costs that accompany each possible action. In fact, they usually are. University-age rugby, basketball or golf players who can earn large sums of money if they opt out of higher education and play professional sport are well aware that their opportunity cost of going to university is very high. It is not surprising that they often decide that the benefit is not worth the cost.

opportunity cost – whatever must be given up to obtain some item; the value of the benefits foregone (sacrificed)

> **SELF TEST** Assume the following costs are incurred by a student over a three-year course at a university:
> ● Tuition fees at €9,000 per year = €27,000 ● Accommodation, based on an average cost of €4,500 a year = €13,500 ● Opportunity cost based on average earnings foregone of €15,000 per year = €45,000 ● Total cost = €85,500 ● Given this relatively large cost why does anyone want to go to university?

Principle 3: Rational People Think at the Margin

Decisions in life are rarely straightforward and usually involve problems. At dinner time, the decision you face is not between fasting or eating as much as you can, but whether to take that extra serving of pizza. When examinations roll around, your decision is not between completely failing them or studying 24 hours a day, but whether to spend an extra hour revising your notes instead of watching TV. Economists use the term **marginal changes** to describe small incremental adjustments to an existing plan of action. Keep in mind that 'margin' means 'edge', so marginal changes are adjustments around the edges of what you are doing.

> **marginal changes** small incremental adjustments to a plan of action

In many situations, people make the best decisions by thinking at the margin. Suppose, for instance, that you were considering whether to study for a Master's degree having completed your undergraduate studies. To make this decision, you need to know the additional benefits that an extra year in education would offer (higher wages throughout your life and the sheer joy of learning) and the additional costs that you would incur (another year of tuition fees and another year of foregone wages). By comparing these *marginal benefits* and *marginal costs*, you can evaluate whether the extra year is worthwhile.

Individuals and firms can make better decisions by thinking at the margin. A rational decision maker takes an action if and only if the marginal benefit of the action exceeds the marginal cost.

Principle 4: People Respond to Incentives

Because people make decisions by comparing costs and benefits, their behaviour may change when the costs or benefits change. That is, people respond to incentives. When the price of an apple rises, for instance, people decide to eat more pears and fewer apples because the cost of buying an apple is higher. At the same time, apple farmers decide to hire more workers and harvest more apples, because the benefit of selling an apple is also higher. As we shall see, the effect of price on the behaviour of buyers and sellers in a market – in this case, the market for apples – is crucial for understanding how the economy works.

Public policymakers should never forget about incentives, because many policies change the costs or benefits that people face and, therefore, alter behaviour. A tax on petrol, for instance, encourages people to drive smaller, more fuel efficient cars. It also encourages people to switch and use public transport rather than drive, or to move closer to where they work. When policymakers fail to consider how their policies affect incentives, they often end up with results they did not intend. For example, the UK government provided tax relief on business premises that were not being used as an incentive to the owners to find new uses or owners for the buildings. The government decided to remove the tax relief and suggested that in doing so there would now be an incentive for owners of premises to get them back into use as quickly as possible so that they avoided losing the tax relief. Unfortunately, as the new policy came into being the economy was going through a severe recession. It was not easy for owners of premises to find new tenants let alone get new businesses created in these empty properties. Some property owners decided that rather than have to pay tax on these properties it was cheaper to demolish them. Is this the outcome the government wanted? Almost certainly not.

This is an example of the general principle that people respond to incentives. Many incentives that economists study are straightforward and others more complex. No one is surprised, for example, that people might switch to driving smaller cars where petrol taxes and thus the price of fuel is relatively high.

Yet, as the example of the removal of tax allowances on empty business premises shows, policies can have effects that are not obvious in advance. When analysing any policy, we must consider not only the direct effects but also the indirect effects that work through incentives. If the policy changes incentives, it will cause people to alter their behaviour.

SELF TEST Many people across the EU are without work and claiming benefits. Governments throughout the EU are trying to cut spending but find themselves having to spend more on welfare benefits for the unemployed. What sort of incentives might governments put in place to encourage workers off welfare and into work? What might be the unintended consequences of the incentives you identify?

HOW PEOPLE INTERACT

The first four principles discussed how individuals make decisions. As we go about our lives, many of our decisions affect not only ourselves but other people as well. The next three principles concern how people interact with one another.

Principle 5: Trade Can Make Everyone Better Off

America and China are competitors to Europe in the world economy. In some ways this is true, because American and Chinese firms produce many of the same goods as European firms. Toy manufacturers compete for the same customers in the market for toys. Fruit farmers compete for the same customers in the market for fruit.

Yet it is easy to be misled when thinking about competition among countries. Trade between Europe and the United States and China is not like a sports contest, where one side wins and the other side loses (a zero-sum game). In fact, the opposite is true: trade between two economies can make each economy better off.

To see why, consider how trade affects your family. When a member of your family looks for a job, he or she competes against members of other families who are looking for jobs. Families also compete against one another when they go shopping, because each family wants to buy the best goods at the lowest prices. So, in a sense, each family in the economy is competing with all other families.

Despite this competition, your family would not be better off isolating itself from all other families. If it did, your family would need to grow its own food, make its own clothes and build its own home. Clearly, your family gains much from its ability to trade with others. Trade allows each person to specialize in the activities he or she does best, whether it is farming, sewing or home building. By trading with others, people can buy a greater variety of goods and services at lower cost.

Countries as well as families benefit from the ability to trade with one another. Trade allows countries to specialize in what they do best and to enjoy a greater variety of goods and services. The Japanese and the Americans, as well as the Koreans and the Brazilians, are as much Europe's partners in the world economy as they are competitors.

Principle 6: Markets Are Usually a Good Way to Organize Economic Activity

The collapse of communism in the Soviet Union and Eastern Europe in the 1980s may be the most important change in the world during the past half century. Communist countries worked on the premise that central planners in the government were in the best position to guide economic activity and answer the three key questions of the economic problem. These planners decided what goods and services were produced, how much was produced, and who produced and consumed these goods and services. The theory behind central planning was that only the government could organize economic activity in a way that promoted economic well-being for the country as a whole.

Today, most countries that once had centrally planned economies such as Russia, Poland, Angola, Mozambique and the Democratic Republic of Congo have abandoned this system and are trying to develop market economies. In a **market economy**, the decisions of a central planner are replaced by the decisions of millions of firms and households. Firms decide whom to hire and what to make. Households decide which firms to work for and what to buy with their incomes. These firms and households interact in the marketplace, where prices and self-interest guide their decisions.

market economy an economy that addresses the three key questions of the economic problem through allocating resources through the decentralized decisions of many firms and households as they interact in markets for goods and services

At first glance, the success of market economies is puzzling. After all, in a market economy, no one is considering the economic well-being of society as a whole. Free markets contain many buyers and sellers of numerous goods and services, and all of them are interested primarily in their own well-being. Yet, despite decentralized decision making and self-interested decision makers, market economies have proven remarkably successful in organizing economic activity in a way that promotes overall economic well-being.

FYI

Adam Smith and the Invisible Hand

Adam Smith's great work An *Inquiry into the Nature and Causes of the Wealth of Nations* was published in 1776 and is a landmark in economics. In its emphasis on the invisible hand of the market economy, it reflected a point of view that was typical of so-called 'enlightenment' writers at the end of the 18th century – that individuals are usually best left to their own devices, without government guiding their actions. This political philosophy provides the intellectual basis for the market economy.

Why do decentralized market economies work so well? Is it because people can be counted on to treat one another with love and kindness? Not at all. Here is Adam Smith's description of how people interact in a market economy:

Man has almost constant occasion for the help of his brethren, and it is vain for him to expect it from their benevolence only. He will be more

likely to prevail if he can interest their self-love in his favour, and show them that it is for their own advantage to do for him what he requires of them. ... It is not from the benevolence of the butcher, the brewer, or the baker that we expect our dinner, but from their regard to their own interest. ...

Every individual ... neither intends to promote the public interest, nor knows how much he is promoting it. ... He intends only his own gain, and he is in this, as in many other cases, led by an invisible hand to promote an end which was no part of his intention. Nor is it always the worse for the society that it was no part of it. By pursuing his own interest he frequently promotes that of the society more effectually than when he really intends to promote it.

Smith is saying that participants in the economy are motivated by self-interest and that the 'invisible hand' of the marketplace guides this

self-interest into promoting general economic well-being.

Many of Smith's insights remain at the centre of modern economics. Our analysis in the coming chapters will allow us to express Smith's conclusions more precisely and to analyse fully the strengths and weaknesses of the market's invisible hand.

One of our goals in this book is to understand how Smith's invisible hand works its magic. As you study economics, you will learn that prices are the instrument with which the invisible hand directs economic activity. Prices reflect both the value of a good to society and the cost to society of making the good. Because households and firms look at prices when deciding what to buy and sell, they unknowingly take into account the social benefits and costs of their actions. As a result, prices guide these individual decision makers to reach outcomes that, in many cases, maximize the welfare of society as a whole.

Principle 7: Governments Can Sometimes Improve Market Outcomes

If the invisible hand of the market is so wonderful, why do we need government? One answer is that the invisible hand needs government to protect it. Markets work only if property rights are enforced. A farmer won't grow food if he expects his crop to be stolen, and a restaurant won't serve meals unless it is assured that customers will pay before they leave. We all rely on government provided police and courts to enforce our rights over the things we produce.

Yet there is another answer to why we need government: although markets are usually a good way to organize economic activity, this rule has some important exceptions. There are two broad reasons for a government to intervene in the economy – to promote efficiency and to promote equity. That is, most policies aim either to enlarge the economic cake or to change the way in which the cake is divided.

Although the invisible hand often leads markets to allocate resources efficiently, that is not always the case. Economists use the term **market failure** to refer to a situation in which the market on its own fails to produce an efficient allocation of resources. One possible cause of market failure is an **externality**, which is the uncompensated impact of one person's actions on the well-being of a bystander (a third party). For instance, the classic example of an external cost is pollution. Another possible cause of market failure is **market power**, which refers to the ability of a single person or business (or group of businesses) to unduly influence market prices. In the presence of market failure, well designed public policy can enhance economic efficiency.

> **market failure** a situation where scarce resources are not allocated to their most efficient use
>
> **externality** the cost or benefit of one person's decision on the well-being of a bystander (a third party) which the decision maker does not take into account in making the decision
>
> **market power** the ability of a single economic agent (or small group of agents) to have a substantial influence on market prices

The invisible hand may also fail to ensure that economic prosperity is distributed equitably. One of the three questions society has to address is who gets what is produced? A market economy rewards people according to their ability to produce things for which other people are willing to pay. The world's best footballer earns more than the world's best chess player simply because people are willing to pay more to watch football than chess. That individual is getting more of what is produced as a result of his earnings. The invisible hand does not ensure that everyone has sufficient food, decent clothing and adequate health care. Many public policies, such as income tax and the social security system, aim to achieve a more equitable distribution of economic well-being.

To say that the government *can* improve on market outcomes at times does not mean that it always *will*. Public policy is made not by angels but by a political process that is far from perfect. Sometimes policies are designed simply to reward the politically powerful. Sometimes they are made by well-intentioned leaders who are not fully informed. One goal of the study of economics is to help you judge when a government policy is justifiable to promote efficiency or equity, and when it is not.

HOW THE ECONOMY AS A WHOLE WORKS

We started by discussing how individuals make decisions and then looked at how people interact with one another. All these decisions and interactions together make up 'the economy'. The last three of our ten principles concern the workings of the economy as a whole.

Microeconomics and Macroeconomics

Economics is studied on various levels. The first seven principles involve the study of the decisions of individual households and firms and the interaction of households and firms in markets for specific goods and services. In the last three principles we are looking at the operation of the economy as a whole, which is just the sum of the activities of all these decision makers in all these markets.

Since roughly the 1930s, the field of economics has traditionally been divided into two broad subfields. **Microeconomics** is the study of how households and firms make decisions and how they interact in specific markets. **Macroeconomics** is the study of economy-wide phenomena. A microeconomist might study the effects of a congestion tax on the use of cars in a city centre, the impact of foreign competition on the European car industry or the effects of attending university on a person's lifetime earnings. A macro-economist might study the effects of borrowing by national governments, the changes over time in an economy's rate of unemployment or alternative policies to raise growth in national living standards.

> **microeconomics** the study of how households and firms make decisions and how they interact in markets
> **macroeconomics** the study of economy-wide phenomena, including inflation, unemployment and economic growth

Microeconomics and macroeconomics are closely intertwined. Because changes in the overall economy arise from the decisions of millions of individuals, it is impossible to understand macroeconomic developments without considering the associated microeconomic decisions. For example, a macro-economist might study the effect of a cut in income tax on the overall production of goods and services in an economy. To analyse this issue, he or she must consider how the tax cut affects the decisions of households concerning how much to spend on goods and services.

Despite the inherent link between microeconomics and macroeconomics, the two fields are distinct. In economics, it may seem natural to begin with the smallest unit and build up. Yet doing so is neither necessary nor always the best way to proceed. Because microeconomics and macroeconomics address different questions, they sometimes take quite different approaches and are often taught in separate courses.

A key concept in macroeconomics is **economic growth** – the percentage increase in the number of goods and services produced in an economy over a period of time, usually expressed over a quarter and annually.

> **economic growth** the increase in the amount of goods and services in an economy over a period of time

Principle 8: An Economy's Standard of Living Depends on its Ability to Produce Goods and Services

Table 1.1 shows **gross domestic product per capita (head)** of the population in a number of selected countries expressed in U.S. dollars. It is clear that many of the advanced economies have a relatively high income per capita; in Norway it is an enviable $98,102, the Netherlands $50,087 and Germany $43,689.

> **gross domestic product per capita (head)** the market value of all goods and services produced within a country in a given period of time divided by the population of a country to give a per capita figure

Moving away from the prosperous economies of Western Europe, we begin to see differences in income and living standards around the world that are quite staggering. For example, average income in Yemen was $1,361 whilst in Afghanistan average income is just over a half a per cent of the size of per-capita income in Norway.

TABLE 1.1	Gross Domestic Product Per Capita, Current Prices US dollars 2011

Afghanistan	576
Austria	49,707
Belgium	46,469
Benin	802
Bolivia	1,421
China	5,445
Estonia	16,556
Finland	49,391
Germany	43,689
Hungary	21,732
Italy	36,116
Japan	45,903
Kenya	808
Netherlands	50,087
Norway	98,102
Portugal	22,330
Russian Federation	13,089
Spain	32,244
Sweden	56,927
Switzerland	80,391
Turkey	10,498
United Kingdom	38,818
United States	48,442
Yemen	1,361

Not surprisingly, this large variation in average income is reflected in various other measures of the quality of life and **standard of living**. Citizens of high-income countries have better nutrition, better health care and longer life expectancy than citizens of low-income countries, as well as more TV sets, more gadgets and more cars.

> **standard of living** refers to the amount of goods and services that can be purchased by the population of a country. Usually measured by the inflation-adjusted (real) income per head of the population

Changes in the standard of living over time are also large. Over the last 5 years, economic growth in Albania has grown at about 4.68 per cent per year, in China at about 10.5 per cent a year but in Latvia the economy has shrunk by around 1.4 per cent over the same time period (Source: World Bank).

What explains these large differences in living standards among countries and over time? The answer is surprisingly simple. Almost all variation in living standards is attributable to differences in countries' **productivity** – that is, the amount of goods and services produced from each hour of a worker's time. In nations where workers can produce a large quantity of goods and services per unit of time, most people enjoy a high standard of living; in nations where workers are less productive, most people must endure a more meagre existence. Similarly, the growth rate of a nation's productivity determines the growth rate of its average income.

> **productivity** the quantity of goods and services produced from each hour of a worker or factor of production's time

The fundamental relationship between productivity and living standards is simple, but its implications are far-reaching. If productivity is the primary determinant of living standards, other explanations must be of secondary importance. For example, it might be tempting to credit trade unions or minimum wage laws for the rise in living standards of workers over the past 50 years. Yet the real hero of workers is their rising productivity.

The relationship between productivity and living standards also has profound implications for public policy. When thinking about how any policy will affect living standards, the key question is how it will affect our ability to produce goods and services. To boost living standards, policymakers need to raise productivity by ensuring that workers are well educated, have the tools needed to produce goods and services, and have access to the best available technology.

Principle 9: Prices Rise When the Government Prints Too Much Money

In Zimbabwe in March 2007 inflation was reported to be running at 2,200 per cent. That meant that a good priced at the equivalent of Z$2.99 in March 2006 would be priced at Z$65.78 just a year later. In February 2008, inflation was estimated at 165,000 per cent. Five months later it was reported as 2,200,000 per cent. In July 2008 the government issued a Z$100 billion note. At that time it was just about enough to buy a loaf of bread. Estimates for inflation in Zimbabwe in July 2008 put the rate of growth of prices at 231,000,000 per cent. In January 2009, the government issued Z$10, 20, 50 and 100 trillion dollar notes – 100 trillion is 100 followed by 12 zeros. This episode is one of history's most spectacular examples of **inflation**, an increase in the overall level of prices in the economy.

> **inflation** an increase in the overall level of prices in the economy

High inflation is a problem because it imposes various costs on society; keeping inflation at a low level is a goal of economic policymakers around the world. What causes inflation? In almost all cases of high or persistent inflation, the culprit turns out to be the same – growth in the quantity of money. When a government creates large quantities of the nation's money, the value of the money falls. As outlined above, the Zimbabwean government was issuing money at ever higher denominations. It is generally accepted that there is a relationship between the growth in the quantity of money and the rate of growth of prices.

Principle 10: Society Faces a Short-run Trade-off Between Inflation and Unemployment

When the government increases the amount of money in the economy, one result is inflation. Another result, at least in the short run, is a lower level of unemployment. The curve that illustrates this short-run trade-off between inflation and unemployment is called the **Phillips curve**, after the economist who first examined this relationship while working at the London School of Economics.

> **Phillips curve** a curve that shows the short run trade-off between inflation and unemployment

The Phillips curve remains a controversial topic among economists, but most economists today accept the idea that society faces a short-run trade-off between inflation and unemployment. This simply means that, over a period of a year or two, many economic policies push inflation and unemployment in opposite directions. Policymakers face this trade-off regardless of whether inflation and unemployment both start out at high levels at low levels or somewhere in-between.

The trade-off between inflation and unemployment is only temporary, but it can last for several years. The Phillips curve is, therefore, crucial for understanding many developments in the economy. In particular, it is important for understanding the **business cycle** – the irregular and largely unpredictable fluctuations in economic activity, as measured by the number of people employed or the production of goods and services.

> **business cycle** fluctuations in economic activity such as employment and production

Policymakers can exploit the short-run trade-off between inflation and unemployment using various policy instruments. By changing the amount that the government spends, the amount it taxes and the amount of money it prints, policymakers can influence the combination of inflation and unemployment that the economy experiences. Because these instruments of monetary and fiscal policy are potentially so powerful, how policymakers should use these instruments to control the economy, if at all, is a subject of continuing debate.

SELF TEST What is the difference between microeconomics and macroeconomics? Write down three questions that the study of microeconomics might be concerned with and three questions that might be involved in the study of macroeconomics

---

CONCLUSION

You now have a taste of what economics is all about. In the coming chapters we will develop many specific insights about people, markets and economies. Mastering these insights will take some effort, but it is not an overwhelming task. The field of economics is based on a few basic ideas that can be applied in many different situations.

Throughout this book we will refer back to the *Ten Principles of Economics* highlighted in this chapter and summarized in Table 1.2 which can be seen as building blocks for your study of the subject; you should keep these building blocks in mind. Even the most sophisticated economic analysis is built using the ten principles introduced here.

TABLE 1.2 **Ten Principles of Economics**

How people make decisions	1. People face trade-offs
	2. The cost of something is what you give up to get it
	3. Rational people think at the margin
	4. People respond to incentives
How people interact	5. Trade can make everyone better off
	6. Markets are usually a good way to organize economic activity
	7. Governments can sometimes improve market outcomes
How the economy as a whole works	8. A country's standard of living depends on its ability to produce goods and services
	9. Prices rise when the government prints too much money
	10. Society faces a short-run trade-off between inflation and unemployment

IN THE NEWS

Latest Thinking in Economics – Incentives

One of the *Ten Principles of Economics* is that people respond to incentives. This should not be an entirely surprising principle and may seem like an example of economists making common sense sound more complex. However, the reality is that the complex nature of human beings does make the introduction and effect of incentives much more challenging than might at first appear.

Gneezy et al. highlight some of these issues (Gneezy, U. Meier, S. and Ray-Biel, P. (2011) 'When and why incentives (don't) work to modify behaviour'. In *Journal of Economic Perspectives*. 25:4, 191–210). They point out that incentives may work better in certain circumstances than in others and policymakers need to consider a wide variety of issues when deciding on putting incentives in place.

First of all, they have to consider the type of behaviour to be changed. For example, society might want to encourage its citizens to do more, what Gneezy et al. call 'prosocial' behaviour such as donating blood, sperm or organs, increasing the amount of waste put out for recycling, attending school, college or university, working harder in education to improve grades, improving the environment such as installing insulation or solar panels in homes to reduce energy waste, or finding ways of encouraging people to stop smoking.

Second, we have to consider the parties involved. This can be expressed as a principal-agent issue. The principal is a person or group for whom another person or group, the agent, is performing some act. In encouraging people to stop smoking, the smoker is the agent and society is the principal. Next, we have to consider the type of incentive offered – often this will be monetary. Monetary incentives have two main types of effects which Gneezy et al. refer to as the direct price effect and the psychological effect. Once the behaviour has been identified, the type of incentive and who the principal and agent are, the next question is to consider how the incentive is framed.

At first the solution might be seen as being simple – provide a monetary incentive; pay people to achieve the desired behaviour. The question is, will the incentive work? Gneezy et al. point to a number of reasons why the outcome might not be as obvious as first hoped. They suggest that in some cases, offering monetary incentives can 'crowd out' the desired behaviour. Offering a monetary incentive to go to school, donate blood or install solar panels might not have the desired effect. The reasons might be that offering a monetary incentive changes the perceptions of agents. People have intrinsic motivations – personal reasons for particular behaviours. Other people also have perceptions about the behaviour of others, for example someone who donates blood might be seen by others as being 'nice'. Social norms may also be affected, for example attitudes to recycling of waste or smoking.

Providing a monetary incentive on these behaviours might not necessarily lead to more blood being donated, more recycling and solar panels or less smoking. Gneezy et al. suggest that the reasons may be that monetizing behaviour in this way changes the psychology and the psychology effect can be greater than the direct price effect. The price effect would suggest that if you pay someone to donate more blood, you should get more people donating blood. The reality might be that such incentives reduce blood donorship. Why? People who donate blood might do so out of a personal conviction – they have intrinsic motivations. By offering monetary incentives, the perception of the donor and others might change so that they are not seen as being 'nice' any more but as being 'mercenary' and not motivated intrinsically but by extrinsic reward – greed, in other words. If the psychological effect outweighs the direct money effect the result could be a reduction in the number of donors.

In the case of cutting smoking, the size of the money effect might be a factor. Principal 5 of *The Ten Principles of Economics* states that rational people think at the margin. With smoking, the marginal decision to have one more cigarette imposes costs and benefits on the smoker – the benefit is the pleasure people get from smoking, the cost the (estimated) 11 minutes of their life that is cut as a result. The problem is that the marginal cost is not tangible at that time and is likely to be outweighed by the marginal benefit (not to mention the addictive qualities of tobacco products). Over time, however, the total benefit of stopping smoking

becomes much greater than the total cost. The incentive offered, therefore, has to be such that it takes into account these marginal decisions and it might be difficult to estimate the size of the incentive needed.

Other issues relating to incentives involve the trust between the principal and agent. If an incentive is provided, for example, then this sends a message that the desired behaviour is not taking place and that there may be a reason for this. This might be that the desired behaviour is not attractive and/or is difficult to carry out. Incentives also send out a message that the principal does not trust the agent's intrinsic motivation, for example that people will not voluntarily give blood or recycle waste effectively. Some incentives may work to achieve the desired behaviour in the short-term but will this lead to the desired behaviour continuing in the long-term when the incentive is removed?

Finally, incentives might be affected by the way they are framed – how the wording or the benefits of the incentive is presented to the agent by the principal. Gneezy et al. use a very interesting example of this. Imagine a situation, they say, where you meet a person and develop a relationship. You want to provide that person with the incentive to have sex. The effect of the way

Providing a monetary incentive on these behaviours might not necessarily lead to more blood being donated

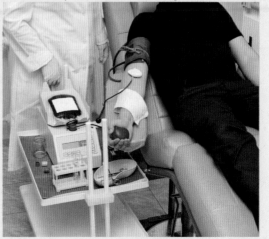

the incentive is framed might have a considerable effect on the outcome. If, for example, you framed your 'offer' by saying 'I would like to make love to you and to incentivize you to do so I will offer you €50', you might get a very different response to that if you framed it by saying: 'I would like to make love to you – I have bought you a bunch of red roses' (the roses just happened to cost €50).

Finally, the cost effectiveness of incentives has to be considered. Health authorities spend millions of euros across Europe on drugs to reduce blood pressure and cholesterol. Getting people to take more exercise will also help achieve the same result. What would be more cost-effective and a more efficient allocation of resources? Providing incentives (assuming they work) to encourage people to exercise more by, for example, paying for gym membership, or spending that same money on drugs but not dealing with some of the underlying causes?

Questions

1 Why should people need incentives to do 'good' things like donating blood or putting out more rubbish for recycling?

2 What is meant by the 'principal-agent' issue?

3 **What might be the price and psychological effect if students were given a monetary incentive to attain top grades in their university exams?**

4 **Why might the size of a monetary incentive be an important factor in encouraging desired behaviour and what side-effects might arise if the size of an incentive was increased?**

5 **What is 'framing' and why might it be important in the way in which an incentive works? Refer to the need to increase the number of organ donors in your answer to this question.**

FYI

How To Read This Book

Economics is fun, but it can also be hard to learn. Our aim in writing this text has been to make it as easy and as much fun as possible. But you, the student, also have a role to play. Experience shows that if you are actively involved as you study this book, you will enjoy a better outcome, both in your exams and in the years that follow. Here are a few tips about how best to read this book.

1. *Summarize, don't highlight.* Running a yellow marker over the text is too passive an activity to keep your mind engaged. Instead, when you come to the end of a section, take a minute and summarize what you have just learnt in your own words, writing your summary in a note book or on your computer. When you've finished the chapter, compare your summary with the one at the end of the chapter. Did you pick up the main points?

2. *Test yourself.* Throughout the book, the Self Test features offer the chance to test your understanding of the subject matter. Take the opportunity to jot down your ideas and thoughts to the Self Test questions. The tests are meant to assess your basic comprehension and application of the ideas and concepts in the chapter. If you aren't sure your answer is right, you probably need to review the section.

3. *Practise, practise, practise.* At the end of each chapter, Questions for Review test your understanding, and Problems and Applications ask you to apply and extend the material. Perhaps your lecturer will assign some of these exercises as work for seminars and tutorials. If so, do them. If not, do them anyway. The more you use your new knowledge, the more solid it becomes.

4. *Study in groups.* After you've read the book and worked through the problems on your own, get together with other students to discuss the material. You will learn from each other – an example of the gains from trade.

5. *Don't forget the real world.* In the midst of all the numbers, graphs and strange new words, it is easy to lose sight of what economics is all about. The Case Studies and In the News boxes sprinkled throughout this book should help remind you. Don't skip them. They show how the theory is tied to events happening in all of our lives and the questions provided with the In the News features will help you think about issues that you have covered in the chapter and also to apply your understanding to specific contexts. As with the Self Test questions, attempt an answer to the questions to help build your understanding.

SUMMARY

- The fundamental lessons about individual decision making are that people face trade-offs among alternative goals, that the cost of any action is measured in terms of foregone opportunities, that rational people make decisions by comparing marginal costs and marginal benefits, and that people change their behaviour in response to the incentives they face.

- The fundamental lessons about interactions among people are that trade can be mutually beneficial, that markets are usually a good way of coordinating trade among people, and that the government can potentially improve market outcomes if there is some market failure or if the market outcome is inequitable.

- The field of economics is divided into two sub-fields: microeconomics and macroeconomics. Microeconomists study decision making by households and firms and the interaction among households and firms in the marketplace. Macroeconomists study the forces and trends that affect the economy as a whole.

- The fundamental lessons about the economy as a whole are that productivity is the ultimate source of living standards, that money growth is the ultimate source of inflation, and that society faces a short-run trade-off between inflation and unemployment.

QUESTIONS FOR REVIEW

1 Give three examples of important trade-offs that you face in your life.

2 What is the opportunity cost of going to a restaurant for a meal?

3 Water is necessary for life. Is the marginal benefit of a glass of water large or small?

4 Why should policymakers think about incentives?

5 Why isn't trade among countries like a game, with some winners and some losers?

6 What does the 'invisible hand' of the marketplace do?

7 Explain the two main causes of market failure and give an example of each.

8 What are the two subfields into which economics is divided? Explain what each subfield studies.

9 Why is productivity important?

10 How are inflation and unemployment related in the short run?

PROBLEMS AND APPLICATIONS

1 Describe some of the trade-offs faced by each of the following.
   a. A family deciding whether to buy a new car.
   b. A member of the government deciding how much to spend on building a new motorway connecting two main cities.
   c. A company chief executive officer deciding whether to recommend the acquisition of a smaller firm.
   d. A university lecturer deciding how much to prepare for her lecture.

2 You are trying to decide whether to take a holiday. Most of the costs of the holiday (airfare, hotel, foregone wages) are measured in euros, but the benefits of the holiday are psychological. How can you compare the benefits to the costs?

3 You were planning to spend an evening working at your part-time job, but a friend asks you to go to a night club. What is the true cost of going to the night club? Now suppose that you had been planning to spend the evening studying in the library. What is the cost of going to the night club in this case? Explain.

4 You win €10,000 on the EuroMillions lottery draw. You have a choice between spending the money now or putting it away for a year in a bank account that pays 5 per cent interest. What is the opportunity cost of spending the €10,000 now?

5 The company that you manage has invested €5 million in developing a new product, but the development is not quite finished. At a recent meeting, your sales people report that the introduction of competing products has reduced the expected sales of your new product to €3 million. If it would cost €1 million to finish development and make the product, should you go ahead and do so? What is the most that you should pay to complete development?

6 Three managers of the van Heerven Coach Company are discussing a possible increase in production. Each suggests a way to make this decision.

FIRST MANAGER: We need to decide how many additional coaches to produce. Personally, I think we should examine whether our company's productivity – number of coaches produced per worker per hour – would rise or fall if we increased output.

SECOND MANAGER: We should examine whether our average cost per worker – would rise or fall.

THIRD MANAGER: We should examine whether the extra revenue from selling the additional coaches would be greater or smaller than the extra costs.

Who do you think is right? Why?

7 Assume a social security system in a country provides income for people over the age of 65. If a recipient decides to work and earn some income, the amount he or she receives in social security benefits is typically reduced.

   a. How does the provision of this grant affect people's incentive to save while working?
   b. How does the reduction in benefits associated with higher earnings affect people's incentive to work past the age of 65?

8 Your flatmate is a better cook than you are, but you can clean more quickly than your flatmate can. If your flatmate did all of the cooking and you did all of the cleaning, would your household chores take you more or less time than if you divided each task evenly? Give a similar example of how specialization and trade can make two countries both better off.

9 Explain whether each of the following government activities is motivated by a concern about equity or a concern about efficiency. In the case of efficiency, discuss the type of market failure involved.

   a. Regulating water prices.
   b. Regulating electricity prices.
   c. Providing some poor people with vouchers that can be used to buy food.
   d. Prohibiting smoking in public places.
   e. Imposing higher personal income tax rates on people with higher incomes.
   f. Instituting laws against driving whilst under the influence of alcohol.

10 In what ways is your standard of living different from that of your parents or grandparents when they were your age? Why have these changes occurred?

2 THINKING LIKE AN ECONOMIST

INTRODUCTION

Every field of study has its own language, its own processes, its methods of discovery and its own way of thinking. Economics is no different. As you embark on your study of economics, the understanding you bring to the discipline is going to be very different to that which your lecturer has. You will have to learn lots of new terms as is the case in any new subject area. You will also have to learn how economists go about their work and how new ideas in the subject are developed and refined over time. One of the challenges facing students of economics is that many terms used are also used in everyday language. In economics, however, these terms mean specific things. The challenge, therefore, is to set aside that everyday understanding and think of the term or concept as economists do.

Many of the concepts you will come across in this book are abstract. Abstract concepts are ones which are not concrete or real – they have no tangible qualities. We will talk about markets, efficiency, comparative advantage and equilibrium, for example, but it is not easy to physically see these concepts. There are also some concepts that are fundamental to the subject – if you master these concepts they act as a portal which enables you to think like an economist. Once you have mastered these concepts you will never think in the same way again and you will never look at an issue in the same way.

These concepts are referred to as *threshold concepts*. You can read about this further in Meyer et al. (Meyer, J.H.F. and Land, R. (2005). 'Threshold concepts and troublesome knowledge 2: epistemological considerations and a conceptual framework for teaching and learning'. *Higher Education,* 49: 373–388). As you work through your modules you will find that it is not always easy to think like an economist and that there will be times when you are confused, find some of the ideas and concepts being presented to you running contrary to common sense (i.e. they are counter intuitive). What you will be experiencing is what is called *troublesome knowledge*. Don't worry about this – what you are experiencing is perfectly normal and a part of the learning journey. As you travel along this learning journey you will be provided with new information and as a result develop new and useful ways of thinking about the world in which you live.

This chapter discusses the field's methodology. What is distinctive about how economists confront a question? What does it mean to think like an economist? What tools do economists use to explain the world we live in?

THE ECONOMIST AS SCIENTIST

Economists try to address their subject with a scientist's objectivity. They approach the study of the economy in much the same way as a physicist approaches the study of matter and a biologist approaches the study of life: they devise theories, collect data and then analyse these data in an attempt to verify or refute their theories.

There is much debate about whether economics can ever be a science – principally because it is dealing with human behaviour. The essence of any science is *scientific method* – the dispassionate development and testing of theories about how the world works. This method of inquiry is as applicable to studying a nation's economy as it is to studying the Earth's gravity or a species' evolution. As Albert Einstein once put it, 'The whole of science is nothing more than the refinement of everyday thinking'.

Empiricism

One of the *Ten Principles of Economics* states that 'prices rise when the government prints too much money'. To make such a statement we have to have some evidence that this is indeed the case. How did economists find out that printing too much money leads to rising prices? The evidence for this principle is empirical. Empirical means that information has been gathered either by observation, experience or experiment of an event or phenomena (such as a period of rising prices), the formulation of a hypothesis (that prices rise when government prints too much money) and the testing of the hypothesis. A hypothesis is an assumption; the word is derived from the Greek (*hypotithenai*) meaning 'to suppose'. A hypothesis can be developed through observation or experience of phenomena or through what we might call 'idle reasoning'. Having developed a hypothesis, the economist might use scientific method to test it to see whether the hypothesis can be supported, rejected or there might be no evidence to support the hypothesis either way, or they might apply inductive reasoning to explain it.

Inductive and Deductive Reasoning Inductive reasoning refers to the process of observation from which patterns might be formed which provides evidence for a hypothesis which may lead to a theory. In contrast, deductive reasoning begins with a theory from which a hypothesis is drawn. The hypothesis is then subject to observation and either confirmation or rejection. One is not any better than the other – they are different ways of approaching research and may be closely linked. What is important is that we always treat any research with a degree of critical awareness – we don't just simply accept the conclusions drawn from the research but question them and subject them to further testing. Through this circular process, refinements and improvements to theories and explanations can be developed which in turn allow us to make more informed decisions.

A classic example of the relationship between inductive and deductive reasoning can be seen in the case of observing swans. The researcher observes a river with swans swimming past. Every swan observed is white. At the end of the observation period the researcher draws a conclusion that 'all swans are white'. The evidence gathered does support the hypothesis that 'all swans are white'. A theory about why swans are always white might be developed to explain this phenomenon. Subsequent testing of the hypothesis might confirm that, based on the evidence, all swans are white and this might be the accepted hypothesis for many years until, one day, someone sees a black swan. At which point the hypothesis is rejected and the theory will have to be modified. This may lead the researcher to begin asking questions about why the majority of swans appear to be white and what reasons there might be for some swans being black which can again be the subject of empirical research.

Theories Throughout this book we will look at theories. Theories can be used to explain something and to make predictions. The theory of indifference curves and budget lines can be used to explain consumer behaviour. Theories, however, can be developed separate to empirical research. In 1982, Nobel prize-winning economist, Wassily Leontif, lamented the lack of systematic empirical enquiry in economics at the expense of too much 'theorizing'. Leontif (Leontif, W. (1982) Academic Economics. In Science 217: 104–107) had looked at articles in the *American Economic Review* and observed that a large proportion of the articles contained models which were not supported by any data and analysed issues without supporting data. In comparison, articles based on primary data generated by the author/s, or on secondary data and which used appropriate statistical tests to arrive at conclusions, represented the minority. Was it wise to base decisions or policy on the knowledge generated by research which was not subject to the rigours of empirical methods?

Theorizing on its own can be said to be a tradition in rationalist economics. Here, the economist uses logic, reason and induction to arrive at conclusions. Much of the logic might be based on assumptions which may not be subject to any supporting data. For example, the theory of consumer behaviour makes assumptions about the way human beings behave when making consumption decisions, such as consumers act rationally, prefer more to less and make purchasing decisions based on pure self-interest.

Empiricist economics starts with observations and data from which models can be developed which reflect the data. These models can be used to arrive at conclusions and to make predictions. Observations of consumer behaviour suggest that humans do not act rationally when making purchasing decisions. Models can be developed which represent the data – how humans *do* behave as consumers – and these models can be used to generate theories which help make predictions about consumer behaviour in different situations.

Even if the hypothesis is supported by the evidence this is not a reason for the economist to sit back and relax, happy in the knowledge they have found 'the truth'. Things change, new information, experience or observations may be made which render the original hypothesis redundant and subject to revision or refinement; there is a process which is never ending.

The Scientific Method: Observation, Theory and More Observation

The interplay between theory and observation is central to the methodology adopted in the field of economics. Let us return to the principle that prices rise when the government prints too much money. How might this principle have arisen? An economist might live in a country experiencing rapid increases in prices and be moved by this observation to develop a theory of inflation. The theory might assert that high inflation arises when the government prints too much money. To test this theory, the economist could collect and analyse data on prices and money from many different countries. If growth in the quantity of money were not at all related to the rate at which prices are rising, the economist would start to doubt the validity of his theory of inflation. If money growth and inflation were strongly correlated in international data, as in fact they are, the economist would become more confident in his theory.

Although economists use theory and observation like other scientists, they do face an obstacle that makes their task especially challenging: experiments are often difficult in economics. Physicists studying gravity can drop many objects in their laboratories to generate data to test their theories. By contrast, economists studying inflation are not allowed to manipulate a nation's monetary policy simply to generate useful data. Economists, like astronomers and evolutionary biologists, usually have to make do with whatever data the world happens to give them.

To find a substitute for laboratory experiments, economists pay close attention to the natural experiments offered by history. When a war in the Middle East interrupts the flow of crude oil, for instance, oil prices shoot up around the world. For consumers of oil and oil products, such an event depresses living standards. For economic policymakers, it poses a difficult choice about how best to respond. But for economic scientists, it provides an opportunity to study the effects of a key natural resource on the world's economies, and this opportunity persists long after the wartime increase in oil prices is over. Throughout this book, therefore, we consider many historical episodes. These episodes are valuable to study because they give us insight into the economy of the past and, more important, because they allow us to illustrate and evaluate economic theories of the present.

Empiricism or Rationalism?

Like many things in economics, there is no right answer to this question. The debate between rationalists is beyond the scope of this introduction. The debate lies in the realm of economic philosophy – about the nature of knowledge, how we acquire knowledge. Some things may seem intuitive and have led to 'laws' or beliefs to be widely held and in some cases entrenched. For example, intuition tells us that if the price of a good rises, people will buy less of that good. Rationally, this would also make sense and logic would tell us that if the price of a good is higher it changes the way people view that good, whether they can now afford it and how they view the good in relation to others that they could buy that are similar. Putting all these things together the conclusion must be that when prices rise, the amount purchased will fall. Such a conclusion can then be seen as being generalizable. This means that we can extend the reasoning for this one good to most others.

Some of these can become self-evident truths which are accepted by the general public. For example, the idea that a large proportion of those who claim welfare benefits are 'scroungers', that an increase in immigration will take jobs away from the indigenous population, that the increase in carbon emissions will cause global warming, or that the way of reducing the budget deficit is to cut taxes, may all be widely accepted 'truths'.

Economists will be mindful of the debate between rationalists and empiricists but the idea that scientific methodology can be applied to economics as a discipline and help to improve the knowledge we have and to build upon this knowledge, regardless of how we arrived at it (whether through initial observation or through theorizing) is now widely accepted as the direction for the subject. The Cambridge economist, Joan Robinson, perhaps captured the debate very well when she wrote [economics] 'limps along with one foot in untested hypotheses and the other in untestable slogans … our task is to sort out as best we may this mixture of ideology and science' (Robinson, J. (1968) *Economic Philosophy*. Pelican).

The Role of Assumptions

If you ask a physicist how long it would take for a cannonball to fall from the top of the Leaning Tower of Pisa, she will probably answer the question by assuming that the cannonball falls in a vacuum. Of course, this assumption is false. In fact, the building is surrounded by air, which exerts friction on the falling cannonball and slows it down. Yet the physicist will correctly point out that friction on the cannonball is so small in relation to its weight that its effect is negligible. Assuming the cannonball falls in a vacuum greatly simplifies the problem without substantially affecting the answer.

Economists make assumptions for the same reason: assumptions can simplify the complex world and make it easier to understand. To study the effects of international trade, for example, we may assume that the world consists of only two countries and that each country produces only two goods. Of course, the real world consists of dozens of countries, each of which produces thousands of different types of goods. But by assuming two countries and two goods, we can focus our thinking. Once we understand international trade in an imaginary world with two countries and two goods, we are in a better position to understand international trade in the more complex world in which we live.

The art in scientific thinking is deciding which assumptions to make. Suppose, for instance, that we were dropping a beach ball rather than a cannonball from the top of the building. Our physicist would realize that the assumption of no friction is far less accurate in this case: friction exerts a greater force on a beach ball than on a cannonball because a beach ball is much larger and, moreover, the effects of air friction may not be negligible relative to the weight of the ball because it is so light. The assumption that gravity works in a vacuum may, therefore, be reasonable for studying a falling cannonball but not for studying a falling beach ball.

Similarly, economists use different assumptions to answer different questions. What happens to demand if price changes but we assume incomes stay constant? If we make an assumption of perfect competition in an industry, what will happen to long-run profits? What will happen to the economy when the government changes the amount of money in circulation if we assume prices do not change much in the short run? How does this differ in the long run if we assume that prices are flexible? As we have seen above, these assumptions have to be used with care and they are also subject to testing to see the extent to which the assumption is reasonable in the same way that it is deemed reasonable by the physicist to drop the assumption of friction when considering the effect of dropping a cannonball from the Leaning Tower of Pisa.

Experiments in Economics

Because economics is a science which is centred on human behaviour, it is not always possible to conduct experiments in the way in which physical sciences like Biology, Chemistry and Physics do. However, there are two major fields of experimentation in economics that are worthy of note. Experiments in economics can be conducted in a 'laboratory' where data can be collected via observations on individual or group behaviour, through questionnaires and surveys, interviews and so on, or through the collection and analysis of data that exists such as wages, prices, stock prices and volumes of trades, unemployment levels, inflation and so on. The data can be analysed in relation to a research question and conclusions drawn which help develop new understanding or refine and improve existing understanding. The conclusions drawn from such experiments may be generalizable; in other words, the findings of the experiment can be extended outside the 'laboratory' to explain behaviour or economic phenomena and provide the basis for prediction.

One example of how such laboratory experiments can help change understanding is the work of people such as Daniel Kahneman, Amos Tversky, Richard Thaler and Cass Sunstein, whose research has helped to provide insights into judgement and decision making and has offered a different perspective on the assumptions of rational decision making. Thaler, for example, conducted a number of experiments to explore how individuals respond when faced with different questions on losses and gains in relation to a reference point. He found that prior ownership of a good, for example a ticket to see a football game, altered people's willingness to sell, even at prices significantly higher than that which they had paid.

Thaler's observations on the consistency of this behaviour across a number of experiments led him to coin the term *endowment effect* to explain the behaviour and it is now widely accepted that the endowment effect does exist and that it runs counter to the assumptions of rational behaviour in economics. Thaler then worked with Kahneman and Tversky and extended the theory to distinguish between goods which are held for trade and those which are held for use. The endowment effect, they suggested, was not universal, it was more powerful when goods were held for use.

A second type of experiment in economics is *natural experiments*. A natural experiment is one where the study of phenomena is determined by natural conditions which are not in the control of the experimenter. Natural experiments can be exploited when some change occurs which allows observation to be carried out on the effects of this change in one population and comparisons made with another population who are not affected. Examples of natural experiments include observing the effects of bans on smoking in public places on the number of people smoking or the possible health benefits, how far a change in the way in which education is financed affects standards, the effect of the length of schooling and income, the effects of a rise in a tax on property on the market for housing, what are the effects on the female labour market of changes in fertility treatment and availability?

Typically, natural experiments make use of the statistical tools of correlation and regression to determine whether there is any relationship between two or more variables, what the strength of the relationship might be, if any such relationship exists and what the nature of the relationship is. From such analysis, a model can be developed which can be used to predict. At the heart of such analysis is the extent to which a relationship between two or more variables can be linked to cause and effect. Just because two variables appear to have some relationship does not necessarily imply cause and effect. For example, a researcher might find that an observation of graduates in the workforce shows that their incomes are generally higher than those of non-graduates; can the researcher conclude that having a degree will lead to higher income? Possibly, but not necessarily. There might be other factors that have an effect on income apart from having a degree and trying to build a model which takes into account these different factors is an important part of the value of natural experiments.

Models in Economics

The image on the right shows a plastic replica of the human body. Anatomical models like the one shown have all the major organs – the heart, liver, kidneys and so on – and are used in teaching anatomy and biology. The models allow teachers to show students in a simple way how the important parts of the body fit together. Of course, these plastic models are not actual human bodies; they are stylized and omit many details. Despite this, using these models is useful for learning how the human body works. Economists also use models to learn about the world, but, instead of being made of plastic, they are most often composed of diagrams and equations. It is important to remember that we should not confuse economic with reality just as no-one would mistake an anatomical model for a real person. Economic models omit many details to allow us to see what is truly important. As we use models to examine various economic issues throughout this book, you will see that all the models are built with assumptions. In making these assumptions we can focus on the specific things that we want to study. For example, if we are studying a model of the market we might make an assumption that supply remains constant and that the factors affecting demand apart from a change in income are also constant. By simplifying reality in this way through the model, we can improve our understanding of it.

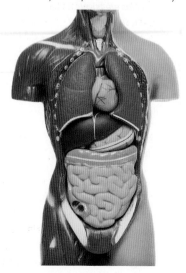

Models are used in many different disciplines. This anatomical model is used to help students understand the workings of the human body and the major organs. In Economics, models are similar stylized representations of reality.

A model will contain a number of variables. In the example above the variables in the market model are demand, supply, incomes, tastes, price and so on. Some of these variables are determined by the model and some are generated within the model. For example, take the market model where the quantity demanded (Q_d) is dependent on the price. Q_d is said to be the dependent variable. Its value, however, will be dependent on the functional relationships in the model (the factors that affect demand) such as incomes, tastes and the prices of other goods. Q_d can be described as an **endogenous variable**. Price, on the other hand, is the independent variable – it affects the model (the quantity demanded) but is not affected by it. The price is not determined by, or dependent on, the quantity demanded. Price would be referred to as an **exogenous variable**.

> **endogenous variable** a variable whose value is determined within the model
> **exogenous variable** a variable whose value is determined outside the model

Understanding the difference between endogenous and exogenous variables is important because it helps us to separate out cause and effect. Does a change in price, for example, cause a change in quantity demanded or does it affect quantity demanded?

Our First Model: The Circular-Flow Diagram

The economy consists of millions of people engaged in many activities – buying, selling, working, hiring, manufacturing and so on. It is extremely complex. It is extremely difficult to intuitively understand how the economy works. A model helps to simplify our thinking about all these activities.

Figure 2.1 presents a visual model of the economy, called a **circular-flow diagram**. In this model, the economy is simplified to include only two types of decision makers – households and firms. Firms produce goods and services using the factor inputs of labour, land and capital. Households own the factors of production and consume all the goods and services that the firms produce.

> **circular-flow diagram** a visual model of the economy that shows how money and production inputs and outputs flow through markets among households and firms

FIGURE 2.1

The Circular Flow
This diagram is a schematic representation or model of the organization of the economy. Decisions are made by households and firms. Households and firms interact in the markets for goods and services (where households are buyers and firms are sellers) and in the markets for the factors of production (where firms are buyers and households are sellers). The outer set of arrows shows the flow of money, and the inner set of arrows shows the corresponding flow of inputs and outputs.

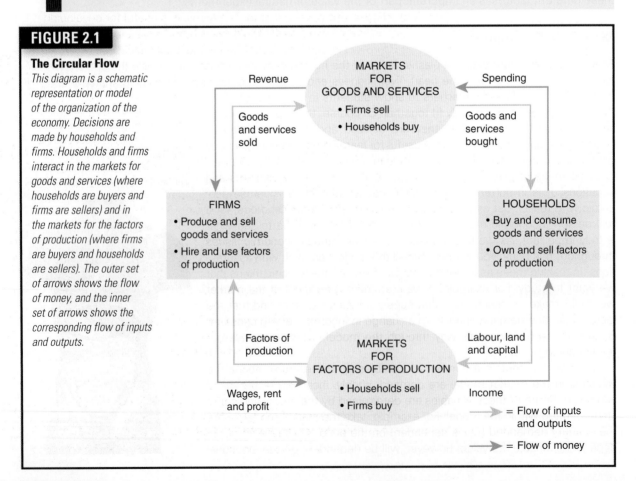

Households and firms interact in two types of markets. In the *markets for goods and services*, households are buyers and firms are sellers. In particular, households buy the output of goods and services that firms produce. In the *markets for the factors of production,* households are sellers and firms are buyers. In these markets, households provide the inputs that the firms use to produce goods and services. The circular-flow diagram offers a simple way of representing the organization of all the economic transactions that occurs between households and firms in the economy.

The inner loop of the circular-flow diagram represents the flows of inputs and outputs. The households sell the use of their labour, land and capital to the firms in the markets for the factors of production. The firms then use these factors to produce goods and services, which in turn are sold to households in the markets for goods and services. Hence, the factors of production flow from households to firms, and goods and services flow from firms to households.

The outer loop of the circular-flow diagram represents the corresponding flows of money. The households spend money to buy goods and services from the firms. The firms use some of the revenue from these sales to pay for the factors of production, such as the wages of their workers. What's left is the profit of the firm's owners, who themselves are members of households. Hence, spending on goods and services flows from households to firms, and income, in the form of wages, rent and profit, flows from firms to households.

Let's take a tour of the circular flow by following a one euro coin as it makes its way from person to person through the economy. Imagine that the euro begins at a household, sitting in, say, your pocket. If you want to buy a cup of coffee, you take the euro to one of the economy's markets for goods and services, such as your local café. There you spend it on your favourite drink: a double espresso. When the euro moves into the café cash register, it becomes revenue for the owner of the café. The euro doesn't stay with the café owner for long, however, because he uses it to buy inputs in the markets for the factors of production. For instance, the café owner might use the euro to pay rent to the owner of the building that the café occupies or to pay the wages of its workers. In either case, the euro enters the income of some household and, once again, is back in someone's pocket. At that point, the story of the economy's circular flow starts once again.

The circular-flow diagram in Figure 2.1 is one simple model of the economy. It is useful for developing some basic ideas about how the economy works. It dispenses with details that, for some purposes, might be significant. We will introduce a more complex circular flow model later in the book which takes account of taxes, government spending, saving, investment and exports and imports.

THE ECONOMIST AS POLICY ADVISOR

Often economists are asked to explain the causes of economic events. Why, for example, is unemployment higher for teenagers than for older workers? Sometimes economists are asked to recommend policies to improve economic outcomes. What, for instance, should the government do to improve the economic well-being of teenagers? When economists are trying to explain the world, they are scientists. When they are trying to help improve it, they are policy advisors.

Positive versus Normative Analysis

To help clarify the two roles that economists play, we begin by examining the use of language. Because scientists and policy advisors have different goals, they use language in different ways.

For example, suppose that two people are discussing minimum wage laws.

Pascale: Minimum wage laws cause unemployment

Sophie: The government should raise the minimum wage

There is a fundamental difference in these two statements. Pascale's statement is spoken like that of a scientist: she is making a claim about how the world works. Sophie is speaking like a policy advisor: she is making a claim about how she would like to change the world.

Pascale's is making a positive statement. **Positive statements** are descriptive. They make a claim about how the world *is*. Positive statements have the property that the claims in them can be tested and confirmed, refuted or shown to not be provable either way. A second type of statement, such as Sophie's, is normative. **Normative statements** are prescriptive. They make a claim about how the world *ought to be.* Normative statements have the property that they include opinion; it is not possible to test opinions and confirm or reject them.

> **Positive statements** claims that attempt to describe the world as it is
> **Normative statements** claims that attempt to prescribe how the world should be

In studying economics (and in everyday life) you will come across many examples of positive and normative statements. In conducting analysis it is important to distinguish between the two. It is perfectly possible to conduct both positive and normative analysis. For example, the statement: *the government should reduce the deficit as this will benefit the economy*, is a normative statement – it contains an opinion that the government ought to reduce the deficit. *A reduction in the government deficit will benefit the economy* is a positive statement, it is capable of being tested. Economists could engage in positive analysis to test whether there is any evidence to support the statement but equally could engage in normative analysis on the basis that there are many people who believe that reducing the deficit will benefit the economy.

A key difference between positive and normative statements, therefore, is how we judge their validity. An economist might evaluate Pascale's statement by analysing data on changes in minimum wages and changes in unemployment over time. By contrast, evaluating normative statements involves values as well as facts. Sophie's statement cannot be judged using data alone. Deciding what is good or bad policy is not merely a matter of science; it also involves our views on ethics, religion and political philosophy.

Of course, positive and normative statements may be related. Our positive views about how the world works affect our normative views about what policies are desirable. Pascale's claim that the minimum wage causes unemployment, if true, might lead us to reject Sophie's conclusion that the government should raise the minimum wage. Yet our normative conclusions cannot come from positive analysis alone; they involve value judgements as well. Normative analysis has its value but it may be necessary to carry out positive analysis first in order to inform the normative.

As you study economics, keep in mind the distinction between positive and normative statements. Much of economics just tries to explain how the economy works. Yet often the goal of economics is to improve how the economy works. When you hear economists making normative statements, you know they have crossed the line from scientist to policy advisor.

WHY ECONOMISTS DISAGREE

There are many jokes about economists and in recent years the profession has come under scrutiny in the wake of the financial crisis. Some of these jokes imply that economists' advice is either contradictory or not definite. One joke about economists concerns the politician who announced that in future she would only employ economists with one hand. The reason being she was tired of receiving advice from her economists which said: 'On the one hand … On the other hand …'

A witticism from the Irish playwright and co-founder of the London School of Economics goes: 'If all economists were laid end to end, they would not reach a conclusion'. Economists as a group are often criticized for giving conflicting advice to policymakers. There are two basic reasons:

● Economists may disagree about the validity of alternative positive theories about how the world works.
● Economists may have different values and, therefore, different normative views about what policy should try to accomplish.

Let's discuss each of these reasons.

Differences in Scientific Judgements

Several centuries ago, astronomers debated whether the Earth or the Sun was at the centre of the solar system. More recently, meteorologists have debated whether the Earth is experiencing global warming and, if so, why. Science is a search for understanding about the world around us. It is not surprising that as the search continues, scientists can disagree about the direction in which truth lies.

Economists often disagree for the same reason. Economics is a young science, and there is still much to be learned. Economists sometimes disagree because they have different beliefs about the validity of alternative theories or about the size of important parameters.

For example, economists disagree about whether the government should levy taxes based on a household's income or based on its consumption (spending). Advocates of a switch from an income tax to a consumption tax believe that the change would encourage households to save more, because income that is saved would not be taxed. Higher saving, in turn, would lead to more rapid growth in productivity and living standards. Advocates of an income tax system believe that household saving would not respond much to a change in the tax laws. These two groups of economists hold different normative views about the tax system because they have different positive views about the responsiveness of saving to tax incentives.

Differences in Values

Anneka and Henrik both take water from the town well. To pay for maintaining the well, the town imposes a property tax on its residents. Anneka lives in a large house worth €2 million and pays a property tax of €10,000 a year. Henrik owns a small cottage worth €20,000 and pays a property tax of €1,000 a year.

Is this policy fair? If not, who pays too much and who pays too little? Would it be better to replace the tax based on the value of the property with a tax that was just a single payment from everyone living in the town (a poll tax) in return for using the well – say, €1,000 a year? After all, Anneka lives on her own and actually uses much less water than Henrik and the other four members of his family who live with him and use more water as a result. Would that be a fairer policy?

This raises two interesting questions in economics – how do we define words like 'fair' and 'unfair', and who holds the power to influence and make decisions? If the power is in the hands of certain groups in government or powerful businesses, the policies may be adopted even if they are widely perceived as being 'unfair'.

What about replacing the property tax not with a poll tax but with an income tax? Anneka has an income of €100,000 a year so that a 5 per cent income tax would present her with a tax bill of €5,000. Henrik, on the other hand, has an income of only €10,000 a year and so would pay only €500 a year in tax and the members of his family who do not work don't pay any income tax. Does it matter whether Henrik's low income is due to his decision not to go to university and take a low paid job? Would it matter if it were due to a physical disability? Does it matter whether Anneka's high income is due to a large inheritance from her family? What if it were due to her willingness to work long hours at a dreary job?

These are difficult questions on which people are likely to disagree. If the town hired two experts to study how the town should tax its residents to pay for the well, we should not be surprised if they offered conflicting advice.

This simple example shows why economists sometimes disagree about public policy. As we learned earlier in our discussion of normative and positive analysis, policies cannot be judged on scientific grounds alone. Economists give conflicting advice sometimes because they have different values. Perfecting the science of economics will not tell us whether it is Anneka or Henrik who pays too much.

Perception versus Reality

Because of differences in scientific judgements and differences in values, some disagreement among economists is inevitable. Yet one should not overstate the amount of disagreement. In many cases, economists do offer a united view.

Table 2.1 contains ten propositions about economic policy. In a survey of economists in business, government and academia, these propositions were endorsed by an overwhelming majority of respondents. Most of these propositions would fail to command a similar consensus among the general public.

One of the propositions in the table concerns tariffs and import quotas, two policies that restrict trade among nations. For reasons we will discuss more fully in later chapters, almost all economists oppose such barriers to free trade. This, in fact, is one of the major reasons why the European Union (EU) was set up and why countries are queuing up to join it: tariffs and quotas are not imposed on trade between EU member countries. Tariffs and quotas *are*, however, often imposed by EU countries on goods coming from outside of the European Union.

TABLE 2.1 | **Ten Propositions About Which Most Economists Agree**

Proposition (and percentage of economists who agree)

1. A ceiling on rents reduces the quantity and quality of housing available. (93%)
2. Tariffs and import quotas usually reduce general economic welfare. (93%)
3. Flexible and floating exchange rates offer an effective international monetary arrangement. (90%)
4. Fiscal policy (e.g., tax cut and/or government expenditure increase) has a significant stimulative impact on a less than fully employed economy. (90%)
5. If the government budget is to be balanced, it should be done over the business cycle rather than yearly. (85%)
6. Cash payments increase the welfare of recipients to a greater degree than do transfers-in-kind of equal cash value. (84%)
7. A large government budget deficit has an adverse effect on the economy. (83%)
8. A minimum wage increases unemployment among young and unskilled workers. (79%)
9. The government should restructure the welfare system along the lines of a 'negative income tax'. (79%)
10. Effluent taxes and marketable pollution permits represent a better approach to pollution control than imposition of pollution ceilings. (78%)

Another of the propositions concerns the imposition of a legal minimum wage – nearly 80 per cent of economists surveyed said that they thought a minimum wage increases unemployment among unskilled and young workers. Nevertheless, the majority of European Union countries now have a statutory minimum wage. Of course, these economists were not necessarily *against* the imposition of a minimum wage. Some of them might argue, for example, that while, on the one hand, introducing a minimum wage above a certain level may affect unemployment, on the other hand it may increase the average quality of goods and services produced in the economy by making it harder for producers of low-quality goods and services to compete by keeping wages and prices low, and this may lead to a net benefit to the economy overall. Remember: people face trade-offs.

Table 2.2 shows another aspect of this same idea. This is based on a paper written by Alan Budd, a former Chief Economic Advisor to HM Treasury in the UK, former Chair of the Office for Budget Responsibility and Provost of the Queen's College, Oxford University until 2008. The paper appeared in the journal *World Economics* in 2004. This table shows a list of things that Sir Alan thinks that economists know and therefore agree on. Most of these things are based on hypotheses that have been tested and observed and which appear to explain key behaviours. It is worth bearing the information in Tables 2.1 and 2.2 in mind as you read through the book.

TABLE 2.2 | **What Economists Know**

Economists know that demand curves slope downwards from left to right.

- This suggests that when prices rise, the quantity demanded of a product (under normal circumstances) will fall and vice versa.

Economists know that supply curves slope upwards from left to right.

- This suggests that when prices rise, the quantity supplied by producers will also rise and vice versa.

Economists know that the proportion of income spent on food falls as income rises.

- This is what is referred to as Engel's law, after the German statistician, Ernst Engel. Budd points out that this law applies not only to studies of the differences in the proportion of income spent on food by the rich and the poor, but also over time. When nations go through economic development and become richer, the proportion of national income spent on food falls.

Economists know that there are gains from trade to be had when countries or individuals have comparative advantage.

- What this means is that one country might be better at producing a number of goods compared to another. However, if it focuses its attention on producing the good in which it has a comparative advantage, both countries can gain from trade and the world economy will be in a better state. By focusing on production of one good at the expense of others, countries move resources from the production of one good to another. By doing so, the country sacrifices the output of this other good that it could have produced. However, the gains made from shifting resources into production of products in which they are more efficient in production helps to raise total output. A mutually beneficial rate of exchange between the two countries means they both are better off than before.

Economists tend to think in terms of general rather than partial equilibrium.

- Economies are made up of millions of interrelated markets. Non-economists, argues Budd, tend to see things from a partial equilibrium point of view. In many cases, this view is based around a zero-sum outcome – the benefit received by one party to an economic decision is offset by a negative impact on someone else. Looking at the big picture gives a more accurate understanding of how economies work and what the consequences of economic policy can be.

Economists know that sunk costs should not affect pricing decisions.

- Sunk costs are those costs that have been spent and cannot be recovered or affected by future economic activity. What this means is that the spending on (for example) major infrastructure projects will be largely academic. Arguments about how much it will cost to build a new high-speed rail link for the eastern half of the UK are simply not relevant. What will be important are the on-going costs of actually running the line and the infrastructure that is built.

There is a difference between what economists know and what non-economists know.

- This can be summarized under the heading 'folk economics'. Folk economics is the intuitive understanding that untrained people have about how the economy operates. If you like, this can be seen as being a novice perspective as opposed to an expert one.

  Budd makes an interesting observation here. If you (as a non-physicist) were engaged in conversation with a physicist who tells you about string theory, you are unlikely to interrupt him or her and disagree with what they were telling you. An economist engaged in a discussion about obesity, for example, with a non-economist would be far more likely to be questioned about the views being put forward. If I, as an economist, told you, a non-economist, that obesity was caused by the rise in poverty levels in countries, it is likely that there would be some disagreement with my view. In short, economists think in the subject, whereas non-economists do not!

SELF TEST Why might economic advisors to the government disagree about a question of policy such as reducing a budget deficit?

Economists as Decision Makers

It could be said that economics is the science of decision making. The way that economists go about making decisions is a specific one. They will initially try to identify the problem or issue related to the decision: for example, will measures to cut greenhouse gas emissions be efficient; or is it worth my while travelling 50 miles to redeem a voucher for €50 at a particular store?

The next stage is to look at the costs and benefits involved in the decision. These costs and benefits are not just the private costs and benefits to the individual concerned; however, they will also include the costs and benefits to third parties who are not directly involved in the actual decision. For example, cutting greenhouse gas emission means that resources will have to be diverted to new ways of production or different ways of producing energy. The private costs will be those borne by the businesses that will have to implement measures to adhere to the limits placed upon them. The social costs might include the impact on local people of the construction of wind farms or new nuclear power stations. If I chose to make the 50-mile journey then I would incur travelling costs – petrol, vehicle depreciation and so on – as well as the cost in terms of the time I have to give to make the journey. The social costs include the addition to possible road congestion that I add, as well as the potential danger to other road users that my being on the road presents.

Having identified the costs and benefits, the economist then seeks to place a value on them in order to get some idea of the relationship between the costs and benefits of making the decision. In some cases, valuing costs and benefits can be easy: in the case of my shopping trip, the benefit is the €50 saved; the costs of petrol used on the journey are easy to calculate. Some costs and benefits are much more difficult to value. The loss of visual amenity for a resident living near a wind turbine or the value of the possible loss of life from a nuclear catastrophe at a power plant may be very difficult to value. Economists have devised ways in which these values can be estimated.

Once the sum of the costs and benefits are calculated, the decision then becomes clearer. If the cost outweighs the benefit then making the decision may be unwise, but if the costs are less than the benefits then it may mean the decision is warranted. Policymakers may want to look at the extent to which the costs outweigh the benefit or the benefit outweighs the costs, however. If the benefit to me of going to redeem the voucher is €50 but the cost of making the trip to do so is valued at €49 then it may not be worth my while going, but if the cost were valued at just €10 then my decision may be more obvious.

Every day millions of decisions are made by individuals, businesses and governments. Whilst not every one of these decisions will be made using the exact processes outlined above, and we certainly do not stop to think about how we rationalize our decisions, nevertheless our brains do engage in computational processes as we make decisions, but they are mostly subconscious. Economists and psychologists are increasingly finding out more about how humans make decisions, which is helping improve our understanding of the models which we use to analyse consumer behaviour.

LET'S GET GOING

The first two chapters of this book have introduced you to the ideas and methods of economics. We are now ready to get to work. In the next chapter we start learning in more detail the principles of economic behaviour and economic policy.

As you proceed through this book, you will be asked to draw on many of your intellectual skills. You might find it helpful to keep in mind some advice from the great John Maynard Keynes:

The study of economics does not seem to require any specialised gifts of an unusually high order. Is it not … a very easy subject compared with the higher branches of philosophy or pure science? An easy subject, at which very few excel! The paradox finds its explanation, perhaps, in that the master-economist must possess a rare combination of gifts. He must be mathematician, historian, statesman, philosopher – in some degree. He must understand symbols and speak in words. He must contemplate the particular in terms of the general, and touch abstract and concrete in the same flight of thought. He must study the present in the light of the past for the purposes of the future. No part of man's nature or his institutions must lie entirely outside his regard. He must be purposeful and disinterested in a simultaneous mood; as aloof and incorruptible as an artist, yet sometimes as near the earth as a politician.

It is a tall order. But with practice you will become more and more accustomed to thinking like an economist.

SUMMARY

- Economists try to address their subject with a scientist's objectivity. Like all scientists, they make appropriate assumptions and build simplified models in order to understand the world around them. One simple economic model is the circular-flow diagram.

- Economists use empirical methods to develop and test hypotheses

- Research can be conducted through using inductive and deductive reasoning – no one way is the 'right way'.

- Economists develop theories which can be used to explain phenomena and make predictions. In developing theories and models, economists have to make assumptions.

- Using theory and observation is part of scientific method but economists always have to remember that they are studying human beings and humans do not always behave in consistent or rational ways.

- A positive statement is an assertion about how the world *is*. A normative statement is an assertion about how the world *ought to be*. When economists make normative statements, they are acting more as policy advisors than scientists.

- Economists who advise policymakers offer conflicting advice either because of differences in scientific judgements or because of differences in values. At other times, economists are united in the advice they offer, but policymakers may choose to ignore it.

QUESTIONS FOR REVIEW

1 How is economics like a science?

2 Why do economists make assumptions?

3 Should an economic model describe reality exactly?

4 What is meant by empirical study in economics?

5 Using an example, explain the difference between inductive and deductive reasoning.

6 Should economic theories be developed as a result of observation or before observation? Explain.

7 What is the difference between a positive and a normative statement? Give an example of each.

8 What is the role of assumptions in economics?

9 Using an example, explain the difference between an endogenous and an exogenous variable.

10 Why do economists sometimes offer conflicting advice to policymakers?

PROBLEMS AND APPLICATIONS

1 Terms like Investment, Capital, Interest, Price and Cost have different meanings in economics than they do in normal everyday usage. Find out what the differences are and explain why economists might have developed these different meanings.

2 One common assumption in economics is that the products of different firms in the same industry are indistinguishable. For each of the following industries, discuss whether this is a reasonable assumption.

a. steel

b. novels

c. wheat

d. fast food

e. mobile phones (think carefully about this one)

f. hairdressers.

3 Draw a circular-flow diagram. Identify the parts of the model that correspond to the flow of goods and services and the flow of euros for each of the following activities.

a. Sam pays a petrol station €60 for filling up his car with petrol.

b. Georgia earns €5.50 per hour working at a fast food restaurant.

c. Millie spends €7 to see a film.

d. Patrick earns €10,000 from his 10 per cent ownership of Pan-European Industrial.

4 A researcher in a university notices that the price of flights to holiday destinations tends to be much higher outside semester dates. He formulates a theory to explain this phenomenon. Has the researcher arrived at the theory by induction or deduction? What steps might the researcher take to apply scientific method to test his theory?

5 A politician makes a speech in which he criticizes the government's immigration policy, saying that it is too loose and encourages too many people to enter the country and take jobs away from local people. How might an economist go about assessing the validity of the politician's comments?

6 If models are not capable of representing the real world in any detail and rely too much on assumptions, then what value can they be? In the wake of the financial crisis, there has been much criticism of economists' models. Does this suggest that economists need to rethink the way they go about seeking to understand and represent the world?

7 Classify each of the following statements as positive or normative. Explain.

a. Society faces a short-run trade-off between inflation and unemployment.

b. A reduction in the rate of growth of money will reduce the rate of inflation.

c. The European Central Bank should reduce the rate of growth of money.

d. Society ought to require welfare recipients to look for jobs.

e. Lower tax rates encourage more work and more saving.

8 Classify each of the statements in Table 2.1 as positive, normative or ambiguous. Explain.

9 If you were prime minister, would you be more interested in your economic advisors' positive views or their normative views? Why?

10 Would you expect economists to disagree less about public policy as time goes on? Why or why not? Can their differences be completely eliminated? Why or why not?

APPENDIX
Graphing and the Tools of Economics: A Brief Review

As you work through this book and in your course, you will come across a number of standard economic methods and processes which economists use in analysing the world. In this appendix we are going to briefly introduce some of these.

Many of the concepts that economists study can be expressed with numbers – the price of bananas, the quantity of bananas sold, the cost of growing bananas and so on. These numbers often represent variables – things that can change. Economists are interested in these variables and in particular are interested in how variables are related to each other. When the price of bananas rises, for example, people buy fewer bananas. Does this mean that there is a relationship between the variable, price and the variable, demand? If there is sufficient proof that not only are the two variables related but that there is a strong relationship between the two then this may help in predicting a more general relationship between two variables. Economists will use maths to represent such relationships and also through graphs.

Functions

In economics a lot of use is made of functions. Demand and supply equations are two examples of functions. Typically, functions are expressed as:

$$y = f(x)$$

or simply $f(x)$.

This means that the value of y is dependent on the value of the terms in the bracket – in our example above there is only one value, x, so the value of y is dependent on the value of x.

In the example above, the value of y is dependent on the value of a single variable x. However, it is quite possible that the value of y could be dependent on a range of different variables. This can also be represented in the form of a function which would look like:

$$y = f(x_1 \ldots \ldots \ldots x_n)$$

where $x_1 \ldots \ldots \ldots x_n$ represents a range of variables.

Linear Equations During your course it is likely that you will have to work with linear equations – equations which are represented graphically as straight lines. A linear equation typically looks like:

$$y = a + bx$$

In this equation, y = the value plotted on the vertical axis (the dependent variable) and x is the value on the horizontal axis (the independent variable).

a is a constant and represents the point where the line cuts the y axis and b is the slope of the line or its gradient. We can plot a linear equation as a graph by assigning different values to x and using the equation to establish the value of y in each case. This is represented in the table for Figure 2A.1 for the linear equation $y = 5 + 2x$.

FIGURE 2A.1

Values of x and y for the linear equation $y = 5 + 2x$ between $x = 0$ and $x = 10$ when

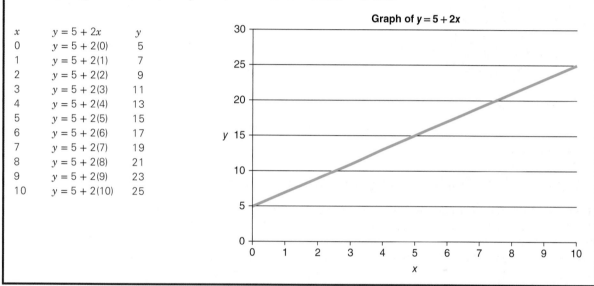

x	$y = 5 + 2x$	y
0	$y = 5 + 2(0)$	5
1	$y = 5 + 2(1)$	7
2	$y = 5 + 2(2)$	9
3	$y = 5 + 2(3)$	11
4	$y = 5 + 2(4)$	13
5	$y = 5 + 2(5)$	15
6	$y = 5 + 2(6)$	17
7	$y = 5 + 2(7)$	19
8	$y = 5 + 2(8)$	21
9	$y = 5 + 2(9)$	23
10	$y = 5 + 2(10)$	25

Graph of $y = 5 + 2x$

Notice that the line intersects the vertical axis where $x = 0$. The value of the constant a in this equation is 5 and represents the vertical intercept, the point where the equation of the line cuts the vertical axis. Next thing to notice is that as we give different values for x we see that the value of y rises by 2 for each increase of x by 1. In the equation, the constant b is 2 and is the slope or gradient of the line. More on slopes later in this appendix.

Types of Graphs The line graph we generated from the equation is one example of a graph that you will use in your study of economics. There are a number of others.

Why use graphs at all? Graphs serve two purposes. First, when developing economic theories, graphs offer a way to express visually ideas that might be less clear if described with equations or words. Secondly, when analysing economic data, graphs provide a way of finding how variables are in fact related in the world. Whether we are working with theory or with data, graphs provide a means by which we can see patterns and relationships. Choosing the appropriate graphical method is important – the aim is to make the information we are trying to view as clear as possible. An effective economist chooses the type of graph that best suits the purpose at hand.

Graphs of a Single Variable

Three common graphs are shown in Figure 2A.2. The *pie chart* in panel (a) shows the proportion of gross domestic product devoted to investment in the so called 'G7 countries'. These countries are Japan, the United States, United Kingdom, France, Germany, Canada and Italy. A slice of the pie represents

FIGURE 2A.2

Types of Graph

The pie chart in panel (a) shows the proportion of GDP devoted to investment in the G7 countries in 2011. The bar graph in panel (b) shows the interest rate set by the ECB. The time-series graph in panel (c) shows the unemployment rate for the 27 EU countries from 2000–2011. Panel (d) shows the same information as panel (c) but uses a different scale for the vertical axis.

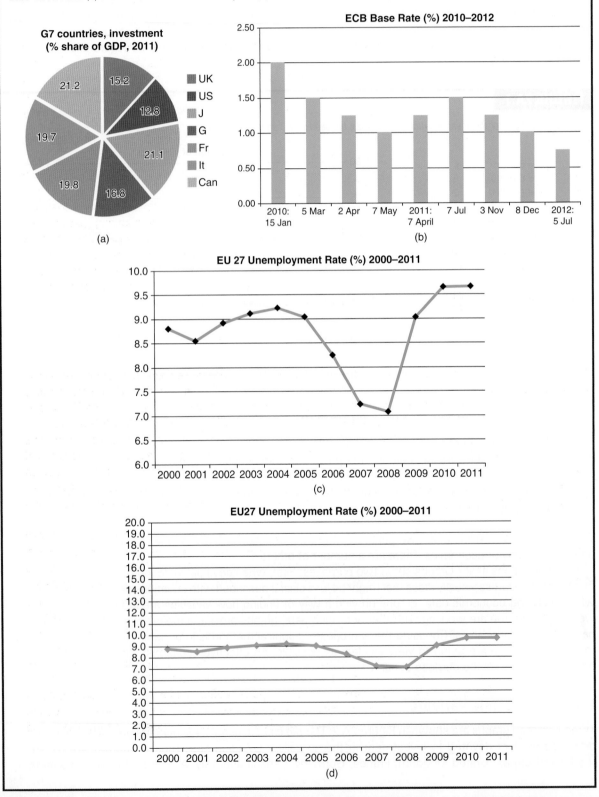

each country's proportion of investment. The *bar graph* in panel (b) shows the interest rate set by the European Central Bank (ECB) between January 2010 and July 2012. The interest rate is on the vertical axis represented as a percentage and the time period is on the horizontal axis. The height of each bar represents the interest rate. The *time-series graph* in panel (c) traces the unemployment rate in the 27 EU countries between 2000 and 2011. The unemployment rate as a percentage is represented on the vertical axis and the year is on the horizontal axis. The height of the line shows the unemployment rate each year.

Interpreting Line Graphs

Look at the line graph in panel (c) of Figure 2A.2. The unemployment rate starts off at about 8.7 per cent in 2000, falls to around 8.5 per cent in 2001 before rising to about 9.2 per cent in 2004. The difference between the unemployment rate in 2001 and 2004 is about 0.7 per cent – a relatively small rise – which is represented by a moderately upward sloping line. From 2004, the unemployment rate falls to around 7.1 per cent in 2008 – a relatively large fall at 2.1 per cent. This is represented by a relatively steep line. Equally, the rise in the unemployment rate after 2008 to around 9.6 per cent in 2010 is represented by a steep rise in the line. Unemployment rose by around 2.5 per cent in just two years compared to the rise in unemployment of just 0.7 per cent in three years between 2001 and 2004. Between 2010 and 2011, the unemployment rate remained at about 9.6 per cent and so we would say that the rate had been 'flat' between those two dates represented by the flat shape of the line.

Looking at the shallowness or steepness of a line graph can tell us a great deal about the rate of change – whether our variable is changing quickly or slowly. However, we must take care in ensuring that we take note of the scale of the graph we are using. Look at the graph in panel (d). This shows exactly the same information as that in panel (c) but the scale on the vertical axis has been changed. The change in the unemployment rate does not look anything like as dramatic in panel (d) and the line appears to be relatively flat. This is a reminder that if we are comparing information on two different line graphs we have to make sure that we take note of the scale before drawing any conclusions.

Graphs of Two Variables: The Coordinate System

Although the three graphs in Figure 2A.2 are useful in showing how a variable changes over time or across individuals, such graphs are limited in how much they can tell us. These graphs display information only on a single variable. Economists are often concerned with the relationships between variables. Thus, they need to be able to display two variables on a single graph. The *coordinate system* makes this possible.

Suppose you want to examine the relationship between study time and examination marks for students attending economics lectures. You could record a pair of numbers: hours per week spent studying and marks obtained in the final course examination. These numbers could then be placed in parentheses as an *ordered pair* and appear as a single point on the graph. Albert, for instance, is represented by the ordered pair (25 hours/week, 70 per cent examination mark), while his classmate Alfred is represented by the ordered pair (5 hours/week, 40 per cent examination mark).

We can graph these ordered pairs on a two-dimensional grid. The first number in each ordered pair, called the *x-coordinate*, tells us the horizontal location of the point. The second number, called the *y-coordinate*, tells us the vertical location of the point. The point with both an x-coordinate and a y-coordinate of zero is known as the *origin*. The two coordinates in the ordered pair tell us where the point is located in relation to the origin: x units to the right of the origin and y units above it.

Figure 2A.3 graphs examination marks against study time for Albert, Alfred and the rest of the students who attended the course. This type of graph is called a *scatterplot* because it plots scattered points. Looking at this graph, we immediately notice that points further to the right (indicating more study time) also tend to be higher (indicating a better examination result). Because study time and examination mark typically move in the same direction, we say that these two variables have a *positive correlation*. By contrast, if we were to graph time spent partying per week and examination marks, we would probably find that higher party time is associated with lower marks; because these variables typically move in opposite directions, we would call this a *negative correlation*. In either case, the coordinate system makes the correlation between the two variables easy to see.

FIGURE 2A.3

Using the Coordinate System

Final examination mark is measured on the vertical axis and study time on the horizontal axis. Albert, Alfred and the other students on their course are represented by various points. We can see from the graph that students who spend more hours studying tend to get higher marks.

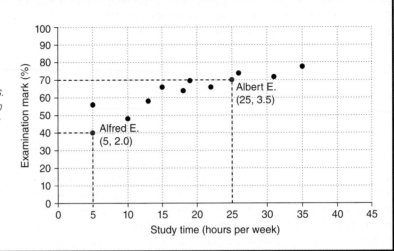

Limitations of Scatter Plot Graphs Looking at the scatter plot in Figure 2A.3, it seems intuitively sensible that more time devoted to study is associated with higher marks. But just because two variables appear to have a relationship does not mean we can simply accept the data at face value. As economists we have to be critical – we have to question what we see. The following example highlights this issue.

Assume that data are released in a particular area which we shall call Region X, which shows a rise in the number of new born babies over a period of time. At the same time, it is observed that the stork population in Region X has also risen over the same period of time. There is a 'theory' that storks bring babies. This 'theory' comes from the belief that storks are a fertility symbol. Storks live in and around marsh and wetland areas. There was also an ancient belief that the souls of unborn babies lived in water and that storks carried these souls to mothers – hence the belief that storks bring babies.

FIGURE 2A.4

The Stork Population and New Born Babies in Region X

The scatter plot of the information in the Table shows the stork population over a period of time in Region X and the number of new born babies over the same time period.

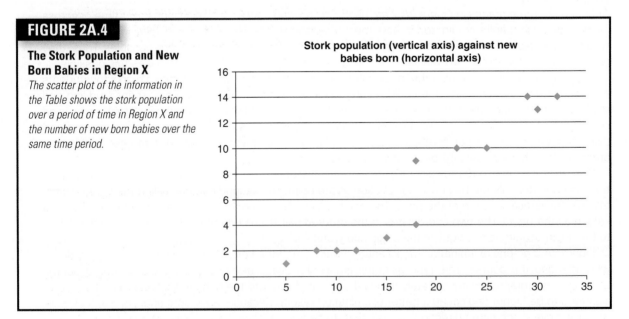

Looking at the scatter plot in Figure 2A.4 it seems clear that there is a correlation between the two variables and one might be drawn to the conclusion that storks do indeed bring babies. However, common sense and biology tell us that what we are seeing is simply a coincidence – two variables which seem to have some correlation but where the correlation is due to chance. To determine whether there is a relationship between variables and the extent to which any relationship is due to chance can be identified by the use of different statistical tests. If the appropriate tests were carried out on this data it is likely to tell us that there is a significant correlation and the extent to which the correlation is due to chance. This example serves as another reminder that economists must always question and never simply accept things at face value.

Curves in the Coordinate System

Students who study more do tend to get higher marks, but other factors also influence a student's marks. Previous preparation is an important factor, for instance, as are talent, attention from teachers and even eating a good breakfast. A scatter plot like Figure 2A.3 does not attempt to isolate the effect that study has on grades from the effects of other variables. Often, however, economists prefer looking at how one variable affects another while holding everything else constant. The principle used here is referred to as *ceteris paribus*, a Latin phrase which roughly translated means 'other things being equal'. Economists analyse problems which they fully understand have multiple factors which could be affecting outcomes being investigated. In order to try and isolate the factors which are the most significant ones, the principle of *ceteris paribus* is used. It enables us to look at how changes in one variable affect outcomes assuming other variables that we know might have an effect are held constant. We can then look at the other variables in turn and build a more complete picture of the effect of changes in variables.

To see how this is done, let's consider one of the most important graphs in economics – the *demand curve*. The demand curve traces out the effect of a good's price on the quantity of the good consumers want to buy. Before showing a demand curve, however, consider Table 2A.1, which shows how the number of novels that Maria buys depends on her income and on the price of novels. When novels are cheap, Maria buys them in large quantities. As they become more expensive, she borrows books from the library instead of buying them or chooses to go to the cinema instead of reading. Similarly, at any given price, Maria buys more novels when she has a higher income. That is, when her income increases, she spends part of the additional income on novels and part on other goods.

TABLE 2A.1	**Novels Purchased by Maria**

This table shows the number of novels Maria buys at various incomes and prices. For any given level of income, the data on price and quantity demanded can be graphed to produce Maria's demand curve for novels, as shown in Figures 2A.5 and 2A.6.

	Income		
Price	**€20,000**	**€30,000**	**€40,000**
€10	2 novels	5 novels	8 novels
€9	6	9	12
€8	10	13	16
€7	14	17	20
€6	18	21	24
€5	22	25	28
	Demand curve, D₃	*Demand curve, D₁*	*Demand curve, D₂*

We now have three variables – the price of novels, income and the number of novels purchased – which is more than we can represent in two dimensions. To put the information from Table 2A.1 in graphical form, we need to hold one of the three variables constant and trace out the relationship between the other two. Because the demand curve represents the relationship between price and quantity demanded, we hold Maria's income constant and show how the number of novels she buys varies with the price of novels.

Suppose that Maria's income is €30,000 per year. If we place the number of novels Maria purchases on the *x*-axis and the price of novels on the *y*-axis, we can graphically represent the middle column of Table 2A.1. When the points that represent these entries from the table – (5 novels, €10), (9 novels, €9) and so on – are connected, they form a line. This line, pictured in Figure 2A.5, is known as Maria's demand curve for novels; it tells us how many novels Maria purchases at any given price. The demand curve is downward sloping, indicating that a higher price reduces the quantity of novels demanded. Because the quantity of novels demanded and the price move in opposite directions, we say that the two variables are *negatively or inversely related*. (Conversely, when two variables move in the same direction, the curve relating them is upward sloping, and we say the variables are *positively related*.)

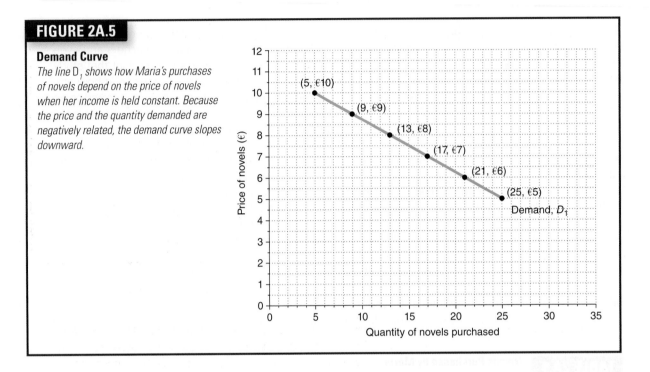

FIGURE 2A.5

Demand Curve
The line D_1 shows how Maria's purchases of novels depend on the price of novels when her income is held constant. Because the price and the quantity demanded are negatively related, the demand curve slopes downward.

Now suppose that Maria's income rises to €40,000 per year. At any given price, Maria will purchase more novels than she did at her previous level of income. Just as earlier we drew Maria's demand curve for novels using the entries from the middle column of Table 2A.1, we now draw a new demand curve using the entries from the right-hand column of the table. This new demand curve (curve D_2) is pictured alongside the old one (curve D_1) in Figure 2A.6; the new curve is a similar line drawn farther to the right. We therefore say that Maria's demand curve for novels *shifts* to the right when her income increases. Likewise, if Maria's income were to fall to €20,000 per year, she would buy fewer novels at any given price and her demand curve would shift to the left (to curve D_3).

In economics, it is important to distinguish between *movements along a curve* and *shifts of a curve*. As we can see from Figure 2A.5, if Maria earns €30,000 per year and novels are priced at €8 apiece, she will purchase 13 novels per year. If the price of novels falls to €7, Maria will increase her purchases of novels to 17 per year. The demand curve, however, stays fixed in the same place. Maria still buys the same number of novels *at each price*, but as the price falls she moves along her demand curve from left to right. By contrast, if the price of novels remains fixed at €8 but her income rises to €40,000, Maria increases her purchases of novels from 13 to 16 per year. Because Maria buys more novels *at each price,* her demand curve shifts out, as shown in Figure 2A.6.

There is a simple way to tell when it is necessary to shift a curve. When a variable that is not named on either axis changes, the curve shifts. Income is on neither the *x*-axis nor the *y*-axis of the graph, so when Maria's income changes, her demand curve must shift. Any change that affects Maria's purchasing habits, besides a change in the price of novels, will result in a shift in her demand curve. If, for instance, the public library closes and Maria must buy all the books she wants to read, she will demand more novels at each price, and her demand curve will shift to the right. Or, if the price of going to the cinema falls and Maria spends more time at the movies and less time reading, she will demand fewer novels at each price, and her demand curve will shift to the left. By contrast, when a variable on an axis of the graph changes, the curve does not shift. We read the change as a movement along the curve.

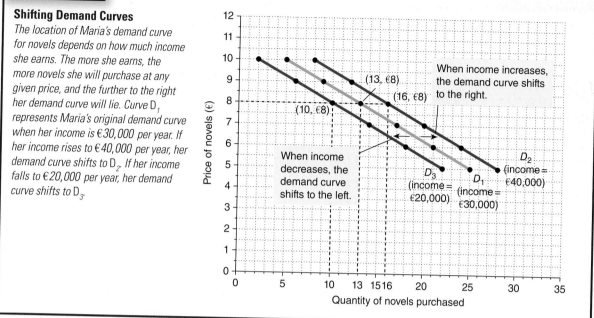

FIGURE 2A.6

Shifting Demand Curves

The location of Maria's demand curve for novels depends on how much income she earns. The more she earns, the more novels she will purchase at any given price, and the further to the right her demand curve will lie. Curve D_1 represents Maria's original demand curve when her income is €30,000 per year. If her income rises to €40,000 per year, her demand curve shifts to D_2. If her income falls to €20,000 per year, her demand curve shifts to D_3.

Slope

One question we might want to ask about Maria is how much her purchasing habits respond to price. Look at the demand curve D_2 pictured in Figure 2A.7. This curve is very steep, Maria purchases nearly the same number of novels regardless of whether they are cheap or expensive. The demand curve D_1 is much flatter, Maria purchases fewer novels when the price rises. To answer questions about how much one variable responds to changes in another variable, we can use the concept of *slope*.

The slope of a line is the ratio of the vertical distance covered to the horizontal distance covered as we move along the line. This definition is usually written out in mathematical symbols as follows:

$$slope = \frac{\Delta y}{\Delta x}$$

where the Greek letter Δ (delta) stands for the change in a variable. In other words, the slope of a line is equal to the 'rise' (change in y) divided by the 'run' (change in x). The slope will be a small positive number for a fairly flat upward sloping line, a large positive number for a steep upward sloping line and a negative number for a downward sloping line. A horizontal line has a slope of zero because in this case the y-variable never changes; a vertical line is said to have an infinite slope because the y-variable can take any value without the x-variable changing at all.

What is the slope of Maria's demand curve for novels? First of all, because the curve slopes down, we know the slope will be negative. To calculate a numerical value for the slope, we must choose two points on the line. With Maria's income at €30,000, she will purchase 21 novels at a price of €6 or 13 novels at a price of €8. When we apply the slope formula, we are concerned with the change between these two points; in other words, we are concerned with the difference between them, which lets us know that we will have to subtract one set of values from the other, as follows:

$$\text{Slope} = \frac{\Delta y}{\Delta x} = \frac{\text{first } y\text{-coordinate} - \text{second } y\text{-coordinate}}{\text{first } x\text{-coordinate} - \text{second } x\text{-coordinate}} = \frac{6-8}{21-13} = \frac{-2}{8} = \frac{-1}{4}$$

Figure 2A.7 shows graphically how this calculation works. Try computing the slope of Maria's demand curve using two different points. You should get exactly the same result, −1/4. One of the properties of a straight line is that it has the same slope everywhere. This is not true of other types of curves, which are steeper in some places than in others.

FIGURE 2A.7

Calculating the Slope of a Line
To calculate the slope of the demand curve, we can look at the changes in the y- and x-coordinates as we move from the point (21 novels, €6) to the point (13 novels, €8). The slope of the line is the ratio of the change in the y-coordinate (−2) to the change in the x-coordinate (+8), which equals −1/4.

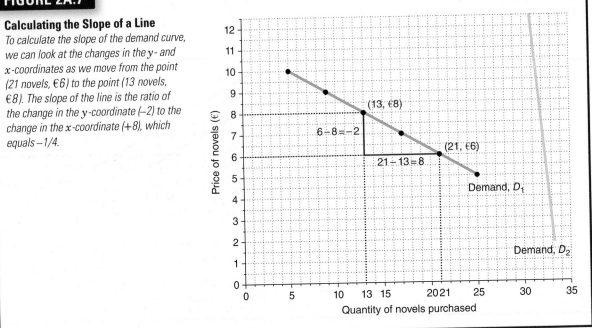

The slope of Maria's demand curve tells us something about how responsive her purchases are to changes in the price. A small slope (a number close to zero) means that Maria's demand curve is relatively flat; in this case, she adjusts the number of novels she buys substantially in response to a price change. A larger slope (a number further from zero) means that Maria's demand curve is relatively steep; in this case she adjusts the number of novels she buys only slightly in response to a price change.

Cause and Effect

Economists often use graphs to advance an argument about how the economy works. In other words, they use graphs to argue about how one set of events *causes* another set of events. With a graph like the demand curve, there is no doubt about cause and effect. Because we are varying price and holding all other variables constant, we know that changes in the price of novels cause changes in the quantity Maria demands. Remember, however, that our demand curve came from a hypothetical example. When graphing data from the real world, it is often more difficult to establish how one variable affects another.

The first problem is that it is difficult to hold everything else constant when measuring how one variable affects another. If we are not able to hold variables constant, we might decide that one variable on our graph is causing changes in the other variable when actually those changes are caused by a third *omitted variable* not pictured on the graph. Even if we have correctly identified the two variables to look at, we might run into a second problem – *reverse causality*. In other words, we might decide that A causes B when in fact B causes A. The omitted variable and reverse causality traps require us to proceed with caution when using graphs to draw conclusions about causes and effects.

Omitted Variables To see how omitting a variable can lead to a deceptive graph, let's consider an example. Imagine that the government, spurred by public concern about the large number of deaths from cancer, commissions an exhaustive study from Big Brother Statistical Services. Big Brother examines many of the items found in people's homes to see which of them are associated with the risk of cancer. Big Brother reports a strong relationship between two variables: the number of cigarette lighters that a household owns and the probability that someone in the household will develop cancer. Figure 2A.8 shows this relationship.

FIGURE 2A.8

Graph With an Omitted Variable

The upward sloping curve shows that members of households with more cigarette lighters are more likely to develop cancer. Yet we should not conclude that ownership of lighters causes cancer, because the graph does not take into account the number of cigarettes smoked.

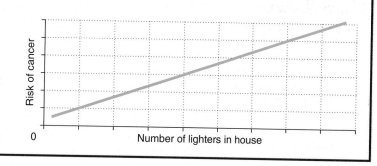

What should we make of this result? Big Brother advises a quick policy response. It recommends that the government discourages the ownership of cigarette lighters by taxing their sale. It also recommends that the government requires warning labels: 'Big Brother has determined that this lighter is dangerous to your health.'

In judging the validity of Big Brother's analysis, one question is paramount: has Big Brother held constant every relevant variable except the one under consideration? If the answer is no, the results are suspect. An easy explanation for Figure 2A.8 is that people who own more cigarette lighters are more likely to smoke cigarettes and that cigarettes, not lighters, cause cancer. If Figure 2A.8 does not hold constant the amount of smoking, it does not tell us the true effect of owning a cigarette lighter.

This story illustrates an important principle: when you see a graph being used to support an argument about cause and effect, it is important to ask whether the movements of an omitted variable could explain the results you see.

Reverse Causality Economists can also make mistakes about causality by misreading its direction. To see how this is possible, suppose the Association of European Anarchists commissions a study of crime in Eurovia and arrives at Figure 2A.9, which plots the number of violent crimes per 1,000 people in major Eurovian cities against the number of police officers per 1,000 people. The anarchists note the curve's upward slope and argue that because police increase rather than decrease the amount of urban violence, law enforcement should be abolished.

If we could run a controlled experiment, we would avoid the danger of reverse causality. To run an experiment, we would set the number of police officers in different cities randomly and then examine the correlation between police and crime. Figure 2A.9, however, is not based on such an experiment. We simply observe that more dangerous cities have more police officers. The explanation for this may be that more dangerous cities hire more police. In other words, rather than police causing crime, crime may cause police. Nothing in the graph itself allows us to establish the direction of causality.

It might seem that an easy way to determine the direction of causality is to examine which variable moves first. If we see crime increase and then the police force expand, we reach one conclusion. If we see the police force expand and then crime increase, we reach the other. Yet there is also a flaw with this approach: often people change their behaviour not in response to a change in their present conditions but

FIGURE 2A.9

Graph Suggesting Reverse Causality

The upward sloping curve shows that Eurovian cities with a higher concentration of police are more dangerous. Yet the graph does not tell us whether police cause crime or crime-plagued cities hire more police.

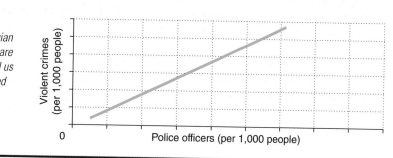

in response to a change in their *expectations* of future conditions. A city that expects a major crime wave in the future, for instance, might well hire more police now. This problem is even easier to see in the case of babies and baby cots. Couples often buy a baby cot in anticipation of the birth of a child. The cot comes before the baby, but we wouldn't want to conclude that the sale of cots causes the population to grow!

There is no complete set of rules that says when it is appropriate to draw causal conclusions from graphs. Yet just keeping in mind that cigarette lighters don't cause cancer (omitted variable) and baby cots do not cause larger families (reverse causality) will keep you from falling for many faulty economic arguments.

Constrained Optimization

Throughout this book we will look at situations where consumers, firms and governments are assumed to exhibit maximizing or minimizing behaviour. Consumers might be assumed to want to maximize the satisfaction (utility) they get from consumption, firms might be assumed to want to maximize profits but minimize costs, and governments might want to maximize tax revenue, for example. In most cases, there will be factors which will limit the extent to which this maximizing or minimizing behaviour can be carried out such as time, income and resources. In the case of consumers, the ability to maximize utility will be subject to a constraint – their income. Firms might want to minimize costs but subject to the constraint of their income (revenue) or the factor inputs that they have at their disposal.

Economists will often carry out analysis under conditions of constrained optimization. Typically this might take the form: maximize x subject to the existence of y constraint. Usually, the constraint is assumed to be fixed and so a calculation can be made which shows the optimizing (maximum or minimum) behaviour given the constraint which exists. We can then change the constraint to see how behaviour would differ and what the outcome would be. You will probably learn some of the mathematical techniques for solving constrained optimization problems in the quantitative methods modules that you will take alongside your Principles of Economics module.

Real versus Nominal Values

Economists deal with numbers but it is important to have some understanding of the numbers we might happen to be working with. Distinguishing between real and nominal values is extremely important. A simple way to understand the difference between nominal and real values is to remember that nominal values are expressed in money terms whereas real values are expressed as quantities. Typically, we will look at values which are affected by price movements over time. For example, if a firm was to tell you that it had sold €1 million worth of extra products over the last year (2014) what does that tell you? The answer is: not very much! If the firm sold €10 million worth of goods the year before (2013) you might be tempted to think that now selling €11 million worth is a 'good' thing and indeed, it might be.

Now assume that you know a little bit more about the situation of the firm in our example. Assume that the firm sold 10 million units in 2013, each priced at €1. Making a judgement on the performance of the firm in 2014 requires we know a little bit more about the extra €1 million worth of sales – the nominal value. If the price of the goods sold in 2014 stayed at €1 then we know that the firm sold an extra 1 million units that year – a 10 per cent increase in sales volumes, which we might conclude is a creditable performance. However, would you come to the same conclusion if you discovered that the price they sold their products at in 2014 was €10, meaning they only sold an extra 100,000 units in that year? Now the increase in sales is only 1 per cent – not such a good performance. The performance of the firm is largely due to the change in price not the amount of goods sold. In this case, nominal sales rose by €1 million but real sales rose by 100,000 units.

Real values, therefore, take into account price changes over time or the adjusting factors such as the seasons, whereas nominal values don't take account of these adjusting factors. For this reason you might see nominal values referred to as *current prices* whereas real values might be referred to as *constant prices*.

PART 2
SUPPLY AND DEMAND: HOW MARKETS WORK

3 THE MARKET FORCES OF SUPPLY AND DEMAND

In April 2012, the price of winter wheat on global markets was around €209 per metric tonne. By September 2012 the price had risen to €277 per metric tonne, a rise of around 33 per cent. One of the reasons for the rise in price was that wheat-producing states in the United States suffered a drought which damaged the wheat crop. Other crops such as corn and soya beans had also been rising in price. One of the consequences of this is that livestock farmers faced increased costs of production – some arable crops are used in livestock feedstuffs. Some farmers had been unable to afford to feed their animals and so had to send them for slaughter which led to beef prices falling.

In November 2006, the average house price in the UK was £200,000 (€250,000). In January 2009, this had fallen to £164,000 (€205,000). When major sporting events are held in a country, such as the World Cup or the Olympics, hotel prices in the areas around the venues tend to rise. In the Holy month of Ramadan, many Muslims find that the price of food rises quite sharply. If you book an airline flight several months in advance of a trip the seat prices tend to be lower than if you try booking two weeks before your trip. What do these events have in common? They all show the workings of supply and demand.

Supply and *demand* are the two words that economists use most often – and for good reason. Supply and demand are the forces that make market economies work. They determine the quantity of each good produced and the price at which it is sold. If you want to know how any event or policy will affect the economy, you must think first about how it will affect supply and demand.

This chapter introduces the theory of supply and demand. It considers how buyers and sellers behave and how they interact with one another. It shows how supply and demand determine prices in a market economy and how prices, in turn, allocate the economy's scarce resources.

MARKETS AND COMPETITION

The terms *supply* and *demand* refer to the behaviour of people as they interact with one another in markets. A **market** is a group of buyers and sellers of a particular good or service. The buyers as a group determine the demand for the product, and the sellers as a group determine the supply of the product. Before discussing how buyers and sellers behave, let's first consider more fully what we mean by a 'market' and the various types of markets we observe in the economy.

> **market** a group of buyers and sellers of a particular good or service

Competitive Markets

Markets take many forms. Sometimes markets are highly organized, such as the markets for many agricultural commodities and for metals. In these markets, buyers and sellers meet at a specific time and place, where an auctioneer helps set prices and arrange sales.

More often, markets are less organized. For example, consider the market for coffee in a particular town. Buyers of coffee do not meet together at any one time. The sellers of coffee are in different locations and offer different products (lattes, Americano, espresso, instant, filter, etc.). There is no auctioneer calling out the price of coffee. Each seller posts a price for a cup of coffee in their shop, and each buyer decides how much coffee to buy at each shop.

Even though it is not organized, the group of coffee buyers and coffee sellers forms a market. Each buyer knows that there are several sellers from which to choose, and each seller is aware that his product is similar to that offered by other sellers. The price of coffee and the quantity of coffee sold are not determined by any single buyer or seller. Rather, price and quantity are determined by all buyers and sellers as they interact in the marketplace.

The market for coffee, like most markets in the economy, is highly competitive. Competition exists when two or more firms are rivals for customers. Each firm strives to gain the attention and custom of buyers in the market. The market for coffee in a town will consist of established chains which are familiar across Europe – Costa, Starbucks, Café Nero, Koffie Café, Lavazza and Coffeeheaven, for example – but there will also be many small independent cafés, bars and restaurants where buyers can get a cup of coffee. Any of these coffee sellers faces competition from other coffee sellers.

In economics, however, there are particular characteristics ascribed to the term 'competitive market'. A **competitive market** is a market in which there are many buyers and many sellers so that each has a negligible impact on the market price. Each seller has limited control over the price because other sellers are offering similar products and each seller only supplies a very small amount in relation to the total supply of the market. In a perfectly competitive market the products are identical (homogenous) so a seller has little reason to charge less than the going price, and if he or she charges more, buyers will make their purchases elsewhere. Similarly, no single buyer can influence the price because each buyer purchases only a small amount relative to the size of the market.

In this chapter, we will look at the model for supply and demand assuming these characteristics; we examine how buyers and sellers interact in competitive markets. We see how the forces of supply and demand determine both the quantity of the good sold and its price. In later chapters we will look at what happens when some of these assumptions are relaxed. By doing this we can see how markets might work differently when there are a few sellers who dominate the market or when they are able to differentiate their product in some way and so the assumption of homogeneity does not hold.

> **competitive market** a market in which there are many buyers and sellers so that each has a negligible impact on the market price

Competition: Perfect and Otherwise

The assumptions of perfect competition outlined above lead us to some important conclusions. Because there are many buyers and sellers in a perfectly competitive market, neither has any power to influence price – they must accept the price the market determines, they are said to be *price takers*.

There are some markets in which the assumption of perfect competition applies to a very large degree. In the EU agriculture market, for example, there are about 14 million farmers who sell cereals, fruit, milk, beef, lamb and so on, and millions of consumers who buy these products. Because no single buyer or seller can influence the price of agricultural products, each takes the price as given.

Not all goods and services, however, are sold in perfectly competitive markets. Some markets have only one seller, and this seller sets the price. Such a seller is called a *monopoly.* Your local water company, for instance, may be a monopoly. Residents in your area probably have only one water company from which to buy this service.

Some markets fall between the extremes of perfect competition and monopoly. One such market, called an *oligopoly,* has a few sellers that do not always compete aggressively. There are many examples of oligopolistic markets across Europe in products like steel, tyre manufacture, retailing (supermarkets), alcoholic beverages, telecommunications, pharmaceuticals, banking and athletic sportswear. Another type of market is *monopolistically competitive*; it contains many sellers but each offers a slightly different product. Because the products are not exactly the same, each seller has some ability to set the price for its own product. An example is the market for magazines. Magazines compete with one another for readers and anyone can enter the market by starting a new one, but each magazine offers different articles and can set its own price.

Despite the diversity of market types we find in the world, we begin by studying perfect competition. Perfectly competitive markets are the easiest to analyse. Moreover, because some degree of competition is present in most markets, many of the lessons that we learn by studying supply and demand under perfect competition apply in more complicated markets as well.

SELF TEST What constitutes a market? List the main characteristics of a competitive market.

DEMAND

We begin our study of markets by examining the behaviour of buyers. To focus our thinking, let's keep in mind a particular good – milk. The market for milk fulfils many of the characteristics of a perfectly competitive market; milk is fairly homogenous, there are about half a million dairy farms across the EU and there are millions of buyers of milk across the EU.

The Demand Curve: The Relationship Between Price and Quantity Demanded

The **quantity demanded** of any good is the amount of the good that buyers are willing and able to purchase at different prices. Many things determine the quantity demanded of any good, but when analysing how markets work, one determinant plays a central role – the price of the good. If the price of milk rose from €0.25 per litre to €0.35 per litre, less milk would be bought. If the price of milk fell to €0.20 per litre more milk would be bought. Because the quantity demanded falls as the price rises and rises as the price falls, we say that the quantity demanded is *negatively or inversely related* to the price. This relationship between price and quantity demanded is true for most goods in the economy and, in fact, is so pervasive that economists call it the **law of demand**: other things equal, when the price of a good rises, the quantity demanded of the good falls, and when the price falls, the quantity demanded rises.

> **quantity demanded** the amount of a good that buyers are willing and able to purchase at different prices
> **law of demand** the claim that, other things equal (*ceteris paribus*) the quantity demanded of a good falls when the price of the good rises

We can represent the relationship between the price and quantity demanded in a table such as the one shown in Figure 3.1. The table shows how many litres of milk Rachel is willing and able to buy each month at different prices for milk. If milk is free, Rachel would be willing to buy 20 litres. At €0.10 per litre, Rachel would be willing to buy 18 litres. As the price rises further, she is willing to buy fewer and fewer litres. When the price reaches €1, Rachel would not be prepared to buy any milk at all. This table is a **demand schedule**, a table that shows the relationship between the price of a good and the quantity demanded, holding constant everything else that influences how much consumers of the good want to buy.

demand schedule a table that shows the relationship between the price of a good and the quantity demanded

The graph in Figure 3.1 uses the numbers from the table to illustrate the law of demand. By convention, price is on the vertical axis, and the quantity demanded is on the horizontal axis. The downwards sloping line relating price and quantity demanded is called the **demand curve**.

demand curve a graph of the relationship between the price of a good and the quantity demanded

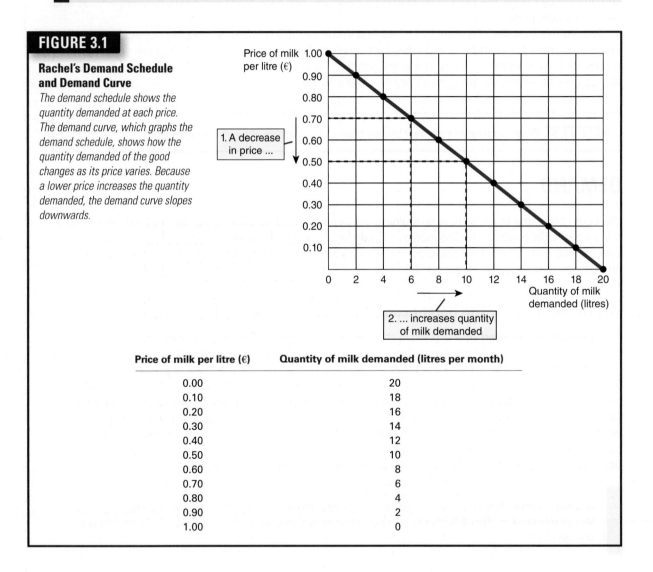

FIGURE 3.1

Rachel's Demand Schedule and Demand Curve

The demand schedule shows the quantity demanded at each price. The demand curve, which graphs the demand schedule, shows how the quantity demanded of the good changes as its price varies. Because a lower price increases the quantity demanded, the demand curve slopes downwards.

Price of milk per litre (€)	Quantity of milk demanded (litres per month)
0.00	20
0.10	18
0.20	16
0.30	14
0.40	12
0.50	10
0.60	8
0.70	6
0.80	4
0.90	2
1.00	0

Market Demand versus Individual Demand

The demand curve in Figure 3.1 shows an individual's demand for a product. To analyse how markets work, we need to determine the *market demand*, which is the sum of all the individual demands for a particular good or service.

The table in Figure 3.2 shows the demand schedules for milk of two individuals – Rachel and Lars. At any price, Rachel's demand schedule tells us how much milk she would like to buy and Lars' demand

FIGURE 3.2

Market Demand as the Sum of Individual Demands

*The quantity demanded in a market is the sum of the quantities demanded by all the buyers at each price. Thus, the market demand curve is found by adding horizontally the individual demand curves. At a price of €0.50, Rachel would like to buy 10 litres of milk but Lars would only be prepared to buy 5 litres at that price. The quantity demanded **in the market** at this price, therefore, is 15 litres.*

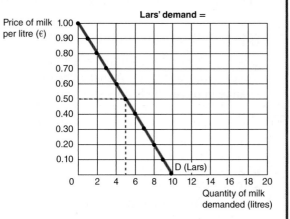

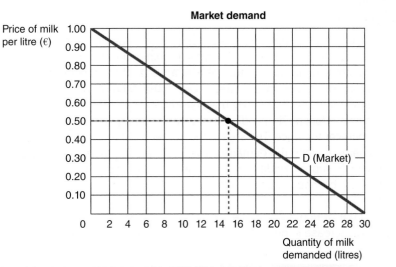

Price of milk per litre (€)	Rachel +	Lars =	Market
0.00	20	10	30
0.10	18	9	27
0.20	16	8	24
0.30	14	7	21
0.40	12	6	18
0.50	10	5	15
0.60	8	4	12
0.70	6	3	9
0.80	4	2	6
0.90	2	1	3
1.00	0	0	0

schedule tells us how much milk he is willing to buy. The market demand at each price is the sum of the two individual demands.

Figure 3.2 shows the demand curves that correspond to these demand schedules. To find the total quantity demanded at any price, we add the individual quantities found on the horizontal axis of the individual demand curves. The market demand curve shows how the total quantity demanded of a good varies as the price of the good varies, while all the other factors that affect how much consumers want to buy, such as incomes and taste, among other things, are held constant.

Shifts versus Movements along the Demand Curve

One important distinction that must be made is between a shift of the demand curve and a movement along the demand curve. A shift in the demand curve is caused by a factor affecting demand **other than a change in price**. The factors affecting demand are outlined below presented as a function written:

$$D = f(P_n, P_1 P_2 ... P_{n-1}, Y, T, P_{LS}, A, E)$$

Where:

- P_n = Price
- $P_1 P_2 ... P_{n-1}$ = Prices of other goods – substitutes and complements
- Y = Incomes – the level and distribution of income
- T = Tastes and fashions
- P_{LS} = The level and structure of the population
- A = Advertising
- E = Expectations of consumers

If any of the variables affecting demand *apart from* price changes then the demand curve will shift, either to the right (an increase in demand) or to the left (a reduction in demand). For example, if the price of milk is €0.30 per litre a family might buy 5 litres of milk a week. If their income rises, they can now afford to buy more milk and so might now buy 7 litres a week. The price of milk has not changed – it is still €0.30 per litre but the amount of milk the family buys has increased.

If any of the factors affecting demand other than price change then the amount consumers wish to purchase changes whatever the price. The shift in the demand curve is referred to as an *increase or decrease in demand.* A movement along the demand curve occurs when there is a change in price. This may occur because of a change in supply conditions. A change in price leads to a movement along the demand curve and is referred to as a *change in quantity demanded.*

Movement Along the Demand Curve Let us assume that the price of milk falls. We know that the fall in price will lead to an increase in quantity demanded. There are two reasons for this increase:

1. **The income effect**. If we assume that incomes remain constant then a fall in the price of milk means that consumers can now afford to buy more with their income. In other words, their *real income*, what a given amount of money can buy at any point in time, has increased and part of the increase in quantity demanded can be put down to this effect.
2. **The substitution effect**. Now that milk is lower in price compared to other products such as fruit juice, some consumers will choose to substitute the more expensive drinks with the now cheaper milk. This switch accounts for the remaining part of the increase in quantity demanded.

A Shift in the Demand Curve The demand curve for milk shows how much milk people are willing to buy at any given price, holding constant the many other factors beyond price that influence consumers' buying decisions. As a result, this demand curve need not be stable over time. If something happens to alter the quantity demanded at any given price, the demand curve shifts. For example, suppose a top European medical school published research findings that suggested people who regularly drink milk live longer, healthier lives. The discovery would raise the demand for milk. At any given price, buyers would now want to purchase a larger quantity of milk and the demand curve for milk would shift.

Figure 3.3 illustrates shifts in demand. Any change that increases the quantity demanded at every price, such as our imaginary research report, shifts the demand curve to the right and is called *an increase in demand*. Any change that reduces the quantity demanded at every price shifts the demand curve to the left and is called *a decrease in demand*.

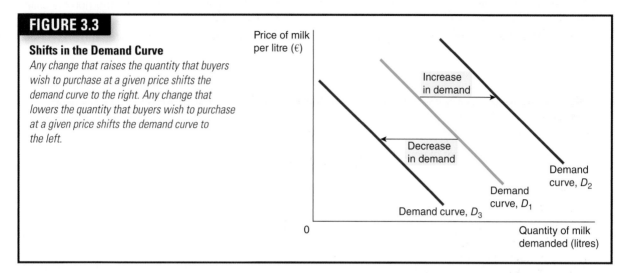

FIGURE 3.3

Shifts in the Demand Curve
Any change that raises the quantity that buyers wish to purchase at a given price shifts the demand curve to the right. Any change that lowers the quantity that buyers wish to purchase at a given price shifts the demand curve to the left.

The following is a short summary of the factors affecting demand, changes in which cause a shift of the demand curve.

Prices of Other (Related) Goods Suppose that the price of milk falls. The law of demand says that you will buy more milk. At the same time, you will probably buy less fruit juice. Because milk and fruit juice are both refreshing drinks, they satisfy similar desires. When a fall in the price of one good reduces the demand for another good, the two goods are called **substitutes**. Substitutes are often pairs of goods that are used in place of each other, such as butter and margarine, pullovers and sweatshirts, and cinema tickets and DVD rentals. The more closely related substitute products are, the more effect we might see on demand if the price of one of the substitutes changes.

> **substitutes** two goods for which an increase in the price of one leads to an increase in the demand for the other

Now suppose that the price of breakfast cereals falls. According to the law of demand, more packets of breakfast cereals will be bought. Yet, in this case, the demand for milk will increase as well, because breakfast cereals and milk are used together. When a fall in the price of one good raises the demand for another good, the two goods are called **complements**. Complements are often pairs of goods that are used together, such as petrol and cars, computers and software, bread and cheese, strawberries and cream, and bacon and eggs.

> **complements** two goods for which an increase in the price of one leads to a decrease in the demand for the other

Income What would happen to your demand for milk if you lost your job? Most likely, it would fall. A lower income means that you have less to spend in total, so you would have to spend less on some – and probably most – goods. If the demand for a good falls when income falls, the good is called a **normal good**.

normal good a good for which, *ceteris paribus*, an increase in income leads to an increase in demand (and vice versa)

Not all goods are normal goods. If the demand for a good rises when income falls, the good is called an **inferior good**. An example of an inferior good might be bus rides. As your income falls, you are less likely to buy a car or take a taxi and more likely to take the bus. As income falls, therefore, demand for bus rides tends to increase.

inferior good a good for which, *ceteris paribus*, an increase in income leads to a decrease in demand (and vice versa)

Tastes A key determinant of your demand is your tastes. If you like milk, you buy more of it. Understanding the role of tastes in consumer behaviour is taking on more importance as research in the fields of psychology and neurology are applied to economics.

Population Because market demand is derived from individual demands, it follows that the more buyers there are the higher the demand is likely to be. The size of the population, therefore, is a determinant of demand. A larger population, *ceteris paribus*, will mean a higher demand for all goods and services. Changes in the way the population is structured also influences demand. Many countries have an ageing population and this leads to a change in demand. If there is an increasing proportion of the population aged 65 and over, the demand for goods and services used by the elderly, such as the demand for retirement homes, insurance policies suitable for older people, the demand for smaller cars and for health care services, etc. is likely to increase in demand as a result.

Advertising Firms advertise their products in many different ways and it is likely that if a firm embarks on an advertising campaign then the demand for that product will increase.

Expectations of Consumers Expectations about the future may affect the demand for a good or service today. For example, if it was announced that the price of milk was expected to rise next month consumers may be more willing to buy milk at today's price.

Summary The demand curve shows what happens to the quantity demanded of a good when its price varies, holding constant all the other variables that influence buyers; when one or more of these other variables changes, the demand curve shifts. Table 3.1 lists all the variables that influence how much consumers choose to buy of a good.

TABLE 3.1   **Variables That Influence Buyers**

This table lists the variables that affect how much consumers choose to buy of any good. Notice the special role that the price of the good plays: a change in the good's price represents a movement along the demand curve, whereas a change in one of the other variables shifts the demand curve.

Variable	A change in this variable . . .
Price	Is represented as a movement along the demand curve
Prices of other, related goods	Shifts the demand curve
Income	Shifts the demand curve
Tastes	Shifts the demand curve
Population	Shifts the demand curve
Advertising	Shifts the demand curve
Expectations	Shifts the demand curve

SELF TEST Make up an example of a demand schedule for pizza and graph the demand curve. Give an example of something that would cause the demand curve to shift to the right. Give a different example of something that would cause the demand curve to shift to the left.

Finding Price and Quantity Using Algebra

In Chapter 2 we looked at linear equations and gave some examples of how demand functions can be expressed as simple linear equations.

Look at the following equation:

$$Qd = 1{,}700 - 3p$$

We can dissect this in a bit more detail in relation to the standard $y = a + bx$ linear equation we covered in Chapter 2.

The quantity demanded is one of the variables in the equation. In this case it is the dependent variable. The quantity demanded depends upon the price and so price is the independent variable.

The equation tells us that the quantity demanded will be 1,700 minus 3 times whatever the price is. If price is €5 then quantity demanded will be $1{,}700 - 3(7) = 1{,}679$. If price is €20 then quantity demanded will be $1{,}700 - 3(20) = 1{,}640$.

Let us take a different example. Given the demand function $p = 760 - 0.3Qd$, if price were €5 the quantity demanded (rounded up) would be:

$$\begin{aligned} 0.3Qd &= 760 - 5 \\ \frac{0.3Qd}{0.3} &= \frac{755}{0.3} \\ Qd &= 2{,}517 \end{aligned}$$

The same process would be used if we knew the quantity but needed to find the price. Using the equation:

$$Qd = 1{,}800 - 3p$$

If we knew the quantity demanded was 1,640 then substituting this into the equation would enable us to find the price:

$$\begin{aligned} Qd &= 1800 - 3p \\ Qd - 1800 &= -3p \\ \frac{Qd}{-3} - \frac{1800}{-3} &= p \\ 600 - \frac{1}{3}Qd &= p \end{aligned}$$

SELF TEST Given the equation $Qd = -8p + 2{,}500$, calculate the quantity demanded for prices increasing in €10 increments from €0 – €100. Plot the resulting demand curve on a piece of graph paper. At what value does the demand curve you have drawn cut the horizontal axis? What is the slope of the demand curve you have drawn? Having worked out these two values, what conclusions can you draw from comparing these values with the equation?

SUPPLY

We now turn to the other side of the market and examine the behaviour of sellers. Once again, to focus our thinking, we will continue to consider the market for milk.

The Supply Curve: The Relationship Between Price and Quantity Supplied

The **quantity supplied** of any good or service is the amount that sellers are willing and able to sell at different prices. There are many determinants of quantity supplied, but once again price plays a special role in our analysis. When the price of milk is high, selling milk is profitable, and so the sellers are willing to supply more. Sellers of milk work longer hours, buy more dairy cows and hire extra workers in order to ensure supplies to the market rise. By contrast, when the price of milk is low, the business is less profitable, and so sellers are willing to produce less milk. At a low price, some sellers may even choose to shut down, and their quantity supplied falls to zero. Because the quantity supplied rises as the price rises and falls as the price falls, we say that the quantity supplied is *positively related* to the price of the good. This relationship between price and quantity supplied is called the **law of supply**: other things equal, when the price of a good rises, the quantity supplied of the good also rises, and when the price falls, the quantity supplied falls as well.

> **quantity supplied** the amount of a good that sellers are willing and able to sell at different prices
> **law of supply** the claim that, *ceteris paribus*, the quantity supplied of a good rises when the price of a good rises

The table in Figure 3.4 shows the quantity, Richard, a milk producer, is willing to supply, at various prices. At a price below €0.10 per litre, Richard does not supply any milk at all. As the price rises, he is willing to supply a greater and greater quantity. This is the **supply schedule**, a table that shows the relationship between the price of a good and the quantity supplied, holding constant everything else that influences how much producers of the good want to sell.

> **supply schedule** a table that shows the relationship between the price of a good and the quantity supplied

The graph in Figure 3.4 uses the numbers from the table to illustrate the law of supply. The curve relating price and quantity supplied is called the **supply curve**. The supply curve slopes upwards because, other things equal, a higher price means a greater quantity supplied.

> **supply curve** a graph of the relationship between the price of a good and the quantity supplied

Market Supply versus Individual Supply

Just as market demand is the sum of the demands of all buyers, market supply is the sum of the supplies of all sellers. The table in Figure 3.5 shows the supply schedules for two milk producers – Richard and Megan. At any price, Richard's supply schedule tells us the quantity of milk Richard is willing to supply, and Megan's supply schedule tells us the quantity of milk Megan is willing to supply. The market supply is the sum of the two individual supplies.

The graph in Figure 3.5 shows the supply curves that correspond to the supply schedules. As with demand curves, we find the total quantity supplied at any price by adding the individual quantities found

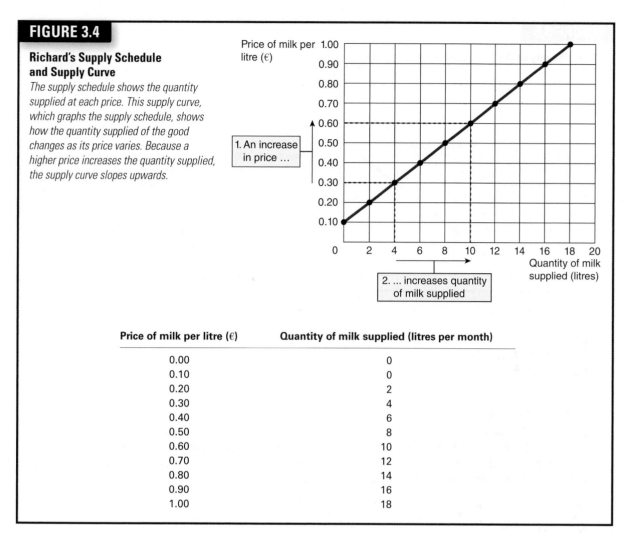

FIGURE 3.4

Richard's Supply Schedule and Supply Curve
The supply schedule shows the quantity supplied at each price. This supply curve, which graphs the supply schedule, shows how the quantity supplied of the good changes as its price varies. Because a higher price increases the quantity supplied, the supply curve slopes upwards.

1. An increase in price ...

2. ... increases quantity of milk supplied

Price of milk per litre (€)	Quantity of milk supplied (litres per month)
0.00	0
0.10	0
0.20	2
0.30	4
0.40	6
0.50	8
0.60	10
0.70	12
0.80	14
0.90	16
1.00	18

on the horizontal axis of the individual supply curves. The market supply curve shows how the total quantity supplied varies as the price of the good varies.

Shifts in the Supply Curve

The supply curve for milk shows how much milk producers are willing to offer for sale at any given price, holding constant all the other factors beyond price that influence producers' decisions about how much to sell. This relationship can change over time, which is represented by a shift in the supply curve. For example, suppose the price of animal feed falls. Because animal feed is an input into producing milk, the fall in the price of animal feed makes selling milk more profitable. This raises the supply of milk: at any given price, sellers are now willing to produce a larger quantity. Thus, the supply curve for milk shifts to the right.

Figure 3.6 illustrates shifts in supply. Any change that raises quantity supplied at every price, such as a fall in the price of animal feed, shifts the supply curve to the right and is called *an increase in supply*. Similarly, any change that reduces the quantity supplied at every price shifts the supply curve to the left and is called *a decrease in supply*.

FIGURE 3.5

Market Supply as the Sum of Individual Supplies

The quantity supplied in a market is the sum of the quantities supplied by all the sellers at each price. Thus, the market supply curve is found by adding horizontally the individual supply curves. At a price of €0.50, Richard is willing to supply 8 litres of milk, and Megan is willing to supply 5 litres. The quantity supplied in the market at this price is 13 litres.

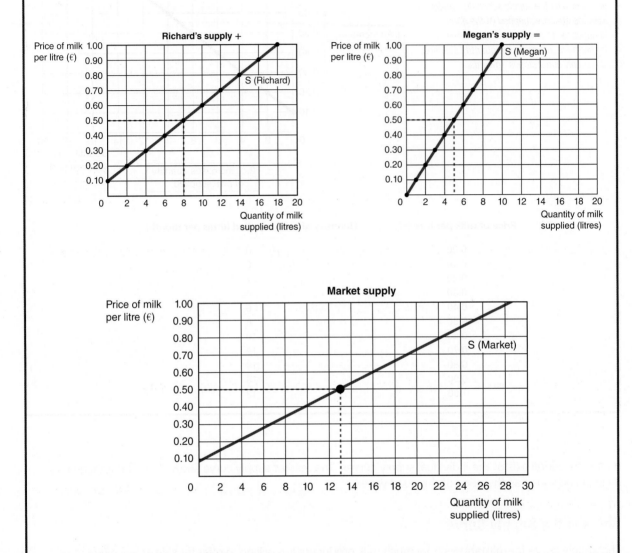

Price of milk per litre (€)	Richard +	Megan =	Market
0.00	0	0	0
0.10	0	1	1
0.20	2	2	4
0.30	4	3	7
0.40	6	4	10
0.50	8	5	13
0.60	10	6	16
0.70	12	7	19
0.80	14	8	22
0.90	16	9	25
1.00	18	10	28

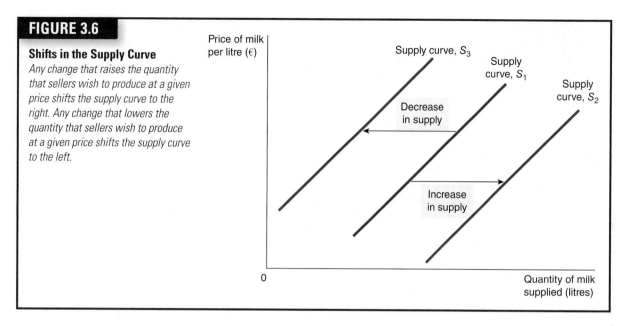

FIGURE 3.6

Shifts in the Supply Curve

Any change that raises the quantity that sellers wish to produce at a given price shifts the supply curve to the right. Any change that lowers the quantity that sellers wish to produce at a given price shifts the supply curve to the left.

Price of milk per litre (€)

Supply curve, S_3

Supply curve, S_1

Supply curve, S_2

Decrease in supply

Increase in supply

0

Quantity of milk supplied (litres)

A shift in the supply curve will be caused by one or more of the factors affecting supply **other than price.** As with demand, we can represent the factors that influence supply in a function:

$$S = f(P_n, P_n ... P_{n-1}, H, N/S_f, F_1 ... F_m, E, S_q)$$

Where:

- P_n = Price
- $P_n ... P_{n-1}$ = Profitability of other goods in production and prices of goods in joint supply
- H = Technology
- N/S_f = Natural shocks/Social factors
- $F_1 ... F_m$ = Costs of production
- E = Expectations of producers
- S_q = Number of sellers

If any of the factors affecting supply other than price changes, the supply curve will shift. The following provides a brief outline of these factors.

Profitability of Other Goods in Production and Prices of Goods in Joint Supply Firms have some flexibility in the supply of products and in some cases can switch production to other goods. For example, motor vehicle manufacturers can use production lines to change production between different models as can other manufacturers. If one product becomes more profitable then it may be that the firm switches to the more profitable product. In other cases, firms may find that products are in joint supply; an increase in the supply of lamb, for example, might also lead to an increase in the supply of wool.

Technology The technology for turning the inputs into milk is yet another determinant of supply. Advances in technology increase productivity allowing more to be produced using fewer factor inputs. As a result costs, both total and unit, may fall and supply increases. The development of fertilizers and more efficient milking parlours, for example, have increased milk yields per cow and helped reduce costs as a result. By reducing firms' costs, the advance in technology raises the supply of milk.

Natural/Social Factors There are often many natural or social factors that affect supply. These include such things as the weather affecting crops, natural disasters, pestilence and disease, changing attitudes and social expectations (for example over the production of organic food, the disposal of waste, reducing carbon emissions, ethical supply sourcing and so on) all of which can have an influence on production decisions. Some or all of these may have an influence on the cost of inputs into production.

Input Prices – the Prices of Factors of Production To produce the output of milk, sellers use various inputs including land, fertilizer, feed, silage, farm buildings, veterinary services and the labour of workers. When the price of one or more of these inputs rises, producing milk is less profitable and firms supply less milk. If input prices rise substantially, a firm might shut down and supply no milk at all. If input prices fall for some reason, then production may be more profitable and there is an incentive to supply more at each price. Thus, the supply of a good is negatively related to the price of the inputs used to make the good.

Expectations of Producers The amount of milk a firm supplies today may depend on its expectations of the future. For example, if it expects the price of milk to rise in the future, the firm might invest in more productive capacity or increase the size of the herd.

Number of Sellers If there are more sellers in the market then it makes sense that the supply would increase. Equally, if a number of dairy farms closed down then it is likely that the amount of milk supplied would also fall.

SELF TEST Make up an example of a supply schedule for pizza and graph the implied supply curve.
Give an example of something that would shift this supply curve.
Would a change in price shift the supply curve?

The Algebra of Supply

The principles we applied to linear demand curves can equally be applied to a linear supply curve of the type:

$$Qs = -15 + 8p$$

The plus sign in front of the price variable in the supply equation tells us that there is a positive relationship between price and quantity supplied. Using this equation, if the price were €10 then the quantity supplied would be $-15 + 8(10) = 65$ and if price were €20 then quantity supplied would be $-15 + 8(20) = 145$.

CASE STUDY   Fracking and the effect on oil prices

Developments in technology have ripple effects on many markets. In the constant search to find new sources of energy, humans have come up with many ingenious ideas and in recent years a process called fracking has caused both excitement and concern. Fracking involves injecting fluid, consisting of water and a number of chemicals, into the shale deposits underground at extremely high pressure. The pressure fractures shale rocks and releases natural gas and oil which can be 'harvested' and used for energy. The possibilities for extracting large quantities of gas and oil from fracking around the world is high but there are some who ask whether the cost in terms of the potential damage to the environment of the large amounts of water needed in the fracking process, the chemical residues left behind, the potential for contamination of drinking water supplies and pollution, not to mention concerns over the increased possibilities of earthquakes in the area around fracking wells, is worth the amount of gas and oil which can be extracted.

The amount of gas and oil that could be extracted is not insignificant. The chief executive officer for the US energy firm Conoco, Ryan Lance, was reported to have predicted that the United States could be self-sufficient in oil and gas by 2025. Estimates are that shale oil and gas could be around 2 million barrels per day by 2020 and could rise to 3 million barrels per day by 2035.

The Organization of Petroleum Exporting Countries (OPEC) is a group of oil-producing countries which act together to manage oil supplies. In our model of demand and supply in this chapter we have assumed that no buyer or seller can individually influence market price. Because a country like Saudi Arabia has massive reserves of oil, it can influence market price by increasing and reducing the supply of oil coming onto the market. Together, OPEC countries can and do manipulate oil supplies to try and keep the market price of oil relatively stable. Even OPEC cannot influence demand, however, and so changes in economic activity, the weather and natural disasters such as hurricanes, earthquakes and tsunamis do cause the demand for oil to change and help account for some of the volatility in market prices.

In November 2012, OPEC acknowledged that the possibilities represented by fracking might have a long-term effect on the price of oil. The predicted output of 2 million barrels per day, for example, is almost equivalent to the daily production of one of the OPEC countries, Nigeria, so the effect on oil and gas supplies in the future is going to be a factor. If fracking expands not only in North America but in the rest of the world, the effect on the supply of oil and gas will be to shift the supply curve to the right and assuming demand is relatively stable, the future oil price could fall. OPEC might choose to respond to this possibility by cutting back its own supply of oil to the market in order to stabilize the price. Because oil produced by fracking is a substitute for crude oil, OPEC expects the demand for crude oil to moderate as consumers switch to oil generated by fracking. All these factors could mean that oil prices remain more stable in the medium to long term and might also fall.

Is this good news for consumers of oil and gas? That depends on whether the concerns of environmentalists over the safety of fracking are real or not. Environmentalists would argue that the true cost of generating shale gas and oil is not being taken into account by firms involved in the process because they are not accounting for the potential environmental damage that they say can be caused by fracking. This represents an excellent example of the working of markets and also the economic problem – are the benefits of generating more oil and gas and helping keep prices more stable, greater than the costs? Can we truly know the real costs of fracking if the companies involved dispute the claims of environmentalists?

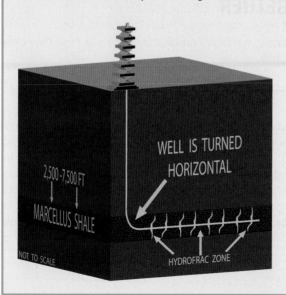

The fracking process is controversial with opponents citing the extensive use of water in the process and the potential to cause local earthquake risks, but proponents say it is a safe and cost-effective method of generating new gas and oil supplies.

Summary The supply curve shows what happens to the quantity supplied of a good when its price varies, holding constant all the other variables that influence sellers. When one of the other variables changes, the supply curve shifts. Table 3.2 lists all the variables that influence how much producers choose to sell of a good.

TABLE 3.2	**Variables That Influence Sellers**

This table lists the variables that affect how much producers choose to sell of any good. Notice the special role that the price of the good plays: a change in the good's price represents a movement along the supply curve, whereas a change in one of the other variables shifts the supply curve.

Variable	A change in this variable . . .
Price	Is represented by a movement along the supply curve
Profitability of goods in production and price of goods in joint supply	Shifts the supply curve
Technology	Shifts the supply curve
Natural/social factors	Shifts the supply curve
Input costs	Shifts the supply curve
Expectations of producers	Shifts the supply curve
Number of sellers	Shifts the supply curve

SELF TEST Using the supply equation:

$$Qs = 2 + 3p$$

Calculate quantity supplied if $p = 40$
Calculate price if $Qs = 88$

SUPPLY AND DEMAND TOGETHER

Having analysed supply and demand separately, we now combine them to see how they determine the quantity of a good sold in a market and its price.

Equilibrium

Figure 3.7 shows the market supply curve and market demand curve together. Equilibrium, remember, is defined as a state of rest, a point where there is no force acting for change. Economists refer to supply and demand as being *market forces*. In any market the relationship between supply and demand exerts force on price. If supply is greater than demand or vice versa, then there is pressure on price to change. Market equilibrium occurs when the amount consumers wish to buy at a particular price is the same as the amount sellers are willing to offer for sale at that price. The price at this intersection is called the **equilibrium or market price**, and the quantity is called the **equilibrium quantity**. In Figure 3.7 the equilibrium price is €0.40 per litre, and the equilibrium quantity is 7,000 litres of milk bought and sold.

equilibrium or market price the price where the quantity demanded is the same as the quantity supplied
equilibrium quantity the quantity bought and sold at the equilibrium price

At the equilibrium price, the quantity of the good that buyers are willing and able to buy exactly balances the quantity that sellers are willing and able to sell. The equilibrium price is sometimes called the *market-clearing price* because, at this price, everyone in the market has been satisfied: buyers have bought all they want to buy, and sellers have sold all they want to sell; there is no shortage in the market where demand is greater than supply and neither is there any surplus where supply is greater than demand.

FIGURE 3.7

The Equilibrium of Supply and Demand

The equilibrium is found where the supply and demand curves intersect. At the equilibrium price, the quantity supplied is the same as the quantity demanded. Here the equilibrium price is €0.40 per litre of milk: at this price, sellers are willing to offer 7,000 litres of milk for sale and buyers wish to purchase 7,000 litres of milk.

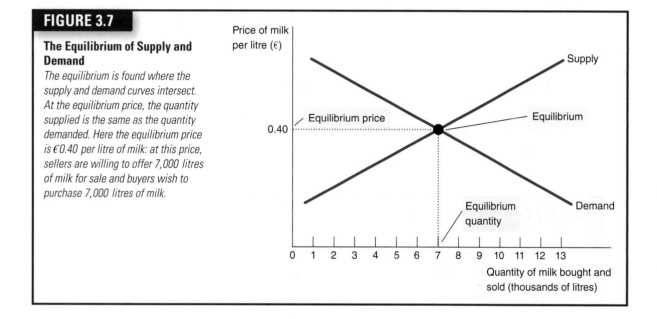

The market will remain in equilibrium until something causes either a shift in the demand curve or a shift in the supply curve (or both). If one or both curves shift, at the existing equilibrium price, there will now be either a **surplus** or a **shortage**. The market mechanism takes time to adjust – sometimes it can be very quick (which tends to happen in highly organized markets like stock and commodity markets) and sometimes it is much slower to react. When the market is in disequilibrium and a shortage or surplus exists, the behaviour of buyers and sellers act as forces on price.

surplus a situation in which the quantity supplied is greater than the quantity demanded at the going market price
shortage a situation in which quantity demanded is greater than quantity supplied at the going market price

When there is a *surplus* or *excess supply* of a good, suppliers are unable to sell all they want at the going price. Sellers find stocks of milk increasing so they respond to the surplus by cutting their prices. As the price falls, some consumers are persuaded to buy more milk and so there is a movement along the demand curve. Equally, some sellers in the market respond to the falling price by reducing the amount they are willing to offer for sale (a movement along the supply curve). Prices continue to fall until the market reaches a new equilibrium. The effect on price and the amount bought and sold depends on whether the demand curve or supply curve shifted in the first place (or whether both shifted). This is why analysis of markets is referred to as comparative statics because we are comparing one initial static equilibrium with another once market forces have worked their way through.

If the shift in demand or supply that causes the equilibrium to be disturbed creates a shortage in the market, buyers' and sellers' behaviour again 'forces' price to change to bring the market back into equilibrium. A *shortage* or situation of *excess demand* occurs where the quantity of the good demanded exceeds the quantity supplied at the going price; buyers are unable to buy all they want at that price. With too many buyers chasing too few goods, sellers can respond to the shortage by raising their prices without losing sales. As the price rises, some buyers will drop out of the market and quantity demanded falls (a movement along the demand curve). Rising prices encourage some farmers to offer more milk for sale as it is now more profitable for them to do so and the quantity supplied rises. Once again this process will continue until the market once again moves toward the equilibrium.

Thus, the activities of the many buyers and sellers 'automatically' push the market price towards the equilibrium price. Individual buyers and sellers don't consciously realize they are acting as forces for change in the market when they make their decisions but the collective act of all the many buyers and sellers does push markets towards equilibrium. This phenomenon is so pervasive that it is called the **law of supply and demand**: the price of any good adjusts to bring the quantity supplied and quantity demanded for that good into balance.

---

law of supply and demand the claim that the price of any good adjusts to bring the quantity supplied and the quantity demanded for that good into balance

---

Prices as Signals

If the government announced that there was going to be a cull of beef cattle because of some disease, if workers at major copper mines go on strike, the chances are that the price of beef and copper would rise. Markets are subject to change and changes in the factors that affect supply and demand other than price cause a shift in the curve and bring about disequilibrium. The many buyers and sellers in a market all make independent decisions which act as forces for changes in price. Why do buyers and sellers react when prices change? The reason is that price acts as a signal to both buyers and sellers.

Economists have conducted extensive research into the nature and determinants of both demand and supply. It is useful to have a little bit of background knowledge on this to help understand markets more effectively. The main function of price in a free market is to act as a signal to both buyers and sellers. For buyers, price tells them something about what they have to give up (usually an amount of money) to acquire the benefits that having the good will confer on them. These benefits are referred to as the utility or satisfaction derived from consumption. If an individual is willing to pay €10 to go and watch a movie then economists will assume that the value of the benefits gained from watching the movie is worth that amount of money to the individual. But what does this mean? How much is €10 worth? Economists would answer this question by saying that if an individual is willing to give up €10 to watch a movie then the value of the benefits gained (the utility) must be greater than the next best alternative that the €10 could have been spent on. Principles 1 and 2 of the *Ten Principles of Economics* states that people face trade-offs and that the cost of something is what you have to give up to acquire it. This is fundamental to the law of demand. At higher prices, the sacrifice being made in terms of the value of the benefits gained from alternatives is greater and so we may be less willing to do so as a result. If the price of a ticket for the movie was €15 then it might have to be a very good movie to persuade me that giving up what else €15 could buy me is worth it. Price also acts as a signal at the margin. Most consumers will recognize the agony they have experienced over making a purchasing decision. Those 'to die for' pair of shoes may be absolutely perfect but at €120 they might make the buyer think twice. If they were €100 then it might be considered a 'no brainer'. That extra €20 might make all the difference to the decision of whether to buy or not.

Economists and those in other disciplines such as psychology are increasingly investigating the complex nature of purchasing decisions that humans make. The development of magnetic resonance imaging (MRI) techniques, for example, has allowed researchers to investigate how the brain responds to different stimuli when making purchasing decisions. This increased understanding is being used by firms to persuade buyers to choose their products over rivals.

For sellers price acts as a signal in relation to the profitability of production. For most sellers, increasing the amount of a good produced will incur some additional input costs. A higher price is required in order to compensate for the additional cost and to also enable the producer to gain some reward from the risk they are taking in production. That reward is termed *profit*.

If prices are rising in a free market then this acts as a different but related signal to buyers and sellers. Rising prices to a seller means that there is a shortage and thus acts as a signal to expand production because the seller knows that s/he will be able to sell what they produce. For buyers, a rising price changes the nature of the trade-off they have to face. Rising prices act as a signal that more will have to be given up in order to acquire the good and they will have to decide whether the value of the benefits they will gain from acquiring the good is worth the extra price they have to pay and the sacrifice of the value of the benefits of the next best alternative.

For example, say the price of going to the movies increases from €10 per ticket to €15 per ticket. Some movie goers will happily pay the extra because they really enjoy a night out at the cinema but some people might start to think that €15 is a bit expensive. They might think that they could have a night out at a restaurant with friends and have a meal and a few drinks for €15 and that would represent more value to them than going to the cinema. Some of these people would, therefore, stop going to the cinema and go to a restaurant instead – the price signal to these people has changed.

What we do know is that for both buyers and sellers, there are many complex processes that occur in decision making. Whilst we do not fully understand all these processes yet, economists are constantly searching for new insights that might help them understand the workings of markets more fully. All of us go through these complex processes every time we make a purchasing decision – we may not realize it but we do! Having some appreciation of these processes is fundamental to thinking like an economist.

The Algebra of Market Equilibrium

We know that in equilibrium, demand equals supply ($D = S$). To find the market equilibrium, therefore, we set the demand and supply equations equal to each other and solve for P and Q by substitution.

Finding Market Equilibrium – The Substitution Method Take the following demand and supply equations assuming all positive quantities are greater than 20:

$$Qd = 32 - 3p$$
$$Qs = 20 + 4p$$

We know that in equilibrium:

$$Qd = Qs$$

So, equilibrium in this market will be where:

$$32 - 3p = 20 + 4p$$

This now allows us to solve for P and so find the equilibrium price:

$$32 - 3p = 20 + 4p$$

Subtract 20 from both sides and add $3p$ to both sides to get:

$$32 - 20 = 4p + 3p$$
$$12 = 7p$$
$$P = €1.71 (rounded\ to\ the\ nearest\ whole\ cent)$$

We can now substitute the equilibrium price into our two equations to find the equilibrium quantity rounded to the nearest whole number:

$$Qd = 32 - 3p$$
$$Qd = 32 - 3(1.71)$$
$$Qd = 32 - 5.13$$
$$Qd = 26.87$$
$$Qd = 27$$

As a check, follow the same process with the supply equation:

$$Qs = 20 + 4p$$
$$Qs = 20 + 4(1.71)$$
$$Qs = 20 + 4(1.71)$$
$$Qs = 26.84$$
$$Qs = 27$$

Note the figures for Qd and Qs before rounding differ slightly because we had to round the price. Now look at this example:

$$P = 3 + 0.25Qs$$
$$P = 15 - 0.75Qd$$

In this case the equations are defined in terms of price but the principle of working out equilibrium is the same as we have used above.

First, set the two equations equal to each other:

$$3 + 0.25Qs = 15 - 0.75Qd$$

Then solve for Q by adding $0.75Qd$ to both sides and then subtract 3 from both sides to get:

$$0.75Qd + 0.25Qs = 15 - 3$$
$$Q = 12$$

Substitute $Q = 12$ into one of the equations to find P.

$$P = 3 + 0.25Qs$$
$$P = 3 + 0.25(12)$$
$$P = 6$$

To check, also substitute into the demand equation:

$$P = 15 - 0.75Qd$$
$$P = 15 - 0.75(12)$$
$$P = 15 - 9$$
$$P = 6$$

Finding Market Equilibrium – The Elimination Method There is another way to find both the quantity and the price and that is through adopting the approach of solving simultaneous equations. Simultaneous equations require us to find two or more unknowns. In our case the two unknowns are price and quantity.

Look at the following two equations:

$$Qd = 20 - 2p$$
$$Qs = 2 + 2p$$

In this case, the terms are all neatly aligned above each other so it is a relatively simple task to add the two together. Note that we are trying to find equilibrium so $Qd = Qs$, thus the value of Q is the same. Adding the two together we get:

$$Qd = 20 - 2p$$
$$Qs = 2 + 2p$$
$$2Q = 22$$
$$Q = 11$$

Notice that in the above equations we have a very convenient fact that the coefficient of p in each case is the same but with opposite signs. This makes this example very easy to eliminate p to isolate the Q value. This is not always the case, however, but it is important to remember that having two equal values with opposite signs allows us to get rid of them! We will come back to this later.

We can now use the fact that we know Q to find the equilibrium price by substituting Q into one of the equations thus:

$$Qd = 20 - 2p$$
$$11 = 20 - 2p$$
$$2p = 20 - 11$$
$$2p = 9$$
$$p = 4.5$$

It is always worth checking your answer to make sure you have made no mistakes along the way so in this case we will substitute our known value of Q into the second equation to check we get the same answer ($p = 4.5$). So:

$$Qs = 2 + 2p$$
$$11 = 2 + 2p$$
$$11 - 2 = 2p$$
$$9 = 2p$$
$$p = 4.5$$

Sometimes we may have equations where the p and Q values are both on the same side of the equation. In this case we have to use a different technique – the elimination method.

Take the following two equations:

$$-3p + 4Q = 5 \tag{1}$$
$$2p - 5Q = -15 \tag{2}$$

We have labelled these two equations (1) and (2) to allow us to keep track of what we are doing and reduce the risk of making an error.

Remember above when we noted the fact that having a nice convenient equation where the coefficient was equal but the signs were opposite, enabling us to be able to eliminate one of the values to help solve the equation for the other unknown? That is what we need to do with these two equations. We have to choose to manipulate the two equations to make either the 'p' terms or the 'Q' terms have the same coefficient but opposite signs. A knowledge of factors and lowest common denominators is useful here.

In this example we are going to manipulate the equations to get rid of the 'p' terms. This allows us to isolate the 'Q' terms and thus solve for Q and then find p.

This is how we do this:

$$-3p + 4Q = 5 \qquad (1)$$
$$2p - 5Q = -15 \qquad (2)$$

To eliminate p, multiply (1) by 2 and (2) by 3

$$-6p + 8Q = 10 \qquad (3)$$
$$6p - 15Q = -45 \qquad (4)$$

Add together (3) and (4)

$$-6p + 8Q = 10 \qquad (3)$$
$$6p - 15Q = -45 \qquad (4)$$
$$-7Q = -35$$

Divide both sides by -7

$$Q = 5$$

We can now substitute Q into equations (1) and (2) to find (and check) p
If $Q = 5$ then:

$$-3p + 4(5) = 5$$
$$-3p + 20 = 5$$
$$20 - 5 = 3p$$
$$15 = 3p$$
$$p = 5$$

As a check:

$$2p - 5(5) = -15$$
$$2p - 25 = -15$$
$$2p = -15 + 25$$
$$2p = 10$$
$$p = 5$$

In this example the equilibrium price is €5 and the equilibrium quantity is 5.

Three Steps to Analysing Changes in Equilibrium

So far we have seen how supply and demand together determine a market's equilibrium, which in turn determines the price of the good and the amount of the good that buyers purchase and sellers produce. Of course, the equilibrium price and quantity depend on the position of the supply and demand curves. We use comparative static analysis to look at what happens when some event shifts one of these curves and causes the equilibrium in the market to change.

To do this we proceed in three steps:

1. We decide whether the event in question shifts the supply curve, the demand curve or, in some cases, both curves.
2. We decide whether the curve shifts to the right or to the left.
3. We use the supply and demand diagram to compare the initial and the new equilibrium, which shows how the shift affects the equilibrium price and quantity.

Remember that the process by which equilibrium changes is not instantaneous – some markets will take longer to adjust to changes than others. To see how these three steps work in analysing market changes, let's consider various events that might affect the market for milk. We begin the analysis by assuming that the market for milk is in equilibrium with the price of milk at €0.50 per litre and 13,000 litres are bought and sold and then follow our three-step approach.

Example: A Change in Demand Suppose that one summer the weather is very hot. How does this event affect the market for milk? To answer this question, let's follow our three steps:

1. The hot weather affects the demand curve by changing peoples' taste for milk. That is, the weather changes the amount of milk that people want to buy at any given price.
2. Because hot weather makes people want to drink more milk, make refreshing milk shakes or producers of ice cream buy more milk to make ice cream, the demand curve shifts to the right. Figure 3.8 shows this increase in demand as the shift in the demand curve from D_1 to D_2. (What you have to remember now is that demand curve D_1 does not exist anymore and so we have shown it as a dashed line.) This shift indicates that the quantity of milk demanded is higher at every price. At the existing market price of €0.50 buyers now want to buy 19,000 litres of milk but sellers are only offering 13,000 litres for sale at this price. The shift in demand has led to a shortage of milk in the market of 6,000 litres represented by the bracket.
3. The shortage encourages producers to increase the output of milk (a movement along the supply curve). There is an *increase in quantity supplied*. But, the additional production incurs extra costs and so a higher price is required to compensate sellers. As sellers increase the amount of milk offered for sale as price rises. Consumers behave differently. Some consumers who were willing to buy milk at €0.50 are not willing to pay more and so drop out of the market. As price creeps up, therefore, there is a movement along the demand curve representing these consumers who drop out of the market. The market forces of supply and demand continue to work through until a new equilibrium is reached. The new equilibrium price is now €0.60 per litre and the equilibrium quantity bought and sold is now 16,000 litres. To compare our starting and finishing positions, the hot weather which caused the shift in the demand curve has led to an increase in the price of milk and the quantity of milk bought and sold.

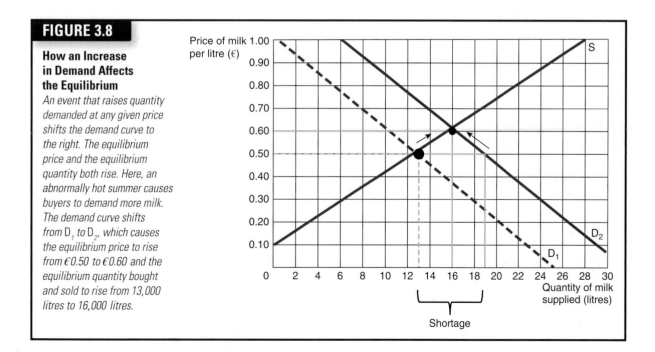

FIGURE 3.8

How an Increase in Demand Affects the Equilibrium
An event that raises quantity demanded at any given price shifts the demand curve to the right. The equilibrium price and the equilibrium quantity both rise. Here, an abnormally hot summer causes buyers to demand more milk. The demand curve shifts from D₁ to D₂, which causes the equilibrium price to rise from €0.50 to €0.60 and the equilibrium quantity bought and sold to rise from 13,000 litres to 16,000 litres.

Example: A Change in Supply Suppose that, during another summer, a drought drives up the price of animal feed for dairy cattle. How does this event affect the market for milk? Once again, to answer this question, we follow our three steps:

1. The change in the price of animal feed, an input into producing milk, affects the supply curve. By raising the costs of production, it reduces the amount of milk that firms produce and sell at any given price. Some farmers may send cattle for slaughter because they cannot afford to feed them anymore and some farmers may simply decide to sell up and get out of farming altogether. The demand curve does not change because the higher cost of inputs does not directly affect the amount of milk consumers wish to buy.

2. The supply curve shifts to the left because, at every price, the total amount that farmers are willing and able to sell is reduced. Figure 3.9 illustrates this decrease in supply as a shift in the supply curve from S_1 to S_2. At a price of €0.50 sellers are now only able to offer 2,000 litres of milk for sale but demand is still 13,000 litres. The shift in supply to the left has created a shortage in the market of 11,000 litres. Once again, the shortage will create pressure on price to rise as buyers look to purchase milk.

3. As Figure 3.9 shows, the shortage raises the equilibrium price from €0.50 to €0.70 per litre and lowers the equilibrium quantity bought and sold from 13,000 to 8,000 litres. As a result of the animal feed price increase, the price of milk rises, and the quantity of milk bought and sold falls.

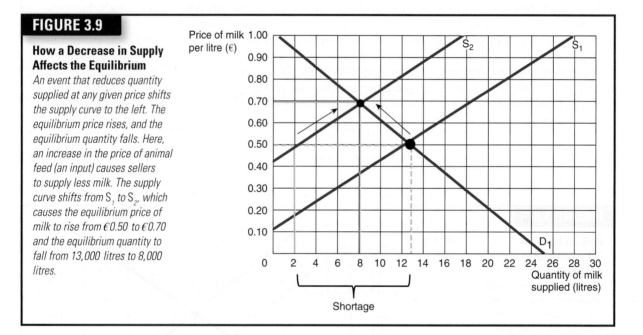

FIGURE 3.9

How a Decrease in Supply Affects the Equilibrium

An event that reduces quantity supplied at any given price shifts the supply curve to the left. The equilibrium price rises, and the equilibrium quantity falls. Here, an increase in the price of animal feed (an input) causes sellers to supply less milk. The supply curve shifts from S₁ to S₂, which causes the equilibrium price of milk to rise from €0.50 to €0.70 and the equilibrium quantity to fall from 13,000 litres to 8,000 litres.

Example: A Change in Both Supply and Demand (i) Now suppose that the hot weather and the rise in animal feed occur during the same time period. To analyse this combination of events, we again follow our three steps:

1. We determine that both curves must shift. The hot weather affects the demand curve for milk because it alter the amount that consumers want to buy at any given price. At the same time, when the rise in animal feed drives up input prices, it alters the supply curve for milk because they change the amount that firms want to sell at any given price.

2. The curves shift in the same directions as they did in our previous analysis: the demand curve shifts to the right, and the supply curve shifts to the left. Figure 3.10 illustrates these shifts.

3. As Figure 3.10 shows, there are two possible outcomes that might result, depending on the relative size of the demand and supply shifts. In both cases, the equilibrium price rises. In panel (a), where demand increases substantially while supply falls just a little, the equilibrium quantity also rises.

By contrast, in panel (b), where supply falls substantially while demand rises just a little, the equilibrium quantity falls. Thus, these events certainly raise the price of milk, but their impact on the amount of milk bought and sold is ambiguous (that is, it could go either way).

FIGURE 3.10

A Shift in Both Supply and Demand (i)

Here we observe a simultaneous increase in demand and decrease in supply. Two outcomes are possible. In panel (a), the equilibrium price rises from P_1 to P_2, and the equilibrium quantity rises from Q_1 to Q_2. In panel (b), the equilibrium price again rises from P_1 to P_2, but the equilibrium quantity falls from Q_1 to Q_2.

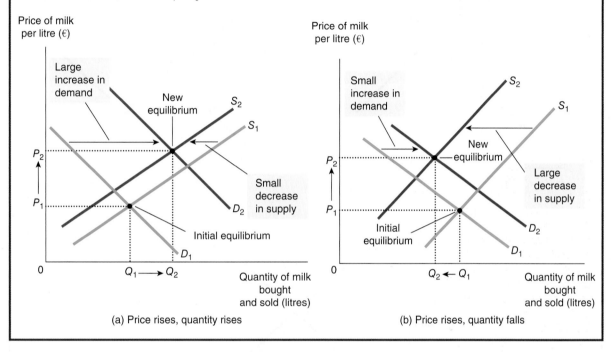

(a) Price rises, quantity rises

(b) Price rises, quantity falls

Example: A Change in Both Supply and Demand (ii) We are now going to look at a slightly different scenario but with both supply and demand changing together. Assume that forecasters have predicted a heatwave for some weeks. We know that the hot weather is likely to increase demand for milk and so the demand curve will shift to the right. However, sellers' expectations that sales of milk will increase as a result of the forecasts mean that they take steps to expand production of milk. This would lead to a shift of the supply curve to the right – more milk is now offered for sale at every price. To analyse this particular combination of events, we again follow our three steps:

1. We determine that both curves must shift. The hot weather affects the demand curve because it alters the amount of milk that consumers want to buy at any given price. At the same time, the expectations of producers alter the supply curve for milk because they change the amount that firms want to sell at any given price.
2. Both demand and supply curves shift to the right: Figure 3.11 illustrates these shifts.
3. As Figure 3.11 shows, there are three possible outcomes that might result, depending on the relative size of the demand and supply shifts. In panel (a), where demand increases substantially while supply rises just a little, the equilibrium price and quantity rises. By contrast, in panel (b), where supply rises substantially while demand rises just a little, the equilibrium price falls but the equilibrium quantity rises. In panel (c) the increases in demand and supply are identical and so equilibrium price does not change. Equilibrium quantity will increase, however. Thus, these events have different effects on the price of milk although the amount bought and sold in each case is higher. In this instance the effect on price is ambiguous.

FIGURE 3.11

A Shift in Both Supply and Demand (ii)

Here, again, we observe a simultaneous increase in demand and supply. Here, three outcomes are possible. In panel (a) the equilibrium price rises from P_1 to P_2 and the equilibrium quantity rises from Q_1 to Q_2. In panel (b), the equilibrium price falls from P_1 to P_2 but the equilibrium quantity rises from Q_1 to Q_2. In panel (c), there is no change to the equilibrium price but the equilibrium quantity rises from Q_1 to Q_2.

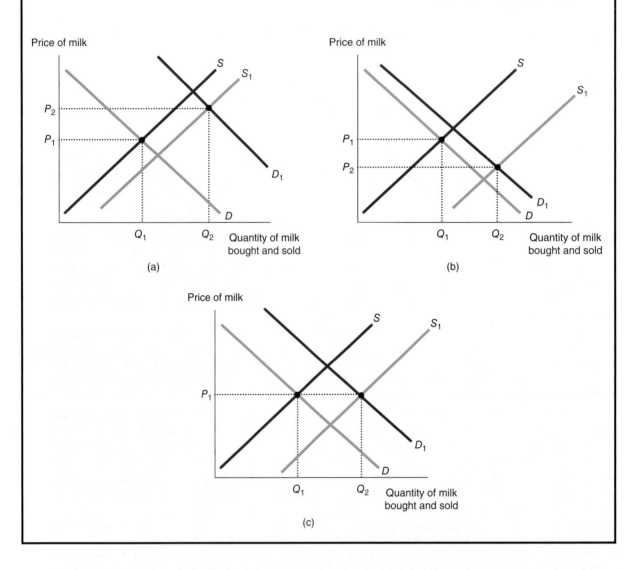

Summary We have just seen four examples of how to use demand and supply curves to analyse a change in equilibrium. Whenever an event shifts the demand curve, the supply curve, or perhaps both curves, you can use these tools to predict how the event will alter the amount bought and sold in equilibrium and the price at which the good is bought and sold. Table 3.3 shows the predicted outcome for any combination of shifts in the two curves. To make sure you understand how to use the tools of supply and demand, pick a few entries in this table and make sure you can explain to yourself why the table contains the prediction it does.

TABLE 3.3	**What Happens to Price and Quantity When Demand or Supply Shifts?**

As a test, make sure you can explain each of the entries in this table using a supply and demand diagram.

	No change in supply	An increase in supply	A decrease in supply
No change in demand	P same	P down	P up
	Q same	Q up	Q down
An increase in demand	P up	P ambiguous	P up
	Q up	Q up	Q ambiguous
A decrease in demand	P down	P down	P ambiguous
	Q down	Q ambiguous	Q down

CONCLUSION: HOW PRICES ALLOCATE RESOURCES

This chapter has analysed demand and supply in a single market. Although our discussion has centred on the market for milk, the lessons learned here apply in most other markets as well. Whenever you go to a shop to buy something, you are contributing to the demand for that item. Whenever you look for a job, you are contributing to the supply of labour services. Because demand and supply are such pervasive economic phenomena, the model of demand and supply is a powerful tool for analysis. We shall be using this model repeatedly in the following chapters. One of the *Ten Principles of Economics* discussed in Chapter 1 is that markets are usually a good way to organize economic activity. Although it is still too early to judge whether market outcomes are good or bad, in this chapter we have begun to see how markets work. In any economic system, scarce resources have to be allocated among competing uses. Market economies harness the forces of demand and supply to serve that end. Demand and supply together determine the prices of the economy's many different goods and services; prices in turn are the signals that guide the allocation of resources.

For example, consider the allocation of property on the beach. Because the amount of this property is limited, not everyone can enjoy the luxury of living by the beach. Who gets this resource? The answer is: whoever is willing and able to pay the price. The price of seafront property adjusts until the quantity of property demanded exactly balances the quantity supplied. Thus, in market economies, prices are the mechanism for rationing scarce resources.

Similarly, prices determine who produces each good and how much is produced. For instance, consider farming. Because we need food to survive, it is crucial that some people work on farms. What determines who is a farmer and who is not? In a free society, there is no government planning agency making this decision and ensuring an adequate supply of food. Instead, the allocation of workers to farms is based on the job decisions of millions of workers. This decentralized system works well because these decisions depend on prices. The prices of food and the wages of farm workers (the price of their labour) adjust to ensure that enough people choose to be farmers.

If a person had never seen a market economy in action, the whole idea might seem preposterous. Economies are large groups of people engaged in many interdependent activities. What prevents decentralized decision making from degenerating into chaos? What coordinates the actions of the millions of people with their varying abilities and desires? What ensures that what needs to get done does in fact get done? The answer, in a word, is *prices.* If market economies are guided by an invisible hand, as Adam Smith famously suggested, then prices are the baton that the invisible hand uses to conduct the economic orchestra.

SELF TEST Analyse what happens to the market for pizza if the price of tomatoes rises. Analyse what happens to the market for pasta if the price of potatoes falls.

IN THE NEWS

Markets in Action

We have seen how we can use supply and demand analysis to begin to understand markets. The real world has examples of markets in action every day. This article highlights an example of markets in action.

The Market for Cotton

Cotton is a commodity – a tradable product – which is used in textiles and clothing manufacture in particular, but is also used in the production of other products such as nets and filters. There are different qualities of cotton but it is reasonably homogenous. There are around 90 countries in the world that produce cotton but the United States, China and India account for around half the world's supply. There are thousands of cotton farmers and large numbers of buyers, and cotton is traded on organized commodity markets to bring together buyers and sellers of cotton.

Changes in the price of cotton present an excellent way to see how markets work in real life. The price of cotton responds to the changes in demand for the commodity and to changes in supply. The supply of cotton can be dependent on factors such as the weather but also on the expectations of farmers about the future price of cotton which may influence how much land they devote to planting cotton.

What might account for these changes in prices? One of the main reasons was changes in the supply of cotton. In the years to 2010, cotton growers had faced increasing challenges making cotton farming profitable. The amount of land given over to growing cotton had declined and so supplies of cotton had been relatively low. In 2010, the weather also played a part in damaging crops and as a result there was a shortage of cotton and this accounted for the rise in price up to March 2011. How might

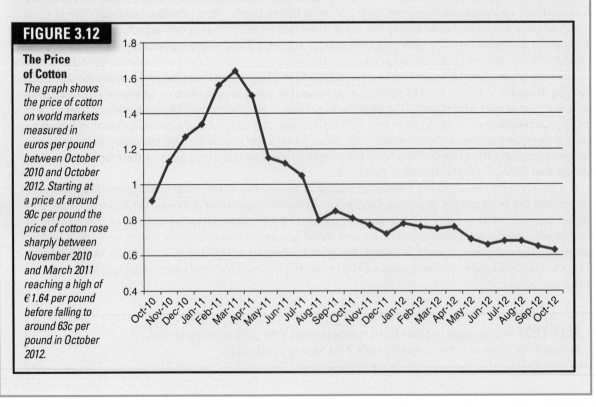

FIGURE 3.12

The Price of Cotton
The graph shows the price of cotton on world markets measured in euros per pound between October 2010 and October 2012. Starting at a price of around 90c per pound the price of cotton rose sharply between November 2010 and March 2011 reaching a high of €1.64 per pound before falling to around 63c per pound in October 2012.

farmers respond to the increased price? For some farmers it will now be worthwhile them planting cotton if the price they get is around €1.50–€1.60 per pound. Each farmer has to make an individual decision about whether to grow cotton but if there are large numbers of farmers across the world all making a decision to devote more land to cotton the result is going to be more cotton supplied.

A look at cotton stocks shows that between 2006 and 2009 world cotton stocks remained fairly stable at around 60 million bales. In 2010 stocks dropped to around 48 million bales. Since that time, however, stocks have risen again

and forecasters were predicting that world cotton stocks would reach around 76 million bales in 2013.

The increase in the supply of cotton has led to prices falling and those in the industry were not predicting any fundamental changes in either supply or demand over the next two years. Of course, no-one can say for sure that prices will remain stable at around 60c per pound. Some of the estimates for future stocks of cotton were based on existing acreage levels devoted to cotton and also on the assumption that nothing would happen to cause cotton harvests to change dramatically. Cotton is a crop, however, and is subject to pests

and diseases and the vagaries of the weather. No-one can tell whether the 2013 or 2014 crops might be affected by drought or flood.

Questions

1. To what extent would you say that the market for cotton was an example of perfect competition? Explain.
2. What makes up the market for cotton?
3. What signal did price send to cotton growers following the rise in cotton prices in the first quarter of 2011? How might farmers respond to this signal and what effect might this have on the future price of cotton? Explain your answer using appropriate demand and supply diagrams.
4. In the article, the principle of *ceteris paribus* was implied; what do you think was assumed to be held constant? Is this a reasonable assumption to make in this instance? Explain.
5. If data are collected which suggests that the amount of land in cotton-growing regions of the world devoted to cotton does not change significantly in the next five years, how useful is the model of demand and supply in predicting price changes in the cotton market in the future? Explain.

Changes in the price of cotton presents an excellent way to see how markets work in real life. The price of cotton responds to the changes in demand for the commodity and to changes in supply.

SUMMARY

- Economists use the model of supply and demand to analyse competitive markets. In a competitive market, there are many buyers and sellers, each of whom has little or no influence on the market price.
- The demand curve shows how the quantity of a good demanded depends on the price. According to the law of demand, as the price of a good falls, the quantity

demanded rises. Therefore, the demand curve slopes downwards.

- In addition to price, other determinants of how much consumers want to buy include income, the prices of substitutes and complements, tastes, expectations, the size and structure of the population and advertising. If one of these factors changes, the demand curve shifts.

The supply curve shows how the quantity of a good supplied depends on the price. According to the law of supply, as the price of a good rises the quantity supplied rises. Therefore, the supply curve slopes upwards.

- In addition to price, other determinants of how much producers want to sell include the price and profitability of goods in production and joint supply, input prices, technology, expectations, the number of sellers and natural and social factors. If one of these factors changes, the supply curve shifts.

- The intersection of the supply and demand curves determines the market equilibrium. At the equilibrium price, the quantity demanded equals the quantity supplied.

- The behaviour of buyers and sellers naturally drives markets towards their equilibrium. When the market price is above the equilibrium price, there is a surplus of the good, which causes the market price to fall. When the market price is below the equilibrium price, there is a shortage, which causes the market price to rise.

- To analyse how any event influences a market, we use the supply and demand diagram to examine how the event affects the equilibrium price and quantity. To do this we follow three steps. First, we decide whether the event shifts the supply curve or the demand curve (or both). Second, we decide which direction the curve shifts. Third, we compare the new equilibrium with the initial equilibrium.

- In market economies, prices are the signals that guide economic decisions and thereby allocate scarce resources. For every good in the economy, the price ensures that supply and demand are in balance. The equilibrium price then determines how much of the good buyers choose to purchase and how much sellers choose to produce.

QUESTIONS FOR REVIEW

1 What is a competitive market? Briefly describe the types of markets other than perfectly competitive markets.

2 What determines the quantity of a good that buyers demand?

3 What are the demand schedule and the demand curve, and how are they related? Why does the demand curve slope downwards?

4 Does a change in consumers' tastes lead to a movement along the demand curve or a shift in the demand curve? Does a change in price lead to a movement along the demand curve or a shift in the demand curve?

5 Francine's income declines and, as a result, she buys more cabbage. Are cabbages an inferior or a normal good? What happens to Francine's demand curve for cabbages?

6 What determines the quantity of a good that sellers supply?

7 What are the supply schedule and the supply curve, and how are they related? Why does the supply curve slope upwards?

8 Does a change in producers' technology lead to a movement along the supply curve or a shift in the supply curve? Does a change in price lead to a movement along the supply curve or a shift in the supply curve?

9 Define the equilibrium of a market. Describe the forces that move a market toward its equilibrium.

10 Describe the role of prices in market economies.

PROBLEMS AND APPLICATIONS

1 Explain each of the following statements using supply and demand diagrams.

  a. When there is a drought in southern Europe, the price of soft fruit rises in supermarkets throughout Europe.

  b. When a report is published linking a product with an increased risk of cancer, the price of the product concerned tends to fall.

  c. When conflict breaks out in the Middle East, the price of petrol in Europe rises and the price of a used Mercedes falls.

2 'An increase in the demand for mozzarella cheese raises the quantity of mozzarella demanded, but not the quantity supplied.' Is this statement true or false? Explain.

3 Technological advances have reduced the cost of producing mobile phones. How do you think this affected the market for mobile phones? For software used on mobile phones? For landlines?

4 Using supply and demand diagrams, show the effect of the following events on the market for sweatshirts.

  a. A drought in Egypt damages the cotton crop.

  b. The price of leather jackets falls.

c. All universities require students to attend morning exercise classes in appropriate attire.

d. New knitting machines are invented.

5 Suppose that in the year 2005 the number of births is temporarily high. How might this baby boom affect the price of baby-sitting services in 2010 and 2020? (Hint: 5-year-olds need babysitters, whereas 15-year-olds can be babysitters.)

6 Think about the market for cigars.

a. Are cigars substitutes or complements for cigarettes?

b. Using a supply and demand diagram, show what happens in the markets for cigars if the tax on cigarettes is increased.

c. If policymakers wanted to reduce total tobacco consumption, what policies could they combine with the cigarette tax?

7 The market for pizza has the following demand and supply schedules:

Price	Quantity demanded	Quantity supplied
€4	135	26
5	104	53
6	81	81
7	68	98
8	53	110
9	39	121

Graph the demand and supply curves. What is the equilibrium price and quantity in this market? If the actual price in this market were above the equilibrium price, what would drive the market towards the equilibrium? If the actual price in this market were below the equilibrium price, what would drive the market towards the equilibrium?

8 Because bacon and eggs are often eaten together, they are complements.

a. We observe that both the equilibrium price of eggs and the equilibrium quantity of bacon have risen. What could be responsible for this pattern – a fall in the price of chicken feed or a fall in the price of pig feed? Illustrate and explain your answer.

b. Suppose instead that the equilibrium price of bacon has risen but the equilibrium quantity of eggs has fallen. What could be responsible for this pattern – a rise in the price of chicken feed or a rise in the price of pig feed? Illustrate and explain your answer.

9 Suppose that the price of tickets to see your local football team play at home is determined by market forces. Currently, the demand and supply schedules are as follows:

Price	Quantity demanded	Quantity supplied
€10	50,000	30,000
20	40,000	30,000
30	30,000	30,000
40	20,000	30,000
50	10,000	30,000

a. Draw the demand and supply curves. What is unusual about this supply curve? Why might this be true?

b. What are the equilibrium price and quantity of tickets?

c. Your team plans to increase total capacity in its stadium by 5,000 seats next season. What admission price should it charge?

10 Market research has revealed the following information about the market for chocolate bars: $Qd = 1,600 - 300p$, and the supply schedule is $Qs = 1,400 + 700p$. Calculate the equilibrium price and quantity in the market for chocolate bars.

PART 3
THE DATA OF MACROECONOMICS

4

MEASURING A NATION'S INCOME

When you finish university and start looking for a full-time job, your experience will, to a large extent, be shaped by prevailing economic conditions. In some years, firms throughout the economy are expanding their production of goods and services, employment is rising, and jobs are relatively easy to find. In other years, firms are cutting back on production, employment is declining, and finding a good job takes a long time. Not surprisingly, any university graduate would rather enter the labour force in a year of economic expansion than in a year of economic contraction.

Because the condition of the overall economy profoundly affects all of us, changes in economic conditions are widely reported by the media. Indeed, it is hard to pick up a newspaper without seeing some newly reported statistic about the economy. The statistic might measure the total income of everyone in the economy called gross domestic product (GDP), the rate at which average prices are rising (inflation), the percentage of the labour force that is out of work (unemployment), total spending in shops (retail sales), or the imbalance of trade between the domestic economy and the rest of the world (the trade deficit). All these statistics are *macroeconomic*. Rather than telling us about a particular household or firm, they tell us something about the entire economy.

Economics is divided into two branches: microeconomics and macroeconomics. Microeconomics is the study of how individual households and firms make decisions and how they interact with one another in markets. Macroeconomics is the study of the economy as a whole. The goal of macroeconomics is to explain the economic changes that affect many households, firms and markets simultaneously. Macroeconomists address diverse questions: why is average income high in some countries while it is low in others? Why do prices rise rapidly in some periods of time while they are more stable in other periods? Why do production and employment expand in some years and contract in others? What, if anything, can the government do to promote rapid growth in incomes, low inflation and stable employment? These questions are all macroeconomic in nature because they concern the workings of the entire economy.

Because the economy as a whole is just a collection of many households and many firms interacting in many markets, microeconomics and macroeconomics are closely linked. The basic tools of supply and demand, for instance, are as central to macroeconomic analysis as they are to microeconomic analysis. Yet studying the economy in its entirety raises some new and intriguing challenges.

In this chapter and the next one, we discuss some of the data that economists and policymakers use to monitor the performance of the overall economy. These data reflect the economic changes that macroeconomists try to explain. This chapter considers *gross domestic product,* or simply GDP, which measures the total income of a nation. GDP is the most closely watched economic statistic because it is thought to be the best single (although not perfect) measure of a society's economic well-being.

THE ECONOMY'S INCOME AND EXPENDITURE

If you were to judge how a person is doing economically, you might first look at his or her income. A person with a high income can more easily afford life's necessities and luxuries. It is no surprise that people with higher incomes enjoy higher standards of living – better housing, better health care, fancier cars, more opulent vacations and so on.

The same logic applies to a nation's overall economy. When judging whether the economy is doing well or poorly, it is natural to look at the total income that everyone in the economy is earning. This is the task of gross domestic product (GDP).

GDP measures two things at once: the total income of everyone in the economy and the total expenditure on the economy's output of goods and services. The reason that GDP can perform the trick of measuring both total income and total expenditure is that these two things are really the same. For an economy as a whole, income must equal expenditure.

Why is this true? An economy's income is the same as its expenditure because every transaction has two parties: a buyer and a seller. Every euro of spending by some buyer is a euro of income for some seller. Suppose, for instance, that Michael pays Astrid €20 to clean the windows at his house. In this case, Astrid is a seller of a service and Michael is a buyer. Astrid earns an income of €20 and Michael spends €20. Thus, the transaction contributes equally to the economy's income and to its expenditure. GDP, whether measured as total income or total expenditure, rises by €20.

Another way to see the equality of income and expenditure is with the circular-flow diagram in Figure 4.1. We presented a simple circular-flow diagram in Chapter 2 but this one includes some additional information. You may remember that this is a model which describes all the transactions between households and firms in a simple economy. In this economy, households buy goods and services from firms; these expenditures flow through the markets for goods and services. The firms in turn use the money they receive from sales to pay workers' wages, landowners' rent and firm owners' profit; this income flows through the markets for the factors of production. In this economy, money flows from households to firms and then back to households. The additional information in this circular flow diagram covers what are termed leakages and injections from and into the circular flow.

When households receive income some of this income is subject to tax. Some households will not spend all the income they receive, some of it is saved and the funds find their way into financial institutions in the form of pension saving, insurance and assurance, and saving in bank accounts. Some of the income spent on goods and services by households leaves the economy in the form of spending on imports. Similarly, some of the income received by firms is paid to the government in business taxes. Taxes (*T*), saving (*S*) and spending on imports (*M*) are leakages to the circular flow.

Governments use the funds received in tax revenue and borrowing from financial institutions to spend on government services and investment on infrastructure, education, health, defence and so on. Firms also make use of the funds provided by savers in financial institutions by borrowing to finance investment spending on new plant, equipment and expansion. This investment finds its way back into the market for goods and services. Firms will also sell some of the goods and services they produce abroad and so the revenue from exports flows back into the system. Financial institutions also lend money overseas and firms overseas invest money into the country which is recorded as net capital outflow.

The injections to the circular flow, therefore, are government spending (*G*), investment spending (*I*) and revenue from exports (*X*). We can compute GDP for this economy by adding the sum of consumer spending, government spending, investment spending and the difference between the amount paid out in imports and that received in exports (net exports). Regardless of whether a household, government or firm buys a good or service, the transaction has a buyer and seller. Thus, for the economy as a whole, expenditure and income are always the same.

FIGURE 4.1

The Circular-Flow Diagram

Households buy goods and services from firms, and firms use their revenue from sales to pay wages to workers, rent to landowners and profit to firm owners. GDP equals the total amount spent by households in the market for goods and services. It also equals the total wages, rent and profit paid by firms in the markets for the factors of production. Leakages to the circular flow include taxes, savings and spending on imports whereas injections to the circular flow include government spending, investment and revenue generated from exports.

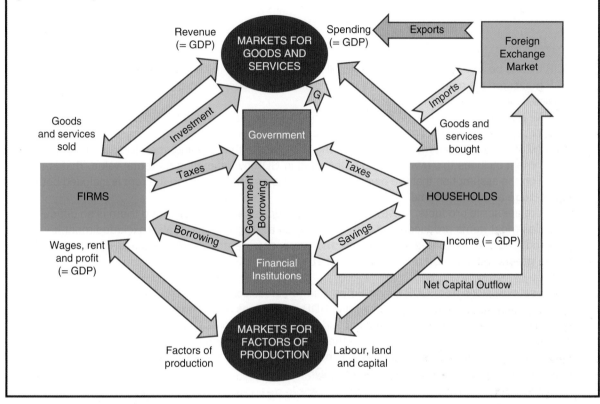

SELF TEST What two things do gross domestic product measure? How can it measure two things at once?

THE MEASUREMENT OF GROSS DOMESTIC PRODUCT

Now that we have discussed the meaning of gross domestic product in general terms, let's be more precise about how this statistic is measured. Here is a definition of GDP:

● **Gross domestic product (GDP)** is the market value of all final goods and services produced within a country in a given period of time.

> **gross domestic product (GDP)** the market value of all final goods and services produced within a country in a given period of time

This definition might seem simple enough. But, in fact, many subtle issues arise when computing an economy's GDP. Let's therefore consider each phrase in this definition with some care.

'GDP Is the Market Value ...'

You have probably heard the adage, 'You can't compare apples and oranges.' Yet GDP does exactly that. GDP adds together many different kinds of products into a single measure of the value of economic activity. To do this, it uses market prices. Because market prices measure the amount people are willing to pay for different goods, they reflect the value of those goods. If the price of an apple is twice the price of an orange, then an apple contributes twice as much to GDP as does an orange.

'... Of All ...'

GDP tries to be comprehensive. It includes all items produced in the economy and sold legally in markets. GDP measures the market value of not just apples and oranges, but also pears and grapefruit, books and movies, haircuts and health care, and so on.

GDP also includes the market value of the housing services provided by the economy's stock of housing. For rental housing, this value is easy to calculate – the rent equals both the tenant's expenditure and the landlord's income. Yet many people own the place where they live and, therefore, do not pay rent. The government includes this owner-occupied housing in GDP by estimating its rental value. That is, GDP is based on the assumption that the owner, in effect, pays rent to himself, so the rent is included both in his expenditure and in his income.

There are some products, however, that GDP excludes because measuring them is so difficult. GDP excludes most items produced and sold illicitly, such as illegal drugs. It also excludes most items that are produced and consumed at home and, therefore, never enter the marketplace. Vegetables you buy at the greengrocer's shop or the supermarket are part of GDP; vegetables you grow in your garden are not.

These exclusions from GDP can at times lead to paradoxical results. The value of work carried out by housewives and husbands is not included in GDP calculations and neither is the value of child care work carried out by grandparents, for example. In addition, when Eva pays Didi to wash her car, that transaction is part of GDP. If Eva were to marry Didi, the situation would change. Even though Didi may continue to wash Eva's car, the value of the car wash is now left out of GDP because Didi's service is no longer sold in a market. Thus, when Eva and Didi marry, GDP falls.

'... Final ...'

When a paper company sells paper to a greetings card company, the paper is called an *intermediate good*, and the card is called a *final good*. GDP includes only the value of final goods. The reason is that the value of intermediate goods is already included in the prices of the final goods. Adding the market value of the paper to the market value of the card would be double counting. That is, it would (incorrectly) count the paper twice.

An important exception to this principle arises when an intermediate good is produced and, rather than being used, is added to a firm's inventory of goods to be used or sold at a later date. In this case, the intermediate good is taken to be 'final' for the moment, and its value as inventory investment is added to GDP. When the inventory of the intermediate good is later used or sold, the firm's inventory investment is negative, and GDP for the later period is reduced accordingly.

'... Goods and Services ...'

GDP includes both tangible goods (food, clothing, cars) and intangible services (haircuts, house cleaning, doctor's visits). When you (legally) download an album by your favourite band, you are buying a good, and the purchase price is part of GDP. When you pay to hear a concert by the same band, you are buying a service, and the ticket price is also part of GDP.

'... Produced ...'

GDP includes goods and services currently produced. It does not include transactions involving items produced in the past. When Aston Martin produces and sells a new car, the value of the car is included in the GDP of the country in which Aston Martin operates. When one person sells a used car to another person, the value of the used car is not included in GDP.

'... Within a Country ...'

GDP measures the value of production within the geographic confines of a country. When an Australian citizen works temporarily in the United Kingdom, his production is part of UK GDP. When a UK citizen owns a factory in Bulgaria, the production at his factory is not part of UK GDP (it's part of Bulgaria's GDP). Thus, items are included in a nation's GDP if they are produced domestically, regardless of the nationality of the producer.

'... In a Given Period of Time'

GDP measures the value of production that takes place within a specific interval of time. Usually that interval is a year or a quarter (three months). GDP measures the economy's flow of income and expenditure during that interval.

When the government reports the GDP for a quarter, it usually presents GDP 'at an annual rate'. This means that the figure reported for quarterly GDP is the amount of income and expenditure during the quarter multiplied by 4. The government uses this convention so that quarterly and annual figures on GDP can be compared more easily.

In addition, when the government reports quarterly GDP, it presents the data after they have been modified by a statistical procedure called *seasonal adjustment.* The unadjusted data show clearly that the economy produces more goods and services during some times of year than during others. (As you might guess, December's holiday shopping season is a high point in many countries whilst the period before Ramadan is a high point for many Muslim countries.) When monitoring the condition of the economy, economists and policymakers often want to look beyond these regular seasonal changes. Therefore, government statisticians adjust the quarterly data to take out the seasonal cycle. The GDP data reported in the news are always seasonally adjusted.

Now let's repeat the definition of GDP:

● Gross domestic product (GDP) is the market value of all final goods and services produced within a country in a given period of time.

It should be apparent that GDP is a sophisticated measure of the value of economic activity. In advanced courses in macroeconomics you will learn more about the subtleties that arise in its calculation. But even now you can see that each phrase in this definition is packed with meaning.

SELF TEST Which contributes more to GDP – the production of €1 of tin or the production of €1 of gold? Why?

THE COMPONENTS OF GDP

Spending in the economy takes many forms. At any moment, the Müller family may be having lunch in a Munich restaurant; Honda may be building a car factory on the banks of the Rhine and the German Army may be procuring weapons from German arms manufacturers. German GDP includes all of these various forms of spending on domestically produced goods and services. Similarly, each country in Europe will monitor the forms of spending and income to arrive at the GDP for that country.

FYI

Other Measures of Income

When the Office for National Statistics (ONS) or Eurostat computes the GDP every three months for the UK and the EU respectively, they also compute various other measures of income to arrive at a more complete picture of what's happening in the economy. These other measures differ from GDP by excluding or including certain categories of income. What follows is a brief description of five of these income measures, ordered from largest to smallest, based on the UK.

- **Gross national product** (GNP) is the total income earned by a nation's permanent residents (called nationals). It differs from GDP by including income that domestic citizens earn abroad and excluding income that foreigners earn in the domestic country, as we saw above. For most countries, domestic residents are responsible for most domestic production, so GDP and GNP are quite close.
- **Net national product** (NNP) is the total income of a nation's residents (GNP) minus losses from depreciation. *Depreciation* is the wear and tear on the economy's stock of equipment and structures, such as lorries rusting and computers becoming obsolete.
- **National income** is the total income earned by a nation's residents in the production of goods and services. It differs from net national product by excluding indirect business taxes (such as sales taxes) and including business subsidies. NNP and national income also differ because of a 'statistical discrepancy' that arises from problems in data collection.
- **Personal income** is the income that households and non-corporate businesses receive. Unlike national income, it excludes *retained earnings*, which is income that corporations have earned but have not paid out to their owners. It also subtracts corporate income taxes and contributions for social insurance. In addition, personal income includes the interest income that households receive from their holdings of government debt and the income that households receive from government transfer programmes, such as welfare and social security payments.
- **Disposable personal income** is the income that households and non-corporate businesses have left after satisfying all their obligations to the government. It equals personal income minus personal taxes and certain non-tax payments (such as parking tickets).

Although the various measures of income differ in detail, they almost always tell the same story about economic conditions. When GDP is growing rapidly, these other measures of income are usually growing rapidly. And when GDP is falling, these other measures are usually falling as well. For monitoring fluctuations in the overall economy, it does not matter much which measure of income we use.

To understand how the economy is using its scarce resources, economists are often interested in studying the composition of GDP among various types of spending as we noted in our look at the circular flow of income. To do this, GDP (which we denote as Y) is divided into four components: consumption (C), investment (I), government purchases (G) and net exports (NX) – the difference of the value of exports minus the value of (expenditure on) imports ($X - M$):

$$Y \equiv C + I + G + NX$$

This equation is an *identity* – an equation that must be true by the way the variables in the equation are defined. (That's why we used the three-bar, 'identically equals' symbol, '$\equiv$', although for the most part we'll follow normal practice in dealing with identities and use the usual equals sign, '='.) In this case, because each pound or euro of expenditure included in GDP is placed into one of the four components of GDP, the total of the four components must be equal to GDP. Let's look at each of these four components more closely.

Consumption

Consumption is spending by households on goods and services. 'Goods' include household spending on durable goods, such as cars and appliances like washing machines and fridges, and non-durable goods, such as food and clothing.

> **consumption** spending by households on goods and services, with the exception of purchases of new housing

'Services' include such intangible items as haircuts, entertainment and medical care. Household spending on education is also included in consumption of services (although one might argue that it would fit better in the next component).

Investment

Investment is the purchase of goods that will be used in the future to produce more goods and services. It is the sum of purchases of capital equipment, inventories and structures. Investment in structures includes expenditure on new housing. By convention, the purchase of a new house is the one form of household spending categorized as investment rather than consumption.

> **investment** spending on capital equipment, inventories and structures, including household purchases of new housing

As mentioned earlier in this chapter, the treatment of inventory accumulation is noteworthy. When Sony produces a phone and, instead of selling it, adds it to its inventory, Sony is assumed to have 'purchased' the phone for itself. That is, the national income accountants treat the phone as part of Sony's investment spending. (If Sony later sells the phone out of inventory, Sony's inventory investment will then be negative, offsetting the positive expenditure of the buyer.) Inventories are treated this way because one aim of GDP is to measure the value of the economy's production, and goods added to inventory are part of that period's production.

Government Purchases

Government purchases include spending on goods and services by local and national governments. It includes the salaries of government workers and spending on public works.

> **government purchases** spending on goods and services by local, state and national governments

The meaning of 'government purchases' requires a little clarification. When the government pays the salary of an army general, that salary is part of government purchases. But what happens when the government pays a social security benefit to one of the elderly? Such government spending is called a **transfer payment** because it is not made in exchange for a currently produced good or service. Transfer payments alter household income, but they do not reflect the economy's production. (From a macroeconomic standpoint, transfer payments are like negative taxes.) Because GDP is intended to measure income from, and expenditure on, the production of goods and services, transfer payments are not counted as part of government purchases.

> **transfer payment** a payment for which no good or service is exchanged

Net Exports

Net exports equal the purchases of domestically produced goods and services by foreigners (exports) minus the domestic purchases of foreign goods (imports). A domestic firm's sale to a buyer in another country, such as the sale of Sony phones to customers in the USA, increases Japanese net exports.

CASE STUDY   Revisions to GDP Figures

National or regional statistical services such as the ONS or Eurostat have very sophisticated systems for collecting and calculating national income data. The European system of national and regional accounts (known as ESA95) compiles data on the structure and developments of member state economies. It uses an agreed accounting framework which is recognized across the world to allow each economy to be described and to be able to draw accurate and reliable comparisons between different regions and economies or groups of economies. It is worth trying to imagine how challenging a task collecting all this data actually is. Just look around you whenever you are out at the amount of economic activity which is taking place – people buying and selling goods and services in shops, online transactions, people travelling on public transport, people using their cars for which they have bought insurance, fuel and paid for maintenance, road sweepers cleaning up litter, emptying bins and removing chewing gum off the pavements, police patrolling the streets and so on. Trying to collect all the data for the expenditures that are taking place is a massive task. Inevitably, any published GDP figure is provisional and statistical services continue to revise the data they receive and publish revised figures on a regular basis.

Providing accurate data is important because business, government and investment decisions are all made with the macroeconomic environment in mind. It is made very clear, therefore, that GDP data when published is subject to revision and these revisions can sometimes be significant. In January 2013, for example, the ONS published provisional GDP statistics for the fourth quarter of 2012. The third quarter figures had provided some good news amidst a year which was generally depressing for the UK. Third quarter GDP was reported as increasing by 0.9 per cent largely due to the effect of the Olympic Games which the UK hosted in the summer of 2012. The fourth quarter figures showed the economy had shrunk by 0.3 per cent. However, the ONS reported that the figures, which are often called 'flash estimates', were based on just 44 per cent of the total data used for final estimate. There will be at least two revisions to this data and it may be that once all the data is in, the 0.3 per cent decrease will be confirmed or revised up or down. Quarter 2 data, for example, was originally published as a contraction of 0.7 per cent in April but then revised to –0.5 per cent and then to –0.4 per cent when all the data were available in September 2012. Announcements on GDP data, therefore, needs to be looked at with some caution – one quarter's figures may not necessarily be a reliable indicator of the pattern of GDP over time.

The complexity of capturing data from all the transactions and trade which takes place in an economy is such that revision to GDP data is a fact of life.

> **net exports** spending on domestically produced goods and services by foreigners (exports) minus spending on foreign goods by domestic residents (imports)

The 'net' in 'net exports' refers to the fact that the value of imports is subtracted from the value of exports. This subtraction is made because imports of goods and services are included in other components of GDP. For example, suppose that a UK household buys a £30,000 car from Volvo, the Swedish car maker. That transaction increases consumption in the UK by £30,000 because car purchases are part of consumer spending in the UK. It also reduces net exports by £30,000 because the car is an import (note it represents an export for Sweden). In other words, net exports include goods and services produced abroad (with a minus sign) because these goods and services are included in consumption, investment and government purchases (with a plus sign). Thus, when a domestic household, firm or government buys a good or service from abroad, the purchase reduces net exports – but because it also raises consumption, investment or government purchases, it does not affect GDP. The above example shows the importance of making sure that we focus on a particular country when discussing imports and exports because of the potential for confusion to arise.

Once GDP figures are published they can be presented in different ways. One of the most common is GDP per capita. **GDP per capita** is found by dividing the GDP of a country by the population of that country to express national income per head of the population. This measure is useful in comparing GDP across different countries.

> **GDP per capita** gross domestic product divided by the population of a country to give a measure of national income per head

> **SELF TEST** List the four components of expenditure. Which of these do you think accounts for the largest proportion of GDP in a country? Why?

REAL VERSUS NOMINAL GDP

As we have seen, GDP measures the total expenditure on goods and services in all markets in the economy. If total spending rises from one year to the next, one of two things must be true (or a combination of the two): (1) the economy is producing a larger output of goods and services (a real increase); or (2) goods and services are being sold at higher prices (a nominal increase). When studying changes in the economy over time, economists want to separate these two effects. In particular, they want a measure of the total quantity of goods and services the economy is producing that is not affected by changes in the prices of those goods and services.

To do this, economists use a measure called **real GDP**. Real GDP answers a hypothetical question: what would be the value of the goods and services produced this year if we valued these goods and services at the prices that prevailed in some specific year in the past? By evaluating current production using prices that are fixed at past levels, real GDP shows how the economy's overall production of goods and services changes over time. The GDP figures produced using this method are called **GDP at constant prices**. GDP figures produced without taking into consideration the change in prices over time are called **GDP at current or market prices** and are calculated by taking the output of goods and services and multiplying by the price of those goods and services in the reporting year.

> **real GDP** the measure of the value of output in the economy which takes into account changes in prices over time
> **GDP at constant prices** gross domestic product calculated using prices that existed at a particular base year which takes into account changes in inflation over time
> **GDP at current or market prices** gross domestic product calculated by multiplying the output of goods and services by the price of those goods and services in the reporting year

To see more precisely how real GDP is constructed, let's consider an example.

A Numerical Example

Table 4.1 shows some data for an economy that produces only two goods – apples and potatoes. The table shows the quantities of the two goods produced and their prices in the years 2013, 2014 and 2015.

To compute total spending in this economy, we would multiply the quantities of apples and potatoes by their prices. In the year 2013, 100 kg of apples are sold at a price of €1 per kg, so expenditure on apples equals €100. In the same year, 50 kg of potatoes are sold for €2 per kg, so expenditure on potatoes also equals €100. Total expenditure in the economy – the sum of expenditure on apples and expenditure on potatoes – is €200. This amount, the production of goods and services valued at current or market prices (i.e. the price existing in the reporting year), is called **nominal GDP**.

> **nominal GDP** the production of goods and services valued at current prices

TABLE 4.1   Real and Nominal GDP

This table shows how to calculate real GDP, nominal GDP and the GDP deflator for a hypothetical economy that produces only apples and potatoes.

	Prices and quantities			
Year	**Price of apples per kg (€)**	**Quantity of apples (kg)**	**Price of potatoes per kg (€)**	**Quantity of potatoes (kg)**
2013	1	100	2	50
2014	2	150	3	100
2015	3	200	4	150

Year	Calculating nominal GDP
2013	(€1 per kg apples × 100 kg) + (€2 per kg potatoes × 50 kg) = €200
2014	(€2 per kg apples × 150 kg) + (€3 per kg potatoes × 100 kg) = €600
2015	(€3 per kg apples × 200 kg) + (€4 per kg potatoes × 150 kg) = €1,200

Year	Calculating real GDP (base year 2013)
2013	(€1 per kg apples × 100 kg) + (€2 per kg potatoes × 50 kg) = €200
2014	(€1 per kg apples × 150 kg) + (€2 per kg potatoes × 100 kg) = €350
2015	(€1 per kg apples × 200 kg) + (€2 per kg potatoes × 150 kg) = €500

Year	Calculating the GDP deflator
2013	(€200/€200) × 100 = 100
2014	(€600/€350) × 100 = 171
2015	(€1,200/€500) × 100 = 240

The table shows the calculation of nominal GDP for these three years. Total spending rises from €200 in 2013 to €600 in 2014 and then to €1,200 in 2015. Part of this rise is attributable to the increase in the quantities of apples and potatoes, and part is attributable to the increase in the prices of apples and potatoes.

To obtain a measure of the amount produced that is not affected by changes in prices, we use real GDP, which is the production of goods and services valued at constant prices. We calculate real GDP by first choosing one year as a *base year*. We then use the prices of apples and potatoes in the base year to compute the value of goods and services in all of the years. In other words, the prices in the base year provide the basis for comparing quantities in different years.

Suppose that we choose 2013 to be the base year in our example. We can then use the prices of apples and potatoes in 2013 to compute the value of goods and services produced in 2013, 2014 and 2015. Table 4.1 shows these calculations. To compute real GDP for 2013 we use the prices of apples and potatoes in 2013 (the base year) and the quantities of apples and potatoes produced in 2013. (Thus, for the base year, real GDP always equals nominal GDP.) To compute real GDP for 2014, we use the prices of apples and potatoes in 2013 (the base year) and the quantities of apples and potatoes produced in 2014. Similarly, to compute real GDP for 2015, we use the prices in 2013 and the quantities in 2015. When we find that real GDP has risen from €200 in 2013 to €350 in 2014 and then to €500 in 2015, we know that the increase is attributable to an increase in the *quantities produced*, because the prices are being held fixed at base-year levels.

To sum up: nominal GDP uses current or market prices to place a value on the economy's production of goods and services, while real GDP uses constant base-year prices to place a value on the economy's production of goods and services. Because real GDP is not affected by changes in prices, changes in real GDP reflect only changes in the amounts being produced. Thus, real GDP is a measure of the economy's production of goods and services.

Our goal in computing GDP is to gauge how well the overall economy is performing. Because real GDP measures the economy's production of goods and services, it reflects the economy's ability to satisfy people's needs and desires. Thus, real GDP is a better gauge of economic well-being than is nominal GDP. When economists talk about the economy's GDP, they usually mean real GDP rather than nominal GDP. And when they talk about growth in the economy, they measure that growth as the percentage change in real GDP from one period to another.

The GDP Deflator

As we have just seen, nominal GDP reflects both the prices of goods and services and the quantities of goods and services the economy is producing. In contrast, by holding prices constant at base-year levels, real GDP reflects only the quantities produced. From these two statistics we can compute a third, called the **GDP deflator**, which reflects the prices of goods and services but not the quantities produced.

> **GDP deflator** a measure of the price level calculated as the ratio of nominal GDP to real GDP times 100

The GDP deflator is calculated as follows:

$$\text{GDP deflator} = \frac{\text{Nominal GDP}}{\text{Real GDP}} \times 100$$

Because nominal GDP and real GDP must be the same in the base year, the GDP deflator for the base year always equals 100. The GDP deflator for subsequent years measures the change in nominal GDP from the base year that cannot be attributable to a change in real GDP.

The GDP deflator measures the current level of prices relative to the level of prices in the base year. To see why this is true, consider a couple of simple examples. First, imagine that the quantities produced in the economy rise over time but prices remain the same. In this case, both nominal and real GDP rise together, so the GDP deflator is constant. Now suppose, instead, that prices rise over time but the quantities produced stay the same. In this second case, nominal GDP rises but real GDP remains the same, so the GDP deflator rises as well. Notice that, in both cases, the GDP deflator reflects what's happening to prices, not quantities.

Let's now return to our numerical example in Table 4.1. The GDP deflator is computed at the bottom of the table. For year 2013, nominal GDP is €200, and real GDP is €200, so the GDP deflator is 100. For the year 2014, nominal GDP is €600, and real GDP is €350, so the GDP deflator is 171. Because the GDP deflator rose in year 2014 from 100 to 171, we can say that the price level increased by 71 per cent.

The GDP deflator is one measure that economists use to monitor the average level of prices in the economy. We examine another – the consumer prices index – in the next chapter, where we also describe the differences between the two measures.

SELF TEST Define real and nominal GDP. Which is a better measure of economic well-being? Why?

FYI

Measuring GDP

We have looked at measuring GDP through income and expenditure methods and said that in theory they are the same. GDP can also be measured by looking at the output method. The price of a product represents the value of the inputs (land, labour and capital) that went into production. At each stage of the production process the value or output can be recorded – the value added. GDP is also a measure of the value of output in the economy. Statistics offices usually classify output according to industry types – construction, agriculture forestry and fisheries, mining, services and so on.

The measure for GDP is essentially what is called a 'volume measure'. In other words, it is measuring 'how much' has been produced. In the UK the ONS has to produce a single measure of GDP and does this by using the three approaches – income, expenditure and output – and balancing the final figure in relation to the three measures. Remember, we said that in theory they should all be the same but the process of collecting information from millions of transactions means that in reality they would never be exact.

Imagine a situation, for example, where someone has some work done on his or her house – say some

plastering of a room. The total price for the work paid by the owner of the house might be £1,500 – this should represent the sum of the resources used in the job. The plasterer may declare to Her Majesty's Revenue and Customs (HMRC), that is responsible for collecting UK taxes, that the work represented income of £1,200 (to evade paying income tax – illegal, but nevertheless it happens!) and the resources used might have included the plasterboard, plaster, electricity, buckets, nails, water, trowels and hawks, the vehicles to get to and from the builders' merchants, etc. It is easy to see how, even in such a simple example, it becomes incredibly difficult to keep track of every item involved!

The choice of which base year to use in calculating real GDP is also important. Up until early 2004, the ONS used a method referred to as 'fixed base aggregations'. For example, they might have compared the data using 1995 as the base year. However, as with any statistical data which use a base year in their compilation, this can lead to inconsistencies in the data because circumstances change. Goods, for example, that were common in 1995 may not exist anymore and there might be some products that were not available at that time – DVDs,

for example. In general, the more you can update the base year, the more accurate the statistics will be. Fixed base aggregations in GDP statistics were used as follows. The growth of the different parts of the economy was given weights when trying to arrive at the final figure for GDP. This takes account of their relative importance in the economy and a base year of 1995 was used to help determine these weights. These base years were updated every five years but, as we have seen, this can lead to problems.

The method known as 'annual chain linking' helps to overcome these problems. Rather than updating the base year every five years, this method does it every year, calculating the prices in previous years' prices (PYPs). You will see GDP tables expressed as 'GDP (CVM)', where CVM means Chained Volume Measures, as opposed to 'GDP in constant prices'. The ONS and other statistical services are constantly looking to update their methods to provide more reliable and accurate data and this is one example of such a revision of methods.

In terms of analysis of the data it should make little difference, but recognizing it enables you to be more confident that the data are more likely to be accurate and reliable compared to the previous measures.

GDP AND ECONOMIC WELL-BEING

Earlier in this chapter, GDP was referred to as the best single measure of the economic well-being of a society. Now that we know what GDP is, we can evaluate this claim.

As we have seen, GDP measures both the economy's total income and the economy's total expenditure on goods and services. Thus, GDP per person tells us the income and expenditure of the average person in the economy. Because most people would prefer to receive higher income and enjoy higher expenditure, GDP per person seems a natural measure of the economic well-being of the average individual.

Yet some people dispute the validity of GDP as a measure of well-being. Surely we should not be obsessed with material things and income? Surely we should value things that are not measured by GDP and that contribute to the quality of life and economic well-being, such as the health of a country's children, or the quality of their education, or even the beauty of the poetry making up our literary heritage?

The answer is that a large GDP does in fact help us to lead a good life. GDP does not measure the health of our children, but nations with larger GDP can afford better health care for their children. GDP does not measure the quality of their education, but nations with larger GDP can afford better educational systems. GDP does not measure the beauty of our poetry, but nations with larger GDP can afford to teach more of their citizens to read and enjoy poetry. GDP does not take account of our intelligence, integrity, courage or wisdom, but all of these laudable attributes are easier to foster when people are less concerned about being able to afford the material necessities of life. In short, GDP does not directly measure those things that make life worthwhile, but it does measure our ability to obtain the inputs into a worthwhile life.

GDP is not, however, a perfect measure of well-being. Some things that contribute to a good life are left out of GDP. One is leisure. Suppose, for instance, that everyone in the economy suddenly started working every day of the week, rather than enjoying leisure on weekends. More goods and services would be produced, and GDP would rise. Yet, despite the increase in GDP, we should not conclude that everyone would be better off. The loss from reduced leisure would offset the gain from producing and consuming a greater quantity of goods and services.

Because GDP uses market prices to value goods and services, it excludes the value of almost all activity that takes place outside of markets. In particular, GDP omits the value of goods and services produced at home. When a chef prepares a delicious meal and sells it at his restaurant, the value of that meal is part of GDP. But if the chef prepares the same meal for his wife, the value he has added to the raw ingredients is left out of GDP. As we saw above, child care provided in day care centres is part of GDP, whereas child care by parents at home is not. Volunteer work also contributes to the well-being of those in society, but GDP does not reflect these contributions.

Another thing that GDP excludes is the quality of the environment. Imagine that the government eliminated all environmental regulations. Firms could then produce goods and services without considering the pollution they create, and GDP might rise. Yet well-being would most likely fall. The deterioration in the quality of air and water would more than offset the gains from greater production.

GDP also says nothing about the distribution of income. A society in which 100 people have annual incomes of €50,000 has GDP of €5 million and, not surprisingly, GDP per capita (person) of €50,000; so does a society in which 10 people earn €500,000 and 90 suffer with nothing at all. Few people would look at those two situations and call them equivalent. GDP per person tells us what happens to the average person, but behind the average lies a large variety of personal experiences.

In the end, we can conclude that GDP is a good measure of economic well-being for most – but not all – purposes. It is important to keep in mind what GDP includes and what it leaves out.

The Economics of Happiness

It does appear that, despite the massive increase in wealth, incomes and access to material goods and services for many people in developed countries over the last 50 years, our perception of happiness has not really changed that much. Increased wealth has not brought with it similar increases in happiness. Numerous surveys have highlighted relatively stable rates of 'happiness' in rich countries. Professor Richard Layard, one of a group of economists including Andrew Oswald, Stephen Nickell, Robert Skidelsky, Tim Besley, Will Hutton and those behavioural economists that we have met before in this book, have studied this apparent paradox. Layard states that in relation to Western societies: 'on average, people are no happier than they were fifty years ago' (see Layard, R. (2005) *Happiness: Lessons from a New Science*. London: Penguin).

Many people perceive January to be a very stressful month. In 2006, a number of newspapers and media organizations ran a story suggesting that 23 January 2006 was going to be the official 'worst day of the year'. How was this arrived at? It appears that someone called Cliff Arnall had devised a formula for calculating it. The formula is: $[W + (D - d)] \times TQM \times NA$, where W is the weather, D is debt, T is time since Christmas, Q the time since failing to keep to our New Year's resolutions, M is motivational levels and NA the need to take action.

This formula was an attempt to quantify a way in which states of happiness (or sadness) can be measured. Its scientific basis has been called into question. Arnall said that it is useful in triggering discussion and debate about what we understand by happiness and to think of ways we can deal with the effects of how we live our lives on our well-being.

What is needed, therefore, is a widely accepted set of criteria that is accepted as constituting happiness. The increased understanding of the brain and neuroscience has helped to shed some light on this but it is a complex area. Psychologists and economists have found that links between how people see their own happiness and other things that might influence, such as judgement, are statistically strong. This also seems to apply across different countries. As a result, we might be able to conclude that there are a range of factors that can contribute to a definition of happiness; that if you are fortunate enough to find yourself being able to boast having these characteristics, or in some cases managing to avoid them, then you are more likely to be happy.

Layard identified some key factors that may contribute to 'happiness'. He suggested that some of the factors associated with promoting happiness, include sex, socializing, relaxing, praying, worshipping or meditating, eating, exercising, watching TV and shopping, among others. Other studies have suggested that an individual's level of education, health, whether they are married, single or divorced, the level of income enjoyed, whether they are working/unemployed/retired, their aspirations and whether they have experienced bereavement can all be contributory factors.

From such characteristics, equations to statistically arrive at measures of well-being can be derived. These have been used by both economists and psychologists and have been found to be surprisingly reliable in statistical terms. One of the leading thinkers on the economics of happiness is Professor Andrew Oswald who is based at the University of Warwick. Oswald offers the following formula:

$$W_{it} = \acute{\alpha} + \beta X_{it} + \varepsilon_{it}$$

In this formula, W_{it} is the reported well-being of an individual at a particular time period, X represents a collection of variables that are known to be characteristics affecting well-being at a particular time period: these could be economic, such as income, or demographic, such as gender, with various points in between. The final term is an error term, which is used to take into account unobserved factors that may have an impact on the final outcome.

One of the factors above that may be affecting happiness levels more than we might expect is aspirations. You are very likely, whatever your age, to have been regaled by your parents that things were different in their day and that people these days have so much more. That is very true but what might also be the case is that different generations are starting to expect more. If your parents have managed to reach middle age and have a comfortable BMW to drive around in, you might start to expect such a vehicle to be the norm and would hope it might be your first car and so on.

Layard suggests that unhappiness results from society viewing how it is developing in terms of a zero-sum game. What he means by this is that we might increasingly view the scramble to gain money and status in terms of a competitive game that has a winner and a loser. If I get a high ranking job with a large salary and lots of status, it means that you somehow lose out – either by not being able to get that same job or in some sort of psychological way. Such a perception of life being a zero-sum game is a source of much unhappiness.

If we know something of the factors that can contribute to making someone 'happy' and also that our current measure is not the best at reflecting this, then it makes sense to look elsewhere for a measure of well-being. One such idea is to use something called the Measure of Domestic Progress (MDP). The MDP looks at many of the factors that we might associate with economic growth but takes into consideration the relative effects of economic growth and factors in other things that GDP calculations do not consider. For example, there is an attempt to place a value on the amount of unpaid domestic work that is carried out, which is taken as being a positive factor in contributing to well-being. It also assigns a negative effect to various social and environmental impacts of growth such as pollution, depletion of natural resources and costs of crime and family breakdown.

Other attempts to suggest more effective measures of improvements in well-being include such things as the Measure of Economic Welfare (MEW) developed by James Tobin and William Nordhaus, the Index of Sustainable Economic Welfare and the Genuine Progress Indicator.

It is proving difficult for any of these alternative measures to make a breakthrough and to be accepted in widespread use as a measure of well-being. The problems of attempting to measure subjective human behaviour and expose it to rigorous science are once again proving a challenge to economists. We might think that having some form of 'happiness index' would be a good thing, but if it does not really tell us what we want it to tell us, it is not very useful. There again, GDP figures do not seem to be telling us the whole story either!

International Differences in GDP and the Quality of Life

One way to gauge the usefulness of GDP as a measure of economic well-being is to examine international data. Rich and poor countries have vastly different levels of GDP per person. If a large GDP leads to a higher standard of living, then we should observe GDP to be strongly correlated with measures of the quality of life. And, in fact, we do.

Table 4.2 shows 13 of the world's countries ranked in order of GDP per person. The table also shows life expectancy (the expected life span at birth) and literacy (the percentage of the adult population who can read). These data show a clear pattern. In rich countries, such as the United Kingdom, the United States, Japan and Germany, people can expect to live into their late seventies or early eighties, and almost all of the population can read. In poor countries, such as Niger, Bangladesh and Pakistan, people typically can expect to live much shorter lives and the proportion of the population which is literate is relatively low.

TABLE 4.2   GDP, Life Expectancy and Literacy

The table shows GDP per person (measured in US dollars) and two measures of the quality of life for 13 countries.

Country	GDP per capita (Current US$) (2011)	Life expectancy at birth (males and females) total years (2011)	Literacy rate (% of people over 15), adult total (2011)
United States	48,112	78 (2010)	99
Japan	45,903	83	99
Germany	44,060	80 (2010)	99
United Kingdom	39,038	80	99
Russia	13,089	69 (2010)	100
Mexico	10,047	77 (2010)	93 (2010)
Brazil	12,594	73	90 (2009)
China	5,445	73 (2010)	94 (2010)
Indonesia	3,495	69	92 (2010)
India	1,489	65	63 (2010)
Pakistan	1,189	65 (2010)	56 (2010)
Bangladesh	743	69	56 (2010)
Niger	374	55	29

Although data on other aspects of the quality of life are less complete, they tell a similar story. Countries with low GDP per person tend to have more infants with low birth weight, higher rates of infant mortality, higher rates of maternal mortality, higher rates of child malnutrition and less common access to safe drinking water. In countries with low GDP per person, fewer school-age children are actually in school, and those who are in school must learn with fewer teachers per student.

These countries also tend to have fewer televisions, fewer telephones, fewer paved roads and fewer households with electricity. International data leave no doubt that a nation's GDP is closely associated with its citizens' standard of living.

SELF TEST Why should policymakers care about GDP?

CONCLUSION

This chapter has discussed how economists measure the total income of a nation. Measurement is, of course, only a starting point. Much of macroeconomics is aimed at revealing the long-run and short-run determinants of a nation's gross domestic product. Why, for example, is GDP higher in the United Kingdom and Japan than in India and Nigeria? What can the governments of the poorest countries do to promote more rapid growth in GDP? Why does GDP in European and North American countries rise rapidly in some years and fall in others? What can policymakers do to reduce the severity of these fluctuations in GDP? These are the questions we will take up shortly.

At this point, it is important to acknowledge the importance of just measuring GDP. We all get some sense of how the economy is doing as we go about our lives. But the economists who study changes in the economy and the policymakers who formulate economic policies need more than this vague sense – they need concrete data on which to base their judgements. Quantifying the behaviour of the economy with statistics such as GDP is, therefore, the first step to developing a science of macroeconomics.

IN THE NEWS

Recession and Recovery

A number of countries in Europe have faced significant economic difficulties in the wake of the financial crisis in 2007–2008. Economic growth in many countries since the crisis has been sluggish with many countries failing to get back to a position they were in prior to the crisis.

Comparing Recessions

At the time of the financial crisis a number of economists predicted that recovery would be long and difficult. Those predictions have proved correct but maybe many people have been surprised by the length of time which has elapsed and for some countries things do not look any brighter. In Greece, for example, the recession which began in 2008 shows no sign of abating and in 2012 the government had to announce

that GDP would shrink by 7 per cent in 2012, 2 per cent more than was originally forecast and that there would be no growth until 2014 at the earliest.

In 2009, the 17 Eurozone countries and the UK experienced negative growth which occurs when the value of output is lower than that in the previous time period. In Estonia the economy shrank by over 14 per cent, in Slovenia by 8 per cent, by 8.4 per cent in Finland, by 7.0 per cent in Ireland and by 5.5 per cent in Italy and 5.2 per cent in Germany. The

other Eurozone countries also saw a contraction in the economy but less severe than those quoted, ranging between 0 per cent and 4.4 per cent. In 2010, 15 of the 17 countries returned to growth although in many cases it was modest. By 2011 the rate of growth for some had slowed considerably with growth rates of less than 1 per cent occurring in five countries, and three countries experiencing negative growth.

In the UK the time it is taking to get the economy back onto a more

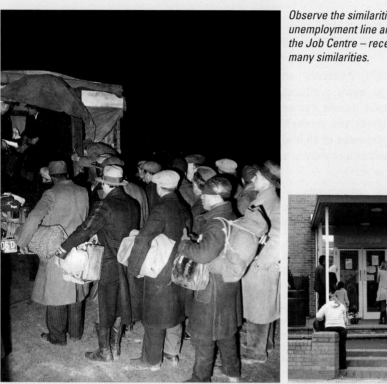

Observe the similarities between this 1930s Depression unemployment line and the present day queue outside the Job Centre – recessions throughout history have many similarities.

long-term growth trend of around 2.0 per cent is taking much longer than many people thought. The problems in the Eurozone have meant that export markets for the UK have shrunk and the Coalition government's austerity measures to try and cut the budget deficit has hit consumer spending. Firms are reluctant to invest in such a depressed climate although many large firms do have lots of spare cash which is adding to the failure of the UK economy to break out of recession.

In comparison to other recessions, the UK is taking much longer to recover. There have been four major recessionary periods in recent UK economic history, 1930–1934, 1973–1976, 1979–1983 and 1990–1993. Almost five years on from the start of the recession in 2008, the UK economy is about

3.35 per cent smaller. At the same time, five years following the start of the 1930–1934 recession, the economy was 3.83 per cent bigger; after the start of the 1973–1976 recession the economy was 5.45 per cent bigger; after the 1979–1983 recession, 3.04 per cent bigger; and the economy was 8.54 per cent bigger five years after the start of the 1990–1993 recession (data source, NIESR).

With Spain, Portugal, Ireland, Italy and Greece all experiencing austerity policies, the chances of the Eurozone growing strongly is unlikely. Most economists see minimal growth at best for these economies and whilst parts of the Eurozone remain depressed, the hope for trading out of recession for other economies becomes less.

Questions

1 Use an example to show how an economy can 'shrink'.

2 What is the difference between a slowdown in GDP and a fall in GDP? Use a suitable example to illustrate your answer.

3 What do you think is meant by an 'export-led recovery'?

4 GDP is the sum of $C + I + G + X - M$. Using the article, explain how the behaviour of each of these components in the UK is affecting GDP.

5 Why do you think the UK economy has failed to recover to at least the size it was prior to the start of the recession in 2008 when in all of the instances of previous recessions noted in the article, the economy has recovered so much quicker after the same length of time?

SUMMARY

- Because every transaction has a buyer and a seller, the total expenditure in the economy must equal the total income in the economy.

- Gross domestic product (GDP) measures an economy's total expenditure on newly produced goods and services and the total income earned from the production of these goods and services. More precisely, GDP is the market value of all final goods and services produced within a country in a given period of time.

- GDP is divided among four components of expenditure: consumption, investment, government purchases and net exports. Consumption includes spending on goods and services by households, with the exception of purchases of new housing. Investment includes spending on new equipment and structures, including households' purchases of new

housing. Government purchases include spending on goods and services by local, state and central governments. Net exports equal the value of goods and services produced domestically and sold abroad (exports) minus the value of goods and services produced abroad and sold domestically (imports).

- Nominal GDP uses current prices to value the economy's production of goods and services. Real GDP uses constant base-year prices to value the economy's production of goods and services. The GDP deflator – calculated from the ratio of nominal to real GDP – measures the level of prices in the economy.

- GDP is a good measure of economic well-being because people prefer higher to lower incomes. But it is not a perfect measure of well-being. For example, GDP excludes the value of leisure and the value of a clean environment.

QUESTIONS FOR REVIEW

1 Explain why an economy's income must equal its expenditure.

2 What is meant by the term GDP per capita and how is it measured?

3 Which contributes more to GDP – the production of an economy car or the production of a luxury car? Why?

4 A farmer sells wheat to a baker for €2. The baker uses the wheat to make bread, which is sold for €3. What is the total contribution of these transactions to GDP?

5 Many years ago, Jamanda paid €500 to put together a record collection. Today she sold her albums at a car boot sale for €100. How does this sale affect current GDP?

6 List the four components of GDP. Give an example of each.

7 Why do economists use real GDP rather than nominal GDP to gauge economic well-being?

8 In the year 2014, the economy produces 100 loaves of bread that sell for €2 each. In the year 2015, the economy produces 200 loaves of bread that sell for €3 each. Calculate nominal GDP, real GDP and the GDP deflator for each year (use 2014 as the base year). By what percentage does each of these three statistics rise from one year to the next?

9 Why is it desirable for a country to have a large GDP? Give an example of something that would raise GDP and yet be undesirable.

10 What are the limitations of using GDP as a measure of well-being for a country?

PROBLEMS AND APPLICATIONS

1 What components of GDP (if any) would each of the following transactions affect? Explain.

  a. A family buys a new refrigerator.
  b. Aunt Jane buys a new house.
  c. Aston Martin sells a DB7 from its inventory.
  d. You buy a pizza.
  e. The government builds a new motorway.
  f. You buy a bottle of Californian wine.
  g. Honda expands its factory in Derby, England.

2 The 'government purchases' component of GDP does not include spending on transfer payments such as social security. Thinking about the definition of GDP, explain why transfer payments are excluded.

3 Why do you think households' purchases of new housing are included in the investment component of GDP rather than the consumption component? Can you think of a reason why households' purchases of

new cars should also be included in investment rather than in consumption? To what other consumption goods might this logic apply?

4   As the chapter states, GDP does not include the value of used goods that are resold. Why would including such transactions make GDP a less informative measure of economic well-being?

5   Below are some data from the land of milk and honey.

Year	Price of milk (€)	Quantity of milk (quarts)	Price of honey (€)	Quantity of honey (quarts)
2013	1	100	2	50
2014	1	200	2	100
2015	2	200	4	100

  a. Compute nominal GDP, real GDP and the GDP deflator for each year, using 2013 as the base year.
  b. Compute the percentage change in nominal GDP, real GDP and the GDP deflator in 2014 and 2015 from the preceding year. For each year, identify the variable that does not change. Explain in words why your answer makes sense.
  c. Did economic well-being rise more in 2014 or 2015? Explain.

6   If prices rise, people's income from selling goods increases. The growth of real GDP ignores this gain, however. Why, then, do economists prefer real GDP as a measure of economic well-being?

7   One day Boris the Barber, plc, collects €400 for haircuts. Over this day, his equipment depreciates in value by €50. Of the remaining €350, Boris sends €30 to the government in sales taxes, takes home €220 in wages, and retains €100 in his business to add new equipment in the future. From the €220 that Boris takes home, he pays €70 in income taxes. Based on this information, compute Boris' contribution to the following measures of income:
  a. gross domestic product
  b. net national product
  c. national income
  d. personal income
  e. disposable personal income.

8   Goods and services that are not sold in markets, such as food produced and consumed at home, are generally not included in GDP. Can you think of how this might cause the numbers in the second column of Table 4.2 to be misleading in a comparison of the economic well-being of the United Kingdom and India? Explain.

9   Economists sometimes prefer to use GNP rather than GDP as a measure of economic well-being. Which measure should we prefer if we are analysing the total income of domestic residents? Which measure should we prefer if we are analysing the total amount of economic activity occurring in the economy?

10 The participation of women in many European and North American economies has risen dramatically over the past three decades.
  a. How do you think this rise affected GDP?
  b. Now imagine a measure of well-being that includes time spent working in the home and taking leisure. How would the change in this measure of well-being compare to the change in GDP?
  c. Can you think of other aspects of well-being that are associated with the rise in women's labour-force participation? Would it be practical to construct a measure of well-being that includes these aspects?

5 MEASURING THE COST OF LIVING

The UK parliament is often referred to as the 'mother of parliaments', by which is meant that it is one of the oldest parliaments and one that has served as a model, to a greater or lesser extent, when parliaments have been established in other countries. The origins of the British parliament, as a meeting place where representatives of the various regions and boroughs throughout the country could influence national policy, can be traced as far back as the early 13th century. It is therefore perhaps strange that members of parliament were paid nothing at all for their trouble until 1911, when they first received a salary of £400 (€460) a year. This amount was decreased to £360 (€414) in 1931, but has generally increased over time, so that, for example, MPs received £600 (€690) in 1937, £6,270 (€7,214) in 1977 and £65,738 (€75,644) in 2012. The 2012 pay doesn't sound too bad (especially as this excludes various allowances to which the MP is also entitled at this time) – it is, after all, over two and a half times what the average bus driver in the UK earns – around £24,000 (€27,616) and double what the average secondary school teacher earns – around £32,000 (€36,822). But the pay of £400 a year – about £8 a week (€9.20) in 1911 seems pretty poor, and it even went down by 10 per cent over the ensuing 20 years.

But, as everyone knows, the prices of goods and services have also changed over time and have for the most part increased. In 1900, a copy of *The Times* was priced at 1.2p, a pint of beer and milk could be bought for less than 1p and a dozen fresh eggs was 6.9p. In 1930, the average house price was £590; a loaf of bread was around 3p (These prices are expressed in decimal currency equivalents). At the turn of the 21st century, the average level of prices was 66 times the level of 1900. Because prices were so much lower in the early 1900s than they are today, it is not clear whether an MP in 1911 enjoyed a higher or lower standard of living than today's MPs.

In the preceding chapter we looked at how economists use gross domestic product (GDP) to measure the quantity of goods and services that the economy is producing. This chapter examines how economists measure the overall cost of living. To compare an MP's salary of £400 in 1911 to salaries from today, we need to find some way of turning money figures into meaningful measures of purchasing power. That is exactly the job of a statistic called the *consumer prices index*. After seeing how the consumer prices index is constructed, we discuss how we can use such a prices index to compare money figures from different points in time.

The consumer prices index is used to monitor changes in the cost of living over time. When the consumer prices index rises, the typical family has to spend more money to maintain the same standard of living. Economists use the term *inflation* to describe a situation in which the economy's overall price level is rising. The *inflation rate* is the percentage change in the price level from the previous period. As we will see in the coming chapters, inflation is a closely watched aspect of macroeconomic performance and is a key variable guiding macroeconomic policy. This chapter provides the background for that analysis by showing how economists measure the inflation rate using the consumer prices index.

THE CONSUMER PRICES INDEX

The **consumer prices index** (CPI) is a measure of the overall prices of the goods and services bought by a typical consumer. Each month, a government bureau – in the UK the Office for National Statistics (ONS) and in Europe, Eurostat – computes and reports the CPI. In this section we discuss how the CPI is calculated and what problems arise in its measurement. We also consider how this index compares to the GDP deflator, another measure of the overall level of prices, which we examined in the preceding chapter.

> **consumer prices index** a measure of the overall prices of the goods and services bought by a typical consumer

How the Consumer Prices Index Is Calculated

When the ONS or Eurostat calculates the CPI and the inflation rate, it uses data on the prices of thousands of goods and services. To see exactly how these statistics are constructed, let's consider a simple economy in which consumers buy only two goods – hot dogs and burgers. Table 5.1 shows the five steps that the ONS and Eurostat follow. (We will use the ONS as the base for the example here but the principle applies to the way price changes are measured in Europe as a whole.)

TABLE 5.1 **Calculating the Consumer Prices Index and the Inflation Rate: An Example**

This table shows how to calculate the CPI and the inflation rate for a hypothetical economy in which consumers buy only hot dogs and burgers.

Step 1: Survey consumers to determine a fixed basket of goods

4 hot dogs, 2 burgers

Step 2: Find the price of each good in each year

Year	Price of hot dogs (€)	Price of burgers (€)
2014	1	2
2015	2	3
2016	3	4

Step 3: Compute the cost of the basket of goods in each year

2014	(€1 per hot dog × 4 hot dogs) + (€2 per burger × 2 burgers) = €8
2015	(€2 per hot dog × 4 hot dogs) + (€3 per burger × 2 burgers) = €14
2016	(€3 per hot dog × 4 hot dogs) + (€4 per burger × 2 burgers) = €20

Step 4: Choose one year as a base year (2014) and compute the consumer prices index in each year

2014	(€8/€8) × 100 = 100
2015	(€14/€8) × 100 = 175
2016	(€20/€8) × 100 = 250

Step 5: Use the consumer prices index to compute the inflation rate from previous year

2015	(175 − 100)/100 × 100 = 75%
2016	(250 − 175)/175 × 100 = 43%

1. *Fix the basket.* The first step in computing the consumer prices index is to determine which prices are most important to the typical consumer. If the typical consumer buys more hot dogs than burgers, then the price of hot dogs is more important than the price of burgers and, therefore, should be given greater weight in measuring the cost of living. The ONS sets these weights by surveying consumers and finding the basket of goods and services that the typical consumer buys. In the example in Table 5.1, the typical consumer buys a basket of 4 hot dogs and 2 burgers.

2. *Find the prices.* The second step in computing the CPI is to find the prices of each of the goods and services in the basket for each point in time. The table shows the prices of hot dogs and burgers for three different years.

3. *Compute the basket's cost.* The third step is to use the data on prices to calculate the cost of the basket of goods and services at different times. The table shows this calculation for each of the three years. Notice that only the prices in this calculation change. By keeping the basket of goods the same (4 hot dogs and 2 burgers), we are isolating the effects of price changes from the effect of any quantity changes that might be occurring at the same time.

4. *Choose a base year and compute the index.* The fourth step is to designate one year as the base year, which is the benchmark against which other years are compared. To calculate the index, the price of the basket of goods and services in each year is divided by the price of the basket in the base year, and this ratio is then multiplied by 100. The resulting number is the CPI.

   In the example in the table, the year 2014 is the base year. In this year, the basket of hot dogs and burgers costs €8. Therefore, the price of the basket in all years is divided by €8 and multiplied by 100. The CPI is 100 in 2014. (The index is always 100 in the base year.) The CPI is 175 in 2015. This means that the price of the basket in 2015 is 175 per cent of its price in the base year. Put differently, a basket of goods that costs €100 in the base year costs €175 in 2015. Similarly, the consumer prices index is 250 in 2016, indicating that the price level in 2016 is 250 per cent of the price level in the base year.

5. *Compute the inflation rate.* The fifth and final step is to use the CPI to calculate the **inflation rate**, which is the percentage change in the price index from the preceding period. That is, the inflation rate between two consecutive years is computed as follows:

$$\text{Inflation rate in year 2} = 100 \times \frac{(\text{CPI in year 2} - \text{CPI in year 1})}{\text{CPI in year 1}}$$

> **inflation rate** the percentage change in the price index from the preceding period

In our example, the inflation rate is 75 per cent in 2015 and 43 per cent in 2016.

Although this example simplifies the real world by including only two goods, it shows how the ONS computes the CPI and the inflation rate. The ONS collects and processes data on the prices of thousands of goods and services every month and, by following the five foregoing steps, determines how quickly the cost of living for the typical consumer is rising. When the ONS makes its monthly announcement of the CPI, you can usually hear the number on the evening television news or see it in the next day's newspaper.

In addition to the CPI for the overall economy, the ONS also calculates price indices for the sub-categories of 'goods' and of 'services' separately, as well as the **producer prices index** (PPI), which measures the prices of a basket of goods and services bought by firms rather than consumers. Because firms eventually pass on their costs to consumers in the form of higher consumer prices, changes in the PPI are often thought to be useful in predicting changes in the CPI.

> **producer prices index** a measure of the prices of a basket of goods and services bought by firms

Problems in Measuring the Cost of Living

The goal of the CPI is to measure changes in the cost of living – how much people have to pay to purchase goods and services. In other words, the CPI tries to gauge how much incomes must rise in order to maintain a constant standard of living. The standard of living is measured by the amount of goods and services people are able to buy. Assume that an individual in 2014 has an income of €100 per week and only buys burgers at €2 each. Their standard of living is 50 burgers a week. In 2015, burgers rise in price to €3 and so the standard of living, assuming income does not change, is now only 33.3 burgers a week. We would say that the individual's standard of living has fallen because he can now afford to consume fewer burgers. To keep his standard of living constant at 50 burgers, the person's income needs to rise from €100 per week to €150 per week. If the rise in incomes keeps pace with the rise in prices then the individual's standard of living will remain constant. If incomes rise by a lower percentage than the CPI then standards of living are being eroded and, if incomes rise at a faster rate than the CPI, standards of living are improving and people are better off.

The CPI, however, is not a perfect measure of the cost of living. Three problems with the index are widely acknowledged but difficult to solve.

Substitution Bias The first problem is called *substitution bias*. When prices change from one year to the next, they do not all change proportionately: some prices rise more than others and some prices fall. Consumers respond to these differing price changes by buying less of the goods whose prices have risen by large amounts and by buying more of the goods whose prices have risen less or perhaps even have fallen (and, of course, different consumers will respond to price changes in different ways because of the price elasticity of demand). That is, consumers substitute towards goods that have become relatively less expensive. If a price index is computed assuming a fixed basket of goods, it ignores the possibility of consumer substitution and, therefore, overstates the increase in the cost of living from one year to the next.

Let's consider a simple example. Imagine that in the base year apples are cheaper than pears, and so consumers buy more apples than pears. When the ONS constructs the basket of goods, it will include more apples than pears. Suppose that next year pears are cheaper than apples. Consumers will naturally respond to the price changes by buying more pears and fewer apples. Yet, when computing the CPI, the ONS uses a fixed basket, which in essence assumes that consumers continue buying the now expensive apples in the same quantities as before. For this reason, the index will measure a much larger increase in the cost of living than consumers actually experience.

The Introduction of New Goods The second problem with the CPI is the *introduction of new goods* as highlighted in the following FYI box. When a new good is introduced, consumers have more variety from which to choose. Greater variety, in turn, makes each pound more valuable, so consumers need fewer pounds to maintain any given standard of living. Yet because the CPI is based on a fixed basket of goods and services, it does not reflect this change in the purchasing power of the pound.

Again, let's consider an example. When video players were introduced, consumers were able to watch their favourite films at home. Compared with going to the cinema, the convenience was greater and the cost was less. A perfect cost of living index would have reflected the introduction of the video player with a decrease in the cost of living. The CPI, however, did not decrease in response to the introduction of the video player. Eventually, the ONS did revise the basket of goods to include video players, and subsequently the index reflected changes in their prices. But the reduction in the cost of living associated with the initial introduction of the video player never showed up in the index. As time has passed the index has to be revised to take account of the decline in video and the rise of DVD, then Blu-ray DVD and more recently the increase in downloading of movies.

Unmeasured Quality Change The third problem with the consumer prices index is *unmeasured quality change*. If the quality of a good deteriorates from one year to the next, the effective value of a pound falls, even if the price of the good stays the same. Similarly, if the quality rises from one year to the next, the effective value of a pound rises. The ONS does its best to account for quality change. When the quality of a good in the basket changes – for example, when a car model has more horsepower or gets better petrol mileage from one year to the next – the ONS adjusts the price of the good to account for the quality change. It is, in essence, trying to compute the price of a basket of goods of constant quality.

FYI

What is in the CPI's Basket?

When constructing the CPI, the UK ONS tries to include all the goods and services that the typical consumer buys. Moreover, it tries to weight these goods and services according to how much consumers buy of each item. Every month the ONS collects around 180,000 prices of 700 goods and services from around 150 areas throughout the UK that are supposed to be representative of the goods and services we use on a regular basis. As buying habits change, the basket of goods and services has to change also. Each year the ONS announces a revision to the basket of goods and services that make up the basis of inflation figures in the UK. The ONS has to take into consideration not only how representative the sample of goods and services is but also any changes in importance in the typical household budget and whether the replacement brands that shops bring in are of comparable quality.

Table 5.2 shows the main groupings of the products included in the index. In this case, the index is the Retail Prices Index (RPI) which is constructed in exactly the same way as the CPI but includes some product areas, notably housing costs, which the CPI does not. The UK adopted the CPI as its official measure of inflation to come into line with the rest of Europe and many other countries around the world in 2003. Each month the ONS announce the CPI and the RPI.

Table 5.2 shows that food is not as important in the typical household budget in 2012 as it was in 1987, and similarly tobacco and alcohol are also less important. Housing, though, has become more important, perhaps reflecting the interest people have in their homes (there is a large proportion of the population in the UK who own their own homes unlike the situation in

other parts of Europe where renting is more common). It is also worth noting the increased importance of leisure services, which includes spending on holidays, which have risen significantly in importance since 1987.

Some goods and services that are not as representative any more are removed from the basket. This is measured by the amount spent on these goods and services. If consumer expenditure on items exceeds £400 million annually then these are normally included in the basket but if expenditure falls below £100 million then there has to be a very good reason put forward to keep these goods in the basket. In recent years this has included microwave ovens which first made an appearance in the index in the 1980s. They are still popular, say the ONS, but their reliability and the falling prices means that the amount spent on them has

TABLE 5.2 Product Group Weightings since 1987

RPI GROUP	1987	1992	1997	2002	2007	2011	2012
Food	167	152	136	114	105	118	114
Catering	46	47	49	52	47	47	47
Alcohol	76	80	80	68	66	60	56
Tobacco	38	36	34	31	29	28	29
Housing	157	172	186	199	238	238	237
Fuel and light	61	47	41	31	39	42	46
Household goods	73	77	72	73	66	65	62
Household services	44	48	52	60	65	63	67
Clothing and footwear	74	59	56	51	44	44	45
Personal goods and services	38	40	40	43	39	38	39
Motoring expenditure	127	143	128	141	133	137	131
Fares and other travel costs	22	20	20	20	20	20	23
Leisure goods	47	47	47	48	41	36	33
Leisure services	30	32	59	69	68	64	71

Weights are specified as parts per 1,000 of the all items' RPI reduced and as such they have been removed from the basket. Other items that have dropped out include film for 35 mm cameras (the cameras themselves dropped out in 2007), top 40 CD singles and television repair, as technology changes the way we live. The ONS says that people prefer to download music rather than buy singles and households tend to replace TVs rather than get them repaired.

The goods and services that have come into the basket are a reflection of the growing 'café culture' in the UK. Muffins have been brought into the basket to represent croissants and cakes that tend to be bought with coffee in cafés. The ONS has also reported that the UK tends to be more health conscious; fruit smoothies are now more popular so they enter the basket as do small fruits such as satsumas and clementines. Perhaps not so healthy are crates of 20 bottles of lager. However, they are now in the basket. The ONS says that the once popular 'stubbie' is now less so and people are tending to buy lager in different ways. Hot rotisserie cooked chickens, Blu-ray discs, bottled rosé wine, MP4 players, baby wipes, television and internet access subscriptions, tablet computers and soft continental cheeses have also made it into the basket but single cream, candy coated chocolates, imported lamb loin chops, glass ovenware casserole dishes, step ladders and wine boxes have been removed.

To take another example, in 2004 the ONS introduced digital cameras into the CPI for the first time. As well as the problems associated with introducing a new good into the index that we discussed earlier, digital cameras are also subject to very rapid technological progress – features such as zoom and the number of megapixels in the pictures taken keep on improving rapidly and the sale of digital cameras has now been impacted by the developments in camera technology which is incorporated in smart phones. Thus, while the average price of a digital camera or a smart phone might remain the same over a period, the average quality may have risen substantially. The ONS attempts to correct for this by a method known as hedonic quality adjustment. This involves working out the average characteristics (e.g. LCD screen size, number of megapixels, zoom features, etc.) of the average digital camera and adjusting the price when one of these average characteristics increases.

Despite these efforts, changes in quality remain a problem, because quality is so hard to measure.

Relevance of the CPI A final problem with the index is that people may not see the reported CPI measure of inflation as relevant to their particular situation. This is because their spending patterns are individual and might not be typical of the representative pattern on which the official figures are based. For example, if an individual spent a high proportion of her income on fuel and her mortgage, the effect of price rises in gas, electricity, petrol and a rise in mortgage rates would have a disproportionate effect on her own experience of inflation. This different perception of inflation can have an effect on expectations, the importance of which we will see in later chapters.

Because of the different perceptions that people have about inflation and how it affects them, the ONS published a Personal Inflation Calculator (PIC) in 2007. The PIC allows users to be able to input their own details such as what their personal monthly expenditure is, how much they spend on food, meals out, alcohol, clothing and footwear, fuel for transport and so on. In addition, the calculator looks at what is spent on utilities such as water, council tax, vehicles, holidays and housing.

The ONS hopes that the PIC will help people to develop more of an interest in how inflation is calculated and be more aware of how the reality of price rises in their lives might differ to the officially published figures.

The CPI, the Harmonized Index of Consumer Prices and the Retail Prices Index

Before the end of 2003, it was more usual in the UK to measure prices using an index known as the retail prices index (RPI). In December 2003, however, the UK Chancellor of the Exchequer announced that all policy announcements concerning inflation and prices would relate to the CPI rather than the RPI, so that movements in the CPI became the main measure of inflation. What is the difference between the CPI and the RPI, and why the switch?

The RPI is a price index constructed in the way described above, and differs from the CPI mainly in the goods and services included in the basket and in the coverage of households. In particular, the CPI excludes a number of items that are included in the RPI, mainly related to housing, such as council tax (a local government tax) and house mortgage interest payments. These items are excluded because if council taxes rise or mortgage payments rise because interest rates have risen, then the inflation rate as measured by the RPI will rise, even though underlying inflationary pressures in the economy may not have changed. Also, the CPI covers all private households, whereas the RPI excludes the top 4 per cent by income and pensioner households who derive at least three-quarters of their income from state benefits. The CPI also includes the residents of institutional households such as student hostels, and also foreign visitors to the UK. This means that it covers some items that are not in the RPI, such as stockbrokers' fees, university accommodation fees and foreign students' university tuition fees. The two indices also differ in some of the very fine details of the way in which prices are measured (such as allowance for quality adjustment).

What were the reasons for introducing the CPI? One reason is that some economists believe that it is closer to the concept of the overall price level employed in macroeconomic analysis – although others would argue that it may be misleading in the way in which it understates housing costs by excluding mortgage interest payments and council taxes. The main reason for its adoption, however, is that the construction of the CPI is identical to that used in the European Union (EU) to construct price indices for

TABLE 5.3	Inflation Rates Across Europe (2005 = 100) October 2013
Belgium	1.4
Bulgaria	1.0
Czech Republic	1.6
Denmark	0.8
Germany (including former GDR from 1991)	1.7
Estonia	3.5
Ireland	0.7
Greece	−0.4
Spain	2.0
France	1.1
Italy	1.6
Cyprus	0.8
Latvia	0.3
Lithuania	1.6
Luxembourg	1.9
Hungary	2.5
Malta	1.4
Netherlands	2.9
Austria	2.3
Poland	1.1
Portugal	0.8
Romania	3.7
Slovenia	2.2
Slovakia	2.0
Finland	2.5
Sweden	0.5
United Kingdom	2.7
Iceland	4.5
Norway	1.8
Switzerland	−0.0
Croatia	2.9
Turkey	7.3

other EU member countries. Because these price indices are harmonized in their construction across countries, they are known in Europe as harmonized indices of consumer prices, or HICPs. This allows direct comparison of inflation rates across EU member states. Such comparisons are not possible using national consumer price indices due to differences in index coverage and construction. The CPI published by the UK Office for National Statistics is in fact the UK HICP.

In Table 5.3 we have listed the HICP as of October 2013 for each of the members of the European Union, and for Switzerland and Turkey. Because we know that the price index has been constructed using the same conventions for each country, we can compare the figures directly.

The GDP Deflator versus the Consumer Prices Index

In the preceding chapter we examined another measure of the overall level of prices in the economy – the GDP deflator. The GDP deflator is the ratio of nominal GDP to real GDP. Because nominal GDP is current output valued at current prices and real GDP is current output valued at base-year prices, the GDP deflator reflects the current level of prices relative to the level of prices in the base year.

Economists and policymakers monitor both the GDP deflator and the CPI to gauge how quickly prices are rising. Usually, these two statistics tell a similar story. Yet there are two important differences that can cause them to diverge.

The first difference is that the GDP deflator reflects the prices of all goods and services *produced domestically*, whereas the CPI reflects the prices of all goods and services *bought by consumers*. For example, suppose that the price of an aeroplane produced by Dassault, a French aerospace firm and sold to the French Air Force rises. Even though the aeroplane is part of GDP in France, it is not part of the basket of goods and services bought by a typical consumer. Thus, the price increase shows up in the GDP deflator for France but not in France's CPI.

As another example, suppose that Volvo raises the price of its cars. Because Volvos are made in Sweden, the car is not part of French GDP. But French consumers buy Volvos, and so the car is part of the typical consumer's basket of goods. Hence, a price increase in an imported consumption good, such as a Volvo, shows up in the CPI but not in the GDP deflator.

This first difference between the CPI and the GDP deflator is particularly important when the price of oil changes. Although the United Kingdom does produce some oil, as with all of Europe and also North America, much of the oil used in the UK is imported from the Middle East. As a result, oil and oil products such as petrol and heating oil comprise a much larger share of consumer spending than they do of GDP. When the price of oil rises, the CPI rises by much more than does the GDP deflator.

The second and subtler difference between the GDP deflator and the CPI concerns how various prices are weighted to yield a single number for the overall level of prices. The CPI compares the price of a *fixed* basket of goods and services with the price of the basket in the base year. Whilst, as we have seen, the ONS revise the basket of goods on a regular basis, in contrast, the GDP deflator compares the price of *currently produced* goods and services with the price of the same goods and services in the base year. Thus, the group of goods and services used to compute the GDP deflator changes automatically over time. This difference is not important when all prices are changing proportionately. But if the prices of different goods and services are changing by varying amounts, the way we weight the various prices matters for the overall inflation rate.

Figure 5.1 shows the UK inflation rate as measured by both the GDP deflator and the CPI for each year from 1996 until 2012. You can see that whilst there are some occasions when the two diverge they do tend to move together. Figure 5.2 shows the GDP deflator for the EU 27 from 2010 to 2012 as a means of comparison.

SELF TEST Explain briefly what the consumer prices index is trying to measure and how it is constructed.

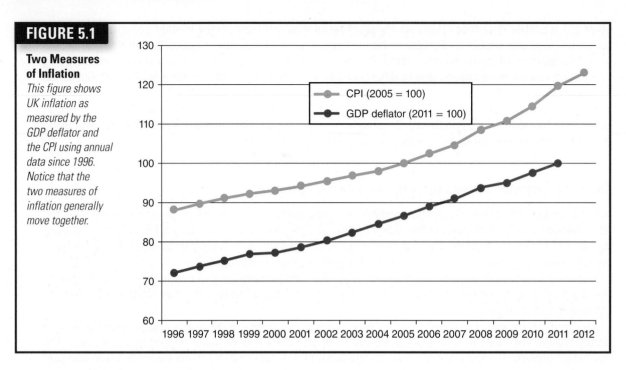

FIGURE 5.1

Two Measures of Inflation
This figure shows UK inflation as measured by the GDP deflator and the CPI using annual data since 1996. Notice that the two measures of inflation generally move together.

FIGURE 5.2

GDP Deflator (EU 27)
This figure shows the GDP deflator for the EU 27 countries by quarter between 2010 and 2012.

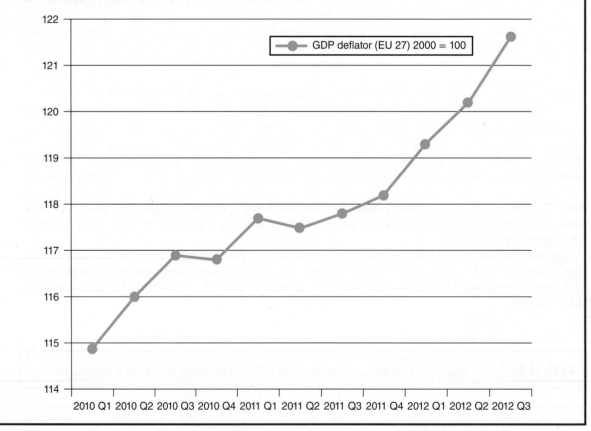

CORRECTING ECONOMIC VARIABLES FOR THE EFFECTS OF INFLATION

The purpose of measuring the overall level of prices in the economy is to permit comparisons of monetary figures from different points in time. Now that we know how price indices are calculated, let's see how we might use such an index to compare a certain figure from the past to a figure in the present.

Money Figures from Different Times

We first return to the issue of MPs' salary. Was the salary of £400 a year, first paid to MPs in 1911, high or low compared to the salaries of today's MPs?

To answer this question, we need to know the level of prices in 1911 and the level of prices today. Part of the increase in salaries merely compensates MPs for the higher level of prices today. To compare the salary to those of today's MPs, we need to inflate the 1911 salary to turn 1911 pounds into today's pounds. A price index determines the size of this inflation correction.

The formula for turning pound figures from *year T* into today's pounds is the following (assuming the price level today and the price level in *year T* are measured against the same base year):

$$\text{Amount in today's pounds} = \text{Amount in } year\ T \text{ pounds} \times \frac{\text{Price level today}}{\text{Price level in } year\ T}$$

A price index such as the CPI measures the price level and determines the size of the inflation correction. Let's apply this formula to MPs' wages. Statistics from the ONS show a price index of 9.6 for 1911 and 973.6 for December 2012. Thus the overall level of prices has risen by a factor of 101.4 (which equals 973.6/9.6). We can use these numbers to measure MP's salary in 2012 pounds, as follows:

$$\text{Salary in December 2012 pounds} = \text{Salary in 1911 pounds} \times \frac{\text{Price level in December 2012}}{\text{Price level in 1911}}$$

$$= £400 \times \left(\frac{973.6}{9.6}\right)$$

$$= £40{,}567$$

We find that the salary paid to an MP in 1911 is equivalent to a salary today of £40,567. This is more than the median annual salary across all occupations in April 2012 of £26,500 and is nearly two-thirds of what MPs were paid in 2012: £65,738. In that sense, MPs have done well.

Indexation

As we have just seen, price indices are used to correct for the effects of inflation when comparing monetary figures from different times. This type of correction shows up in many places in the economy. When some money amount is automatically corrected for inflation by law or contract, the amount is said to be **indexed** for inflation.

> **indexed** the automatic correction of a money amount for the effects of inflation by law or contract

For example, many long-term contracts between firms and unions include partial or complete indexation of the wage to the CPI. Such a provision is called a *cost-of-living allowance*, or COLA. A COLA automatically raises the wage each year based on the CPI or other measure such as the RPI, at a particular point in time.

Income tax brackets – the income levels at which the tax rates change – are also often moved annually in line with inflation, although, in most countries, they are not formally indexed. Indeed, there are many

CASE STUDY   Adjusting for Inflation: Use the Force

What was the most popular film of all time? The answer might surprise you. Film popularity is usually gauged by worldwide box office receipts. By that measure, as of the end of 2012, *Avatar* (released in 2009) was the number one film of all time grossing $2.78 billion, followed by *Titanic* (1993 – $2.19 billion); *Marvel's the Avengers* (2012 – $1.5 billion); *Harry Potter and the Deathly Hallows, Part 2* (2011 – $1.33 billion); *Lord of the Rings: Return of the King* (2003 – $1.19 billion); *The Dark Knight Rises* (2012 – $1.08 billion); and *Skyfall* (2012 – $1.08 billion). But this ranking ignores an obvious but important fact: prices, including those of cinema tickets, have been rising over time. When we correct box office receipts for the effects of inflation, the story is very different.

Table 5.4 shows the top ten films of all time ranked by inflation-adjusted worldwide box office receipts in US dollars. The original *Star Wars,* released in 1977, moves up to number two, while *The Sound of Music* takes the number three spot and the number one film of all time is the American Civil War drama, *Gone with the Wind* ($1.64 billion adjusted) which was released in 1939 and is well ahead of *Avatar* ($533 million adjusted), which doesn't even make the top ten (appearing at number 14). In the 1930s, before everyone had televisions in their homes, cinema attendance was about three or four times what it is today. But the films from that era rarely show up in popularity rankings because ticket prices were only a fraction of what they are today. Scarlett and Rhett, the main characters in *Gone with the Wind*, fare a lot better once we correct for the effects of inflation, as do Mowgli, Balou and King Louie of *The Jungle Book* fame (number 9 in the inflation-adjusted list). However, television ownership (indeed multiple television ownership) was widespread by 1977 when *Star Wars* was released, and so the ranking of this film as number two in the inflation-adjusted table perhaps makes Luke Skywalker an even more impressive figure.

The number one film of all time is the American Civil War drama, Gone with the Wind *($1.64 billion adjusted) which was released in 1939.*

TABLE 5.4   **The Most Popular Films of All Time, Inflation-Adjusted**

Film	Year of release
1. *Gone with the Wind*	1939
2. *Star Wars*	1977
3. *The Sound of Music*	1965
4. *E.T.*	1982
5. *Titanic*	1997
6. *The Ten Commandments*	1956
7. *Jaws*	1975
8. *Doctor Zhivago*	1965
9. *The Jungle Book*	1967
10. *Snow White and the Seven Dwarfs*	1937

ways in which the tax system is not indexed for inflation, even when perhaps it should be. We discuss these issues more fully when we discuss the costs of inflation later in this book.

Real and Nominal Interest Rates

Correcting economic variables for the effects of inflation is particularly important, and somewhat tricky, when we look at data on interest rates. When you deposit your savings in a bank account, you will earn interest on your deposit. Conversely, when you borrow from a bank in order to buy a car, you will pay interest on the loan. Interest represents a payment in the future for a transfer of money in the past. As a result, interest rates always involve comparing amounts of money at different points in time. To fully understand interest rates, we need to know how to correct for the effects of inflation.

Let's consider an example. Suppose that Carla deposits €1,000 in a bank account that pays an annual interest rate of 10 per cent. After a year passes, Carla has accumulated €100 in interest. Carla then withdraws her €1,100. Is Carla €100 richer than she was when she made the deposit a year earlier?

The answer depends on what we mean by 'richer'. Carla does have €100 more than she had before. In other words, the number of euros has risen by 10 per cent. But if prices have risen at the same time, each euro now buys less than it did a year ago. Thus, her purchasing power has not risen by 10 per cent. If the inflation rate was 4 per cent, then the amount of goods she can buy has increased by only 6 per cent. And if the inflation rate was 15 per cent, then the price of goods has increased proportionately more than the number of euros in her account. In that case, Carla's purchasing power has actually fallen by 5 per cent.

The interest rate that the bank pays is called the **nominal interest rate**, and the interest rate corrected for inflation is called the **real interest rate**. We can write the relationship among the nominal interest rate, the real interest rate and inflation as follows:

> **nominal interest rate** the interest rate as usually reported without a correction for the effects of inflation
> **real interest rate** the interest rate corrected for the effects of inflation

Real interest rate = Nominal interest rate − Inflation rate

The real interest rate is the difference between the nominal interest rate and the rate of inflation. The nominal interest rate tells you how fast the number of pounds or euros in your bank account rises over time. The real interest rate tells you how fast the purchasing power of your bank account rises over time.

Figure 5.3 shows the nominal interest rate (measured as the average rate of discount on three-month Treasury bills), the inflation rate (measured by the RPI) and the real interest rate (the difference between the two). You can see that real and nominal interest rates do not always move together. For example, in the late 1970s, nominal interest rates were high, but because inflation was higher, real interest rates were low. It is noticeable that since the financial crisis in 2008, real interest rates have been negative with inflation eroding people's savings more quickly than nominal interest payments increased them. By contrast, in the 1990s, nominal interest rates were low but because inflation was also low, real interest rates were relatively high. In the coming chapters, when we study the causes and effects of changes in interest rates, it will be important for us to keep in mind the distinction between real and nominal interest rates.

> **SELF TEST** Why is it important to adjust for inflation when considering wage increases and the returns from any financial investment?

FIGURE 5.3

Real and Nominal Interest Rates

This figure shows the inflation rate (RPI), nominal and real interest rates using average annual changes since 1976. The nominal interest rate is the rate on a three-month Treasury bill. The real interest rate is the nominal interest rate minus the annual inflation rate as measured by the retail prices index. Notice that nominal and real interest rates do not always move together.

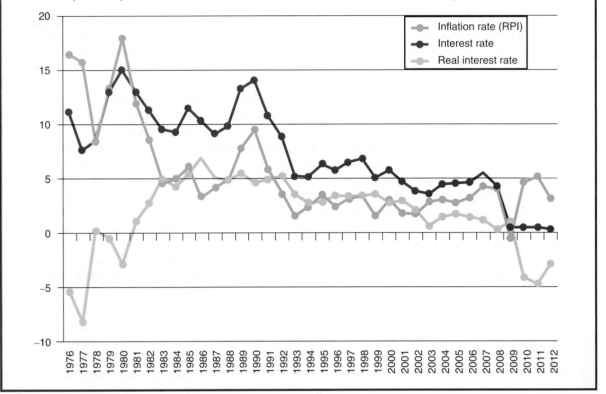

CONCLUSION

Throughout recent history, the real values behind the currencies of most major industrialized countries, such as the pound, euro and dollar, have not been stable. Persistent increases in the overall level of prices in advanced economies such as those of the UK, the other countries of Europe and of the USA have been the norm. Such inflation reduces the purchasing power of each unit of money over time. When comparing figures in monetary or nominal terms from different times, it is important to keep in mind that a pound or euro today is not the same as a pound or euro ten years ago or, most likely, ten years from now.

This chapter has discussed how economists measure the overall level of prices in the economy and how they use price indices to correct economic variables for the effects of inflation. This analysis is only a starting point. We have not yet examined the causes and effects of inflation or how inflation interacts with other economic variables. To do that, we need to go beyond issues of measurement. Indeed, that is our next task. Having explained how economists measure macroeconomic quantities and prices in the past chapter, we are now ready to develop the models that explain long-run and short-run movements in these variables.

IN THE NEWS

Accounting for Quality Change

Economists and statisticians are always looking to find ways of improving data, which is so crucial to decision making and policy. Accurate and reliable inflation data are one of the areas that have been subject to considerable review. In particular the issue of how changes in quality affect measures of inflation has been at the forefront of debate for a number of years. This article looks at the use of hedonics in the calculation of price indices.

Hedonics and Price Indices

We all know that prices change over time. The reason for price changes can be varied but some price changes may reflect improvements in the quality of a product as technology advances ever more rapidly. Does this mean that a TV bought in 2012 for €600 represents better value for money (and therefore a lower price) than one priced at €450 in 2009? Taking into account this issue is the subject of hedonics. Hedonics is a statistical device to account for the changing quality of products when calculating price movements. It has stirred some debate on both sides of the Atlantic. In the United States for example, the *Wall Street Journal* reported on the case of 27-inch TV sets. Tim LaFleur, a commodity specialist for televisions working with the US Bureau of Labor Statistics, the body which compiles CPI data, estimated that the price of a TV set with a nominal price of $329.99 had improved in terms of the quality of the screen, among other things, which increased its value by $135. When running the data through a computer program, LaFleur concluded that the price of the TV had actually fallen by 29 per cent.

There are other aspects to the issue as well. The increasing concern with the effects of humans on the planet means that there is a

drive to improve energy efficiency. Developments in technology are also helping to improve health and safety, the improvements in safety records of cars being one example of this. If manufacturers produce a washing machine that improves the efficiency of energy use by 10 per cent, for example, then even if the nominal price of the product rose, the use of hedonics might show that the price of washing machines did not rise at all. Equally, if a car is now safer to use and protects the driver and passengers, then the value of this is far greater than any increase in price to cover the cost of fitting such features. The adjusted price of the car, therefore, falls.

The ONS has been using hedonics as part of its calculation of price indices since 2004. One news report at the time suggested that the use of hedonics could save the Chancellor around £100 million a year, as a result of having to pay less to savers and pensioners. Initially the technique was applied to the RPI relating to digital cameras and computers. It led to a cut in the RPI by around 0.05 per cent, according to the ONS, but this equates to a saving for the government of £50 million in payments to those on index linked benefits, £45 million on interest payments for index linked gilts and further savings on tax allowances which may not be uprated. Whilst the initial

introduction of hedonics at the ONS caused a relatively small change in the RPI, there have been suggestions that a wider application of the technique across more goods could reduce the annual rate of inflation by between 0.25 and 0.5 per cent.

There have been concerns expressed, therefore, that the use of this technique presents a distorted picture of how price changes affect the economy. A report published in the US in 1996 suggested that underestimation of the improvements in quality might mean that price indices were overstated by as much as 0.6 per cent per year. There are some concerns, however, that the technique could be exploited for political purposes; whilst hedonics has a firm root in statistical methodology there is some judgement applied about the nature of the quality improvements and there are concerns that these might be used to artificially lower published inflation rates. Given that inflation figures are used to index link certain payments from government and as the basis for wage claims, any depression in the index might be viewed with some suspicion.

Proponents of the use of hedonics argue that far from distorting the picture, the use of the technique gives a far more accurate picture of what is going on in the economy. They point out that bodies such as

(Continued)

the Royal Statistical Society make observations on the way the ONS gathers and interprets data and that it is an important way of measuring quality changes in relation to prices. Technology is improving so rapidly that a failure to do so would over inflate prices. They point to the way in which products like digital cameras, mobile phones, TVs and computers have changed in recent years. In many cases, improvements in technology also lead to a reduction in price which will affect price indices. The question is should these price indices be even lower? Take tablet computers, which at the time of writing have the computing power to run advanced, high-quality graphics games, have massive memory, roaming internet access, extensive music and video files, cameras and video recorders and players, and are priced at around £500 in comparison to bulky, low graphics, slow machines that basically ran word-processing and other office applications but which were priced over £1,000 five years ago. Surely the improvements in speed, quality, capacity and flexibility are worth more to consumers than the change in price of £500?

Ultimately the debate comes down to the accuracy of the judgements made by statisticians in being able to accurately account for the improvements in quality of products. If these judgements are accurate and widely accepted then incorporating hedonics into the index could improve its accuracy. If, however, such judgements are subject to political interference then some sections of society could be made worse off.

Questions

1 Why is it important to take changes in quality into account when measuring price changes over time?

2 What sort of quality improvements do you think statisticians ought to account for in generating more accurate measures of price changes over time?

3 Why is index linking important to people whose incomes are 'fixed' (i.e. not subject to increases linked to productivity improvements)?

4 Why might the incorporation of hedonics into measurement of prices over time affect those whose incomes are index linked?

5 Do you think that incorporating hedonics into measurement of price changes is a good thing or too likely to be subject to political interference?

Technology changes over time as do prices but how can we take into account changes in quality over time? Hedonics may provide the answer.

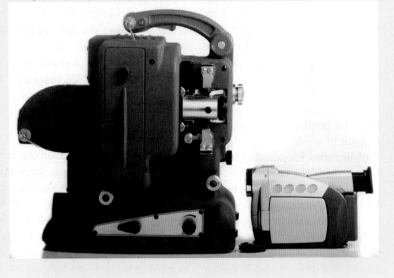

SUMMARY

- The CPI shows the changes in the prices of a basket of goods and services relative to the prices of the same basket in the base year. The index is used to measure the overall level of prices in the economy. The percentage change in the CPI measures the inflation rate.

- The CPI is an imperfect measure of the cost of living for three reasons. First, it does not take into account consumers' ability to substitute towards goods that become relatively cheaper over time. Second, it does not take into account increases in the purchasing power of money due to the introduction of new goods. Third, it is distorted by unmeasured changes in the quality of goods and services. Because of these measurement problems, the CPI overstates true inflation.

- Although the GDP deflator also measures the overall level of prices in the economy, it differs from the CPI because it includes goods and services produced rather than goods and services consumed. As a result, imported goods affect the CPI but not the GDP deflator. In addition, while the CPI uses a fixed basket of goods, the GDP deflator automatically changes the group of goods and services over time as the composition of GDP changes.

● Money figures (e.g. in euros) from different points in time do not represent a valid comparison of purchasing power. To compare a money figure from the past to a money figure today, the older figure should be inflated using a price index.

● Various laws and private contracts use price indices to correct for the effects of inflation.

● A correction for inflation is especially important when looking at data on interest rates. The nominal interest rate is the interest rate usually reported; it is the rate at which the amount of money in a savings account increases over time. In contrast, the real interest rate takes into account changes in the value of the money over time. The real interest rate equals the nominal interest rate minus the rate of inflation.

QUESTIONS FOR REVIEW

1 What are the five stages of constructing a price index?

2 Why do statisticians use weighting in constructing price indices?

3 Which do you think has a greater effect on the consumer prices index: a 10 per cent increase in the price of chicken or a 10 per cent increase in the price of caviar? Why?

4 Describe the three problems that make the CPI an imperfect measure of the cost of living.

5 Why do statisticians change the composition of the basket of goods used in constructing a price index from time to time?

6 Assume that the price of a bottle of wine in 1990 was €3.50 and in 2012 it is €8.50. Further assume that the price index in 1990 was 95 and in 2012 was 160. Was wine cheaper in 1990 than in 2012? Explain.

7 If the price of a French Navy submarine rises, is the French consumer prices index or the French GDP deflator affected more? Why?

8 Over a long period of time, the price of a box of chocolates rose from €1 to €6. Over the same period, the CPI rose from 150 to 300. Adjusted for overall inflation, how much did the price of the box of chocolates change?

9 Explain the meaning of nominal interest rate and real interest rate. How are they related?

10 Why is knowledge of real interest rates of importance to people who rely on their savings for their income?

PROBLEMS AND APPLICATIONS

1 Suppose that people consume only three goods, as shown in this table:

	Tennis balls	Tennis racquets	Cola
2014 price (€)	2	40	1
2014 quantity	100	10	200
2015 price (€)	2	60	2
2015 quantity	100	10	200

a. What is the percentage change in the price of each of the three goods? What is the percentage change in the overall price level?

b. Do tennis racquets become more or less expensive relative to cola? Does the well-being of some people change relative to the well-being of others? Explain.

2 Suppose that the residents of Vegopia spend all of their income on cauliflower, broccoli and carrots. In 2014 they buy 100 heads of cauliflower for €200, 50 bunches of broccoli for €75 and 500 carrots for €50. In 2015 they buy 75 heads of cauliflower for €225, 80 bunches of broccoli for €120 and 500 carrots for €100. If the base year is 2014, what is the CPI in both years? What is the inflation rate in 2015?

3 Go to the website of the UK Office for National Statistics (http://www.statistics.gov.uk) or Eurostat (http://epp.eurostat.ec.europa.eu/portal/page/portal/eurostat/home) and find data on the CPI. By how much has the index including all items risen over the past year for your country? For which categories of spending have prices risen the most? The least? Have any categories experienced price declines? Can you explain any of these facts?

4 Which of the problems in the construction of the CPI might be illustrated by each of the following situations? Explain.

a. the increase in downloading movies

b. the introduction of air bags in cars

c. increased personal computer purchases in response to a decline in their price

d. increased use of digital cameras in smart phones

e. greater use of fuel-efficient cars after petrol prices increase.

5 Suppose the government were to determine the level of the state retirement pension in the UK so that it increased each year in proportion to the increase in the

CPI (even though most economists believe that the CPI overstates actual inflation).

a. If the elderly consume the same market basket as other people, would such a policy provide the elderly with an improvement in their standard of living each year? Explain.

b. In fact, the elderly consume more health care than younger people, and health care costs tend to rise faster than overall inflation. What would you do to determine whether the elderly are actually better off from year to year?

6 How do you think the basket of goods and services you buy differs from the basket bought by the typical household? Do you think you face a higher or lower inflation rate than is indicated by the CPI? Why?

7 In some years in some countries, income tax brackets are not increased in line with inflation. Why do you think the government might do this? (Hint: this phenomenon is known as 'bracket creep'.)

8 When deciding how much of their income to save for retirement, should workers consider the real or the nominal interest rate that their savings will earn? Explain.

9 Suppose that a borrower and a lender agree on the nominal interest rate to be paid on a loan. Then inflation turns out to be higher than they both expected.

a. Is the real interest rate on this loan higher or lower than expected?

b. Does the lender gain or lose from this unexpectedly high inflation? Does the borrower gain or lose?

10 Explain why nominal and real interest rates might vary over time.

PART 4
THE REAL ECONOMY IN THE LONG RUN

6 PRODUCTION AND GROWTH

When you travel around the world, you see tremendous variation in the standard of living. The average person in a rich country, such as the countries of Western Europe, has an income more than ten times as high as the average person in a poor country, such as India, Indonesia or Nigeria. These large differences in income are reflected in large differences in the quality of life. Richer countries have more cars, more smart phones, more televisions, better nutrition, safer housing, better health care and longer life expectancy.

Even within a country, there are large changes in the standard of living over time. In the United Kingdom over the past century or so, average income as measured by real GDP per person has grown by about 1.3 per cent per year. Although 1.3 per cent might seem small, this rate of growth implies that average income doubles about every 50 years. Because of this growth, average UK income today is about four times as high as average income a century ago. As a result, the typical Brit enjoys much greater economic prosperity than did his or her parents, grandparents and great-grandparents. The story is similar for many other European countries. Figure 6.1 shows GDP per person in the EU 27 since 2003. The trend has been upwards until the recession struck but despite this the average person in the EU 27 is still better off in 2011 than they were in 2003.

Growth rates vary substantially from country to country. In some East Asian countries, such as Singapore, South Korea and Taiwan, average income has risen about 7 per cent per year in recent decades. At this rate, average income doubles about every ten years. These countries have, in the length of one generation, gone from being among the poorest in the world to being among the richest. In contrast, in some African countries, such as Chad, Ethiopia and Nigeria, average income has been stagnant for many years.

What explains these diverse experiences? How can the rich countries be sure to maintain their high standard of living? What policies should the poor countries pursue to promote more rapid growth in order to join the developed world? These are among the most important questions in macroeconomics. As the Nobel Prize winning economist, Robert Lucas, once put it, 'The consequences for human welfare in questions like these are simply staggering: once one starts to think about them, it is hard to think about anything else.'

In the previous two chapters we discussed how economists measure macroeconomic quantities and prices. In this chapter we start studying the forces that determine these variables. As we have seen, an economy's gross domestic product (GDP) measures both the total income earned in the economy and the total expenditure on the economy's output of goods and services. The level of real GDP is a good gauge of economic prosperity, and the growth of real GDP is a good gauge of economic progress. Here we focus on the long-run determinants of the level and growth of real GDP. Later in this book we study the short-run fluctuations of real GDP around its long-run trend.

We proceed here in three steps. First, we examine international data on real GDP per person. These data will give you some sense of how much the level and growth of living standards vary around the world. Second, we examine the role of *productivity* – the amount of goods and services produced for each hour of a worker's time. In particular, we see that a nation's standard of living is determined by the productivity of its workers, and we consider the factors that determine a nation's productivity. Third, we consider the link between productivity and the economic policies that a nation pursues.

FIGURE 6.1

EU 27 GDP at Market Prices, Purchasing Power Standard Per Capita, 2003–2011 (€)

The figure shows GDP per person for the 27 EU countries over the period 2003–2011. Average incomes rose up to 2009 after which the recession led to a fall in GDP per capita.

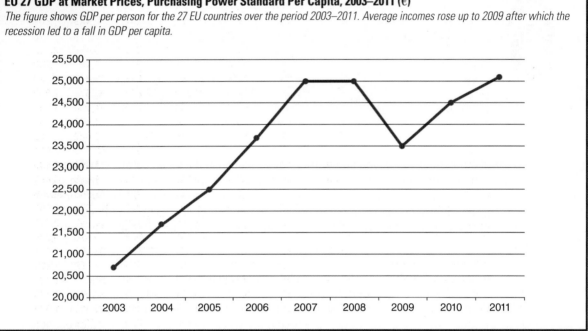

ECONOMIC GROWTH AROUND THE WORLD

As a starting point for our study of long-run growth, let's look at the experiences of some of the world's economies. Table 6.1 shows real GDP per person in 31 selected countries.

The data in the table show that living standards vary widely from country to country and have changed at very different rates over the last 50 years. Income per person in the United States, for instance, is about 32 times that in India even though India's per capita income has increased by almost 2,405 per cent since 1961. The poorest countries have very low average levels of income; the per capita income in the Democratic Republic of Congo has only increased by 18 per cent since 1961. Japan is one of the countries that has seen some of the most significant increases in per capita income rising by over 8,000 per cent since 1961 but Norway, Ireland and Brazil have also seen notable increases in per capita income which have been over 6,000 per cent. In 1961 Japan was not a rich country. Japan's average income is lower than Greece and not that much higher than Mexico's. Data from Barro and Xavier Sala-i-Martin published in 1995 (Robert J. Barro and Xavier Sala-i-Martin (1995). *Economic Growth*. New York: McGraw-Hill) suggested that

Japan's income in 1890 was less than in India today. But because of its spectacular growth, Japan is now an economic superpower, with average income more than 4.5 times that of Mexico, almost 1.8 times that of Greece and similar to that of France and Germany. The typical resident of many African countries continues to live in abject poverty, with average incomes in countries like Burkina Faso, Burundi and the Central African Republic at very low levels.

TABLE 6.1 **Real GDP Per Capita, Current US$, Selected Countries**

Country Name	1961	1971	1981	1991	2001	2011	% change
Algeria	221	358	2,281	1,763	1,781	5,244	2,271
Australia	1,874	3,490	11,850	18,873	19,541	60,979	3,153
Bangladesh	93	129	238	287	356	743	695
Barbados	403	851	3,792	6,480	9,524	13,453	3,242
Bolivia	179	254	1,077	784	960	2,374	1,229
Brazil	203	500	2,115	2,677	3,130	12,594	6,097
Burkina Faso	71	81	240	327	222	600	750
Burundi	68	71	228	204	127	271	300
Central African Republic	81	108	297	467	247	489	507
Congo, Dem. Rep.	196	268	451	240	92	231	18
Congo, Rep.	146	234	1,076	1,110	870	3,485	2,289
Egypt, Arab Rep.	151	225	509	638	1,417	2,781	1,738
Finland	1,327	2,684	10,790	24,991	24,025	48,823	3,578
France	1,446	3,126	10,917	21,270	21,812	42,377	2,830
Germany	–	3,089	9,879	22,604	22,840	44,060	1,326
Ghana	187	271	375	434	271	1,570	739
Greece	597	1,576	5,130	9,776	11,858	25,622	4,190
Iceland	1,418	3,204	14,913	26,406	27,803	43,969	3,001
India	59	120	275	308	460	1,489	2,405
Ireland	739	1,652	5,804	13,659	27,340	48,423	6,450
Japan	564	2,234	10,212	28,541	32,716	45,903	8,045
Luxembourg	2,222	4,397	13,718	35,439	45,743	114,508	5,053
Mexico	357	734	3,556	3,660	6,139	10,047	2,717
Netherlands	1,159	3,130	10,671	20,131	24,969	50,076	4,219
Norway	1,560	3,709	15,335	28,077	37,867	98,102	6,187
Pakistan	86	174	337	395	490	1,189	1,280
Saudi Arabia	–	1,127	17,617	7,879	8,849	20,540	1,722
United Kingdom	1,453	2,526	9,142	18,387	24,836	39,038	2,588
United States	2,935	5,360	13,526	23,443	35,912	48,112	1,539
Zambia	218	386	672	419	350	1,425	555
Zimbabwe	283	405	1,058	804	539	757	168

Because of differences in growth rates, the ranking of countries by income changes substantially over time. As we have seen, Japan is a country that has risen relative to others. One country that has fallen behind is the United Kingdom. In 1870, the United Kingdom was the richest country in the world, with average income about 20 per cent higher than that of the United States and more than twice that of Canada. Today, average income in the United Kingdom is 20 per cent below that of the United States and similar to Canada's. Looking at how the change in per capita income has changed over the past 50 years is one way to look at how countries have grown but it is also usual to look at economic growth from the perspective of the change in GDP over a year. Typical growth rates for developed countries might be between 1 and 2 per cent a year, which may not sound that much but over time can lead to major improvements in standards of living (see the FYI on Compounding). For emerging countries like China, growth rates of between 7 and 12 per cent have been recorded over a period but it has to be remembered that these rates are being recorded from a relatively low base.

These data show that the world's richest countries have no guarantee that they will stay the richest and that the world's poorest countries are not doomed forever to remain in poverty. But what explains these changes over time? Why do some countries zoom ahead while others lag behind? These are precisely the questions that we take up next.

SELF TEST Find out the approximate growth rate of real GDP per person in your country. Find a country that has had faster growth and a country that has had slower growth.

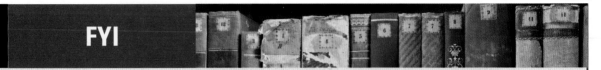

FYI

The Magic of Compounding and the Rule of 70

Suppose you observe that one country has an average growth rate of 1 per cent per year while another has an average growth rate of 3 per cent per year. At first, this might not seem like a big deal. What difference can 2 per cent make?

The answer is, a big difference. Even growth rates that seem small when written in percentage terms seem large after they are compounded for many years.

Consider an example. Suppose that two economics graduates – Milton and Maynard – both take their first jobs at the age of 22 earning €20,000 a year. Milton lives in an economy where all incomes grow at 1 per cent per year, while Maynard

lives in one where incomes grow at 3 per cent per year. Calculations using the principle of compounding show what happens. For Milton, after the first year he earns an additional 1 per cent of €20,000 (€200). In year 2 he earns an additional 1 per cent of €20,200 (€22,402) and so on. To calculate compound figures over time we use the formula $M = P(1 + i)^n$ where M is the total value at the end of the period, P is the initial value, i is the rate of interest (or rate of growth) and n the number of years. After 40 years, therefore, Milton earns $20,000 (1 + 0.01)^{40}$ which equals €29,777 a year.

Maynard, on the other hand, earns $€20,000 (1 + 0.03)^{40}$ and earns

€65,240 40 years later. Because of that difference of 2 percentage points in the growth rate, Maynard's salary is more than twice Milton's.

An old rule of thumb, called the *rule of 70*, is helpful in understanding growth rates and the effects of compounding. According to the rule of 70, if some variable grows at a rate of x per cent per year, then that variable doubles in approximately $\frac{70}{x}$ years. In Milton's economy, incomes grow at 1 per cent per year, so it takes about 70 years for incomes to double. In Maynard's economy, incomes grow at 3 per cent per year, so it takes about, $\frac{70}{3}$ or a little over 23 years for incomes to double.

GROWTH THEORY

Over time, economic growth in any country varies. Sometimes the economy experiences strong periods of growth and at other times growth is slower and sometimes the economy shrinks. But over a period of time, a trend can be established which is usually expressed in percentage terms. Trend growth can be found using the following formula:

$$\text{Trend growth} = \frac{\text{GDP}_{t2} - \text{GDP}_{t1}}{\text{GDP}_{t1}} \times 100$$

Which states the trend growth is found by taking GDP in some time period, subtracting GDP from an earlier time period, dividing the result by the value in the initial time period and expressing the figure as a percentage. If we took GDP of the, UK for example, in 1860 as time period$_{t1}$ and then the GDP in 2012 as time period$_{t2}$, and did the calculation the answer would give trend growth over that period. Trend growth and actual growth are important factors when we look at business cycles later in the book. Different countries have different trend growth rates. What determines trend growth over time? Why do some countries seem to be able to grow at fast rates and lift their citizens out of poverty whilst others struggle to generate any growth and as a result successive generations of people live in abject poverty? Why is the trend rate in developed countries relatively low?

There have been different theories of economic growth put forward over time, one of the most popular has been that advanced by Robert. M. Solow and Trevor Swan in 1956. They identified the rate of human and physical capital and population growth as being key determinants of economic growth. Over the years, economists have looked at other factors that may influence economic growth including the level of macroeconomic stability in an economy (don't worry too much about what this means at this stage, it will become clearer as you read the relevant section of this book), the type of trade policy that exists in a country (is the country outward looking or does it tend to be insular?), the nature and quality of institutions and governance (i.e. how effectively the rule of law operates and how well governments are able to control corruption) in the country concerned, the extent to which violence, war and conflict exist in a country, regional characteristics such as whether the country is part of Europe, North America, Asia or sub-Saharan Africa, geographical factors such as physical resource endowments and climate, the extent to which the country is competitive in international markets, and internal factors such as the amount of productive land available.

You will need to keep in mind that theories of growth are changing as economists carry out more research and have access to more data. The next section will cover the role of productivity in growth which can be referred to as the *neoclassical theory of growth*. Other theories, such as endogenous growth theory, argue that investment in a nation's human capital will be a key driver of economic growth. The reason being that investment in human capital is more likely to lead to increases in technology which in turn help promote efficiency and increases in productivity. This is the main driver of growth rather than trade. The debates surrounding these different theories are beyond the scope of this book but are something that you need to be aware of.

PRODUCTIVITY: ITS ROLE AND DETERMINANTS

If you have any knowledge of the production function and the concepts of marginal and diminishing marginal product, it will be useful in this section; the main difference is that we are thinking on a macroeconomic level rather than a microeconomic one.

Explaining the large variation in living standards around the world is, in one sense, very easy. As we will see, the explanation can be summarized in a single word – *productivity*. But, in another sense, the international variation is deeply puzzling. To explain why incomes are so much higher in some countries than in others, we must look at the many factors that determine a nation's productivity.

Why Productivity is So Important

Let's begin our study of productivity and economic growth by developing a simple model based on an individual who finds himself shipwrecked on a desert island, who we will call Fernando. Because Fernando lives alone, he catches his own fish, grows his own vegetables and makes his own clothes. We can think of Fernando's activities – his production and consumption of fish, vegetables and clothing – as being a simple economy. By examining Fernando's economy, we can learn some lessons that also apply to more complex and realistic economies.

What determines Fernando's standard of living? The answer is obvious. If Fernando is good at catching fish, growing vegetables and making clothes, he lives well. If he is bad at doing these things, he lives poorly. Because Fernando can consume only what he produces, his living standard is tied to his productive ability.

Remember that *productivity* refers to the quantity of goods and services that a worker can produce per specified time period. In the case of Fernando's economy, it is easy to see that productivity is the key determinant of living standards and that growth in productivity is the key determinant of growth in living standards. The more fish Fernando can catch per hour, the more he eats for dinner. If Fernando finds a better place to catch fish, his productivity rises. This increase in productivity makes Fernando better off: he could eat the extra fish, or he could spend less time fishing and devote more time to making other goods he enjoys.

The key role of productivity in determining living standards is as true for nations as it is for Fernando. Recall that an economy's gross domestic product (GDP) measures two things at once: the total income earned by everyone in the economy and the total expenditure on the economy's output of goods and services. The reason why GDP can measure these two things simultaneously is that, for the economy as a whole, they must be equal. Put simply, an economy's income is the economy's output.

Like Fernando, a nation can enjoy a high standard of living only if it can produce a large quantity of goods and services. Western Europeans live better than Nigerians because western European workers are more productive than Nigerian workers. The Japanese have enjoyed more rapid growth in living standards than Mexicans because Japanese workers have experienced more rapidly growing productivity. Indeed, one of the *Ten Principles of Economics* is that a country's standard of living depends on its ability to produce goods and services.

Hence, to understand the large differences in living standards we observe across countries or over time, we must focus on the production of goods and services. But seeing the link between living standards and productivity is only the first step. It leads naturally to the next question: why are some economies so much better at producing goods and services than others?

The Determinants of Economic Growth

Solow and Swan established some key elements of the determinants of economic growth. GDP in any country can be assumed to be an extension of a firm's production function where the level of output is dependent on the factors of production employed. In the analysis that follows we are going to assume just two factors, capital (K) and labour (L) are employed. At a macroeconomic level, therefore, the GDP of a country (Y) is a function of the capital stock (K) and the supply of human capital (L). We will express this as follows:

$$Y = f(K, L)$$

Remember also that the total product curve gets flatter as the amount of each factor input is increased due to the law of diminishing marginal product. The marginal product of labour is the change in output (GDP) which results from the change in labour inputs: MP_L

$$MP_L = \frac{\Delta Y}{\Delta L}$$

And the marginal product of capital is the change in output (GDP) which results from the change in capital inputs:

$$MP_K = \frac{\Delta Y}{\Delta K}$$

The factor endowments that exist in many countries are closely interlinked. There is some criticism of the principle of comparative advantage on the basis that countries with large amounts of cheap labour at their disposal, which should give them a comparative advantage, do not always experience the sort of growth that the theory might suggest. It is not just the amount of labour that is important but the productivity of labour and this is determined by many other factors, not least the amount and quality of capital.

We can do some rearranging of the production function to derive average labour productivity to see how this is dependent on the capital stock. If we take our production function $Y = f(K, L)$ and divide both sides by L we get:

$$\frac{Y}{L} = f\left(\frac{K}{L}, 1\right)$$

$\frac{Y}{L}$ is average labour productivity – the amount of output per worker. Average labour productivity is dependent on the ratio of capital to labour $\frac{K}{L}$. The number 1 is a constant derived from dividing the equation by L which we can ignore. The amount and quality of the capital stock in relation to the labour force is an important determinant of labour productivity. Labour productivity will rise if the capital stock increases but it must also be remembered that because of diminishing marginal product the rate of increase in average labour productivity will decline as the capital stock per worker increases. Economic growth, therefore, is dependent on the capital stock per worker and on average labour productivity.

How Does the Stock of Physical Capital Grow? Think back to Chapter 4 when we introduced a more complex circular flow diagram of the economy. We introduced withdrawals from and injections to the circular flow. When households receive income not all of it is spent, some of it is saved. The proportion of income saved is called the savings ratio. The Solow–Swan model noted the importance of the savings ratio in determining investment. Investment is spending on physical capital in the economy – on future productive capacity. Investment is financed by saving (we will look at the relationship between investment and saving in more detail in later chapters).

The level of investment in an economy is an important factor in determining the capital/labour ratio. Over time, economies will experience increases in population and in addition the existing capital stock will be subject to depreciation – machines wear out or become obsolete, plant will rust or break and so will need replacing. If capital is not replaced and the population increased, the capital/labour ratio will decline. Investment spending can be classified in two ways, gross investment and net investment. **Gross investment** is the total amount spent on capital stock in a period; **net investment** is spending on the capital stock minus the amount spent on replacing existing stock – in other words, spending on new capital and not on depreciation. The depreciation rate and the rate of growth of population will be key factors in determining the investment required to keep the capital/labour ratio constant. If the rate of depreciation of capital in an economy was 5 per cent a year and the population was rising at a rate of 1.5 per cent a year, then the economy would need investment to increase at a rate of 6.5 per cent a year to keep the capital/labour ratio constant.

> **gross investment** the total spending on capital stock per period of time in an economy
> **net investment** spending on the capital stock taking into account spending on depreciation of the existing capital stock

The ratio of capital to labour is one aspect, therefore, of how productive labour can be. One of the reasons put forward for the rapid growth in countries like Korea and Vietnam is that not only have they a supply of relatively cheap labour but both countries have invested in capital and as a result labour productivity is relatively high. Compare this to the various African countries we saw in Table 6.1 where average incomes remain very low, and the main difference is that in these African countries investment in capital stock is extremely low and so labour productivity is also very low.

We will now look further at how productivity of factors of production is determined.

How Productivity is Determined

Let us return to our example of Fernando. Although productivity is uniquely important in determining Fernando's standard of living, many factors determine Fernando's productivity. Fernando will be better at catching fish, for instance, if he has more fishing rods, if he has been trained in the best fishing techniques, if his island has a plentiful fish supply, and if he invents a better fishing lure. Each of these determinants of Fernando's productivity – which we can call *physical capital*, *human capital*, *natural resources* and *technological knowledge* – has a counterpart in more complex and realistic economies. Let's consider each of these factors in turn.

Physical Capital As we have seen, workers are more productive if the capital stock is high. The stock of equipment and structures that are used to produce goods and services is called **physical capital**, or just *capital*. For example, when carpenters make furniture, they use saws, lathes and drill presses. More tools allow work to be done more quickly and more accurately. That is, a carpenter with only basic hand tools can make less furniture each week than a carpenter with sophisticated and specialized woodworking equipment.

> **physical capital** the stock of equipment and structures that are used to produce goods and services

An important feature of capital is that it is a *produced* factor of production. That is, capital is an input into the production process that in the past was an output from the production process. The carpenter uses a lathe to make the leg of a table. Earlier the lathe itself was the output of a firm that manufactures lathes. The lathe manufacturer in turn used other equipment to make its product. Thus, capital is a factor of production used to produce all kinds of goods and services, including more capital.

Human Capital A second determinant of productivity is human capital. Human capital is the economist's term for the knowledge and skills that workers acquire through education, training and experience. Human capital includes the skills accumulated in early childhood programmes, primary school, secondary school, university or college, and on-the-job training for adults in the labour force.

Although education, training and experience are less tangible than lathes, bulldozers and buildings, human capital is like physical capital in many ways. Like physical capital, human capital raises a nation's ability to produce goods and services. Also like physical capital, human capital is a produced factor of production. Producing human capital requires inputs in the form of teachers, lecturers, libraries and student time. Indeed, students can be viewed as 'workers' who have the important job of producing the human capital that will be used in future production.

Natural Resources A third determinant of productivity is **natural resources**. Natural resources are inputs into production that are provided by nature, such as land, rivers and mineral deposits. Natural resources take two forms: renewable and non-renewable. A forest is an example of a renewable resource. When one tree is cut down, a seedling can be planted in its place to be harvested in the future. Oil is an example of a non-renewable resource. Because oil is produced by nature over many thousands or even millions of years, there is only a limited supply. Once the supply of oil is depleted, it is impossible to create more (at least not for thousands of years).

natural resources the inputs into the production of goods and services that are provided by nature, such as land, rivers and mineral deposits

Differences in natural resources are responsible for some of the differences in standards of living around the world. The historical success of the United States was driven in part by the large supply of land well suited for agriculture. Today, some countries in the Middle East, such as Kuwait and Saudi Arabia, are rich simply because they happen to be on top of some of the largest pools of oil in the world.

Although natural resources can be important, they are not necessary for an economy to be highly productive in producing goods and services. Japan, for instance, is one of the richest countries in the world, despite having few natural resources. International trade makes Japan's success possible. Japan imports many of the natural resources it needs, such as oil, and exports its manufactured goods to economies rich in natural resources.

Technological Knowledge A fourth determinant of productivity is **technological knowledge** – the understanding of the best ways to produce goods and services. (Technology is defined as the application of knowledge to the environment to enable people to exercise greater control over that environment.) A hundred years ago, most Europeans and North Americans worked on farms, because farm technology required a high input of labour in order to feed the entire population. Today, thanks to advances in the technology of farming, a small fraction of the populations of western Europe, the USA and Canada can produce enough food to feed their entire population. This technological change made labour available to produce other goods and services.

technological knowledge society's understanding of the best ways to produce goods and services

Technological knowledge takes many forms. Some technology is common knowledge – after it starts to be used by one person, everyone becomes aware of it. For example, once Henry Ford successfully introduced production in assembly lines in the USA, other car makers and industrial producers throughout the world quickly followed suit. Other technology is proprietary – it is known only by the company that discovers it. Only the Coca-Cola Company, for instance, knows the secret recipe for making its famous soft drink. Still other technology is proprietary for a short time. When a pharmaceutical company discovers a new drug, the patent system gives that company a temporary right to be its exclusive manufacturer. When the patent expires, however, other companies are allowed to make the drug. All these forms of technological knowledge are important for the economy's production of goods and services.

It is worthwhile to distinguish between technological knowledge and human capital. Although they are closely related, there is an important difference. Technological knowledge refers to *society's* understanding about how the world works. Human capital refers to the resources expended transmitting this understanding to the *labour force*. To use a relevant metaphor, knowledge is the quality of society's textbooks, whereas human capital is the amount of time that the population has devoted to reading them. Workers' productivity depends on both the quality of textbooks they have available and the amount of time they have spent studying them.

We have noted that investment is required in order to maintain the capital/labour ratio but in order to achieve growth, it is not simply sufficient to keep things in a constant state – this is where technical progress is so important. Technical progress means that the *quality* of physical and human capital is improved so for any given quantity of capital and labour, the average productivity of both is higher so that a higher output can be produced from the economy's factors of production. In essence, technical progress can help to counterbalance the effects of diminishing marginal product. If additional factors are employed but the total productivity of those factors increases then the economy can experience growth.

The production function can be written as:

$$\frac{Y}{L} = \beta f\left(\frac{K}{L}, 1\right)$$

where β (beta) is the rate of technological progress. Even if the capital/labour ratio is constant, this factor productivity can increase by whatever the increase in technological progress is. For example, if technological progress increases by 0.5 per cent a year, then $\beta = (1 + 0.005)$. Average labour productivity can increase by 0.5 per cent even if the ratio of capital to labour stays constant. If this is the case then the production function will actually shift upwards will shift outwards reflecting the ability of the economy to produce more of every good.

We can summarize this analysis through the use of the following production function:

$$Y = \beta f(K, L, H, N)$$

Where Y denotes the quantity of output, K the quantity of physical capital, L the quantity of labour, H the quantity of human capital and N the quantity of natural resources. β is a variable that reflects the available production technology. As technology improves, β rises, so the economy produces more output from any given combination of inputs.

Many production functions have a property called *constant returns to scale*. If a production function has constant returns to scale, then a doubling of all the inputs causes the amount of output to double as well. Mathematically, we write that a production function has constant returns to scale if, for any positive number x:

$$xY = \beta f(xK, xL, xH, xN)$$

A doubling of all inputs is represented in this equation by $x = 2$. The right-hand side shows the inputs doubling, and the left-hand side shows output doubling.

If we set $x = 1/L$, the equation above becomes:

$$Y/L = \beta f\left(1, \frac{K}{L}, \frac{H}{L}, \frac{N}{L}\right)$$

Remember that Y/L is output per worker, a measure of productivity. This equation says that productivity depends on physical capital per worker $\left(\frac{K}{L}\right)$, human capital per worker $\left(\frac{H}{L}\right)$, and natural resources per worker $\left(\frac{N}{L}\right)$. Productivity also depends on the state of technology, as reflected by the variable β. Thus, this equation provides a mathematical summary of the four determinants of productivity that we have just discussed.

> **SELF TEST** List and describe four determinants of a country's productivity.

Are Natural Resources a Limit to Growth?

Today the world's population is over 6 billion, about four times what it was a *century* ago. At the same time, many people are enjoying a much higher standard of living than did their great-grandparents. A perennial debate concerns whether this growth in population and living standards can continue in the future.

Many commentators have argued that natural resources provide a limit to how much the world's economies can grow. At first, this argument might seem hard to ignore. If the world has only a fixed supply of non-renewable natural resources, how can population, production and living standards continue to grow over time? Eventually, won't supplies of oil and minerals start to run out? When these shortages start to occur, won't they stop economic growth and, perhaps, even force living standards to fall?

Despite the apparent appeal of such arguments, most economists are less concerned about such limits to growth than one might imagine. They argue that technological progress often yields ways to avoid these limits. If we compare the economy today to the economy of the past, we see various ways in which the use of natural resources has improved. Modern cars have better petrol mileage. New houses have better insulation and require less energy to heat and cool them. More efficient oil rigs waste less oil in the process of extraction. Recycling allows some non-renewable resources to be reused. The development of alternative fuels, such as ethanol instead of petrol, allows us to substitute renewable for non-renewable resources.

Copper prices fluctuate over short periods of time but over longer periods of time are relatively stable. This might imply that supplies from mines like these are not running out as quickly as some people have predicted.

Fifty years ago, some conservationists were concerned about the excessive use of tin and copper. At the time, these were crucial commodities: tin was used to make many food containers, and copper was used to make telephone wire. Some people advocated mandatory recycling and rationing of tin and copper so that supplies would be available for future generations. Today, however, plastic has replaced tin as a material for making many food containers, and telephone calls often travel over fibre-optic cables, which are made from sand. Technological progress has made once-crucial natural resources less necessary.

But are all these efforts enough to permit continued economic growth? One way to answer this question is to look at the prices of natural resources. In a market economy, scarcity is reflected in market prices. If the world were running out of natural resources, then the prices of those resources would be rising over time. But, in fact, the opposite is more nearly true. Natural resource prices exhibit substantial short-run price fluctuations, but over long spans of time, the prices of most natural resources (adjusted for overall inflation) are stable or falling. It appears that our ability to conserve these resources is growing more rapidly than their supplies are dwindling. Market prices give no reason to believe that natural resources are a limit to economic growth.

ECONOMIC GROWTH AND PUBLIC POLICY

So far, we have determined that a society's standard of living depends on its ability to produce goods and services and that its productivity depends on physical capital, human capital, natural resources and technological knowledge. Let's now turn to the question faced by policymakers around the world: what can government policy do to raise productivity and living standards?

The Importance of Saving and Investment

We introduced the role of the savings ratio in relation to investment earlier in the chapter. Investment is necessary to sustain and increase the capital stock. Because capital is a produced factor of production, a society can change the amount of capital it has. If today the economy produces a large quantity of new capital goods, then tomorrow it will have a larger stock of capital and be able to produce more of all types of goods and services. Thus, one way to raise future productivity is to invest more current resources in the production of capital.

One of the *Ten Principles of Economics* is that people face trade-offs. This principle is especially important when considering the accumulation of capital. Because resources are scarce, devoting more resources to producing capital requires devoting fewer resources to producing goods and services for current consumption. That is, for society to invest more in capital, it must consume less and save more of its current income (the savings ratio must rise). The growth that arises from capital accumulation is not a free lunch: it requires that society sacrifice consumption of goods and services in the present in order to enjoy higher consumption in the future.

In the 1930s, the rulers of Russia deliberately diverted resources to the production of capital goods in an attempt to try to catch up with the richer and more industrialized Western countries such as Germany, the United States and the United Kingdom. It managed to expand production in core industries such as coal and steel significantly which in turn increased its capacity to produce other capital goods (and military equipment). The trade-off for the Russian people at the time was fewer consumer goods and a harsh life. It could be argued that whilst this represented significant short-term hardship for many of its people, the decision helped Russia to be in a position to fight off the Germans in World War II and emerge to be one of the planet's superpowers.

In later chapters we examine in more detail how the economy's financial markets coordinate saving and investment. We also examine how government policies influence the amount of saving and investment that takes place. At this point it is important to note that encouraging saving and investment is one way that a government can encourage growth and, in the long run, raise the economy's standard of living.

To see the importance of investment for economic growth, consider Figure 6.2, which displays data on 19 countries. Panel (a) shows each country's average growth rate between 1961 and 2011. The countries are ordered by their average annual growth rates, from most to least rapid. Panel (b) shows the percentage of GDP that each country devoted to investment as an average over the period 1961–2011. Note that some data for some countries in both cases are not complete – there are gaps in data for Afghanistan, in particular.

The correlation between growth and investment is strong. Countries that devote a large share of GDP to investment, such as China, Japan and Australia, also have a stronger average growth rate. Countries that devote a small share of GDP to investment, such as the Central African Republic, Zimbabwe and Bangladesh, tend to have low growth rates. Drilling down more deeply into the figures shows that there are a number of years where investment in the Central African Republic and Bangladesh has been in single digits, whereas in China, investment began to increase from around 1978 to over 30 per cent and in the early 1990s to over 44 per cent. Investment hovered in the upper 30 per cents until the early part of the new century when investment was consistently above 44 per cent and reached over 48 per cent from 2009. In the 1970s and 1980s, Japan consistently allocated over 30 per cent of GDP to investment and growth during those years was generally high at around 5.0 per cent. In the last ten years, Japan has experienced considerable economic problems, its growth rates have stagnated but so has the proportion of GDP accounted for by investment – under 20 per cent from 2009 onwards.

Studies that examine a more comprehensive list of countries confirm this strong correlation between investment and growth. It should also be noted that the figures can be affected by the starting base; countries such as China now devote over a third of GDP to investment whereas in the early 1960s it hovered between 10.5 per cent and 22.08 per cent.

There is, however, a problem in interpreting these data. As the appendix to Chapter 2 discussed, a correlation between two variables does not establish which variable is the cause and which is the effect. It is possible that high investment causes high growth, but it is also possible that high growth causes high investment. (Or, perhaps, high growth and high investment are both caused by a third variable that has been omitted from the analysis.) The data by themselves cannot tell us the direction of causation. Nevertheless, because capital accumulation affects productivity so clearly and directly, many economists interpret these data as showing that high investment leads to more rapid economic growth.

FIGURE 6.2

Growth and Investment

Panel (a) shows the average growth rate of GDP for 19 countries over the period 1961–2011. Panel (b) shows the average percentage of GDP that each country devoted to investment over this period. The figure suggests that investment and growth are positively correlated.

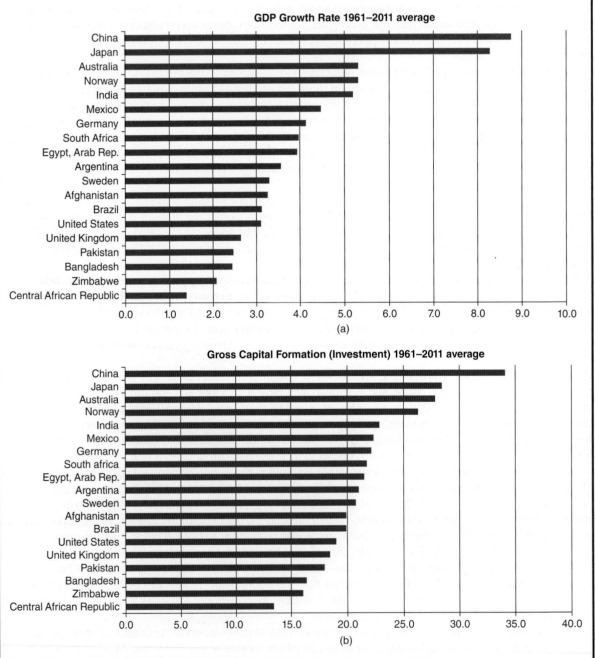

Diminishing Returns and the Catch-Up Effect

Suppose that a government, convinced by the evidence in Figure 6.2, pursues policies that raise the nation's saving rate. What happens? With the nation saving more, fewer resources are needed to make consumption goods, and more resources are available to make capital goods. As a result, the capital stock increases, leading to rising productivity and more rapid growth in GDP. But how long does this higher rate of growth last? Assuming that the saving rate remains at its new higher level, does the growth rate of GDP stay high indefinitely or only for a period of time?

We know that the traditional view of the production process is that capital is subject to diminishing returns: as the stock of capital rises, the extra output produced from an additional unit of capital falls. In other words, when workers already have a large quantity of capital to use in producing goods and ser- vices, giving them an additional unit of capital increases their productivity only slightly. This is illustrated in Figure 6.3, which shows how the amount of capital per worker determines the amount of output per worker, holding constant all the other determinants of output. Because of diminishing returns, an increase in the saving rate leads to higher growth only for a while. As the higher saving rate allows more capital to be accumulated, the benefits from additional capital become smaller over time, and so growth slows down. In the long run, the higher saving rate leads to a higher level of productivity and income, but not to higher growth in these variables. Reaching this long run, however, can take quite a while. According to studies of international data on economic growth, increasing the saving rate can lead to substantially higher growth for a period of several decades.

The diminishing returns to capital has another important implication: other things equal, it is easier for a country to grow fast if it starts out relatively poor.

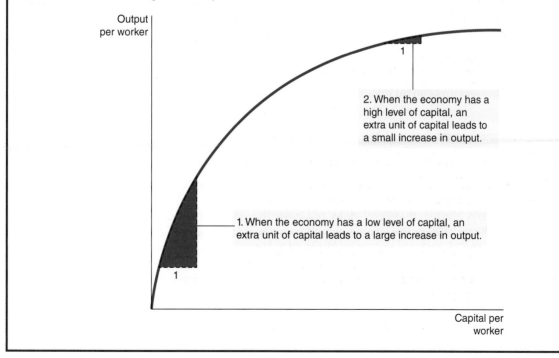

FIGURE 6.3

Illustrating the Production Function
This figure shows how the amount of capital per worker influences the amount of output per worker. Other determinants of output, including human capital, natural resources and technology are held constant. The curve becomes flatter as the amount of capital increases because of diminishing returns to capital.

Output per worker

2. When the economy has a high level of capital, an extra unit of capital leads to a small increase in output.

1. When the economy has a low level of capital, an extra unit of capital leads to a large increase in output.

Capital per worker

This effect of initial conditions on subsequent growth is sometimes called the **catch-up effect**. In poor countries, workers lack even the most rudimentary tools and, as a result, have low productivity. Small amounts of capital investment would substantially raise these workers' productivity. By contrast, workers in rich countries have large amounts of capital with which to work, and this partly explains their high productivity. Yet with the amount of capital per worker already so high, additional capital investment has a relatively small effect on productivity. Studies of international data on economic growth confirm this catch-up effect: controlling for other variables, such as the percentage of GDP devoted to investment, poor countries do tend to grow at a faster rate than rich countries.

> **catch-up effect** the property whereby countries that start off poor tend to grow more rapidly than countries that start off rich

This catch-up effect can help explain variations in observations on average investment as a proportion of GDP and average growth rates over time. Between 1961 and 2011, Japan allocated around 10 per cent more to investment as a proportion of GDP compared to China, but China grew at an average rate 1.7 times the Japanese annual average growth rate. The explanation is the catch-up effect. In 1961 Japan had GDP per person about 15 times that of China, in part because investment in China up to the end of the 1960s had been so low. With a small initial capital stock, the benefits to capital accumulation were much greater in China, and this gave China a higher subsequent growth rate.

Investment from Abroad

So far we have discussed how policies aimed at increasing a country's saving rate can increase investment and, thereby, long-term economic growth. Yet saving by domestic residents is not the only way for a country to invest in new capital. The other way is investment by foreigners.

Investment from abroad takes several forms. BMW might build a car factory in Portugal. A capital investment that is owned and operated by a foreign entity is called **foreign direct investment**. Alternatively, a German might buy equity in a Portuguese corporation (that is, buy a share in the ownership of the corporation); the Portuguese corporation can use the proceeds from the equity sale to build a new factory. An investment that is financed with foreign money but operated by domestic residents is called **foreign portfolio investment**. In both cases, Germans provide the resources necessary to increase the stock of capital in Portugal. That is, German saving is being used to finance Portuguese investment.

> **foreign direct investment** capital investment that is owned and operated by a foreign entity
> **foreign portfolio investment** investment that is financed with foreign money but operated by domestic residents

When foreigners invest in a country, they do so because they expect to earn a return on their investment. BMW's car factory increases the Portuguese capital stock and, therefore, increases Portuguese productivity and Portuguese GDP. Yet BMW takes some of this additional income back to Germany in the form of profit. Similarly, when a German investor buys Portuguese equity, the investor has a right to a portion of the profit that the Portuguese corporation earns.

Investment from abroad, therefore, does not have the same effect on all measures of economic prosperity. Recall that GDP is the income earned within a country by both residents and non-residents, whereas GNP is the income earned by residents of a country both at home and abroad. When BMW opens its car factory in Portugal, some of the income the factory generates accrues to people who do not live in Portugal. As a result, foreign investment in Portugal raises the income of the Portuguese (measured by GNP) by less than it raises the production in Portugal (measured by GDP).

Nevertheless, investment from abroad is one way for a country to grow. Even though some of the benefits from this investment flow back to the foreign owners, this investment does increase the economy's stock of capital, leading to higher productivity and higher wages. Moreover, investment from abroad is one way for poorer countries to learn the state-of-the-art technologies developed and used in richer countries. For these reasons, many economists who advise governments in less developed economies advocate policies that encourage investment from abroad. Often this means removing restrictions that governments have imposed on foreign ownership of domestic capital.

An organization that tries to encourage the flow of capital to poor countries is the World Bank. This international organization obtains funds from the world's advanced industrialized countries, and uses these resources to make loans to less developed countries so that they can invest in roads, sewage systems, schools and other types of capital. It also offers the countries advice about how the funds might best be used. The World Bank, together with its sister organization, the International Monetary Fund (IMF), was set up after World War II. One lesson from the war was that economic distress often leads to political turmoil, international tensions and military conflict. Thus, every country has an interest in promoting economic prosperity around the world. The World Bank and the IMF were set up to achieve that common goal.

Education

Education – investment in human capital – is at least as important as investment in physical capital for a country's long-run economic success. In the developed economies of Western Europe and North America, each extra year of schooling raises a worker's income by about 10 per cent on average. In less developed countries, where human capital is especially scarce, the gap between the wages of educated and uneducated workers is even larger. Thus, one way in which government policy can enhance the standard of living is to provide good schools and to encourage the population to take advantage of them.

Investment in human capital, like investment in physical capital, has an opportunity cost. When students are in school, they forgo the wages they could have earned. In less developed countries, children often drop out of school at an early age, even though the benefit of additional schooling is very high, simply because their labour is needed to help support the family.

Some economists have argued that human capital is particularly important for economic growth because human capital conveys positive externalities. An *externality*, remember, is the effect of one person's actions on the well-being of a third party. An educated person, for instance, might generate new ideas about how best to produce goods and services. If these ideas enter society's pool of knowledge, so that everyone can use them, then the ideas are an external benefit of education. In this case, the return to schooling for society is even greater than the return for the individual. This argument would justify the large subsidies to human capital investment that we observe in the form of public education.

One problem facing some poor countries is the **brain drain** – the emigration of many of the most highly educated workers to rich countries where these workers can enjoy a higher standard of living. If human capital does have positive externalities, then this brain drain makes those people left behind poorer than they otherwise would be. This problem offers policymakers a dilemma. On the one hand, rich countries like those of western Europe and North America have the best systems of higher education, and it would seem natural for poor countries to send their best students abroad to earn higher degrees. On the other hand, those students who have spent time abroad may choose not to return home, and this brain drain will reduce the poor nation's stock of human capital even further.

> **brain drain** the emigration of many of the most highly educated workers to rich countries

Health and Nutrition

The term *human capital* usually refers to education, but it can also be used to describe another type of investment in people: expenditures that lead to a healthier population. Other things equal, healthier workers are more productive. The right investments in the health of the population provide one way for a nation to increase productivity and raise living standards.

Economic historian, Robert Fogel, has suggested that a significant factor in long-run economic growth is improved health from better nutrition. He estimates that in Great Britain in 1780 about one in five people were so malnourished that they were incapable of manual labour. Among those who could work, insufficient intake of calories substantially reduced the work effort they could carry out. As nutrition improved so did workers' productivity.

Fogel studies these historical trends in part by looking at the height of the population. Short stature can be an indicator of malnutrition, especially during gestation and the early years of life. Fogel finds that as nations develop economically, people eat more and the population gets taller. From 1775 to 1975, the average caloric intake in Great Britain rose by 26 per cent and the height of the average man rose by 3.6 inches (around 10 cm). Similarly, during the spectacular economic growth in the Republic of Korea from 1962 to 1995, caloric consumption rose by 44 per cent and, average male height rose by 2 inches (5 cm). Of course, a person's height is determined by a combination of genetic predisposition and environment. But because the genetic make-up of a population is slow to change, such increases in average height are likely due to changes in the environment – nutrition being the obvious explanation.

Moreover, studies have found that height is an indicator of productivity. Looking at data on a large number of workers at a point in time, researchers have found that taller workers tend to earn more. Because wages reflect a worker's productivity, this finding suggests that taller workers tend to be more productive. The effect of height on wages is especially pronounced in poorer countries, where malnutrition is a bigger risk.

Fogel won the Nobel Prize in Economics in 1993 for his work in economic history, which includes not only his studies on nutrition but also work on American slavery and the role of the railroads in the development of the American economy. In the lecture he gave when awarded the Prize, he surveyed the evidence on health and economic growth. He concluded that 'improved gross nutrition accounts for roughly 30 per cent of the growth of per capita income in Britain between 1790 and 1980'.

Today malnutrition is fortunately rare in developed nations (obesity is a more widespread problem). But for people in developing nations, poor health and inadequate nutrition remain obstacles to higher productivity and improved living standards. The United Nations estimates that almost a third of the population in sub-Saharan Africa is undernourished.

The causal link between health and wealth runs in both directions. Poor countries are poor, in part, because their populations are not healthy, and their populations are not healthy, in part, because they are poor and cannot afford adequate health care and nutrition. It is a vicious circle. But this fact opens the possibility of a virtuous circle. Policies that lead to more rapid economic growth would naturally improve health outcomes, which in turn would further promote economic growth.

Property Rights, Political Stability and Good Governance

Other ways in which policymakers can foster economic growth are by protecting property rights, promoting political stability and maintaining good governance. As noted when we discussed economic interdependence, production in market economies arises from the interactions of millions of individuals and firms. When you buy a car, for instance, you are buying the output of a car dealer, a car manufacturer, a steel company, an iron ore mining company and so on. This division of production among many firms allows the economy's factors of production to be used as effectively as possible. To achieve this outcome, the economy has to coordinate transactions among these firms, as well as between firms and consumers. Market economies achieve this coordination through market prices. That is, market prices are the instrument with which the invisible hand of the marketplace brings supply and demand into balance.

An important prerequisite for the price system to work is an economy-wide respect for *property rights*. A mining company will not make the effort to mine iron ore if it expects the ore to be stolen. The company mines the ore only if it is confident that it will benefit from the ore's subsequent sale. For this reason, courts serve an important role in a market economy: they enforce property rights. Through the criminal justice system, the courts discourage direct theft. In addition, through the civil justice system, the courts ensure that buyers and sellers live up to their contracts.

Although people in developed countries tend to take property rights for granted, those living in less developed or emerging countries understand that lack of property rights can be a major problem. In many countries, the system of justice does not work well. Contracts are hard to enforce, and fraud often goes unpunished. In more extreme cases, the government not only fails to enforce property rights but actually infringes upon them. To do business in some countries, firms are expected to bribe powerful government officials. Such corruption impedes the coordinating power of markets. It also discourages domestic saving and investment from abroad. The problem of corruption and bribery is extensive. Transparency International is a pressure group that exists to advance the cause of anti-corruption. Each year it publishes an index showing perceptions of corruption across the world. Countries are scored on a scale of 0–100 with 0 being highly corrupt and 10 being highly clean. Around two-thirds of the 176 countries in the ranking fall below 50. The extent of the problem is highlighted in the map produced by Transparency International reproduced in Figure 6.4.

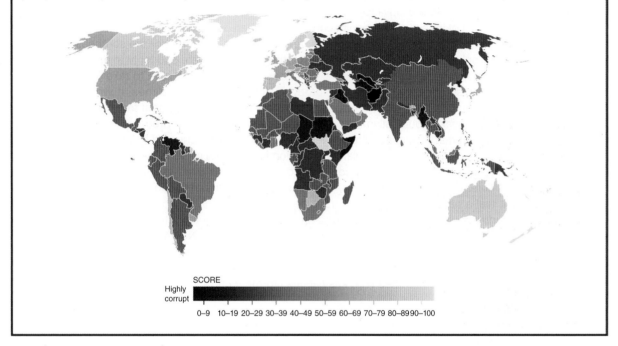

FIGURE 6.4

Corruption Perceptions Index 2012
The map shows the perceptions of corruption across 176 countries around the world. The darker the red on the map, the more there is a perception of corruption and the more yellow, the cleaner the perception.

One threat to property rights is political instability. When revolutions and coups are common, there is doubt about whether property rights will be respected in the future. If a revolutionary government might confiscate the capital of some businesses, as was often true after communist revolutions, domestic residents have less incentive to save, invest and start new businesses. At the same time, foreigners have less incentive to invest in the country. Even the threat of revolution can act to depress a nation's standard of living. It is no coincidence that countries with a strong military power, who are subject to frequent coups, are ones that are at the bottom of any standard of living league table.

Thus, economic prosperity depends in part on political prosperity. A country with an efficient court system, honest government officials and a stable constitution will enjoy a higher economic standard of living than a country with a poor court system, corrupt officials and frequent revolutions and coups. These are the key features of good governance – the extent to which a country is ruled by sound democracies, where the rule of law, the authority of law, the absence of corruption and independent judicial processes are in existence. If these things are in place then it means that contracts and property rights can be enforced and free markets can operate effectively to allocate scarce resources. Without good governance, many economists believe that economic development will be compromised.

Free Trade

Some of the world's poorest countries have tried to achieve more rapid economic growth by pursuing *inward-oriented policies*. These policies are aimed at raising productivity and living standards within the country by avoiding interaction with the rest of the world. This approach gets support from some domestic firms, which claim that they need protection from foreign competition in order to compete and grow. This infant-industry argument, together with a general distrust of foreigners, has at times led policymakers in less developed countries to impose tariffs and other trade restrictions.

Most economists today believe that poor countries are better off pursuing *outward-oriented policies* that integrate these countries into the world economy. When we studied international trade earlier in the book, we showed how international trade can improve the economic well-being of a country's citizens. Trade is, in some ways, a type of technology. When a country exports wheat and imports steel, the country benefits in the same way as if it had invented a technology for turning wheat into steel. A country that eliminates trade restrictions will, therefore, experience the same kind of economic growth that would occur after a major technological advance.

The adverse impact of inward orientation becomes clear when one considers the small size of many less developed economies. The total GDP of Argentina, for instance, is about that of the southeast of England (if we include London). Imagine what would happen if the southeast were suddenly to declare that it was illegal to trade with anyone beyond the regional boundaries. Without being able to take advantage of the gains from trade, the southeast would need to produce all the goods it consumes. It would also have to produce all its own capital goods, rather than importing state-of-the-art equipment from other cities. Living standards in the southeast would fall immediately, and the problem would probably only get worse over time. This is precisely what happened when Argentina pursued inward-oriented policies throughout much of the 20th century and can also partly explain the economic problems in North Korea which has effectively cut itself off from the rest of the world. By contrast, countries pursuing outward-oriented policies, such as the Republic of Korea, Singapore and Taiwan, have enjoyed high rates of economic growth.

The amount that a nation trades with others is determined not only by government policy but also by geography. Countries with good natural seaports find trade easier than countries without this resource. It is not a coincidence that many of the world's major cities, such as Paris, New York, Hong Kong and London, are located either next to oceans or on the banks of a major river giving easy access for seafaring trade vessels. Similarly, because landlocked countries find international trade more difficult, they tend to have lower levels of income than countries with easy access to the world's waterways.

Research and Development

The primary reason that living standards are higher today than they were a century ago is that technological knowledge has advanced. The telephone, the transistor, the computer and the internal combustion engine, are among the thousands of innovations that have improved the ability to produce goods and services.

Although most technological advance comes from private research by firms and individual inventors, there is also a public interest in promoting these efforts. To a large extent, knowledge is a *public good*: once one person discovers an idea, the idea enters society's pool of knowledge and other people can freely use it (subject to any legal restrictions such as those imposed by intellectual property rights). Just as government has a role in providing a public good such as national defence, it also has a role in encouraging the research and development of new technologies. The governments in most advanced countries do this in a number of ways, for example through science research laboratories owned and funded by the government, or through a system of research grants offered to promising researchers. It may also offer tax breaks and concessions for firms engaging in research and development.

Yet another way in which government policy encourages research is through the patent system. When a person or firm invents a new product, such as a new drug, the inventor can apply for a patent. If the product is deemed truly original, the government awards the patent, which gives the inventor the exclusive right to make the product for a specified number of years. In essence, the patent gives the inventor a property right over his invention, turning his new idea from a public good into a private good. By allowing inventors to profit from their inventions – even if only temporarily – the patent system enhances the incentive for individuals and firms to engage in research.

Population Growth

Economists and other social scientists have long debated how population growth affects a society. The most direct effect is on the size of the labour force: a large population means more workers to produce goods and services. At the same time, it means more people to consume those goods and services. Beyond these obvious effects, population growth interacts with the other factors of production in ways that are less obvious and more open to debate.

Stretching Natural Resources Thomas Robert Malthus (1766–1834), an English minister and early economic thinker, is famous for his book entitled *An Essay on the Principle of Population as It Affects the Future Improvement of Society*. In it, Malthus offered what may be history's most chilling forecast. Malthus argued that an ever-increasing population would continually strain society's ability to provide for itself. As a result, mankind was doomed to forever live in poverty.

Malthus's logic was simple. He began by noting that 'food is necessary to the existence of man' and that 'the passion between the sexes is necessary and will remain nearly in its present state'. He concluded that 'the power of population is infinitely greater than the power in the earth to produce subsistence for man'. According to Malthus, the only check on population growth was 'misery and vice'. Attempts by charities or governments to alleviate poverty were counterproductive, he argued, because they merely allowed the poor to have more children, placing even greater strains on society's productive capabilities.

Fortunately, Malthus's dire forecast was far off the mark. Although the world population has increased about six-fold over the past two centuries, living standards around the world are on average much higher. As a result of economic growth, chronic hunger and malnutrition are less common now than they were in Malthus's day. Famines occur from time to time, but they are more often the result of an unequal income distribution or political instability than an inadequate production of food.

Thomas Robert Malthus

Where did Malthus go wrong? He assumed – correctly – that world population would rise exponentially, since as more people are born and survive, more and more people are born as their children, and so on. But he also assumed – incorrectly – that the amount of food produced could rise only linearly, by increasing the amount of land under cultivation with productivity remaining constant. But growth in mankind's ingenuity over the years has offset the effects of a larger population. Pesticides, fertilizers, mechanized farm equipment, new crop varieties and other technological advances that Malthus never imagined have allowed each farmer to feed ever greater numbers of people. Even with more mouths to feed, fewer farmers are necessary because each farmer is so much more productive than Malthus ever imagined.

Diluting the Capital Stock Whereas Malthus worried about the effects of population on the use of natural resources, some modern theories of economic growth emphasize its effects on capital accumulation. According to these theories, high population growth reduces GDP per worker because rapid growth in the number of workers forces the capital stock to be spread more thinly. In other words, when population growth is rapid, each worker is equipped with less capital. A smaller quantity of capital per worker leads to lower productivity and lower GDP per worker.

This problem is most apparent in the case of human capital. Countries with high population growth have large numbers of school-age children. This places a larger burden on the educational system. It is not surprising, therefore, that educational attainment tends to be low in countries with high population growth.

The differences in population growth around the world are large. In developed countries, such as the United States, the United Kingdom and the other countries of western Europe, the population has risen only about 1 per cent per year in recent decades and is expected to rise even more slowly in the future. In contrast, in many poor African countries, population grows at about 3 per cent per year. At this rate, the population doubles every 23 years (remember the rule of 70). This rapid population growth makes it harder to provide workers with the tools and skills they need to achieve high levels of productivity.

Although rapid population growth is not the main reason that less developed countries are poor, some analysts believe that reducing the rate of population growth would help these countries raise their standards of living. In some countries, this goal is accomplished directly with laws that regulate the number of children families may have. China, for instance, allows only one child per family living in urban areas; couples who violate this rule are subject to substantial fines. (In 2008, the National Population and Family Planning Commission announced that there were no planned changes to the policy for 'at least another decade'.) In countries with greater freedom, the goal of reduced population growth is accomplished less directly by increasing awareness of birth control techniques.

Another way in which a country can influence population growth is to apply one of the *Ten Principles of Economics*: people respond to incentives. Bearing a child, like any decision, has an opportunity cost. When the opportunity cost rises, people will choose to have smaller families. In particular, women with the opportunity to receive good education and desirable employment tend to want fewer children than those with fewer opportunities outside the home. Hence, policies that foster equal treatment of women are one way for less developed economies to reduce the rate of population growth and, perhaps, raise their standards of living.

Promoting Technological Progress Although rapid population growth may depress economic prosperity by reducing the amount of capital each worker has, it may also have some benefits. Some economists have suggested that world population growth has been an engine of technological progress and economic prosperity. The mechanism is simple: if there are more people, then the greater the probability that some of those people will come up with new ideas that will lead to technological progress, which benefits everyone.

Economist Michael Kremer has provided some support for this hypothesis in an article titled 'Population Growth and Technological Change: One Million BC to 1990', which was published in the *Quarterly Journal of Economics* in 1993. Kremer begins by noting that over the broad span of human history, world growth rates have increased as world population has. For example, world growth was more rapid when the world population was 1 billion (which occurred around the year 1800) than it was when the population was only 100 million (around 500 BC). This fact is consistent with the hypothesis that having more people induces more technological progress.

Kremer's second piece of evidence comes from comparing regions of the world. The melting of the polar ice caps at the end of the ice age around 10,000 BC flooded the land bridges and separated the world into several distinct regions that could not communicate with one another for thousands of years. If technological progress is more rapid when there are more people to discover things, then larger regions should have experienced more rapid growth.

According to Kremer, that is exactly what happened. The most successful region of the world in 1500 (when Columbus re-established technological contact) comprised the 'Old World' civilizations of the large Eurasia-Africa region. Next in technological development were the Aztec and Mayan civilizations in the Americas, followed by the hunter-gatherers of Australia, and then the primitive people of Tasmania, who lacked even fire-making and most stone and bone tools.

The smallest isolated region was Flinders Island, a tiny island between Tasmania and Australia. With the smallest population, Flinders Island had the fewest opportunities for technological advance and, indeed, seemed to regress. Around 3000 BC, human society on Flinders Island died out completely. A large population, Kremer concludes, is a prerequisite for technological advance.

At first sight this conclusion does seem to be at odds with casual empirical observation of the modern world: as we previously noted, in many rich, developed countries population growth has been only about 1 per cent per year in recent decades, while in many poor countries, such as those of sub-Saharan Africa, population growth is much higher. So why doesn't this higher population growth help these poor countries to grow, if Kremer's argument is right? The point is that Kremer was really analysing *world* economic growth, or rather, economic growth in isolated regions of the world. Nowadays, in a very poor country, it is unlikely that technological advances will be made that are not already known in developed countries; the problem is not lack of technological progress but difficulty in applying technology because of the scarcity of human capital and perhaps because of problems arising from political instability and corruption, as we discussed earlier. Moreover, because many talented people from less developed countries tend to emigrate to richer, developed countries where they may work, for example, as scientists or entrepreneurs – a phenomenon we referred to earlier as the *brain drain* – population growth in less developed countries may actually enhance economic growth in developed countries.

> **SELF TEST** Describe three ways in which a government policymaker can try to raise the growth in living standards in a society. Are there any drawbacks to these policies?

CONCLUSION: THE IMPORTANCE OF LONG-RUN GROWTH

In this chapter we have discussed what determines the standard of living in a nation and how policymakers can endeavour to raise the standard of living through policies that promote economic growth. Most of this chapter is summarized in one of the *Ten Principles of Economics*: a country's standard of living depends on its ability to produce goods and services. Policymakers who want to encourage growth in standards of living must aim to increase their nation's productive ability by encouraging rapid accumulation of the factors of production and ensuring that these factors are employed as effectively as possible.

Economists differ in their views of the role of government in promoting economic growth. At the very least, government can lend support to the invisible hand by maintaining property rights and political stability. More controversial is whether government should target and subsidize specific industries that might be especially important for technological progress. There is no doubt that these issues are among the most important in economics. The success of one generation's policymakers in learning and heeding the fundamental lessons about economic growth determines what kind of world the next generation will inherit.

IN THE NEWS

Economic Growth in China

Just as there were eyebrows raised for the way in which Japan transformed itself in the post-war period, in the last 20 years growth in China has been nothing short of remarkable. In Japan, economic growth has ground to a halt and the country is struggling with a number of problems. How long can China's growth continue?

How Sustainable is Economic Growth in China?

To many people outside China, the economic growth that has projected the country onto the world economic stage, as well as its political one, has been remarkable and generated primarily by having a very large supply of labour willing to work for low wages to manufacture goods at low cost which have been bought by countries throughout the world. Professor Justin Yifu Lin, former Chief Economist and Senior Vice President of the World Bank, has spoken at length about China's capacity to continue growing at high rates in a series of speeches at prominent higher education institutions including the London School of Economics in December 2012 where he spoke on 'Demystifying the Chinese Economy'.

(Continued)

Lin noted that in 1979 China had a per capita income of just $182 which was less than a third of the average of Sub-Saharan African countries. Over the last 30 years economic growth has averaged over 9 per cent, 600 million people have been raised out of poverty and per capita income is now over $4,000. In 2009, China became the world's second largest economy and many predict that it will become the largest in the next ten years. Lin referred to studies by economic historian, Angus Maddison (2001) which showed that average annual per capita income growth in the West was around 0.05 per cent prior to the 18th century, meaning it took 1,400 years for European per capita income to double, rising to 1 per cent in the 19th century (taking 70 years for per capita income to double) and 2 per cent in the 20th century (35 years for per capita income to double).

The industrial revolution led to millions of people moving from rural

Professor Justin Yifu Lin, former Chief Economist and Senior Vice President of the World Bank believes that the Chinese economy can continue to grow strongly but that it will have to change its focus as its comparative advantage changes.

occupations to manufacturing and infrastructure but the risks involved in the process were huge. China, Lin argues, has been able to take advantage of what he calls 'backwardness' – the ability to 'borrow' technology, innovation and institutions at relatively low risk and cost from advanced nations. The World Bank Commission noted this as the ability for developing countries to 'import what the rest of the world knew and export what it wanted'. This ability is one factor that can help a developing nation to secure sustained per-capita growth at high levels for a considerable period of time.

The early stages of China's growth were characterized by the setting up of heavy industry but in the context of very limited trade with the outside world. In the 1980s and beyond, the Chinese government began to exploit the advantages it had in labour supply, developing more modern industries and adopting some market-based reforms within the framework of a single-party state. The development of a more market-led economy enabled China to be able to become more outward-facing and export growth began to fuel economic growth.

Lin notes, however, that economic growth in China was not without its costs as rising inequality being a consequence. However, large companies and a rump of very rich people are able to access funds for investment at relatively favourable rates and because rich people and corporations tend to have a relatively high savings ratio, funds for further investment in improving the capital stock and productivity in China are available more freely than in more developed nations.

Some of these distortions will, however, have to be tackled by the Chinese government as it moves

ever further towards a fully functioning market economy. This includes the necessity to improve the quality of the banking sector to ensure finance is available for the development of small firms and for supplying credit to the consumer markets, tackle corporate governance and property rights and further improving infrastructure.

Lin believes that China can continue to grow at rates in excess of 8 per cent or more for the next 20 years. He bases this conclusion on the continued benefits the country can gain from 'backwardness' and the fact that there is still a massive gap to make up before China matches the per-capita income of country's like the United States. However, China will have to move to exploiting technological change rather than relying on its supply of cheap labour because this comparative advantage is already beginning to narrow as other low wage economies develop. China will need to move from absorbing technology, therefore, to being an innovator.

Questions

1 China's population is in excess of 1 billion. Is this natural factor endowment a key reason why China has been able to generate such remarkable economic growth in the last 30 years? If so, why can't other countries with very large populations also grow at such rates?

2 Lin notes that 60 million people have been lifted out of poverty in China. The industrial revolution also meant millions across Europe were able to leave the grind of agricultural poverty and find work in new industries. Does such a transition come with its own challenges to a country like China?

3 If China has been growing at an average of 9 per cent in the last ten years, how long will it take for per capita incomes to double?

4 Explain how the idea of 'backwardness' allows China to be able to generate rapid and sustained economic growth over a period.

5 Lin has warned that China cannot rely on its comparative advantage in low-wage labour and on backwardness for much longer. Why do you think he believes this and why has he urged the Chinese government to push China to pursue innovation?

SUMMARY

- Economic prosperity, as measured by GDP per person, varies substantially around the world. The average income in the world's richest countries is more than ten times that in the world's poorest countries. Because growth rates of real GDP also vary substantially, the relative positions of countries can change dramatically over time.

- The standard of living in an economy depends on the economy's ability to produce goods and services. Productivity, in turn, depends on the amounts of physical capital, human capital, natural resources and technological knowledge available to workers.

- Government policies can try to influence the economy's growth rate in many ways: by encouraging saving and investment, encouraging investment from abroad, fostering education, maintaining property rights and political stability, allowing free trade, promoting the research and development of new technologies, and controlling population growth.

- The accumulation of capital is subject to diminishing returns: the more capital an economy has, the less additional output the economy gets from an extra unit of capital. Because of diminishing returns, higher saving leads to higher growth for a period of time, but growth eventually slows down as the economy approaches a higher level of capital, productivity and income. Also because of diminishing returns, the return to capital is especially high in poor countries. Other things equal, these countries can grow faster because of the catch-up effect.

QUESTIONS FOR REVIEW

1 What does the level of a nation's GDP measure? What does the growth rate of GDP measure? Would you rather live in a nation with a high level of GDP and a low growth rate, or in a nation with a low level of GDP and a high growth rate?

2 What is the difference between the terms 'productivity' and 'production'?

3 List and describe four determinants of productivity.

4 In what way is a university degree a form of capital?

5 Explain how higher saving leads to a higher standard of living. What might deter a policymaker from trying to raise the rate of saving?

6 Does a higher rate of saving lead to higher growth temporarily or indefinitely?

7 Why is technological progress important in improving growth rates in any economy?

8 Why would removing a trade restriction, such as a tariff, lead to more rapid economic growth?

9 How does the rate of population growth influence the level of GDP per person?

10 Describe two ways in which the government can try to encourage advances in technological knowledge.

PROBLEMS AND APPLICATIONS

1 Most countries import substantial amounts of goods and services from other countries. Yet the chapter says that a nation can enjoy a high standard of living only if it can produce a large quantity of goods and services itself. Can you reconcile these two facts?

2   List the capital inputs necessary to produce each of the following:

   a. cars

   b. secondary education

   c. air travel

   d. fruit and vegetables.

3   UK income per person today is roughly four times what it was a century ago. Many other countries have also experienced significant growth over that period. What are some specific ways in which your standard of living is likely to differ from that of your great-grandparents?

4   The chapter discusses how employment in developed economies has declined relative to output in the agricultural sector. Can you think of another sector of the economy where the same phenomenon has occurred more recently? Would you consider the change in employment in this sector to represent a success or a failure from the standpoint of society as a whole?

5   Suppose that society decided to reduce consumption and increase investment.

   a. How would this change affect economic growth?

   b. What groups in society would benefit from this change? What groups might be hurt?

6   Societies choose what share of their resources to devote to consumption and what share to devote to investment. Some of these decisions involve private spending; others involve government spending.

   a. Describe some forms of private spending that represent consumption, and some forms that represent investment.

   b. Describe some forms of government spending that represent consumption, and some forms that represent investment.

7   What is the opportunity cost of investing in capital? Do you think a country can 'over-invest' in capital? What is the opportunity cost of investing in human capital? Do you think a country can 'over-invest' in human capital? Explain.

8   Suppose that a car company owned entirely by South Korean citizens opens a new factory in the north of England.

   a. What sort of foreign investment would this represent?

   b. What would be the effect of this investment on UK GDP? Would the effect on UK GNP be larger or smaller?

9   In the countries of South Asia in 1992, only 56 young women were enrolled in secondary school for every 100 young men. Describe several ways in which greater educational opportunities for young women could lead to faster economic growth in these countries.

10 International data show a positive correlation between political stability and economic growth.

   a. Through what mechanism could political stability lead to strong economic growth?

   b. Through what mechanism could strong economic growth lead to political stability?

7 UNEMPLOYMENT

Losing a job can be the most distressing economic event in a person's life. Most people rely on their labour earnings to maintain their standard of living, and many people get from their work not only income but also a sense of personal accomplishment. A job loss means a lower living standard in the present, anxiety about the future and reduced self-esteem. It is not surprising, therefore, that politicians campaigning for office often speak about how their proposed policies will help create jobs.

A major determinant of a country's standard of living is the amount of unemployment it typically experiences. People who would like to work but cannot find a job are not contributing to the economy's production of goods and services. Although some degree of unemployment is inevitable in a complex economy with thousands of firms and millions of workers, the amount of unemployment varies substantially over time and across countries. When a country keeps its workers as fully employed as possible, it achieves a higher level of GDP than it would if it left many of its workers standing idle.

This chapter begins our study of unemployment. The problem of unemployment is usefully divided into two categories – the long-run problem and the short-run problem. In this chapter we discuss the determinants of the long-run problem – an economy's *natural rate of unemployment*. As we will see, the designation *natural* does not imply that this rate of unemployment is desirable. Nor does it imply that it is constant over time or impervious to economic policy. It merely means that this unemployment does not go away on its own, even in the long run.

We begin the chapter by looking at three questions: how does the government measure the economy's rate of unemployment? What problems arise in interpreting the unemployment data? How long are the unemployed typically without work?

We then turn to the reasons why economies always experience some unemployment and the ways in which policymakers can help the unemployed. We discuss four explanations for the economy's natural rate of unemployment: job search, minimum wage laws, unions and efficiency wages. As we will see, long-run unemployment does not arise from a single problem that has a single solution. Instead, it reflects a variety of related problems. As a result, there is no easy way for policymakers to reduce the economy's natural rate of unemployment and, at the same time, to alleviate the hardships experienced by the unemployed.

We finish the chapter by looking at some of the costs of unemployment.

IDENTIFYING UNEMPLOYMENT

We begin this chapter by examining more precisely what the term *unemployment* means. We consider how governments measure unemployment, what problems arise in interpreting the unemployment data, how long the typical spell of unemployment lasts and why there will always be some people unemployed.

What is Unemployment?

The answer to this question may seem obvious: an unemployed person is someone who does not have a job. But as economists we need to be precise and careful in our definitions of economic categories. If you are in full-time education, for example, you do not have a full-time job in the usual sense of the word, i.e. you are not in full-time paid employment. And there is a good reason: you are studying. Hence you are not available for work. What if you were not a student but were suffering from some long-term illness that meant that you were unfit for work? Again, although you would not have a job, we would not say that you were unemployed because you would not be available for work. From these two examples, it seems clear that we need to qualify our original definition of an unemployed person as 'someone who does not have a job' to 'someone who does not have a job and who is available for work'.

But we still need to be clear as to what we mean by 'available for work'. Suppose you were not in full-time employment and were looking for a job and I offered you a job as my research assistant for €1 a day. Would you take it? If we ignore for a moment the complication that economic research is so interesting that it is its own reward, you would probably not take the job because the wage rate offered is so low. At another extreme, suppose you won so much money on the Euro Millions Lottery that you decided you would leave university and live off your winnings for the rest of your life. Would you be unemployed? No, because you would still be unavailable for work, no matter what wage rate you were offered. Thus, being unemployed also depends upon whether you are willing to work (whether you are 'available for work') at going wage rates.

We are now in a position to give a more precise definition of what it means to be unemployed: the number unemployed in an economy is the number of people of working age who are able and available for work at current wage rates and who do not have a job.

Normally, economists find it more convenient to speak of the *unemployment rate*. This expresses the number unemployed as a percentage of the *labour force*, which in turn can be defined as the total number of people who could possibly be employed in the economy at any given point in time. If you think about it, this must be equal to the total number of people who are employed plus the total number of people who are unemployed.

How is Unemployment Measured?

How do government agencies go about measuring the unemployment rate in the economy? There are two basic ways.

The Claimant Count One simple way is to count the number of people who, on any given day, are claiming unemployment benefit payments from the government – the so-called *claimant count*. Since a government agency is paying out the benefits, it will be easy to gather data on the number of claimants. The government also has a good idea of the total labour force in employment, since it is receiving income tax payments from them. Adding to this the number of unemployment benefit claimants is a measure of the total labour force, and expressing the claimant count as a proportion of the labour force is a measure of the unemployment rate.

Since the government already has all the data necessary to compute the unemployment rate based on the claimant count, it is relatively cheap and easy to do. Unfortunately, there are a number of important drawbacks with the claimant count method.

One obvious problem is that it is subject to changes in the rules the government applies for eligibility to unemployment benefit. Suppose the government gets tougher and changes the rules so that fewer people are now entitled to unemployment benefit. The claimant count will go down and so will the measured unemployment rate, even though there has been no change in the number of people with or without work! The opposite would happen if the government became more lenient and relaxed the rules so that more people became eligible.

As it happens, governments do often change the rules on unemployment benefit eligibility. In the UK, for example, there have been about 30 changes to the eligibility rules over the past 25 years, all but one of which have reduced the claimant count and so reduced the unemployment rate based on this measure. The following are examples of categories of people who are excluded from the UK claimant count: people over the age of 55 who are without a job; those on government training programmes (largely school-leavers who have not found a job); anyone looking for part-time work; and people who have left the workforce for a while and now wish to return to employment (for example, women who have raised a family). Many – if not all – of the people in these categories would be people who do not have a job, are of working age and are able and available for work at current wage rates; yet they would be excluded from measured unemployment in the UK using the claimant count method.

Labour Force Surveys The second, and probably more reliable method of measuring unemployment is through the use of surveys – in other words, going out and asking people questions – based on an accepted definition of unemployment. Questions then arise as to whom to speak to, how often (since surveys use up resources and are costly) and what definition of unemployment to use. Although the definition of unemployment that we developed earlier seems reasonable enough, the term 'available for work at current wage rates' may be too loose for this purpose. In the UK and many other countries, the government carries out Labour Force Surveys (LFS) based on the standardized definition of unemployment from the International Labour Office, or ILO. The ILO definition of an unemployed person is someone who is without a job and who is willing to start work within the next two weeks and either has been looking for work within the past four weeks or was waiting to start a job.

The Labour Force Survey is carried out quarterly throughout Europe. National statistical services collect the data which are then processed by Eurostat. The surveys are published in different languages but scrutinized by statisticians to ensure comparability between the surveys carried out in each member state. In the UK, the survey is based on a sample of about 60,000 households and across Europe as a whole the sample size is around 1.5 million. Based on the answers to survey questions, the government places each adult (aged 16 and older) in each surveyed household into one of three categories:

● employed
● unemployed
● not in the labour force (or 'economically inactive').

A person is considered employed if he or she spent some of the previous week working at a paid job. A person is unemployed if he or she fits the ILO definition of an unemployed person. A person who fits neither of the first two categories, such as a full-time student, homemaker or retiree, is not in the labour force (or, to use ILO terminology, is economically inactive).

Once the government has placed all the individuals covered by the survey in a category, it computes various statistics to summarize the state of the labour market. The **labour force** is defined as the sum of the employed and the unemployed:

> **labour force** the total number of workers, including both the employed and the unemployed

$$\text{Labour force} = \text{Number of employed} + \text{Number of unemployed}$$

Then the **unemployment rate** can be measured as the percentage of the labour force that is unemployed:

> **unemployment rate** the percentage of the labour force that is unemployed:

$$\text{Unemployment rate} = \left(\frac{\text{Number of unemployed}}{\text{Labour force}}\right) \times 100$$

Unemployment rates are computed for the entire adult population and for more narrowly defined groups – men, women, youths and so on.

The same survey results are used to produce data on labour force participation. The **labour force participation rate** measures the percentage of the total adult population of the country that is in the labour force:

$$\text{Labour force participation rate} = \left(\frac{\text{Labour force}}{\text{Adult population}}\right) \times 100$$

> **labour force participation rate (or economic activity rate)** the percentage of the adult population that is in the labour force

This statistic tells us the fraction of the population that has chosen to participate in the labour market. The labour force participation rate, like the unemployment rate, is computed both for the entire adult population and for more specific groups.

To see how these data are computed, consider the UK figures for January 2013. According to the *Labour Market Statistics*, 29.68 million people were employed and 2.49 million people were unemployed. The labour force was:

$$\text{Labour force} = 29.68 + 2.49 = 32.17 \text{ million}$$

The unemployment rate was:

$$\text{Unemployment rate} = \left(\frac{2.49}{32.17}\right) \times 100 = 7.74 \text{ per cent}$$

Because the adult population (the number of people aged between 15 and 65) was 41.7 million, the labour force participation rate was:

$$\text{Labour force participation rate} = (32.17/41.7) \times 100 = 77.14 \text{ per cent}$$

Hence, in January 2013, just over three-quarters of the UK adult population were participating in the labour market, and 7.74 per cent of those labour market participants were without work.

Table 7.1 shows the unemployment rate across the EU.

TABLE 7.1

Unemployment Rates in European Union (November 2012)

Country	Unemployment rate (%)
Austria	4.5
Belgium	7.4
Bulgaria	12.4
Cyprus	14.0
Czech Republic	7.4
Denmark	7.9
Estonia	9.5
Finland	7.9
France	10.5
Germany	5.4
Greece	26.0
Hungary	10.9
Ireland	14.6
Italy	11.1
Latvia	14.1
Lithuania	12.5
Luxembourg	5.1
Malta	6.9
Netherlands	5.6
Poland	10.6
Portugal	16.3
Romania	6.7
Slovak Republic	14.5
Slovenia	9.6
Spain	26.6
Sweden	8.1

The Natural Rate of Unemployment

Data on the labour market also allow economists and policymakers to monitor changes in the economy over time. Figure 7.1 shows the unemployment rate in the UK since 1971. The figure shows that the economy always has some unemployment and that the amount changes – often considerably – from year to year.

The normal rate of unemployment, around which the unemployment rate fluctuates is called the **natural rate of unemployment** and the deviation of unemployment from its natural rate is called **cyclical unemployment**. Figure 7.1 shows that the economy always has some unemployment; a trend line has been added to give some indication of the natural rate of unemployment (around 7.2 per cent).

> **natural rate of unemployment** the normal rate of unemployment around which the unemployment rate fluctuates
> **cyclical unemployment** the deviation of unemployment from its natural rate

FIGURE 7.1

UK Unemployment Rate Since 1971

This graph uses annual data on the unemployment rate to show the fraction of the labour force without a job, calculated by the LFS definition. A trend line has been added to show the natural rate of unemployment, the normal level of unemployment around which the unemployment rate fluctuates.

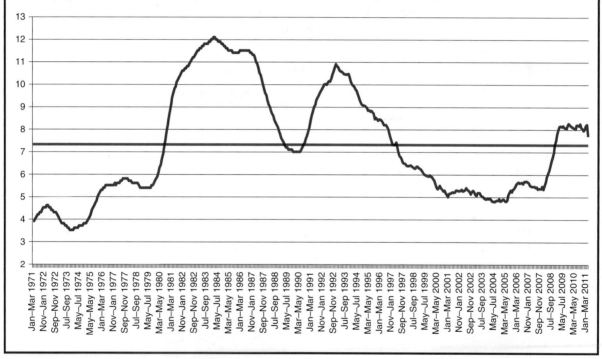

Later in this book we discuss short-run economic fluctuations, including the year-to-year fluctuations in unemployment. In the rest of this chapter, however, we ignore the short-run fluctuations and examine why there is always some unemployment in market economies.

How Long Are the Unemployed without Work?

In judging how serious the problem of unemployment is, one question to consider is whether unemployment is typically a short-term or long-term condition. If unemployment is short term, one might conclude that it is not a big problem. Workers may require a few weeks between jobs to find the openings that best suit their tastes and skills. Yet if unemployment is long term, one might conclude that it is a serious problem. Workers unemployed for many months are more likely to suffer economic and psychological hardship.

CASE STUDY Long-Term Unemployment in the European Union

A report published by the European Employment Observatory Review (see European Employment Observatory Review *Long Term Unemployment 2012. September 2012*) highlights some key trends in long-term unemployment in the EU. The report notes the significant costs both to the individual and to society of long-term unemployment which include loss of self-esteem, increasing difficulties of finding work because of the erosion of skills, damage to health, material deprivation, social exclusion and the cost of supporting the long-term unemployed.

Some 10 million people in the EU have been unemployed for longer than a year. Of these, 1.9 million have not had a job for over two years, 3 million have not had jobs for up to 17 months and 3.2 million have been out of work for between 24 and 47 months. The overall rate of long-term unemployment (LTU) in the EU sits at around 4.1 per cent in 2011 but some countries are faring better than others. In Spain the LTU rate has risen from 2 per cent in 2008 to 9 per cent in 2011 whereas in Germany the rate has decreased from 4.9 per cent in 2007 to 2.8 per cent in 2011.

The countries which have the lowest rates of LTU tend to be the more developed countries of northern Europe such as Norway, Sweden, Luxembourg, the Netherlands, Austria and Denmark, all of whom have LTU rates under 2.0 per cent, whereas the former Soviet Bloc countries have the highest: Latvia, Hungary, Estonia and Slovakia all have rates in excess of 8.0 per cent. Ireland too has a LTU rate of over 8.0 per cent, largely due to the effects of the financial crisis in 2007–2008 which led to the rate increasing from under 2.0 per cent to around 8.5 per cent.

One of the dangers of long-term unemployment is that workers find it impossible to find work because the longer they are out of work the less likely it is that firms will see these people as being serious contenders for jobs. The result is what is called **hysteresis** – the lagging effects of past economic events on future ones. Those who are unemployed for long periods gradually adjust to a lower standard of living, they also find it increasingly harder to get work and so may lose interest in returning to the labour market.

hysteresis the lagging effects of past economic events on future ones

When looking at the breakdown of the LTU, it seems that older people are more likely to be victims of LTU but a worrying trend is the increasing number of young people across the EU who are falling into the LTU bracket. Prior to the financial crisis it was women who were more likely to be LTU but this has now shifted and more men are now LTU.

The rise in youth unemployment across Europe is a grave concern. For many young people without jobs, the future looks bleak.

Because the duration of unemployment can affect our view about how big a problem it is, economists have devoted much energy to studying data on the duration of unemployment spells. In this work, they have uncovered a result that is important, subtle and seemingly contradictory: most spells of unemployment are short, and most unemployment observed at any given time is long term.

To see how this statement can be true, consider an example. Suppose that you visited the government's unemployment office every week for a year to survey the unemployed. Each week you find that there are four unemployed workers. Three of these workers are the same individuals for the whole year, while the fourth person changes every week. Based on this experience, would you say that unemployment is typically short term or long term?

Some simple calculations help answer this question. In this example, you meet a total of 55 unemployed people: 52 of them are unemployed for one week, and three are unemployed for the full year. This means that 52/55, or 95 per cent, of unemployment spells end in one week. Thus, most spells of unemployment are short. Yet consider the total amount of unemployment. The three people unemployed for one year (52 weeks) make up a total of 156 weeks of unemployment. Together with the 52 people unemployed for one week, this makes 208 weeks of unemployment. In this example, 156/208, or 75 per cent, of unemployment is attributable to those individuals who are unemployed for a full year. Thus, most unemployment observed at any given time is long term.

This subtle conclusion implies that economists and policymakers must be careful when interpreting data on unemployment and when designing policies to help the unemployed. Most people who become unemployed will soon find jobs. Yet most of the economy's unemployment problem is attributable to the relatively few workers who are jobless for long periods of time.

Why are There Always Some People Unemployed?

In most markets in the economy, prices adjust to bring quantity supplied and quantity demanded into balance. In an ideal labour market, wages would adjust to balance the quantity of labour supplied and the quantity of labour demanded. This adjustment of wages would ensure that all workers are always fully employed.

Of course, reality does not resemble this ideal. There are always some workers without jobs, even when the overall economy is doing well. In other words, the unemployment rate never falls to zero; instead, it fluctuates around the natural rate of unemployment. To understand this natural rate, we will examine the reasons why actual labour markets depart from the ideal of full employment.

To preview our conclusions, we will find that there are four ways to explain unemployment in the long run.

The first explanation is that it takes time for workers to search for the jobs that are best suited for them. The unemployment that results from the process of matching workers and jobs is sometimes called **frictional unemployment**, and it is often thought to explain relatively short spells of unemployment.

> **frictional unemployment** unemployment that results because it takes time for workers to search for the jobs that best suit their tastes and skills

The next three explanations for unemployment suggest that the number of jobs available in some labour markets may be insufficient to give a job to everyone who wants one. This occurs when the quantity of labour supplied exceeds the quantity demanded. Unemployment of this sort is sometimes called **structural unemployment**, and it is often thought to explain longer spells of unemployment. As we will see, this kind of unemployment results when wages are, for some reason, set above the level that brings supply and demand into equilibrium. We will examine three possible reasons for an above-equilibrium wage: minimum wage laws, unions and efficiency wages.

> **structural unemployment** unemployment that results because the number of jobs available in some labour markets is insufficient to provide a job for everyone who wants one

---

SELF TEST How is the unemployment rate measured? ● How might the unemployment rate overstate the amount of joblessness? How might it understate it?

In Chapter 15 we will introduce the ideas of John Maynard Keynes whose ideas on unemployment changed the nature of economics. Since the 1930s there has been an ongoing debate in economics about the principal causes of unemployment and the extent to which these causes stem from the supply side of the economy or the demand side. That debate has continued and has been brought into sharper focus with the rise in unemployment in many European countries during the first decade of the new century. Policies designed to improve the workings of the supply side of the economy which includes cutting taxes, investing in training an education, changing the benefits system and improving incentives to get work, have to be viewed alongside those which affect the level of aggregate demand in the economy. In essence, the debate centres on the extent to which unemployment is cyclical or structural – the latter accounting for the level of unemployment not due to changes in the economic cycle. As we build the theoretical building blocks of macroeconomics it must be remembered that policies to cut unemployment still deeply divide opinion in the economics profession.

JOB SEARCH

One reason why economies always experience some unemployment is job search. **Job search** is the process of matching workers with appropriate jobs. If all workers and all jobs were the same, so that all workers were equally well suited for all jobs, job search would not be a problem. Laid-off workers would quickly find new jobs that were well suited for them. But, in fact, workers differ in their tastes and skills, jobs differ in their attributes, and information about job candidates and job vacancies is disseminated slowly among the many firms and households in the economy.

job search the process by which workers find appropriate jobs given their tastes and skills

Why Some Frictional Unemployment Is Inevitable

Frictional unemployment is often the result of changes in the demand for labour among different firms. When consumers decide that they prefer Brand X to Brand Y, the company producing Brand X increases employment, and the other firm lays off workers. The former Brand Y workers must now search for new jobs, and the Brand X producer must decide which new workers to hire for the various jobs that have opened up. The result of this transition is a period of unemployment.

Similarly, because different regions of the country produce different goods, employment can rise in one region while it falls in another. Consider, for instance, what happens when the world price of oil falls. Firms extracting oil from the fields below the North Sea, off the coast of Scotland, respond to the lower price by cutting back on production and employment. At the same time, cheaper petrol stimulates car sales, so car manufacturing firms in northern and central England raise production and employment. Changes in the composition of demand among industries or regions are called *sectoral shifts*. Because it takes time for workers to search for jobs in the new sectors, sectoral shifts temporarily cause unemployment.

Frictional unemployment is inevitable simply because the economy is always changing. In 1960, manufacturing as a percentage of GDP was 38 per cent in the UK; it now accounts for around 15 per cent. The number of people employed in manufacturing in 1960 was around 9 million compared to about 3 million today. The gross value added by industry (where gross value added is defined as the value of newly generated goods and services) in the EU 27 (which includes manufacturing) fell from 23.1 per cent in 1998 to 18.7 per cent in 2010. Even Germany, traditionally heavily reliant on industry for its export earnings, has seen the value added by industry fall from 25.0 per cent in 2001 to 23.8 per cent in 2010.

On the other hand, business services and finance contributed only about 3 per cent of UK GDP in the mid-1950s but contribute more than a quarter today. The EU 27 has seen gross value added by business activities and financial services increasing from 23.1 per cent of GDP in 1998 to 29.0 per cent in 2010. As these transitions take place, jobs are created in some firms and destroyed in others. The end result of this process has been higher productivity and higher living standards. But, along the way, workers in declining industries found themselves out of work and searching for new jobs.

In addition to the effects of sectoral shifts on unemployment, workers will leave their jobs sometimes because they realize that the jobs are not a good match for their tastes and skills and they wish to look for a better job. Many of these workers, especially younger ones, find new jobs at higher wages, although given the vast improvements in information technology in recent years (especially the Internet) it is likely that many people search for new jobs without actually quitting their current job. Nevertheless, this churning of the labour force is normal in a well-functioning and dynamic market economy, and the result is some amount of frictional unemployment.

Public Policy and Job Search

Even if some frictional unemployment is inevitable, the precise amount is not. The faster information spreads about job openings and worker availability, the more rapidly the economy can match workers and firms. The Internet, for instance, may help facilitate job search and reduce frictional unemployment. In addition, public policy may play a role. If policy can reduce the time it takes unemployed workers to find new jobs, it can reduce the economy's natural rate of unemployment.

Government policies try to facilitate job search in various ways. One way is through government-run employment agencies or job centres, which give out information about job vacancies. Another way is through public training schemes, which aim to ease the transition of workers from declining to growing industries and to help disadvantaged groups escape poverty. Advocates of these policies believe that they make the economy operate more efficiently by keeping the labour force more fully employed, and that they reduce the inequities inherent in a constantly changing market economy.

Critics of these policies question whether the government should get involved with the process of job search. They argue that it is better to let the private market match workers and jobs. In fact, most job search in the economy takes place without intervention by the government. Newspaper advertisements, internet job sites, head-hunters and word of mouth all help spread information about job openings and job candidates. Similarly, much worker education is done privately, either through schools or through on-the-job training. These critics contend that the government is no better – and most likely worse – at disseminating the right information to the right workers and deciding what kinds of worker training would be most valuable. They claim that these decisions are best made privately by workers and employers.

Unemployment Insurance

One government policy that increases the amount of frictional unemployment, without intending to do so, is **unemployment insurance** (or, as it is called in the UK, national insurance). This policy is designed to offer workers partial protection against job loss. The unemployed who quit their jobs, were fired for just cause or who have just entered the labour force are not eligible. Benefits are paid only to the unemployed who were laid off because their previous employers no longer needed their skills.

> **unemployment insurance** a government programme that partially protects workers' incomes when they become unemployed

While unemployment insurance reduces the hardship of unemployment, it is argued that it can also increase the amount of unemployment. This explanation is based on one of the *Ten Principles of Economics*: people respond to incentives. Because unemployment benefits stop when a worker takes a new job, the unemployed, it is argued, devote less effort to job search and are more likely to turn down unattractive job offers. In addition, because unemployment insurance makes unemployment less onerous, workers are less likely to seek guarantees of job security when they negotiate with employers over the terms of employment. However, research on unemployment insurance in Europe gives a different perspective. In a paper by Konstantinos Tatsiramos (Tatsiramos, K. (2006) *Unemployment Insurance in Europe: Unemployment Duration and Subsequent Employment Stability*. Institute for the Study of Labor Discussion Paper no. 2280) the benefits to workers searching for jobs and receiving unemployment insurance is greater than the costs:

> *This paper provides evidence on the effect of unemployment benefits on unemployment and employment duration in Europe, using individual data from the European Community Household Panel for eight countries. Even if receiving benefits has a direct negative effect increasing the duration of unemployment spells, there is also a positive indirect effect of benefits on subsequent employment duration. This indirect effect is pronounced in countries with relatively generous benefit systems, and for recipients who have remained unemployed for at least six months. In terms of the magnitude of the effect, recipients remain employed on average two to four months longer than non-recipients. This represents a 10 to 20 per cent increase relative to the average employment duration, compensating for the additional time spent in unemployment.*

The effect of unemployment insurance is likely to be related to the way the scheme is designed and operated. In one US study, when unemployed workers applied to collect unemployment insurance benefits, some of them were randomly selected and offered each a $500 bonus if they found new jobs within 11 weeks. This group was then compared with a control group not offered the incentive. The average spell of unemployment for the group offered the bonus was 7 per cent shorter than the average spell for the control group. This experiment shows that the design of the unemployment insurance system influences the effort that the unemployed devote to job search.

Several other studies examined search effort by following a group of workers over time. Unemployment insurance benefits, rather than lasting forever, usually run out after six months or a year. These studies found that when the unemployed become ineligible for benefits, the probability of their finding a new job rises markedly. Thus, receiving unemployment insurance benefits does reduce the search effort of the unemployed.

Even though unemployment insurance reduces search effort and raises unemployment, we should not necessarily conclude that the policy is a bad one. The policy does achieve its primary goal of reducing the income uncertainty that workers face. In addition, when workers turn down unattractive job offers, they have the opportunity to look for jobs that better suit their tastes and skills. Some economists have argued that unemployment insurance improves the ability of the economy to match each worker with the most appropriate job.

The study of unemployment insurance shows that the unemployment rate is an imperfect measure of a nation's overall level of economic well-being. Most economists agree that eliminating unemployment insurance would reduce the amount of unemployment in the economy. Yet economists disagree on whether economic well-being would be enhanced or diminished by this change in policy.

SELF TEST How would an increase in the world price of oil affect the amount of frictional unemployment? Is this unemployment undesirable? What public policies might affect the amount of unemployment caused by this price change?

MINIMUM WAGE LAWS

Having seen how frictional unemployment results from the process of matching workers and jobs, let's now examine how structural unemployment results when the number of jobs is insufficient for the number of workers.

To understand structural unemployment, we begin by reviewing how unemployment arises from minimum wage laws. Although minimum wages are not the predominant reason for unemployment in an economy, they have an important effect on certain groups with particularly high unemployment rates. Moreover, the analysis of minimum wages can be used to understand some of the other reasons for structural unemployment.

Figure 7.2 reviews the basic economics of a minimum wage. When a minimum wage law forces the wage to remain above the level that balances supply and demand, it raises the quantity of labour supplied and reduces the quantity of labour demanded compared to the equilibrium level. There is a surplus of labour. Because there are more workers willing to work than there are jobs, some workers are unemployed.

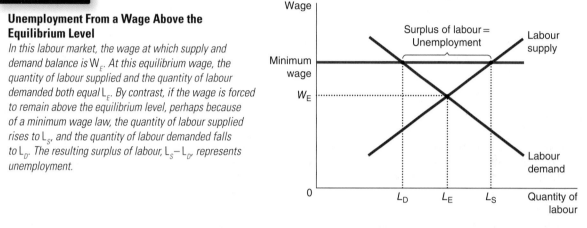

FIGURE 7.2

Unemployment From a Wage Above the Equilibrium Level

In this labour market, the wage at which supply and demand balance is W$_E$. At this equilibrium wage, the quantity of labour supplied and the quantity of labour demanded both equal L$_E$. By contrast, if the wage is forced to remain above the equilibrium level, perhaps because of a minimum wage law, the quantity of labour supplied rises to L$_S$, and the quantity of labour demanded falls to L$_D$. The resulting surplus of labour, L$_S$–L$_D$, represents unemployment.

We will not discuss minimum wage laws here. It is, however, important to note why minimum wage laws are not a predominant reason for unemployment: most workers in the economy have wages well above the legal minimum. Minimum wage laws are binding most often for the least skilled and least experienced members of the labour force, such as teenagers. It is only among these workers that minimum wage laws explain the existence of unemployment.

Although Figure 7.2 is drawn to show the effects of a minimum wage law, it also illustrates a more general lesson: if the wage is kept above the equilibrium level for any reason, the result is unemployment. Minimum wage laws are just one reason why wages may be 'too high'. In the next two sections of this chapter, we consider two other reasons why wages may be kept above the equilibrium level – unions and efficiency wages. The basic economics of unemployment in these cases is the same as that shown in Figure 7.2, but these explanations of unemployment can apply to many more of the economy's workers.

At this point, however, we should stop and notice that the structural unemployment that arises from an above-equilibrium wage is, in an important sense, different from the frictional unemployment that arises from the process of job search. The need for job search is not due to the failure of wages to balance labour supply and labour demand. When job search is the explanation for unemployment, workers are *searching* for the jobs that best suit their tastes and skills. By contrast, when the wage is above the equilibrium level, the quantity of labour supplied exceeds the quantity of labour demanded, and workers are unemployed because they are *waiting* for jobs to open up.

SELF TEST Draw the supply curve and the demand curve for a labour market in which the wage is fixed above the equilibrium level. Show the quantity of labour supplied, the quantity demanded and the amount of unemployment.

UNIONS AND COLLECTIVE BARGAINING

A union is a worker association that bargains with employers over wages and working conditions. **Union density** measures the proportion of the workforce that is unionized, excluding people who cannot, for legal or other reasons, be members of a union – for example, members of the armed forces.

> **union density** a measure of the proportion of the workforce that is unionized

Broadly speaking, this amounts to expressing the number of union members as a proportion of civilian employees plus the unemployed. In the UK in 2011, union density was 23.8 per cent, and has been steadily falling since 1995 when it stood at around 32.4 per cent and an even greater marked fall from the beginning of the 1980s, when it was over 50 per cent. In other European countries there is a similar trend of falling union density. In Germany density has fallen from 23.3 per cent in 1999 to 18.5 per cent in 2010, in the Netherlands the fall has been from 24.6 per cent to 18.2 per cent in 2011. However, there are exceptions with countries like Finland, Denmark, Iceland and Sweden having densities between 68 per cent and 79 per cent, however even in these countries the density is gradually falling. In the United States, by comparison, density was around 11.3 per cent and in Australia 18.0 per cent (both in 2011, data from the OECD).

The Economics of Unions

A union is a type of cartel. Like any cartel, a union is a group of sellers acting together in the hope of exerting their joint market power. Workers in a union act as a group when discussing their wages, benefits and working conditions with their employers. The process by which unions and firms agree on the terms of employment is called **collective bargaining**.

> **collective bargaining** the process by which unions and firms agree on the terms of employment

When a union bargains with a firm, it asks for higher wages, better benefits and better working conditions than the firm would offer in the absence of a union. If the union and the firm do not reach agreement, the union can take various steps to put pressure on employers to come to an agreement including working to rule (doing only what is agreed in the contract of employment) and as a last resort organizing a withdrawal of labour from the firm, called a strike. Because a strike reduces production, sales and profit, a firm facing a strike threat is likely to agree to pay higher wages than it otherwise would. Economists who study the effects of unions typically find that union workers earn significantly more than similar workers who do not belong to unions.

When a union raises the wage above the equilibrium level, it raises the quantity of labour supplied and reduces the quantity of labour demanded, resulting in unemployment. Those workers who remain employed are better off, but those who were previously employed and are now unemployed are worse off. Indeed, unions are often thought to cause conflict between different groups of workers – between the *insiders* who benefit from high union wages and the *outsiders* who do not get the union jobs.

The outsiders can respond to their status in one of two ways. Some of them remain unemployed and wait for the chance to become insiders and earn the high union wage. Others take jobs in firms that are not unionized. Thus, when unions raise wages in one part of the economy, the supply of labour increases in other parts of the economy. This increase in labour supply, in turn, reduces wages in industries that are not unionized. In other words, workers in unions reap the benefit of collective bargaining, while workers not in unions bear some of the cost.

The role of unions in the economy depends in part on the laws that govern union organization and collective bargaining. Normally, explicit agreements among members of a cartel are illegal. If firms that sell a common product were to agree to set a high price for that product, they would generally be held to be in breach of competition law and the government would prosecute these firms in the civil and criminal courts. In contrast, unions are given exemption from these laws in the belief that workers need greater market power as they bargain with employers.

Legislation affecting the market power of unions is a perennial topic of political debate. Members of parliament sometimes debate *right-to-work laws*, which give workers in a unionized firm the right to choose whether to join the union. In the absence of such laws, unions can insist during collective bargaining that firms make union membership a requirement for employment.

Are Unions Good or Bad for the Economy?

Economists disagree about whether unions are good or bad for the economy as a whole. Let's consider both sides of the debate.

Critics of unions argue that unions are merely a type of cartel. When unions raise wages above the level that would prevail in competitive markets, they reduce the quantity of labour demanded, cause some workers to be unemployed and reduce the wages in the rest of the economy. The resulting allocation of labour is, critics argue, both inefficient and inequitable. It is inefficient because high union wages reduce employment in unionized firms below the efficient, competitive level. It is inequitable because some workers benefit at the expense of other workers.

Advocates of unions contend that unions are a necessary antidote to the market power of the firms that hire workers. In some regions where one particular company is the dominant employer, if workers do not accept the wages and working conditions that the firm offers, they may have little choice but to move or stop working. In the absence of a union, therefore, the firm could use its market power to pay lower wages and offer worse working conditions than would prevail if it had to compete with other firms for the same workers. In this case, a union may balance the firm's market power and protect the workers from being at the mercy of the firm owners.

Advocates of unions also claim that unions are important for helping firms respond efficiently to workers' concerns. Whenever a worker takes a job, the worker and the firm must agree on many attributes of the job in addition to the wage: hours of work, overtime, holidays, sick leave, health benefits, promotion schedules, job security and so on. By representing workers' views on these issues, unions allow firms to provide the right mix of job attributes. In many countries unions have now taken on additional roles in supporting workers with respect to offering legal support in the event of an individual dispute at work, advice on pensions, financial services such as insurance, and support for those who have been injured or disabled at work and have to retire early. Even if unions have the adverse effect of pushing wages above the equilibrium level and causing unemployment, they have the benefit of helping firms keep a happy and productive workforce.

In the end, there is no consensus among economists about whether unions are good or bad for the economy. Like many institutions, their influence is probably beneficial in some circumstances and adverse in others.

SELF TEST How does a union in the car industry affect wages and employment at Ford and Nissan plants in the UK? How might it affect wages and employment in other industries?

THE THEORY OF EFFICIENCY WAGES

A fourth reason why economies always experience some unemployment is suggested by the theory of efficiency wages. According to this theory, firms operate more efficiently if wages are above the equilibrium level. Therefore, it may be profitable for firms to keep wages high even in the presence of a surplus of labour.

In some ways, the unemployment that arises from efficiency wages is similar to the unemployment that arises from minimum wage laws and unions. In all three cases, unemployment is the result of wages above the level that balances the quantity of labour supplied and the quantity of labour demanded. Yet there is also an important difference. Minimum wage laws and unions prevent firms from lowering wages in the presence of a surplus of workers. Efficiency wage theory states that such a constraint on firms is unnecessary in many cases because firms may be better off keeping wages above the equilibrium level.

Why should firms want to keep wages high? This decision may seem odd at first, for wages are a large part of firms' costs. Normally, we expect profit-maximizing firms to want to keep costs – and therefore wages – as low as possible. The novel insight of efficiency wage theory is that paying high wages might be profitable because they might raise the efficiency of a firm's workers.

There are several types of efficiency wage theory. Each type suggests a different explanation for why firms may want to pay high wages. Let's now consider four of these types.

Worker Health

The first and simplest type of efficiency wage theory emphasizes the link between wages and worker health. Better paid workers eat a more nutritious diet, and workers who eat a better diet are healthier and more productive. A firm may find it more profitable to pay high wages and have healthy, productive workers than to pay lower wages and have less healthy, less productive workers.

This type of efficiency wage theory is not relevant for firms in rich countries such as the United Kingdom and many of those in Europe. In these countries, the equilibrium wages for most workers are well above the level needed for an adequate diet. Firms are not concerned that paying equilibrium wages would place their workers' health in jeopardy.

This type of efficiency wage theory is more relevant for firms in less developed countries where inadequate nutrition is a more common problem. Unemployment is high in the cities of many poor African countries, for example. In these countries, firms may fear that cutting wages would, in fact, adversely influence their workers' health and productivity. In other words, concern over nutrition may explain why firms do not cut wages despite a surplus of labour.

Worker Turnover

A second type of efficiency wage theory emphasizes the link between wages and worker turnover. Workers quit jobs for many reasons – to take jobs in other firms, to move to other parts of the country, to leave the labour force and so on. The frequency with which they quit depends on the entire set of incentives they face, including the benefits of leaving and the benefits of staying. The more a firm pays its workers, the less often its workers will choose to leave. Thus, a firm can reduce turnover among its workers by paying them a high wage.

Why do firms care about turnover? The reason is that it is costly for firms to hire and train new workers. Moreover, even after they are trained, newly hired workers are not as productive as experienced workers. Firms with higher turnover, therefore, will tend to have higher production costs. Firms may find it profitable to pay wages above the equilibrium level in order to reduce worker turnover.

Worker Effort

A third type of efficiency wage theory emphasizes the link between wages and worker effort. In many jobs, workers have some discretion over how hard to work. As a result, firms monitor the efforts of their workers, and workers caught shirking their responsibilities can be disciplined and possibly dismissed. But not all shirkers are caught immediately because monitoring workers is costly and imperfect. A firm can respond to this problem by paying wages above the equilibrium level. High wages make workers more eager to keep their jobs and, thereby, give workers an incentive to put forward their best effort.

This particular type of efficiency wage theory is similar to the old Marxist idea of the 'reserve army of the unemployed'. Marx thought that employers benefited from unemployment because the threat of unemployment helped to discipline those workers who had jobs. In the worker effort variant of efficiency wage theory, unemployment fills a similar role. If the wage were at the level that balanced supply and demand, workers would have less reason to work hard because if they were fired, they could quickly find new jobs at the same wage. Therefore, firms raise wages above the equilibrium level, causing unemployment and providing an incentive for workers not to shirk their responsibilities.

Worker Quality

A fourth and final type of efficiency wage theory emphasizes the link between wages and worker quality. When a firm hires new workers, it cannot perfectly gauge the quality of the applicants. By paying a high wage, the firm attracts a better pool of workers to apply for its jobs.

To see how this might work, consider a simple example. Waterwell Company owns one well and needs one worker to pump water from the well. Two workers, Jekyll and Hyde, are interested in the job. Jekyll, a proficient worker, is willing to work for €10 per hour. Below that wage, he would rather start his own car-washing business. Hyde, a complete incompetent, is willing to work for anything above €2 per hour. Below that wage, he would rather sit on the beach. Economists say that Jekyll's *reservation wage* – the lowest wage he would accept – is €10 per hour, and Hyde's reservation wage is €2 per hour.

What wage should the firm set? If the firm was interested in minimizing labour costs, it would set the wage at €2 per hour. At this wage, the quantity of workers supplied (one) would balance the quantity demanded. Hyde would take the job, and Jekyll would not apply for it. Yet suppose Waterwell knows that only one of these two applicants is competent, but it does not know whether it is Jekyll or Hyde. If the firm hires the incompetent worker, he may damage the well, causing the firm huge losses. In this case, the firm has a better strategy than paying the equilibrium wage of €2 per hour and hiring Hyde. It can offer €10 per hour, inducing both Jekyll and Hyde to apply for the job. By choosing randomly between these two applicants and turning the other away, the firm has a 50:50 chance of hiring the competent one. By contrast, if the firm offers any lower wage, it is sure to hire the incompetent worker.

This story illustrates a general phenomenon. When a firm faces a surplus of workers, it might seem profitable to reduce the wage it is offering. But by reducing the wage, the firm induces an adverse change in the mix of workers. In this case, at a wage of €10 per hour, Waterwell has two workers applying for one job. But if Waterwell responds to this labour surplus by reducing the wage, the competent worker (who has better alternative opportunities) will not apply. Thus, it is profitable for the firm to pay a wage above the level that balances supply and demand.

SELF TEST Give four explanations for why firms might find it profitable to pay wages above the level that balances quantity of labour supplied and quantity of labour demanded.

THE COST OF UNEMPLOYMENT

We mentioned at the outset of this chapter that unemployment can be one of the most distressing things to happen to anyone in their lives. Unemployment imposes costs on the individual and their family and friends but there is also a wider cost of unemployment which affects government, the taxpayer and the economy as a whole.

The Costs of Unemployment to the Individual

Loss of Earnings One of the first and perhaps most obvious costs of unemployment to an individual is the loss of earnings that results from being unemployed. Many countries provide some form of unemployment insurance as we have seen but the sums given to the unemployed are relatively small and in most cases nowhere near the earnings that the individual would have earned in work. In some countries there might be other state benefits that an unemployed worker can claim which can mean that in the case of workers in low-skilled, low-paid industries the incentive to take work can be reduced as we have seen. In many other cases, however, unemployment means that individuals have to re-evaluate their household spending budgets.

This might mean that households cut back on certain luxuries like spending on leisure activities, going to the cinema, going out to eat and so on, but might also cut down on luxuries such as clothing, furniture, electrical goods, having extensions built on a house and so on. We will see shortly how this has an effect on society as a whole.

The unemployed and their families are more likely to be at risk of slipping into poverty. Remember, the definition of poverty is a household income less than 60 per cent below the median income. It is unlikely that welfare support from the state is ever going to be, on its own, sufficient to put families above this level so unless the unemployed have savings to draw upon it is more likely that they will fall into poverty. The Trades Union Congress (TUC) in the UK estimate that around 60 per cent of working age adults in families where there is unemployment are likely to be in poverty.

In addition, some families will find that unemployment means that they face problems in paying for rent or mortgages and this can result in the loss of homes. The unemployed are more likely to have to go into debt in order to pay bills and this can add to the problems highlighted in our next section.

Stress, Self-Esteem and Health Problems Being unemployed can lead to significant mental health problems. The process of becoming unemployed is stressful, it can be a life-changing event for some people. Having to adjust to claiming benefits, applying for other jobs, possibly getting additional training and the chances of having repeated experiences of either not having any replies to applications or in the event of unsuccessful interviews, the feeling of rejection, is not only stressful in itself but can lead to feelings of guilt and the reduction in self-esteem. These experiences can bring on stress-related illnesses and the incidences of health problems in the unemployed can increase the longer that the unemployment continues.

Drug and Alcohol Abuse and Crime Closely linked to the self-esteem problems, the boredom that can result from being unemployed and the feeling of worthlessness that many unemployed people say they experience, is the increased potential to turn to alcohol and illegal drugs as a means of escape. In 2010, a survey by the Prince's Trust Youth Index reported that over 10 per cent of young people experiencing unemployment had abused drugs and alcohol.

When people move from being employed and having an income to be able to afford a reasonable standard of living, to experiencing tight restrictions on incomes and spending, the feeling of social exclusion and deprivation can be acute and cause some to turn to crime as a means of maintaining what they see as a reasonable standard of living. Indeed, the correlation between crime rates and drug abuse is very high; once people get involved with a drug or alcohol habit it becomes expensive and one way of funding this habit is to turn to crime.

Family Breakdown Families who have an experience of unemployment are more prone to break-up. Divorce rates amongst the unemployed are higher as the stresses of coping with adjusting to new income levels, trying to find work and so on take their toll.

De-Skilling The longer someone is out of work the more likely it is that they will lose touch with changes in the workplace and the labour market in general and the more likely it is that they might be viewed as being unemployable or not favourable candidates for employment. Changes in the workplace, in technology and in the skills needed for employment change rapidly. Those in work are able to take advantage of training – both off-the-job and on-the-job, to maintain their skill levels, but the unemployed may be excluded from being able to maintain or improve their skill levels and as a result find it even harder to find work. This can lead to the hysteresis effect as outlined above.

The Costs of Unemployment to Society and the Economy

The Opportunity Cost of Unemployment
An individual who is willing and able to work represents a unit of productive output. If that person is unemployed the opportunity cost to society is the value of the goods and services that the individual could have produced. This 'lost output' can be considerable and represents a lower standard of living for society as a whole. If there is unemployment in society which is not simply frictional unemployment then society will not be operating on the production possibilities frontier (PPF) but instead somewhere inside it which represents an inefficient use of resources.

The Tax and Benefits Effect
People who are unemployed have lower incomes and may rely solely on government welfare payments to support their standard of living. If people lose their jobs then they do not pay as much in income taxes and if they also reduce spending they then do not pay consumption taxes at the same level as if they were in employment. The higher the level of unemployment in a country the greater the impact on tax revenue for the government. Not only is government revenue adversely affected but government spending is also likely to be higher. The unemployed will claim additional benefits and in addition, governments may also incur additional costs in having to deal with the social problems caused by unemployment such as drug and alcohol abuse, family breakdown and the increase in crime.

If government income is reduced through lower tax receipts and there is also a requirement to increase spending because of higher welfare spending, the pressure on government budgets can increase and it is more likely that the government experience a budget deficit – a situation where its spending is higher than its revenue from taxation. If governments experience a budget deficit then the deficit has to be funded by additional borrowing. If governments have to borrow more then this can not only cause crowding out but also puts upward pressure on interest rates, which in turn might affect investment decisions by firms. The knock-on effects can have ripples throughout the economy as our next point highlights.

The Reverse Multiplier Effect
We have seen that when people experience unemployment they cut back their spending on luxuries and may also switch their spending to substitute goods which may be seen as inferior goods. Firms who produce these different goods may see a change in spending patterns which can have an effect on cash flows and ultimately profits.

Goods with a relatively high income elasticity of demand are likely to be affected more significantly. If sales fall firms earn lower incomes and may have to adjust their business to manage cash flows. This might involve cutting back on orders from suppliers, building up stocks as goods remain unsold and in some cases firms may have to either lay-off workers or even make workers redundant or close down the business if it becomes insolvent. If workers are made redundant or lose their jobs in this way this then means those workers receive lower incomes and so the process continues.

Not all firms will be affected in such an extreme way but it is the case that in periods of high unemployment, firms may see falling profit levels and this in turn means they pay lower corporate taxes which puts further pressure on government budgets. Some firms might see demand for their services actually increase in periods of high unemployment. If the unemployed switch spending to inferior goods, the producers of those goods might see demand rise. In the aftermath of the financial crisis and beyond, low-cost supermarkets across the UK and Europe reported seeing an increase in sales whilst traditional supermarkets reported reduced sales.

The effect of unemployment if more than simply frictional unemployment is to produce a multiplied impact on economic activity as a whole. If there are concentrated pockets of workers losing their jobs such as a major employer in an area, then the effect of this reverse multiplier effect can be considerable. Indeed, there are areas of the UK and Europe where the decline in industries concentrated in particular areas has led to considerable regional deprivation which has lasted for many years. Once an area is caught in the cycle of economic decline it is extremely hard to recover.

CONCLUSION

In this chapter we discussed the measurement of unemployment, the reasons why economies always experience some degree of unemployment and some of the costs of unemployment to society and the economy as a whole. We have seen how job search, minimum wage laws, unions and efficiency wages can all help explain why some workers do not have jobs. Which of these four explanations for the natural rate of unemployment are the most important? Unfortunately, there is no easy way to tell. Economists differ in which of these explanations of unemployment they consider most important.

The analysis of this chapter yields an important lesson: although the economy will always have some unemployment, its natural rate is not immutable. Many events and policies can change the amount of unemployment the economy typically experiences. As the information revolution changes the process of job search, as government adjusts the minimum wage, as workers form or quit unions, and as firms alter their reliance on efficiency wages, the natural rate of unemployment evolves. Unemployment is not a simple problem with a simple solution. But how we choose to organize our society can profoundly influence how prevalent a problem it is. The costs of unemployment are significant not only to individuals but also to the economy and society which is why so many governments around the world are highly sensitive to the problem and look to develop policies to deal with unemployment. It is worth noting that when high unemployment persists, the potential for social disorder and political upheaval is greater. It might not be surprising, therefore, that governments are keen to ensure that the problems which can arise from unemployment are given due consideration in policy formulation.

IN THE NEWS

Unemployment and Vacancies

You may sometimes hear news reports of the number of vacancies in the economy and wonder why unemployment is so high when there are seemingly a large number of jobs available. This article looks at this in more detail.

Search Costs in the Labour Market

According to the Organization of Economic Co operation and Development (OECD), in December 2012 there were around 28,045 job vacancies in Austria against a registered unemployment level (the claimant count) of 273,615 (10.2 per cent of the unemployed), in the UK, 494,000 vacancies against a claimant count of 1,557,100 (31.7 per cent), in Switzerland 16,866 against 131,509 (12.8 per cent) and in Sweden 45,132 against 217,187 (20.7 per cent). In theory, if the unemployed could fill the vacancies that exist then unemployment would

be lower and the costs to individuals and society would be less.

The relationship between vacancies and unemployment does tend to be regional in many countries. In some parts of the UK, the number of people chasing each job vacancy is high with figures from a job search website, Adzuna, suggesting around 80 applicants for every vacancy in some cities such as Hull in the north of England, 73 per job in Stoke-on-Trent and 53 in Sunderland, while in parts of the south east, such as Reading, Cambridge, London and Milton Keynes, the number of applicants per vacancy was under two.

Why are there people who are unemployed when there are

sometimes large numbers of vacant positions waiting to be filled? This was a question asked by three economists who were awarded the Nobel Prize for Economics in 2010. Peter A. Diamond, Date T. Mortenson and Christopher A. Pissarides developed a theory known as 'search and matching theories'.

Under normal circumstances, markets are assumed to be in equilibrium when supply equals demand. When something happens to disturb that equilibrium, market forces work to restore equilibrium. The work of these three economists has shown how labour markets can operate differently and that unemployment can remain at high levels even though there are plenty of vacancies. Government policy and labour market regulation may have important consequences for labour markets and can contribute to the disequilibrium rather than helping to clear the market.

Some of the reasons include the time it takes for those who are unemployed to find work – there are search costs involved. For employers there are transaction costs to hiring labour and whilst there may be employers looking for labour and labour looking for work, both parties need to be put in touch with each other and agree to a transaction. Even if the two parties do come together a transaction may not be guaranteed (i.e. the supplier of labour gets a job) because there may be incentives for both sides to see if they can get a better outcome for themselves. In addition, policies regulating the ease with which employers can hire or fire workers and the benefits or unemployment insurance that exists in a country can also influence when labour

In reality the labour market is not perfect and is subject to a number of frictions. The development of job search sites on the Internet may be one way in which search costs for employers and employees can be reduced and help match workers to available jobs.

becomes unemployed and how long they stay unemployed. If for example, unemployment benefit is relatively generous then it may be that workers take more time to find work because they have some degree of support to live on whilst they find 'the right job'. It is entirely possible, therefore, that vacancies can remain unfilled even when there are high levels of unemployment and that the more generous unemployment benefits are the higher unemployment might be.

The search process, therefore, involves both time and resources for both employers and the unemployed looking for work and these create frictions in the market which mean that the wants of both employers and the unemployed remain unmet. Both could agree on a price if they were able to meet and thus fulfil one of the basic requirements for a functioning market, but the search frictions mean that the labour market will fail to clear at particular points in time. Search theory provides a departure point from the assumptions of perfect competition in the labour market. The theory further suggests that when the economy is subject to a shock, such as the financial crisis or recession, it will take much longer for unemployment to return to pre-shock levels even though firms may be looking to hire workers once again.

The research carried out by the laureates is helping economists and policymakers gain a better understanding of policies to help reduce high levels of

unemployment. They have brought a different perspective to the debate on how best to deal with the frictional aspects of structural unemployment, which seems to be a problem for a number of countries following the financial crisis where jobs have been lost in one sector but workers have found difficulty moving to other sectors of the economy where vacancies exist.

Questions

1 **What do you think is the main cause of the differences in regional unemployment implied by the different applicant to vacancy rates quoted for the UK: frictional or structural? Explain.**

2 **Why is it important to identify the type of unemployment and the nature of the unemployed when looking at levels of unemployment?**

3 **The number of unemployed is much higher in the UK than the other countries quoted in the article and the proportion of vacancies to the unemployed also much higher. What questions would you ask if analysing these data to discover why this is the case?**

4 **Why might search costs render some of the assumptions of perfect competition redundant and thus result in the labour market not clearing?**

5 **To what extent can governments reduce search costs or does government intervention simply exacerbate frictions in the market?**

SUMMARY

- The unemployment rate is the percentage of those who would like to work who do not have jobs. The government calculates this statistic monthly based on a survey of thousands of households.

- The unemployment rate is an imperfect measure of joblessness. Some people who call themselves unemployed may actually not want to work, and some people who would like to work have left the labour force after an unsuccessful search.

- In many advanced economies, most people who become unemployed find work within a short period of time. Nevertheless, most unemployment observed at any given time is attributable to the few people who are unemployed for long periods of time.

- One reason for unemployment is the time it takes for workers to search for jobs that best suit their tastes and skills. Unemployment insurance is a government policy that, while protecting workers' incomes, increases the amount of frictional unemployment.

- A second reason why an economy may always have some unemployment is if there is a minimum wage that exceeds the wage that would balance supply and demand for the workers who are eligible for the minimum wage. By raising the wage of unskilled and inexperienced workers above the equilibrium level, minimum wage laws raise the quantity of labour supplied and reduce the quantity demanded. The resulting surplus of labour represents unemployment.

- A third reason for unemployment is the market power of unions. When unions push the wages in unionized industries above the equilibrium level, they create a surplus of labour.

- A fourth reason for unemployment is suggested by the theory of efficiency wages. According to this theory, firms find it profitable to pay wages above the equilibrium level. High wages can improve worker health, lower worker turnover, increase worker effort and raise worker quality.

- The costs of unemployment to individuals include lower incomes, loss of self-esteem, de-skilling, an increase in the possibility of mental health problems, family breakdown and crime.

- The costs of unemployment to society as a whole includes the opportunity cost of lost output which reduces potential growth, the impact on government income and expenditure, the social costs of dealing with unemployment and its effects, the underuse of resources and the reverse multiplier effect.

QUESTIONS FOR REVIEW

1 Why might a person who does not have a job not be unemployed?

2 How do national statistical offices compute the labour force, the unemployment rate and the labour force participation rate?

3 Is unemployment typically short term or long term? Explain.

4 Why is frictional unemployment inevitable? How might the government reduce the amount of frictional unemployment?

5 Are minimum wage laws a better explanation for structural unemployment among teenagers or among university graduates? Why?

6 How do unions affect the natural rate of unemployment?

7 What is the hysteresis effect?

8 What claims do advocates of unions make to argue that unions are good for the economy?

9 Explain four ways in which a firm might increase its profits by raising the wages it pays.

10 Outline three costs of unemployment to (a) an individual and (b) to society.

PROBLEMS AND APPLICATIONS

1 Assume that in a country, of all adult people, 29,500,000 were employed, 1,120,000 were unemployed and 11,000,000 were not in the labour force. How big was the labour force? What was the labour force participation rate? What was the unemployment rate?

2 Go to the website of the UK Office for National Statistics (http://www.statistics.gov.uk) or Eurostat (http://epp.eurostat.ec.europa.eu/portal/page/portal/eurostat/home) or the statistics office for the country in which you are studying. What is the national unemployment rate right now? Find the unemployment rate for the demographic

group that best fits a description of you (for example, based on age, sex and ethnic group). Is it higher or lower than the national average? Why do you think this is so?

3 According to a Labour Force Survey in a country, total employment increased by around 1.35 million workers between 2010 and 2016, but the number of unemployed workers increased by 350,000.

a. How are these numbers consistent with each other?

b. In some cases, there can be an increase in the number of people employed but the number of unemployed people declines by a smaller amount. Why might one expect a reduction in the number of people counted as unemployed to be smaller than the increase in the number of people employed?

4 Are the following workers more likely to experience short-term or long-term unemployment? Explain.

a. A construction worker laid off because of bad weather.

b. A manufacturing worker who loses her job at a plant in an isolated area.

c. A bus industry worker laid off because of competition from the railway.

d. A short-order cook who loses his job when a new restaurant opens across the street.

e. An expert welder with little formal education who loses her job when the company installs automatic welding machinery.

5 Using a diagram of the labour market, show the effect of an increase in the minimum wage on the wage paid to workers, the number of workers supplied, the number of workers demanded and the amount of unemployment.

6 Do you think that firms in small towns or in cities have more market power in hiring? Do you think that firms generally have more market power in hiring today than 50 years ago, or less? How do you think this change over time has affected the role of unions in the economy? Explain.

7 Consider an economy with two labour markets, neither of which is unionized. Now suppose a union is established in one market.

a. Show the effect of the union on the market in which it is formed. In what sense is the quantity of labour employed in this market an inefficient quantity?

b. Show the effect of the union on the non-unionized market. What happens to the equilibrium wage in this market?

8 Some workers in the economy are paid a flat salary and some are paid by commission. Which compensation scheme would require more monitoring by supervisors? In which case do firms have an incentive to pay more than the equilibrium level (as in the worker effort variant of efficiency wage theory)? What factors do you think determine the type of compensation firms choose?

9 Suppose that the government passes a law requiring employers to provide employees some benefit (such as a guaranteed pension) that raises the cost of an employee by €4 per hour.

a. What effect does this new law have on the demand for labour? (In answering this and the following questions, be quantitative when you can.)

b. If employees place a value on this benefit exactly equal to its cost, what effect does the new law have on the supply of labour?

c. If the wage is free to balance supply and demand, how does this law affect the wage and the level of employment? Are employers better or worse off? Are employees better or worse off?

d. If a minimum wage law prevents the wage from balancing supply and demand, how does the new law affect the wage, the level of employment and the level of unemployment? Are employers better or worse off? Are employees better or worse off?

e. Now suppose that workers do not value the benefit arising from the new law at all. How does this alternative assumption change your answers to parts (b), (c) and (d) above?

10 Statistics from the International Labour Organization in 2011, suggest that there are 75 million young people (those aged between 16 and 23) unemployed worldwide. Young people are three times more likely to be unemployed than those in other age groups and each month out of work prior to age 23 increases the likelihood that they will experience longer periods of unemployment later in life.

a. Why are such statistics of importance to policymakers?

b. What specific costs might be associated with youth unemployment to young people and to society?

c. Should policymakers devote more resources to dealing with youth unemployment compared to other groups in society? Justify your response.

PART 5
INTEREST RATES, MONEY AND PRICES IN THE LONG RUN

8 SAVING, INVESTMENT AND THE FINANCIAL SYSTEM

Imagine that you have just graduated from university (with a degree in economics, of course) and you decide to start your own business – an economic forecasting firm. Before you make any money selling your forecasts, you have to incur substantial costs to set up your business. You have to buy computers with which to make your forecasts, as well as desks, chairs and filing cabinets to furnish your new office. Each of these items is a type of capital that your firm will use to produce and sell its services.

How do you obtain the funds to invest in these capital goods? Perhaps you are able to pay for them out of your past savings. More likely, however, like most entrepreneurs, you do not have enough money of your own to finance the start of your business. As a result, you have to get the money you need from other sources.

There are various ways for you to finance these capital investments. You could borrow the money, perhaps from a bank or from a friend or relative. In this case, you would promise not only to return the money at a later date but also to pay interest for the use of the money. Alternatively, you could convince someone to provide the money you need for your business in exchange for a share of your future profits, whatever they might happen to be. In either case, your investment in computers and office equipment is being financed by someone else's saving.

The **financial system** consists of those institutions in the economy that help to match one person's saving with another person's investment. As we discussed in the previous chapter, saving and investment are key ingredients to long-run economic growth: when a country saves a large portion of its GDP, more resources are available for investment in capital, and higher capital raises a country's productivity and living standard. The previous chapter, however, did not explain how the economy coordinates saving and investment. At any time, some people want to save some of their income for the future, and others want to borrow in order to finance investments in new and growing businesses. What brings these two groups of people together? (Not physically of course!) What ensures that the supply of funds from those who want to save balances the demand for funds from those who want to invest?

financial system the group of institutions in the economy that help to match one person's saving with another person's investment

This chapter examines how the financial system works. First, we discuss the large variety of institutions that make up the financial system. Second, we discuss the relationship between the financial system and some key macroeconomic variables – notably saving and investment. Third, we develop a model of the supply and demand for funds in financial markets. In the model, the interest rate is the price that adjusts to balance supply and demand. The model shows how various government policies affect the interest rate and, thereby, society's allocation of scarce resources.

FINANCIAL INSTITUTIONS IN THE ECONOMY

At the broadest level, the financial system moves the economy's scarce resources from savers (people who spend less than they earn) to borrowers (people who spend more than they earn). Savers save for various reasons – to help put a child through university in several years or to retire comfortably in several decades. Similarly, borrowers borrow for various reasons – to buy a house in which to live or to start a business with which to make a living. Savers supply their money to the financial system with the expectation that they will get it back with interest at a later date. The expectation that the reward for saving will be the receipt of interest is not universal – Islamic finance has a very different approach to finance but in this chapter we will be focusing on what might be called 'traditional' financial institutions. Borrowers demand money from the financial system with the knowledge that they will be required to pay it back with interest at a later date.

The financial system is made up of various financial institutions that help coordinate savers and borrowers. Financial institutions can be grouped into two categories – financial markets and financial intermediaries. We consider each category in turn.

Financial Markets

Financial markets are the institutions through which a person who wants to save can directly supply funds to a person who wants to borrow. Two of the most important financial markets in advanced economies are the bond market and the stock market.

> **financial markets** financial institutions through which savers can directly provide funds to borrowers

The Bond Market When BP, the oil company, wants to borrow to finance a major new oil exploration project, it can borrow directly from the public. It does this by selling bonds. A **bond** is a certificate of indebtedness that specifies the obligations of the borrower to the holder of the bond. Put simply, a bond is an IOU. It identifies the time at which the loan will be repaid, called the *date of maturity*, and the rate of interest that will be paid periodically (called the *coupon*) until the loan matures. The buyer of a bond gives his or her money to BP in exchange for this promise of interest and eventual repayment of the amount borrowed (called the *principal*). The buyer can hold the bond until maturity or can sell the bond at an earlier date to someone else.

> **bond** a certificate of indebtedness

There are literally millions of bonds traded in advanced economies. When large corporations or the national government, or even local governments need to borrow in order to finance the purchase of a new factory, a new jet fighter or a new school, they often do so by issuing bonds. If you look at the *Financial Times* or the business section of any national newspaper, you will find a listing of the prices and interest rates on some of the most important bond issues. Although these bonds differ in many ways, two characteristics of bonds are most important.

The first characteristic is a bond's *term* – the length of time until the bond matures. Some bonds have short terms, such as a few months, while others have terms as long as 30 years. (The British government has even issued a bond that never matures, called a *perpetuity*. This bond pays interest forever, but the principal is never repaid.) The interest rate on a bond depends, in part, on its term. Long-term bonds are riskier than short-term bonds because holders of long-term bonds have to wait longer for repayment of the principal. If a holder of a long-term bond needs his money earlier than the distant date of maturity, he has no choice but to sell the bond to someone else, perhaps at a reduced price. To compensate for this risk, long-term bonds usually (but not always) pay higher interest rates than short-term bonds.

The second important characteristic of a bond is its *credit risk* – the probability that the borrower will fail to pay some of the interest or principal. Such a failure to pay is called a *default*. Borrowers can (and sometimes do) default on their loans by declaring bankruptcy. When bond buyers perceive that the probability of default is high, they demand a higher interest rate to compensate them for this risk. When national governments want to borrow money to finance public spending, they issue bonds. You will hear this referred to as *sovereign debt*. Some government bonds are considered a safe credit risk, such as those from Germany, for example, and tend to pay low interest rates. UK government bonds have come to be referred to as *gilt-edged* bonds, or more simply as *gilts*, reflecting that, in terms of credit risk, they are 'as good as gold' (early bond certificates had a gold edge – hence the term 'gilt edged'). In contrast, financially shaky corporations raise money by issuing *junk bonds*, which pay very high interest rates; in recent years some countries' debt has been graded as 'junk'. Buyers of bonds can judge credit risk by checking with various private agencies, such as Standard & Poor's, which rate the credit risk of different bonds. Sometimes, these bonds are referred to euphemistically but less graphically as *below investment grade bonds*.

One important point to note is the relationship between a bond's price and its yield. Assume that a corporation issues a €1,000 bond over a ten-year period with a coupon of 3.5 per cent. For the duration of the ten years, the corporation will pay the bond holder €35 a year in interest and when the bond matures the corporation will pay back the bond holder the €1,000 principal. At any time during the ten-year period the bond holder can sell the bond on the bond market. The price she gets will depend on the supply and demand of those bonds on the market. The yield of the bond (in simple terms) is given by the coupon/price × 100. Price is quoted as a percentage of the principal. Assume the bond holder needs to get access to cash (liquidity) quickly – they decide to sell their bond. The price of the bond on the market is €995.

The yield on this bond, therefore, is 35/995 × 100 = 3.52 per cent. If the seller was able to sell the bond for €1,050, the yield would be 35/1050 × 100 = 3.33 per cent. This is an important point about the price and yield of a bond – there is an inverse relationship between price and yield. As bond prices rise, the yield falls and vice versa. Why might bond prices rise and fall on the markets? The demand and supply of bonds (the number of people wanting to buy bonds and the number of people wanting to sell bonds) is made up of existing bonds and the availability of new bonds. Bond prices (and, therefore, yields) are affected by existing bonds in the market, the issue of new bonds, the likelihood of the bond issuer defaulting and the interest rates on other securities. The issue of a new bond is also affected by these factors. If current interest rates are high, new issues have to have a coupon which will compete and vice versa.

The Stock Market Another way for BP to raise funds for its oil exploration project is to sell stock in the company. **Stock** represents ownership in a firm and is, therefore, a claim to the future profits that the firm makes. For example, if BP sells a total of 1,000,000 shares of stock, then each share represents ownership of 1/1,000,000 of the business. A stock is also commonly referred to as a *share* or as an *equity*. In this book, we'll use the terms 'share' and 'stock' (and 'stockholder' and 'shareholder') more or less interchangeably.

> **stock (or share or equity)** a claim to partial ownership in a firm

The sale of stock to raise money is called *equity finance,* whereas the sale of bonds is called *debt finance*. Although corporations use both equity and debt finance to raise money for new investments, stocks and bonds are very different. The owner of BP shares is a part owner of BP; the owner of a BP bond is a creditor of the corporation. If BP is very profitable, the shareholders enjoy the benefits of these profits, whereas the bondholders get only the interest on their bonds. And if BP runs into financial difficulty, the bondholders are paid what they are due before shareholders receive anything at all. Compared to bonds, stocks offer the holder both higher risk and potentially higher return.

As we noted just now, stocks are also called shares or equities. In the UK, bonds are also, confusingly, referred to as 'stock'. This term for government bonds has been in use in England since the late 17th century and is well established. In order to avoid confusion, however, the term is often qualified as *government stock* or *gilt-edged stock*. In general, though, despite the confusing use of language, the term *stock* refers to ownership of a firm.

After a corporation issues stock by selling shares to the public, these shares trade among stockholders on organized stock exchanges. In these transactions, the corporation itself receives no money when its stock changes hands. Most of the world's countries have their own stock exchanges on which the shares of national companies trade.

The prices at which shares trade on stock exchanges are determined by the supply and demand for the stock in these companies. Because stock represents ownership in a corporation, the demand for a stock (and thus its price) reflects people's perception of the corporation's future profitability. When people become optimistic about a company's future, they raise their demand for its stock and thereby bid up the price of a share of stock. Conversely, when people come to expect a company to have little profit or even losses, the price of a share falls.

Various stock indices are available to monitor the overall level of stock prices for any particular stock market. A *stock index* is computed as an average of a group of share prices. The Dow Jones Industrial Average has been computed regularly for the New York Stock Exchange since 1896. It is now based on the prices of the shares of 30 major US companies. The Financial Times Stock Exchange (FTSE) 100 Index, is based on the top 100 companies (according to the total value of their shares) listed on the London Stock Exchange (LSE), while the FTSE All-Share Index is based on all companies listed on the LSE. Indices of prices on the Frankfurt stock market, based on 30 and 100 companies respectively, are the DAX 30 and DAX 100. The NIKKEI 225 (or just plain NIKKEI Index) is based on the largest 225 companies, in terms of market value of shares, traded on the Tokyo Stock Exchange.

Because share prices reflect expected profitability, stock indices are watched closely as possible indicators of future economic conditions.

Financial Intermediaries

Financial intermediaries are financial institutions through which savers can indirectly provide funds to borrowers. The term *intermediary* reflects the role of these institutions in standing between savers and borrowers. Here we consider two of the most important financial intermediaries – banks and investment funds.

> **financial intermediaries** financial institutions through which savers can indirectly provide funds to borrowers

Banks If the owner of a small business wants to finance an expansion of his business, he probably takes a strategy quite different from BP. Unlike BP, a small businessman would find it difficult to raise funds in the bond and stock markets. Most buyers of stocks and bonds prefer to buy those issued by larger, more familiar companies. The small businessman, therefore, most likely finances his business expansion with a loan from a bank.

Banks are the financial intermediaries with which people are most familiar. A primary function of banks is to take in deposits from people who want to save and use these deposits to make loans to people who want to borrow. Banks pay depositors interest on their deposits and charge borrowers slightly higher interest on their loans. The difference between these rates of interest covers the banks' costs and returns some profit to the owners of the banks.

Besides being financial intermediaries, banks play a second important role in the economy: they facilitate purchases of goods and services by allowing people to write cheques against their deposits (although cheques are being phased out in many countries as digital payment systems become more common), or to use debit cards to transfer money electronically from their account to the account of the person or corporation they are buying something from. In other words, banks help create a special asset that people can use as a *medium of exchange*. A medium of exchange is an item that people can easily use to engage in transactions. A bank's role in providing a medium of exchange distinguishes it from many other financial institutions. Stocks and bonds, like bank deposits, are a possible *store of value* for the wealth that people have accumulated in past saving, but access to this wealth is not as easy, cheap and immediate as just writing a cheque or swiping a debit card. For now, we ignore this second role of banks, but we will return to it when we discuss the monetary system later in the book.

Investment Funds A financial intermediary of increasing importance is the investment fund. An **investment fund** is an institution that sells shares to the public and uses the proceeds to buy a selection, or *portfolio,* of various types of shares, bonds, or both shares and bonds. The shareholder of the investment fund accepts all the risk and return associated with the portfolio. If the value of the portfolio rises, the shareholder benefits; if the value of the portfolio falls, the shareholder suffers the loss.

> **investment fund** an institution that sells shares to the public and uses the proceeds to buy a portfolio of stocks and bonds

The primary advantage of investment funds is that they allow people with small amounts of money to diversify. Buyers of shares and bonds are well advised to heed the adage, 'Don't put all your eggs in one basket.' Because the value of any single stock or bond is tied to the fortunes of one company, holding a single kind of stock or bond is very risky. By contrast, people who hold a diverse portfolio of shares and bonds face less risk because they have only a small stake in each company. Investment funds make this diversification easy. With only a few hundred euros, a person can buy shares in an investment fund and, indirectly, become the part owner or creditor of hundreds of major companies. For this service, the company operating the investment fund charges shareholders a fee, usually between 0.5 and 2.0 per cent of assets each year. Closely related to investment funds are unit trusts, the difference being that when people put money into a unit trust, more 'units' or shares are issued, whereas the only way to buy into an investment fund is to buy existing shares in the fund. For this reason, unit trusts are sometimes referred to as 'open-ended'.

A second advantage claimed by investment fund companies is that investment funds give ordinary people access to the skills of professional money managers. The managers of most investment funds pay close attention to the developments and prospects of the companies in which they buy stock. These managers buy the stock of those companies that they view as having a profitable future and sell the stock of companies with less promising prospects. This professional management, it is argued, should increase the return that investors in investment funds earn on their savings.

Financial economists, however, are often sceptical of this second argument. With thousands of money managers paying close attention to each company's prospects, the price of a company's stock could be seen as being a good reflection of the company's true value. As a result, it is hard to 'beat the market' by buying good stocks and selling bad ones. In fact, investment funds called *index funds* or *tracker trusts* which buy all (or the large majority of) the stocks in a given stock index, perform somewhat better on average than investment funds that take advantage of active management by professional money managers. The explanation for the superior performance of tracker trusts is that they keep costs low by buying and selling very rarely and by not having to pay the salaries of the professional money managers.

> **SELF TEST** What is stock? What is a bond? How are they different? How are they similar?

Credit Default Swaps (CDS)

The financial crisis of 2007–2009 highlighted the role of the range of financial instruments traded in the financial system. These instruments play a role in the financial system but have become increasingly complex; indeed, there were some senior bankers who were accused of not fully understanding what they were trading! The first of these instruments are credit default swaps or CDS. A **credit default swap** is a means by which bondholders can insure themselves against the risk of default.

> **credit default swap (CDS)** a means by which a bondholder can insure against the risk of default

Whenever a bond is sold there is an associated risk attached to it. In the case of bonds backed by a pool of mortgage debt, the risk is that the mortgage payer defaults on the payment in some way. CDS are a means of insuring against the risk involved. To see how this works let us take an example.

Assume a bank has bought a bond in an asset-backed security (in reality of course it might be many bonds) worth €5 million. The bond has a principal, therefore, of €5 million. The coupon payment (the interest on the bond) is 10 per cent. The bond is backed by the stream of cash flows being paid by mortgage holders – the underlying asset to the bond. The bondholder knows that there is a risk that some mortgage holders might default and as a result the bond return might also be in default – i.e. it does not pay the coupon or possibly the principal. If mortgage holders all meet their obligations and pay the money back (the principal) the bank will have earned interest for as long as it held the bond. If the bond was a ten-year bond with a coupon of 10 per cent then the bondholder would have earned a 10 per cent return on the bond for ten years (€500,000 per year for ten years).

The bondholder can go to an insurance company (which could also be another bank or a hedge fund) and take out a policy on the risk. The bank seeking to insure the risk is referred to as the *protection buyer* and the insurance company or other financial institution, the *protection seller*. The policy will agree to restore the bondholder to their original position should the bond default. The bondholder pays the insurance company premiums over the life of the policy, let us assume this is €500,000 a year over ten years, and in return the insurance company would agree to pay the bondholder €5 million if the bond defaults in some way during the period of the agreement.

What the bondholder has done is to swap the risk in the bond with the insurance company. In the event of the bond defaulting then the protection seller pays out to the protection buyer. These CDS could also be traded and in many cases the protection buyer might take out a number of such hedges against its risk.

The price of a CDS is quoted in terms of basis points where a basis point is $\frac{1}{100}$th of 1 per cent. The price quoted reflects the cost of protecting debt for a period of time. In May 2010, for example, the price of a CDS for BP was quoted at 255 bps suggesting that the cost of protecting €10 million of BP debt for five years was €255,000 a year.

If the bond was subject to default this would trigger a payment called a *credit event*. If a credit event occurs then there are two ways in which the contract could be closed. One was through a physical settlement. In this case the protection buyer would deliver the bond to the seller who would give the buyer the value of the bond, called par. The CDS market expanded rapidly throughout the 'noughties' leading to multiple trading. The holder of the CDS might not actually own the bond in question and so this method of settlement clearly does not work. The growth in the market meant that the number of contracts far outweighed the number of bonds on which they were based. To settle the claims of contract holders through physical means would not be possible. As a consequence, protection sellers undertook to settle the contract claim through cash settlement where the positions were cleared by the transfer of cash.

The protection seller would also have to put up some form of collateral to cover its exposure to the possible default as part of the CDS agreement. The size of the exposure in the example above would be €5 million. This would be part of the contract between the insurance seller and the buyer. The amount of the collateral required would depend on the market value of the bond and the credit rating of the protection seller. The market value of the bond can change because the bondholder can sell their bond.

If a bond associated with a mortgage pool is deemed a higher risk then it may become more difficult to sell it and its price would fall. At a lower price the risk involved for the protection buyer is higher and they can exercise a call (known as a collateral call) on the protection seller to increase the collateral supplied. If, for example, the price of the bond in the example above fell to 40 cents in the euro, the insurance company would have to find 0.60 × €500,000 in additional collateral (€3 million). This process is known as collateral calls. Equally, if the rating of the protection seller is downgraded then the risk to the protection buyer also rises – the seller may be not be able to meet its obligations. Once again, the protection buyer can call the seller to ask for more collateral to be provided. The insurance company would then have to find more funds to top up the collateral it has to provide to reflect the lower value of the bond.

If the seller was unable to meet its obligations at least the buyer would have some protection in the form of the collateral supplied by the seller. If the bond runs its course and matures without any credit event then the collateral is returned to the seller (who also, remember, receives premiums from the buyer).

CDS represent sound business principles when the risk of default is very low, which was the case when they were first developed in the late 1990s and when the bonds being insured were corporate bonds with a low risk attached to them. The expansion of CDS presented a different challenge to the financial markets when the housing market collapse occurred from around 2007.

CASE STUDY   **Ireland and the Financial Crisis**

One of the first countries to be affected by the financial crisis of 2007/08 was Ireland. In the 1990s and early part of the 2000s, Ireland's economy grew at rates of between 4.4 per cent and 6.5 per cent throughout the years from 2000 to 2007, fuelled in part by boom in property prices (the construction industry accounted for around a quarter of Ireland's GDP in 2007), advantageous tax rates and the benefits it was gaining from being a member of the European Union. When the financial crisis struck, the Irish economy was hit hard, shrinking by 3 per cent in 2008 and 7 per cent in 2009. The Irish banking system was particularly badly hit and the Irish government had to ask the EU for a bailout to help support the banking system.

Support from the EU and the International Monetary Fund (IMF) has amounted to some €85 billion but securing this support has come at a price – the cuts in government spending and austerity measures that the government has put in place have increased unemployment to a peak of 15 per cent and seen many people suffer as property prices collapsed. As the austerity plans have taken effect the prospects for the Irish economy were starting to look a little brighter in the latter half of 2012 and into 2013. One example of this brighter future was the re-entry of the Irish government into the sovereign bond market. In July 2012, the Irish government managed to raise €500 million in an auction that was oversubscribed by 2.8 times and represented the first time the Irish government has ventured into the capital markets to borrow money since 2010. At the auction, the government borrowed through the issue of three-month treasury bills with a yield of 1.8 per cent.

In early 2013, Ireland managed to raise €2.5 billion through a bond sale, which was again oversubscribed by more than two-and-a-half-times, at a yield of around 3.35 per cent. Irish bond yields had been gradually falling since 2011 when a peak of 14 per cent was reached suggesting that investors have more confidence in the Irish government and the economy. The Irish government will see the support from the capital markets as encouraging because it was planning to raise €10 billion in bond issues in 2013 to help fund government spending and emerge from the funding support it has received from the EU and IMF. In the early part of 2013, the Irish government was on course to meet the projected targets for reducing its budget deficits and this has helped boost confidence in the markets along with the gradual improvement in the economy as a whole.

Austerity policies have affected a lot of people in Ireland but the economy showed signs of improvement in 2013. The cost of turning round the economy has been very high for many individuals and businesses, however.

Collateralized Debt Obligations (CDOs)

CDOs are pools of asset-backed securities which are dependent on the value of the asset that backs them up and the stream of income that flows from these assets. Essentially, CDOs work in the following way. In setting up a CDO, a manager encourages investors to buy bonds, the funds of which are used to buy pools of debt – mortgage debt. This debt is split and rated according to its risk into tranches; low-risk tranches attract low interest rates whilst the riskier tranches attract higher interest rates. Under '*normal*' circumstances (the relevance of the emphasis will become clear later) the payments by mortgage holders provide sufficient income each month to pay the interest to each of the tranche holders. There is a risk, of course, that some of the mortgage holders in the initial debt could default on payment but historical data enable investors to have some idea of what this risk will be. In the event of default, some of the riskier tranches may not get paid – that is the risk they take and why they get a higher interest rate.

The development of new approaches to risk management enabled these structures to be extended further into second and third 'waves' of securitized debt. Asset managers could buy particular tranches of debt (backed, remember, by mortgages ultimately) and mix them with other types of debt and sell them on to other investors. Investors in these higher risk tranches are assured by the ratings on the investment. Calculation of default correlations during the latter part of the 1990s and into the first years of the 2000s was relatively low but when times were not '*normal*' the correlations could start to become far more unstable. Problems for CDOs began when holders of sub-prime mortgages began to default on payments. The **sub-prime market** offered mortgage opportunities to those not traditionally seen as being part of the financial markets because of their high credit risk and was part of the way in which banks and other lenders sought to increase their lending. Individuals seen as being a relatively low credit risk for mortgage lending were known as the prime market; the term is said to have derived from analogy with the best cuts of meat from an animal. It followed that there was a sub-prime group for whom access to mortgages was altogether more difficult.

> **sub-prime market** individuals not traditionally seen as being part of the financial markets because of their high credit risk

Some of these people had credit histories that were very poor, some did not have jobs, but in an atmosphere of risk seeking and changed priorities this group provided lenders with a market opportunity because they were willing to pay high rates of interest on their mortgages. At first these defaults might have been 'pin pricks' in the structure but as the number increased the payments to the first tranches began to reduce. Those at the top of the ratings list may have still got paid but the riskier lower tranches began to see their payments dry up. In turn, the asset-backed securities sold in the second and subsequent 'waves' began to see their payments cease and as the sub-prime problem became worse it became clear that it was likely that these subsequent 'waves' would not be paid back and were thus worthless. Holders of this debt (including banks, governments and local governments around the world) found that they had to write-off large assets. The term 'toxic assets' became familiar to many who may never have thought they were affected by high finance. These were mortgage-backed securities and other debt (such as bonds) that are not able to be repaid in many cases because the value of the assets against which they are secured have fallen significantly.

Summing Up

An advanced economy contains a large variety of financial institutions. In addition to the bond market, the stock market, banks and investment funds, there are also pension funds, insurance companies and – notably in the UK and USA – even the local pawnbroker's shop: places where people who might be deemed bad credit risks can borrow money and leave some valuable item such as a watch or a piece of jewellery as security in case the loan is not repaid. Clearly, these institutions differ in many ways and the products they sell have become more complex in lots of cases. When analysing the macroeconomic role of the financial system, however, it is more important to keep in mind the similarity of these institutions than the differences. These financial institutions all serve the same goal – directing the resources of savers into the hands of borrowers.

FYI

Dark Pools

Despite having a rather sinister sounding name, dark pools are just an electronic network which puts buyers of shares in touch with sellers. However, the nature of dark pools has raised some concerns and is currently being looked at by the Securities and Exchange Commission (SEC) in the United States (which may account for why the volume of shares traded through these systems fell in 2012). Dark pools are not widespread in the UK and Europe at the time of writing, but are likely to become more significant in the future.

How do dark pools work? Under normal circumstances, trades in shares are carried out via a number of exchanges such as the London and New York stock exchanges. Traders on those exchanges can see who is doing the buying and who is doing the selling. Any transaction that goes through, therefore, can affect the market and traders will be able to amend their positions accordingly. Dark pools allow trades to be carried out anonymously so the trade can go through but no one knows – crucially at the time of the trade – who is doing the buying and selling. Dark pools tend to be used for trades where significant volumes of shares are transacted. The following is an outline of how it works.

Assume an institutional investor, such as a pension fund or insurance company, has $1 billion worth of shares in ExxonMobil that it wants to sell. It knows that if it attempts to trade this amount it is likely to affect the market. Typically, this sort of volume would have to be broken up and sold in chunks. If the price of ExxonMobil shares was currently $500 each, then as the sale progresses, the insurance company would end up with lower prices for the latter chunks of shares than the first lots. The average price it gains from the sale would, therefore, be less than $500 each.

The price would fall because the supply of ExxonMobil shares would be rising, traders would see the trades going through and adjust their positions accordingly. If the insurance company carries out the trade via a dark pool it places the shares into an electronic exchange. In the pool there are buyers and sellers all looking for trades, but anonymously. The use of algorithms to improve the efficiency of the trades in dark pools is common. The algorithm is programmed to search for buyers who want to purchase $1 billion of ExxonMobil shares, for example, and matches the two together. At this point in the trade no-one knows who the traders are. Once the trade is completed then it is announced.

The announcement may, or may not, have an effect on the market. The advantage for the pension fund or insurance company is that it completes the trade for the volume of shares it wants to deal and the use of dark pools prevents the market reacting to the sale at the time it is happening and thus affecting the price the seller gets.

There has been some criticism of dark pools mainly because of two key issues. It is feared that dark pools may take too much trade away from traditional exchanges. As they develop, more trading will be conducted in secret and in some cases, even though the trades are announced, the identity of the trader is not revealed. Dark pools may discriminate against individual investors who can be affected by the price changes that result from the activity which they could not foresee because of the very nature of the anonymous transactions.

Despite the criticism, proponents of dark pools point to the efficiency with which they operate and the fact that they help liquidity in the markets. The bank Goldman Sachs has been criticized for its use of dark pools but has defended the practice and suggested that enhanced transparency post-trade is an obvious way to offset concern about secrecy.

SAVING AND INVESTMENT IN THE NATIONAL INCOME ACCOUNTS

Events that occur within the financial system are central to understanding developments in the overall economy. As we have just seen, the institutions that make up this system – the bond market, the stock market, banks and investment funds – have the role of coordinating the economy's saving and investment. And as we saw in the previous chapter, saving and investment are important determinants of long-run growth in GDP and living standards. As a result, macroeconomists need to understand how financial markets work and how various events and policies affect them.

As a starting point for an analysis of financial markets, we discuss in this section the key macroeconomic variables that measure activity in these markets. Our emphasis here is not on behaviour but on accounting. *Accounting* refers to how various numbers are defined and added up. A personal accountant might help an individual add up his income and expenses. A national income accountant does the same thing for the economy as a whole. The national income accounts include, in particular, GDP and the many related statistics.

The rules of national income accounting include several important identities. Recall that an *identity* is an equation that must be true because of the way the variables in the equation are defined. Identities are useful to keep in mind, for they clarify how different variables are related to one another. Here we consider some accounting identities that shed light on the macroeconomic role of financial markets.

Some Important Identities

Recall that GDP is both total income in an economy and the total expenditure on the economy's output of goods and services. GDP (denoted as Y) is divided into four components of expenditure: consumption (C), investment (I), government purchases (G) and net exports (NX). We write:

$$Y = C + I + G + NX$$

This equation is an identity because every euro of expenditure that shows up on the left-hand side also shows up in one of the four components on the right-hand side. Because of the way each of the variables is defined and measured, this equation must always hold. Sometimes we make this clear by using an identity sign, with three bars, instead of the usual equals sign with two bars:

$$Y \equiv C + I + G + NX$$

In general, though, we can use the usual equality sign.

In this chapter, we simplify our analysis by assuming that the economy we are examining is closed. A *closed economy* is one that does not interact with other economies. In particular, a closed economy does not engage in international trade in goods and services, nor does it engage in international borrowing and lending. Of course, actual economies are *open economies* – that is, they interact with other economies around the world. Nevertheless, assuming a closed economy is a useful simplification with which we can learn some lessons that apply to all economies. Moreover, this assumption applies perfectly to the world economy (since interplanetary trade is not yet common).

Because a closed economy does not engage in international trade, imports and exports are exactly zero. Therefore, net exports (NX) are also zero. In this case, we can write:

$$Y = C + I + G$$

This equation states that GDP is the sum of consumption, investment and government purchases. Each unit of output sold in a closed economy is consumed, invested or bought by the government.

To see what this identity can tell us about financial markets, subtract C and G from both sides of this equation. We obtain:

$$Y - C - G = (C - C) + I + (G - G)$$
$$Y - C - G = I$$

The left-hand side of this equation ($Y - C - G$) is the total income in the economy that remains after paying for consumption and government purchases: this amount is called **national saving**, or just saving, and is denoted S. Recall from the more complex circular flow of income diagram in Chapter 4, that there are withdrawals and injections from the circular flow. Saving is one of the withdrawals from the circular flow but reappears in the economy in the form of investment when savings are channelled by financial institutions.

national saving (saving) the total income in the economy that remains after paying for consumption and government purchases

Substituting S for $Y - C - G$, we can write the last equation as:

$$S = I$$

This equation states that saving equals investment.

To understand the meaning of national saving, it is helpful to manipulate the definition a bit more. Let T denote the amount that the government collects from households in taxes (a withdrawal from the circular flow) minus the amount it pays back to households in the form of transfer payments (such as social security payments). We can then write national saving in either of two ways:

$$S = Y - C - G$$

or

$$S = (Y - T - C) + (T - G)$$

These equations are the same, because the two Ts in the second equation cancel each other, but each reveals a different way of thinking about national saving. In particular, the second equation separates national saving into two pieces: private saving $(Y - T - C)$ and public saving $(T - G)$.

Consider each of these two pieces. **Private saving** is the amount of income that households have left after paying their taxes and paying for their consumption. In particular, because households receive income of Y, pay taxes of T and spend C on consumption, private saving is $Y - T - C$. **Public saving** is the amount of tax revenue that the government has left after paying for its spending. The government receives T in tax revenue and spends G on goods and services. If T exceeds G, the government runs a budget surplus because it receives more money than it spends. This surplus of $T - G$ represents public saving. If the government spends more than it receives in tax revenue, then G is larger than T. In this case, the government runs a budget deficit, and public saving $T - G$ is a negative number. In this case the government has to borrow money to fund spending by issuing sovereign debt in the form of bonds.

> **private saving** the income that households have left after paying for taxes and consumption
> **public saving** the tax revenue that the government has left after paying for its spending

Now consider how these accounting identities are related to financial markets. The equation $S = I$ reveals an important fact: for the economy as a whole, saving must be equal to investment. Yet this fact raises some important questions: what mechanisms lie behind this identity? What coordinates those people who are deciding how much to save and those people who are deciding how much to invest? The answer is the financial system. The bond market, the stock market, banks, investment funds, and other financial markets and intermediaries, stand between the two sides of the $S = I$ equation. They take in the nation's saving and direct it to the nation's investment.

The Meaning of Saving and Investment

The terms *saving* and *investment* can sometimes be confusing. Most people use these terms casually and sometimes interchangeably. In contrast, the macroeconomists who put together the national income accounts use these terms carefully and distinctly.

Consider an example. Suppose that Connah earns more than he spends and deposits his unspent income in a bank or uses it to buy a bond or some stock from a corporation. Because Connah's income exceeds his consumption, he adds to the nation's saving. Connah might think of himself as 'investing' his money, but a macroeconomist would call Connah's act saving rather than investment.

In the language of macroeconomics, investment refers to the purchase of new capital, such as equipment or buildings. When Gerry borrows from the bank to build himself a new house, he adds to the nation's investment. Similarly, when the O'Connell Corporation issues some new shares and uses the proceeds to build a new brass doorknocker factory, it also adds to the nation's investment.

Although the accounting identity $S = I$ shows that saving and investment are equal for the economy as a whole, this does not have to be true for every individual household or firm. Connah's saving can be greater than his investment, and he can deposit the excess in a bank. Gerry's saving can be less than his investment, and he can borrow the shortfall from a bank. Banks and other financial institutions make these individual differences between saving and investment possible by allowing one person's saving to finance another person's investment.

SELF TEST Define private saving, public saving, national saving and investment. How are they related?

THE MARKET FOR LOANABLE FUNDS

Having discussed some of the important financial institutions in the economy and the macroeconomic role of these institutions, we are ready to build a model of financial markets. Our purpose in building this model is to explain how financial markets coordinate the economy's saving and investment. The model also gives us a tool with which we can analyse various government policies that influence saving and investment.

To keep things simple, we assume that the economy has only one financial market, called the **market for loanable funds**. All savers go to this market to deposit their saving, and all borrowers go to this market to get their loans. Thus, the term *loanable funds* refers to all income that people have chosen to save and lend out, rather than use for their own consumption. In the market for loanable funds, there is one interest rate, which is both the return to saving and the cost of borrowing.

> **market for loanable funds** the market in which those who want to save supply funds and those who want to borrow to invest demand funds

The assumption of a single financial market, of course, is not literally true. As we have seen, the economy has many types of financial institutions. But, as we discussed in Chapter 2, the art in building an economic model is simplifying the world in order to explain it. For our purposes here, we can ignore the diversity of financial institutions and assume that the economy has a single financial market.

Supply and Demand for Loanable Funds

The economy's market for loanable funds, like other markets in the economy, is governed by supply and demand. To understand how the market for loanable funds operates, therefore, we first look at the sources of supply and demand in that market.

The supply of loanable funds comes from those people who have some extra income they want to save and lend out. This lending can occur directly, such as when a household buys a bond from a firm, or it can occur indirectly, such as when a household makes a deposit in a bank, which in turn uses the funds to make loans. In both cases, saving is the source of the supply of loanable funds.

The demand for loanable funds comes from households and firms who wish to borrow to make investments. This demand includes families taking out mortgages to buy homes. It also includes firms borrowing to buy new equipment or build factories. In both cases, investment is the source of the demand for loanable funds.

The interest rate is the price of a loan. It represents the amount that borrowers pay for loans and the amount that lenders receive on their saving. Because a high interest rate makes borrowing more expensive, the quantity of loanable funds demanded falls as the interest rate rises. Similarly, because a high interest rate makes saving more attractive, the quantity of loanable funds supplied rises as the interest rate rises. In other words, the demand curve for loanable funds slopes downwards, and the supply curve for loanable funds slopes upwards.

Figure 8.1 shows the interest rate that balances the supply and demand for loanable funds. In the equilibrium shown, the interest rate is 5 per cent, and the quantity of loanable funds demanded and the quantity of loanable funds supplied both equal €500 billion.

The adjustment of the interest rate to the equilibrium level occurs for the usual reasons. If the interest rate was lower than the equilibrium level, the quantity of loanable funds supplied would be less than the quantity of loanable funds demanded. The resulting shortage of loanable funds would encourage lenders to raise the interest rate they charge. A higher interest rate would encourage saving (thereby increasing the quantity of loanable funds supplied) and discourage borrowing for investment (thereby decreasing the quantity of loanable funds demanded). Conversely, if the interest rate was higher than the equilibrium level, the quantity of loanable funds supplied would exceed the quantity of loanable funds demanded. As lenders competed for the scarce borrowers, interest rates would be driven down. In this way, the interest rate approaches the equilibrium level at which the supply and demand for loanable funds exactly balance.

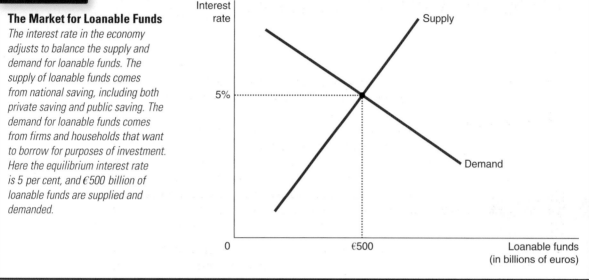

FIGURE 8.1

The Market for Loanable Funds
The interest rate in the economy adjusts to balance the supply and demand for loanable funds. The supply of loanable funds comes from national saving, including both private saving and public saving. The demand for loanable funds comes from firms and households that want to borrow for purposes of investment. Here the equilibrium interest rate is 5 per cent, and €500 billion of loanable funds are supplied and demanded.

Recall that economists distinguish between the real interest rate and the nominal interest rate. The nominal interest rate is the interest rate as usually reported – the monetary return to saving and cost of borrowing. The real interest rate is the nominal interest rate corrected for inflation; it equals the nominal interest rate minus the inflation rate. Because inflation erodes the value of money over time, the real interest rate more accurately reflects the real return to saving and cost of borrowing. Therefore, the supply and demand for loanable funds depends on the real (rather than nominal) interest rate, and the equilibrium in Figure 8.1 should be interpreted as determining the real interest rate in the economy. For the rest of this chapter, when you see the term *interest rate*, you should remember that we are talking about the real interest rate.

This model of the supply and demand for loanable funds shows that financial markets work much like other markets in the economy. Once we realize that saving represents the supply of loanable funds and investment represents the demand, we can see how the invisible hand coordinates saving and invest-ment. When the interest rate adjusts to balance supply and demand in the market for loanable funds, it coordinates the behaviour of people who want to save (the suppliers of loanable funds) and the behaviour of people who want to invest (the demanders of loanable funds).

We can now use this analysis of the market for loanable funds to examine various government policies that affect the economy's saving and investment. Because this model is just supply and demand in a particular market, we analyse any policy using the three steps discussed in Chapter 3. First, we decide whether the policy shifts the supply curve or the demand curve. Second, we determine the direction of the shift. Third, we use the supply-and-demand diagram to see how the equilibrium changes.

Policy 1: Saving Incentives

We know from Chapter 6 that saving is an important long-run determinant of a nation's productivity. Hence if a country can raise its saving rate, the growth rate of GDP should increase and, over time, the citizens of that country should enjoy a higher standard of living.

Many economists have used the principle that people respond to incentives to suggest that the savings rates in some countries are depressed because of tax laws that discourage saving. Governments collect revenue by taxing income, including interest and dividend income. To see the effects of this policy, consider a 25-year-old who saves €1,000 and buys a 30-year bond that pays an interest rate of 9 per cent. In the absence of taxes, the €1,000 grows to €13,268 when the individual reaches age 55. Yet if that interest is taxed at a rate of, say, 33 per cent, then the after-tax interest rate is only 6 per cent. In this case, the €1,000 grows to only €5,743 after 30 years. The tax on interest income substantially reduces the future pay-off from current saving and, as a result, reduces the incentive for people to save.

In response to this problem, many economists and some politicians have sometimes advocated replacing the current income tax with a consumption tax. Under a consumption tax, income that is saved would not be taxed until the saving is later spent; in essence, a consumption tax is like the value-added tax (VAT) that European countries impose on many goods and services. VAT is an indirect tax, however, levied on a good or service at the time it is purchased by a final consumer, whereas a consumption tax could also be a direct tax levied on an individual by calculating how much consumer expenditure they carried out over the year and taxing them on that, perhaps at higher and higher rates as the level of consumer expenditure rises.

A more modest proposal is to expand eligibility for special savings accounts that allow people to shelter some of their saving from taxation. Let's consider the effect of such a saving incentive on the market for loanable funds, as illustrated in Figure 8.2.

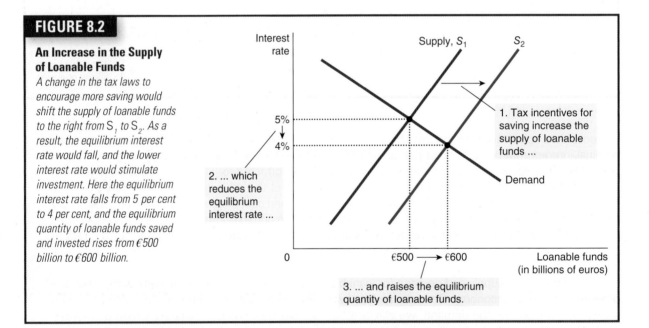

FIGURE 8.2

An Increase in the Supply of Loanable Funds

A change in the tax laws to encourage more saving would shift the supply of loanable funds to the right from S_1 to S_2. As a result, the equilibrium interest rate would fall, and the lower interest rate would stimulate investment. Here the equilibrium interest rate falls from 5 per cent to 4 per cent, and the equilibrium quantity of loanable funds saved and invested rises from €500 billion to €600 billion.

First, which curve would this policy affect? Because the tax change would alter the incentive for households to save *at any given interest rate*, it would affect the quantity of loanable funds supplied at each interest rate. Thus, the supply of loanable funds would shift. The demand for loanable funds would remain the same, because the tax change would not directly affect the amount that borrowers want to borrow at any given interest rate.

Second, which way would the supply curve shift? Because saving would be taxed less heavily, households would increase their saving by consuming a smaller fraction of their income. Households would use this additional saving to increase their deposits in banks or to buy more bonds. The supply of loanable funds would increase, and the supply curve would shift to the right from S_1 to S_2, as shown in Figure 8.2.

Finally, we can compare the old and new equilibria. In the figure, the increased supply of loanable funds reduces the interest rate from 5 per cent to 4 per cent. The lower interest rate raises the quantity of loanable funds demanded from €500 billion to €600 billion. That is, the shift in the supply curve moves the market equilibrium along the demand curve. With a lower cost of borrowing, households and firms are motivated to borrow more to finance greater investment. Thus, if a reform of the tax laws encouraged greater saving, the result would be lower interest rates and greater investment.

Although this analysis of the effects of increased saving is widely accepted among economists, there is less consensus about what kinds of tax changes should be enacted. Many economists endorse tax reform aimed at increasing saving in order to stimulate investment and growth. Yet others are sceptical that these tax changes would have much effect on national saving. These sceptics also doubt the equity of the proposed reforms. They argue that, in many cases, the benefits of the tax changes would accrue primarily to the wealthy, who are least in need of tax relief.

Policy 2: Investment Incentives

Suppose that the government passed a tax reform aimed at making investment more attractive. In essence, this is what the government does when it institutes an *investment tax credit*, which it does from time to time. An investment tax credit gives a tax advantage to any firm building a new factory or buying a new piece of equipment. Let's consider the effect of such a tax reform on the market for loanable funds, as illustrated in Figure 8.3.

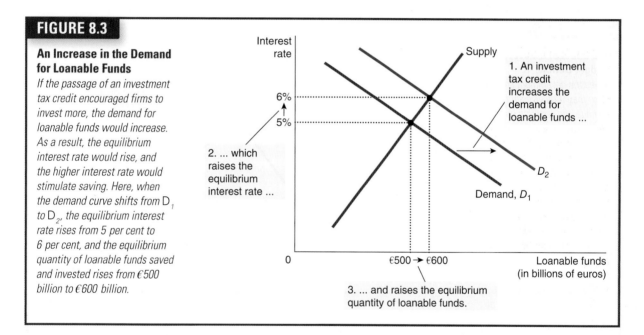

FIGURE 8.3

An Increase in the Demand for Loanable Funds

If the passage of an investment tax credit encouraged firms to invest more, the demand for loanable funds would increase. As a result, the equilibrium interest rate would rise, and the higher interest rate would stimulate saving. Here, when the demand curve shifts from D₁ to D₂, the equilibrium interest rate rises from 5 per cent to 6 per cent, and the equilibrium quantity of loanable funds saved and invested rises from €500 billion to €600 billion.

1. An investment tax credit increases the demand for loanable funds ...

2. ... which raises the equilibrium interest rate ...

3. ... and raises the equilibrium quantity of loanable funds.

First, would the reform affect supply or demand? Because the tax credit would reward firms that borrow and invest in new capital, it would alter investment at any given interest rate and, thereby, change the demand for loanable funds. By contrast, because the tax credit would not affect the amount that households save at any given interest rate, it would not affect the supply of loanable funds.

Second, which way would the demand curve shift? Because firms would have an incentive to increase investment at any interest rate, the quantity of loanable funds demanded would be higher at any given interest rate. Thus, the demand curve for loanable funds would move to the right, as shown by the shift from D_1 to D_2 in the figure.

Third, consider how the equilibrium would change. In Figure 8.3, the increased demand for loanable funds raises the interest rate from 5 per cent to 6 per cent, and the higher interest rate in turn increases the quantity of loanable funds supplied from €500 billion to €600 billion, as households respond by increasing the amount they save. This change in household behaviour is represented here as a movement along the supply curve. Thus, if a reform of the tax system encouraged greater investment, the result would be higher interest rates and greater saving.

Policy 3: Government Budget Deficits and Surpluses

A perpetual topic of political debate is the status of the government budget. Recall that a *budget deficit* is an excess of government spending over tax revenue. Governments finance budget deficits by borrowing in the bond market, and the accumulation of past government borrowing is called the *government debt*. A *budget surplus,* an excess of tax revenue over government spending, can be used to repay some of the government debt. If government spending exactly equals tax revenue, the government is said to have a *balanced budget.*

Imagine that the government starts with a balanced budget and then, because of a tax cut or a spending increase, starts running a budget deficit. We can analyse the effects of the budget deficit by following our three steps in the market for loanable funds, as illustrated in Figure 8.4.

First, which curve shifts when the government starts running a budget deficit? Recall that national saving – the source of the supply of loanable funds – is composed of private saving and public saving. A change in the government budget balance represents a change in public saving and, thereby, in the supply of loanable funds. Because the budget deficit does not influence the amount that households and firms want to borrow to finance investment at any given interest rate, it does not alter the demand for loanable funds.

FIGURE 8.4

The Effect of a Government Budget Deficit

When the government spends more than it receives in tax revenue, the resulting budget deficit lowers national saving. The supply of loanable funds decreases, and the equilibrium interest rate rises. Thus, when the government borrows to finance its budget deficit, it crowds out households and firms who otherwise would borrow to finance investment. Here, when the supply shifts from S₁ to S₂, the equilibrium interest rate rises from 5 per cent to 6 per cent, and the equilibrium quantity of loanable funds saved and invested falls from €500 billion to €300 billion.

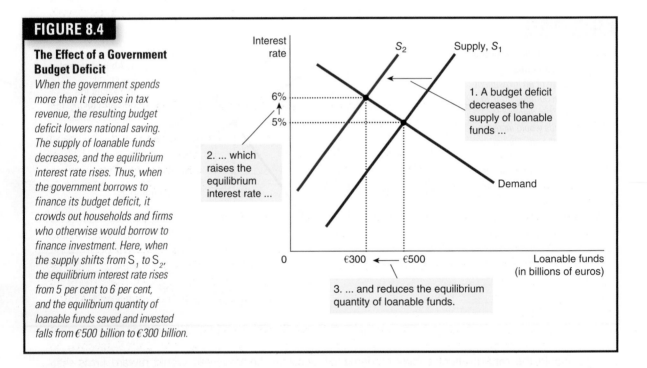

1. A budget deficit decreases the supply of loanable funds ...

2. ... which raises the equilibrium interest rate ...

3. ... and reduces the equilibrium quantity of loanable funds.

Second, which way does the supply curve shift? When the government runs a budget deficit, public saving is negative, and this reduces national saving. In other words, when the government borrows to finance its budget deficit, it reduces the supply of loanable funds available to finance investment by households and firms. Thus, a budget deficit shifts the supply curve for loanable funds to the left from S_1 to S_2, as shown in Figure 8.4.

Third, we can compare the old and new equilibria. In the figure, when the budget deficit reduces the supply of loanable funds, the interest rate rises from 5 per cent to 6 per cent. This higher interest rate then alters the behaviour of the households and firms that participate in the loan market. In particular, many demanders of loanable funds are discouraged by the higher interest rate. Fewer families buy new homes, and fewer firms choose to build new factories. The fall in investment because of government borrowing is called **crowding out** and is represented in the figure by the movement along the demand curve from a quantity of €500 billion in loanable funds to a quantity of €300 billion. That is, when the government borrows to finance its budget deficit, it crowds out private borrowers who are trying to finance investment.

crowding out a decrease in investment that results from government borrowing

Thus, the most basic lesson about budget deficits follows directly from their effects on the supply and demand for loanable funds: when the government reduces national saving by running a budget deficit, the interest rate rises and investment falls. Because investment is important for long-run economic growth, government budget deficits reduce the economy's growth rate.

Government budget surpluses work just the opposite way to budget deficits. When government collects more in tax revenue than it spends, its saves the difference by retiring some of the outstanding government debt. This budget surplus, or public saving, contributes to national saving. Thus, a budget surplus increases the supply of loanable funds, reduces the interest rate and stimulates investment. Higher investment, in turn, means greater capital accumulation and more rapid economic growth.

CONCLUSION

'Neither a borrower nor a lender be', Polonius advises his son in Shakespeare's *Hamlet*. If everyone followed this advice, this chapter would have been unnecessary.

Few economists would agree with Polonius. In our economy, people borrow and lend often, and usually for good reason. You may borrow one day to start your own business or to buy a home. And people may lend to you in the hope that the interest you pay will allow them to enjoy a more prosperous retirement. The financial system has the job of coordinating all this borrowing and lending activity.

In many ways, financial markets are like other markets in the economy. The price of loanable funds – the interest rate – is governed by the forces of supply and demand, just as other prices in the economy are. And we can analyse shifts in supply or demand in financial markets as we do in other markets. One of the *Ten Principles of Economics* is that markets are usually a good way to organize economic activity. This principle applies to financial markets as well. When financial markets bring the supply and demand for loanable funds into balance, they help allocate the economy's scarce resources to their most efficient use.

In one way, however, financial markets are special. Financial markets, unlike most other markets, serve the important role of linking the present and the future. Those who supply loanable funds – savers – do so because they want to convert some of their current income into future purchasing power. Those who demand loanable funds – borrowers – do so because they want to invest today in order to have additional capital in the future to produce goods and services. Thus, well-functioning financial markets are important not only for current generations but also for future generations who will inherit many of the resulting benefits.

IN THE NEWS

Borrowing in Developing Countries

The growth of developing countries has been the subject of a large amount of interest amongst economists and politicians. These countries may provide the markets for the developed countries in the future but the speed at which they develop may be influenced by a number of factors as outlined in this article.

The BNDES and Crowding Out

Brazil is one of the so-called BRIC countries – countries which are developing strongly and include Russia, China and India in addition to Brazil. In 1952, the Brazilian government set up a development bank called Banco Nacional de Desenvolvimento Econômico e Social (BNDES) as a vehicle to help with the development of the country. As Brazil has grown, the BNDES has become more powerful and a bigger player in the capital markets, so much so that some critics are now claiming that it is taking too big a role in borrowing for investment and is crowding out long-term lending of the sort required for key infrastructure projects by private-sector banks in Brazil.

To put the potential problem into context, the BNDES lent almost $47 billion (€35 billion) more than the World Bank in 2009–2010 to Brazilian corporations. It lent $76.3 billion (€57 billion) in 2012, 12 per cent up on the previous year and was the major investor in a number of share offerings, one of the most notable being a $70.1 billion (€52.5 billion) share offering by Brazil's oil company, Petrobras.

The sheer size of the involvement of the BNDES in investment in Brazil has raised concerns that private investment is being crowded out. When corporations borrow from the BNDES, they have to pay the Taxa de Juros de Longo Prazo (TJLP), a long-term interest rate set by the Brazilian central bank's monetary policy committee. This rate is lower than the rate at which corporations can borrow from the commercial banking sector by, in some cases, 2.5 per cent. In other cases, firms can borrow for capital investment at even lower rates which, when inflation is taken into account (which in early 2013 was running at over 6 per cent), means that corporations can borrow at negative interest rates. Corporations, therefore, are able to access loans for investment at subsidized rates. With that sort of incentive, the opportunity for commercial lenders to be able to compete is limited, given that the BNDES accounts for over 75 per cent of long-term loans (defined as in excess of three years). When the BNDES is so dominant in the market for funds, it is likely to be a barrier to Brazil's future ongoing development if a thriving private sector capital market such as those which operate in developed countries is not allowed to grow. For those corporations which are not able to access BNDES funding, the additional cost of securing private lending is much higher and as a result they are less competitive.

Questions

1 Why is the development of infrastructure projects so vital for a developing country like Brazil?
2 In what sense is the involvement of the BNDES crowding out investment from private lenders?
3 What do you think might be the advantages and disadvantages of the subsidized interest rates offered by the BNDES to Brazilian corporations and the economy as a whole?
4 In the context of corporations borrowing from the BNDES and from other private sector sources what is the relevance of the real interest rate?
5 Why might the continued involvement of the BNDES in lending in Brazil be a barrier to the country's growth prospects in the future?

An offshore oil rig in the Campos Basin in Rio de Janeiro, state owned by Petrobras, one of the companies raising capital for expansion from BNDES.

SUMMARY

- The financial system of an advanced economy is made up of many types of financial institutions, such as the bond market, the stock market, banks and investment funds. All of these institutions act to direct the resources of households, who want to save some of their income, into the hands of households and firms who want to borrow.

- National income accounting identities reveal some important relationships among macroeconomic variables. In particular, for a closed economy, national saving must equal investment. Financial institutions are the mechanism through which the economy matches one person's saving with another person's investment.

- The interest rate is determined by the supply and demand for loanable funds. The supply of loanable funds comes from households who want to save some of their income and lend it out. The demand for loanable funds comes from households and firms who want to borrow for investment. To analyse how any policy or event affects the interest rate, one must consider how it affects the supply and demand for loanable funds.

- National saving equals private saving plus public saving. A government budget deficit represents negative public saving and, therefore, reduces national saving and the supply of loanable funds available to finance investment. When a government budget deficit crowds out investment, it reduces the growth of productivity and GDP.

QUESTIONS FOR REVIEW

1 What is the role of the financial system?

2 Name and describe two markets that are part of the financial system in the economy of the country in which you are studying.

3 What is a financial intermediary? Name and describe two financial intermediaries.

4 Why is it important for people who own stocks and bonds to diversify their holdings? What type of financial institution makes diversification easier?

5 What is national saving? What is private saving? What is public saving? How are these three variables related?

6 How do credit default swaps help reduce the risk involved in buying bonds?

7 What is a collateralized debt obligation?

8 What is investment? How is it related to national saving?

9 Describe a change in the tax system that might increase private saving. If this policy were implemented, how would it affect the market for loanable funds?

10 What is a government budget deficit? How does it affect interest rates, investment and economic growth?

PROBLEMS AND APPLICATIONS

1 For each of the following pairs, which bond would you expect to pay a higher interest rate? Explain.

   a. A bond of the UK government or a bond of an east European government.

   b. A bond that repays the principal in year 2020 or a bond that repays the principal in year 2035.

   c. A bond from BP or a bond from a software company operating from a business park on the outskirts of a large city.

   d. A bond issued by the national government or a bond issued by a local authority.

2 What is the difference between gambling at cards or in lotteries or on the race track and gambling on the stock market? What social purpose do you think is served by the existence of the stock market?

3 Declines in share prices are sometimes viewed as harbingers of future declines in real GDP. Why do you suppose that might be true?

4 When the Greek government asked for support from the European Union to repay bonds that were coming up for maturity between 2008 and 2010, interest rates rose on bonds issued by a number of other EU countries like Portugal, Spain and Ireland also rose. Why do you suppose this happened? What can you predict happened to the price of bonds from these countries during this period?

5 Many workers hold large amounts of stock issued by the firms at which they work. Why do you suppose companies encourage this behaviour? Why might a person not want to hold stock in the company where he works?

6 Explain the difference between saving and investment as defined by a macroeconomist. Which of the following situations represent investment? Saving? Explain.

a. Your family takes out a mortgage and buys a new house.

b. You use your €500 wage payment to buy stock in BP.

c. Your flatmate earns €200 and deposits it in her account at a bank.

d. You borrow €5,000 from a bank to buy a car to use in your pizza delivery business.

7 Suppose GDP is €5 trillion, taxes are €1.5 trillion, private saving is €0.5 trillion and public saving is €0.2 trillion. Assuming this economy is closed, calculate consumption, government purchases, national saving and investment.

8 Suppose that BP is considering exploring a new oil field.

a. Assuming that BP needs to borrow money in the bond market to finance the purchase of new oil rigs and drilling machinery, why would an increase in interest rates affect BP's decision about whether to carry out the exploration?

b. If BP has enough of its own funds to finance the development of the new oil field without borrowing, would an increase in interest rates still affect BP's decision about whether to undertake the new project? Explain.

9 Suppose the government borrows €5 billion more next year than this year.

a. Use a supply-and-demand diagram to analyse this policy. Does the interest rate rise or fall?

b. What happens to investment? To private saving? To public saving? To national saving? Compare the size of the changes to the €5 billion of extra government borrowing.

c. How does the elasticity of supply of loanable funds affect the size of these changes?

d. How does the elasticity of demand for loanable funds affect the size of these changes?

e. Suppose households believe that greater government borrowing today implies higher taxes to pay off the government debt in the future. What does this belief do to private saving and the supply of loanable funds today? Does it increase or decrease the effects you discussed in parts (a) and (b)?

10 This chapter explains that investment can be increased both by reducing taxes on private saving and by reducing the government budget deficit.

a. Why is it difficult to implement both of these policies at the same time?

b. What would you need to know about private saving in order to judge which of these two policies would be a more effective way to raise investment?

9 THE BASIC TOOLS OF FINANCE

You will almost certainly have had to deal with the economy's financial system already in your life and this will only increase as you leave education and move into work. You will deposit your savings in a bank account, or you might take out a loan to buy a car or a mortgage to buy a house. Once you take a job, you will have to decide whether to invest your retirement account in company shares, bonds or other financial instruments (or you may buy a personal pension and let the pension company do this for you). You may try to put together your own share portfolio, and then you will have to decide between betting on established companies or newer ones. You will have to take out assurance and insurance policies to cover various risks such as death, fire and theft to property, vehicle insurance and so on. And whenever you watch the evening news, you will hear reports about whether the stock market is up or down, together with the attempts to explain why the market behaves as it does.

If you reflect for a moment on the many financial decisions you will make through your life, you will see two related elements in almost all of them – time and risk. As we saw in the preceding chapter, the financial system coordinates the economy's saving and investment. Thus, it concerns decisions we make today that will affect our lives in the future. But the future is unknown. When a person decides to allocate some saving, or a firm decides to undertake an investment, the decision is based on a guess (albeit an often informed guess) about the likely future result – but the actual result could end up being very different.

This chapter introduces some tools that help us understand the decisions that people make as they participate in financial markets. The field of **finance** – a sub-discipline of economics – develops these tools in great detail, and you may choose to take courses that focus on this topic. But because the financial system is so important to the functioning of the economy, many of the basic insights of finance are central to understanding how the economy works. The tools of finance may also help you think through some of the decisions that you will make in your own life.

> **finance** the field of economics that studies how people make decisions regarding the allocation of resources over time and the handling of risk

This chapter takes up three topics. First, we discuss how to compare sums of money at different points in time. Second, we discuss how to manage risk. Third, we build on our analysis of time and risk to examine what determines the value of an asset, such as a share of stock.

PRESENT VALUE: MEASURING THE TIME VALUE OF MONEY

Imagine that someone offered to give you €100 today or €100 in ten years. Which would you choose? The answer to this question should be easy. Getting €100 today is better, because you can always deposit the money in a bank, still have it in ten years and earn interest on the €100 along the way. The lesson: money today is more valuable than the same amount of money in the future.

Now consider a harder question: imagine that someone offered you €100 today or €200 in ten years. Which would you choose? To answer this question, you need some way to compare sums of money from different points in time. Economists do this with a concept called *present value*. The **present value** of any future sum of money is the amount today that would be needed, at current interest rates, to produce that future sum.

> **present value** the amount of money today that would be needed to produce, using prevailing interest rates, a given future amount of money

To learn how to use the concept of present value, let's work through a couple of simple examples.

Question: If you put €100 in a bank account today, how much will it be worth in *N* years? That is, what will be the **future value** of this €100?

> **future value** the amount of money in the future that an amount of money today will yield, given prevailing interest rates

Answer: Let's use *r* to denote the interest rate expressed in decimal form (so an interest rate of 5 per cent means $r = 0.05$). Suppose that interest is paid annually and that the interest paid remains in the bank account to earn more interest – a process called **compounding**. Then the €100 will become:

$(1 + r) \times €100$	after one year
$(1 + r) \times (1 + r)€100$	after two years
$(1 + r) \times (1 + r)(1 + r)€100$	after three years
$(1 + r)^N \times €100$	after *N* years

For example, if we are investing at an interest rate of 5 per cent for ten years, then the future value of the €100 will be $(1.05)^{10} \times €100$, which is €163 (rounded up to the nearest whole euro. Note: we will follow this rounding up for the remainder of the chapter).

> **compounding** the accumulation of a sum of money in, say, a bank account, where the interest earned remains in the account to earn additional interest in the future

Question: Now suppose you are going to be paid €200 in *N* years. What is the *present value* of this future payment? That is, how much would you have to deposit in a bank right now to yield €200 in *N* years?

Answer: To answer this question, just turn the previous answer on its head. In the first question, we computed a future value from a present value by *multiplying* by the factor $(1 + r)^N$. To compute a present value from a future value, we *divide* by the factor $(1 + r)^N$. Thus, the present value of €200 in *N* years is $€200/(1 + r)^N$. If that amount is deposited in a bank today, after *N* years it would become $(1 + r)^N \times [€200/(1 + r)^N]$, which is €200. For instance, if the interest rate is 5 per cent, the present value of €200 in ten years is $€200/(1.05)^{10}$, which is €123.

This illustrates the general formula: if *r* is the interest rate, then an amount *X* to be received in *N* years has present value of $X/(1 + r)^N$.

Let's now return to our earlier question: should you choose €100 today or €200 in ten years? We can infer from our calculation of present value that if the interest rate is 5 per cent, you should prefer the €200 in ten years. The future €200 has a present value of €123, which is greater than €100. You are better off waiting for the future sum.

Notice that the answer to our question depends on the interest rate. If the interest rate were 8 per cent, then the €200 in ten years would have a present value of $€200/(1.08)^{10}$, which is only €93. In this case, you should take the €100 today. Why should the interest rate matter for your choice? The answer is that the higher the interest rate, the more you can earn by depositing your money at the bank, so the more attractive getting €100 today becomes.

Applying the Concept of Present Value

The concept of present value is useful in many applications, including the decisions that companies face when evaluating investment projects. For instance, imagine that Citroën is thinking about building a new car factory. Suppose that the factory will cost €100 million today and will yield the company €200 million in ten years. Should Citroën undertake the project? You can see that this decision is exactly like the one we have been studying. To make its decision, the company will compare the present value of the €200 million return to the €100 million cost.

The company's decision, therefore, will depend on the interest rate. If the interest rate is 5 per cent, then the present value of the €200 million return from the factory is €123 million, and the company will choose to pay the €100 million cost. By contrast, if the interest rate is 8 per cent, then the present value of the return is only €93 million, and the company might decide to forgo the project. Thus, the concept of present value helps explain why investment – and thus the quantity of loanable funds demanded – declines when the interest rate rises.

Here is another application of present value: suppose you win the Euro Millions Lottery and you are given a choice between €20,000 a year for 50 years (totalling €1,000,000) or an immediate payment of €400,000. Which would you choose? To make the right choice, you need to calculate the present value of the stream of payments. After performing 50 calculations similar to those above (one calculation for each payment) and adding up the results, you would learn that the present value of this million-euro prize at a 7 per cent interest rate is only €256,000. You are better off picking the immediate payment of €400,000. The million euros may seem like more money, but the future cash flows, once discounted to the present, are worth far less.

> **SELF TEST** The interest rate is 7 per cent. What is the present value of €150 to be received in ten years?

MANAGING RISK

Life is full of gambles. When you go skiing, you risk breaking your leg in a fall. When you cycle to work or university, you risk being knocked off your bike by a car. When you put some of your savings in the stock market, you risk a fall in prices. **Risk** is the probability of something happening which results in a loss or some degree of hazard or damage. The rational response to risk is not necessarily to avoid it at any cost, but to take it into account in your decision-making. Let's consider how a person might do that.

> **risk** the probability of something happening which results in a loss or some degree of hazard or damage

Risk Aversion

Most people are **risk averse**. This means more than simply people dislike bad things happening to them. It means that they dislike bad things more than they like comparable good things. (This is also reflected in *loss aversion* – research suggests that losing something makes people twice as miserable as gaining something makes them happy!)

> **risk averse** exhibiting a dislike of uncertainty

For example, suppose a friend offers you the following opportunity. He will flip a coin. If it comes up heads, he will pay you €1,000. But if it comes up tails, you will have to pay him €1,000. Would you accept the bargain? You wouldn't if you were risk averse, even though the probability of winning is the same as the probability of losing (50 per cent). For a risk-averse person, the pain from losing the €1,000 would exceed the gain from winning €1,000.

Economists have developed models of risk aversion using the concept of *utility*, which is a person's subjective measure of well-being or satisfaction. Every level of wealth provides a certain amount of utility, as shown by the utility function in Figure 9.1. But the function exhibits the property of diminishing marginal utility: the more wealth a person has, the less utility he gets from an additional euro. Thus, in the figure, the utility function gets flatter as wealth increases. Because of diminishing marginal utility, the utility lost from losing the €1,000 bet is more than the utility gained from winning it. As a result, people are risk averse.

FIGURE 9.1

The Utility Function
This utility function shows how utility, a subjective measure of satisfaction, depends on wealth. As wealth rises, the utility function becomes flatter, reflecting the property of diminishing marginal utility. Because of diminishing marginal utility, a €1,000 loss decreases utility by more than a €1,000 gain increases it.

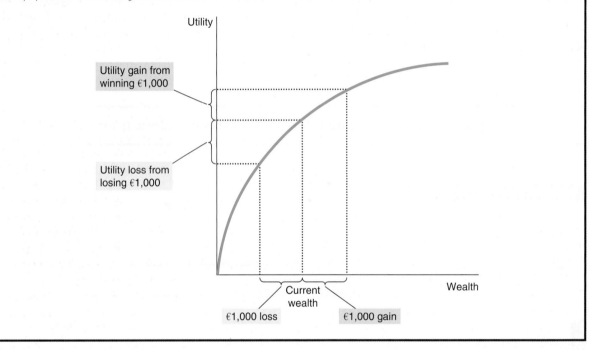

Risk aversion provides the starting point for explaining various things we observe in the economy. Let's consider three of them: insurance, diversification and the risk–return trade-off.

The Markets for Insurance

One way to deal with risk is to buy insurance. The general feature of insurance contracts is that a person facing a risk pays a fee to an insurance company, which in return agrees to accept all or part of the risk. There are many types of insurance. Car insurance covers the risk of your being in a car accident, fire insurance covers the risk that your house will burn down, and life assurance covers the risk that you will die and leave your family without your income. There is also insurance against the risk of living too long and running out of money: for a fee paid today, an insurance company will pay you an *annuity* – a regular income every year until you die (otherwise known as a pension).

In a sense, every insurance contract is a gamble. It is possible that you will not be in a car accident or that your house will not burn down. In most years, you will pay the insurance company the premium and get nothing in return except peace of mind. Indeed, the insurance company is counting on the fact that most people will not make claims on their policies; otherwise, it couldn't pay out the large claims to those few who are unlucky and still stay in business.

From the standpoint of the economy as a whole, the role of insurance is not to eliminate the risks inherent in life but to spread them around more efficiently. Consider fire insurance, for instance. Owning fire insurance does not reduce the risk of losing your home in a fire. But, if that unlucky event occurs, the insurance company compensates you. The risk, rather than being borne by you alone, is shared among the thousands of insurance company shareholders. Because people are risk averse, it is easier for 10,000 people to bear 1/10,000 of the risk than for one person to bear the entire risk themself.

The markets for insurance suffer from two types of problems that impede their ability to spread risk. One problem is *adverse selection*: a high-risk person is more likely to apply for insurance than a low-risk person. A second problem is *moral hazard*: after people buy insurance, they have less incentive to be careful about their risky behaviour. Insurance companies are aware of these problems, and the price of insurance reflects the actual risks that the insurance company will face after the insurance is bought. The high price of insurance is why some people, especially those who know themselves to be low risk, decide against buying insurance and, instead, endure some of life's uncertainty on their own.

FYI

Pricing Risk

We have seen how bond issues are a means by which firms can borrow money. The buyer has to have confidence that she will get her money back and also receive an appropriate reward for lending the money in the first place. There is a risk involved that the issuer will not be able to pay back the money and that risk is associated with a probability. If the issuer is very sound then the probability of default may be close to zero, but if the issuer is extremely weak then the probability is closer to 1. We saw in Chapter 8 how financial markets now deal in pools of debt (collections of different types of loans sold to an investor). As debt is pooled the outcomes become more varied. In any given pool of mortgage debt, for example, there will be some borrowers who will default and not be able to pay off their mortgages – possibly because of family bereavement or loss of their job. Other mortgage holders may look to pay off their mortgages early, some may move house and thus settle their mortgage, some will increase monthly payments or pay lump sums to help reduce the repayment period of their mortgage and so on.

Assessing probabilities with such a wide range of outcomes becomes difficult.

The risk involved with such debt is therefore difficult to assess with any certainty. However, investors want to price risk as part of their decision-making so that they can judge the value of an asset. If an asset is very risky then the returns expected will be higher and vice versa. In order to have an efficient market, that risk has to be priced and the information on which the risk is based has to be reliable, accurate – and understood.

Let's consider an example. In your class there may be a number of students that you associate with every day. Take any one individual and we can identify a number of 'risks' for that person. For example, there is a risk that the individual:

- fails his exams and has to leave the course
- will be involved in a car crash
- will travel on an aircraft more than five times a year
- may be mugged
- may get flu.

What are the chances of these events happening? The analysis of

such outcomes is what actuaries in the insurance industry have to do. An estimate of the probability of such events happening can be derived from analysis of data, specifically historical data. It is possible, therefore, to gather data on the average 19-year-old student coming from a particular area and with a particular background, and use this data to arrive at the probability of the event occurring. Historical data tell us, for example that young people aged between 18 and 24 are more likely to be mugged than the elderly, despite popular perception. If we are able to identify these probabilities then they can be priced. Securities can be issued based on the chances of these things happening – the more likely the event to occur, the higher the price and vice versa.

Whilst it may be possible to identify probabilities for an individual it may be more problematic when looking at relationships between individuals. For example, if person X fails her exams what is the probability that you will also fail your exams? If that individual gets flu what are the chances that you also get flu? In both cases the probability might depend on your relationship with that person. If you spend a lot of time with that person then it may be that you share similar distractions – going out every night instead of studying, skipping lectures to play pool and so on. If this were the case then the probability of you also failing your exams and getting flu might be high, but if you have no relationship at all then the chance of you sharing bad habits which lead you to also failing your exams are lower. However, given that you share some time with that person in a lecture hall or seminar room, for example, might mean that the probability of also getting swine flu is relatively high.

Looking at such relationships involves the concept of correlation – the extent to which there is any statistical relationship between two variables. If person X is involved in a car crash (and you were not in the car with him) what is the chance of you also being involved in a car crash? The chances are the correlation is very low; the probability of you both getting mugged is higher regardless of the relationship between you and so there will be a stronger correlation in this instance. The correlation is likely to become more and more unstable the more variables are introduced (number of students in this example). In the case of pools of debt, the same problems arise and the efficiency of the information on which investors are basing their decision becomes ever more complex; probabilities become very difficult to assess and therefore to price.

Actuaries have been studying these types of correlations for some years. Issuing life assurance involves a risk. Life assurance means that the event covered – the death of an individual – will occur at some point in the future (unlike insurance where the event might never happen). The job of the actuary is to provide information to the insurer on the chances of death occurring under different situations. Where information becomes available which indicates risk factors change, actuaries have to incorporate this into models to help insurers price the risk adequately (i.e. set the premiums for the policy). In the 1980s much work was done on studying a phenomenon known as stress cardiomyopathy, a condition for which, in the wake of some exceptional emotional trauma, the human brain releases chemicals into the bloodstream that leads to a weakening of the heart and an increased chance of death. The condition has been referred to as a 'broken heart' because it seemed to manifest itself in particular where one partner died soon after the death of the other. A study by Spreeuw, J. and Wang, X. (2008), *'Modelling the short-term dependence between two remaining lifetimes'*, showed that following the death of a female partner, a male was over six times more likely to die than normal and women more than twice as likely. The conclusion for the insurance industry is to take such information and build it into the pricing of offering joint-life policies.

Diversification of Idiosyncratic Risk

In 2009 thousands of investors lost their savings as a result of fraud committed by former stock broker Bernard Madoff in the United States. The fraud, known as a Ponzi scheme, involved Madoff taking money from investors on the promise of high returns through a supposedly sophisticated trading and hedging strategy with little apparent risk to the investor. Madoff did not invest the money he received but instead relied on attracting new investors, whose money was used to pay existing investors and hence maintain the fraud. Madoff eventually received a prison sentence of 150 years for crimes such as serious fraud, lying to federal securities regulators and money laundering. The saddest part of the story, however, involved the thousands of investors. The estimated value of the fraud was some $65 billion. Some of the victims were wealthy film stars but there were also many who had saved hard for their future and charities, all of whom lost their life savings. At least two suicides have been linked with the fraud.

If there is one piece of practical advice that finance offers to risk-averse people, it is this: 'Don't put all your eggs in one basket.' You may have heard this before, but finance has turned this traditional wisdom into a science. It goes by the name **diversification**.

diversification the reduction of risk achieved by replacing a single risk with a large number of smaller unrelated risks

The market for insurance is one example of diversification. Imagine a town with 10,000 homeowners, each facing the risk of a house fire. If someone starts an insurance company and each person in town becomes both a shareholder and a policyholder of the company, they all reduce their risk through diversification. Each person now faces 1/10,000 of the risk of 10,000 possible fires, rather than the entire risk of a single fire in his own home. Unless the entire town catches fire at the same time, the downside that each person faces is much smaller.

When people use their savings to buy financial assets, they can also reduce risk through diversification. A person who buys stock in a company is placing a bet on the future profitability of that company. That bet is often quite risky because companies' fortunes are hard to predict. Microsoft evolved from a start-up by some geeky teenagers into one of the world's most valuable companies in only a few years; Enron, a former US energy company which became insolvent with the loss of millions to investors and the jobs of workers because of fraud, went from one of the world's most respected companies to an almost worthless one in only a few months. Fortunately, a shareholder need not tie his own fortune to that of any single company. Risk can be reduced by placing a large number of small bets, rather than a small number of large ones.

Figure 9.2 shows how the risk of a portfolio of shares depends on the number of shares in the portfolio. Risk is measured here with a statistic called *standard deviation*, which you may have learned about in a mathematics or statistics course. Standard deviation measures the volatility of a variable – that is, how much the variable is likely to fluctuate. The higher the standard deviation of a portfolio's return, the more volatile and riskier it is.

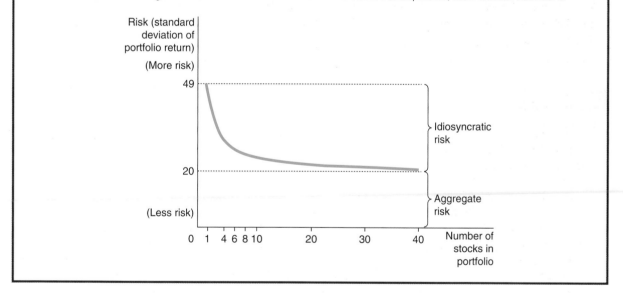

FIGURE 9.2

Diversification Reduces Risk

This figure shows how the risk of a portfolio, measured here with a statistic called standard deviation (a measure of the variability about the mean), depends on the number of shares in the portfolio. The investor is assumed to put an equal percentage of his portfolio in each of the shares. Increasing the number of shares reduces the amount of risk in a stock portfolio, but it does not eliminate it.

The figure shows that the risk of a stock portfolio reduces substantially as the number of shares increase. For a portfolio with a single share, the standard deviation is 49 per cent. Going from 1 share to 10 shares eliminates about half the risk. Going from 10 to 20 shares reduces the risk by another 13 per cent. As the number of shares continues to increase, risk continues to fall, although the reductions in risk after 20 or 30 shares are small.

Notice that it is impossible to eliminate all risk by increasing the number of stocks or shares in the portfolio. Diversification can eliminate **idiosyncratic risk** – the uncertainty associated with the specific companies. But diversification cannot eliminate **aggregate risk** – the uncertainty associated with the entire economy, which affects all companies. For example, when the economy goes into a recession, most companies experience falling sales, reduced profit and low stock returns. Diversification reduces the risk of holding stocks, but it does not eliminate it.

> **idiosyncratic risk** risk that affects only a single economic actor
> **aggregate risk** risk that affects all economic actors at once

The Trade-Off Between Risk and Return

One of the *Ten Principles of Economics* is that people face trade-offs. The trade-off that is most relevant for understanding financial decisions is the trade-off between risk and return.

As we have seen, there are risks inherent in holding shares, even in a diversified portfolio. But risk-averse people are willing to accept this uncertainty because they are compensated for doing so. Historically, shares have offered much higher rates of return than alternative financial assets, such as bonds and bank savings accounts. Over the past two centuries, stocks have offered an average real return of about 8 per cent per year, while short-term government bonds paid a real return of only 3 per cent per year.

When deciding how to allocate their savings, people have to decide how much risk they are willing to undertake to earn the higher return. Figure 9.3 illustrates the risk-return trade-off for a person choosing to allocate his portfolio between two asset classes:

- The first asset class is a diversified group of risky stocks, with an average return of 8 per cent and a standard deviation of 20 per cent. (You may recall from mathematics or statistics courses that a normal random variable stays within two standard deviations of its average about 95 per cent of the time. Thus, while actual returns are centred around 8 per cent, they typically vary from a gain of 48 per cent to a loss of 32 per cent.)
- The second asset class is a safe alternative. With a return of 3 per cent and a standard deviation of zero. The safe alternative can be either a bank savings account or a government bond.

FIGURE 9.3

The Trade-Off Between Risk and Return

When people increase the percentage of their savings that they have invested in shares, they increase the average return they can expect to earn, but they also increase the risks they face.

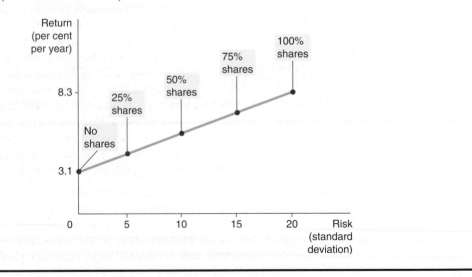

Each point in this figure represents a particular allocation of a portfolio between risky shares and the safe asset. The figure shows that the more a person puts into stock, the greater is both the risk and the return.

Acknowledging the risk–return trade-off does not, by itself, tell us what a person should do. The choice of a particular combination of risk and return depends on a person's risk aversion, which reflects a person's own preferences. But it is important for shareholders to realize that the higher average return that they enjoy comes at the price of higher risk.

SELF TEST Describe three ways that a risk-averse person might reduce the risk she faces.

CASE STUDY The Quants and Zero Risk

Having an economics degree may give you an advantage in the employment stakes but many financial institutions have also found highly skilled mathematicians and physicists extremely useful. They became known as 'the quants'. One such 'quant' was David Li, a talented mathematician who worked on quantitative analysis at the Wall Street investment bank J.P. Morgan Chase. In 2000 he published a paper in the *Journal of Fixed Income* entitled 'On Default Correlation: A Copula Function Approach'.

Li had some background in actuarial science as well as business and in his role within J.P. Morgan Chase, he was part of a growing number of highly qualified mathematical and statistical individuals being employed by financial institutions to identify risk and find ways of reducing it to a minimum – if not eliminating it totally. The basis behind this 'quantitative finance' was that the market could be beaten. What quantitative finance provided was the possibility of improved information that enabled decision-makers to invest with significantly reduced risk.

The basis of Li's paper in 2000 focused on the problems of probabilities and correlation of events. For example, a company in the southwest of England sources animal hide and processes it into a range of different quality leather for sale to manufacturers of leather products. It sources its hides from a company in Kenya. Analysis of data can give reasonably reliable estimates of the probability of both these businesses' chances of failure. The probability of the UK company failing might be 0.3 and the probability of the Kenyan company failing, 0.4. However, given the relationship between the two, if the Kenyan company did fail then there is a relatively high probability that the UK company might also fail if it cannot source the same high-quality hides elsewhere quickly. The correlation between the two companies failing, therefore, is quite high.

What is the correlation between the chances of the UK company failing and an Icelandic tourism operator also failing? Intuition might suggest that the correlation would be weak given the fact that the two companies are operating in different markets and are not related. However, they may be related by the fact that they have both acquired loans from a bank based in Germany. If that bank suffered problems then the chance of the two companies failing would be relatively high. Li attempted to apply his skills to the effect of the default of one business on another. If this could be modelled then it could help decision-makers to reduce the risk of investing.

One of the statistical devices used for modelling linked events is a copula. The chances of two or more events occurring together can be modelled through the use of a copula which produces a distribution. The specific distribution that Li used was a Gaussian Copula, which to many students is the familiar 'bell curve' given by a normal distribution. Li looked at the probability of any two or more elements in a pool of debt defaulting and his formula showed that this was equal to the normal distribution (the copula) times the probabilities of the time taken for the elements to default (referred to as survival times) multiplied by a correlation constant. The survival time aspect of the formula was derived from Li's knowledge of the work of actuaries in looking at survival rates of partners following the death of one of them. In this scenario events (in this case death) tend to an average and, as mentioned earlier, in this scenario there are certainties – death will occur at some point in the future. With assets the outcomes were not so clear cut and while Li's formula looked 'elegant' it was not able to take into account the range and randomness of

(continued)

events which were not so clear cut. Indeed, Li appeared to recognize (as any good scientist would claim to do) that his formula did have limitations. In 2005, he is quoted as saying 'Very few people understand the essence of the model'.

For those in the financial world, the model was useful in that it appeared to be able to reduce risk to a 'simple' number and thus help price that risk. It told decision-makers what effect the default of one company might have on another regardless of the knowledge of either company. Li's formula gained some currency in financial markets to the extent that ratings agencies such as Moody's and Standard & Poor's incorporated it into their methodology. In particular the formula could be used to assess risk on collateralized debt obligations (CDOs).

Li's formula may have provided investors with new information which they could use to factor in when making decisions – it became part of the set of 'relevant generally available information'. The problem was that, despite having this information, those using it may not have fully understood the information which they were exploiting. The whole point of employing top-ranked mathematicians, statisticians and physicists in the world of finance since the latter part of the 1990s was that their skills were very special – it was simply not something that anybody else but these brilliant minds could do; if it had have been possible then others would have done it!

The problem of employing such minds to try and beat the market is that the new information they bring to the market is highly technical, is based on assumptions that are standard in science but which are recognized in that discipline as 'provisional', and that any theory or model is simply there to be taken apart and either destroyed or improved upon. The information we now have on the financial crisis, some of the causes of which were laid at the feet of these 'quants', is something that markets can now factor into decision-making. There are a great many things in economics that can be modelled and mathematics can be very useful in helping to provide the means to analyse and to predict, but ultimately economics is about human behaviour. Despite such rigorous analysis, the old adage about baskets and eggs still applies!

David Li was referred to by some media outlets as the man who was responsible for the credit crunch and subsequent recession.

ASSET VALUATION

Now that we have developed a basic understanding of the two building blocks of finance – time and risk – let's apply this knowledge. This section considers a simple question: what determines the price of a share of stock? Like most prices, the answer is supply and demand. But that is not the end of the story. To understand share prices, we need to think more deeply about what determines a person's willingness to pay for a share of stock.

Fundamental Analysis

Let's imagine that you have decided to put 60 per cent of your savings into company shares and, to achieve diversification, you have decided to buy 20 different shares. How should you pick the 20 for your portfolio?

When you buy company shares, you are buying shares in a business. When deciding which businesses you want to own, it is natural to consider two things: the value of the business and the price at which the shares are being sold. If the price is less than the value, the stock is said to be *undervalued*. If the price is more than the value, the stock is said to be *overvalued*. If the price and the value are equal, the stock is said to be *fairly valued*. When choosing 20 stocks for your portfolio, you should prefer undervalued stocks. In these cases, you are getting a bargain by paying less than the business is worth.

This is easier said than done. Learning the price is easy: you can just look it up in the newspaper or online or have it downloaded to an app on your mobile device. Determining the value of the business is the hard part. The term **fundamental analysis** refers to the detailed analysis of a company to determine its value. Many financial sector firms hire stock price analysts to conduct such fundamental analysis and offer advice about which stocks to buy.

> **fundamental analysis** the study of a company's accounting statements and future prospects to determine its value

The value of a stock to a shareholder is what he gets out of owning it, which includes the present value of the stream of dividend payments and the final sale price. Recall that *dividends* are the cash payments that a company makes to its shareholders. A company's ability to pay dividends, as well as the value of the stock when the shareholder sells his shares, depends on the company's ability to earn profits. Its profitability, in turn, depends on a large number of factors – the demand for its product, how much competition it faces, how much capital it has in place, whether its workers are unionized, how loyal its customers are, what kinds of government regulations and taxes it faces, and so on. The job of fundamental analysts is to take all these factors into account to determine how much a share of stock in the company is worth.

If you want to rely on fundamental analysis to pick a stock portfolio, there are three ways to do it. One way is to do all the necessary research yourself, by reading through companies' annual reports and so forth. A second way is to rely on the advice of financial analysts. A third way is to buy into an investment fund, which has a manager (sometimes called a fund manager) who conducts fundamental analysis and makes the decision for you.

The Efficient Markets Hypothesis

There is another way to choose 20 shares for your portfolio: pick them randomly by, for instance, putting the stock pages of the *Financial Times* on your notice board and throwing darts at the page. This may sound crazy, but there is reason to believe that it won't lead you too far astray. That reason is called the **efficient markets hypothesis**.

> **efficient markets hypothesis** the theory that asset prices reflect all publicly available information about the value of an asset

To understand this theory, the starting point is to acknowledge that each company listed on a major stock exchange is followed closely by many fund managers, such as the individuals who run investment funds. Every day, these managers monitor news stories and conduct fundamental analysis to try to determine the fund's value. Their job is to buy a share when its price falls below its value, and to sell it when its price rises above its value.

The second piece to the efficient markets hypothesis is that the equilibrium of supply and demand sets the market price. This means that, at the market price, the number of shares being offered for sale exactly equals the number of shares that people want to buy. In other words, at the market price, the number of people who think the share is overvalued exactly balances the number of people who think it's undervalued. As judged by the typical person in the market, all shares are fairly valued all the time.

According to this theory, the stock market is **informationally efficient**: It reflects all available information about the value of the asset. Share prices change when information changes. When the good news about the company's prospects become public, the value and the stock price both rise. When the company's prospects deteriorate, the value and price both fall. But at any moment in time, the market price is the best guess of the company's value based on available information.

> **informationally efficient** reflecting all available information in a rational way

One implication of the efficient markets hypothesis is that stock prices should follow a **random walk**. This means that changes in stock prices are impossible to predict from available information. If, based on publicly available information, a person could predict that a stock price would rise by 10 per cent tomorrow, then the stock market must be failing to incorporate that information today. According to this theory, the only thing that can move stock prices is news that changes the market's perception of the company's value. But news must be unpredictable – otherwise, it wouldn't really be news. For the same reason, changes in stock prices should be unpredictable.

> **random walk** the path of a variable whose changes are impossible to predict

If the efficient markets hypothesis is correct, then there is little point in spending many hours studying the business page to decide which 20 shares to add to your portfolio. If prices reflect all available information, no stock is a better buy than any other. The best you can do is buy a diversified portfolio.

Efficient Markets Hypothesis: Dead and Buried or Just Resting? Any theory is a framework for analysing the world and which allows us to be able to make predictions. Theories are subject to testing and can be found to be inaccurate, limited in understanding or just plain wrong! One of the problems with economic theories, unlike those of the hard sciences, is that they are not easily testable in a laboratory environment where experiments can be repeated in order to establish the reliability or otherwise of a theory. Economic theories are used as the basis for policy making and if a theory is inaccurate or unreliable then policies and decisions can be undermined. The assumption of efficient markets and the belief that markets self-correct and revert to reflect true market value was the basis of the regulatory framework that underpinned the financial system in most major centres of the world.

New information comes out all the time but to the extent that this information really is new, it is unpredictable. In hindsight it always seems that we could have foreseen events after they have arisen; a chain of causality can invariably be established. However, if humans were able to predict future events with any certainty or predict the news it would not be news, by definition!

Much of the above reasoning, however, is based on the principle of rational behaviour. The question raised in the wake of the financial crisis was the extent to which the 'bubbles' which occurred in asset prices represented rational behaviour as opposed to a herd mentality or mass psychology as proposed by the Yale economist and 2013 Nobel Prize winner, Robert Shiller, and Richard Thaler at the University of Chicago, who are leading behavioural economists. The existence of speculative bubbles suggests that markets react to what Alan Greenspan, a former chair of the US Federal Reserve, called 'irrational exuberance' and what Keynes referred to as 'animal spirits'. In speculative bubbles, asset prices rise, not because of the stream of income that flows from them and the price when sold, but solely because of an expectation of what others will think the asset will be worth in the future. It is worth pausing on this for a moment, because there is a subtle difference between valuing an assert based on fundamental analysis – the present value of future dividends – and valuing it based on an assumption that people will bid up the price *regardless of expected future dividends*. It is when the price gets detached from the fundamentals and starts to be contingent only on what everyone in the market expects everyone else will think that a bubble starts to form.

Keynes believed that, given the fact that most investors would sell shares they own at some point in the future, it was not unreasonable to have some concern about others' valuation of that asset. Such views could lead to irrational waves of optimism and pessimism. The efficient markets hypothesis (EMH) is based on an assumption that there are a sufficient number of people in the market who act rationally to counter the few that do not.

Central to the EMH is the role of information. Information is necessary to value anything, to enable the valuer to make judgements. This information could include data of different kinds. It might include statistical data based on historical records or on reliable forecasting techniques; data can be gained from official statements from a business, from trends, market research, financial audits, analyst reports on the business in relation to its market and the economy, from government and its agencies on economic performance, from other specialist market analysts such as Mintel and Experian, representatives of retail trades and so on. In valuing the price of an asset, therefore, the assumption is that the market is informationally efficient in that it reflects all available information about the value of that asset.

The extent to which this assumption can be accepted is open to question. Access to information and the speed at which information travels is now greater than ever before. Despite the growth in technology, information transfer is not instantaneous nor is it assimilated and understood by all at the same speed and with the same depth. There is, therefore, a time lag involved with information transfer. As we have seen above, if individuals are able to exploit that time lag they can use this to their advantage to make profits; this is the basis of arbitrage. A conclusion from this might be that EMH implies that markets will clear and that most of the time, or on average, that they are efficient. The remaining time periods, when they are not efficient, may be where problems can arise.

A belief in the fundamentals of EMH led even revered financial luminaries such as Alan Greenspan to have to admit that he may have been wrong in some of his assumptions.

In testimony given to the Committee of Government Oversight and Reform in the US on 23 October 2008 in the wake of the financial crisis, Greenspan said:

… those of us who have looked to the self-interest of lending institutions to protect shareholders' equity (myself especially) are in a state of shocked disbelief. Such counterparty surveillance is a central pillar of our financial markets' state of balance. If it fails, as occurred this year, market stability is undermined.

In response to a further question from Committee Chairman, Henry Waxman, who asked:

You found that your view of the world, your ideology, was not right, it was not working?

Greenspan replied:

That's precisely the reason I was shocked because I'd been going for 40 years or so with considerable evidence that it was working exceptionally well.

Information may be widely available and extensive but it does not mean that it is always understood. Decision-makers may have access to a wide range of information but some vital part of that information may be missed if understanding is not complete. Greenspan alluded to this in his testimony. Information may not only be misunderstood but also be partial; gathering information requires some investment in terms of research (information gathering and processing) on the part of decision-makers and this investment can be expensive. In any decision-making, therefore, research costs have to be built in. One very good example of this principle will be considered in the next section. It looks at the way in which information can be made available to decision-makers, can be used and exploited but without critical acceptance may provide the basis for erroneous judgements, as we saw in our outline of the role of 'the quants' in the Case Study earlier in this chapter.

Faith in markets is fundamental to economic growth in most of the world and the financial crisis of 2007–2009 has shaken this faith to the core. There have been many who have consigned EMH to the 'dustbin of history' but there are others that suggest that the events since the early 2000s are testament to the robustness of EMH – that the market cannot be beaten and that attempts to try and do so will ultimately fail. The development of sophisticated information to try and beat the market is one example of how this has happened. The use of such techniques to make 'superrational' valuations of assets is impossible, its supporters would argue.

What may come out of the analysis of the financial crisis is a better understanding of how markets work, especially in a rapidly changing world. The assumptions that have been made about how markets work, the variables that are considered, the effect of external shocks and the extent to which humans may act irrationally, are risk seeking or risk averse and more, may all be revisited, revised and re-interpreted. Ultimately we may be in a better position to understand the complexity of markets but to arrive at the conclusion that our understanding and our mastery is complete is akin to a pronouncement by physicists that they understand every aspect of the physical world and the universe; in short it is not going to happen!

Minsky's Financial Instability Hypothesis There are some, therefore, who suggest that the EMH has been found wanting. Some have suggested an alternative and referred to the idea of American 20th-century economists, Hyman Minsky and Irving Fisher, of the financial instability hypothesis (FIH). This suggests that the idea that markets always move to an equilibrium position and remain in that position pending some external shock may have some resonance in commodities or goods markets but that financial markets are not subject to the same forces. Minsky and Fisher argue that financial markets create their own internal forces which create periods of asset inflation and credit expansion. This will be followed by contraction in credit and asset deflation. Financial markets, they conclude, are not self-optimizing or stable and far from allocating resources efficiently the outcome may be sub-optimal. Minsky suggests that some of these internal forces relate to the lack of supply of assets which drive demand in those markets. For example, the lack of supply of housing drives demand for housing and forces prices upwards creating a bubble. Changing asset prices (such as houses) in turn act as a driver for demand for those assets. If house prices are rising quickly there is an incentive for buyers to want to get into the market quickly to avoid having to pay higher prices and also to benefit from rising prices once they have purchased. This simply fuels demand further in the face of limited supply and so drives price up higher.

Maybe the last word on this issue can be with Burton G. Malkiel from Princeton who, in a paper in 2003, concluded:

> As long as stock markets exist, the collective judgment of investors will sometimes make mistakes. Undoubtedly, some market participants are demonstrably less then rational. As a result, pricing irregularities and predictable patterns in stock returns can appear over time and even persist for short periods. Moreover, the market cannot be perfectly efficient or there would be no incentive for professionals to uncover the information that gets so quickly reflected in market prices, a point stressed by Grossman and Stiglitz (1980). Undoubtedly, with the passage of time and with the increasing sophistication of our databases and empirical techniques, we will document further apparent departures from efficiency and further patterns in the development of stock returns.
>
> But I suspect that the end result will not be an abandonment of the belief of many in the profession that the stock market is remarkably efficient in its utilization of information. Periods such as 1999 where 'bubbles' seem to have existed, at least in certain sectors of the market, are fortunately the exception rather than the rule. Moreover, whatever patterns or irrationalities in the pricing of individual stocks that have been discovered in a search of historical experience are unlikely to persist and will not provide investors with a method to obtain extraordinary returns. If any $100 bills are lying around the stock exchanges of the world, they will not be there for long.

Malkiel, B.G. (2003). 'The Efficient Market Hypothesis and its Critics'. CEPS Working Paper no. 91.

Market Irrationality

The efficient markets hypothesis assumes that people buying and selling stock rationally process the information they have about the stocks' underlying value. But is the stock market really that rational? Or do share prices sometimes deviate from reasonable expectations of their true value?

There is a long tradition suggesting that fluctuations in share prices are partly psychological. In the 1930s, British economist John Maynard Keynes suggested that asset markets are driven by the 'animal spirits' of investors – irrational waves of optimism and pessimism. Alan Greenspan's reference to 'irrational exuberance' became popular in describing stock market behaviour, especially when it was used as the title of a book on stock market behaviour by Robert Shiller that successfully predicted a large fall in US stock prices. Nevertheless, whether the exuberance of stock markets in the USA and around the world in the 1990s and the middle of the noughties was irrational given the information available at the time remains debatable.

Sustained and sometimes rapid rises in stock prices are called speculative bubbles, since often the price rise comes to an end and share prices fall abruptly, just as a soap bubble will rise and rise until it suddenly bursts. The possibility of such speculative bubbles arises in part because the value of a share to a stockholder depends not only on the stream of dividend payments but also on the final sale price of the share. Thus, a person might be willing to pay more than a stock is worth today if he expects another person to pay even more for it tomorrow. When you evaluate a stock, you have to estimate not only the value of the business but also what other people will think the business is worth in the future.

There is much debate among economists about whether departures from rational pricing are important or rare. Believers in market irrationality point out (correctly) that the stock market often moves in ways that are hard to explain on the basis of news that might alter a rational valuation. We have already described a number of examples where disciplines such as biology and psychology are helping to contribute to our understanding of human behaviour. The growth in 'neuroeconomics' is one example of where such information is helping to push the boundaries of our understanding and is being applied to finance. Believers in the efficient markets hypothesis point out (correctly) that it is impossible to know the correct, rational valuation of a company, so one should not quickly jump to the conclusion that any particular valuation is irrational. Moreover, if the market were irrational, a rational person should be able to take advantage of this fact; yet, as we have seen, beating the market is nearly impossible.

SELF TEST Investors sometimes refer to 'highly respected' companies as 'blue chip companies'. These are usually large, national or multinational corporations with a reputation for high-quality management or products. Examples of blue chip companies quoted on the London Stock Exchange would be Rolls-Royce, Unilever and BP. According to the efficient markets hypothesis, if you restrict your stock portfolio to blue chip companies, would you earn a better than average return? Explain.

FYI

Keynes's View of Stock Markets

As well as being the most influential economist of the 20th century, Keynes was also a successful stock market investor and considerably enriched his college in Cambridge by managing its investment portfolio. Yet his opinion of professional investment managers was notoriously low. In his *Treatise on Money* (1930), he wrote:

... the vast majority of those who are concerned with the buying and selling of securities know almost nothing whatever about what they are doing. They do not possess even the rudiments of what is required for a valid judgment, and are the prey of hopes and fears easily aroused by transient events and as easily dispelled. This is one of the odd characteristics of the capitalist system under which we live, which, when we are dealing with the real world, is not to be overlooked.

Keynes was not known for his modesty, but, even so, one suspects that he may have been overstating his case somewhat for the sake of emphasis. In *The General Theory of Employment, Interest and Money* (1936), he sketched out a more balanced view that amounts to a simple theory of speculative bubbles in a very famous passage in which he compares the stock market to a beauty contest:

... professional investment may be likened to those newspaper competitions in which the competitors have to pick out the six prettiest faces from a hundred photographs, the prize being awarded to the competitor whose choice most nearly corresponds to the average preferences of the competitors as a whole; so that each competitor has to pick, not

those faces which he himself finds prettiest, but those which he thinks likeliest to catch the fancy of the other competitors, all of whom are looking at the problem from the same point of view. It is not a case of choosing those which, to the best of one's judgment, are really the prettiest, nor even those which average opinion genuinely thinks the prettiest. We have reached the third degree where we devote our intelligences to anticipating what average opinion expects the average opinion to be.

For these reasons, a person who believes that departures from rational pricing are the rule rather than the exception in the stock market are sometimes referred to as having a Keynesian view of financial markets.

CONCLUSION

This chapter has developed some of the basic tools that people should (and often do) use as they make financial decisions. The concept of present value reminds us that a euro in the future is less valuable than a euro today, and it gives us a way to compare sums of money at different points in time. The theory of risk management reminds us that the future is uncertain and that risk-averse people can take precautions to guard against this uncertainty. The study of asset valuation tells us that the stock price of any company should reflect its expected future profitability.

Although most of the tools of finance are well established, there is more controversy about the validity of the efficient markets hypothesis and whether stock prices are, in practice, rational estimates of a company's true worth. Rational or not, the large movements in stock prices that we observe have important macroeconomic implications. Stock market fluctuations often go hand in hand with fluctuations in the economy more broadly. We will look at the stock market again when we study economic fluctuations later in the book.

IN THE NEWS

The Efficient Markets Hypothesis

The financial crisis of 2007–2009 led to a number of economists and commentators being fiercely critical of the EMH. Amidst this criticism, what did the founder of the EMH think? Eugene Fama, a professor of finance at the University of Chicago Booth School of Business and joint-winner of the Nobel Prize for Economists in 2013, developed portfolio theory and is credited with developing the theory that markets are efficient.

EMH in Hindsight

Since the financial crisis it has been fashionable to criticize the efficient markets hypothesis as being incorrect. The founder of the EMH, Eugene Fama, has been asked about whether his view of the EMH has changed in the wake of the crisis. In various interviews he has offered a robust and objective analysis of the crisis and what it means for the theory he developed. It is worthwhile clarifying a point that is sometimes missed – in the period leading up to the crisis, people may have assumed that prices being quoted on stock markets reflected the fundamental value of corporations. Quants were employed by finance houses across the world to find ways to beat the market and the development of highly sophisticated statistical and mathematical models were supposed to help exploit informational inefficiency in markets to give dealers an edge over their rivals. Perhaps one thing that has not been made clear in the wake of the crisis is that in market trades there will always be a winner and a loser. If one trader manages to exploit undervaluation, someone on the opposite side of the trade must have been overvaluing that same trade in order for the exchange to take place.

Hindsight is always an impressive thing – we look back on price rises in the housing market and in asset prices around 2004–2007 and can confidently state that this was an example of an asset and credit bubble. Fama recognizes the importance of hindsight. If investors are living through a period of a bubble and can identify this *at the time*, then this will be part of known information and so investors would respond in kind. During a credit bubble it makes sense to sell when prices are high in the expectation and knowledge that prices are going to fall. So, if a credit bubble did exist at the time, someone, somewhere would have made a great deal of money. Fama argues that there are always instances where people are going to say that asset prices are too high and that the markets are experiencing a bubble. Equally, there are those who present an opposing argument and both cannot be correct. If prices do collapse then it is relatively easy to pick out the individuals who warned of a bubble and laud them whilst we castigate those who provided an opposing point of view. At the time of writing (February 2013), stock prices have been rising on world markets – are stock markets experiencing a bubble?

A search of the financial media at this time suggested that there are those who believe in a bubble and those who scoff at the very idea. By the time this book is published we may know who was right and who was wrong – or indeed if both were incorrect. Fama's view is that the word 'bubble' has little meaning and that observations on whether markets are experiencing a bubble are right and wrong in equal measures.

Observers might question this view and note that there was never any rationality to lending money to people with very poor credit ratings. Fama counters that part of the sub-prime problems was down to US government policy to promote home ownership among all classes of society and that it was not just the collapse in sub-prime house prices that caused the financial crisis, but a global fall in house prices which took place across most house price bands, not simply those linked to sub-prime. The consequences of the decline in global house prices were problems for the banking sector and a lack of availability of credit in markets. Fama points to the cause being an economic one – a global downturn in economic activity which led to people in all walks of life being unable to meet their credit (and mortgage) commitments. There is always going to be a group of people who are at the margin – just able to afford their commitments provided things don't change – but when they do these people at the margin are the first to default; they are literally living on the edge. Fama's view is that the downturn in economic activity started to show itself before the financial crisis and that there was a worldwide fall in house prices that pre-dated the financial crisis. What actually causes recessions is something Fama thinks is still very much

a mystery to macroeconomists and that it can be argued that the financial markets were a victim of the recession and not the cause of it.

Fama is still a passionate believer in the role of financial markets providing a conduit from those who wish to save to those who wish to borrow – including corporates – and that financial innovation of the type that generated CDOs and CDS have contributed much to the development of countries across the globe and to the welfare of millions of people over the last 30 years. If the EMH is about valuing stock prices using all available information, there is an assumption that markets will understand completely the models which they are working with and the information which they have available to price assets. It is highly unlikely that every decision-maker in financial markets knows everything about what they are working with and so there is always some element

of unknown information. Those fund managers working with David Li's formula may not have fully understood the model but chose to use it anyway, and, as such, decisions are being made with less than complete information.

So, when financial markets get into trouble Fama does not believe that the finger should be solely pointed at the markets themselves or any underlying theory of market efficiency, but he does think that the idea that financial institutions can be 'too big to fail' is of real concern because it creates moral hazard and adverse selection. Financial institutions should be allowed to fail and that would be an ultimate regulation.

So, despite the criticism that has been levelled against the EMG, Fama still believes that the fundamental conclusion of the theory, you cannot beat the market, still holds and that financial markets can be described as 'efficient'. Fama does

Eugene Fama was acknowledged for his work on the empirical analysis of asset prices when he shared the Nobel Prize for Economic Sciences in 2013, along with Robert Shiller and Lars Peter Hansen.

(*Continued*)

think that the developments in other parts of the University of Chicago on behavioural explanations is an interesting development and, if empirical evidence can be put forward, has much to contribute to the efficient markets debate.

Questions

1 One of the key conclusions of the EMH is that 'you can't beat the market'. Is the fact that financial institutions employed highly qualified maths, physics and statistics graduates to develop ways to exploit information asymmetries testament to the view that few working in financial markets believed in the EMH? Explain your reasoning.

2 Must there always be a winner and a loser in financial transactions? Explain.

3 Do you think that the word 'bubble' is only ever useful in hindsight? Explain.

4 'Lending to the sub-prime market must have been a rational thing to do at the time otherwise people would not have done it'. Comment on this view.

5 Fama argues that economists have been researching the cause of the Great Depression in the 1930s for many years but have not yet managed to come up with a definitive conclusion about its causes. Can economists ever identify cause and effect when analysing financial crises such as that in 2007–2009?

SUMMARY

- Because savings can earn interest, a sum of money today is more valuable than the same sum of money in the future. A person can compare sums from different times using the concept of present value. The present value of any future sum is the amount that would be needed today, given prevailing interest rates, to produce that future sum.

- Because of diminishing marginal utility, most people are risk averse. Risk-averse people can reduce risk using insurance, through diversification, and by choosing a portfolio with lower risk and lower return.

- The value of an asset, such as a share of stock, equals the present value of the cash flows the owner of the share will receive, including the stream of dividends and the final sale price. According to the efficient markets hypothesis, financial markets process available information rationally, so a stock price always equals the best estimate of the value of the underlying business. Some economists question the efficient markets hypothesis, however, and believe that irrational psychological factors also influence asset prices.

QUESTIONS FOR REVIEW

1 Outline the concept of present value.

2 The interest rate is 7 per cent. Use the concept of present value to compare €200 to be received in ten years and €300 to be received in 20 years.

3 What benefit do people get from the market for insurance? What two problems impede the insurance company from working perfectly?

4 What is meant by the term 'fundamental analysis'?

5 What is diversification? Does a shareholder get more diversification going from 1 to 10 stocks or going from 100 to 120 stocks?

6 Comparing company shares and government bonds, which has more risk? Which pays a higher average return?

7 What factors should a stock analyst think about in determining the value of a share of stock?

8 Describe the efficient markets hypothesis, and give a piece of evidence consistent with this theory.

9 Explain the view of those economists who are sceptical of the efficient markets hypothesis.

10 Why is knowledge of whether people are risk averse or risk seeking important in financial markets?

PROBLEMS AND APPLICATIONS

1 About 400 years ago, Native Americans sold the island of Manhattan for $24. If they had invested this money at an interest rate of 7 per cent per year, how much would they have today?

2 A company has an investment project that would cost €10 million today and yield a payoff of €15 million in four years.

   a. Should the firm undertake the project if the interest rate is 11 per cent? 10 per cent? 9 per cent? 8 per cent?

   b. Can you figure out the exact cut-off for the interest rate between profitability and non-profitability?

3 For each of the following kinds of insurance, give an example of behaviour that can be called *moral hazard* and another example of behaviour that can be called *adverse selection*:

   a. health insurance
   b. car insurance.

4 Imagine that you intend to buy a portfolio of ten shares with some of your savings. Should the shares be of companies in the same industry? Should the shares be of companies located in the same country? Explain.

5 For which kind of stock would you expect to pay the higher average return: stock in an industry that is very sensitive to economic conditions (such as a car manufacturer) or stock in an industry that is relatively insensitive to economic conditions (such as a water company)? Why?

6 A company faces two kinds of risk. An idiosyncratic risk is that a competitor might enter its market and take some of its customers. An aggregate risk is that the economy might enter a recession, reducing sales. Which of these two risks would more likely cause the company's shareholders to demand a higher return? Why?

7 You have two flatmates who invest in the stock market.

   a. One flatmate says she buys stock only in companies that everyone believes will experience big increases in profits in the future. How do you suppose the price – earnings ratio of these companies compares to the price – earnings ratio of other companies? What might be the disadvantage of buying stock in these companies?

   b. Another flatmate says she only buys stock in companies that are cheap, which she measures by a low price-earnings ratio. How do you suppose the earnings prospects of these companies compare to those of other companies? What might be the disadvantage of buying stock in these companies?

8 When company executives buy and sell stock based on private information they obtain as part of their jobs, they are engaged in *insider trading*.

   a. Give an example of inside information that might be useful for buying or selling stock.

   b. Those who trade shares based on inside information usually earn very high rates of return. Does this fact violate the efficient market hypothesis?

   c. Insider trading is illegal. Why do you suppose that is?

9 Financial markets in the early years of the 21st century were heavily influenced by the work of quantitative analysts ('quants') who looked at ways to reassess the pricing of risk. Discuss some of the advantages and disadvantages of pricing risk using mathematics and mathematical models.

10 How might you go about pricing the risk on the following:

   a. the price of a ten-year bond from the Portuguese government

   b. the price of a ten-year bond from the German government

   c. the construction of a new oil well off the South African coast.

10 THE MONETARY SYSTEM

When you walk into a restaurant to buy a meal, you receive something of value: the enjoyment of the food together with the experience of eating the meal in a pleasant environment and being waited upon. To pay for this service, you might hand the restaurateur several pieces of brightly coloured paper decorated with strange symbols, buildings and maps of Europe (or even a portrait of a monarch). Or you might hand him a small, rectangular piece of coloured plastic with a magnetic strip and a small computer chip set into it, which the restaurateur will later return to you. Whether you pay by cash, debit card or credit card, the restaurateur is happy to work hard to satisfy your gastronomic desires either in exchange for pieces of paper that, in and of themselves, are worthless, or in exchange for borrowing an equally worthless small piece of plastic from you for a few minutes.

To anyone who has lived in a modern economy, this social custom is not at all odd. Even though paper money has no intrinsic value, the restaurateur is confident that, in the future, some third person will accept it in exchange for something that the restaurateur does value. And that third person is confident that some fourth person will accept the money, with the knowledge that yet a fifth person will accept the money … and so on. To the restaurateur and to other people in our society, your cash represents a claim to goods and services in the future. If you paid by debit card, the restaurateur is happy because he knows that money has been transferred more or less instantly to his bank account from your bank account, and the figures on his bank balance also represent a claim to goods and services produced by the economy. If you paid with a credit card, he knows that his account has been credited with the money that you have borrowed on the credit card in order to pay the restaurant bill.

The social custom of using money for transactions is extraordinarily useful in a large, complex society. Imagine, for a moment, that there was no item in the economy widely accepted in exchange for goods and services. People would have to rely on **barter** – the exchange of one good or service for another – to obtain the things they need. To get your restaurant meal, for instance, you would have to offer the restaurateur something of immediate value. You could offer to wash some dishes, clean his car or give him the secret recipe for your family's favourite dish. An economy that relies on barter will have trouble allocating its scarce resources efficiently. In such an economy, trade is said to require the **double coincidence of wants** – the unlikely occurrence that two people each have a good or service that the other wants.

> **barter** the exchange of one good or service for another
> **double coincidence of wants** a situation in exchange where two people each have a good or service that the other wants and can thus enter into an exchange

The existence of money makes trade easier. The restaurateur does not care whether you can produce a valuable good or service for him. He is happy to accept your money, knowing that other people will do the same for him. Such a convention allows trade to be roundabout. The restaurateur accepts your money and uses it to pay his chef; the chef uses her salary to send her child to the crèche; the crèche uses this money to pay a teacher; and the teacher hires you to child-mind when he goes to the cinema on a Saturday evening. As money flows from person to person in the economy, it facilitates production and trade, thereby allowing each person to specialize in what he or she does best and raising everyone's standard of living.

In this chapter we begin to examine the role of money in the economy. We discuss what money is, the various forms that money takes, how the banking system helps create money, and how the central bank controls the quantity of money in circulation. Because money is so important in the economy, we devote much effort in the rest of this book to learning how changes in the quantity of money affect various economic variables, including inflation, interest rates, production and employment. Consistent with our long-run focus in the previous three chapters, in the next chapter we will examine the long-run effects of changes in the quantity of money. The short-run effects of monetary changes are a more complex topic, which we will take up later in the book. This chapter provides the background for all of this further analysis.

THE MEANING OF MONEY

Economists use the word in a specific sense: **money** is the set of assets in the economy that people regularly use to buy goods and services from other people. The cash in your wallet is money because you can use it to buy a meal at a restaurant or a shirt at a clothes shop. By contrast, if you happened to own part of Facebook, as Mark Zuckerberg does, you would be wealthy, but this asset is not considered a form of money. You could not buy a meal or a shirt with this wealth without first obtaining some cash. According to the economist's definition, money includes only those few types of wealth that are regularly accepted by sellers in exchange for goods and services.

> **money** the set of assets in an economy that people regularly use to buy goods and services from other people

The Functions of Money

Money has three functions in the economy: it is a medium of exchange; a unit of account; and a store of value. These three functions together distinguish money from other assets in the economy, such as stocks, bonds, residential property and art. Let's examine each of these functions of money in turn.

A Medium of Exchange A **medium of exchange** is an item that buyers give to sellers when they purchase goods and services. When you buy a shirt at a clothes shop, the shop gives you the shirt and you give the shop your money. This transfer of money from buyer to seller allows the transaction to take place. When you walk into a shop, you are confident that the shop will accept your money for the items it is selling because money is the commonly accepted medium of exchange.

> **medium of exchange** an item that buyers give to sellers when they want to purchase goods and services

A Unit of Account A **unit of account** is the yardstick people use to post prices and record debts. When you go shopping, you might observe that a shirt is priced at €20 and a ham-and-cheese sandwich at €2. Even though it would be accurate to say that the price of a shirt is 10 sandwiches and the price of a sandwich is 1/10 of a shirt, prices are never quoted in this way. Similarly, if you take out a loan in euros from a bank, the size of your future loan repayments will be measured in euros, not in a quantity of goods and services. When we want to measure and record economic value, we use money as the unit of account.

> **unit of account** the yardstick people use to post prices and record debts

A Store of Value A **store of value** is an item that people can use to transfer purchasing power from the present to the future. When a seller accepts money today in exchange for a good or service, that seller can hold the money and become a buyer of another good or service at another time. Of course, money is not the only store of value in the economy, for a person can also transfer purchasing power from the present to the future by holding other assets. The term **wealth** is used to refer to the total of all stores of value, including both money and non-monetary assets.

> **store of value** an item that people can use to transfer purchasing power from the present to the future
> **wealth** the total of all stores of value, including both money and non-monetary assets

Liquidity

Economists use the term **liquidity** to describe the ease with which an asset can be converted into the economy's medium of exchange. Because money is the economy's medium of exchange, it is the most liquid asset available. Other assets vary widely in their liquidity. Most stocks and bonds can be sold easily with small cost, so they are relatively liquid assets. By contrast, selling a car or a Rembrandt painting requires more time and effort, so these assets are less liquid.

> **liquidity** the ease with which an asset can be converted into the economy's medium of exchange

When people decide in what form to hold their wealth, they have to balance the liquidity of each possible asset against the asset's usefulness as a store of value. Money is the most liquid asset, but it is far from perfect as a store of value. When prices rise, the value of money falls. In other words, when goods and services become more expensive, each euro or pound in your pocket can buy less. This link between the price level and the value of money will turn out to be important for understanding how money affects the economy.

The Kinds of Money

When money takes the form of a commodity with intrinsic value, it is called **commodity money**. The term *intrinsic value* means that the item would have value even if it were not used as money. One example of commodity money is gold. Gold has intrinsic value because it is used in industry and in the making of jewellery. Although today we no longer use gold as money, historically gold has been a common form of money because it is relatively easy to carry, measure, and verify for impurities. When an economy uses gold as money (or uses paper money that is convertible into gold on demand), it is said to be operating under a *gold standard*.

> **commodity money** money that takes the form of a commodity with intrinsic value

Although gold has, historically, been the most common form of commodity money, other commodity monies have been used from time to time. For example, in the hyperinflation in Zimbabwe in the early 2000s the country's people began to lose faith in the Zimbabwean dollar; people began to trade goods and services with one another using cigarettes as the store of value, unit of account and medium of exchange.

Money without intrinsic value is called **fiat money**. A fiat is simply an order or decree, and fiat money is established as money by government decree. For example paper euros are able to circulate as legal tender in 18 European countries because the governments of those countries have decreed that the euro be valid currency in each of their economies.

> **fiat money** money without intrinsic value that is used as money because of government decree

Although governments are central to establishing and regulating a system of fiat money (by prosecuting counterfeiters, for example), other factors are also required for the success of such a monetary system. To a large extent, the acceptance of fiat money depends as much on expectations and social convention as on government decree. Zimbabweans preferred to accept cigarettes (or American dollars) in exchange for goods and services, because they were more confident that these alternative monies would be accepted by others in the future.

Money in the Economy

As we will see, the quantity of money circulating in the economy, called the **money stock**, has a powerful influence on many economic variables. But before we consider why that is true, we need to ask a preliminary question: what is the quantity of money? In particular, suppose you were given the task of measuring how much money there is in the economy of a country like the United Kingdom, or in the economies of the 18 countries that make up the euro area. What would you include in your measure?

> **money stock** the quantity of money circulating in the economy

The most obvious asset to include is **currency** – the paper notes and metal coins in the hands of the public. Currency is clearly the most widely accepted medium of exchange in a modern economy. There is no doubt that it is part of the money stock.

> **currency** the paper banknotes and coins in the hands of the public

Yet currency is not the only asset that you can use to buy goods and services. Most businesses also accept payment by debit card, which allows money to be transferred electronically between your current account and the current account of the business. Another, more old-fashioned way of transferring money between current accounts is to write a personal cheque, and personal cheques are still accepted as a means of payment although being phased out in many countries.

So is a debit card or a cheque money? Not really – it is the bank account on which the cheque or debit card draws which contains the money. A debit card is just a *means* of transferring money between accounts. The same is true of a cheque because it is simply a *means* of transferring money from one bank account to another.

What about credit cards? We need to think about these even more carefully, because credit cards are not really a method of payment but a method of *deferring* payment. When you buy a meal with a credit card, the bank that issued the card pays the restaurant what it is due – you have effectively borrowed from the bank. At a later date, you will have to repay the bank (perhaps with interest). When the time comes to pay your credit card bill, you will probably do so by direct transfer from your current account. The balance in this current account is part of the economy's stock of money. Notice that credit cards are very different from debit cards, which automatically withdraw funds from a bank account to pay for items bought. Why does the restaurateur accept payment by credit card? Because he gets his money immediately by having his bank account credited for the price of the meal even though you do not have to pay the credit card company back immediately. Again, however, it is the underlying movement in the restaurateur's bank balance that matters.

Thus, although a debit card and a credit card can each be used to settle the restaurant bill, none of them are money – they are each a method of transferring money between bank accounts. In the case of a debit card or a cheque, money is transferred from your account to the restaurateur's account more or less immediately or with a very short lag. In the case of a credit card, the restaurateur gets his money in his account more or less immediately and you will then have to settle up with the bank issuing the credit card later by drawing on your bank account. In every case, the true movement in money occurs when bank balances change.

Wealth held in your current account is almost as convenient for buying things as wealth held in your wallet. To measure the money stock, therefore, you might want to include **demand deposits** – balances in bank accounts that depositors can access *on demand* simply by using their debit card. Once you start to consider balances in current accounts as part of the money stock, you are led to consider the large variety of other accounts that people hold at banks and other financial institutions. Bank depositors usually cannot use their debit cards against the balances in their savings accounts, but they can (mostly) easily transfer funds from savings into current accounts. In addition, depositors in money market funds can often use debit cards against their balances. Thus, these other accounts should plausibly be counted as part of the money stock.

> **demand deposits** balances in bank accounts that depositors can access on demand by using a debit card or writing a cheque

In a complex economy, it is in general not easy to draw a line between assets that can be called 'money' and assets that cannot. The coins in your pocket are clearly part of the money stock, and your car clearly is not, but there are many assets for which the choice is less clear. Therefore, various measures of the money stock are available for advanced economies. Panel (a) of Figure 10.1 shows the three most important measures for the euro area, designated M1 (a 'narrow' measure), M2 (an 'intermediate' measure) and M3 (a 'broad' measure). Each of these measures uses a slightly different criterion for distinguishing between monetary and non-monetary assets. In the UK, the most widely observed measures of the money stock are M0 (a narrower measure than the European M1 and corresponding to notes and coins in circulation plus bankers' balances held with the Bank of England) and M4 (a broad measure, similar – but not identical to – the European M3). Panel (b) of Figure 10.1 shows a breakdown of the various components of the money stock.

For our purposes in this book, we need not dwell on the differences between the various measures of money. The important point is that the money stock for an advanced economy includes not just currency but also deposits in banks and other financial institutions that can be readily accessed and used to buy goods and services.

FIGURE 10.1

Three Measures of the Money Stock for the Euro Area (billions of euro)

Panel (a) shows the three measures of euro area money stock are M1 (a 'narrow' monetary aggregate that comprises currency in circulation and overnight deposits), M2 (an 'intermediate' monetary aggregate that comprises M1 plus deposits with an agreed maturity of up to two years and deposits redeemable at notice of up to three months) and M3 (a 'broad' monetary aggregate that comprises M2 plus repurchase agreements, money market fund shares and units as well as debt securities with a maturity of up to two years). Panel (b) shows the size of the different components of the money stock. This figure shows the size of each measure in December 2012.

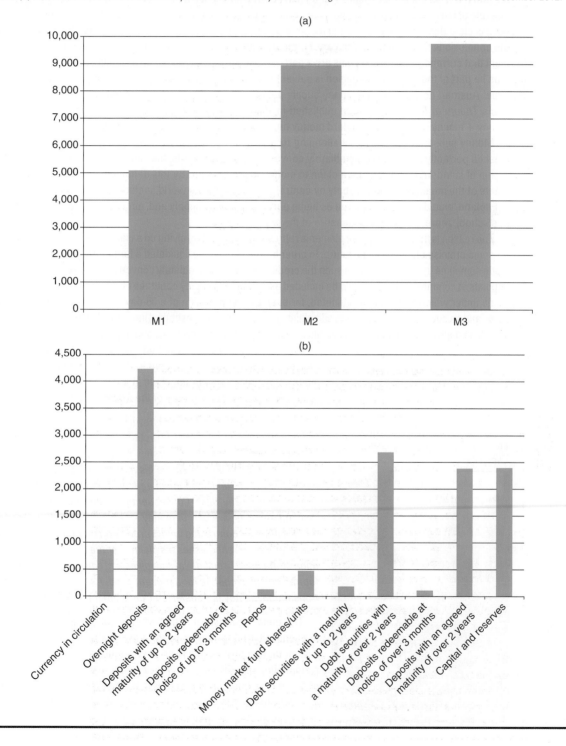

SELF TEST List and describe the three functions of money.

As with many aspects of economics, definitions of the money supply are open to different interpretations. The role of the money supply is going to be central too much of the analysis in the rest of this book as noted but it is clear that if the measure of the money supply being used varies then it is likely that the analysis and the conclusions that result will also vary. Fortunately, economists of almost every persuasion are in agreement that currency – notes and coins are a part of the money supply. What else should count as money and thus be part of the accepted definition is subject to different interpretations. One example is the so-called 'True' Austrian definition of the money supply put forward by the Austrian economist Ludwig von Mises in his *Theory of Money and Credit* published in 1953. von Mises defined the money supply as standard money + money substitutes. Standard money he defined as notes and coins in circulation or currency.

Money substitutes are more challenging to define but von Mises suggested that money substitutes must be perfectly secure and immediately convertible. In other words, they must be evidence of the ownership of standard money and be a claim to money in the present. By this definition, a number of the elements of the measured money supply by central banks across the world, including the ECB and the Bank of England, would not be considered as being part of the money supply and, according to economists from this school, represent a flawed measure of the money supply.

The reason is that some of these elements represent the individual giving up a claim to money in the present for some promise of money in the future. In order for the claim to be liquidated a further transaction has to be made sometime in the future and as such the credit claim is not immediately convertible. For example, savings deposits at commercial banks would be included as part of M2 in many countries but such deposits have legal terms under which they can be liquidated, for example the provision of a 30-day notice period given to the bank, and as such they represent a credit claim and not a money substitute. Under the Austrian school definition, time deposits and money funds would also be classed as credit claims and thus not money substitutes.

An economist at the Mises Institute in the United States, Dr Frank Shostak, provides some clarification of the difference between a money substitute and a credit claim in an essay published in 2000 (Shostak, F. (2000) *'The Mystery of the Money Supply'*):

Ludwig von Mises, founder of the so-called Austrian school of economics proposes a different view of the money supply which would impact on policy decisions. An example of where economists disagree as outlined in Chapter 2.

Once an individual places his money in a bank's warehouse he is in fact engaging in a claim transaction. In depositing his money, he never relinquishes his ownership. No one else is expected to make use of it. When Joe stores his money with a bank, he continues to have an unlimited claim against it and is entitled to take charge of it at any time. Consequently, these deposits, labelled demand deposits, are part of money …

This must be contrasted with a credit transaction, in which the lender of money relinquishes his claim over the money for the duration of the loan. Credit always involves a creditor's purchase of a future good in exchange for a present good. As a result, in a credit transaction, money is transferred from a lender to a borrower.

The debate over what is and what is not money is not simply academic, it is important for policy making; after all, we would not use an unaccepted measure of temperature in situations where maintaining specific level of heat or cold are required because of the disastrous consequences that could result so if we use incorrect measures of the money supply it follows that the consequences could be equally serious.

THE ROLE OF CENTRAL BANKS

Whenever an economy relies on a system of fiat money – as all modern advanced economies do – some agency must be responsible for regulating the system. This agency is generally known as the **central bank** – an institution designed to regulate the quantity of money made available in the economy, called the **money supply**. Two of the most important central banks in Europe are the European Central Bank and the Bank of England. Other major central banks around the world include the US central bank – the Federal Reserve – the Bank of Japan and the People's Bank of China. We'll take a closer look at the European Central Bank and the Bank of England in a moment. Before then, however, we can look at some features of central banks in general.

> **central bank** an institution designed to regulate the quantity of money in the economy
> **money supply** the quantity of money available in the economy

The central bank of an economy has the power to increase or decrease the amount of currency in that economy. The set of actions taken by the central bank in order to affect the money supply is known as **monetary policy**. In simple metaphorical terms, you can imagine the central bank printing banknotes and dropping them by helicopter. Similarly, you can imagine the central bank using a giant vacuum cleaner to suck banknotes out of people's wallets. Although in practice the central bank's methods for changing the money supply are more complex and subtle than this, the helicopter-vacuum metaphor is a good first approximation to the meaning of monetary policy.

> **monetary policy** the set of actions taken by the central bank in order to affect the money supply

We discuss later in this chapter how the central bank actually changes the money supply, but it is worth noting here that an important tool the central bank can use is **open-market operations** – the purchase and sale of non-monetary assets from and to the banking sector. For example, if the central bank decides to increase the money supply, it can do this by creating currency and using it to buy bonds from the public in the bond market. After the purchase, the extra currency is in the hands of the public. Thus, an open-market purchase of bonds by the central bank increases the money supply. Conversely, if the central bank decides to decrease the money supply, it can do this by selling bonds from its portfolio to the public. After the sale, the currency it receives for the bonds is out of the hands of the public. Thus, an open-market sale of bonds by the central bank decreases the money supply.

> **open-market operations** the purchase and sale of non-monetary assets from and to the banking sector by the central bank

The central bank of an economy is an important institution because changes in the money supply can profoundly affect the economy. One of the *Ten Principles of Economics* is that prices rise when too much money is printed. Another of the *Ten Principles of Economics* is that society faces a short-run trade-off between inflation and unemployment. The power of the central bank rests on these principles. For reasons we discuss more fully in the coming chapters, the central bank's policy decisions have an important influence on the economy's rate of inflation in the long run and the economy's employment and production in the short run. In particular, because of the link between the amount of money in the economy and the inflation rate (the rate of increase of prices), the central bank is often seen as the guardian of price stability in a modern economy charged with the duty to maintain inflation at or near an inflation target – a policy we'll discuss more fully in the coming chapters. To be precise, the central bank should perhaps be thought of as the guardian of inflation stability, rather than price stability, since even with a constant, low rate of inflation, prices are by definition rising. Still, if inflation is low and stable, prices might be said to be rising in a stable fashion – and, in any case, this usage is now well established, so we'll follow suit.

THE EUROPEAN CENTRAL BANK AND THE EUROSYSTEM

The **European Central Bank (ECB)**, located in Frankfurt, Germany, was officially created on 1 June 1998 as a number of European countries had decided that they wished to enter European Monetary Union (EMU) and have the same currency – the euro – circulating among them. We'll discuss the pros and cons of monetary union in a later chapter. For now, though, we just note that if a group of countries has the same currency, then it makes sense for the countries in the group to have a common monetary policy, and the ECB was set up for precisely this purpose. There were originally 11 countries making up the euro area: Austria, Belgium, Germany, Spain, France, Ireland, Italy, Luxembourg, the Netherlands, Portugal and Finland. By 2010, there were 16 countries, the new additions being Greece, Cyprus, Slovakia, Slovenia and Malta, Estonia adopted the euro in 2011 and Latvia adopted the euro in January 2014 to make the euro area currently consist of 18 countries.

> **European Central Bank (ECB)** the overall central bank of the 18 countries comprising the European Monetary Union

The primary objective of the ECB is to promote price stability throughout the euro area and to design and implement monetary policy that is consistent with this objective. The ECB operates with the assistance of the national central banks in each of the euro area countries, such as the Banque de France, the Banca d'Italia, the Bank of Greece and the German Bundesbank. The network made up of the ECB together with the 18 euro area national central banks is termed the **Eurosystem**.

> **Eurosystem** the system made up of the ECB plus the national central banks of each of the 18 countries comprising the European Monetary Union

The implementation of monetary policy by the ECB is under the control of the Executive Board, which comprises the President and Vice-President of the ECB and four other people of high standing in the banking profession. While the Executive Board – as the name suggests – is responsible for *executing* monetary policy, the monetary policy of the ECB is actually designed by the Governing Council, which comprises the whole of the Executive Board plus the governors of the national central banks in the Euro system (22 people in total). The Governing Council, which meets twice a month in Frankfurt, is the most important decision-making body of the ECB and decides, for example, on the level of the ECB's key interest rate, the refinancing rate. The Governing Council also decides how to interpret its duty to achieve price stability. In October 1998 it agreed that price stability should be defined as a 'year-on-year increase in prices of less than 2 per cent as measured by the annual change in a harmonized index of consumer prices throughout the euro area'. A problem with this definition of price stability, however, is that 'less than 2 per cent' is a little vague – an annual inflation rate of 1 per cent and an annual inflation rate of 0 per cent are both less than 2 per cent. In fact, some people were worried that the ECB might even aim for falling prices or negative inflation in order to achieve its target of less than 2 per cent. As we discuss more fully in the coming chapters, this would tend sharply to reduce output and employment in the economy, especially in the short to medium run. In May 2003, therefore, the Governing Council confirmed its official definition thus:

> in the pursuit of price stability, it aims to maintain inflation rates below but close to 2 per cent over the medium term.

An important feature of the ECB and of the Euro system in general is its independence. When performing Euro system-related tasks, neither the ECB, nor a national central bank, nor any member of their decision-making bodies is allowed to seek or take instructions from any external body, including any member governments or any European Union institutions.

The President of the ECB and other members of the Executive Board are appointed for a minimum non-renewable term of office of eight years (although a system of staggered appointments was used for the first Executive Board for members other than the President in order to ensure continuity) and the governors of the 18 national central banks in the Euro system are appointed for a minimum renewable term of office of five years.

THE BANK OF ENGLAND

The **Bank of England** was founded in 1694, although it is not the oldest European central bank (the Swedish Riksbank was founded in 1668). Arguably the most significant event in the Bank of England's 300-year history was when the UK government granted it independence in the setting of interest rates in 1997, which was formalized in an Act of Parliament in 1998. The important body within the Bank that makes the decision on the level at which to set the Bank's key interest rate, the repo rate, is the Monetary Policy Committee (MPC). The MPC consists of the Governor and two Deputy Governors of the Bank of England, two other members appointed by the Bank after consultation with the Chancellor of the Exchequer (the UK finance minister) and four other members appointed by the Chancellor. The Governor and the two Deputy Governors serve five-year renewable terms of office, while other MPC members serve three-year renewable terms. The MPC meets monthly and its interest rate decision is announced immediately after the meeting.

Bank of England the central bank of the United Kingdom

Like the ECB, one of the Bank of England's primary duties is to deliver price stability. Also in common with the ECB, it enjoys independence in the setting of monetary policy – and in particular interest rates – in order to achieve the objective of price stability. Unlike the ECB, however, the Bank of England does not have the freedom to define for itself precisely what 'price stability' means in this context. This is done by the UK government and, in particular, by the Chancellor of the Exchequer. In fact, the 1998 Bank of England Act requires that the Chancellor write to the Governor of the Bank of England once a year to specify what price stability is to be defined as. Currently, the inflation target of 2 per cent is expressed in terms of an annual rate of inflation based on the consumer prices index (CPI). If the target is missed by more than 1 percentage point on either side, i.e. if the annual rate of CPI inflation is more than 3 per cent or less than 1 per cent, the Governor of the Bank of England must write an open letter to the Chancellor explaining the reasons why inflation has increased or fallen to such an extent and what the Bank proposes to do to ensure inflation comes back to the target.

In changes made to financial regulation in the UK in June 2010, the Chancellor of the Exchequer announced that the Bank of England would have new responsibilities focusing on monetary policy and financial stability which have been confirmed in the Financial Services Bill 2012. The new system led to the Bank of England getting additional responsibilities for financial stability, macro-prudential supervision and oversight of micro-prudential supervision. These regulatory functions are overseen by three main groups, the Prudential Regulatory Authority (PRA), which is responsible for day-to-day supervision of bank safety and soundness (micro-prudential policy), the Financial Policy Committee (FPC), charged with 'identifying, monitoring and addressing systemic risks to the UK financial system' and the Financial Conduct Authority (FCA) which manages protection of investors, market supervision and regulation and the conduct of banks and financial services.

SELF TEST If the central bank wants to increase the supply of money, how may it do so?

BANKS AND THE MONEY SUPPLY

So far we have introduced the concept of 'money' and discussed how the central bank controls the supply of money by buying and selling government bonds and other assets in open-market operations. Although this explanation of the money supply is correct, it is not complete. In particular, it omits the central role that banks play in the monetary system.

Recall that the amount of money you hold includes both currency (the banknotes in your wallet and coins in your pocket) and demand deposits (the balance in your current account). Because demand deposits are held in banks, the behaviour of banks can influence the quantity of demand deposits in the economy and, therefore, the money supply. This section examines how banks affect the money supply and how they complicate the central bank's job of controlling the money supply.

The Simple Case of 100 Per Cent Reserve Banking

To see how banks influence the money supply, it's useful to imagine first a world without any banks at all. In this simple world, currency is the only form of money. To be concrete, let's suppose that the total quantity of currency is €100. The supply of money is, therefore, €100.

Now suppose that someone opens a bank, appropriately called First European Bank. First European Bank is only a depository institution – that is, it accepts deposits but does not make loans. The purpose of the bank is to give depositors a safe place to keep their money. Whenever a person deposits some money, the bank keeps the money in its vault until the depositor comes to withdraw it or writes a cheque against his or her balance. Deposits that banks have received but have not lent out are called **reserves**. In this imaginary economy, all deposits are held as reserves, so this system is called 100 per cent reserve banking.

---

reserves deposits that banks have received but have not loaned out

---

We can express the financial position of First European Bank with a T-account, which is a simplified accounting statement that shows changes in a bank's assets and liabilities. Here is the T-account for First European Bank if the economy's entire €100 of money is deposited in the bank:

FIRST EUROPEAN BANK

Assets	Liabilities
Reserves €100.00	Deposits €100.00

On the left-hand side of the T-account are the bank's assets of €100 (the reserves it holds in its vaults). On the right-hand side of the T-account are the bank's liabilities of €100 (the amount it owes to its depositors). Notice that the assets and liabilities of First European Bank exactly balance.

Now consider the money supply in this imaginary economy. Before First European Bank opens, the money supply is the €100 of currency that people are holding. After the bank opens and people deposit their currency, the money supply is the €100 of demand deposits. (There is no longer any currency outstanding, for it is all in the bank vault.) Each deposit in the bank reduces currency and raises demand deposits by exactly the same amount, leaving the money supply unchanged. Thus, *if banks hold all deposits in reserve, banks do not influence the supply of money.*

Money Creation With Fractional-Reserve Banking

Eventually, the bankers at First European Bank may start to reconsider their policy of 100 per cent reserve banking. Leaving all that money sitting idle in their vaults seems unnecessary. Why not use some of it to make loans? Families buying houses, firms building new factories and students at university would all be happy to pay interest to borrow some of that money for a while. Of course, First European Bank has to keep some reserves so that currency is available if depositors want to make withdrawals. But if the flow of new deposits is roughly the same as the flow of withdrawals, First European needs to keep only a fraction of its deposits in reserve. Thus, First European adopts a system called **fractional-reserve banking**.

> **fractional-reserve banking** a banking system in which banks hold only a fraction of deposits as reserves

The fraction of total deposits that a bank holds as reserves is called the **reserve ratio**. This ratio is determined by a combination of government regulation and bank policy. As we discuss more fully later in the chapter, the European Central Bank place a minimum on the amount of reserves that banks hold, called a *reserve requirement* (although, unusually among central banks, the Bank of England does not impose reserve requirements). In addition, banks may hold reserves above the legal minimum, called *excess reserves*, so they can be more confident that they will not run short of cash. Even when there are no minimum reserve requirements at all (as in the UK), banks will set their own reserve ratio at which they deem it is prudent to operate. For our purpose here, we just take the reserve ratio as given and examine what fractional-reserve banking means for the money supply.

> **reserve ratio** the fraction of deposits that banks hold as reserves

Let's suppose that First European has a reserve ratio of 10 per cent. This means that it keeps 10 per cent of its deposits in reserve and lends out the rest. Now let's look again at the bank's T-account:

FIRST EUROPEAN BANK

Assets		Liabilities	
Reserves	€10.00	Deposits	€100.00
Loans	€90.00		

First European still has €100 in liabilities because making the loans did not alter the bank's obligation to its depositors. But now the bank has two kinds of assets: it has €10 of reserves in its vault, and it has loans of €90. (These loans are liabilities of the people taking out the loans but they are assets of the bank making the loans, because the borrowers will later repay the bank.) In total, First European's assets still equal its liabilities.

Once again consider the supply of money in the economy. Before First European makes any loans, the money supply is the €100 of deposits in the bank. Yet when First European makes these loans, the money supply increases. The depositors still have demand deposits totalling €100, but now the borrowers hold €90 in currency. The money supply (which equals currency plus demand deposits) equals €190. Thus, *when banks hold only a fraction of deposits in reserve, banks create money.*

At first, this creation of money by fractional-reserve banking may seem too good to be true because it appears that the bank has created money out of thin air. To make this creation of money seem less miraculous, note that when First European Bank lends out some of its reserves and creates money, it does not create any wealth (wealth, as a concept, is a 'stock' as opposed to a flow). Loans from First European give the borrowers some currency and thus the ability to buy goods and services. Yet the borrowers are also taking on debts, so the loans do not make them any richer. In other words, as a bank creates the asset of money, it also creates a corresponding liability for its borrowers. At the end of this process of money creation, the economy is more liquid in the sense that there is more of the medium of exchange, but the economy is no wealthier than before.

The Money Multiplier

The creation of money does not stop with First European Bank. Suppose the borrower from First European uses the €90 to buy something from someone who then deposits the currency in Second European Bank. Here is the T-account for Second European Bank:

SECOND EUROPEAN BANK

Assets		Liabilities	
Reserves	€9.00	Deposits	€90.00
Loans	€81.00		

After the deposit, this bank has liabilities of €90. If Second European also has a reserve ratio of 10 per cent, it keeps assets of €9 in reserve and makes €81 in loans. In this way, Second European Bank creates an additional €81 of money. If this €81 is eventually deposited in Third European Bank, which also has a reserve ratio of 10 per cent, this bank keeps €8.10 in reserve and makes €72.90 in loans. Here is the T-account for Third European Bank:

THIRD EUROPEAN BANK

Assets		Liabilities	
Reserves	€8.10	Deposits	€81.00
Loans	€72.90		

The process goes on and on. Each time that money is deposited and a bank loan is made, more money is created. How much money is eventually created in this economy? Let's add it up:

Original deposit	= €100.00
First European lending	= €90.00 [= 0.9 × €100.00]
Second European lending	= €81.00 [= 0.9 × €90.00]
Third European lending	= €72.90 [= 0.9 × €81.00]
.	.
.	.
.	.
Total money supply	= €1,000.00

It turns out that even though this process of money creation can continue forever, it does not create an infinite amount of money. If you laboriously add the infinite sequence of numbers in the foregoing example, you find the €100 of reserves generates €1,000 of money. The amount of money the banking system generates with each euro of reserves is called the **money multiplier**. In this imaginary economy, where the €100 of reserves generates €1,000 of money, the money multiplier is 10. It is important to remember that there is no new cash being created in this process – banks do not print more notes and press more coins. Most transactions in modern economies are simply 'book entries'; when you get a bank statement telling you that there is a balance of €1,500 in your current account there is not a box with this sum of money stored somewhere in the bank's vault. However, the banking system is such that we have trust that if we did wish to withdraw all that money in cash the bank would have sufficient funds to be able to meet our demand. This is where a 'run on banks' causes so many problems; if a large number of account holders all wanted to withdraw their money as cash the bank is unlikely to have the funds to give to everyone and it would effectively be 'bankrupt'.

money multiplier the amount of money the banking system generates with each unit of reserves

What determines the size of the money multiplier? It turns out that the answer is simple: the money multiplier is the reciprocal of the reserve ratio. If R is the reserve ratio for all banks in the economy, then each euro of reserves generates $1/R$ euros of money. In our example, $R = 1/10$, so the money multiplier is 10.

This reciprocal formula for the money multiplier makes sense. If a bank holds €1,000 in deposits, then a reserve ratio of 1/10 (10 per cent) means that the bank must hold €100 in reserves. The money multiplier just turns this idea around: if the banking system as a whole holds a total of €100 in reserves, it can have only €1,000 in deposits. In other words, if R is the ratio of reserves to deposits at each bank (that is, the reserve ratio), then the ratio of deposits to reserves in the banking system (that is, the money multiplier) must be $1/R$.

This formula shows how the amount of money banks create depends on the reserve ratio. If the reserve ratio were only 1/20 (5 per cent), then the banking system would have 20 times as much in deposits as in reserves, implying a money multiplier of 20. Each euro of reserves would generate €20 of money. Similarly, if the reserve ratio were 1/5 (20 per cent), deposits would be 5 times reserves, the money multiplier would be 5, and each euro of reserves would generate €5 of money. Thus, the higher the reserve ratio, the less of each deposit banks lend out, and the smaller the money multiplier. In the special case of 100 per cent reserve banking, the reserve ratio is 1, the money multiplier is 1, and banks do not make loans or create money.

The Central Bank's Tools of Monetary Control

As we have already discussed, the central bank is responsible for controlling the supply of money in the economy. Now that we understand how fractional-reserve banking works, we are in a better position to understand how the central bank carries out this job. Because banks create money in a system of fractional-reserve banking, the central bank's control of the money supply is indirect. When the central bank decides to change the money supply, it must consider how its actions will work through the banking system.

In general, a central bank has three main tools in its monetary toolbox: open-market operations, the refinancing rate and reserve requirements.

Open-market Operations We introduced the idea of open-market operations earlier through two simple examples. Let's look at these again. If the central bank wants to increase the money supply, it can create currency and use it to buy bonds from the public in the bond market. After the purchase, the extra currency is in the hands of the public. Thus, an open-market purchase of bonds by the central bank increases the money supply. If, on the other hand, the central bank wants to decrease the money supply, it can sell bonds from its portfolio to the public. After the sale, the currency it receives for the bonds is out of the hands of the public. Thus an open-market sale of bonds by the central bank decreases the money supply. To be precise, the open-market operations discussed in these simple examples are called **outright open-market operations**, because they each involve an outright sale or purchase of non-monetary assets to or from the banking sector without a corresponding agreement to reverse the transaction at a later date.

> **outright open-market operations** the outright sale or purchase of non-monetary assets to or from the banking sector by the central bank without a corresponding agreement to reverse the transaction at a later date

The Refinancing Rate The central bank of an economy will set an interest rate at which it is willing to lend to commercial banks on a short-term basis. As we shall see, the name of this interest rate differs across central banks, although in general in this book we'll follow the practice of the European Central Bank and refer to it as the refinancing rate.

The way in which the central bank lends to the banking sector is through a special form of open-market operations. In the previous section we discussed the use of *outright* open-market operations. Although outright open-market operations have traditionally been used by central banks to regulate the money supply, central banks nowadays more often use a slightly more sophisticated form of open-market operations that involves buying bonds or other assets from banks and at the same time agreeing to sell them back later. When it does this, the central bank has effectively made a loan and taken the bonds or other assets as collateral or security on the loan. The central bank will have a list of eligible assets that it will accept as collateral – 'safe' assets such as government bonds or assets issued by large corporations, on which the risk of default by the issuer is negligible. The interest rate that the central bank charges on the loan is the refinancing rate. Because the central bank has bought the assets but the seller has agreed to buy them back later at an agreed price, this kind of open-market operation is often called a **repurchase agreement** or 'repo' for short. To see how central bank's use repos as a means of controlling the money supply and how this is affected by the refinancing rate, we need to look a little more closely at the way commercial banks lend money to one another and borrow from the central bank.

> **repurchase agreement** the sale of a non-monetary asset together with an agreement to repurchase it at a set price at a specified future date

As we discussed earlier, banks need to carry enough reserves to cover their lending and will generally aim for a certain ratio of reserves to deposits, known as the reserve ratio. The minimum reserve ratio may be set by the central bank, but even if it isn't, banks will still have a reserve ratio that they consider prudent. Now, because deposits and withdrawals at banks can fluctuate randomly, some banks may find that they have an excess of reserves one day (i.e. their reserve ratio is above the level the bank considers prudent or above the minimum reserve ratio, or both), while other banks may find that they are short of reserves and their reserve ratio is too low. Therefore, the commercial banks in an economy will generally lend money to one another on a short-term basis – overnight to a couple of weeks – so that banks with excess reserves can lend them to banks that have inadequate reserves to cover their lending. This market for short-term reserves is called the **money market**. If there is a *general* shortage of liquidity in the money market (because the banks together have done a lot of lending), then the short-term interest rate at which they lend to one another will begin to rise, while it will begin to fall if there is excess liquidity among banks. The central bank closely monitors the money market and may intervene in it in order to affect the supply of liquidity to banks, which in turn affects their lending and hence affects the money supply.

> **money market** the market in which the commercial banks lend money to one another on a short-term basis

Suppose, for example, that there is a shortage of liquidity in the market because the banks have been increasing their lending and they need to increase their reserves. A commercial bank may then attempt to obtain liquidity from the central bank by selling assets to the central bank and at the same time agreeing to purchase them back a short time later. As we said before, in this type of open-market operation the central bank effectively lends money to the bank and takes the assets as collateral on the loan. Because the commercial bank is legally bound to repurchase the assets at a set price, this is called a 'repurchase agreement' and the difference between the price the bank sells the assets to the central bank and the price at which it agrees to buy them back, expressed as an annualized percentage of the selling price, is called the repurchase or repo rate by the Bank of England and the refinancing rate by the European Central Bank. The ECB's **refinancing rate** is thus the rate at which it will lend to the banking sector of the euro area, while the **repo rate** is the rate at which the Bank of England lends short term to the UK banking sector.

> **refinancing rate** the interest rate at which the European Central Bank lends on a short-term basis to the euro area banking sector
> **repo rate** the interest rate at which the Bank of England lends on a short-term basis to the UK banking sector

In the example given, the central bank added liquidity to the banking system by lending reserves to banks. This would have the effect of increasing the money supply. Because the loans made through open-market operations are typically very short term, with a maturity of at most two weeks, however, the banks are constantly having to repay the loans and borrow again, or 'refinance' the loans. If the central bank wants to mop up liquidity it can simply decide not to renew some of the loans. In practice, however, the central bank will set a reference rate of interest – the Bank of England's repo rate or the ECB's refinancing rate – and will conduct open-market operations, adding to or mopping up liquidity, close to this reference rate.

In the USA the interest rate at which the Federal Reserve lends to the banking sector (corresponding to the ECB's refinancing rate or the Bank of England's repo rate) is called the **discount rate**.

> **discount rate** the interest rate at which the Federal Reserve lends on a short-term basis to the US banking sector

Now we can see why the setting of the central bank's refinancing rate is the key instrument of monetary policy. If the central bank raises the refinancing rate, commercial banks will try and pull in their lending rather than borrow reserves from the central bank, and so the money supply will fall. If the central bank lowers the refinancing rate, banks will feel freer to lend, knowing that they will be able to borrow more cheaply from the central bank in order to meet their reserve requirements, and so the money supply will tend to rise.

Reserve Requirements   The central bank may also influence the money supply with **reserve requirements**, which are regulations on the minimum amount of reserves that banks must hold against deposits. Reserve requirements influence how much money the banking system can create with each euro of reserves. An increase in reserve requirements means that banks must hold more reserves and, therefore, can lend out less of each euro that is deposited; as a result, it raises the reserve ratio, lowers the money multiplier and decreases the money supply. Conversely, a decrease in reserve requirements lowers the reserve ratio, raises the money multiplier and increases the money supply.

> **reserve requirements** regulations on the minimum amount of reserves that banks must hold against deposits

Central banks have traditionally tended to use changes in reserve requirements only rarely because frequent changes would disrupt the business of banking. When the central bank increases reserve requirements, for instance, some banks find themselves short of reserves, even though they have seen no change in deposits. As a result, they have to curtail lending until they build their level of reserves to the new required level.

As we have noted, the Bank of England no longer sets minimum reserve requirements but the European Central Bank does set minimum reserve requirements. The ECB applies reserves to the average reserve ratio over a specified period rather than at a single point in time. It does this to stop the amount of lending fluctuating wildly, in order to maintain stability in the money market. Hence, the ECB uses reserve requirements in order to maintain stability in the money market rather than as an instrument of policy by which to increase or decrease the money supply. Following the financial crisis, negotiations have taken place on improving banks' reserves to avoid the problems faced during the crisis. The so-called Basel III negotiations between 27 countries set new reserve requirements in September 2010. The new rules came into force in 2013 and are to be phased in over a period of six years (although some relaxation to the requirements on the capital reserves needed to survive a 30-day crisis was agreed in 2013 and will be phased in from 2015). The regulations mean that banks will have to have higher reserves to support lending; for every €50 of lending banks will have to have €3.50 of reserves compared to €1 prior to the Basel III agreement. This obviously more than triples the amount of reserves that banks will have to keep. If banks do not adhere to the new regulations then they risk seeing the authorities placing restrictions on their activities including paying out dividends to shareholders and bonuses to staff.

Quantitative Easing

During the financial crisis of 2007–2009, central banks adopted new tactics to try and support the economy, which involve market operations. One of the methods adopted was an asset purchasing facility (APF) or quantitative easing (QE). In the UK the Bank of England cut interest rates to 0.5 per cent and in the US rates fell to a target of between 0 and 0.25 per cent. Having effectively exhausted the use of lowering the price of money in the economy, central banks have looked at affecting the supply of money as part of their armoury in triggering economic activity. QE was the method adopted by the UK (authority to carry out QE was given in January 2009, although the first purchase was 11 March 2009) and the US (from March 2009).

All banks have accounts at the central bank, which are classed as 'reserves'. The process of QE involves the central bank buying assets from private sector institutions. These might include banks, pension funds and insurance companies. The type of assets purchased varies from bonds and gilt-edged stock to commercial paper (short-term promissory notes issued by companies with a maturity ranging up to 270 days but with an average of 30 days), equities and possibly toxic assets. When the central bank buys assets, these reserves increase.

In buying these assets, the central bank is effectively increasing the amount of money in the accounts of those who sell these assets. The purpose of the policy is to encourage banks and other financial institutions, who are the recipients of this additional money, to lend it out to businesses and consumers thus stimulating demand. An example may serve to help understand the process (we will use pounds in this example and assume the central bank is the Bank of England). Assume a bank has £1 billion worth of gilt-edged stock. It decides that it wants to sell £500 million worth. The Bank of England announces that it intends to purchase gilts at an auction and sets a specific date for the auction (normally a Monday and Wednesday each week for a specified period of time). The process takes place via what is called a 'reverse auction'. Rather than the buyer putting in bids for what they would be willing to pay for the item, the seller submits an electronic bid to the Bank stating what they would like to sell and at what price they would be willing to sell at. The Bank itself has a specified amount that it intends to buy at that time and the bids coming in from banks and other institutions may mean that the auction is oversubscribed (i.e. more bids to sell are received than the Bank intends to buy) and as a result the Bank is able to select which offers it will accept and at what price.

Assume our bank has been successful in its bid. It transfers the gilts to the Bank of England and in return receives a credit for £500 million. It can use this £500 million to lend to businesses for investment into equipment and machinery and consumers for mortgages or personal loans for cars, students loans, new furniture and so on. The additional spending on investment and consumer goods helps boost aggregate demand and so trigger economic growth. Given that the central bank is actively participating in the bond market we can also expect some effects through this market action. Remember, companies use the bond market as a means of raising funds. Over a period of time these bonds will mature and firms may issue new bonds to replace them. These new bond issues may have different coupon rates to existing ones depending on current conditions in the bond market. Assume that a company has issued a ten-year bond with a coupon, on issue, of 5 per cent. The price at which the bond sells on the market will not necessarily be the same as its par value (what it was originally issued at). The ratio of coupon in relation to the price gives investors the yield $\left(Yield = \dfrac{Coupon}{Price} \right)$. For example, if the company issues a €100 bond, with a coupon (interest) rate of 5 per cent, the yield will also be 5 per cent. However, if demand for this bond rises then its price may rise (to €105 for example) and as a result the yield will fall:

$$\left(\frac{5\ per\ cent}{105} = 4.76\ per\ cent \right).$$

This is the inverse relationship between bond prices and yield we introduced in an earlier chapter.

If the central bank intervenes to buy bonds the supply of bonds will fall and bond prices will rise. As bond prices rise, yields fall. If our company now issues a new bond it can offer that bond at a lower coupon (there is no incentive not to buy it since buying existing bonds does not give any better return). Using the example above, if our company wanted to issue a new bond to replace the matured €100 bond, then it could offer the bond at a coupon of 4.76 per cent (or slightly higher) and have every chance of raising the finance. For the company it is now raising funds at 4.76 per cent rather than 5 per cent. This means that firms are now able to borrow at cheaper rates. The rise in price of gilts and subsequent fall in yields reduces the spread (the difference between the interest rate on borrowed money and the return on the gilt). As the spread falls there is more incentive for the bank to look for improved returns elsewhere and it is hoped that it will consider lending to consumers and businesses (who may have been seen as being too risky previously) because the return is now greater.

QE, therefore, works in a variety of ways to influence incentives as highlighted in Principle 4 of the *Ten Principles of Economics*. In essence, therefore, the principle of QE is simple; the acid test is whether it works or not. The central bank is in a position to monitor the effects of the process as it collects data about money flows in the economy, the effect on the money supply, credit flows in corporate markets, interest rates on different types of lending (for example on mortgages) and the amount and type of lending taking place.

The type of debt bought by the central bank is critical to the success of the policy. Given the situation that many banks found themselves in as a result of the financial crisis, it was possible that if the central bank focused its purchases of assets from these institutions, then rather than lending out the money again and freeing up credit markets, banks may simply have used the receipts to build up their balance sheets. As a result the effect would be weaker than planned.

The Bank of England has admitted that it is difficult to know whether QE is working or how long it would take to see any measurable effects. One of the problems is something called the *counterfactual* – what the situation would have been if QE was not implemented. By the end of December 2012, the Bank of England had spent £375 billion on QE. If it had not spent this £375 billion on QE what state would the economy be in? Would it have been in a much worse state and if so how much worse?

Problems in Controlling the Money Supply

Through the setting of its refinancing rate and the associated open-market operations, the central bank can exert an important degree of control over the money supply. Yet the central bank's control of the money supply is not precise. The central bank must wrestle with two problems, each of which arises because much of the money supply is created by the system of fractional-reserve banking.

The first problem is that the central bank does not control the amount of money that households choose to hold as deposits in banks. The more money households deposit, the more reserves banks have, and the more money the banking system can create. And the less money households deposit, the less reserves banks have, and the less money the banking system can create. To see why this is a problem, suppose that one day people begin to lose confidence in the banking system and, therefore, decide to withdraw deposits and hold more currency. When this happens, the banking system loses reserves and creates less money. The money supply falls, even without any central bank action.

The second problem of monetary control is that the central bank does not control the amount that bankers choose to lend. When money is deposited in a bank, it creates more money only when the bank lends it out. Because banks can choose to hold excess reserves instead, the central bank cannot be sure how much money the banking system will create. For instance, suppose that one day bankers become more cautious about economic conditions and decide to make fewer loans and hold greater reserves. In this case, the banking system creates less money than it otherwise would. Because of the bankers' decision, the money supply falls.

Hence, in a system of fractional-reserve banking, the amount of money in the economy depends in part on the behaviour of depositors and bankers. Because the central bank cannot control or perfectly predict this behaviour, it cannot perfectly control the money supply.

SELF TEST Describe how banks create money. ● If the ECB wanted to use three of its policy tools to decrease the money supply, what would it do?

Changes in Banking and the Financial Crisis

A traditional view of banking is closely allied with the idea of prudence. Being prudent may make for safe banking but it does not necessarily satisfy the demands of shareholders for ever larger profits. In the latter part of the 1990s and through to 2008, banks broadened the scope of their activities to generate higher profits. The financial crisis of 2007–2009 was due, in part, to banks taking on riskier activities and an increasingly blurred demarcation from a bank's retail (their dealings with members of the public) and wholesale operations (where the bank deals with corporate and other financial institutions). We have seen how financial institutions used 'quants' to try and reduce risk. This was part of the process that led to the growth of sub-prime lending. With the benefit of hindsight it might seem rather foolish for anyone, let alone a bank, to have contemplated lending money to people with bad credit histories and low incomes.

The growth in the housing market during this period along with the changes brought about by deregulation of financial markets in North America, Europe and the UK created the circumstances which allowed banks and other mortgage lenders to expand the amount of loans they made. Under 'traditional' lending regimes banks would have had to have set aside reserves to cover the loans that they had made. That assumes, of course, that such loans appeared on the bank's balance sheet. Innovation in the financial services industry and deregulation coupled with some ingenious thinking by the quants led to ways being developed which allowed banks to lend funds without it appearing on their balance sheets and as a result they were able to offload the risk to others as well as allow more and more lending to be possible.

In our example of reserve banking, reserves were assumed to be 10 per cent. Banks do not simply wait for deposits to be made and then use those deposits as reserves against loan multiples. Banks want to make loans as this is one key way in which they can make profits. If they want to increase lending, therefore, they have to attract sufficient deposits to provide the reserves needed. For example, assume a bank wants to increase lending by €1 billion. It knows that it has to have cash reserves to cover such lending of €100 million (10 per cent of €1 billion). If it set reserves lower, say at 8 per cent, then it would only have to attract €80 million in deposits. The bank therefore has to manage the risks inherent in its balance sheet. It has to make sure that any loan defaults are not more than the amount it has in reserve. Under normal circumstances it will have to market its services and products aggressively in order to attract deposits of €100 million. In doing so it will have to offer more attractive interest rates and this will cut the profitability of its loans.

However, if the bank can make €1 billion of loans without the loans appearing on its balance sheet then it does not have to attract the deposits to act as reserves. These off-balance sheet loans attract income in the form of interest and fees. The result is a greater capacity for lending whilst increasing potential profits for the bank. Banks found that they could put together collections of debt and sell them on. These parcels of debt did have risk attached to them but this risk could be reduced by taking out credit default swaps. This securitization of assets represented one of the innovations in banking that grew with the expansion of sub-prime lending.

Securitization of Assets The basis of the process lay in the fact that the assets involved generated cash flows over a period of time. Securitization takes loans off the balance sheet and so the bank does not have to set aside reserves to cover those loans. This means that the bank has more scope for increasing lending. Assume a bank has agreed to lend 1,000 individuals mortgages for property with each individual borrowing €100,000. The bank is known as the *originator*. These mortgages could be bundled up to form €1 billion worth of debt. Mathematicians analyse the debt and make an assessment that the debt has a 1 per cent chance of default. That is to say, of the 1,000 individuals associated with this debt, ten are likely to default at some point over the lifetime of the debt. The bank can present the debt package to a credit rating agency and, given the limited risk involved as a result of the pooling of the debt, is able to access a favourable credit rating.

Having secured an appropriate credit rating for the package of debt the bank then sets up what is called a *special purpose vehicle* or SPV. The establishment of an SPV allows the bank to separate its financial obligations. Rather than buyers of the debt having a claim on the bank as a whole in case of default, the setting up of an SPV means that the investor has a claim against the SPV but not the bank. Equally, the investor has the right to receive payments first by dealing with an SPV. The SPV buys the collection of debt and will sell it to investors which may be other banks and financial institutions. The funds raised by the SPV allow it to be able to buy the debt from the bank. The SPV will issue bonds for this purpose. For the prospective investor the bond is associated with the stream of cash flows from the package of loans which also have a relatively high rate of interest attached to them. Given that the debt package has been given a high credit rating, the risk associated with the investment is considered relatively low. The investor is protected by the value of the underlying assets. If there was a default on any of the loans the bank had the option of seizing the properties which are the security for the original loan.

The SPV will issue bonds for a total value lower than the package of debt. The difference is the first-loss position of the originator (the bank in this example). The aim is to ensure that the potential loss on the pool of debt is not greater than the difference between the total value of the pool and the value of the bonds issued to sell on the debt. In our example, the pool of debt, the collection of mortgages, is worth €1 billion. The SPV will receive the mortgage payments and uses the cash flows to pay the bond interest and the principal. The debt is sold by the SPV for €950 million – the difference, therefore being €50 million. Analysis shows that the likely default losses on this package of debt would be no more than €30 million. This means that the cash inflows from mortgage owners is sufficient to pay the investors their money back – €950 million This represents a 3 per cent loss rate based on the total value of the debt package.

The SPV issues shares in itself and, therefore, becomes a subsidiary company of the bank (or originator) with its own legal status. Shares may be bought by the originator and by other parties in the financial community. The attraction of doing so is that the SPV generates high returns based on the flow of cash of the underlying asset (the mortgage). The benefit of setting up an SPV for the bank is that it transfers liabilities to the SPV and therefore these do not appear on its balance sheet. As a result the bank does not have to set aside reserves to cover these loans and this leaves it free to increase lending or engage in deals which further expand its earnings and profits. Such activity may include providing finance for acquisitions or making loans to hedge funds. The setting up of an SPV also protects investors. If the bank (which originated the debt) fails, then creditors of the bank (those to whom the bank owes money) cannot make any claim against investors given that the SPV is a separate legal entity. Equally, if the SPV fails in some way then the investor does not have recourse to any claim against the bank or the originator. The bank can also earn commission on the sale of the debt to the SPV.

The issue of bonds by the SPV would be in bundles, called *tranches*, which reflect different levels of risk. Given these different levels of risk, different types of investors would be attracted for any particular tranche. Each tranche might relate to the maturity date of the mortgages in the pool or be associated with a different rate of interest, but typically in sub-prime securitization there were six tranches (known as '6-pack deals'). Each tranche can be sold separately and much of this bundled debt could be 'insured' using CDS.

The global nature of the financial system meant that what was created was a complex web of financial transactions that built high levels of interdependence among those involved but where few had any real knowledge of the extent of this interdependence. In essence, the whole structure of mortgage lending was dependent on the ability of those who had taken out mortgages (including sub-prime) to be able to pay the principal and interest on their loans. When the number of borrowers defaulting on their repayments started to rise in the middle of the 2000s, the structure began to become unstable and the full extent of the interdependence began to reveal itself.

Mortgages with rates that can change are referred to as variable rate or adjustable rate mortgages. Most of these mortgages are linked not simply to central bank base rate but to 'LIBOR', the London Interbank Offered Rate, which is a benchmark set of interest rates which determine other interest rates in the economy and is the rate at which banks will lend to each other in the London money markets. In the United States around $350 trillion of loans are based on LIBOR.

Each morning the British Bankers' Association gets quotes from 16 major banks on the rates at which they are prepared to borrow ten currencies with 15 different maturities. These maturities are the spot/overnight next (i.e. for loans made today and repaid tomorrow), one week, two weeks, one month, two months and so on up to a maximum of 12 months. Whilst ten currencies are quoted, the four main ones are the dollar, British pound, euro and Japanese yen.

The quotes are ranked in order of size and an average of the middle two quantities taken to give the LIBOR for that currency. The details are published at 11.30 a.m. every morning and form the basis of short-term lending. If LIBOR rates rise then adjustable rate mortgages that are tied to it also rise. Some

73 per cent of adjustable rate sub-prime mortgages in the US were based on six-month LIBOR and not the Federal Funds rate in the period April–September 2007.

From around 2005, central banks began pushing up interest rates to counter inflationary pressures. As interest rates rose, borrowers, especially those on sub-prime mortgages, began to feel the pressure and reports of the number of defaults on sub-prime loans began to rise. Once mortgage defaults began to rise faster the number of financial institutions affected and their exposure became clearer. The whole edifice was based on the expectation that the underlying assets would continue to generate the income stream over time – in other words, that the very large majority of mortgage holders would continue to pay their monthly mortgage repayments. As mortgage rates rose borrowers found it increasingly difficult to meet their monthly payments.

If mortgage payers default on loans then banks who lent money to SPVs can call in that debt. Banks who set up the SPV may then have to take the assets of the SPV back onto its balance sheet. This not only limits their ability to lend further because they now have to put aside reserves to cover these liabilities which are now on their balance sheet, but they may also have to write down the value of the assets, further damaging their balance sheet and ability to lend. Every day, banks have obligations to meet – loans they have taken out that need paying off, interest payments, CDS that mature, bonds that need to be paid, etc. They must have sufficient liquid funds to be able to meet these obligations. Many banks borrow the funds they need from the interbank market. As the sub-prime market collapsed, the exposure to bad debt started to become more obvious and a number of banks reported significant write-downs and losses. Confidence in the banking system, so important to its functioning, began to fall. Banks were not sure of their own exposure to these bad debts (referred to as **toxic debt**) and so were also unsure about the extent of other banks' exposure. Interbank lending began to become much tighter as banks were unwilling to lend to each other and they also faced the task of trying to shore up their own balance sheets.

> **toxic debt** mortgage-backed securities and other debt (such as bonds) that are not able to be repaid in many cases because the value of the assets against which they are secured have fallen significantly

A significant proportion of the funds that banks borrow are from each other. As mentioned above, the rate at which they borrow from each other is LIBOR. Under normal circumstances, the difference between bank rate and LIBOR is small and stable. In times when credit is scarce, the supply of loans falls and as a result the price rises. Between March 2008 and October 2008 LIBOR rose sharply. Central banks around the world responded to the tightness in the credit market, now termed the 'credit crunch', by cutting interest rates and injecting funds in to the markets. It took until June 2008 for LIBOR gradually to fall back to the Fed Funds level, reflecting the continued tightness in the credit market. Accessing credit was, therefore, far more expensive and limited in nature and the higher price of borrowing was passed onto the consumer – individuals and businesses. As business loans are less easy to obtain or more expensive, businesses find it difficult to manage their cash flow and insolvency can result.

Around this time, regulators began investigating reports of irregularities in the way in which LIBOR was being set. Subsequent investigations uncovered that traders at a number of banks had systematically attempted to fix LIBOR rates. Rates were being set artificially low with the result being that the true cost of money in the markets was not being reflected in the interest rate. The scandal raised serious issues for the necessity of trust in the banking and financial system so that decisions can be based on accurate market data. In the wake of the investigations a number of banks were fined, senior executives of some banks resigned and legal action is being taken against traders involved in the scandal.

The Crisis Unfolds In August 2008, the problems facing banks began to mount – how far the attempts to fix LIBOR contributed to the problems is still being debated. However, in March 2008, the US investment bank Bear Stearns' exposure to sub-prime markets led it to seek support from the US Federal Reserve (the Fed); a year before, New Century Financial had sought protective bankruptcy and needed financial assistance. Other banks with a heavy exposure to sub-prime began to announce losses and write-downs only to have to issue worse revised figures a short time later. Bear Stearns was rescued by being acquired by J.P. Morgan Chase. In the UK, Northern Rock suffered a run on its assets as account holders queued to get their money before the bank collapsed – the first run on a UK bank for more than a hundred years. The UK government had to step in to take Northern Rock into public hands and nationalize it.

In the US, it became obvious that two of the major players in the mortgage market: the Federal National Mortgage Association, commonly known as 'Fannie Mae'; and the Federal Home Loan Mortgage Corporation, known as 'Freddie Mac', were facing deep financial problems. Their business involved buying mortgages from lenders and then selling on the debt to investors. They effectively guaranteed the borrowing for millions of mortgage owners and accounted for around half of the US mortgage market which was worth $12 trillion. Such was their importance that the US authorities stepped in to support them. As in the UK with Northern Rock, the US government announced in early September 2008 that it was going to take temporary ownership of the two companies to save them from collapse. If the two had become insolvent, house prices in the US, which were falling at rates of around 15 per cent in some areas, would have been likely to have fallen even further, and a larger number of people would have fallen into negative equity. It was estimated at the time that up to around 10 per cent of US homeowners were facing difficulties in meeting their mortgage payments, and risked having their homes repossessed.

CONCLUSION

In *Le Bourgeois Gentilhomme,* a play by the French playwright Molière, a character called Monsieur Jourdain finds out what prose is and then exclaims, 'Good heavens! For more than 40 years I have been speaking prose without knowing it!' In the same way, newcomers to economics may sometimes be surprised to find that they have been participating in the monetary system of their economy for years without realizing it. Ever since you got your first pocket money you have been using fiat money. Ever since you got your first bank account you have been participating in fractional-reserve banking and the creation of money. Whenever we buy or sell anything, we are relying on the extraordinarily useful social convention called 'money'. Now that we know what money is and what determines its supply, we can discuss how changes in the quantity of money affect the economy. We begin to address that topic in the next chapter.

IN THE NEWS

Open Market Operations

Whilst it is difficult for central banks to control the money supply in precise ways, the use of open market operations can be a useful tool in managing relatively short-term interest rates.

China's Central Bank in Record Market Intervention

In February 2013, it was announced that The People's Bank of China (PBOC), the country's central bank, had engaged in open market operations creating a record in the process. The PBOC bought 450 billion yuan (€54 billion) worth of assets which represented the largest single day injection into the money markets beating the previous record of 395 billion yuan (€47.4 billion) in October 2012. The operation involved the purchase of 14-day reverse bond repurchase agreements. The PBOC purchased securities from the money markets with the agreement to sell them back at a higher price in 14 days (this is the opposite to a repo and so for money market institutions selling the securities and buying them back in 14 days it is a repo). In the first instance, therefore, the PBOC had injected funds into the money markets but sucked out more funds when it sold the securities back.

Part of the reason for doing this was to meet liquidity needs in the markets prior to the Spring Festival Holiday period in China. Around this time, Chinese citizens tend to withdraw more cash to spend on gifts, food, travel and entertainment for the holiday period. The open market operations will provide the liquidity to be able to cope with this demand rather than having to adjust bank reserve requirements. Chinese officials expressed some concern that cutting reserve requirements for banks might stimulate inflation and so using open market operations in this way helps to reduce the threat of rising inflation and keeps interest rates under control. If repo rates are rising, it is a sign that demand for money is higher than supply and in the past, observers have noted that there were spikes in repo rates when holiday periods approached or as the month or quarter approached. By using open market operations in this way, the PBOC sent a signal to the markets that it intends to manage interest rates. When the demand for money increases as during holiday periods, the injection of funds into the system helps reduce the pressure on interest rates to rise and when demand falls back, the selling back of the securities reduces the supply of funds and thus maintains interest rates at a more stable level than without the operation.

Questions

1 **What is meant by the term open market operations?**

2 **What is a repurchase agreement and why was the action of the PBOC termed a 'reverse repurchase agreement'?**

3 **Assume no intervention in the money markets by the PBOC. Use a supply and demand diagram with interest rates on the vertical axis (the price of money) to show how spikes in interest rates can occur in times when the demand for money rises.**

4 **Why might Chinese officials be concerned that a cut in reserve requirements cause inflation?**

5 **Again, using a supply and demand diagram, explain how the open market operations of the PBOC can help to stabilize interest rates.**

The People's Bank of China, the central bank of China is likely to become an increasingly important player in global financial markets as China's economy continues to grow.

SUMMARY

- The term *money* refers to assets that people regularly use to buy goods and services.

- Money serves three functions. As a medium of exchange, it provides the item used to make transactions. As a unit of account, it provides the way in which prices and other economic values are recorded. As a store of value, it provides a way of transferring purchasing power from the present to the future.

- Commodity money, such as gold, is money that has intrinsic value: it would be valued even if it were not used as money. Fiat money, such as paper euros or pounds, is money without intrinsic value: it would be worthless if it were not used as money.

- In an advanced economy, money takes the form of currency and various types of bank deposits, such as current accounts.

- A central bank is an institution designed to regulate the quantity of money in an economy.

- The European Central Bank is the overall central bank for the 18 countries participating in European Monetary Union. The Euro system is made up of the European Central Bank plus the corresponding 18 national central banks.

- The UK central bank is the Bank of England. It was granted independence in the setting of interest rates in 1997.

- Central banks control the money supply primarily through the refinancing rate and the associated open-market operations. An increase in the refinancing rate means that it is more expensive for banks to borrow from the central bank on a short-term basis if they are short of reserves to cover their lending, and so they will tend to reduce their lending and the money supply will contract. Conversely, a reduction in the refinancing rate will tend to expand the money supply.

- The central bank can also use outright open-market operations to affect the money supply: a purchase of government bonds and other assets from the banking sector increases the money supply, and the sale of assets decreases the money supply. The central bank can also expand the money supply by lowering minimum reserve requirements and it can contract the money supply by raising minimum reserve requirements.

- When banks lend out some of their deposits, they increase the quantity of money in the economy. Because banks may choose to hold excess reserves, they can affect the supply of money beyond the control of the central bank. When households deposit money in banks, banks can use these deposits to create money. But the central bank cannot control exactly how much money that households wish to deposit. Because of these two factors, the central bank's control of the money supply is imperfect.

- Central banks adopted quantitative easing as a means of easing the financial crisis and stimulating the economy through buying assets from the banking sector and expanding the money supply.

- A bank run occurs when depositors suspect that a bank may go bankrupt and, therefore, 'run' to the bank to withdraw their deposits. Many countries have a system of deposit insurance and central banks are lenders of last resort so bank runs can be managed more effectively.

- The financial crisis revealed the extent to which banking has changed in the last 30 years and in response to the crisis, governments have attempted to impose more stringent regulations on banks.

QUESTIONS FOR REVIEW

1 What distinguishes money from other assets in the economy?

2 What is commodity money? What is fiat money? Which kind do we use?

3 What are demand deposits, and why should they be included in the stock of money?

4 Who is responsible for setting monetary policy at the European Central Bank? How is this group chosen? Who is responsible for setting monetary policy at the Bank of England? How is this group chosen?

5 If the central bank wants to increase the money supply with outright open-market operations, what does it do?

6 Why don't banks hold 100 per cent reserves? How is the amount of reserves banks hold related to the amount of money the banking system creates?

7 What is the refinancing rate? What happens to the money supply when the European Central Bank raises its refinancing rate?

8 What are reserve requirements? What happens to the money supply when the ECB raises reserve requirements?

9 What is quantitative easing and in what way does it help to counter slow economic growth in an economy?

10 Why can't central banks control the money supply perfectly?

PROBLEMS AND APPLICATIONS

1 What characteristics of an asset make it useful as a medium of exchange? As a store of value?

2 Suppose that someone in one of the euro area countries discovered an easy way to counterfeit €100 banknotes. How would this development affect the monetary system of the euro area? Explain.

3 Your uncle repays a €100 loan from Tenth European Bank (TEB) by writing a €100 cheque from his TEB current account. Use T-accounts to show the effect of this transaction on your uncle and on TEB. Has your uncle's wealth changed? Explain.

4 Beleaguered European Bank (BEB) holds €250 million in deposits and maintains a reserve ratio of 10 per cent.

　a. Show a T-account for BEB.

　b. Now suppose that BEB's largest depositor withdraws €10 million in cash from her account. If BEB decides to restore its reserve ratio by reducing the amount of loans outstanding, show its new T-account.

　c. Explain what effect BEB's action will have on other banks.

　d. Why might it be difficult for BEB to take the action described in part (b)? Discuss another way for BEB to return to its original reserve ratio.

5 You take €100 you had kept under your pillow and deposit it in your bank account. If this €100 stays in the banking system as reserves and if banks hold reserves equal to 10 per cent of deposits, by how much does the total amount of deposits in the banking system increase? By how much does the money supply increase?

6 The European Central Bank conducts a €10 million open market purchase of eligible assets from the banking sector. If the required reserve ratio is 10 per cent, what is the largest possible increase in the money supply that could result? Explain. What is the smallest possible increase? Explain.

7 Suppose that the T-account for First European Bank is as follows:

Assets		Liabilities	
Reserves	€100,000	Deposits	€500,000
Loans	€400,000		

　a. If the ECB requires banks to hold 5 per cent of deposits as reserves, how much in excess reserves does First European now hold?

　b. Assume that all other banks hold only the required amount of reserves. If First European decides to reduce its reserves to only the required amount, by how much would the economy's money supply increase?

8 Suppose that the reserve requirement for current deposits is 10 per cent and that banks do not hold any excess reserves.

　a. If the ECB decides not to renew €1 million of loans it previously made to the euro area banking sector, what is the effect on the economy's reserves and money supply?

　b. Now suppose the ECB lowers the reserve requirement to 5 per cent, but banks choose to hold another 5 per cent of deposits as excess reserves. Why might banks do so? What is the overall change in the money multiplier and the money supply as a result of these actions?

9 The economy of Elmendyn contains 2,000 €1 coins.

　a. If people hold all money as currency, what is the quantity of money?

　b. If people hold all money as demand deposits, and banks maintain 100 per cent reserves, what is the quantity of money?

　c. If people hold equal amounts of currency and demand deposits, and banks maintain 100 per cent reserves, what is the quantity of money?

　d. If people hold all money as demand deposits, and banks maintain a reserve ratio of 10 per cent, what is the quantity of money?

　e. If people hold equal amounts of currency and demand deposits, and banks maintain a reserve ratio of 10 per cent, what is the quantity of money?

10 A bank bundles up €1 billion of mortgage debt with a forecast default ratio of 5 per cent. The debt is sold via an SPV to a group of investors for €800 million.

　a. The group of investors wish to reduce their risk. Explain how a credit default swap with an insurance company might help them to do this.

　b. There is a credit event and the original debt suffers a default ratio of 50 per cent. Explain how the originator and the investors might be affected by such an event.

11 MONEY GROWTH AND INFLATION

In 1930, the Lyons Maid company produced choc ices – which they described as chocolate-coated vanilla and coffee flavoured ice-cream bars – which were sold in UK confectionery shops for two old pence. Given that before the UK currency was decimalized in 1970 there were 240 old pence to the pound, this means that £1 would have bought you 120 choc ices in 1927. Today, a Wall's 'Chunky' choc ice – a chocolate-coated vanilla flavoured ice-cream bar – is priced at about 70p, so £1 today will buy you only 1.4 choc ices. This represents quite a substantial price rise.

You are probably not surprised at the increase in the price of ice cream. In advanced economies, most prices tend to rise over time. This increase in the overall level of prices is called *inflation*. Inflation may seem natural and inevitable to a person who has grown up in an advanced economy in western Europe or North America at the end of the 20th century, but in fact it is not inevitable at all. There were long periods in the 19th century during which, in some economies, most prices fell – a phenomenon called *deflation*.

Although inflation has been the norm in more recent history, there has been substantial variation in the rate at which prices rise. Inflation in the UK during the late 1990s and the first half of the 2000s was low and stable at round 2 per cent or so. However, in the mid-1970s, annual UK inflation, as measured by increases in the retail prices index, exceeded 20 per cent.

International data show an even broader range of inflation experiences. Germany after World War I experienced a spectacular example of inflation. The price of a newspaper rose from 0.3 marks in January 1921 to 70,000,000 marks less than two years later. Other prices rose by similar amounts. An extraordinarily high rate of inflation such as this is called *hyperinflation*. The German hyperinflation had such an adverse effect on the German economy that it is often viewed as one contributor to the rise to power of the National Socialists (Nazis) and, as a result, World War II. Over the past 50 years, with this episode still in mind, German policymakers have been extraordinarily averse to inflation, and Germany has had much lower inflation than most other countries of the world.

In more recent times there have been episodes of hyperinflation in the former Yugoslavia and in Zimbabwe. Inflation in Yugoslavia ran at 5 quadrillion per cent (5 with 15 zeros after it) between October 1993 and January 1995. The Zimbabwean authorities announced that inflation had reached 231,000,000 per cent in June 2008. However, the prices of some goods rose by considerably more. The Zimbabwean central bank reported that some goods on the black market had risen by 70,000,000 per cent. Laundry soap was one of the goods that had risen by this much, but cooking oil also rose by 60,000,000 per cent and sugar by 36,000,000 per cent. Inflation made almost every Zimbabwean a billionaire. Unskilled workers earned around Z$200,000,000,000 a month – at the time, equivalent to about US$10. In July 2008 the government issued a Z$100 billion note. If you had one it would just about have bought you a loaf of bread.

What determines whether an economy experiences inflation and, if so, how much? This chapter answers the question by developing the quantity theory of money. Chapter 1 summarized this theory as one of the *Ten Principles of Economics*: prices rise when the government prints too much money. This insight has a long and venerable tradition among economists. The quantity theory was discussed by the famous 18th-century British philosopher and economist, David Hume, and was advocated in the latter part of the 20th century by the prominent American economist Milton Friedman. This theory of inflation can explain both moderate inflations, such as those experienced in the United States, and hyperinflations, such as those outlined above.

After developing a theory of inflation, we turn to a related question: why is inflation a problem? At first glance, the answer to this question may seem obvious: inflation is a problem because people don't like it. In the 1970s, when the United Kingdom (along with many other economies) was experiencing a relatively high rate of inflation, opinion polls placed inflation as the most important issue facing the nation.

But what, exactly, are the costs that inflation imposes on a society? The answer may surprise you. Identifying the various costs of inflation is not as straightforward as it first appears. As a result, although all economists decry hyperinflation, some economists argue that the costs of moderate inflation are not nearly as large as the general public believes.

THE CLASSICAL THEORY OF INFLATION

We begin our study of inflation by developing the quantity theory of money. This theory is often called 'classical' because it was developed by some of the earliest thinkers about economic issues back in the 18th century such as David Hume, who are often referred to as the 'classical economists'. Most economists today rely on this theory to explain the long-run determinants of the price level and the inflation rate.

The Level of Prices and the Value of Money

Suppose over some period of time we observe a ten-fold increase in the price of an ice cream. What conclusion should we draw from the fact that people are willing to give up so much more money in exchange for an ice cream? It is possible that people have come to enjoy ice cream more. Yet, even if people's enjoyment of ice cream has increased, a large amount of the price rise is probably due to the fact that, over time, the money used to buy ice cream has become less valuable. Indeed, the first insight about inflation is that it is more about the value of money (the goods and services any given amount of money can be exchanged for) than about the value of goods.

This insight helps point the way towards a theory of inflation. When the consumer prices index (CPI) and other measures of the price level rise, commentators are often tempted to look at the many individual prices that make up these price indices: 'The CPI rose by 3 per cent last month, led by a 20 per cent rise in the price of coffee and a 27 per cent rise in the price of electricity.' Although this approach does contain some interesting information about what's happening in the economy, it also misses a key point: inflation is an economy-wide phenomenon that concerns, first and foremost, the value of the economy's medium of exchange.

The economy's overall price level can be viewed in two ways. So far, we have viewed the price level as the price of a basket of goods and services. When the price level rises, people have to pay more for the goods and services they buy. Alternatively, we can view the price level as a measure of the value of money. A rise in the price level means a lower value of money because each unit of money now buys a smaller quantity of goods and services.

It may help to express these ideas mathematically. Suppose P is the price level as measured, for instance, by the CPI or the GDP deflator. Then P measures the number of euros needed to buy a basket of goods and services. Now turn this idea around: the quantity of goods and services that can be bought with €1 equals $1/P$. In other words, if P is the price of goods and services measured in terms of money, $1/P$ is the value of money measured in terms of goods and services. Thus, when the overall price level rises, the value of money falls. We gave an example of this in relation to choc ices above.

Money Supply, Money Demand and Monetary Equilibrium

What determines the value of money? The answer to this question, like many in economics, is supply and demand. Just as the supply and demand for bananas determines the price of bananas, the supply and demand for money determines the value of money. Thus, our next step in developing the quantity theory of money is to consider the determinants of money supply and money demand.

First, consider money supply. In the preceding chapter we discussed how the central bank, together with the banking system, determines the supply of money. When the central bank sells bonds in open-market operations, it receives money in exchange and contracts the money supply. When the central bank buys government bonds, it pays out money and expands the money supply. In addition, if any of this money is deposited in banks which then hold it as reserves, the money multiplier swings into action, and these open-market operations can have an even greater effect on the money supply. For our purposes in this chapter, we ignore the complications introduced by the banking system and simply take the quantity of money supplied as a policy variable that the central bank controls.

Now consider money demand. Most fundamentally, the demand for money reflects how much wealth people want to hold in liquid form. Many factors influence the quantity of money demanded. The amount of currency that people hold in their wallets, for instance, depends on how much they rely on credit cards and on whether an automatic cash dispenser is easy to find. And, as we will emphasize later in the book, the quantity of money demanded depends on the interest rate that a person could earn by using the money to buy an interest-bearing bond rather than leaving it in their pocket or low-interest bank account.

Although many variables affect the demand for money, one variable stands out in importance: the average level of prices in the economy. People hold money because it is the medium of exchange. Unlike other assets, such as bonds or stocks, people can use money to buy the goods and services on their shopping lists. How much money they choose to hold for this purpose depends on the prices of those goods and services. The higher prices are, the more money the typical transaction requires, and the more money people will choose to hold in their pockets and bank accounts. That is, a higher price level (a lower value of money) increases the quantity of money demanded.

What ensures that the quantity of money the central bank supplies balances the quantity of money people demand? The answer, it turns out, depends on the time horizon being considered. Later in this book we will examine the short-run answer, and we will see that interest rates play a key role. In the long run, however, the answer is different and much simpler. *In the long run, the overall level of prices adjusts to the level at which the demand for money equals the supply.* Figure 11.1 illustrates this idea. The horizontal axis of this graph shows the quantity of money. The left-hand vertical axis shows the value of money $1/P$, and the right-hand vertical axis shows the price level P. Notice that the price level axis on the right is inverted: a low price level is shown near the top of this axis, and a high price level is shown near the bottom. This inverted axis illustrates that when the value of money is high (as shown near the top of the left axis), the price level is low (as shown near the top of the right axis).

FIGURE 11.1

How the Supply and Demand for Money Determine the Equilibrium Price Level
The horizontal axis shows the quantity of money. The left vertical axis shows the value of money, and the right vertical axis shows the price level. The supply curve for money is vertical because the quantity of money supplied is fixed by the central bank. The demand curve for money is downward sloping because people want to hold a larger quantity of money when each euro buys less. At the equilibrium, point A, the value of money (on the left axis) and the price level (on the right axis) have adjusted to bring the quantity of money supplied and the quantity of money demanded into balance.

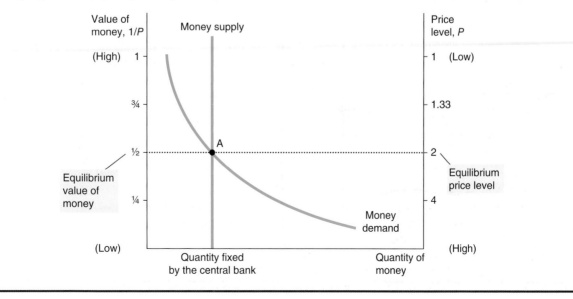

The two curves in this figure are the supply and demand curves for money. The supply curve is vertical because the central bank has fixed the quantity of money available. The demand curve for money is downwards sloping, indicating that when the value of money is low (and the price level is high), people demand a larger quantity of it to buy goods and services. At the equilibrium, shown in the figure as point A, the quantity of money demanded balances the quantity of money supplied. This equilibrium of money supply and money demand determines the value of money and the price level.

To summarize, if the price level is above the equilibrium level, people will want to hold more money than the central bank has created, so the price level must fall to balance supply and demand. If the price level is below the equilibrium level, people will want to hold less money than the central bank has created, and the price level must rise to balance supply and demand. At the equilibrium price level, the quantity of money that people want to hold exactly balances the quantity of money supplied by the central bank.

The Effects of a Monetary Injection

Let's now consider the effects of a change in monetary policy. To do so, imagine that the economy is in equilibrium and then, suddenly, the central bank doubles the supply of money by printing large amounts of money and dropping it around the country from helicopters (this analogy was first drawn by Milton Friedman and later echoed by the Federal Reserve chair, at the time of writing Ben Bernanke, which earned him the nickname 'Helicopter Ben'). Or, less dramatically and more realistically, the central bank could inject money into the economy by buying some government bonds from the public in open-market operations. What happens after such a monetary injection? How does the new equilibrium compare to the old one?

Figure 11.2 shows what happens. The monetary injection shifts the supply curve to the right from MS_1 to MS_2, and the equilibrium moves from point A to point B. As a result, the value of money (shown on the left axis) decreases from ½ to ¼, and the equilibrium price level (shown on the right axis) increases from 2 to 4. In other words, when an increase in the money supply makes euros more plentiful, the result is an increase in the price level that makes each euro less valuable.

FIGURE 11.2

An Increase in the Money Supply

When the central bank increases the supply of money, the money supply curve shifts from MS_1 to MS_2. The value of money (on the left axis) and the price level (on the right axis) adjust to bring supply and demand back into balance. The equilibrium moves from point A to point B. Thus, when an increase in the money supply makes euros more plentiful, the price level increases, making each euro less valuable.

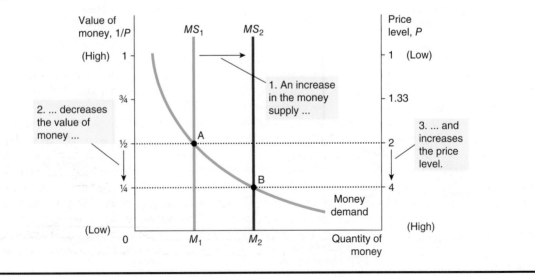

This explanation of how the price level is determined and why it might change over time is called the **quantity theory of money**. According to the quantity theory, the quantity of money available in the economy determines the value of money, and growth in the quantity of money is the primary cause of inflation. As Milton Friedman once put it, 'Inflation is always and everywhere a monetary phenomenon.'

---

quantity theory of money a theory asserting that the quantity of money available determines the price level and that the growth rate in the quantity of money available determines the inflation rate

---

A Brief Look at the Adjustment Process

So far we have compared the old equilibrium and the new equilibrium after an injection of money. How does the economy get from the old to the new equilibrium? A complete answer to this question requires an understanding of short-run fluctuations in the economy, which we examine later in this book. Yet, even now, it is instructive to consider briefly the adjustment process that occurs after a change in money supply.

The immediate effect of a monetary injection is to create an excess supply of money. Before the injection, the economy was in equilibrium (point A in Figure 11.2). At the prevailing price level, people had exactly as much money as they wanted. But after the helicopters drop the new money and people pick it up off the streets, people have more euros in their pockets than they need to buy goods and services. At the prevailing price level, the quantity of money supplied now exceeds the quantity demanded.

People try to get rid of this excess supply of money in various ways. They might buy goods and services with their excess holdings of money. Or they might use this excess money to make loans to others by buying bonds or by depositing the money in a bank savings account (remember the relationship between saving and investment outlined in Chapter 8). These loans allow other people to buy goods and services. In either case, the injection of money increases the demand for goods and services.

The economy's ability to supply goods and services, however, has not changed. As we saw in Chapter 6, the economy's output of goods and services is determined by the available labour, physical capital, human capital, natural resources and technological knowledge. None of these is altered by the injection of money.

Thus, the greater demand for goods and services causes the prices of goods and services to increase. The increase in the price level, in turn, increases the quantity of money demanded because people are using more euros for every transaction. Eventually, the economy reaches a new equilibrium (point B in Figure 11.2) at which the quantity of money demanded again equals the quantity of money supplied. In this way, the overall price level for goods and services adjusts to bring money supply and money demand into balance.

The Classical Dichotomy and Monetary Neutrality

We have seen how changes in the money supply lead to changes in the average level of prices of goods and services. How do these monetary changes affect other important macroeconomic variables, such as production, employment, real wages and real interest rates? This question has long intrigued economists. Indeed, the great classical economist and philosopher David Hume wrote about it in the 18th century. The answer we give today owes much to Hume's analysis.

Hume and his contemporaries suggested that all economic variables should be divided into two groups. The first group consists of **nominal variables** – variables measured in monetary units. The second group consists of **real variables** – variables measured in physical units. For example, the income of corn farmers is a nominal variable because it is measured in euros, whereas the quantity of corn they produce is a real variable because it is measured in kilos. Similarly, nominal GDP is a nominal variable because it measures the euro value of the economy's output of goods and services; real GDP is a real variable because it measures the total quantity of goods and services produced and is not influenced by the current prices of those goods and services. This separation of variables into these groups is now called the **classical dichotomy**. (A *dichotomy* is a division into two groups, and *classical* refers to the earlier economic thinkers or classical economists.)

> **nominal variables** variables measured in monetary units
> **real variables** variables measured in physical units
> **classical dichotomy** the theoretical separation of nominal and real variables

Application of the classical dichotomy is somewhat tricky when we turn to prices. Prices in the economy are normally quoted in terms of money and, therefore, are nominal variables. For instance, when we say that the price of corn is €2 a kilo or that the price of wheat is €1 a kilo, both prices are nominal variables. But what about a *relative* price – the price of one thing compared to another? In our example, we could say that the price of a kilo of corn is two kilos of wheat. Notice that this relative price is no longer measured in terms of money. When comparing the prices of any two goods, the euro signs cancel, and the resulting number is measured in physical units. The lesson is that money prices (e.g. in pounds, euros or dollars) are nominal variables, whereas relative prices are real variables.

This lesson has several important applications. Think about wages. Imagine that a consumer only ever buys bananas and that the price of a banana is €2. If the consumer's wage is €10 per hour then the consumer can buy five bananas with their wage. Ten euro per hour is the nominal wage rate measured in money terms. The **real wages** rate is given by the ratio of the wage rate to the price of bananas $\frac{W}{P}$. In this example the real wage rate is the number of bananas the consumer can buy with their wage, $\frac{10}{2} = 5$ bananas per hour. In order to be able to afford five bananas the consumer has to work for an hour. If the wage rate and prices change then the real wage rate gives a more accurate reflection of how the consumer has been affected. If the wage rate increases to €12 per hour and the price of bananas rises to €3 is the consumer better off or worse off? The real wage is now $\frac{12}{3} = 4$ bananas per hour. We can say that the worker is now worse off since they can now only buy four bananas for every hour they work rather than five. The real wage (the money wage adjusted for inflation) is a real variable because it measures the rate at which the economy exchanges goods and services for each unit of labour. Similarly, the real interest rate (the nominal interest rate adjusted for inflation) is a real variable because it measures the rate at which the economy exchanges goods and services produced today for goods and services produced in the future.

> **real wages** the money wage adjusted for inflation measured by the ratio of the wage rate to price $\frac{W}{P}$

Why bother separating variables into these two groups? Hume suggested that the classical dichotomy is useful in analysing the economy because different forces influence real and nominal variables. In particular, he argued, nominal variables are heavily influenced by developments in the economy's monetary system, whereas the monetary system is largely irrelevant for understanding the determinants of important real variables.

Notice that Hume's idea was implicit in our earlier discussions of the real economy in the long run. In previous chapters we examined how real GDP, saving, investment, real interest rates and unemployment are determined without any mention of the existence of money. As explained in that analysis, the economy's production of goods and services depends on productivity and factor supplies, the real interest rate adjusts to balance the supply and demand for loanable funds, the real wage adjusts to balance the supply and demand for labour, and unemployment results when the real wage is for some reason kept above its equilibrium level. These important conclusions have nothing to do with the quantity of money supplied.

Changes in the supply of money, according to Hume, affect nominal variables but not real variables. When the central bank doubles the money supply, the price level doubles, the euro wage doubles, and all other euro values double. Real variables, such as production, employment, real wages and real interest rates, are unchanged. This irrelevance of monetary changes for real variables is called **monetary neutrality**.

> **monetary neutrality** the proposition that changes in the money supply do not affect real variables

An analogy sheds light on the meaning of monetary neutrality. Recall that, as the unit of account, money is the yardstick we use to measure economic transactions. When a central bank doubles the money supply, all prices double, and the value of the unit of account falls by half. A similar change would occur if a European Union directive reduced the definition of the metre from 100 to 50 centimetres: as a result of the new unit of measurement, all *measured* distances (nominal variables) would double, but the *actual* distances (real variables) would remain the same. The euro, like the metre, is merely a unit of measurement, so a change in its value should not have important real effects.

Is this conclusion of monetary neutrality a realistic description of the world in which we live? The answer is, not completely. A change in the length of the metre from 100 to 50 centimetres would not matter much in the long run, but in the short run it would certainly lead to confusion and various mistakes. Similarly, most economists today believe that over short periods of time – within the span of a year or two – there is reason to think that monetary changes do have important effects on real variables. Hume himself also doubted that monetary neutrality would apply in the short run. (We will turn to the study of short-run non-neutrality later in the book, and this topic will shed light on the reasons why central banks change the supply of money over time.)

Most economists today accept Hume's conclusion as a description of the economy in the long run. Over the course of a decade, for instance, monetary changes have important effects on nominal variables (such as the price level) but only negligible effects on real variables (such as real GDP). When studying long-run changes in the economy, the neutrality of money offers a good description of how the world works.

Velocity and the Quantity Equation

We can obtain another perspective on the quantity theory of money by considering the following question: how many times per year is the typical €1 coin used to pay for a newly produced good or service? The answer to this question is given by a variable called the **velocity of money**. In physics, the term *velocity* refers to the speed at which an object travels. In economics, the velocity of money refers to the speed at which money changes hands as it moves around the economy.

> **velocity of money** the rate at which money changes hands

To calculate the velocity of money, we divide the nominal value of output (nominal GDP) by the quantity of money. If P is the price level (the GDP deflator), Y the quantity of output (real GDP) and M the quantity of money, then velocity is:

$$V = \frac{(P \times Y)}{M}$$

To see why this makes sense, imagine a simple economy that produces only pizza. Suppose that the economy produces 100 pizzas in a year, that a pizza sells for €10, and that the quantity of money in the economy is €50, made up of fifty €1 coins. Then the velocity of money is:

$$V = \frac{(€10 \times 100)}{€50}$$
$$= 20$$

In this economy, people spend a total of €1,000 per year on pizza. For this €1,000 of spending to take place with only €50 of money, each euro coin must be spent (i.e. change hands) on average 20 times per year.

With slight algebraic rearrangement, this equation can be rewritten as:

$$M \times V = P \times Y$$

This equation states that the quantity of money (M) times the velocity of money (V) equals the price of output (P) times the amount of output (Y). It is called the **quantity equation** because it relates the quantity of money (M) to the nominal value of output ($P \times Y$). The quantity equation (which is an identity or a truism) shows that an increase in the quantity of money in an economy must be reflected in one of the other three variables: the price level must rise, the quantity of output must rise or the velocity of money must fall.

> **quantity equation** the equation $M \times V = P \times Y$, which relates the quantity of money, the velocity of money, and the currency value of the economy's output of goods and services

We now have all the elements necessary to explain the equilibrium price level and inflation rate. Here they are:

1. Assume that the velocity of money is relatively stable over time.
2. Because velocity is stable, when the central bank changes the quantity of money (M), it causes proportionate changes in the nominal value of output ($P \times Y$).
3. The economy's output of goods and services (Y) is primarily determined by factor supplies (labour, physical capital, human capital and natural resources) and the available production technology. In particular, because money is neutral, money does not affect output.
4. With output (Y) determined by factor supplies and technology, when the central bank alters the money supply (M) and induces proportional changes in the nominal value of output ($P \times Y$), these changes are reflected in changes in the price level (P).
5. Therefore, when the central bank increases the money supply rapidly, the result is a high rate of inflation.

These five steps are the essence of the quantity theory of money.

CASE STUDY   The Velocity of Circulation

The discussion of the quantity theory of money above makes an important assumption – that the velocity of circulation of money (V) is stable over time. How accurate is such an assumption? One part of the answer might be to consider what is meant by 'stable' and over what time period we are looking. Stable does not mean constant but what degree of volatility is acceptable to describe V as 'stable'?

Using the quantity theory equation, it can be seen that if V is not assumed constant then changes in the money stock have different implied effects on inflation. If we observe that the money stock has increased by (say) 10 per cent but the price level remained unchanged then either the velocity of circulation must have slowed down or output might have fallen. The more stable V is, the more powerful is the quantity theory in helping to monitor the behaviour of the economy and the role of monetary policy.

Figure 11.3 shows a measure of V in the United States taken by taking US GDP and dividing by the Federal Reserve's M2 measure of the money supply from 1959 to 2013. The figure shows V fluctuating between a corridor of 1.6 and 1.9 between 1959 and 1993 but appearing to be a lot more volatile in the subsequent 20 years. Overall, V appears to have varied between a corridor of 1.5 and 2.10 over the time period shown – a variation of around 0.6 over the period. Can this degree of fluctuation be defined as 'stable'?

Is the argument about the stability of V actually relevant? Whilst many economists do place some value in the quantity theory, there are some who cast doubt on it and they do so because of the velocity of circulation which they believe is a fallacy. In Chapter 10 we noted that the Austrian school of economists had a definition of the true money supply. It is the Austrian school who cast doubt on the validity of V.

Their argument is as follows. When individuals make market transactions they pay through the value of the goods and services they produce themselves. A university lecturer, in reality, pays for the food she consumes with the value of the lecture services she produces. Money is merely the means to facilitate

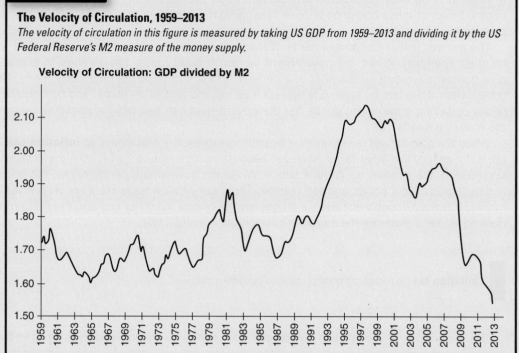

FIGURE 11.3

The Velocity of Circulation, 1959–2013

The velocity of circulation in this figure is measured by taking US GDP from 1959–2013 and dividing it by the US Federal Reserve's M2 measure of the money supply.

Velocity of Circulation: GDP divided by M2

the exchange – the medium of exchange. The number of times a €10 note changes hands has nothing to do with the lecturer's ability to be able to fund her desired purchase of food; it is the lecturer's ability to provide teaching services which determines her ability to buy food. What happens, so the argument goes, is that the lecturer is exchanging her services for money which then enables her to make transactions. The food retailer is exchanging the services he provides for money and using that money to buy the goods and services he needs. In making these transactions both parties are assigning a value to the transactions they make in relation to their own particular well-being. The Austrian school argues that it is individuals' actions that determine the prices of goods and services and not the speed at which money changes hands. V cannot, therefore, say anything about the average price level or the average purchasing power of money. V is simply the value of transactions, the price multiplied by output, divided by the money stock $V = P\left(\frac{Y}{M}\right)$ and as such is a truism which is not helpful and V cannot be defined independently of the rest of the equation – it needs P, Y and M to give it any meaning and as such V in itself cannot be a causal factor of anything. This implies that if M is rising then if V was declining it cannot offset the growth in the price level.

The Austrian school link V to the demand for money. If V is unstable does that also mean that the demand for money is unstable? The Austrian school see this statement as rather absurd – if individuals change their decisions to hold more or less money over time as a result of changes in their personal circumstances, why would this be an issue? Their view would be that over time the demand for money changes – in the same way that over time the demand for any good or service changes. It would be absurd to expect the demand for fish to be stable over time so why should we treat the demand for money in any different way?

This case study reflects the fact that different economists look at theories in different ways. The Austrian school does not deny a link between the money supply and prices but questions the quantity theory (or the equation of exchange) as being an accurate way of looking at the economy. In doing so, they argue, false conclusions may be drawn.

The Inflation Tax

If inflation is so easy to explain, why do countries experience hyperinflation? That is, why do the central banks of these countries choose to print so much money that its value is certain to fall rapidly over time?

The answer is that the governments of these countries are using money creation as a way to pay for their spending. When the government wants to build roads, pay salaries to police officers, or give transfer payments to the poor or elderly, it first has to raise the necessary funds. Normally, the government does this by levying taxes, such as income and sales taxes, and by borrowing from the public by selling government bonds. Yet the government can also pay for spending by simply printing the money it needs.

When the government raises revenue by printing money, it is said to levy an **inflation tax**. The inflation tax is not exactly like other taxes, however, because no one receives a bill from the government for this tax. Instead, the inflation tax is more subtle. When the government prints money, the price level rises, and the euros in your pocket are less valuable. Thus, the inflation tax is like a tax on everyone who holds money. It is even, roughly speaking, a progressive tax since the richer you are, the more money you are likely to hold and therefore the more the inflation tax will affect you.

> **inflation tax** the revenue the government raises by creating money

The importance of the inflation tax varies from country to country and over time. In the early 21st century, most advanced economies have been enjoying very low rates of inflation, so that the inflation tax has been a trivial source of revenue for the government, amounting to only a few per cent of government revenue. In periods of hyperinflation in Germany of the 1920s, in various Latin American countries during the 1970s and 1980s and in Yugoslavia and Zimbabwe more recently, the inflation tax would have been quite considerable.

Nearly all hyperinflations follow the same pattern: the government has high spending, limited ability to borrow, inadequate tax revenue (perhaps because the level of income in the economy is low, or there is widespread tax evasion or a poorly developed tax system, or a combination of all these factors) and, as a result, it turns to the printing press to pay for its spending. The massive increases in the quantity of money lead to massive inflation. The inflation ends when the government institutes fiscal reforms – such as cuts in government spending – that eliminate the need for the inflation tax.

As the economist John Maynard Keynes once pointed out, the temptation to just print money to pay for government spending through the inflation tax may be hard for a government to resist in such circumstances: 'The burden of the tax is well spread, cannot be evaded, costs nothing to collect, and falls, in a rough sort of way, in proportion to the wealth of the victim. No wonder its superficial advantages have attracted Ministers of Finance.' Of course, Keynes also recognized the great damage that high inflation can do to an economy, which is why he referred to the advantages of an inflation tax as 'superficial'.

The Fisher Effect

According to the principle of monetary neutrality, an increase in the rate of money growth raises the rate of inflation but does not affect any real variable. An important application of this principle concerns the effect of money on interest rates. Interest rates are important variables for macroeconomists to understand because they link the economy of the present and the economy of the future through their effects on saving and investment.

To understand the relationship between money, inflation and interest rates, recall the distinction between the nominal interest rate and the real interest rate.

The *nominal interest rate* is the interest rate you hear about at your bank. If you have a savings account, for instance, the nominal interest rate tells you how fast the number of euros in your account will rise over time. The *real interest rate* corrects the nominal interest rate for the effect of inflation in order to tell you how fast the purchasing power of your savings account will rise over time. The real interest rate is the nominal interest rate minus the inflation rate:

$$\text{Real interest rate} = \text{Nominal interest rate} - \text{Inflation rate}$$

For example, if the bank posts a nominal interest rate of 7 per cent per year and the inflation rate is 3 per cent per year, then the real value of the deposits grows by 4 per cent per year.

We can rewrite this equation to show that the nominal interest rate is the sum of the real interest rate and the inflation rate:

$$\text{Nominal interest rate} = \text{Real interest rate} + \text{Inflation rate}$$

This way of looking at the nominal interest rate is useful because different economic forces determine each of the two terms on the right-hand side of this equation. As we discussed earlier in the book, the supply and demand for loanable funds determine the real interest rate. And, according to the quantity theory of money, growth in the money supply determines the inflation rate.

Let's now consider how the growth in the money supply affects interest rates. In the long run over which money is neutral, a change in money growth should not affect the real interest rate. The real interest rate is, after all, a real variable. For the real interest rate not to be affected, the nominal interest rate must adjust one-for-one to changes in the inflation rate. Thus, when the central bank increases the rate of money growth, the result is both a higher inflation rate and a higher nominal interest rate. This adjustment of the nominal interest rate to the inflation rate is called the **Fisher effect**, after the American economist Irving Fisher (1867–1947), who first studied it.

Fisher effect the one-for-one adjustment of the nominal interest rate to the inflation rate

Keep in mind that our analysis of the Fisher effect has maintained a long-run perspective. The Fisher effect does not hold in the short run to the extent that inflation is unanticipated. A nominal interest rate is a payment on a loan, and it is typically set when the loan is first made. If inflation catches the borrower and lender by surprise, the nominal interest rate they set will fail to reflect the rise in prices. To be precise, the Fisher effect states that the nominal interest rate adjusts to expected inflation. Expected inflation moves with actual inflation in the long run but not necessarily in the short run.

The Fisher effect is crucial for understanding changes over time in the nominal interest rate. Figure 11.4 shows the nominal interest rate and the inflation rate in the UK economy since 1976. The close association between these two variables is clear. The nominal interest rate tends to rise when inflation rises and fall when inflation falls. This is true both in high-inflation periods, such as during the late 1970s and the late 1980s, as well as during low-inflation periods, such as the period between 1992 and 2002.

SELF TEST The government of a country increases the growth rate of the money supply from 5 per cent per year to 50 per cent per year. ● What happens to prices? ● What happens to nominal interest rates? ● Why might the government be doing this?

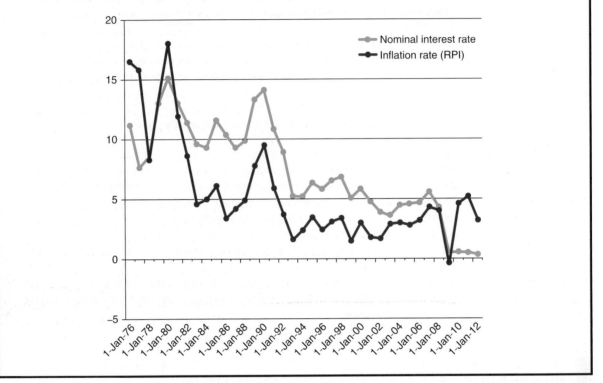

FIGURE 11.4

The UK Nominal Interest Rate and the Inflation Rate

This figure uses annual data since 1976 to show the nominal interest rate on three-month UK Treasury bills (measured as the annual average rate of discount) and the inflation rate (as measured by the retail prices index). The close association between these two variables is evidence for the Fisher effect: when the inflation rate rises, so does the nominal interest rate.

THE COSTS OF INFLATION

In the mid-1970s, when the UK inflation rate reached a peak of about 24 per cent a year, inflation dominated debates over economic policy. And, even though inflation was low during the 1990s, it remained a closely watched macroeconomic variable.

Inflation is closely watched and widely discussed because it is thought to be a serious economic problem. But is that true? And if so, why?

A Fall in Purchasing Power? The Inflation Fallacy

If you ask the typical person why inflation is bad, he will tell you that the answer is obvious: inflation robs him of the purchasing power of his hard-earned money. When prices rise, each euro of income buys fewer goods and services. Thus, it might seem that inflation directly lowers living standards.

Yet further thought reveals a fallacy in this answer. When prices rise, buyers of goods and services pay more for what they buy. At the same time, however, sellers of goods and services get more for what they sell. Because most people earn their incomes by selling their services, such as their labour, inflation in incomes goes hand in hand with inflation in prices. *Thus, inflation does not in itself reduce people's real purchasing power.*

People believe the inflation fallacy because they do not appreciate the principle of monetary neutrality. A worker who receives an annual rise of 10 per cent in her salary tends to view that rise as a reward for her own talent and effort. When an inflation rate of 6 per cent reduces the real value of that pay rise to only 4 per cent, the worker might feel that she has been cheated of what is rightfully her due. In fact, as we discussed in Chapter 6, real incomes are determined by real variables, such as physical capital, human capital, natural resources and the available production technology. Nominal incomes are determined by those factors and the overall price level. If the central bank were to succeed in lowering the inflation rate from 6 per cent to zero, our worker's annual rise would fall from 10 per cent to 4 per cent. She might feel less robbed by inflation, but her real income would not rise more quickly.

If nominal incomes tend to keep pace with rising prices, why then is inflation a problem? It turns out that there is no single answer to this question. Instead, economists have identified several costs of inflation. Each of these costs shows some way in which persistent growth in the money supply does, in fact, have some effect on real variables.

Shoeleather Costs

As we have discussed, inflation is like a tax on the holders of money. The tax itself is not a cost to society: it is only a transfer of resources from households to the government. Yet most taxes give people an incentive to alter their behaviour to avoid paying the tax, and this distortion of incentives causes deadweight losses for society as a whole. Like other taxes, the inflation tax also causes deadweight losses because people waste scarce resources trying to avoid it.

How can a person avoid paying the inflation tax? Because inflation erodes the real value of the money in your pocket, you can avoid the inflation tax by holding less money. One way to do this is to go to the bank more often. For example, rather than withdrawing €400 every four weeks, you might withdraw €100 once a week. By making more frequent trips to the bank, you can keep more of your wealth in your interest-bearing savings account and less in your pocket, where inflation erodes its value.

The cost of reducing your money holdings is called the **shoeleather cost** of inflation because making more frequent trips to the bank causes your shoes to wear out more quickly. Of course, this term is not to be taken literally: the actual cost of reducing your money holdings is not the wear and tear on your shoes but the time and convenience you must sacrifice to keep less money on hand than you would if there were no inflation – it is in effect a **transaction cost**, the opportunity cost of carrying out the trips to the bank.

> **shoeleather cost** the resources wasted when inflation encourages people to reduce their money holdings
> **transaction cost** the opportunity cost of carrying out a transaction in any market

Shoeleather costs of inflation may seem trivial. And, in fact, they are in countries experiencing only moderate inflation. But this cost is magnified in countries experiencing hyperinflation. In conditions of hyperinflation, shoeleather costs can be substantial. With a high inflation rate, individuals do not have the luxury of holding the local money as a store of value. Instead, they are forced to convert the domestic currency quickly into goods or into another currency, often the US dollar, which offer a more stable store of value. The time and effort that individuals expend to reduce their money holdings are a waste of resources. If monetary authorities pursued a low-inflation policy, individuals would be happy to hold the domestic currency, and they could put time and effort to more productive use.

Menu Costs

Most firms do not change the prices of their products every day. Instead, firms often announce prices and leave them unchanged for weeks, months or even years.

Firms change prices infrequently because there are costs involved in changing prices. Costs of price adjustment are called **menu costs**, a term derived from a restaurant's cost of printing a new menu. Menu costs include the cost of deciding on new prices, the cost of printing new price lists and catalogues, the cost of sending these new price lists and catalogues to dealers and customers, the cost of advertising the new prices, and even the cost of dealing with customer annoyance over price changes.

> **menu costs** the costs of changing prices

Inflation increases the menu costs that firms must bear. In an economy with low inflation of just a few percentage points a year, annual price adjustment is an appropriate business strategy for many firms. But when high inflation makes firms' costs rise rapidly, annual price adjustment is impractical. During hyperinflations, for example, firms must change their prices daily or even more often just to keep up with all the other prices in the economy. At the height of the German hyperinflation in the 1920s, people eating in restaurants would sometimes insist on paying the bill at the beginning of the meal rather than at the end, because the price of the food would rise while they were eating!

Relative Price Variability and the Misallocation of Resources

Suppose that a fast food restaurant prints a new menu with new prices every January and then leaves its prices unchanged for the rest of the year. If there is no inflation, the restaurant's relative prices – the prices of its meals compared with other prices in the economy – would be constant over the course of the year. By contrast, if the inflation rate is 12 per cent per year, the restaurant's relative prices will automatically fall by 1 per cent each month. The restaurant's relative prices (that is, its prices compared with others in the economy) will be high in the early months of the year, just after it has printed a new menu, and low in the later months. And the higher the inflation rate, the greater is this automatic variability. Thus, because prices change only once in a while, inflation causes relative prices to vary more than they otherwise would.

Why does this matter? The reason is that market economies rely on relative prices to allocate scarce resources. Consumers decide what to buy by comparing the quality and prices of various goods and services. Through these decisions, they determine how the scarce factors of production are allocated among industries and firms. When inflation distorts relative prices, consumer decisions are distorted, and markets are less able to allocate resources to their best use.

Inflation-Induced Tax Distortions

Almost all taxes distort incentives, cause people to alter their behaviour, and lead to a less efficient allocation of the economy's resources. Many taxes, however, become even more problematic in the presence of inflation. The reason is that politicians often fail to take inflation into account when writing the tax laws. Economists who have studied the tax system conclude that inflation tends to raise the tax burden on income earned from savings.

One example of how inflation discourages saving is the tax treatment of *capital gains* – the profits made by selling an asset for more than its purchase price. Suppose that in 2005 you used some of your savings to buy stock in Apple for €10 and that in 2015 you sold the stock for €50. According to the tax system, you have earned a capital gain of €40, which you must include in your income when computing how much income tax you owe. But suppose the overall price level doubled from 2005 to 2015. In this case, the €10 you invested in 2005 is equivalent (in terms of purchasing power) to €20 in 2015. When you sell your Apple shares for €50, you have a real gain (an increase in purchasing power) of only €30. The tax system, however, does not take account of inflation and assesses you a tax on a gain of €40. Thus, inflation exaggerates the size of capital gains and inadvertently increases the tax burden on this type of income.

Another example is the tax treatment of interest income. The income tax treats the *nominal* interest earned on savings as income, even though part of the nominal interest rate merely compensates for inflation. To see the effects of this policy, consider the numerical example in Table 11.1. The table compares two economies, both of which tax interest income at a rate of 25 per cent. In economy A, inflation is zero, and the nominal and real interest rates are both 4 per cent. In this case, the 25 per cent tax on interest income reduces the real interest rate from 4 per cent to 3 per cent. In economy B, the real interest rate is again 4 per cent, but the inflation rate is 8 per cent. As a result of the Fisher effect, the nominal interest rate is 12 per cent. Because the income tax treats this entire 12 per cent interest as income, the government takes 25 per cent of it, leaving an after-tax nominal interest rate of only 9 per cent and an after-tax real interest rate of only 1 per cent. In this case, the 25 per cent tax on interest income reduces the real interest rate from 4 per cent to 1 per cent. Because the after-tax real interest rate provides the incentive to save, saving is much less attractive in the economy with inflation (economy B) than in the economy with stable prices (economy A).

TABLE 11.1	How Inflation Raises the Tax Burden on Saving

In the presence of zero inflation, a 25 per cent tax on interest income reduces the real interest rate from 4 per cent to 3 per cent. In the presence of 8 per cent inflation, the same tax reduces the real interest rate from 4 per cent to 1 per cent.

	Economy A (price stability)	**Economy B** (inflation)
Real interest rate	4%	4%
Inflation rate	0	8
Nominal interest rate (real interest rate + inflation rate)	4	12
Reduced interest due to 25 per cent tax (.25 × nominal interest rate)	1	3
After-tax nominal interest rate (.75 × nominal interest rate)	3	9
After-tax real interest rate (after-tax nominal interest rate − inflation rate)	3	1

The taxes on nominal capital gains and on nominal interest income are two examples of how the tax system interacts with inflation. There are many others. Because of these inflation-induced tax changes, higher inflation tends to discourage people from saving. Recall that the economy's saving provides the resources for investment, which in turn is a key ingredient to long-run economic growth. Thus, when inflation raises the tax burden on saving, it tends to depress the economy's long-run growth rate. There is, however, no consensus among economists about the size of this effect.

One solution to this problem, other than eliminating inflation, is to index the tax system. That is, the tax laws could be rewritten to take account of the effects of inflation. In the case of capital gains, for example, the tax code could adjust the purchase price using a price index and assess the tax only on the real gain. In the case of interest income, the government could tax only real interest income by excluding that portion of the interest income that merely compensates for inflation.

In an ideal world, tax laws would be written so that inflation would not alter anyone's real tax liability. In the world in which we live, however, tax laws are far from perfect. More complete indexation would probably be desirable, but it would further complicate a tax system that many people already consider too complex.

Confusion and Inconvenience

Imagine that we took a poll and asked people the following question: 'This year the metre is 100 centimetres. How long do you think it should be next year?' Assuming we could get people to take us seriously, they would tell us that the metre should stay the same length – 100 centimetres. Anything else would just complicate life needlessly.

What does this finding have to do with inflation? Recall that money, as the economy's unit of account, is what we use to quote prices and record debts. In other words, money is the yardstick with which we measure economic transactions. The job of the central bank is a little like the job of the government department that deals with weights and measurements, i.e. to ensure the reliability of a commonly used unit of measurement. When the central bank increases the money supply and creates inflation, it erodes the real value of the unit of account.

It is difficult to judge the costs of the confusion and inconvenience that arise from inflation. Earlier we discussed how the tax system incorrectly measures real incomes in the presence of inflation. Similarly, accountants incorrectly measure firms' earnings when prices are rising over time. Because inflation causes money at different times to have different real values, computing a firm's profit – the difference between its revenue and costs – is more complicated in an economy with inflation. Therefore, to some extent, inflation makes investors less able to sort out successful from unsuccessful firms, which in turn impedes financial markets in their role of allocating the economy's saving to alternative types of investment.

A Special Cost of Unexpected Inflation: Arbitrary Redistributions of Wealth

So far, the costs of inflation we have discussed occur even if inflation is steady and predictable. Inflation has an additional cost, however, when it comes as a surprise. Unexpected inflation redistributes wealth among the population in a way that has nothing to do with either merit or need. These redistributions occur because many loans in the economy are specified in terms of the unit of account – money.

Consider an example. Suppose that Lars, a student, takes out a €20,000 loan at a 7 per cent interest rate from Bigbank to attend university. In ten years the loan will have to be repaid. After his debt has compounded for ten years at 7 per cent, Lars will owe Bigbank €40,000 (rounded). The real value of this debt will depend on inflation over the decade. If Lars is lucky, the economy will have hyperinflation. In this case, wages and prices will rise so high that Lars will be able to pay the €40,000 debt out of pocket change. In contrast, if the economy goes through a major deflation, then wages and prices will fall, and Lars will find the €40,000 debt a greater burden than he anticipated.

This example shows that unexpected changes in prices redistribute wealth among debtors and creditors. A hyperinflation enriches Lars at the expense of Bigbank because it diminishes the real value of the debt; Lars can repay the loan in less valuable euros than he anticipated. Deflation enriches Bigbank at Lars' expense because it increases the real value of the debt; in this case, Lars has to repay the loan in more valuable euros than he anticipated. If inflation were predictable, then Bigbank and Lars could take inflation into account when setting the nominal interest rate (recall the Fisher effect). But if inflation is hard to predict, it imposes risk on Lars and Bigbank that both would prefer to avoid.

This cost of unexpected inflation is important to consider together with another fact: inflation is especially volatile and uncertain when the average rate of inflation is high. This is seen most simply by examining the experience of different countries. Countries with low average inflation, such as Germany, tend to have stable inflation. Countries with high average inflation, such as many countries in Latin America, tend also to have unstable inflation. There are no known examples of economies with high, stable inflation. This relationship between the level and volatility of inflation points to another cost of inflation. If a country pursues a high-inflation monetary policy, it will have to bear not only the costs of high expected inflation but also the arbitrary redistributions of wealth associated with unexpected inflation.

The Price of Ice Cream

To return to our starting point – an important discussion of the value of ice cream – how does the price of the 1930 choc ice compare to one you could buy today? Remember that in the 1930s you could have bought 120 choc ices for a pound. Earlier in the book we examined how economists measure the inflation rate as the percentage change in the CPI, the GDP deflator, or some other index of the overall price level. These price indices show that, over the past 70 years or so, UK prices have risen on average about 5 per cent per year. Accumulated over so many years, a 5 per cent annual inflation rate leads to something like a 30-fold increase in the price level, so that £1 in 1930s money is equivalent to about £30 in today's money. With a small amount of mental arithmetic, we can see that the price of a Lyons Maid choc ice in the 1930s would be about 25p in today's money. The retail price of about 70p for a Wall's 'Chunky' choc ice nowadays therefore represents a substantial real increase in the price of a chocolate-coated ice-cream bar, even allowing for the possibility of higher quality. Perhaps people have indeed come to enjoy ice cream more.

SELF TEST List and describe six costs of inflation.

Deflation

The majority of this chapter has focused on inflation – a period of generally rising prices. Economists generally see some inflation in the economy as being desirable (provided it is stable and manageable). The opposite of inflation is deflation where the price level actually falls – not to be confused with a slowdown in the rate of growth of prices. It might sound intuitive that falling prices would be a good thing but that is not necessarily the case.

The post-war period saw unprecedented economic growth in Japan as it grew to become the second biggest economy in the world. Its methods and models were copied and applied in most Western economies; they looked enviously at the consistently high levels of productivity and quality of goods coming out of Japan as its exports flooded the globe.

In the last 15 years, however, the Japanese economy has suffered a number of problems, not least a prolonged recession and deflation. Corporate profits have been low and wage levels falling as business tries to adjust to the new market situation. The result of this is that there is little growth, little incentive to invest, low levels of spending and an increased likelihood of rising unemployment.

Some inflation in any economy is seen as being desirable because it is a sign that demand is present, that there is a reason to produce and invest and that there will be reward to be gained from enterprise. For a number of years in the first decade of the 21st century, interest rates in Japan remained at zero in an effort to help stimulate consumer spending. As with any price in any market, the function of the interest rate is to act as a signal and as such provide incentives that allocate scarce resources. When interest rates are zero, there is very little incentive for institutions to lend money; for businesses it might be good news if money can be raised so cheaply for investment but then again, what is there to invest in? Part of the deflation problem in Japan is that consumers were not spending at the levels that would provide a reason for investing in new capacity. Why spend or invest today when you expect prices to be cheaper tomorrow? If consumers cut back spending then firms see order books shrinking and so cut back on production and lay off staff. Prices fall further as the economy falls into a deflationary spiral.

Deflation, therefore, can be as damaging as inflation and this is the reason why central banks are invariably charged with maintaining targets for inflation at or around 2 per cent. Some inflation is considered good for the economy, when prices rise rapidly it causes the problems outlined in this chapter but this does not mean that falling prices is any better.

CONCLUSION

This chapter discussed the causes and costs of inflation. The primary cause of inflation is simply growth in the quantity of money. When the central bank creates money in large quantities, the value of money falls quickly. To maintain stable prices, the central bank must maintain strict control over the money supply.

The costs of inflation are more subtle. They include shoeleather costs, menu costs, increased variability of relative prices, unintended changes in tax liabilities, confusion and inconvenience, and arbitrary redistributions of wealth. Are these costs, in total, large or small? All economists agree that they become huge during hyperinflation. But their size for moderate inflation – when prices rise by less than 10 per cent per year – is more open to debate.

Although this chapter presented many of the most important lessons about inflation, the discussion is incomplete. When the central bank reduces the rate of money growth, prices rise less rapidly, as the quantity theory suggests. Yet as the economy makes the transition to this lower inflation rate, the change in monetary policy will have disruptive effects on production and employment. That is, even though monetary policy is neutral in the long run, it has profound effects on real variables in the short run. Later in this book we will examine the reasons for short-run monetary non-neutrality in order to enhance our understanding of the causes and costs of inflation.

IN THE NEWS

The Money Supply and Inflation

It is often the case in economics that disagreements about policy options arise not because of whether a particular policy will work but what its consequences will be and the extent to which it will have a beneficial effect.

Helicopter Money or Quantitative Easing – Just a Question of Semantics?

The financial crisis precipitated a period of economic slowdown across the globe which has persisted for far longer than other similar recessionary periods. Calls for growth strategies from governments across Europe and the United States, in addition to the need to get government deficits under control have been made, but exactly what form will these growth strategies take? One policy adopted by central banks has been quantitative easing (QE), which has been popularly reported as 'the government printing money'.

One concern that has been raised with such a policy is the possible long-term effect on prices – if billions of euros, pounds or dollars are being pumped into the economy then the money supply will surely rise and as the quantity theory suggests, will make it more likely that inflation will accelerate in the future. Some, therefore, question whether QE is actually any different to the idea of 'helicopter money'.

Consider the following two scenarios. 1. Each individual in a country is given cash. Some of this cash will be spent and some of it will be saved. 2. If that same amount of cash was given to the government, it could use the money to provide tax cuts, be spent on new infrastructure projects or pay off its debts.

If a government chose a helicopter drop, it is in effect giving its citizens cash to spend. The government flies around the country scattering money out of its helicopter, the cash floats down onto the streets for anyone to pick up. Once people pick it up they then spend it but what they spend it on is not under the government's control. What it does do, however, is to provide a much needed boost to demand in the economy (it increases consumption, C, and so boosts aggregate demand). Would such a boost to aggregate demand be sustainable and significant to help get the economy out of the doldrums? The danger is that if the country's capacity to expand output to meet this increased demand does not expand also then aggregate demand will be greater than aggregate supply and inflation will be the result. The government cannot go round the towns and cities of the country asking people to give back the money it has scattered in order to control inflation. In terms of the quantity theory, if governments print more money through a helicopter drop it will lead to inflation.

Is QE any different to scattering money out of a helicopter? QE involves the central bank buying bonds and the money paid ends up in the financial system in the hope that banks and financial institutions will lend to businesses and consumers thus boosting demand. The end result is meant to be the same but

the long-run effects are different. Crucially, it is argued that QE does not lead to a long-run increase in the money supply.

However, part of QE involves the central bank buying government bonds and this has led to some concern that the difference between QE and a helicopter drop is actually very fine. In addition, there has been concern that QE is being used as a tool of monetary financing – in other words, the central bank giving money to government to finance spending, which is inflationary because it increases the money supply.

Why? Well, government bonds are issued to fund government deficits – the difference between tax receipts and government expenditure. The questions being asked, therefore, are whether QE is financing government spending which would be akin to overt monetary financing (OMF) and whether QE is the same as a helicopter drop. With governments struggling to manage deficits, it is possible to propose an argument along the lines of the following: if the central bank buys government bonds the interest rate on government bonds falls and as a result government borrowing costs are lower. In addition, if the central bank is buying government bonds, what happens to the interest on these bonds – should the interest be accounted for on the central bank's accounts or on the government's (since it has issued the bonds)? When central banks print money to finance government spending this is called monetary financing. The European Central Bank (ECB) is forbidden under its charter to engage in monetary financing. Monetary financing is also frowned upon by many other countries but where is the tipping point? There is a fine line between central bank open market operations involving government bonds and monetary financing largely depending on how different transactions are defined.

In the UK, for example, the Treasury announced in November 2012 that it intended to credit accumulated interest payments on UK government bonds bought by the Bank of England under QE to its account. The total sum was estimated as being some £35 billion over two years – a not unhelpful amount when the government is trying to cut its budget deficit. Such an accounting procedure could be looked at as being pretty much the same as scenario 2 above. If the central bank did engage in monetary financing then the result would be a rise in the money supply and, given the quantity theory, a rise in inflation.

Some question whether quantitative easing is actually any different to the idea of 'helicopter money'.

The counter argument is that QE requires money to be 'printed' by central banks but not for handing to people to spend but for the purchase of securities in financial markets. In this way, what is happening is that assets are being transferred within the financial system – in some cases, private firms are transferring bonds to the central bank's accounts and receiving cash in return which is recorded in its account. In other cases, it is a transfer of assets between the government and the central bank – the central bank is acquiring government bonds and cash is indirectly going to the government. This might be seen as being pretty much the same as monetary financing except that in the long run the monetary base need not rise and as a result inflation may not result unlike overt monetary financing (helicopter drops).

In a helicopter drop, assume the government instructs the central bank to send every individual in the country a cheque for €5,000. This can be seen as being exactly the same as a one-off tax rebate by the government (or a temporary tax cut). How is this financed? The government issues bonds equivalent to the total amount given out to its citizens and the central bank buys up those bonds and the interest on the bonds and the principal when the bond is redeemed on maturity all goes back the government.

QE might be seen as being something very similar but the government does have to pay interest on the bonds it issues and which the central bank buys. In the economic climate in which QE is being used, interest rates happen to be very low but nevertheless, there is a cost to the government unlike a pure helicopter drop. Whilst interest rates remain low (close to zero) it does not look as though there is a great deal of difference between a helicopter drop and QE but at some point in the future, interest rates will rise when economies begin to grow more strongly again and then the government will incur a higher cost of issuing bonds.

With QE, the central bank may have bought bonds and expanding the money supply but at some point in the future, when the economic climate is much better, QE can be unwound in that the central bank can sell back the bonds. The central bank could begin to sell bonds if inflationary pressures started to build and in doing so could take money out of the economy thus reducing the money supply. Proponents of QE argue that unlike a helicopter drop, it is a more flexible policy which allows the central bank to monitor inflationary pressures and adjust its asset purchasing programme to ensure that if it is perceived that the programme is ceasing to add to aggregate demand and boosting economic activity but instead is starting to have an impact on prices, it can be reversed.

Whether QE has the same impact on aggregate demand in a period of economic downturn that a helicopter drop would have is another matter. Critics of QE have argued that the billions spent by central banks have not found their way through to the real economy (to people who spend more money on consumption) but instead have just been absorbed by the financial system to correct balance sheets. Ultimately the question is, do we want to boost the economy at a risk of much higher inflation in the future or do we take a more risk averse approach and try and boost the economy to a lesser extent but have more control in the long run over inflation?

(Continued)

Questions

1 What effect would an increase in the money supply of 10 per cent have on the price level? On what does your answer depend?

2 If helicopter money is dropped, why might the way in which it was handled by those who 'pick it up' be important in determining the extent to which such a policy would boost aggregate demand?

3 Why would government borrowing costs fall if the central bank buys government bonds as part of an asset purchasing programme (QE)?

4 Why do proponents of QE argue that the policy is not inflationary in the same way as a helicopter drop?

5 If you were a policymaker in a period of severe economic decline, would you favour a helicopter drop or a programme of QE? Justify your reasoning.

SUMMARY

- The overall level of prices in an economy adjusts to bring money supply and money demand into balance. When the central bank increases the supply of money, it causes the price level to rise. Persistent growth in the quantity of money supplied leads to continuing inflation.

- The principle of monetary neutrality asserts that changes in the quantity of money influence nominal variables but not real variables. Most economists believe that monetary neutrality approximately describes the behaviour of the economy in the long run.

- A government can pay for some of its spending simply by printing money. When countries rely heavily on this 'inflation tax', the result is hyperinflation.

- One application of the principle of monetary neutrality is the Fisher effect. According to the Fisher effect, when the inflation rate rises, the nominal interest rate rises by the same amount, so that the real interest rate remains the same.

- Many people think that inflation makes them poorer because it raises the cost of what they buy. This view is a fallacy, however, because inflation also raises nominal incomes.

- Economists have identified six costs of inflation: shoeleather costs associated with reduced money holdings; menu costs associated with more frequent adjustment of prices; increased variability of relative prices; unintended changes in tax liabilities due to non-indexation of the tax system; confusion and inconvenience resulting from a changing unit of account; and arbitrary redistributions of wealth between debtors and creditors. Many of these costs are large during hyperinflation, but the size of these costs for moderate inflation is less clear.

- Deflation occurs when prices actually fall and the effects on the economy and on incentives can be as damaging as when inflation is rising too quickly.

QUESTIONS FOR REVIEW

1 Explain how an increase in the price level affects the real value of money.

2 In one month, the CPI is reported as being 5.5 per cent and in the following month is reported as 5.0 per cent. Does this mean prices have fallen? Explain.

3 According to the quantity theory of money, what is the effect of an increase in the quantity of money?

4 Explain the difference between nominal and real variables, and give two examples of each. According to the principle of monetary neutrality, which variables are affected by changes in the quantity of money?

5 In what sense is inflation like a tax? How does thinking about inflation as a tax help explain hyperinflation?

6 What is meant by the velocity of money and what is its relevance to the Fisher equation?

7 According to the Fisher effect, how does an increase in the inflation rate affect the real interest rate and the nominal interest rate?

8 What are the costs of inflation? Which of these costs do you think are most important for your economy?

9 If inflation is less than expected, who benefits – debtors or creditors? Explain.

10 Why is deflation a potentially damaging phenomenon?

PROBLEMS AND APPLICATIONS

1 Suppose that this year's money supply is €500 billion, nominal GDP is €10 trillion and real GDP is €5 trillion.

   a. What is the price level? What is the velocity of money?

   b. Suppose that velocity is constant and the economy's output of goods and services rises by 5 per cent each year. What will happen to nominal GDP and the price level next year if the central bank keeps the money supply constant?

   c. What money supply should the central bank set next year if it wants to keep the price level stable?

   d. What money supply should the central bank set next year if it wants inflation of 10 per cent?

2 Suppose that changes in bank regulations expand the availability of credit cards, so that people need to hold less cash.

   a. How does this event affect the demand for money?

   b. If the central bank does not respond to this event, what will happen to the price level?

   c. If the central bank wants to keep the price level stable, what should it do?

3 It is often suggested that central banks should try to achieve zero inflation. If we assume that velocity is constant, does this zero inflation goal require that the rate of money growth equal zero? If yes, explain why. If no, explain what the rate of money growth should equal.

4 The economist John Maynard Keynes wrote: 'Lenin is said to have declared that the best way to destroy the capitalist system was to debauch the currency. By a continuing process of inflation, governments can confiscate, secretly and unobserved, an important part of the wealth of their citizens.' Justify Lenin's assertion.

5 Suppose that a country's inflation rate increases sharply. What happens to the inflation tax on the holders of money? Why is wealth that is held in savings accounts not subject to a change in the inflation tax? Can you think of any way in which holders of savings accounts are hurt by the increase in the inflation rate?

6 Hyperinflations are extremely rare in countries whose central banks are independent of the rest of the government. Why might this be so?

7 Let's consider the effects of inflation in an economy composed only of two people: Michael, a bean farmer, and Dorothy, a rice farmer. Michael and Dorothy both always consume equal amounts of rice and beans. In year 2014, the price of beans was €1, and the price of rice was €3.

   a. Suppose that in 2015 the price of beans was €2 and the price of rice was €6. What was inflation? Was Michael better off, worse off or unaffected by the changes in prices? What about Dorothy?

   b. Now suppose that in 2015 the price of beans was €2 and the price of rice was €4. What was inflation? Was Michael better off, worse off or unaffected by the changes in prices? What about Dorothy?

   c. Finally, suppose that in 2015 the price of beans was €2 and the price of rice was €1.50. What was inflation? Was Michael better off, worse off or unaffected by the changes in prices? What about Dorothy?

   d. What matters more to Michael and Dorothy – the overall inflation rate or the relative price of rice and beans?

8 If the tax rate is 40 per cent, compute the before-tax real interest rate and the after-tax real interest rate in each of the following cases.

   a. The nominal interest rate is 10 per cent and the inflation rate is 5 per cent.

   b. The nominal interest rate is 6 per cent and the inflation rate is 2 per cent.

   c. The nominal interest rate is 4 per cent and the inflation rate is 1 per cent.

9 Suppose that people expect inflation to equal 3 per cent, but in fact prices rise by 5 per cent. Describe how this unexpectedly high inflation rate would help or hurt the following:

   a. the government

   b. a homeowner with a fixed-rate mortgage

   c. a union worker in the second year of a labour contract

   d. a retired person who has invested their savings in government bonds.

10 Explain whether the following statements are true, false or uncertain.

   a. 'Inflation hurts borrowers and helps lenders, because borrowers must pay a higher rate of interest.'

   b. 'If prices change in a way that leaves the overall price level unchanged, then no one is made better or worse off.'

   c. 'Inflation does not reduce the purchasing power of most workers.'

PART 6
THE MACROECONOMICS OF OPEN ECONOMIES

12 OPEN-ECONOMY MACROECONOMICS: BASIC CONCEPTS

When you next buy some fruit in the supermarket, the chances are that you will have a choice between a domestically produced fruit – perhaps apples – and fruit produced abroad, such as mangoes or bananas. When you take your next holiday, you may consider spending it in one of the cultural capitals of Europe or taking a trip to Disney World in Florida. When you start saving for your retirement, you may choose between a unit trust that buys mainly shares in domestic companies or one that buys shares of US or Japanese companies instead. In all of these cases, you are participating not just in the economy of your own country but in economies around the world.

There are clear benefits to being open to international trade: trade allows people to produce what they produce best and to consume the great variety of goods and services produced around the world. Indeed, one of the *Ten Principles of Economics* is that trade can make everyone better off. International trade can raise living standards in all countries by allowing each country to specialize in producing those goods and services in which it has a comparative advantage.

So far our development of macroeconomics has largely ignored the economy's interaction with other economies around the world. For most questions in macroeconomics, international issues are peripheral. For instance, when we discussed the natural rate of unemployment and the causes of inflation, the effects of international trade could safely be ignored. Indeed, to keep their analysis simple, macroeconomists often assume a closed economy – an economy that does not interact with other economies.

Yet some new macroeconomic issues arise in an open economy – an economy that interacts freely with other economies around the world. This chapter and the next one, therefore, provide an introduction to open-economy macroeconomics. We begin in this chapter by discussing the key macroeconomic variables that describe an open economy's interactions in world markets. You may have noticed mention of these variables – exports, imports, the trade balance and exchange rates – when reading the newspaper or watching the evening news. Our first job is to understand what these data mean. In the next chapter we develop a model to explain how these variables are determined and how they are affected by various government policies.

THE INTERNATIONAL FLOWS OF GOODS AND CAPITAL

An open economy interacts with other economies in two ways: it buys and sells goods and services in world product markets, and it buys and sells capital assets such as stocks and bonds in world financial markets. Here we discuss these two activities and the close relationship between them.

The Flow of Goods and Services: Exports, Imports and Net Exports

Exports are domestically produced goods and services that are sold abroad, and imports are foreign-produced goods and services that are sold domestically. When Lloyd's of London insures a building in Munich, it is paid an insurance premium for this service by the owner of the building. The sale of the insurance service provided by Lloyd's is an export for the United Kingdom and an import for Germany. When Volvo, the Swedish car manufacturer, makes a car and sells it to a Swiss resident, the sale is an import for Switzerland and an export for Sweden.

The net exports of any country are the value of its exports minus the value of its imports. The sale of insurance services abroad by Lloyd's raises UK net exports, and the Volvo sale reduces Swiss net exports. Because net exports tell us whether a country is, in total, a seller or a buyer in world markets for goods and services, net exports are also called the **trade balance**. If net exports are positive, exports are greater than imports, indicating that the country sells more goods and services abroad than it buys from other countries. In this case, the country is said to run a **trade surplus**. If net exports are negative, exports are less than imports, indicating that the country sells fewer goods and services abroad than it buys from other countries. In this case, the country is said to run a **trade deficit**. If net exports are zero, its exports and imports are exactly equal, and the country is said to have **balanced trade**.

> **trade balance** the value of a nation's exports minus the value of its imports; also called net exports
> **trade surplus** an excess of exports over imports
> **trade deficit** an excess of imports over exports
> **balanced trade** a situation in which exports equal imports

In the next chapter we develop a theory that explains an economy's trade balance, but even at this early stage it is easy to think of many factors that might influence a country's exports, imports and net exports. Those factors include the following:

- The tastes of consumers for domestic and foreign goods.
- The prices of goods at home and abroad.
- The exchange rates at which people can use domestic currency to buy foreign currencies.
- The incomes of consumers at home and abroad.
- The cost of transporting goods from country to country.
- The policies of the government towards international trade.

As these variables change over time, so does the amount of international trade.

The Flow of Financial Resources: Net Capital Outflow

So far we have been discussing how residents of an open economy participate in world markets for goods and services. In addition, residents of an open economy participate in world financial markets. A UK resident with £20,000 could use that money to buy a car from BMW, but he could instead use that money to buy stock in the German BMW corporation. The first transaction would represent a flow of goods, whereas the second would represent a flow of capital.

The term **net capital outflow** refers to the purchase of foreign assets by domestic residents minus the purchase of domestic assets by foreigners. (It is sometimes called *net foreign investment*.) When a

UK resident buys shares in BMW, the purchase raises UK net capital outflow. When a Japanese resident buys a bond issued by the UK government, the purchase reduces UK net capital outflow.

net capital outflow the purchase of foreign assets by domestic residents minus the purchase of domestic assets by foreigners

Recall that the flow of capital abroad takes two forms. If the French car manufacturer Renault opens up a factory in Romania, that is an example of *foreign direct investment*. Alternatively, if a French citizen buys shares in a Romanian company, that is an example of *foreign portfolio investment*. In the first case, the French owner is actively managing the investment, whereas in the second case the French owner has a more passive role. In both cases, French residents are buying assets located in another country, so both purchases increase French net capital outflow.

We develop a theory to explain net capital outflow in the next chapter. Here, let's consider briefly some of the more important variables that influence net capital outflow:

- The real interest rates being paid on foreign assets.
- The real interest rates being paid on domestic assets.
- The perceived economic and political risks of holding assets abroad.
- The government policies that affect foreign ownership of domestic assets.

For example, consider German investors deciding whether to buy Mexican government bonds or German government bonds. (Recall that a bond is, in effect, an IOU of the issuer.) To make this decision, German investors compare the real interest rates offered on the two bonds. The higher a bond's real interest rate, the more attractive it is. While making this comparison, however, German investors must also take into account the risk that one of these governments might *default* on its debt (that is, not pay interest or principal when it is due), as well as any restrictions that the Mexican government has imposed, or might impose in the future, on foreign investors in Mexico.

The Equality of Net Exports and Net Capital Outflow

We have seen that an open economy interacts with the rest of the world in two ways – in world markets for goods and services and in world financial markets. Net exports and net capital outflow each measure a type of imbalance in these markets. Net exports measure an imbalance between a country's exports and its imports. Net capital outflow measures an imbalance between the amount of foreign assets bought by domestic residents and the amount of domestic assets bought by foreigners.

An important but subtle fact of accounting states that, for an economy as a whole, these two imbalances must offset each other. That is, net capital outflow (*NCO*) always equals net exports (*NX*):

$$NCO = NX$$

This equation holds because every transaction that affects one side of this equation must also affect the other side by exactly the same amount. This equation is an *identity* – an equation that must hold because of the way the variables in the equation are defined and measured.

To see why this accounting identity is true, consider an example. Suppose that BP sells some aircraft fuel to a Japanese airline. In this sale, a UK company (BP) gives aircraft fuel to a Japanese company, and a Japanese company gives yen to a UK company. Notice that two things have occurred simultaneously. The United Kingdom has sold to a foreigner some of its output (the fuel), and this sale increases UK net exports. In addition, the United Kingdom has acquired some foreign assets (the yen), and this acquisition increases UK net capital outflow.

Although BP most probably will not hold on to the yen it has acquired in this sale, any subsequent transaction will preserve the equality of net exports and net capital outflow. For example, BP may exchange its yen for pounds with a UK investment fund that wants the yen to buy shares in Sony Corporation, the Japanese maker of consumer electronics. In this case, BP's net export of aircraft fuel equals the investment fund's net capital outflow in Sony shares. Hence, *NX* and *NCO* rise by an equal amount.

Alternatively, BP may exchange its yen for pounds with another UK company that wants to buy computers from Toshiba, the Japanese computer maker. In this case, UK imports (of computers) exactly offset UK exports (of aircraft fuel). The sales by BP and Toshiba together affect neither UK net exports nor UK net capital outflow. That is, *NX* and *NCO* are the same as they were before these transactions took place.

The equality of net exports and net capital outflow follows from the fact that every international transaction is an exchange. When a seller country transfers a good or service to a buyer country, the buyer country gives up some asset to pay for this good or service. The value of that asset equals the value of the good or service sold. When we add everything up, the net value of goods and services sold by a country (*NX*) must equal the net value of assets acquired (*NCO*). The international flow of goods and services and the international flow of capital are two sides of the same coin.

Saving and Investment, and their Relationship to the International Flows

A nation's saving and investment are, as we have seen in earlier chapters, crucial to its long-run economic growth. Let's therefore consider how these variables are related to the international flows of goods and capital as measured by net exports and net capital outflow. We can do this most easily with the help of some simple mathematics.

As you may recall, the term net exports first appeared earlier in the book when we discussed the components of gross domestic product. The economy's gross domestic product (*Y*) is divided among four components: consumption (*C*), investment (*I*), government purchases (*G*) and net exports (*NX*). We write this as:

$$Y = C + I + G + NX$$

Total expenditure on the economy's output of goods and services is the sum of expenditure on consumption, investment, government purchases and net exports. Because each pound or euro of expenditure is placed into one of these four components, this equation is an accounting identity: it must be true because of the way the variables are defined and measured.

Recall that national saving is the income of the nation that is left after paying for current consumption and government purchases. National saving (*S*) equals $Y - C - G$. If we rearrange the above equation to reflect this fact, we obtain:

$$Y - C - G = I + NX$$
$$S = I + NX$$

Because net exports (*NX*) also equal net capital outflow (*NCO*), we can write this equation as:

$$
\begin{array}{ccccc}
S & = & I & + & NCO \\
\text{Saving} & = & \text{Domestic} & + & \text{Net capital} \\
& & \text{investment} & & \text{outflow}
\end{array}
$$

This equation shows that a nation's saving must equal its domestic investment plus its net capital outflow. In other words, when UK citizens save a pound of their income for the future, that pound can be used to finance accumulation of domestic capital or it can be used to finance the purchase of capital abroad.

This equation should look somewhat familiar. Earlier in the book, when we analysed the role of the financial system, we considered this identity for the special case of a closed economy. In a closed economy, net capital outflow is zero (*NCO* = 0), so saving equals investment (*S* = *I*). In contrast, an open economy has two uses for its saving: domestic investment and net capital outflow.

As before, we can view the financial system as standing between the two sides of this identity. For example, suppose the Singh family decides to save some of its income for retirement. This decision contributes to national saving, the left-hand side of our equation. If the Singh's deposit their saving in an investment fund, the fund may use some of the deposit to buy shares issued by BP, which uses the proceeds to build an oil refinery in Aberdeen. In addition, the investment fund may use some of the Singh's deposit to buy shares issued by Toyota, which uses the proceeds to build a factory in Osaka. These transactions show up on the right-hand side of the equation. From the standpoint of UK accounting, the BP expenditure on a new oil refinery is domestic investment, and the purchase of Toyota stock by a UK resident is net capital outflow. Thus, all saving in the UK economy shows up as investment in the UK economy or as UK net capital outflow.

Summing Up

Table 12.1 summarizes many of the ideas presented so far in this chapter and will be important for later chapters. It describes the three possibilities for an open economy: a country with a trade deficit, a country with balanced trade and a country with a trade surplus.

TABLE 12.1   International Flows of Goods and Capital: Summary

This table shows the three possible outcomes for an open economy.

Trade deficit	Balanced trade	Trade surplus
Exports < Imports	Exports = Imports	Exports > Imports
Net exports < 0	Net exports = 0	Net exports > 0
$Y < C + I + G$	$Y = C + I + G$	$Y > C + I + G$
Saving < Investment	Saving = Investment	Saving > Investment
Net capital outflow < 0	Net capital outflow = 0	Net capital outflow > 0

Consider first a country with a trade surplus. By definition, a trade surplus means that the value of exports exceeds the value of imports. Because net exports are exports minus imports, net exports (NX) are greater than zero. As a result, income ($Y = C + I + G + NX$) must be greater than domestic spending ($C + I + G$). But if Y is more than spending $C + I + G$, then saving $S = Y - G - G$ must be more than investment, I. Because the country is saving more than it is investing, it must be sending some of its saving abroad. That is, the net capital outflow must be greater than zero.

The converse logic applies to a country with a trade deficit. By definition, a trade deficit means that the value of exports is less than the value of imports. Because net exports are exports minus imports, net exports (NX) are negative. Thus, income ($Y = C + I + G + NX$) must be less than domestic spending ($C + I + G$). But if Y is less than $C + I + G$, then $S = Y - C - G$ must be less than I. That is, saving must be less than investment. The net capital outflow must be negative.

A country with balanced trade is between these cases. Exports equal imports, so net exports are zero. Income equals domestic spending, and saving equals investment. The net capital outflow equals zero.

SELF TEST Define net exports and net capital outflow. ● Explain how they are related.

THE PRICES FOR INTERNATIONAL TRANSACTIONS: REAL AND NOMINAL EXCHANGE RATES

So far we have discussed measures of the flow of goods and services and the flow of capital across a nation's border. In addition to these quantity variables, macroeconomists also study variables that measure the prices at which these international transactions take place. Just as the price in any market serves the important role of coordinating buyers and sellers in that market, international prices help coordinate the decisions of consumers and producers as they interact in world markets. Here we discuss the two most important international prices – the nominal and real exchange rates.

Nominal Exchange Rates

The **nominal exchange rate** is the rate at which a person can trade the currency of one country for the currency of another. For example, if you go to a bank, you might see a posted exchange rate of 125 yen per euro. If you give the bank one euro, it will give you 125 Japanese yen; and if you give the bank 125 Japanese yen, it will give you one euro. (In fact, the bank will post slightly different prices for buying and selling yen. The difference gives the bank some profit for offering this service. For our purposes here, we can ignore these differences.)

> **nominal exchange rate** the rate at which a person can trade the currency of one country for the currency of another

An exchange rate can always be expressed in two ways. If the exchange rate is 125 yen per euro, it is also $\frac{1}{125}$ (= 0.008) euro per yen. If a euro is worth £0.88, a pound is worth $\frac{1}{0.88}$ (= 1.136) euros. This can be a source of confusion, and there is no real hard and fast convention that people use. For example, it is customary to quote the US dollar–pound exchange rate as dollars per pound, e.g. $1.50 if 1 pound exchanges for 1.50 dollars. On the other hand, the pound–euro exchange rate can be quoted either way, as pounds per euro or euros per pound. In this book we shall for the most part think of the exchange rate as being the quantity of foreign currency that exchanges for one unit of domestic currency, or the foreign price of a unit of domestic currency. For example, if we are thinking of the UK as the domestic economy and the USA as the foreign economy, then the exchange rate is $1.50 per pound. If we are thinking of, say, Germany as the domestic economy, then we could express the exchange rate as dollars per euro, e.g. $1.33 dollars per euro.

If the exchange rate changes so that a euro buys more of another currency, that change is called an **appreciation** of the euro. If the exchange rate changes so that a euro buys less of another currency, that change is called a **depreciation** of the euro. For example, when the exchange rate rises from 125 to 127 yen per euro, the euro is said to appreciate (you get a larger amount of yen in return for every euro). At the same time, because a Japanese yen now buys less of the European currency, the yen is said to depreciate (you have to give up more yen to buy one euro). When the exchange rate falls from 125 to 123 yen per euro, the euro is said to depreciate, and the yen is said to appreciate. (It is sometimes helpful to think how much of the domestic currency an individual has to give up to get the required amount of the foreign currency and vice versa.)

> **appreciation** an increase in the value of a currency as measured by the amount of foreign currency it can buy
> **depreciation** a decrease in the value of a currency as measured by the amount of foreign currency it can buy

At times you may have heard the media report that the pound or the euro is either 'strong' or 'weak'. These descriptions usually refer to recent changes in the nominal exchange rate. When a currency appreciates, it is said to *strengthen* because it can then buy more foreign currency. Similarly, when a currency depreciates, it is said to *weaken*. If the individual gets more of the foreign currency in exchange for the same amount of the domestic currency, the domestic currency is stronger. If the individual has to give up more of the domestic currency to get the same amount of the foreign currency then the domestic currency is weaker.

For any currency, there are many nominal exchange rates. The euro can be used to buy US dollars, Japanese yen, British pounds, Mexican pesos and so on. When economists study changes in the exchange rate, they often use indices that average these many exchange rates. Just as the consumer prices index turns the many prices in the economy into a single measure of the price level, an exchange rate index turns these many exchange rates into a single measure of the international value of the currency. So when economists talk about the euro or the pound appreciating or depreciating, they often are referring to an exchange rate index that takes into account many individual exchange rates.

Real Exchange Rates

The **real exchange rate** is the rate at which a person can trade the goods and services of one country for the goods and services of another. For example, suppose that you go shopping and find that a kilo of Swiss cheese is twice as expensive as a kilo of English cheddar cheese. We would then say that the real exchange rate is a $\frac{1}{2}$ kilo of Swiss cheese per kilo of English cheese. Notice that, like the nominal exchange rate, we express the real exchange rate as units of the foreign item per unit of the domestic item. But in this instance the item is a good rather than a currency.

> **real exchange rate** the rate at which a person can trade the goods and services of one country for the goods and services of another

Real and nominal exchange rates are closely related. To see how, consider an example. Suppose that a kilo of British wheat sells for £1 and a kilo of European wheat sells for €3. What is the real exchange rate between British and European wheat? To answer this question, we must first use the nominal exchange rate to convert the prices into a common currency. If the nominal exchange rate is €2 per pound, then a price for British wheat of £1 per kilo is equivalent to €2 per kilo. European wheat, however, sells for €3 a kilo, so British wheat is only $\frac{2}{3}$ as expensive as European wheat. The real exchange rate is $\frac{2}{3}$ of a kilo of European wheat per kilo of British wheat.

We can summarize this calculation for the real exchange rate with the following formula, where we are measuring the exchange rate as the amount of foreign currency needed to buy 1 unit of domestic currency:

$$\text{Real exchange rate} = \frac{(\text{Nominal exchange rate} \times \text{Domestic price})}{(\text{Foreign price})}$$

Using the numbers in our example, the formula applies as follows:

$$\text{Real exchange rate} = \frac{(\text{€2 per pound}) \times (\text{€1 per kilo of UK wheat})}{\text{€3 per kilo of European wheat}}$$
$$= \frac{\text{€2 per kilo of UK wheat}}{\text{€3 per kilo of European wheat}}$$
$$= \frac{2}{3} \text{ kilo of European wheat per kilo of UK wheat}$$

Thus, the real exchange rate depends on the nominal exchange rate and on the prices of goods in the two countries measured in the local currencies.

Why does the real exchange rate matter? As you might guess, the real exchange rate is a key determinant of how much a country exports and imports. For example, when a British bread company is deciding whether to buy British or European wheat to make into flour and use in making its bread, it will ask which wheat is cheaper. The real exchange rate gives the answer. As another example, imagine that you are deciding whether to take a holiday in the Dordogne, France, or in Cancun, Mexico. You might ask your travel agent the price of a hotel room in the Dordogne (measured in euros), the price of a hotel room in Cancun (measured in pesos) and the exchange rate between pesos and euros. If you decide where to go on holiday by comparing costs, you are basing your decision on the real exchange rate.

When studying an economy as a whole, macroeconomists focus on overall prices rather than the prices of individual items. That is, to measure the real exchange rate, they use price indices, such as the consumer prices index, which measure the price of a basket of goods and services. By using a price index for a UK or European basket (P), a price index for a foreign basket (P^*) and the nominal exchange rate between the UK pound or euro and foreign currencies (e = foreign currency per pound or euro), we can compute the overall real exchange rate between the United Kingdom or Europe and other countries as follows:

$$\text{Real exchange rate} = (e \times P)/P^*$$

This real exchange rate measures the price of a basket of goods and services available domestically relative to a basket of goods and services available abroad.

As we examine more fully in the next chapter, a country's real exchange rate is a key determinant of its net exports of goods and services. A depreciation (fall) in the real exchange rate of the euro means that EU goods have become cheaper relative to foreign goods. This change encourages consumers both at home and abroad to buy more EU goods and fewer goods from other countries. As a result, EU exports rise and EU imports fall, and both of these changes raise EU net exports. Conversely, an appreciation (rise) in the euro real exchange rate means that EU goods have become more expensive compared to foreign goods, so EU net exports fall. It is important to remember that whilst we are talking about the prices of exports and imports changing, the domestic price for these goods and services may not change. For example, a French wine producer may have wine for sale priced at €10 per bottle. If the exchange rate between the euro and the UK pound is £1 = €1.2 then a UK buyer of wine will have to give up £8.33 to buy a bottle of wine $\left(\frac{€10}{1.2}\right)$. If the UK exchange rate appreciates to £1 = €1.4 then the UK buyer now has to give up only £7.14 $\left(\frac{€10}{1.4}\right)$ to buy the bottle of wine. The euro price of the wine has not changed but to the UK buyer the price has fallen. Equally, if the pound exchange rate depreciated from £1 = €1.2 to £1 = €1.00 then the UK buyer would now have to give up £10 to buy the wine. Again, the euro price of the wine has not changed but the price to the UK buyer has risen because the exchange rate between the pound and the euro has changed.

SELF TEST Define nominal exchange rate and real exchange rate, and explain how they are related. ● If the nominal exchange rate goes from 100 to 120 yen per euro, has the euro appreciated or depreciated?

A FIRST THEORY OF EXCHANGE RATE DETERMINATION: PURCHASING POWER PARITY

Exchange rates vary substantially over time. In 1970, one UK pound could buy 2.4 US dollars (i.e. the pound–dollar exchange rate was $2.40), but in 1985 the pound was only worth about half this amount of dollars (the exchange rate was about $1.25), in March 2008 one pound could buy over $2 but by March 2013 the rate stood at around £1 = $1.50. So over this 40-year period, the pound first almost halved in value from $2.40 to $1.25 and then increased by over 50 per cent from $1.25 to over $2. On the other hand, if we consider the value of the US dollar against the German and Italian currencies, we see that in 1970, a US dollar could be used to buy 3.65 German marks or 627 Italian lira, while in 1998, as both Germany and Italy were getting ready to adopt the euro as their common currency, a US dollar bought 1.76 German marks or 1,737 Italian lira. In other words, over this period the value of the dollar fell by more than half compared to the mark, while it more than doubled compared to the lira.

What explains these large changes? Economists have developed many models to explain how exchange rates are determined, each emphasizing just some of the many forces at work. Here we develop the simplest theory of exchange rates, called purchasing power parity (PPP). This theory states that a unit of any given currency should be able to buy the same quantity of goods in all countries. Many economists believe that **purchasing power parity** describes the forces that determine exchange rates in the long run. We now consider the logic on which this long-run theory of exchange rates is based, as well as the theory's implications and limitations.

purchasing power parity a theory of exchange rates whereby a unit of any given currency should be able to buy the same quantity of goods in all countries

The Basic Logic of Purchasing Power Parity

The theory of purchasing power parity is based on a principle called the *law of one price*. This law asserts that a good must sell for the same price in all locations. Otherwise, there would be opportunities for profit left unexploited. For example, suppose that coffee beans sold for less in Munich than in Frankfurt. A person could buy coffee in Munich for, say, €4 a kilo and then sell it in Frankfurt for €5 a kilo, making a profit of €1 per kilo from the difference in price. The process of taking advantage of differences in prices in different markets is called **arbitrage**. In our example, as the coffee buyer took advantage of the arbitrage opportunity, it would increase the demand for coffee in Munich and increase the supply in Frankfurt. The price of coffee would rise in Munich (in response to greater demand) and fall in Frankfurt (in response to greater supply). This process would continue until, eventually, the prices were the same in the two markets.

> **arbitrage** a trade which seeks to exploit price differences in order to make profit

Now consider how the law of one price applies to the international marketplace. If a euro (or any other currency) could buy more coffee in Germany than in Japan, international traders could profit by buying coffee in Germany and selling it in Japan. This export of coffee from Germany to Japan would drive up the German price of coffee and drive down the Japanese price. Conversely, if a euro could buy more coffee in Japan than in Germany, traders could buy coffee in Japan and sell it in Germany. This import of coffee into Germany from Japan would drive down the German price of coffee and drive up the Japanese price. In the end, the law of one price tells us that a euro must buy the same amount of coffee in all countries.

This logic leads us to the theory of purchasing power parity. According to this theory, a currency must have the same purchasing power in all countries. That is, a euro must buy the same quantity of goods in Germany and Japan, and a Japanese yen must buy the same quantity of goods in Japan as in Germany. Indeed, the name of this theory describes it well. *Parity* means equality, and *purchasing power* refers to the value of money. *Purchasing power parity* states that a unit of all currencies must have the same real value in every country.

Implications of Purchasing Power Parity

What does the theory of purchasing power parity say about exchange rates? It tells us that the nominal exchange rate between the currencies of two countries depends on the price levels in those countries. If a euro buys the same quantity of goods in Germany (where prices are measured in euros) as in Japan (where prices are measured in yen), then the number of yen per euro must reflect the prices of goods in Germany and Japan. For example, if a kilo of coffee is priced at 500 yen in Japan and €5 in Germany, then the nominal exchange rate must be 100 yen per euro $\left(\frac{500 \text{ yen}}{€5 = 100 \text{ yen per euro}}\right)$. Otherwise, the purchasing power of the euro would not be the same in the two countries.

To see more fully how this works, it is helpful to use just a little mathematics. Think of Germany as the home or domestic economy. Suppose that P is the price of a basket of goods in Germany (measured in euros), P^* is the price of a basket of goods in Japan (measured in yen) and e is the nominal exchange rate (the number of yen needed to buy one euro). Now consider the quantity of goods a euro can buy at home (in Germany) and abroad. At home, the price level is P, so the purchasing power of €1 at home is $1/P$. Abroad, a euro can be exchanged into e units of foreign currency, which in turn have purchasing power e/P^*. For the purchasing power of a euro to be the same in the two countries, it must be the case that:

$$1/P = e/P^*$$

With rearrangement, this equation becomes:

$$1 = eP/P^*$$

Notice that the left-hand side of this equation is a constant, and the right-hand side is the real exchange rate. Thus, if the purchasing power of the euro is always the same at home and abroad, then the real exchange rate – the relative price of domestic and foreign goods – cannot change.

To see the implication of this analysis for the nominal exchange rate, we can rearrange the last equation to solve for the nominal exchange rate:

$$e = P^*/P$$

That is, the nominal exchange rate equals the ratio of the foreign price level (measured in units of the foreign currency) to the domestic price level (measured in units of the domestic currency). According to the theory of purchasing power parity, the nominal exchange rate between the currencies of two countries must reflect the different price levels in those countries.

A key implication of this theory is that nominal exchange rates change when price levels change. As we have seen earlier in the book, the price level in any country adjusts to bring the quantity of money supplied and the quantity of money demanded into balance. Because the nominal exchange rate depends on the price levels, it also depends on the money supply and money demand in each country. When a central bank in any country increases the money supply and causes the price level to rise, it also causes that country's currency to depreciate relative to other currencies in the world. In other words, when the central bank prints large quantities of money, that money loses value both in terms of the goods and services it can buy and in terms of the amount of other currencies it can buy.

Referring back to the beginning of this section, why did the UK pound lose value compared to the US dollar between 1970 and 1985? A good deal of the answer certainly relates to differences in inflation between the two countries. Between 1970 and 1985, the USA pursued, on average, a less inflationary monetary policy than the United Kingdom. Average price inflation in the UK over these 15 years was very high – about 10.5 per cent a year, while in the United States it was only about 6.5 per cent a year on average. This meant that between 1970 and 1985 the UK price level rose an average of 4 per cent a year faster than the US price level. As UK prices rose relative to US prices, the value of the pound fell relative to the dollar.

What about the movements in the exchange rate between the Italian lira and the dollar or the German mark and the dollar? Again, in large measure these movements reflect the relative stance of monetary policy in the countries concerned: Germany pursued a less inflationary monetary policy than the United States, and Italy pursued a more inflationary monetary policy. From 1970 to 1998, inflation in the United States was about 5.3 per cent per year on average. By contrast, average inflation was 3.5 per cent in Germany and 9.6 per cent in Italy. As US prices rose relative to German prices, the value of the dollar fell relative to the mark. Similarly, as US prices fell relative to Italian prices, the value of the dollar rose relative to the lira.

Germany and Italy are now part of a **common currency area**, and the common currency is the euro. This means that the two countries share a single monetary policy and that the inflation rates in the two countries will be closely linked. But the historical lessons of the lira and the mark will apply to the euro as well. Whether the UK pound or the US dollar buy more or fewer euros 20 years from now than they do today depends on whether the European Central Bank oversees more or less inflation in Europe than the Bank of England does in the United Kingdom or the Federal Reserve does in the United States.

---

common currency area a geographical area, possibly covering several countries, in which a common currency is used

FYI

Purchasing Power Standard (PPS)

If you look at statistics produced by Eurostat, the EU's statistical office, you are likely to see data expressed in *purchasing power standard (PPS)*. This is an extension of the PPP idea but applied to the EU. PPS is an artificial currency which expresses the purchasing power of the EU 28 against the euro. In theory, therefore, one PPS would buy the same amount of goods in each EU country and so 1PPS = €1. In reality there will be price differences between European countries so different amounts of euro will be needed to buy the same goods and services in different countries. PPS takes account of these differences. The PPS is found by taking any national economic aggregate, such as GDP, for example, and dividing by its PPP. Thus PPPs can be seen as the exchange rate of the PPS against the euro and allows for more accurate comparisons between data from different EU countries. The PPS for the EU 28 as a whole would be 100. If GDP per capita was expressed in PPS, then any figure above 100 would show GDP per capita in that country above the EU 28 average and any figure below 100 would indicate GDP per capita below the EU average. In 2011, Switzerland had GDP per capita at 157 and Norway was 186, both considerably higher than the EU 27 average at the time, whereas Poland at 64 and Romania at 49 were well below the EU 27 average.

Limitations of Purchasing Power Parity

Purchasing power parity provides a simple model of how exchange rates are determined. For understanding many economic phenomena, the theory works well. In particular, it can explain many long-term trends, such as the examples discussed earlier. It can also explain the major changes in exchange rates that occur during hyperinflations.

Yet the theory of purchasing power parity is not completely accurate. That is, exchange rates do not always move to ensure that a euro has the same real value in all countries all the time. There are two reasons why the theory of purchasing power parity does not always hold in practice.

The first reason is that many goods are not easily traded. Imagine, for instance, that haircuts are more expensive in Paris than in New York. International travellers might avoid getting their haircuts in Paris, and some haircutters might move from New York to Paris. Yet such arbitrage would probably be too limited to eliminate the differences in prices. Thus, the deviation from purchasing power parity might persist, and a euro (or dollar) would continue to buy less of a haircut in Paris than in New York.

The second reason that purchasing power parity does not always hold is that even tradable goods are not always perfect substitutes when they are produced in different countries. For example, some consumers prefer German cars, and others prefer Japanese cars. Moreover, consumer tastes can change over time. If German cars suddenly become more popular, the increase in demand will drive up the price of German cars compared to Japanese cars. But despite this difference in prices in the two markets, there might be no opportunity for profitable arbitrage because consumers do not view the two cars as equivalent.

Thus, both because some goods are not tradable and because some tradable goods are not perfect substitutes with their foreign counterparts, purchasing power parity is not a perfect theory of exchange rate determination. For these reasons, real exchange rates fluctuate over time. Nonetheless, the theory of purchasing power parity does provide a useful first step in understanding exchange rates. The basic logic is persuasive: as the real exchange rate drifts from the level predicted by purchasing power parity, people have greater incentive to move goods across national borders. Even if the forces of purchasing power parity do not completely fix the real exchange rate, they provide a reason to expect that changes in the real exchange rate are most often small or temporary. As a result, large and persistent movements in nominal exchange rates typically reflect changes in price levels at home and abroad.

CASE STUDY | **The Hamburger Standard**

When economists apply the theory of purchasing power parity to explain exchange rates, they need data on the prices of a basket of goods available in different countries. One analysis of this sort is conducted by *The Economist*. This newspaper occasionally collects data on a basket of goods consisting of 'two all-beef patties, special sauce, lettuce, cheese, pickles, onions, on a sesame seed bun.' It's called the 'Big Mac' and is sold by McDonald's around the world.

Once we have the prices of Big Macs in two countries denominated in the local currencies, we can compute the exchange rate predicted by the theory of purchasing power parity. The predicted exchange rate is the one that makes the price of the Big Mac the same in the two countries. For example, assume that the price of a Big Mac in the United States is $3.57 and in the UK, a Big Mac is £2.29. Purchasing power parity would predict an exchange rate of £1 = $1.56.

$$\text{PPP£/\$} = \frac{\text{Price in dollars}}{\text{Price in pounds}}$$

$$\text{PPP£/\$} = \frac{3.57}{2.29}$$

$$\text{PPP£/\$} = 1.56 \text{ (rounded up)}$$

If, however, the actual exchange rate quoted on the foreign exchanges was £1 = $1.60 then the pound would be overvalued – you have to pay 4 cents more to acquire each pound than PPP implies. The extent of the overvaluation can be expressed as a percentage:

$$\% \text{ over or undervaluation} = \frac{\text{Implied PPP rate} - \text{Market rate}}{\text{Market rate}} \times 100$$

$$= \left[\frac{(1.56 - 1.60)}{1.60}\right] \times 100$$

$$= \left(\frac{-0.04}{1.6}\right) \times 100$$

$$= -2.5\%$$

In this example, the pound is overvalued against the dollar by 2.5 per cent and we might expect the pound to depreciate in the future.

If the market exchange rate was £1 = $1.40, then the pound would be undervalued.

$$= \left[\frac{(1.56 - 1.40)}{1.40}\right] \times 100$$

$$= \left(\frac{0.16}{1.4}\right) \times 100$$

$$= 11.43\%$$

In this example, you have to pay 16 cents less than the PPP implies to buy a pound. It might be expected that the pound would appreciate in the future.

How well does purchasing power parity work when applied using Big Mac prices? Here are some examples from January 2013, when the price of a Big Mac was $4.37 in the United States. The price of a Big Mac in China at this time was yuan 16.00. The implied PPP exchange rate therefore would be $1 = yuan 3.66. The actual exchange rate was $1 = yuan 6.22 which suggests that the yuan was under-valued by 41.1 per cent. Table 12.2 shows similar information for a range of other countries.

TABLE 12.2 Purchasing Parity Using the Big Mac Index

Country	Price of a Big Mac	Actual exchange rate	Predicted exchange rate	US Dollar under or overvalued
Chile	2,050 pesos	471.75 US$/peso	469.39 US$/peso	Undervalued by 0.5%
United Kingdom	£2.69	0.63 US$/pound	0.62 US$/pound	Undervalued by 2.7%
Sweden	48.40 kronor	6.35 US$/kronor	11.08 US$/kronor	Overvalued by 74.5%
Russia	Roubles 72.88	30.05 US$/Roubles	16.69 US$/Roubles	Undervalued by 44.5%
Japan	320 yen	91.06 US$/yen	73.27 US$/yen	Undervalued by 19.5%
Mexico	37 pesos	12.74 US$/peso	8.47 US$/pesos	Undervalued by 33.5%
Norway	43.00 Krona	5.48 US$/krona	9.85 US$/krona	Overvalued by 79.6%

You can see that the predicted and actual exchange rates are not exactly the same. After all, international arbitrage in Big Macs is not easy.

Purchasing power parity is not a precise theory of exchange rates (and Big Mac purchasing power parity even less so) and for some countries it does not always work well (it always tends to do badly, for example, for Scandinavian countries), but nevertheless it often provides a reasonable first approximation.

Wherever you go in the world the Big Mac is the same. This provides the standard for applying purchasing power parity to compute the Big Mac Index.

SELF TEST Over the past 20 years, Venezuela has had high inflation and Japan has had low inflation. What do you predict has happened to the number of Venezuelan bolivars a person can buy with a Japanese yen?

CONCLUSION

The purpose of this chapter has been to develop some basic concepts that macroeconomists use to study open economies. You should now understand why a nation's net exports must equal its net capital outflow, and why national saving must equal domestic investment plus net capital outflow. You should also understand the meaning of the nominal and real exchange rates, as well as the implications and limitations of purchasing power parity as a theory of how exchange rates are determined.

The macroeconomic variables defined here offer a starting point for analysing an open economy's interactions with the rest of the world. In the next chapter we develop a model that can explain what determines these variables. We can then discuss how various events and policies affect a country's trade balance and the rate at which nations make exchanges in world markets.

IN THE NEWS

Exchange Rates

One of the reasons for analysing macroeconomics from the perspective of an open economy is that decisions made within a country by policymakers can have repercussions across markets which affect different people in different ways.

Monetary Policy, Quantitative Easing and Exchange Rates

In the early part of 2013, the UK government faced a number of economic challenges, not least trying to reduce borrowing and the deficit, whilst at the same time facing the possibility of economic growth shrinking leading to a third period of recession in three years. Confidence in the UK economy at this time had an effect on the exchange rate. If investors feel that the UK economy is going to shrink there is an incentive to sell pounds on the foreign exchanges and buy a currency that gives a better return. What this does is cause the pound to depreciate.

The UK central bank, the Bank of England, meanwhile is tasked with keeping inflation under control at a target level of 2.0 per cent. In January 2013, the consumer prices index (CPI) was 2.7 per cent, the fourth month in a row that it had stood at this level. The Bank of England had noted that it expected inflation to accelerate in 2013. In minutes of the meeting of the Bank of England's Monetary Policy Committee (MPC), published in February 2013, it became clear that the MPC had discussed cutting interest rates further although in the end the MPC voted to keep the repo rate at 0.5 per cent. There were also discussions about the possibility of extending quantitative easing. In the event, the MPC voted not to expand QE but, given

this was not the first time the issue had been discussed, the markets made an assumption that it was highly likely that it was just a matter of time before QE was expanded further. If the Bank of England extends its asset purchasing facility then the demand for bonds increases and as prices rise, yields fall (remember there is an inverse relationship between the price and the yield of a bond). Falling interest rates do not provide much of an incentive for foreign investors to put their money into the UK.

Then, on 22 February 2013, it was announced that one of the ratings agencies that values credit worthiness had cut the UK government's rating from the highest level of AAA to AA1. The agency,

Moody's, said that the economic climate was still highly uncertain and that the government's debt reduction measures still had a long way to go.

All this news compounded the lack of confidence in the UK economy and led to a further depreciation of the pound against key currencies, the US dollar and the euro. In the six months to February 2013, the pound fell by 10 per cent against the euro and was heading towards parity (£1 = €1). The pound had also slipped from over £1 = \$1.60 to around £1 = \$1.52 over this period. Analysts at the time expected the value of the pound to depreciate further.

A declining value of the pound might reflect a lack of confidence in the UK economy by the financial markets but it could be good news for exporters. As sterling weakens against major trading nations in the EU and the United States, it means that exporters become more competitive and this could mean a boost in exports. This could help the UK economy to recover but exactly how far will depend on a variety of factors, not least the price elasticity of demand for exports.

On the other hand, firms importing raw materials and semi-finished products will see costs rising. Some might pass on those costs to consumers in the form of higher prices but in a difficult economic climate that might not be easy. For those importing raw materials and semi-finished products and then exporting the resulting finished goods, the effect will depend on the balance between the rise in import costs and the benefits from lower export prices.

Questions

1 It has been suggested that quantitative easing is a back-door method of manipulating currencies to help engineer an export-led recovery. Explain.
2 Use a supply and demand diagram to show the effect on the exchange rate between the UK pound and the euro of a decision by investors to pull out of UK investments.
3 Why would a cut in the UK government's credit rating lead to a depreciation of the pound?
4 Explain, using appropriate examples, how a depreciation of a currency affects exporters and importers and the relevance of the price elasticity of demand for imports and exports.
5 To what extent is a depreciation of the currency likely to help a country to turn economic stagnation into economic growth?

The Bank of England – sometimes referred to as the Grand Old Lady of Threadneedle Street – has to balance managing the need to maintain price stability and the external effects of its policies.

SUMMARY

- Net exports are the value of domestic goods and services sold abroad minus the value of foreign goods and services sold domestically. Net capital outflow is the acquisition of foreign assets by domestic residents minus the acquisition of domestic assets by foreigners. Because every international transaction involves an exchange of an asset for a good or service, an economy's net capital outflow always equals its net exports.

- An economy's saving can be used either to finance investment at home or to buy assets abroad. Thus, national saving equals domestic investment plus net capital outflow.

- The nominal exchange rate is the relative price of the currency of two countries, and the real exchange rate is the relative price of the goods and services of two

countries. When the nominal exchange rate changes so that each unit of domestic currency buys more foreign currency, the domestic currency is said to *appreciate* or *strengthen*. When the nominal exchange rate changes so that each unit of domestic currency buys less foreign currency, the domestic currency is said to *depreciate* or *weaken*.

- According to the theory of purchasing power parity, a unit of currency should be able to buy the same quantity of goods in all countries. This theory implies that the nominal exchange rate between the currencies of two countries should reflect the price levels in those countries. As a result, countries with relatively high inflation should have depreciating currencies, and countries with relatively low inflation should have appreciating currencies.

QUESTIONS FOR REVIEW

1 Why do economists sometimes conduct analysis under assumptions of a closed economy?

2 What do you understand by the term an 'open economy'?

3 If a British citizen visits the French Alps to go for a skiing holiday, is this an import for France or an export? Explain.

4 What is a trade deficit and why is it important?

5 Define net exports and net capital outflow. Explain how and why they are related.

6 Explain the relationship between saving, investment and net capital outflow.

7 If a Japanese car is priced at 500,000 yen, a similar German car is priced at €10,000, and a euro can buy 100 yen, what are the nominal and real exchange rates?

8 Describe the economic logic behind the theory of purchasing power parity.

9 If the European Central Bank started printing large quantities of euros, what would happen to the number of Japanese yen a euro could buy?

10 Explain the effect of an appreciation of the euro on German exporters and German importers.

PROBLEMS AND APPLICATIONS

1 How would the following transactions affect UK exports, imports and net exports?

   a. A British art lecturer spends the summer touring museums in Italy.
   b. Students in Paris flock to see the latest Royal Shakespeare Company perform *King Lear* on tour.
   c. The British art lecturer buys a new Volvo.
   d. A student in Munich buys a Manchester United official team shirt (in Munich).
   e. A British citizen goes to Calais for the day to stock up on cheap wine.

2 International trade in each of the following products has increased over time. Suggest some reasons why this might be so:

   a. wheat
   b. banking services

   c. computer software
   d. automobiles.

3 Describe the difference between foreign direct investment and foreign portfolio investment. Who is more likely to engage in foreign direct investment – a corporation or an individual investor? Who is more likely to engage in foreign portfolio investment?

4 How would the following transactions affect UK net capital outflow? Also, state whether each involves direct investment or portfolio investment.

   a. A British mobile telephone company establishes an office in the Czech Republic.
   b. A US company's pension fund buys shares in BP.
   c. Toyota expands its factory in Derby, England.
   d. A London-based investment trust sells its Volkswagen shares to a French investor.

5 Holding national saving constant, does an increase in net capital outflow increase, decrease or have no effect on a country's accumulation of domestic capital?

6 The business section of most major newspapers contains a table showing exchange rates amongst many countries, as does *The Economist*. Find such a table (or find *The Economist* table on its website) and use it to answer the following questions.

   a. Does this table show nominal or real exchange rates? Explain.
   b. What are the exchange rates between the euro and the UK pound, and between the UK pound and the US dollar? Calculate the exchange rate between the euro and the dollar.
   c. If UK inflation exceeds European inflation over the next year, would you expect the UK pound to appreciate or depreciate relative to the euro?

7 Would each of the following groups be happy or unhappy if the euro appreciated? Explain.

   a. US pension funds holding French government bonds.
   b. German manufacturing industries.
   c. Australian tourists planning a trip to Europe.
   d. A British firm trying to purchase property overseas.

8 What is happening to the Swiss real exchange rate in each of the following situations? Explain.

   a. The Swiss nominal exchange rate is unchanged, but prices rise faster in Switzerland than abroad.
   b. The Swiss nominal exchange rate is unchanged, but prices rise faster abroad than in Switzerland.
   c. The Swiss nominal exchange rate declines, and prices are unchanged in Switzerland and abroad.
   d. The Swiss nominal exchange rate declines, and prices rise faster abroad than in Switzerland.

9 List three goods for which the law of one price is likely to hold, and three goods for which it is not. Justify your choices.

10 A can of lemonade is priced at €0.75 in Europe and 12 pesos in Mexico. What would the peso–euro exchange rate be if purchasing power parity holds? If a monetary expansion caused all prices in Mexico to double, so that lemonade rose to 24 pesos, what would happen to the peso–euro exchange rate?

13 A MACROECONOMIC THEORY OF THE OPEN ECONOMY

Over the past two decades, the United Kingdom and United States have persistently imported more goods and services than they have exported. That is, UK and US net exports have been negative. Japan and Germany, on the other hand, have persistently exported more than they have imported (although since 2008 Japan has experienced negative net exports).

If the government of a country wants to reduce trade deficits, what should it do? Should it try to limit imports, perhaps by imposing a quota on the import of cars from Japan or Germany? Or should it try to influence the country's trade deficit in some other way?

To understand what factors determine a country's trade balance and how government policies can affect it, we need a macroeconomic theory of the open economy. The preceding chapter introduced some of the key macroeconomic variables that describe an economy's relationship with other economies – including net exports, net capital outflow, and the real and nominal exchange rates. This chapter develops a model that identifies the forces that determine these variables and shows how these variables are related to one another.

To develop this macroeconomic model of an open economy, we build on our previous analysis in two important ways. First, the model takes the economy's GDP as given. We assume that the economy's output of goods and services, as measured by real GDP, is determined by the supplies of the factors of production and by the available production technology that turns these inputs into output. Second, the model takes the economy's price level as given. We assume that the price level adjusts to bring the supply and demand for money into balance. In other words, this chapter takes as a starting point the lessons learned in Chapters 6 and 11 about the determination of the economy's output and price level.

The goal of the model in this chapter is to highlight the forces that determine the economy's trade balance and exchange rate. In one sense, the model is simple: it applies the tools of supply and demand to an open economy. Yet the model is also more complicated than others we have seen because it involves looking simultaneously at two related markets – the market for loanable funds and the market for foreign currency exchange. After we develop this model of the open economy, we use it to examine how various events and policies affect the economy's trade balance and exchange rate. We shall then be able to determine the government policies that are most likely to reverse trade deficits.

SUPPLY AND DEMAND FOR LOANABLE FUNDS AND FOR FOREIGN CURRENCY EXCHANGE

To understand the forces at work in an open economy, we focus on supply and demand in two markets. The first is the market for loanable funds, which coordinates the economy's saving, investment and the flow of loanable funds abroad (called the net capital outflow). The second is the market for foreign currency exchange, which coordinates people who want to exchange the domestic currency for the currency of other countries. In this section we discuss supply and demand in each of these markets. In the next section we put these markets together to explain the overall equilibrium for an open economy.

The Market for Loanable Funds

When we first analysed the role of the financial system in Chapter 8, we made the simplifying assumption that the financial system consists of only one market, called the *market for loanable funds*. All savers go to this market to deposit their saving and all borrowers go to this market to get their loans. In this market, there is one interest rate, which is both the return to saving and the cost of borrowing.

To understand the market for loanable funds in an open economy, the place to start is the identity discussed in the preceding chapter:

$$S = I + NCO$$
$$\text{Saving} = \text{Domestic investment} + \text{Net capital outflow}$$

Whenever a nation saves some of its income, it can use that money to finance the purchase of domestic capital or to finance the purchase of an asset abroad. The two sides of this identity represent the two sides of the market for loanable funds. The supply of loanable funds comes from national saving (S). The demand for loanable funds comes from domestic investment (I) and net capital outflow (NCO). Note that the purchase of a capital asset adds to the demand for loanable funds, regardless of whether that asset is located at home or abroad. Because net capital outflow can be either positive or negative, it can either add to or subtract from the demand for loanable funds that arises from domestic investment.

As we learned in Chapter 8, the quantity of loanable funds supplied and the quantity of loanable funds demanded depend on the real interest rate. A higher real interest rate encourages people to save and, therefore, raises the quantity of loanable funds supplied. A higher interest rate also makes borrowing to finance capital projects more costly; thus, it discourages investment and reduces the quantity of loanable funds demanded.

In addition to influencing national saving and domestic investment, the real interest rate in a country affects that country's net capital outflow. To see why, consider two investment funds – one in the United Kingdom and one in Germany – deciding whether to buy a UK government bond or a German government bond. The investment funds would make this decision in part by comparing the real interest rates in the United Kingdom and Germany. When the UK real interest rate rises, the UK bond becomes more attractive to both investment funds. Thus, an increase in the UK real interest rate discourages Brits from buying foreign assets and encourages people living in other countries to buy UK assets. For both reasons, a high UK real interest rate reduces UK net capital outflow.

We represent the market for loanable funds on the familiar supply-and-demand diagram in Figure 13.1. As in our earlier analysis of the financial system, the supply curve slopes upward because a higher interest rate increases the quantity of loanable funds supplied, and the demand curve slopes downward because a higher interest rate decreases the quantity of loanable funds demanded.

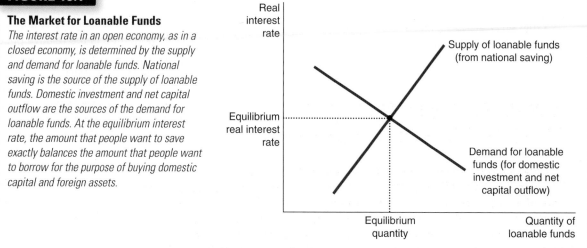

FIGURE 13.1

The Market for Loanable Funds

The interest rate in an open economy, as in a closed economy, is determined by the supply and demand for loanable funds. National saving is the source of the supply of loanable funds. Domestic investment and net capital outflow are the sources of the demand for loanable funds. At the equilibrium interest rate, the amount that people want to save exactly balances the amount that people want to borrow for the purpose of buying domestic capital and foreign assets.

Unlike the situation in our previous discussion, however, the demand side of the market now represents the behaviour of both domestic investment and net capital outflow. That is, in an open economy, the demand for loanable funds comes not only from those who want loanable funds to buy domestic capital goods but also from those who want loanable funds to buy foreign assets.

The interest rate adjusts to bring the supply and demand for loanable funds into balance. If the interest rate were below the equilibrium level, the quantity of loanable funds supplied would be less than the quantity demanded. The resulting shortage of loanable funds would push the interest rate upward. Conversely, if the interest rate were above the equilibrium level, the quantity of loanable funds supplied would exceed the quantity demanded. The surplus of loanable funds would drive the interest rate downward. At the equilibrium interest rate, the supply of loanable funds exactly balances the demand. That is, at the equilibrium interest rate, the amount that people want to save exactly balances the desired quantities of domestic investment and net capital outflow.

The Market for Foreign Currency Exchange

The second market in our model of the open economy is the market for foreign currency exchange. Let's think of the UK as the domestic economy. Participants in this market trade UK pounds in exchange for foreign currencies. To understand the market for foreign currency exchange, we begin with another identity from the last chapter:

$$NCO = NX$$
$$\text{Net capital outflow} = \text{Net exports}$$

This identity states that the imbalance between the purchase and sale of capital assets abroad (NCO) equals the imbalance between exports and imports of goods and services (NX). For example, when the UK economy is running a trade surplus ($NX > 0$), foreigners are buying more UK goods and services than UK residents are buying foreign goods and services. What are Brits doing with the foreign currency they are getting from this net sale of goods and services abroad? They must be buying foreign assets, so UK capital is flowing abroad ($NCO > 0$). Conversely, if the UK is running a trade deficit ($NX < 0$), Brits are spending more on foreign goods and services than they are earning from selling abroad. Some of this spending must be financed by selling UK assets abroad, so foreign capital is flowing into the UK ($NCO < 0$).

Our model of the open economy treats the two sides of this identity as representing the two sides of the market for foreign currency exchange. Net capital outflow represents the quantity of pounds supplied for the purpose of buying foreign assets. For example, when a UK investment fund wants to buy a Japanese government bond, it needs to change pounds into yen, so it supplies pounds in the market for foreign currency exchange. Net exports represent the quantity of pounds demanded for the purpose of buying UK net exports of goods and services. For example, when a Japanese airline wants to buy aircraft fuel produced by BP, it needs to change its yen into pounds, so it demands pounds in the market for foreign currency exchange.

What price balances the supply and demand in the market for foreign currency exchange? The answer is the real exchange rate. As we saw in the preceding chapter, the real exchange rate is the relative price of domestic and foreign goods and, therefore, is a key determinant of net exports. When the UK real exchange rate appreciates, UK goods become more expensive relative to foreign goods, making UK goods less attractive to consumers abroad (exports would rise) and foreign goods more attractive to domestic consumers (imports would rise). For both reasons, net UK exports fall. Hence, an appreciation of the real exchange rate reduces the quantity of pounds demanded in the market for foreign currency exchange.

Figure 13.2 shows supply and demand in the market for foreign currency exchange. The demand curve slopes downward for the reason we just discussed: a higher real exchange rate makes UK goods more expensive and reduces the quantity of pounds demanded to buy those goods. The supply curve is vertical because the quantity of pounds supplied for net capital outflow does not depend on the real exchange rate. (As discussed earlier, net capital outflow depends on the real interest rate. When discussing the market for foreign currency exchange, we take the real interest rate and net capital outflow as given.)

The real exchange rate adjusts to balance the supply and demand for pounds just as the price of any good adjusts to balance supply and demand for that good. If the real exchange rate were below the equilibrium level, the quantity of pounds supplied would be less than the quantity demanded. The resulting shortage of pounds would push the value of the pound upwards. Conversely, if the real exchange rate were above the equilibrium level, the quantity of pounds supplied would exceed the quantity demanded. The surplus of pounds would drive the value of the pound downward. At the equilibrium real exchange rate, the demand for pounds by non-UK residents arising from the UK net exports of goods and services exactly balances the supply of pounds from UK residents arising from UK net capital outflow.

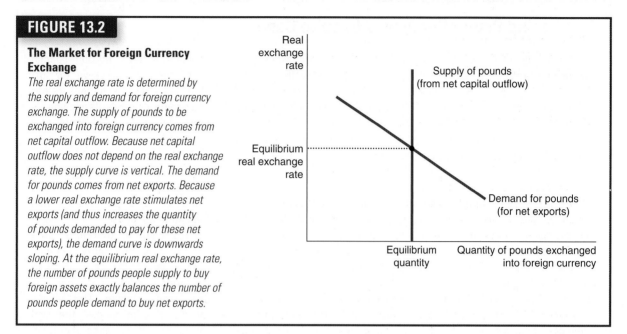

FIGURE 13.2

The Market for Foreign Currency Exchange
The real exchange rate is determined by the supply and demand for foreign currency exchange. The supply of pounds to be exchanged into foreign currency comes from net capital outflow. Because net capital outflow does not depend on the real exchange rate, the supply curve is vertical. The demand for pounds comes from net exports. Because a lower real exchange rate stimulates net exports (and thus increases the quantity of pounds demanded to pay for these net exports), the demand curve is downwards sloping. At the equilibrium real exchange rate, the number of pounds people supply to buy foreign assets exactly balances the number of pounds people demand to buy net exports.

At this point, it is worth noting that the division of transactions between 'supply' and 'demand' in this model is somewhat artificial. In our model, net exports are the source of the demand for pounds, and net capital outflow is the source of the supply. Thus, when a UK resident imports a car made in Japan, our model treats that transaction as a decrease in the quantity of pounds demanded (because net exports fall) rather than an increase in the quantity of pounds supplied. Similarly, when a Japanese citizen buys a UK government bond, our model treats that transaction as a decrease in the quantity of pounds supplied (because net capital outflow falls) rather than an increase in the quantity of pounds demanded. This use of language may seem somewhat unnatural at first, but it will prove useful when analysing the effects of various policies.

SELF TEST Describe the sources of supply and demand in the market for loanable funds and the market for foreign currency exchange.

EQUILIBRIUM IN THE OPEN ECONOMY

So far we have discussed supply and demand in two markets – the market for loanable funds and the market for foreign currency exchange. Let's now consider how these markets are related to each other.

Net Capital Outflow: The Link Between the Two Markets

We begin by recapping what we've learned so far in this chapter. We have been discussing how the economy coordinates four important macroeconomic variables: national saving (S), domestic investment (I), net capital outflow (NCO) and net exports (NX). Keep in mind the following identities:

$$S = I + NCO$$

and

$$NCO = NX$$

FYI

Purchasing Power Parity as a Special Case

An alert reader of this book might ask: why are we developing a theory of the exchange rate here? Didn't we already do that in the preceding chapter?

As you may recall, the preceding chapter developed a theory of the exchange rate called purchasing power parity. This theory asserts that a euro (or any other currency) must buy the same quantity of goods and services in every country. As a result, the real exchange rate is fixed, and all changes in the nominal exchange rate between two currencies reflect changes in the price levels in the two countries.

The model of the exchange rate developed here is related to the theory of purchasing power parity. According to the theory of purchasing power parity, international trade responds quickly to international price differences. If goods were cheaper in one country than in another, they would be exported from the first country and imported into the second until the price difference disappeared. In other words, the theory of purchasing power parity assumes that net exports are highly responsive to small changes in the real exchange rate. If net exports were in fact so responsive, the demand curve in Figure 13.2 would be horizontal.

Thus, the theory of purchasing power parity can be viewed as a special case of the model considered here. In that special case, the demand curve for foreign currency exchange, rather than being downwards sloping, is horizontal at the level of the real exchange rate that ensures parity of purchasing power at home and abroad. That special case is a good place to start when studying exchange rates, but it is far from the end of the story.

This chapter, therefore, concentrates on the more realistic case in which the demand curve for foreign currency exchange is downwards sloping. This allows for the possibility that the real exchange rate changes over time, as in fact it sometimes does in the real world.

In the market for loanable funds, supply comes from national saving, demand comes from domestic investment and net capital outflow, and the real interest rate balances supply and demand. In the market for foreign currency exchange, supply comes from net capital outflow, demand comes from net exports, and the real exchange rate balances supply and demand.

Net capital outflow is the variable that links these two markets. In the market for loanable funds, net capital outflow is part of demand. A person who wants to buy an asset abroad must finance this purchase by obtaining resources in the market for loanable funds. In the market for foreign currency exchange, net capital outflow is the source of supply. A person who wants to buy an asset in another country must supply pounds in order to exchange them for the currency of that country.

The key determinant of net capital outflow, as we have discussed, is the real interest rate. When the UK interest rate is high, owning UK assets is more attractive, and UK net capital outflow is low. Figure 13.3 shows this negative relationship between the interest rate and net capital outflow. This net capital outflow curve is the link between the market for loanable funds and the market for foreign currency exchange.

Simultaneous Equilibrium in Two Markets

We can now put all the pieces of our model together in Figure 13.4. This figure shows how the market for loanable funds and the market for foreign currency exchange jointly determine the important macroeconomic variables of an open economy.

Panel (a) of the figure shows the market for loanable funds (taken from Figure 13.1). As before, national saving is the source of the supply of loanable funds. Domestic investment and net capital outflow are the source of the demand for loanable funds. The equilibrium real interest rate (r_1) brings the quantity of loanable funds supplied and the quantity of loanable funds demanded into balance.

FIGURE 13.3

How Net Capital Outflow Depends on the Interest Rate

Because a higher domestic real interest rate makes domestic assets more attractive, it reduces net capital outflow. Note the position of zero on the horizontal axis: net capital outflow can be positive or negative. A negative value of net capital outflow means that the economy is experiencing a net inflow of capital.

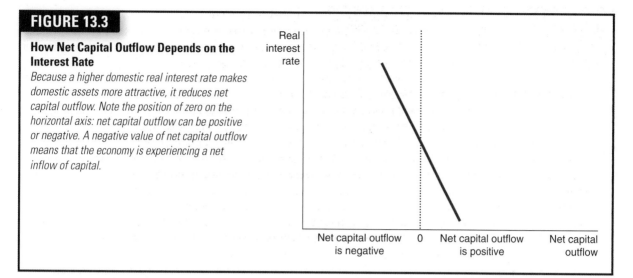

FIGURE 13.4

The Real Equilibrium in an Open Economy

In panel (a), the supply and demand for loanable funds determine the real interest rate. In panel (b), the interest rate determines net capital outflow, which provides the supply of pounds in the market for foreign currency exchange. In panel (c), the supply and demand for pounds in the market for foreign currency exchange determine the real exchange rate.

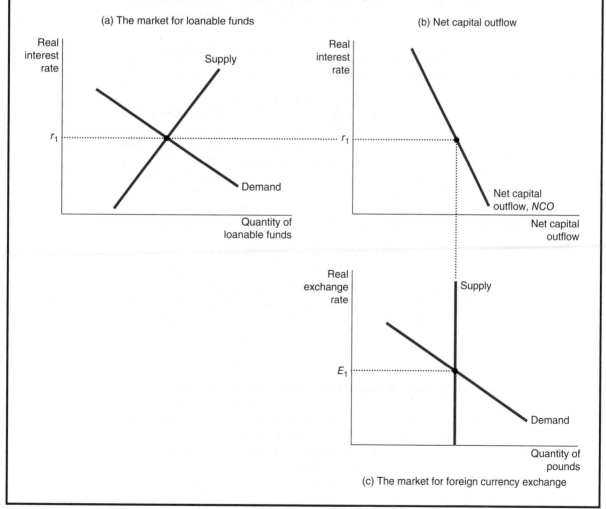

Panel (b) of the figure shows net capital outflow (taken from Figure 13.3). It shows how the interest rate from panel (a) determines net capital outflow. A higher interest rate at home makes domestic assets more attractive, and this in turn reduces net capital outflow. Therefore, the net capital outflow curve in panel (b) slopes downward.

Panel (c) of the figure shows the market for foreign currency exchange (taken from Figure 13.2). Because foreign assets must be purchased with foreign currency, the quantity of net capital outflow from panel (b) determines the supply of pounds to be exchanged into foreign currencies. The real exchange rate does not affect net capital outflow, so the supply curve is vertical. The demand for pounds comes from net exports. Because a depreciation of the real exchange rate increases net exports, the demand curve for foreign currency exchange slopes downward. The equilibrium real exchange rate (E_1) brings into balance the quantity of pounds supplied and the quantity of pounds demanded in the market for foreign currency exchange.

The two markets shown in Figure 13.4 determine two relative prices – the real interest rate and the real exchange rate. The real interest rate determined in panel (a) is the price of goods and services in the present relative to goods and services in the future. The real exchange rate determined in panel (c) is the price of domestic goods and services relative to foreign goods and services. These two relative prices adjust simultaneously to balance supply and demand in these two markets. As they do so, they determine national saving, domestic investment, net capital outflow and net exports. In a moment, we will use this model to see how all these variables change when some policy or event causes one of these curves to shift.

SELF TEST In the model of the open economy just developed, two markets determine two relative prices.
● What are the markets? ● What are the two relative prices?

HOW POLICIES AND EVENTS AFFECT AN OPEN ECONOMY

Having developed a model to explain how key macroeconomic variables are determined in an open economy, we can now use the model to analyse how changes in policy and other events alter the economy's equilibrium. As we proceed, keep in mind that our model is just supply and demand in two markets – the market for loanable funds and the market for foreign currency exchange and as such can be analysed using the three-step approach outlined in Chapter 3.

Government Budget Deficits

When we first discussed the supply and demand for loanable funds earlier in the book, we examined the effects of government budget deficits, which occur when government spending exceeds government revenue. Because a government budget deficit represents *negative* public saving, it reduces national saving (the sum of public and private saving). Thus, a government budget deficit reduces the supply of loanable funds, drives up the interest rate and crowds out investment.

Now let's consider the effects of a budget deficit in an open economy. First, which curve in our model shifts? As in a closed economy, the initial impact of the budget deficit is on national saving and, therefore, on the supply curve for loanable funds. Second, which way does this supply curve shift? Again as in a closed economy, a budget deficit represents *negative* public saving, so it reduces national saving and shifts the supply curve for loanable funds to the left. This is shown as the shift from S_1 to S_2 in panel (a) of Figure 13.5.

Our third and final step is to compare the old and new equilibria. Panel (a) shows the impact of a French budget deficit on the French market for loanable funds. With fewer funds available for borrowers in French financial markets, the interest rate rises from r_1 to r_2 to balance supply and demand.

FIGURE 13.5

The Effects of a Government Budget Deficit

If the French government runs a budget deficit, it reduces the supply of loanable funds from S$_1$ to S$_2$ in panel (a). The interest rate rises from r$_1$ to r$_2$ to balance the supply and demand for loanable funds. In panel (b), the higher interest rate reduces net capital outflow. Reduced net capital outflow, in turn, reduces the supply of euros in the market for foreign currency exchange from S$_1$ to S$_2$ in panel (c). This fall in the supply of euros causes the real exchange rate to appreciate from E$_1$ to E$_2$. The appreciation of the exchange rate pushes the trade balance towards deficit.

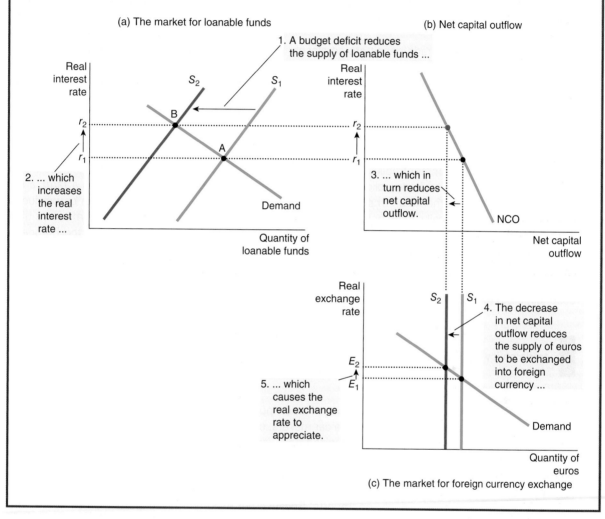

Faced with a higher interest rate, borrowers in the market for loanable funds choose to borrow less. This change is represented in the figure as the movement from point A to point B along the demand curve for loanable funds. In particular, households and firms reduce their purchases of capital goods. As in a closed economy, budget deficits crowd out domestic investment.

In an open economy, however, the reduced supply of loanable funds has additional effects. Panel (b) shows that the increase in the interest rate from r_1 to r_2 reduces net capital outflow. (This fall in net capital outflow is also part of the decrease in the quantity of loanable funds demanded in the movement from point A to point B in panel (a).) Because saving kept at home now earns higher rates of return, investing abroad is less attractive, and domestic residents buy fewer foreign assets. Higher interest rates also attract foreign investors, who want to earn the higher returns on French assets. Thus, when budget deficits raise interest rates, both domestic and foreign behaviour cause French net capital outflow to fall.

Panel (c) shows how budget deficits affect the market for foreign currency exchange. Because net capital outflow is reduced, people need less foreign currency to buy foreign assets, and this induces a leftward shift in the supply curve for euros from S_1 to S_2. The reduced supply of euros causes the real exchange rate to appreciate from E_1 to E_2. That is, the euro becomes more valuable compared to foreign currencies. This appreciation, in turn, makes French goods more expensive compared to foreign goods. Because people both at home and abroad switch their purchases away from the more expensive French goods, exports from France fall, and imports into France rise. For both reasons, French net exports fall. Hence, in an open economy, government budget deficits raise real interest rates, crowd out domestic investment, cause the currency to appreciate and push the trade balance toward deficit.

The budget deficit and trade deficit are so closely related in both theory and practice that, especially when they are both large, they are often referred to by the nickname of the *twin deficits*. We should not, however, view these twins as identical, for many factors beyond fiscal policy can influence the trade deficit.

Trade Policy

A **trade policy** is a government policy that directly influences the quantity of goods and services that a country imports or exports. Trade policy takes various forms. One common trade policy is a *tariff*, a tax on imported goods. Another is an *import quota*, a limit on the quantity of a good that can be produced abroad and sold domestically. Trade policies are common throughout the world, although sometimes they are disguised. For example, before 2000 there was an understanding between Japan and the European Union that Japan would voluntarily limit its sales of cars into the UK, France, Italy, Portugal and Spain to a maximum of 1.1 million (excluding cars produced at factories owned by Japanese companies but located within the European Union). These so-called 'voluntary export restrictions' are not really voluntary and, in essence, are a form of import quota.

> **trade policy** a government policy that directly influences the quantity of goods and services that a country imports or exports

Let's consider the macroeconomic impact of trade policy. Suppose that the European car industry, concerned about competition from Japanese car makers, convinces the European Union (EU) to impose a quota on the number of cars that can be imported from Japan into the EU. In making their case, lobbyists for the car industry assert that the trade restriction would improve the overall EU trade balance. Are they right? Our model, as illustrated in Figure 13.6, offers an answer.

The first step in analysing the trade policy is to determine which curve shifts. The initial impact of the import restriction is, not surprisingly, on imports. Because net exports equal exports minus imports, the policy also affects net exports. And because net exports are the source of demand for euros in the market for foreign currency exchange, the policy affects the demand curve in this market.

The second step is to determine which way this demand curve shifts. Because the quota restricts the number of Japanese cars sold in the EU, it reduces imports at any given real exchange rate. Net exports, which equal exports minus imports, will therefore *rise* for any given real exchange rate. Because non-Europeans need euros to buy EU net exports, there is an increased demand for euros in the market for foreign currency exchange. This increase in the demand for euros is shown in panel (c) of Figure 13.6 as the shift from D_1 to D_2.

The third step is to compare the old and new equilibria. As we can see in panel (c), the increase in the demand for euros causes the real exchange rate to appreciate from E_1 to E_2. Because nothing has happened in the market for loanable funds in panel (a), there is no change in the real interest rate. Because there is no change in the real interest rate, there is also no change in net capital outflow, shown in panel (b). And because there is no change in net capital outflow, there can be no change in net exports, even though the import quota has reduced imports.

FIGURE 13.6

The Effects of an Import Quota

When the EU imposes a quota on the import of Japanese cars, nothing happens in the market for loanable funds in panel (a) or to net capital outflow in panel (b). The only effect is a rise in net exports (exports minus imports) for any given real exchange rate. As a result, the demand for euros in the market for foreign currency exchange rises, as shown by the shift from D_1 to D_2 in panel (c). This increase in the demand for euros causes the value of the euro to appreciate from E_1 to E_2. This appreciation of the euro tends to reduce net exports, offsetting the direct effect of the import quota on the trade balance.

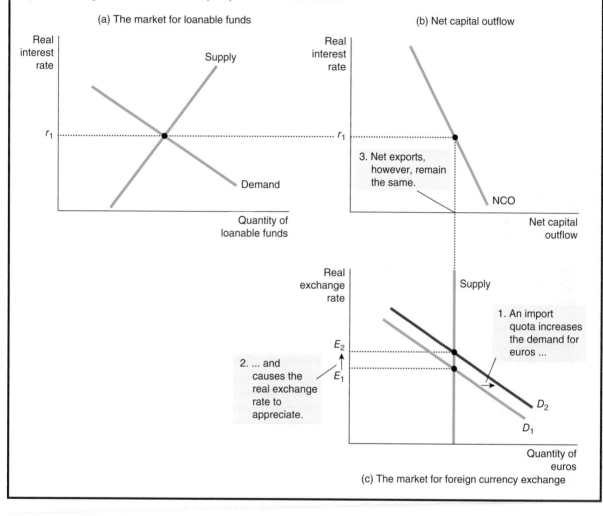

The reason why net exports can stay the same while imports fall is explained by the change in the real exchange rate: when the euro appreciates in value in the market for foreign currency exchange, European goods become more expensive relative to non-European goods. This appreciation encourages imports and discourages exports – and both of these changes work to offset the direct increase in net exports due to the import quota. In the end, an import quota reduces both imports and exports, but net exports (exports minus imports) are unchanged.

We have thus come to a surprising implication: trade policies do not affect the trade balance. That is, policies that directly influence exports or imports do not alter net exports. This conclusion seems less surprising if one recalls the accounting identity:

$$NX = NCO = S - I$$

Net exports equal net capital outflow, which equals national saving minus domestic investment. Trade policies do not alter the trade balance because they do not alter national saving or domestic investment.

For given levels of national saving and domestic investment, the real exchange rate adjusts to keep the trade balance the same, regardless of the trade policies the government puts in place.

Although trade policies do not affect a country's overall trade balance, these policies do affect specific firms, industries and countries. When the EU imposes an import quota on Japanese cars, European car makers have less competition from abroad and will sell more cars. At the same time, because the euro has appreciated in value, Airbus, the European aircraft maker, will find it harder to compete with Boeing, the US aircraft maker. European exports of aircraft will fall, and European imports of aircraft will rise. In this case, the import quota on Japanese cars will increase net exports of cars and decrease net exports of aeroplanes. In addition, it will increase net exports from the EU to Japan and decrease net exports from the EU to the United States. The overall trade balance of the EU economy, however, stays the same.

The effects of trade policies are, therefore, more microeconomic than macroeconomic. Although advocates of trade policies sometimes claim (incorrectly) that these policies can alter a country's trade balance, they are usually more motivated by concerns about particular firms or industries. One should not be surprised, for instance, to hear an executive from BMW advocating import quotas for Japanese cars. Economists almost always oppose such trade policies. Free trade allows economies to specialize in doing what they do best, making residents of all countries better off. Trade restrictions interfere with these gains from trade and, thus, reduce overall economic well-being.

Capital Flight

Large and sudden movement of funds out of a country is called **capital flight**. To see the implications of capital flight for an economy, we again follow our three steps for analysing a change in equilibrium.

> **capital flight** a large and sudden reduction in the demand for assets located in a country

Consider first which curves in our model capital flight affects. We will use France as an example here because in early 2013 it was reported that the country had experienced a considerable outflow of funds amounting to €53 billion in the two months to February 2013. If investors around the world decide to sell some of their assets in France and use the proceeds to buy assets in other countries, this increases French net capital outflow and, therefore, affects both markets in our model. Most obviously, it affects the net capital outflow curve, and this in turn influences the supply of euros in the market for foreign currency exchange. In addition, because the demand for loanable funds comes from both domestic investment and net capital outflow, capital flight affects the demand curve in the market for loanable funds.

Now consider which way these curves shift. When net capital outflow increases, there is greater demand for loanable funds to finance these purchases of capital assets abroad. Thus, as panel (a) of Figure 13.7 shows, the demand curve for loanable funds shifts to the right from D_1 to D_2. In addition, because net capital outflow is higher for any interest rate, the net capital outflow curve also shifts to the right from NCO_1 to NCO_2, as in panel (b).

To see the effects of capital flight on the economy, we compare the old and new equilibria. Panel (a) of Figure 13.7 shows that the increased demand for loanable funds causes the interest rate in France to rise from r_1 to r_2. Panel (b) shows that French net capital outflow increases. (Although the rise in the interest rate does make French assets more attractive, this only partly offsets the impact of capital flight on net capital outflow.) Panel (c) shows that the increase in net capital outflow raises the supply of euros in the market for foreign currency exchange from S_1 to S_2. That is, as people try to get out of French assets, there is a large supply of euros to be converted into other currencies such as dollars and pounds. This increase in supply causes the euro to depreciate from E_1 to E_2. Thus, capital flight from France increases French interest rates and decreases the value of the euro in the market for foreign currency exchange.

These price changes that result from capital flight influence some key macroeconomic quantities. The depreciation of the currency makes exports cheaper and imports more expensive, pushing the trade balance towards surplus. At the same time, the increase in the interest rate reduces domestic investment, which slows capital accumulation and economic growth.

FIGURE 13.7

The Effects of Capital Flight

If people decide that France is a risky place to keep their savings, they will move their capital to safer havens, resulting in an increase in French net capital outflow. Consequently, the demand for loanable funds in France rises from D_1 to D_2, as shown in panel (a), and this drives up French real interest rate from r_1 to r_2. Because net capital outflow is higher for any interest rate, that curve also shifts to the right from NCO_1 to NCO_2 in panel (b). At the same time, in the market for foreign currency exchange, the supply of euros rises from S_1 to S_2, as shown in panel (c). This increase in the supply of euros causes the euro to depreciate from E_1 to E_2, so the euro becomes less valuable compared to other currencies.

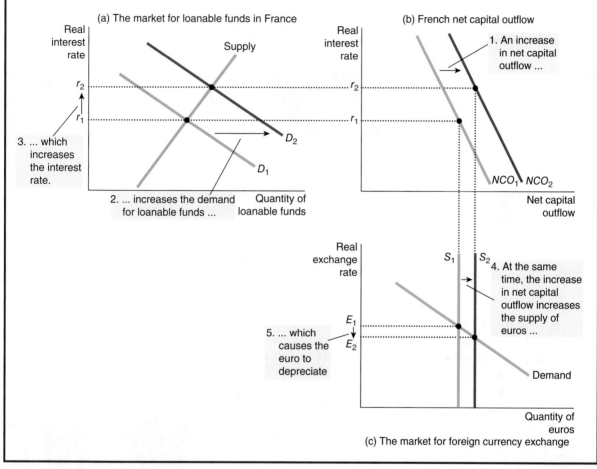

Although capital flight has its largest impact on the country from which capital is fleeing, it also affects other countries. When capital flows out of France into the United States, for instance, it has the opposite effect on the US economy as it has on the French economy. In particular, the rise in French net capital outflow coincides with a fall in US net capital outflow. As the euro depreciates in value and French interest rates rise, the dollar appreciates in value and US interest rates fall. The size of this impact on the US economy is dependent on the relative size of the economy of the United States compared to that of France, and in turn the extent to which the change in the supply of euros from France affects the euro exchange rate as a whole, given that France is just one of 18 countries which make up the euro area.

SELF TEST Suppose that Europeans decided to spend a smaller fraction of their incomes. ● What would be the effect on saving, investment, interest rates, the real exchange rate and the trade balance in the European Union?

CONCLUSION

Historically, international trade has always played a very important role in most European economies. In the past two centuries or so, international finance has also become increasingly important. The typical modern European country consumes a high proportion of goods produced abroad and exports a significant amount of its output to other European countries and to countries outside Europe. In addition, through investment funds and other financial institutions, Europeans borrow and lend in world financial markets, as indeed do the citizens of all advanced industrialized economies.

It is clear, therefore, that a proper understanding of macroeconomics requires a study of the workings of the open economy. This chapter has provided a basic model for thinking about the macroeconomics of open economies.

IN THE NEWS

Capital Flight

Capital flight can be caused by a lack of confidence in an economy or by political instability but it can also manifest itself in funds leaving a country illegally and possibly linked to criminal activity.

Billions Leaving Russia Illegally

The economy of Russia has changed considerably since the early 1990s as the move to a more market-based economy has taken hold. However, the country does suffer from illegal flights of capital both in and out of the country. Estimates put the illegal capital flight since 1994 at some $782.5 billion (€593.2 billion) and in early 2013 the governor of Russia's central bank, Sergei Ignatiev, said that some $49 billion (€37.1 billion) had left the country illegally in 2012. To put this in context, the sum represents around 2.5 per cent of Russia's GDP.

The Russian government claimed that the figure was exaggerated but a study by a US research organization, Global Financial Integrity, in 2013 suggested that on average, some $64 billion (€48.5 billion) had entered or left Russia every year since 2004. Much of this money, it claims, is

income generated from criminal activities which include weapons smuggling, prostitution, people trafficking, drugs and corruption.

The central bank governor noted that the figure he had announced was arrived at by looking at 'payments made by Russian organizations to non-residents, the stated aims of which are clearly false'. In addition, Mr Ignatiev noted that the country also faced problems from so-called 'one-day firms' which are commercial organizations set up to act as channels for illegal funds but which are closed down immediately the funds have been channelled and therefore avoid paying any taxes.

Finding ways to combat this illegal flight is one of the major challenges facing the Russian government. If flows of capital out of the country are as large as were being suggested then the opportunity cost to the country in terms of what the funds could have been used for – investment in infrastructure, health

and education – is extremely high. Some inside Russia have noted that if the country fails to get to grips

Money from criminal gangs involved with prostitution and drugs, among other things, may be part of the funds entering and leaving Russia every year – capital flight has a cost beyond the purely economic.

with the problem and reduces the incidences of corruption which are alleged to be at high levels within the government, the development of the economy would be held back.

Questions

1 Assuming the amount of money leaving Russia is greater than that coming in, what happens to the demand for loanable funds and the interest rate in Russia?

2 What effect would you expect capital flight of the size outlined in the article to have on the exchange rate between the Russian rouble and other currencies?

3 What effect is the capital flight likely to have on Russia's trading partners given the size of the sums quoted in the article?

4 Does the fact that the flows are illegal make any difference to your analysis in the previous questions?

5 Why is clamping down on illegal capital flight and corruption important to Russia's continued economic development?

SUMMARY

- To analyse the macroeconomics of open economies, two markets are central – the market for loanable funds and the market for foreign currency exchange. In the market for loanable funds, the interest rate adjusts to balance the supply of loanable funds (from national saving) and the demand for loanable funds (from domestic investment and net capital outflow). In the market for foreign currency exchange, the real exchange rate adjusts to balance the supply of domestic currency (for net capital outflow) and the demand for domestic currency (for net exports). Because net capital outflow is part of the demand for loanable funds and provides the supply of domestic currency for foreign currency exchange, it is the variable that connects these two markets.

- A policy that reduces national saving, such as a government budget deficit, reduces the supply of loanable funds and drives up the interest rate. The higher interest rate reduces net capital outflow, which reduces the supply of domestic currency in the market

for foreign currency exchange. The domestic currency appreciates and net exports fall.

- Although restrictive trade policies, such as tariffs or quotas on imports, are sometimes advocated as a way to alter the trade balance, they do not necessarily have that effect. A trade restriction increases net exports for a given exchange rate and, therefore, increases the demand for the domestic currency in the market for foreign currency exchange. As a result, the domestic currency appreciates in value, making domestic goods more expensive relative to foreign goods. This appreciation offsets the initial impact of the trade restriction on net exports.

- When investors change their attitudes about holding assets of a country, the ramifications for the country's economy can be profound. In particular, political instability or a lack of confidence in an economy can lead to capital flight, which tends to increase interest rates and causes the currency to depreciate.

QUESTIONS FOR REVIEW

1 Why do we describe the formula $S = I + NCO$ as 'an identity'?

2 How is the interest rate in an open economy determined?

3 Describe supply and demand in the market for loanable funds and the market for foreign currency exchange. How are these markets linked?

4 What effect does a government budget deficit have on the interest rate? Draw a diagram to illustrate your answer.

5 What effect would you expect a government budget surplus to have on the exchange rate? Explain.

6 Why are budget deficits and trade deficits sometimes called the twin deficits?

7 What is 'trade policy'?

8 Suppose that a steel workers' union encourages people to buy only European steel. What would this policy do to the European overall trade balance and the real exchange rate? What is the impact on the European steel industry? What is the impact on the European textile industry?

9 What effect would you expect a tariff to have on the real exchange rate? Explain using appropriate diagrams.

10 What is capital flight? When a country experiences capital flight, what is the effect on its interest rate and exchange rate?

PROBLEMS AND APPLICATIONS

1 Germany generally runs a trade surplus. Do you think this is most related to high foreign demand for German goods, low German demand for foreign goods, a high German saving rate relative to German investment, or structural barriers against imports into Germany? Explain your answer.

2 If the UK prime minister announces that the government are solidly on a course of deficit reduction, which should make the pound more attractive to investors, would such a deficit reduction in fact raise the value of the pound? Explain.

3 Suppose that the government passes an investment tax credit, which subsidizes domestic investment. How does this policy affect national saving, domestic investment, net capital outflow, the interest rate, the exchange rate and the trade balance?

4 Assume that there is a rise in the trade deficit of a country due largely to the rise in a government budget deficit. Assume also that some commentators in the popular press claim that the increased trade deficit resulted from a decline in the quality of the country's products relative to foreign products.

a. Assume that the country's products did decline in relative quality during this period. How might this affect net exports *at any given exchange rate*?

b. Use a three-panel diagram to show the effect of this shift in net exports on the country's real exchange rate and trade balance.

c. Does a decline in the quality of the country's products have any effect on standards of living for its residents? (Hint: when a country's residents sell goods to non-country residents, what do they receive in return?)

5 Explain in words why European *export* industries would benefit from a reduction in restrictions on *imports* into the European Union.

6 Suppose the French suddenly develop a strong taste for British wine. Answer the following questions in words and using a diagram.

a. What happens to the demand for pounds in the market for foreign currency exchange?

b. What happens to the value of pounds in the market for foreign currency exchange?

c. What happens to the quantity of UK net exports?

7 Suppose your country is running a trade deficit and you hear your trade minister on the radio, saying: 'The trade deficit must be reduced, but import quotas only annoy our trading partners. If we subsidize our exports instead, we can reduce the deficit by increasing our competitiveness.' Using a three-panel diagram, show the effect of an export subsidy on net exports and the real exchange rate. Do you agree with the trade minister?

8 Suppose that real interest rates increase across Europe. Explain how this development will affect UK net capital outflow. Then explain how it will affect UK net exports by using a formula from the chapter and by using a diagram. What will happen to the UK real interest rate and real exchange rate?

9 Suppose that Germans decide to increase their saving.

a. If the elasticity of German net capital outflow with respect to the real interest rate is very high, will this increase in private saving have a large or small effect on German domestic investment?

b. If the elasticity of German exports with respect to the real exchange rate is very low, will this increase in private saving have a large or small effect on the German real exchange rate?

10 Assume that saving in China has been used to finance investment into the EU. That is, the Chinese have been buying European capital assets.

a. If the Chinese decided they no longer wanted to buy European assets, what would happen in the European market for loanable funds? In particular, what would happen to European interest rates, European saving and European investment?

b. What would happen in the market for foreign currency exchange? In particular, what would happen to the value of the euro and the European trade balance?

PART 7
SHORT-RUN ECONOMIC FLUCTUATIONS

14 BUSINESS CYCLES

The majority of you reading this chapter will have lived through a period of economic change. Many of you will have been born in the mid-1990s. Between this time and the middle part of the first decade of the 2000s, many countries in Europe experienced a period of prosperity, relatively strong economic growth, relatively low and stable inflation, unemployment rates which were not too high and interest rates which were at relatively low levels.

From about 2007 onwards, things changed. The financial crisis led to serious economic problems in many countries and a global recession. A **recession** is characterized by a period of falling incomes and rising unemployment and technically occurs after two successive quarters of negative growth. If such a contraction in growth continues and is more severe it might be described as a **depression**.

> **recession** a period of declining real incomes and rising unemployment. The technical definition gives recession occurring after two successive quarters of negative economic growth
> **depression** a severe recession

Whilst many countries came out of recession around 2009–2010, economic growth in many European countries has been weak. Interest rates in many developed countries have been at virtually zero rates for a number of years, unemployment has risen to alarming levels in some countries but inflation has been stuck at levels above the target rate for many countries. At the time of writing, the economic prospects do not look good but by the time you read this chapter things may be improving in your country. By 2016 it could be that many economies in Europe return once again to a period of stronger growth and an increase in prosperity.

Your instructors will have experienced the ups and downs of economic activity over a longer period but they too will have experienced periods of considerable economic problems and periods of strong growth. The latter part of the 1970s and into the early part of the 1980s was characterized by severe economic problems in the UK but by the mid-1980s, things improved only to slump again in the early 1990s.

It is clear that the level of economic activity, the amount of buying and selling (the number of transactions) changes over time. Economic activity is an important factor in determining economic growth and in turn the level of employment, unemployment, inflation and other macroeconomic variables. Economists are pretty much agreed on the causes of long-run changes in macroeconomic equilibrium but there is more disagreement about what causes short-run variations in economic activity. The short-run swings in economic activity vary in size and time-span. In the UK, the recession of 1920–1924, for example, saw GDP fall by about 9 per cent from its peak over the first 18 months and then take a further 27 months to get back to its pre-recession peak, and in the next 12 months rise to around 4 per cent above its pre-recession peak. In 1930–1934, the length of time for the economy to recover to its pre-recession peak was around 48 months but the economy 'only' fell to around 7 per cent below its pre-recession peak. In the 1990–1993 recession, the economy took around 32 months to recover but thereafter rose by over 8 per cent above its pre-recession peak and only fell to around 3 per cent of its pre-recession peak. The post-financial crisis of 2008 until the time of writing has seen the economy falling to around 6 per cent below its pre-recession peak and has been below the peak consistently for over 60 months. You may be reading this now and the UK economy has still not managed to reach its pre-recession peak. The **business cycle** refers to the study of the fluctuations in economic growth around the trend growth.

business cycle the fluctuations in economic growth around trend growth

TREND GROWTH RATES

Most of the data we will be looking at in this chapter is classed as **time series data**, observations on a variable over a time-period and which are ordered over time.

time series data observations on a variable over a time-period and which are ordered over time

Central to the analysis of business cycles is GDP over time. Figure 14.1 shows two graphs: panel (a) shows GDP in the UK from 1960–2011. The value of GDP is given on the vertical axis in current US dollars and the horizontal axis is the time period in years. Panel (b) shows GDP across the European Union over the same time period.

Panel (a) shows that the value of the UK economy in 1960 was around $72 billion but by 2011 the UK economy was worth around $2.4 trillion. Panel (b) shows the economy of the EU was worth around $365 billion in 1960 but has grown to some $17.5 trillion in 2011. A trend line has been added in both cases and this shows how over time the GDP of both the UK and the EU has risen. It also shows how actual GDP fluctuates around the trend and that there are similarities in these fluctuations. For example, between 1960 and 1976, trend growth and actual GDP were similar but from around 1977 to the early 1980s growth was above trend but then started to decline and in the mid-1980s was below trend. This sort of pattern has been repeated with some periods above trend and some below and it is noticeable that in the period up to 2008, growth was significantly above trend but was followed by a sharp fall and growth is currently below trend. The pattern is almost the same as that for the EU as a whole.

The question arises as to what causes these fluctuations and, ever since the Great Depression in the 1930s, economists have sought to offer models to explain these macroeconomic variations. It is safe to say that there is disagreement among economists about the cause of these fluctuations and what or indeed whether any policy measures need to be put in place to deal with the welfare issues that arise. Welfare issues arise if it is assumed that the economy is deviating in some way from its equilibrium. Policy is put in place to address the welfare issues that arise. Some economists, however, believe that the economy may not be deviating from its equilibrium but instead the economy is moving from one equilibrium point to another, in which case policy is not required because there are no welfare issues arising if the economy is in equilibrium. We shall explore these differences later in the chapter.

FIGURE 14.1

GDP in the UK and Europe, 1960–2011

Panel (a) shows UK GDP, measured in current US dollars on the vertical axis over the period 1960–2011. Panel (b) shows GDP across the European Union (also in current US dollars) over the same time period. A trend line has been added in both panels.

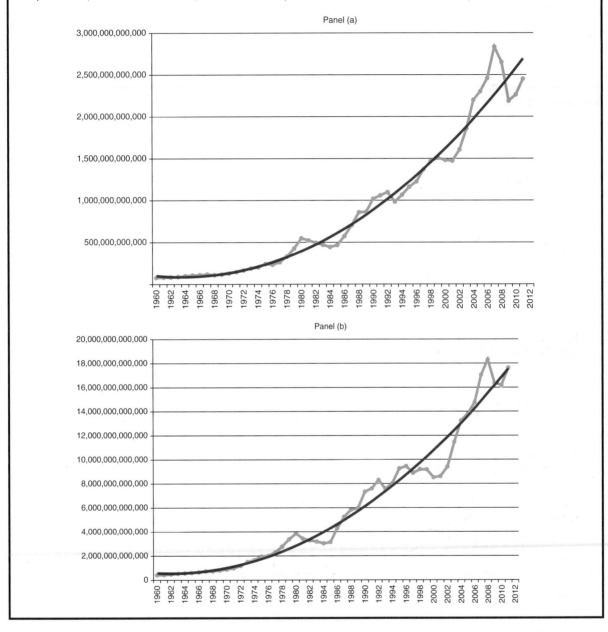

Data Concepts

When dealing with macroeconomic variables there are a number of concepts that we will utilize over the coming chapters which need to be understood. Figure 14.2 shows the rate of growth of UK GDP between 1960 and 2011. It is clear from this figure that the rate of growth fluctuates over the time period. From 1962, growth accelerated and reached 5 per cent in 1964 before slowing down to between 2.8 and 2.0 per cent up to 1968. Thereafter growth accelerated again reaching 7.3 per cent in 1973 before the economy slumped dramatically and economic activity actual shrank in 1974 and 1975. The pattern of rise and fall is repeated in the time period shown thereafter.

GDP shows a pattern of peaks and troughs and periods where growth is accelerating, decelerating and in some cases is declining. The **peak** is where economic activity reaches a high and real output begins to decline. A **trough** is where economic activity reaches a low and the decline ends. These are both turning points in economic activity.

peak where economic activity reaches a high and real output begins to decline
trough where economic activity reaches a low and the decline ends

FIGURE 14.2

UK GDP Growth Rate, 1960–2011 (%)

UK GDP fluctuates between various peaks and troughs over the period. In some cases, GDP growth is positive for a number of years and so the economy is growing during that time, but in other years GDP growth is negative and the economy shrinks.

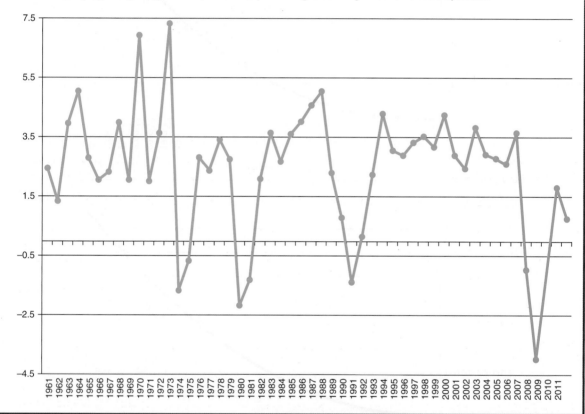

When economic activity is accelerating and the rate of growth is rising each year this represents a period of expansion. Depending on the rate at which real output is accelerating, it may be referred to as a *boom*. In 2003, UK GDP grew at 3.8 per cent, in 2004 it grew at 2.9 per cent. It is important to note that economic activity slowed down in 2004 but still continued to grow. Taking a simple example to illustrate this, if economic activity is measured in terms of the number of tonnes of steel produced, if output was 10 million tonnes in 2002 and 12 million tonnes in 2003, then the growth rate is 2 per cent. If output is 13.5 million tonnes in 2004, the growth rate is now 1.25 per cent; growth has slowed compared to 2003 but the economy is still producing more steel than the year before. This is why we use the terms 'accelerating' and 'decelerating' to describe changes in the rate of growth of GDP when it is positive.

However, when real output actually shrinks then there is a **contraction** in the economy. If output of steel in 2005 was 13 million tonnes, the economy would have shrunk; less steel is being produced compared to 2004 and growth will be –3.8 per cent.

> **contraction** when real output is lower than the previous time period

If expansion is considerably above trend then the term 'boom' might be appropriate but if growth is only just above trend then that term may not be applicable. It is important to be aware of the language used when discussing economic growth; the news media are keen to use emotive words such as 'boom', 'bust' and 'slump' when reporting growth data. Is a growth rate of 0.25 per cent 'a slump' for example?

In Figure 14.2 we can find the mean of the data represented by adding the sum of the annual growth rates (124) and dividing by the number of years (51). The mean growth rate over this period is 2.4 per cent. In describing periods of accelerating and decelerating growth, therefore, we can compare the growth rate at a particular time period with the mean growth rate. The period from 1970 to 1973 might reasonably be called a period of boom given that the rate of growth of GDP averaged almost 5 per cent during that time reaching a peak of 7.3 per cent in 1973. In 2008 and 2009, GDP growth was –1.0 and –4.0 per cent respectively, considerably below the mean growth rate for the whole period of 2.4 per cent.

The difference between a peak and a trough in the business cycle and trend output is called the **amplitude**. Figure 14.2 shows that this can vary considerably. In 1973 the amplitude was 4.9 but in 1984 was 0.3 and in 1981 was –3.7. The length of the time between peaks and troughs in economic activity also varies considerably. Between 1993 and 2008, the UK enjoyed a period of persistent growth. The difference between peak and trough was 16 years. Prior to this, the difference between peak and trough (1988–1991) was just four years.

> **amplitude** the difference between peak and trough and trend output

> **SELF TEST** What are the main phases of the business cycle?

Trends

An important point of disagreement about economic time series data is the existence of trends. A **trend** is the underlying long-term movement in a data series. The trend can be upwards over time, downwards or constant. Earlier we took the mean (average) of the growth rate in UK GDP between 1960 and 2011 as being 2.4 per cent. The mean of a set of time series data can be used as the trend.

> **trend** the underlying long term movement in a data series

Figure 14.1 showed UK and EU GDP between 1960 and 2011 and a trend line was added to the data showing very clearly that the trend was upwards over the time period shown. Trends can demonstrate patterns over a period which can be described as *stationary* and *nonstationary*. **Stationary data** are time series data that have a constant mean value over time, whereas **nonstationary data** are time series data where the mean value can either rise or fall over time. The data in Figure 14.1 would suggest that GDP is non-stationary data rising over time. Other economic variables might exhibit the characteristic of stationary data; unemployment, for example, tends to be more characteristic of stationary data. In the period 1993 to 2003, UK unemployment averaged 1.92 million whereas in the period from 2004–2011, unemployment averaged 1.99 million. As with any statistical analysis, care has to be taken to consider what data have been included, how the data have been constructed, what time period is involved and what test has been applied, and there is often disagreement about appropriate statistical tests and measurements used in economic analysis.

> **stationary data** time series data that has a constant mean value over time
> **nonstationary data** time series data where the mean value can either rise or fall over time

The disagreement about how statistical tests are used and applied is beyond the scope of this book, but understanding that disagreement between economists on vital issues, such as the path of business cycles and the policy options that might be applied, is derived in large part from different interpretations of the reliability and validity of different statistical methods. A trend over time has implications. For example, looking at Figure 14.1, would there be any reason to assume that the level of economic growth for the next 10 years will not continue to be positive and increasing in the UK and EU? Nonstationary data can be assumed to have what are called **deterministic trends** – trends that are constant, positive or negative independent of time for the series being analysed and which change by a constant amount each period. GDP might deviate from trend over short-term periods but when looked at over longer time periods will revert to the mean. In contrast, a **stochastic trend** is one where the trend variable changes by some random amount in each time period. If macroeconomic variables are analysed assuming they exhibit a deterministic trend, for example that GDP will rise by 2.4 per cent on average, then the implication is that policy measures can be applied when GDP deviates from this average. What has caused GDP to deviate from the mean must be a transitory phenomenon (is temporary and only lasting for a short period of time) and this further implies that the cause of the deviation must also be temporary and can be influenced.

> **deterministic trends** trends that are constant, positive or negative independent of time for the series being analysed
> **stochastic trend** where trend variables change by some random amount in each time period

What if the deterministic trend is illusory and we have applied an inappropriate statistical test to the time series data we are looking at? If the data exhibit a trend that is stochastic, then policy measures might be applied that are unnecessary and possibly distorting. If the deviations are removed the variable does not, unlike a deterministic trend, revert to the mean. Instead, the variable might move from its mean and stay away from that mean over the next time period. The law of large numbers states that, as the number of observations increases, the average of the observations is likely to be the mean of the whole population of observations. For example, if we toss a fair coin ten times, we might observe six instances of heads and four of tails. The mean of these observations in terms of the ratio heads to tails is 6:10 or 0.6. If we toss the coin a further 90 times we might observe 42 heads and 48 tails, a mean of 0.46. When we look at the mean of the population as a whole (100 observations) the mean is 0.48. If we toss the coin a further 10,000 times the chances are that the mean is likely to be close to 0.5. If we continued to toss the coin and observe the trend, it is likely that it would continue to be 0.5. Taking any selection of data from the total number of observations, the mean might be different as shown above but the greater the number of observations we observe the more likely it is that we will get the mean. It would not be unreasonable to assume that in future time periods the mean is going to continue to be 0.5.

If, however, something changes in the nature of the coin or the friction exerted by air, the surface on which the coin lands, etc., which affects the coin tossing outcomes, then the trends (mean) we observe might be completely random for every time period we observe and so when looking at the population as a whole the consistency of the law of large numbers is destroyed.

This summary of statistical arguments is important to bear in mind as we look at short-run variations in macroeconomic variables. The study of time series data is complex and it is important to take into account as we look at different schools of thought in economics, that many of the differences of opinion arise from different interpretations and use of statistics.

Procyclical and Countercyclical Movements in Macroeconomic Data

Let us assume that GDP of a country exhibits a deterministic trend and that the trend growth over a period is 2.4 per cent. If GDP over an 18-month period is reported as 1.3 per cent, what might we expect to happen to key macroeconomic variables? If GDP has slowed from trend it might be expected that the number of people out of work would has fallen, that inflation would have slowed, the money supply contracted and that real wages would has fallen. Observations over time do show that, when economic activity slows, unemployment rises and the rate at which prices rise slows. This makes intuitive sense. If firms are cutting back production, as a slowing of GDP implies, then they might not need as many employees and so some might be let go and, at the same time, firms may think twice about increasing prices when economic activity is slowing for fear of losing sales. They may decide to keep prices constant or even lower them in an attempt to try and boost demand.

Economists will often look at the movement of pairs of variables which are called **comovements**. Typically, one of these variables is GDP. Economists will then compare another economic variable such as inflation or employment with GDP over time and see if any relationship can be determined.

> **comovement** the movement of pairs of variables over time

Comovements may exhibit certain relationships. When a variable is above trend when GDP is above trend the variable is said to be **procyclical**. When GDP is above trend, inflation and employment also tend to be above trend and so are classed as procyclical. Real wages and nominal interest rates are also classed as procyclical. If a variable is below trend when GDP is above trend the variable is described as **countercyclical**. Unemployment can be classed as countercyclical because it tends to be below trend when GDP is above trend.

> **procyclical** a variable that is above trend when GDP is above trend
> **countercyclical** a variable that is below trend when GDP is above trend

> **SELF TEST** Would you expect inflation to be procyclical or countercyclical in a period when economic activity is declining? Explain.
> What would you expect real wages to be in a period of rising economic activity? Explain.

Variables as Indicators

Economists are not fortune tellers but, in trying to understand business cycles and whether it is possible to predict changes in economic activity, they have looked at the extent to which economic variables or collections of economic variables over time give any clue to deviations from trend. Research by Wesley C. Mitchell and Arthur F. Burns in the United States in the 1930s led to an index of cyclical indicators which is now utilized by the Organization of Economic Cooperation and Development (OECD) to try and identify potential turning points in economic activity. Figure 14.3 shows the composite leading indicators index between 2003 and 2013 for the OECD area. The arrows show turning points. It is clear that the index began to decline in the middle of 2007. The global recession followed. In early 2009, the index began to rise and this indicated a turning point to suggest economic activity would begin to improve.

Cyclical indicators can have three characteristics. They can be **leading indicators** where the indicator tends to foretell future changes in economic activity, a **lagging indicator** which occurs after changes in economic activity have occurred and **coincident indicators** occur at the same time as changes in economic activity. The OECD's composite leading indicators (CLI) index is classed as a leading indicator. Figure 14.4 shows the CLI index for the UK and the Euro Area 17 from February 2011 to December 2012 (note, Latvia joined the Euro Area in January 2014). The index suggests that the UK economy might expect to see some improvement but that the situation in the Euro Area continues to be challenging.

> **leading indicator** an indicator which can be used to foretell future changes in economic activity
> **lagging indicator** an indicator which occurs after changes in economic activity have occurred
> **coincident indicator** an indicator which occurs at the same time as changes in economic activity

FIGURE 14.3

OECD Area Composite Leading Indicators (CLI) Index, 2003–2013
The CLI index shows key turning points in the global economy since 2003.

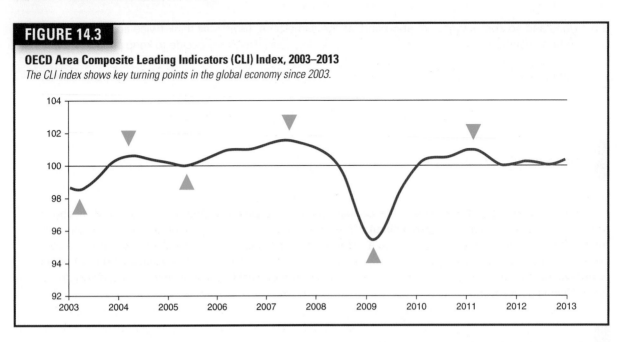

FIGURE 14.4

OECD Composite Leading Indicators Index, February 2011–December 2012 for the UK and the Euro Area 17
The upturn in the CLI index since November 2011 suggests that the UK economy is likely to improve but a softening of the index in December 2012 suggests that growth is still likely to be weak. The Euro Area 17 index has been falling for most of the period, although a slight upturn from September 2012 suggests an improvement in economic activity in the EU 17 in the future.

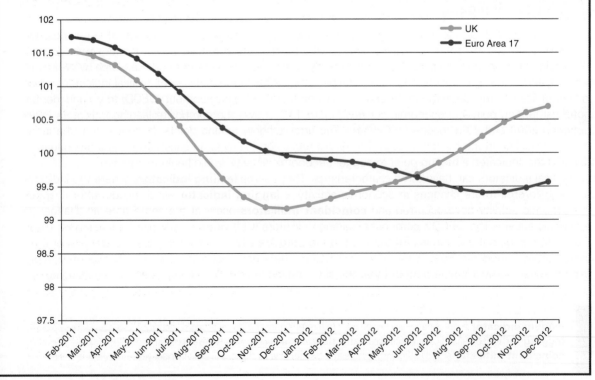

CAUSES OF CHANGES IN THE BUSINESS CYCLE

Having looked at some of the ways in which the data in macroeconomic time series are used and some background to the study of the business cycle, we now turn to asking questions about what causes changes in economic activity. We know that the economy is made up of households and firms and so it is reasonable to expect that the behaviour of these two elements of the economy have a role to play in how economic activity changes. Firms and households make decisions.

Household Spending Decisions

Households make decisions on how much labour to supply. The amount of labour supplied depends in part on the real wage rate. The rate of growth of wages in relation to prices affects consumers' purchasing power. How consumers perceive changes in real wages is an important factor in decision-making. Households also make consumption decisions on everyday goods and services, leisure and entertainment and also on what are sometimes called 'big-ticket' items such as durable household goods (TVs, washing machines, cars, fridge freezers etc.) not to mention decisions on purchasing houses or flats. Purchasing decisions on these items may in themselves be cyclical; if a newly-wed couple buys a house, for example, it may be that in the next year they spend considerable amounts on furniture, decorating and household goods. It then may be several years before goods begin to wear out and need replacing or the house needs decorating again.

Households will also make decisions based on changes in interest rates, house prices and taxation. Increases in interest rates may encourage a rise in saving and a reduction in consumption; changes in house prices affect people's wealth and the effect can lead to changes in spending, especially if people are able to borrow on the strength of the value of their property. Changes in tax rates affect different people in different ways and can have a considerable impact on behaviour.

Firms' Decision-Making

Firms make decisions about production levels – how much output to produce – based on what they think they can sell. If firms face strong demand they are likely to increase output and may have to take on more workers and buy more raw materials and semi-finished goods in order to satisfy demand. Some firms may look to expand by investing in new equipment and machinery or by acquiring new premises or even other firms. Firms also make decisions about how many workers to hire (or release) based on the real wage rate and productivity levels. If the real wage rate falls then firms can afford to hire more workers; if productivity levels rise then costs can be lowered and firms can be more competitive. Firms will also monitor stock levels (stock is often referred to as inventories). If stocks are building up then it may be that sales are slowing down, whereas if stocks are falling demand may be strong and sales rising. Firms will respond to changes in inventory levels by expanding or contracting output as necessary or investing in new plant and equipment or on mergers and acquisitions. The government is also a key economic actor; it makes decisions on taxes and spending and how much to borrow to finance its activities.

External Forces

Economic activity is also affected by events abroad. In an open economy, movements in exchange rates affect the competitiveness of domestic and foreign firms through changes in import and export prices. Economic activity abroad can also have an impact on countries as consumption and investment decisions by firms and consumers abroad change. The UK Chancellor of the Exchequer in 2012 regularly pointed to the problems in the euro area as a reason why the UK economy had not recovered from recession as quickly as had originally been predicted.

We also have to take into account the effect of events which are often totally unpredictable such as drought, flood, tsunamis, hurricanes, extreme cold or earthquakes, through to events such as political upheaval, war, terrorism and conflict which can have far-reaching effects on individual countries and the global economy.

Government Policy

Governments have control over a considerable amount of economic activity. Governments make decisions about tax rates and have to try and consider the incentive effects of changes in tax rates. Decisions about major infrastructure investment can be made by governments which can have ripple effects throughout an economy. Government agents can also have an effect on economic activity. Central banks are independent of most governments but have links with government. In the UK, for example, the government sets the target for inflation which the Bank of England is responsible for. The Bank of England then sets monetary policy to meet the target the government has set. Changes in interest rates will affect both households and firms through policy decisions like quantitative easing and measures designed to help ease credit flows to business and households.

Confidence and Expectations

Households and firms not only make decisions based on current needs but also on the future. It is unlikely that an individual will make a decision to take out a loan for €15,000 to buy a car if that person believes the security of their job is in question. The news media provide information on the state of the economy, governments make pronouncements, senior finance ministers and banking officials are interviewed about their forecasts for the economy. Employees will get a sense of how the firms they work for are performing and those in the public sector may take close note of government policy decisions. Workers may look at current inflation rates and their wage rise and may make judgements about inflation in the future and therefore what sort of wage rise they need to maintain their standard of living. Firms may also look at inflation rates and make judgements about price rises to consumers based on what they expect inflation to be in the future and how inflation in raw materials might affect their costs.

Our expectations of the future shape our decisions, and confidence of firms and households to make decisions is something that is very difficult to quantify and equally difficult to know when it changes. At what point does any individual begin to believe that stock or house prices have reached a peak, at what point does a firm make the decision to make redundancies and why does confidence begin to decline or to pick up? These are all difficult questions to answer but confidence and expectations play a significant part in swings in economic activity.

SELF TEST A country's finance minister presents the government's annual financial statement and advises that she expects GDP to contract sharply in the coming year because of adverse international economic conditions. How might such a speech influence confidence and expectations of households and firms?

BUSINESS CYCLE MODELS

Attempts to try and understand how business cycles occur have led to different models which differ in the assumptions that are made. On the one hand there are models which assume that markets clear quickly and as a result the welfare of economic actors (firms and households) is maximized and there are no reasons why economic actors should change their behaviour. On the other hand there are models which assume that markets do not always clear quickly and that rigidities are present in the market, particularly with regard to prices and wages which mean that for a time, economic actors will not be maximizing welfare.

We will provide an overview of the different business cycle models with perspectives that consider the supply side of the economy and then we will look at models associated with the demand side of the economy.

Supply Side – The New Classical Model

This model is based around analysis of the supply side of the economy and the operation of the labour market. It is assumed that the labour market clears but that workers have imperfect information. The model highlights the importance of anticipated and unanticipated price changes. If workers correctly anticipate price changes they can change their behaviour such that real wages and the amount of labour they supply adjust to clear the market. For example, if the price level rises, the real wage will fall and firms will be encouraged to hire more labour. If the price change is anticipated, workers will recognize that real wages will fall and will supply less labour. The demand for labour will be greater than the supply of labour so the nominal wage will rise. However, the real wage at the new equilibrium will be constant.

If workers do not anticipate the change in prices, the real wage will fall, firms will demand more labour but workers continue to offer the same amount of labour hours so the demand for labour will be in excess of the supply and the nominal wage will rise but the rise will be less than the price rise. The result is that output will rise but the real wage will fall. The increase in output will be above trend GDP. In this model there has been a deviation from equilibrium output because workers have incomplete information and are not aware of the impact of changes in the price level.

Aggregate Supply Shocks A further aspect of the new classical model looks at how shocks to aggregate supply can cause deviations from trend output. These shocks can affect the productivity of factors of production and can be temporary such as the effect of natural disasters, or permanent such as can happen when new technologies are developed. The developments in computer technology over the last 30 years, for example, have had a permanent impact on productivity which few would have envisaged.

If supply shocks are temporary, such as the effect of an earthquake, productivity declines and demand for labour and other factors will fall which will also leads to a fall in output below trend GDP. It is possible to observe aspects of this argument in events which have occurred in the last ten years. An earthquake in Northern Japan in 2011 caused extensive damage and disruption to supply chains across the globe. Firms found that component parts were in short supply and some firms had to lay off workers and suspend production until the supply chains were re-established. The global nature of business means that such natural disasters can have far-reaching effects.

Supply Side – The Keynesian Model

In the next chapter we will look in more detail at the contribution of John Maynard Keynes to macroeconomics. One of the main propositions that Keynes put forward was that markets do not clear as quickly as classical economists believed. The Keynesian assumption is that the ability of the goods and labour market to clear are impaired by the existence of *sticky prices* and *sticky wages*.

In labour markets, firms enter into contractual agreements with workers and are also constrained by labour market legislation and regulation which means that it is not always easy to adjust the labour force to changed economic circumstances. Excess demand or supply in the labour market will not be eliminated quickly by changes in wages because of these wage rigidities, and in particular wages tend to be sticky downwards in that it is difficult for firms to adjust wages down when there is an excess supply of labour as a result of changing economic conditions, such as a change in the price level.

Sticky prices occur where there are costs to firms of changing prices. We introduced the idea of menu costs in Chapter 11. Changing economic conditions in the goods market may warrant a change in price to clear the market but because firms face costs in changing prices it may be that prices are changed infrequently. In addition to the internal costs to firms of diverting labour resources to changing prices, firms will have agreements with suppliers and retailers about prices built into contracts which may not be capable of being re-negotiated for some time. The existence of menu costs mean that prices will be sticky and prevent markets from clearing in the short run.

Demand Side – The New Classical Model

We have noted in earlier chapters that aggregate demand is composed of consumption spending, investment spending, government spending and net exports. Changes to any or all of the components of aggregate demand could cause a deviation of output from trend. Later in the book we will look at causes of shifts in aggregate demand but in this section we are going to trace through the effect of an assumed change in aggregate demand. A rise in aggregate demand, for example, will, *ceteris paribus*, lead to a rise in the price level. A rise in the price level reduces real wages and firms look to hire more workers with the result that the nominal wage will rise. The rise in aggregate demand will lead to an increase in output and the price level increases. The increase in the number of workers hired causes a fall in unemployment. The New Classical interpretation rests on workers misinterpreting a rise in nominal wages as a rise in real wages, in other words, they do not fully take into account the effect on wages of the price rise. We referred to this in Chapter 11 as the *inflation fallacy.*

The result of this is that the economy moves to a temporary equilibrium where the expectations of some economic actors are not fully incorporated because they are incorrect. However, over time, workers will begin to realize that real wages have changed and as a result begin to change their behaviour. As workers negotiate for wage rises that maintain their standard of living, firms' costs rise and some firms will cut back supply with the result that the economy returns to trend output but with a higher price level once expectations have fully adjusted.

If aggregate demand falls then the economy will enter a period of contraction with output and prices falling in the short run. The reverse process to the one outlined above will take place. Real wages rise and firms begin to cut back on output which increases unemployment. The demand for labour will be in excess of the supply of labour and nominal wage rates will fall. Workers see the fall in nominal wages as a fall in the standard of living but over time their expectations will adjust to take into account the fall in the price level and output will return to trend.

Cyclical Implications The analysis provided above has implications for the nature of the cyclicality of key macroeconomic variables. In the new classical model, when output is above trend, unemployment is countercyclical and employment will be above trend and so be procyclical. Inflation will be procyclical but real wages will be countercyclical because as output rises real wages fall.

Demand Side – The Keynesian Model

Remember that the Keynesian model assumes sticky prices and wages. If there is an increase in aggregate demand then wages and prices will take time to adjust. The increase in demand will mean firms' stocks begin to decline and so they will take steps to increase output and in so doing increase employment. In the short run, therefore, output increases above trend but the price level does not change because of sticky prices.

Over time, however, the economy will return to trend because firms will eventually be able to raise prices and nominal wages will also increase. The rise in nominal wages affects firms' costs and some will begin to cut back output which returns to trend but with a higher price level (which is the same outcome as that given in the new classical model above), but the way in which the economy has adjusted to the deviation from trend has differed. If aggregate demand is reduced, the reverse situation will apply and explains why recessions occur.

The speed with which the economy returns to trend after an aggregate demand shock will depend on the time it takes for prices and wages to adjust to the changed economic conditions. In this model, employment, real wages and inflation are procyclical and unemployment is countercyclical.

Real Business Cycles

At the heart of the model of real business cycles is the belief that changes in technology, both positive and negative technology shocks, affect productivity regardless of the real wage rate. The model assumes that there are no market imperfections, that firms and households are profit and utility maximizing and that markets clear. Against the background of these assumptions, if there is a negative technology shock then labour productivity falls and the demand for labour falls. Output will fall as a result and unemployment will increase. Output falls because aggregate supply falls, which creates excess demand in the economy. An excess of aggregate demand will lead to a rise in the price level. If the price level increases this affects the real interest rate. Recall that the real interest rate is the nominal interest rate minus inflation. If inflation rises and the nominal interest rate is constant then the real interest rate will rise. A rise in the real interest rate would lead to a fall in investment by firms.

The causes of business cycles, therefore, are technology shocks that cause permanent shifts in aggregate supply, but when aggregate supply shifts the expectations of economic actors are still correct and so there is no reason for governments or central banks to intervene and apply policy prescriptions. The real business cycle model, therefore, does not see growth over time as being a deterministic trend but a stochastic one. In real business cycle models, employment, labour productivity and real wages are procyclical.

Finn E. Kydland and Edward C. Prescott won the Nobel Prize for Economics in 2004 and their award was based on the work they had done on business cycles. Their work became associated with real business cycles because of the focus on real shocks to the economy as opposed to nominal shocks as the key driver of deviations in output. The question Kydland and Prescott were interested in was not measuring business cycles but focusing on the *pattern* of output and employment around the trend and asking why this seemed to happen in a repeated fashion over time.

Many textbooks explain the business cycle in terms of four phases – boom, slowdown, recession, upturn. The term 'cycle' implies a 'what goes around comes around' type of approach to an economy. Such a view of cycles implies an almost inevitable trend where growth turns into boom, which in turn leads to the start of decline that leads to recession before the process begins again. However, Kydland and Prescott used a generally agreed scientific definition of 'cycles' that makes reference to a point of departure – in this case the trend of economic growth. Kydland and Prescott refer to these recurrent departures as 'deviations'.

They argue that business cycles must be seen as periodic deviations from trend growth and that business cycles are neither inevitable nor evolutionary. As such the explanation for a downturn in economic activity cannot, in itself, be found in the reasons why growth occurred in the first place. Equally, the seeds of an expansion in growth are not to be found in a recession.

In analysing the behaviour of these deviations from trend they sought to challenge some conventional wisdom that had grown up around business cycles. For example, in times of economic downturn the expectation would be that the price level would fall and in times of strong economic growth it would be anticipated that prices would rise – in other words, inflation is procyclical. This implies that in a downturn firms seek to reduce prices to encourage sales and are prevented from increasing prices to improve margins because of the lack of demand. Similarly, in times of economic growth, firms experience rising demand and possibly wage and other costs. They are able to increase prices to improve margins without too much damage to business because of the strong growth in demand.

Kydland and Prescott argued that, in fact, price showed a countercyclical behaviour – when economic growth slowed down, prices rose and when economic growth was strong, prices fell. They further argued that real wages fall as growth increases and vice versa (or are not related to the business cycle) and that the money supply was an important factor in leading economic growth.

Price procyclicality is important because if we are looking for the causes of changes in economic activity as a whole, we would presume to be looking for something fairly major as being the cause – large price rises, for example, or shocks caused by changes in things like the money supply. If price procyclicality is a myth then research into the causes of changes in cycles might be misguided. Think of it in terms of a thermometer in a room. The thermometer tells us what the temperature of the room is but is not a cause of the temperature. Looking at the properties of the thermometer to explain the temperature of the room would lead us down the wrong path.

Kydland and Prescott argue that an important factor in explaining business cycles is the decisions people make about how they devote their time between leisure (non-market activities) and income-earning activities. After analysing the factors that may influence business cycles they come to the following conclusions:

- Aggregate hours worked (a measure of labour input) is strongly correlated with changes in GDP. The problem with this is that the contributions to GDP for all workers are considered the same. Kydland and Prescott point out that the contribution by the hours worked by a brain surgeon is not the same as that of a porter in a hospital. With some consideration of this, Kydland and Prescott conclude that real wages are more procyclical and something which traditional literature on business cycles would not suggest.
- The capital stock is largely unrelated to real GDP but is closely correlated if a time lag of about one year is included.
- With regard to the factors affecting aggregate demand – consumption, investment and government spending – Kydland and Prescott report that consumption and investment are highly procyclical whereas government spending does not seem to be correlated with growth.

(Continued)

- They also comment that imports are procyclical as are exports but with a six-month to a year time lag.
- Labour and capital income is strongly procyclical.
- They find no evidence that narrow money (M1) leads the business cycle. In other words, they do not find evidence that a rise in M1 will lead to a spurt in growth.
- Credit arrangements are likely to play a significant role in future analysis of business cycle theory.
- The price level is countercyclical.

Kydland and Prescott's work has prompted considerable research not least the necessity to look at what might be happening in the macroeconomy. It might be necessary to look at factors other than those that simply describe the data. This emphasis on the quantitative features rather than qualitative features (what it tells us rather than what we think it might signify) has been a feature of a re-assessment of statistical analysis in economics, particularly the analysis of time series data. What do long-term time series tell us in relation to short-term series?

Real business cycle theory does not view a recession as a 'failure' in the economy nor might a boom also be seen as a failure. (A boom might be interpreted as a failure in economic management because it is unsustainable which is why politicians often refer to the 'bad old days of boom and bust'.) Kydland and Prescott see business cycles as explanations of shock to the economy that are understandable reactions rather than failures. Their work tends to dismiss the 'sticky prices' explanation for a slowdown in growth and also the mismatch between investment and consumption and the monetarist argument of market failure in price signals. Instead they look at real shocks to the economy and the adjustment process to those shocks, which could last for some time after. Essentially, Kydland and Prescott argued that business cycles could occur perfectly naturally within a competitive environment despite the implication in traditional theory that, for example, perfect competition would not result in long periods of unemployment.

Real business cycle theory is not without its critics. In particular, the implication that shocks to supply tend to be permanent rather than transitory has been questioned as an explanation of recessions, and empirical studies have also questioned the extent to which the assumptions of the model and the predictions about the cyclicality of economic variables match the evidence.

Finn E. Kydland (left) and Edward C. Prescott (right); winners of the Nobel Prize for Economics in 2004.

CONCLUSION

In this chapter we have provided some background to the more extensive analysis of short-term economic fluctuations in the coming chapters. We have introduced a number of key concepts which need to be borne in mind as we tackle the next chapters, not least building a familiarity with the behaviour of key macroeconomic variables over time.

We have also learned that economists have different interpretations of business cycles based on different assumptions about how the economy works and the extent to which markets clear and how economic actors behave. Models of business cycles focus on both the supply side and demand side of the economy and it is likely that the answers to the questions surrounding policy decisions to help smooth out deviations in trend growth are to be found in a combination of these different models. The model of the real business cycle raises questions about whether the trends that we 'see' in time series data, which form the basis of analysis, are actually present and if trends do not exist then policy measures designed to reduce deviations from trend are misguided.

IN THE NEWS

Employment and Unemployment in an Economic Downturn

We have seen that key macroeconomic variables such as employment and unemployment behave in particular ways during periods of deviation of output from trend. However, the experience of the UK economy in recent years has caused economists to re-assess their assumptions about cyclicality and seek explanations for observed events.

Weak Growth and Rising Employment

In the time period between the three months to December 2011 and the same period in 2012 the number of people working full-time in the UK rose by 394,000 and the number of people working part-time rose by 190,000. This represented the largest increase since 2005 and meant that the number of people employed in the UK was recorded as 29.73 million or an employment rate of 71.5 per cent of the population aged 16–64. The number of people unemployed in the three months to December 2011 stood at 2.66 million and in the same period in 2012 the figure was 2.51 million. The claimant count in January 2012 stood at 1.60 million and in December 2012 at 1.55 million.

In themselves, these figures might not seem particularly remarkable but when set against the performance of the economy during a similar time period they do raise some interesting questions which have led economists to look closer at the data to find answers. Gross domestic product (GDP) during this period has been sluggish at best. During 2011, growth was reported at under 1.0 per cent for three of the four quarters, at just 0.4 per cent in the first quarter of 2012, –0.8 per cent in the second quarter, a bounce back due to the Olympic Games effect in the third quarter of 1.6 per cent and a 0.1 per cent rise in the fourth quarter. The Office for National Statistics reported that GDP in volume terms shrank by 0.3 per cent in the fourth quarter of 2012 and Her Majesty's Treasury (HMT) reported real GDP in 2010 as £1,427 billion in 2010 and £1,440 billion in 2011.

In a time, therefore, when the economy of the UK is performing poorly, it might be expected that if employment is procyclical and unemployment countercyclical, why are both behaving contrary to expectations? For some time, economists and analysts have been asked to explain what is happening. The answers might lie in a number of areas.

Employers know that making staff redundant would help to cut costs in the short run but they might also be looking at the type of employees they have. If these employees have important skills it might not be cost-effective to lose them only to have to suffer the cost of having to recruit staff when the upturn comes and possibly train up staff to the levels of those they have already. As a result, some firms may be playing a waiting game and making a judgement that short-term benefits in terms of cost saving might be outweighed by the medium-term disadvantages of not having the right staff at the right time and so are holding onto employees.

It might also be the case that employees are taking into account the prospects facing them in a tough economic environment and agreeing far more flexible working conditions with employers in an effort to hold onto their jobs. This might

(*Continued*)

include accepting reduced working hours or agreeing cuts in pay to help employers to continue to afford to keep workers on. Average earnings growth was under 2 per cent in 2011 and slowed from 1.7 per cent to 1.4 per cent in 2012. With inflation running above 2.5 per cent over these two years, real wages fell which may also help to explain why employment rose or why unemployment did not rise as much as might be expected in an economic downturn.

The number of people accepting part-time work or being employed in jobs for which they are over-skilled (a situation termed under-employment) has also risen. Those getting part-time jobs might prefer full time work but are willing to take part-time jobs rather than have to claim benefits and might also believe that having some job puts them in a better position to apply for full time work when it becomes

available. There has also been an increase in the number of people becoming self-employed with some 367,000 registering as self-employed between 2008 and 2012 according to the ONS. If people are working part-time or are self-employed then they are not unemployed even though they might not be in a 'first choice' employment position.

The Institute for Fiscal Studies (IFS) in the UK published a report in February 2013 which suggested that there was little evidence for the idea that firms were 'hoarding' staff in the expectation of an upturn in the economy. Whilst employment levels have remained 'robust' and the unemployment 'mercifully low', contrary to other periods of recession experienced in the UK, it is productivity which has suffered. The IFS suggests that productivity per hour per worker declined by 2.6 per cent in 2013 compared to the beginning of

2008. What this means is that the UK is producing 12.8 per cent less than it would have been if pre-recession levels of productivity growth had been maintained. The reasons why employment has been rising and unemployment rising by less than expected is that real wages are low, business investment has been weak (16 per cent lower than its pre-recession peak) and capital is misallocated. Capital is misallocated because banks are being more sympathetic to firms who might be in financial trouble or who are suffering from lower productivity and are also more risk averse in their investment strategies which together reduce the entry and exit of firms from industry.

Questions

1 **What is meant by the terms 'procyclical' and 'countercyclical'.**

2 **Why would you expect employment to fall and unemployment to rise during an economic downturn?**

3 **What economic arguments are there for firms to 'hoard' workers in anticipation of better economic times to come? How persuasive do you find these arguments?**

4 **What effect do falling real wages have on firms' decisions on the demand for labour?**

5 **The IFS report noted that whilst both employment and unemployment had not been affected in the same way as in previous UK recessions, the cost has been a sharp fall in productivity. What might be the consequences of the fall in productivity for the UK economy?**

Productivity is a measure of output per worker per period of time. Unemployment may not be rising as fast in the UK as expected in a recession but how productive are those that are employed?

SUMMARY

- Economies experience periods of changing levels of economic activity.

- Key macroeconomic data are often time series data which raises questions about the validity and reliability of statistical tests applied to data sets.

- Economic growth appears to follow a trend which rises over a period of time.

- Deviations from this trend are known as the business cycle.

- The business cycle has characteristic features which include peaks in economic activity, slowdown, troughs and upturns with key turning points.

- Trends can be stationary and nonstationary. Non-stationary data can exhibit deterministic trends which change by a constant amount independent of time or be stochastic where the trend variable changes by a random amount.

- Macroeconomic data can be viewed in pairs with one of the pairs generally GDP. The variable compared may be either procyclical or countercyclical.

- Collecting macroeconomic data can allow economists to view certain indicators as leading, coincident or lagging.

- Changes in the business cycle can be caused by changes in decision-making by households and firms, by external shocks, government policy and changes in confidence or expectations of the future.

- Business cycle models differ in the assumptions they make about the extent to which markets clear and the relationship between the supply side and demand side of the economy.

- Real business cycles emphasize the effects of changes in technology as causes of changes in economic activity.

QUESTIONS FOR REVIEW

1 What is time series data? Give three examples of key macroeconomic variables that are examples of time series data.

2 What are the main stages of a typical business cycle and how long do these stages last?

3 What is the difference between a deterministic trend and a stochastic trend?

4 Would you expect the following variables to be procyclical or countercyclical if GDP was above trend? Explain.

   a. inflation
   b. unemployment
   c. employment
   d. real wages
   e. nominal interest rates.

5 Unemployment is classified as a lagging indicator. Explain what this means and why unemployment is classed as such.

6 Why might changes in household decision-making cause a deviation in GDP from trend?

7 What role does household and firms' confidence play in business cycles?

8 What is the role of unanticipated price changes in the new classical model of business cycles?

9 Why do Keynesian models of the business cycle emphasize that markets do not always clear immediately?

10 What is the key difference between real business cycle models and other business cycle models?

PROBLEMS AND APPLICATIONS

1 Look at Figure 14.1. For either the UK or the EU:

   a. estimate the amplitude of the deviations from trend over the period shown

   b. estimate the length of time between the beginning of the deviation from trend and the return to trend in each case.

2 In one time period the growth rate of GDP of a country is recorded as 3.4 per cent against a trend growth rate of output of 2.8 per cent. In the next two time periods,

the growth rate of GDP is recorded as 2.8 per cent and 2.0 per cent respectively. Is the country experiencing a recession? Explain.

3 Go to the national statistics office website for your country (this could be the Office for National Statistics in the UK or Eurostat for the EU) and look up unemployment and inflation figures over the last 30 years. Plot the data on a spreadsheet, graph it and identify the trend. Is the trend stationary, nonstationary or indeterminate? Explain.

4 Is it always possible to discern a trend in any time series data? What problems might arise if trends are apportioned to time series data that are not really present?

5 Look up the following comovements for the country in which you are studying on an appropriate website. Explain whether the comovements are procyclical or countercyclical:

   a. GDP and inflation
   b. GDP and employment
   c. GDP and unemployment
   d. GDP and the money supply (M1).

6 Firms experience a rise in stocks. Explain why this might have occurred and what you expect firms' response to this event might be and how this might affect output.

7 Why might household and firms' confidence and expectations change leading to deviations in output from trend? Is there any way in which changes in confidence can be measured to provide an indicator of changes in economic activity?

8 There is a fall in the price level which workers do not anticipate. Explain what effect such a scenario will have on output.

9 To what extent do you think that workers are always fooled by the inflation fallacy?

10 Which business cycle model do you find the most compelling and why?

15 KEYNESIAN ECONOMICS AND IS-LM ANALYSIS

The next four chapters will cover different aspects of macroeconomic policy, in particular the role of fiscal and monetary policy. The framework for analysing the effects of these two policies is developed through a series of steps leading to the model of aggregate demand and aggregate supply.

In 1936, economist John Maynard Keynes published a book entitled *The General Theory of Employment, Interest and Money*, which attempted to explain short-run economic fluctuations in general and the Great Depression in particular. In the last chapter we looked at models which explained the business cycle. Prior to *The General Theory*, the classical assumption of market clearing was prevalent and it can be argued that the development of macroeconomics as a separate path of economic research stemmed from the experiences of the Great Depression and a desire to try to understand why it had appeared that the classical model had gone so spectacularly wrong. Keynes was not the first to question classical paradigms; in the preceding chapter the work of Wesley C. Mitchell in the United States was alluded to. Mitchell published research on business cycles some 20 years before the Great Depression. Keynes picked up this tradition and helped create interest in the analysis of aggregate phenomena.

Keynes' primary message was that recessions and depressions can occur because of inadequate aggregate demand for goods and services. Keynes had long been a critic of classical economic theory because it could explain only the long-run effects of policies. A few years before offering *The General Theory*, Keynes had written the following about classical economics: 'The long run is a misleading guide to current affairs. In the long run we are all dead. Economists set themselves too easy, too useless a task if in tempestuous seasons they can only tell us that when the storm is long past, the ocean will be flat.'

Keynes' message was aimed at policymakers as well as economists. As the world's economies suffered with high unemployment, Keynes advocated policies to increase aggregate demand, including government spending on public works. Keynes argued for the necessity of short-run interventions in the economy. He argued that such intervention could lead to improvements in the economy that would be beneficial rather than waiting for the long run equilibrium to establish itself – hence the famous quote 'In the long run we are all dead'.

The focus on monetary and supply-side policy as the main ways of controlling the economy in most developed countries in Europe had largely consigned Keynesian demand management to the economic history books. However, the financial crisis and subsequent recession of 2007–2009 has reignited the debate about the role of Keynesian economics in macro policy. Keynes' contribution to economic thinking is widely acknowledged and it is valuable to have some insight into Keynesian economics. This chapter will begin this process.

THE KEYNESIAN CROSS

Classical economics placed a fundamental reliance on the efficiency of markets and the assumption that they would clear. At a macro level, this meant that if the economy was in disequilibrium and unemployment existed, wages and prices would adjust to bring the economy back into equilibrium at full employment. **Full employment** is defined as a point where those people who want to work at the going market wage level are able to find a job. Any unemployment that did exist would be classed as voluntary unemployment. The experience of the Great Depression of the 1930s brought the classical assumptions under closer scrutiny; the many millions suffering from unemployment could not all be volunteering to not take jobs at the going wage rates so some must, therefore, be involuntarily unemployed. We have also seen in the preceding chapter that prices can also be sticky, meaning markets may not always adjust to clear surpluses and shortages quickly.

> **full employment** a point where those people who want to work at the going market wage level are able to find a job

Planned and Actual Spending

Fundamental to Keynesian analysis is the distinction between *planned* and *actual* decisions by households and firms. **Planned spending, saving or investment** refers to the desired or intended actions of firms and households. A publisher may plan to sell 100,000 copies of a textbook in the first three months of the year; an individual may plan to go on holiday to Turkey in the summer and save up to finance the trip; a person may intend to save €1,000 over the year to put towards paying for a wedding next year.

> **planned spending, saving or investment** the desired or intended actions of households and firms

Actual spending, saving or investment refers to the realized, *ex post* (after the event) outcome. The publisher may only sell 80,000 copies in the first three months and so has a build-up of stock (inventories) of 20,000 more than planned; the holidaymaker may fall ill and is unable to go on holiday and so their actual consumption is lower than planned (whereas actual saving is more than planned because they have not spent what they intended) and the plans for saving for the wedding may be compromised by the need to spend money on repairing a house damaged by a flood.

> **actual spending, saving or investment** the realized or *ex post* outcome resulting from actions of households and firms

Planned and actual outcomes might be very different as briefly outlined above. As a result Keynes argued that there was no reason why equilibrium national income would coincide with full employment output. Wages and prices might not adjust in the short run because of sticky wages and prices, and so the economy could be at a position where the level of demand in the economy was insufficient to bring about full employment. The mass unemployment of the 1930s could be alleviated, he argued, by governments intervening in the economy to manage demand to achieve the desired level of employment.

The Equilibrium of the Economy

Recall the identity describing how a country's gross domestic product (which we will refer to as national income, Y) is divided among four components: consumption spending, investment spending, spending by government and net exports – the difference between the funds received from selling exports minus the expenditure on imports.

Imagine a situation where, at every point, total expenditure in the economy given by $C + I + G + NX$ was exactly the same as national income. We could represent this in diagrammatic form as a 45° line such as the one in Figure 15.1.

FIGURE 15.1

Deflationary and Inflationary Gaps

The 45° line shows all the points where consumption spending equals income. The vertical intercept of the expenditure line shows autonomous expenditure. The economy is in equilibrium where the expenditure line, C + I + G + NX cuts the 45° line. In panel (a) this equilibrium is lower than full employment output (Y_f) at Y_1– there is insufficient demand to maintain full employment output. The government would need to shift the expenditure line up to C + I + G + NX_1 to eliminate the deflationary gap as shown. In panel (b) the equilibrium is higher than full employment output – the economy does not have the capacity to meet demand. In this case the government needs to shift the C + I + G + NX line down to C + I + G + NX_2 to eliminate the inflationary gap.

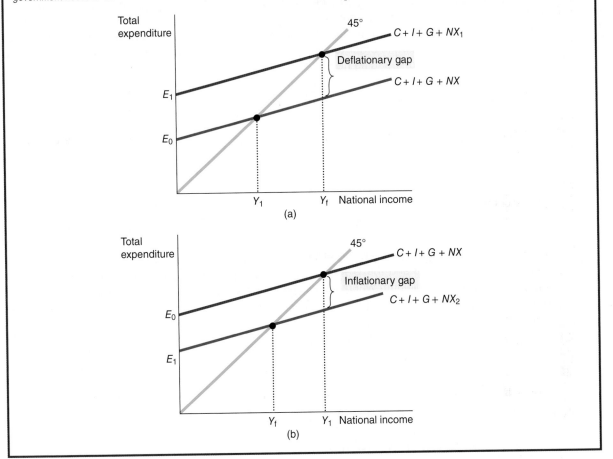

In panels (a) and (b), the 45° line connects all points where consumption spending (actual expenditure) would be equal to national income (planned expenditure). This line can be thought of as the equivalent of the capacity of the economy – the aggregate supply (AS) curve.

The $C + I + G + NX$ line is a function of income – in other words, spending depends on income. If income is higher, spending will also be higher and so the $C + I + G + NX$ line has a positive slope. The vertical intercept of the $C + I + G + NX$ line given as E_0, is termed **autonomous spending** or **autonomous expenditure**. This is the component of expenditure which does not depend on income/ output – government spending being a key element of this expenditure.

autonomous spending or **autonomous expenditure** spending which is not dependent on income/output

Where actual spending is equal to planned spending is the short-run equilibrium of the economy. Note that the use of the term 'equilibrium' in this context does not mean the 'best' or 'desired' equilibrium – it is simply a point where actual spending is equal to planned spending. The economy is in equilibrium where the $C + I + G + NX$ line cuts the 45° line. This is referred to as the *Keynesian cross*. In panel (a) the economy is in equilibrium at a national income of Y_1. However, full employment national income is at Y_f. Actual spending of $C + I + G + NX$ in panel (a) gives an equilibrium which is less than that required for full employment output (Y_f). At the equilibrium Y_1 there is spare capacity in the economy – some resources are not being used to their full extent, capital may be underused and unemployment will exist. This is the equivalent to an economy being at a point inside its production possibilities frontier. The difference between full employment output and the expenditure required to meet it is termed the **deflationary gap** (you may sometimes see this also referred to as the **output gap**). Expenditure needs to rise to $C + I + G + NX_1$ in order to eliminate the deflationary gap which is the vertical distance between actual spending and spending necessary to achieve full employment.

> **deflationary gap** or **output gap** the difference between full employment output and expenditure when expenditure is less than full employment output

In panel (b) the $C + I + G + NX$ line cuts the 45° line at an output level Y_1 which is higher than full employment output, Y_f. In this situation the economy does not have the capacity to meet actual spending. This will trigger inflationary pressures in the economy. The difference between full employment output and the expenditure line here is called the **inflationary gap**. Actual spending needs to be reduced to eradicate the inflationary gap and the $C + I + G + NX$ line needs to be reduced to $C + I + G + NX_2$ to bring the economy to an equilibrium where actual spending equals full employment output.

> **inflationary gap** the difference between full employment output and actual expenditure when actual expenditure is greater than full employment output

Demand Management The deviations in the business cycle in Keynesian analysis are primarily due to demand side factors. The principle behind Keynesian economics is at its heart: very simple and intuitive. Downturns in economic activity occur because firms fail to sell all the goods and services they planned to sell. If customers (and of course we are not only talking about final consumers, we are also talking about other businesses as customers of firms) are not buying as many goods and services, firms will not need to produce as many and so cut back production as stocks rise. If production is cut back then firms do not need as many workers and either do not replace workers when they retire, make some workers redundant or lay-off workers by reverting to shorter working weeks or even ceasing production temporarily for a time period. Unemployment rises and the cause is due to *demand deficiency*. The affected workers now see a fall in their incomes and so cut back on spending which exacerbates the problem.

The cause of a fall in consumption in the first place is often difficult to pinpoint as noted in the preceding chapter. It could be due to confidence and expectations; it could be due to the way in which the public respond to news items (the more the news media refer to the possibility of slowdown or recession it might become a self-fulfilling prophecy); it could be due to a change in patterns of consumption with some firms seeing a decline in demand for their goods whilst others see an increase but the structural change causes a disruption in demand. Workers who are made redundant from the declining industries may not have the skills to move to jobs being created in the growth industries and as a result, regardless of the wage rate, they remain unemployed.

Keynes argued that governments can use the tools of fiscal and monetary policy, and in particular fiscal policy, to influence demand in the economy and reduce deflationary and inflationary gaps. Recall in

Chapter 4 we introduced a more detailed circular flow of income diagram which included leakages and injections. Taxation is a leakage from the circular flow but can be manipulated by the government. Equally, government can vary its own expenditure and the combinations of changes in tax and government spending can be used as levers to manage demand to bring the economy into equilibrium at a point nearer to full employment output. If the value of full employment output, the amount the economy is capable of producing if all existing resources are used fully (planned spending) is €1 trillion, (€1,000,000,000,000) for example, but actual spending is only €800 billion (€800,000,000,000). The deflationary or output gap would be €200 billion. The government might introduce policy levers which lead to a cut in taxes and a boost to government spending to generate this additional €200 billion in spending. The use of these 'levers' has some interesting features which we will describe in the next section.

SELF TEST Why might actual spending differ from planned spending?
If planned spending in an economy is €500 billion but actual spending €400 billion, is there an inflationary gap or a deflationary gap? Explain.
What might the government do in this situation to bring spending more in line with full employment output?

THE MULTIPLIER EFFECT

The $C + I + G + NX$ line is referred to as the expenditure function. Planned expenditure (E) is dependent on the level of consumption, plus investment, plus government spending plus net exports and can be written:

$$E = C + I + G + NX$$

Actual expenditure/output (remember that expenditure is one way of measuring output – these two things are the same) will be denoted as (Y). The economy will be in equilibrium, therefore, when planned expenditure is equal to actual expenditure ($E = Y$).

The positive slope of the expenditure function implies that planned spending rises as income rises. What determines the slope of the expenditure function? This is what we will explore in this next section.

When a government makes a purchase, say it enters into a contract for €10 billion to build three new nuclear power generating stations, that purchase has repercussions. The immediate impact of the higher demand from the government is to raise employment and profits at the construction company (which we shall call Nucelec). Nucelec, in turn, has to buy resources from other contractors to carry out the job and so these suppliers also experience an increase in orders. Then, as the workers see higher earnings and the firm owners see higher profits, they respond to this increase in income by raising their own spending on consumer goods. As a result, the government purchase from Nucelec raises the demand for the products of many other firms in the economy. Because each euro spent by the government can raise the aggregate demand for goods and services by more than a euro, government purchases are said to have a **multiplier effect** on aggregate demand.

multiplier effect the additional shifts in aggregate demand that result when expansionary fiscal policy increases income and thereby increases consumer spending

The multiplier effect continues even after this first round. When consumer spending rises, the firms that produce these consumer goods hire more people and experience higher profits. Higher earnings and profits stimulate consumer spending once again, and so on. Thus, there is positive feedback as higher demand leads to higher income, which in turn leads to even higher demand. Once all these effects are added together, the total impact on the quantity of goods and services demanded can be much larger than the initial impulse from higher government spending.

The multiplier effect arising from the response of consumer spending can be strengthened by the response of investment to higher levels of demand. For instance, Nucelec might respond to the higher demand for building services by buying more cranes and other mechanized building equipment. In this case, higher government demand spurs higher demand for investment goods. This positive feedback from demand to investment is sometimes called the *investment accelerator*.

CASE STUDY   **The Accelerator Principle**

The accelerator principle relates the *rate of change* of aggregate demand to the *rate of change* in investment. To produce goods, a firm needs equipment. Imagine that a machine is capable of producing 1,000 tablet computers per week. Demand for computer tablets is currently 800. A rise in demand for computer tablets of up to 200 is capable of being met without any further investment in new machinery. However, if the rate of growth of demand continues to rise, it may be necessary to invest in a new machine.

Imagine that in year 1, demand for computer tablets rises by 10 per cent to 880. The business can meet this demand through existing equipment. In year 2, demand increases by 20 per cent and is now 1,056. The existing capacity of the machine means that this demand cannot be met but the shortage is only 56 units so the firm decides that it might increase price rather than invest in a new machine. In year 3, demand rises by a further 25 per cent. Demand is now 1,320 but the machine is only capable of producing a maximum of 1,000 tablet computers. The firm decides to invest in a new machine. The manufacturers of the new machine will therefore see a rise in their order books as a result of the increase in demand. An increase in demand of 25 per cent has led to an 'accelerated' rise in investment of 100 per cent. Investment is a component of aggregate demand and so economists are interested in the way investment adjusts to changes in demand in the economy. As this brief example shows, the relationship between an increase in demand and an increase in investment is not a simple one.

To produce goods, a firm needs equipment which can meet customer demands. For example, the rate of growth of demand for tablet computers continues to rise, firms producing them may find it necessary to invest in a new machine – this is called the 'accelerator principle'.

A Formula for the Spending Multiplier

A little algebra permits us to derive a formula for the size of the multiplier effect that arises from consumer spending. An important number in this formula is the **marginal propensity to consume** (*MPC*) – the fraction of extra income that a household consumes rather than saves. For example, suppose that the marginal propensity to consume is ¾. This means that for every extra pound or euro that a household earns, the household spends ¾ of it and saves ¼. The **marginal propensity to save** (*MPS*) is the fraction of extra income that a household saves rather than consumes. With an *MPC* of ¾, when the workers and owners of Nucelec earn €10 billion from the government contract, they increase their consumer spending

marginal propensity to consume (*MPC*) the fraction of extra income that a household consumes rather than saves
marginal propensity to save the fraction of extra income that a household saves rather than consumes

by ¾ × €10 billion, or €7.5 billion. (You should see from the above that the $MPC + MPS = 1$. The formula below can also be expressed in terms of the MPS as a result.)

To gauge the impact on spending of a change in government purchases, we follow the effects step-by-step. The process begins when the government spends €10 billion, which implies that national income (earnings and profits) also rises by this amount. This increase in income in turn raises consumer spending by MPC × €10 billion, which in turn raises the income for the workers and owners of the firms that produce the consumption goods. This second increase in income again raises consumer spending, this time by MPC × (MPC × €10 billion). These feedback effects go on and on.

To find the total impact on the demand for goods and services, we add up all these effects:

Change in government purchases	= €10 billion
First change in consumption	= MPC × €10 billion
Second change in consumption	= $(MPC)^2$ × €10 billion
Third change in consumption	= $(MPC)^3$ × €10 billion
•	•
•	•
•	•
Total change in demand	= $(1 + MPC + MPC^2 + MPC^3 = ...)$ × €10 billion

Below, '...' represents a pattern of similar terms. Thus, we can write the multiplier as follows:

$$\text{Multiplier} = (1 + MPC + MPC^2 + MPC^3 + ...)$$

This multiplier tells us the demand for goods and services that each euro of government purchases generates.

To simplify this equation for the multiplier, recall from your school algebra that this expression is an infinite geometric series. For x between −1 and 1:

$$1 + x + x^2 + x^3 + ...$$

The sum of this series as the number of terms tends to infinity is given by:

$$\frac{1}{1 - x}$$

In our case, $x = MPC$. Thus:

$$\text{Multiplier} = \frac{1}{(1 - MPC)}$$

We have said that the $MPC + MPS = 1$ so the multiplier can also be expressed as:

$$\text{Multiplier} = \frac{1}{MPS}$$

For example, if the MPC is ¾, the multiplier is $\frac{1}{(1 - ¾)}$, which is 4. In this case, the €10 billion of government spending generates €40 billion of demand for goods and services.

This formula for the multiplier shows an important conclusion: the size of the multiplier depends on the marginal propensity to consume. While an MPC of ¾ leads to a multiplier of 4, an MPC of ½ leads to a multiplier of only 2. Thus, a larger MPC means a larger multiplier. To see why this is true, remember that the multiplier arises because higher income induces greater spending on consumption. The larger the MPC is, the greater is this induced effect on consumption, and the larger is the multiplier.

The MPC determines the slope of the consumption element of the planned expenditure function.

Other Applications of the Multiplier Effect

Because of the multiplier effect, a euro of government purchases can generate more than a euro of aggregate demand. The logic of the multiplier effect, however, is not restricted to changes in government purchases. Instead, it applies to any event that alters spending on any component of planned expenditure – consumption, investment, government purchases or net exports.

For example, suppose that a recession overseas reduces the demand for Ireland's net exports by €1 billion. This reduced spending on Irish goods and services depresses Ireland's national income, which reduces spending by Irish consumers. If the marginal propensity to consume is ¾ and the multiplier is 4, then the €1 billion fall in net exports means a €4 billion contraction in output.

As another example, suppose that a stock market boom increases households' wealth and stimulates their spending on goods and services by €2 billion. This extra consumer spending increases national income, which in turn generates even more consumer spending. If the marginal propensity to consume is ¾ and the multiplier is 4, then the initial impulse of €2 billion in consumer spending translates into an €8 billion increase in aggregate demand.

The multiplier is an important concept in macroeconomics because it shows how the economy can amplify the impact of changes in spending. A small initial change in consumption, investment, government purchases or net exports can end up having a large effect on aggregate demand and, therefore, on the economy's production of goods and services.

Autonomous spending is also an important concept in this analysis. The amount spent in each successive 'round' of spending is termed *induced expenditure*. The multiplier showed how the eventual change in income would be determined by the size of the *MPC* and the *MPS*. The higher the MPC the greater the multiplier effect.

However, in an open economy with government, any extra €1 is not simply either spent or saved, some of the extra income may be spent on imported goods and services or go to the government in taxation – withdrawals from the circular flow. Withdrawals (*W*) from the circular flow are classed as endogenous as they are directly related to changes in income. Withdrawals are saving (*S*), taxation (*T*) and imports (*M*).

We also have to take into consideration injections to the circular flow of income. Governments receive tax revenue (a withdrawal from the circular flow) but use it to spend on the goods and services they provide for citizens (an injection into the circular flow); firms earn revenue from selling goods abroad (exports) which are an injection into the circular flow and firms, as we have seen in Chapter 7, use savings (a withdrawal) as a source of funds to borrow for investment (an injection). Injections into the circular flow are exogenous – they are not related to the level of output or income – and are investment (*I*), government spending (*G*) and export earnings (*X*).

The slope of the expenditure line as a whole, therefore, will be dependent on how much of each extra €1 is withdrawn. For each additional €1 of income, some will exit the circular flow of income in taxation, some through savings and some through spending on imports. The marginal propensity to taxation (*MPT*) is the proportion of each additional €1 of income taken in taxation by the government and the marginal propensity to import (*MPM*) the proportion of each additional €1 of income spent on goods from abroad. When we take into consideration the fact that each extra €1 in income is not disposable income, i.e. not all available for consumption, the multiplier effect when considering the *marginal propensity to withdraw* (*MPW*) will be much lower than if we were simply considering the *MPC* alone in any increase in income.

We can restate the formula for the multiplier (*k*) in an open economy with a government as:

$$k = \frac{1}{MPS + MPT + MPM}$$

Or:

$$k = \frac{1}{MPW}$$

The size of the MPW will determine the slope of the expenditure line: the steeper the slope of the expenditure line the greater the size of the multiplier, as shown in Figure 15.2.

FIGURE 15.2

The Slope of the Expenditure Line and Changes in Autonomous Expenditure

Panel (a) shows a relatively shallow expenditure line which would mean that the marginal propensity to withdraw would be high and the value of the multiplier was relatively low. The impact on national income (ΔY) of a change in government spending (ΔG) would be more limited in comparison to the effect as shown in panel (b) where the expenditure line is much steeper reflecting a higher value of the multiplier where the MPW was relatively low. In this case it takes a smaller rise in government spending to achieve the same increase in national income.

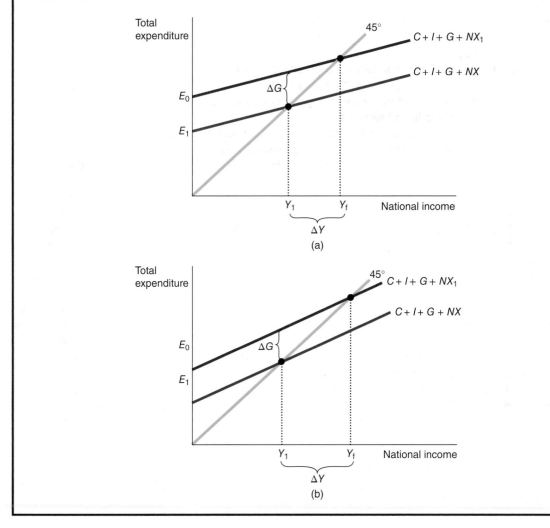

Equilibrium of Planned Withdrawals and Injections

Seeing the economy from the perspective of withdrawals and injections is helpful to understand how demand management might work. Let us start with the national income identity:

$$Output \equiv Expenditure \equiv Income$$

We know from Chapter 7 that in a closed economy $S = I$ with savings a withdrawal and investment an injection. We can also extend this analysis to state that in equilibrium, in an open economy with a government, that planned withdrawals would equal planned injections:

$$Planned \ S + T + M = Planned \ I + G + X$$

At this point all the output being produced by the economy would be 'bought' by households and firms. However, if actual withdrawals are greater than planned injections then the economy would be experiencing a deficiency in demand. For example, assume that full employment output, (Y), is €120 billion. Withdrawals are a function of income; assume that S, T and M have the following values:

$$S = 0.1Y$$
$$T = 0.2Y$$
$$M = 0.2Y$$

Such that if income increased by €1, savings would change by $0.1 \times 1 = 10$ cents and so on.

Now assume that investment was €20 billion, government spending also €20 billion and the value of exports was €10 billion.

Given these figures the equilibrium level of national income would be:

$$\text{Planned } S + T + M = \text{Planned } I + G + X$$
$$0.1Y + 0.2Y + 0.2Y = 20 + 20 + 10$$
$$0.5Y = 50$$
$$Y = 100$$

This equilibrium is below the level of full employment output by €20 billion. The government could manage demand to achieve full employment output in different ways. It could increase its spending by €10 billion and through the multiplier effect see Y rise to €120 billion.

$$\text{Planned } S + T + M = \text{Planned } I + G + X$$
$$0.1Y + 0.2Y + 0.2Y = 20 + 30 + 10$$
$$0.5Y = 60$$
$$Y = 120$$

In an open economy, the government might not simply target full employment but might wish to reduce net exports. For example, assume $Y = $ €120 billion, the value of exports is given as €10 billion but the value of imports would be $0.2Y$ and so would be €24 billion (0.2×120). If the government wanted to reduce net exports to zero it might cut government spending but change tax rates so that the marginal propensity to tax increased. If government spending was cut to 5 and the marginal propensity to tax raised to 0.4 then the government could achieve zero net exports:

$$\text{Planned } S + T + M = \text{Planned } I + G + X$$
$$0.1Y + 0.4Y + 0.2Y = 20 + 5 + 10$$
$$0.7Y = 35$$
$$Y = 50$$

It is clear that the policy to reduce net exports has had a severe effect on national income. One of the features of demand management is that it is possible for governments to use fiscal policy to achieve desired output levels but there will be consequences for other areas of the economy which may have more long-term effects. If government sets policy to achieve a reduction in unemployment through boosting the economy, then net exports would fall and the country would be running a trade deficit ($NX < 0$). We saw in Chapter 13 that trade influences net capital outflow and the exchange rate. Changes in the exchange rate affect the competitiveness of firms in the economy and so even though the government might reduce unemployment, its policy causes longer term effects which might cause it to have to alter policy to deal with these effects (such as a currency crisis) which in turn might reduce income and increase unemployment again.

Demand management seemed to work in many countries in the period following World War II up to the mid-1960s but from that point other problems emerged which cast doubt on the viability of demand management which led to Keynesian policies falling out of favour.

THE IS AND LM CURVES

The Keynesian cross gives us a picture of the economy in short-run equilibrium. (Note, if you access a copy of Keynes' *General Theory* you might be surprised to see a complete absence of Keynesian cross diagrams. The use of these diagrams to explain Keynesian ideas was developed by later economists to help portray Keynes' ideas.) In equilibrium, planned expenditure equals income, $(E = Y)$. This equilibrium is referred to as equilibrium in the *goods market*. We have also seen, in Chapter 11, how equilibrium in the money market is given by the intersection of the demand for money and the supply of money. We need to consider here the concept of **real money balances** – what money can actually buy or the real value of money given the ratio of the money supply (M) to the price level $P\left(\dfrac{M}{P}\right)$

> **real money balances** what money can actually buy given the ratio of the money supply to the price level M/P

The goods market and the money market are both interrelated with the linking factor being the interest rate. Following Keynes' analysis of the goods market and the money market (via the liquidity preference theory which we will look at in more detail in a later chapter), Nobel Prize winning economist John Hicks developed a theory that described the links between the two and showed how changes in both fiscal and monetary policy could be analysed. The framework for this analysis is known as the IS-LM model.

IS-LM describes equilibrium in these two markets and together determines a *general equilibrium* in the economy. General equilibrium in the economy occurs at the point where the goods market and money market are both in equilibrium at a particular interest rate and level of income. The remainder of this chapter will provide an introduction to the IS-LM model. The model forms the basis of many intermediate courses in macroeconomics although some have argued that it is now outdated and fails to represent how the modern economy works, particularly since the financial crisis. We will look at an alternative representation of the model that seeks to take into account some of these objections.

Regardless of the debates about the validity of the model, it does represent a useful way of understanding how the goods and money markets interact and as an exercise in analytical thinking is helpful in seeing the effects of monetary and fiscal policy on the macroeconomy.

IS stands for investment and saving; LM stands for liquidity and money. The thing linking these two markets is the rate of interest (i).

The IS Curve

The IS curve shows the relationship between the interest rate and level of income (Y) in the goods market. In Figure 15.3, panel (a) shows the Keynesian cross diagram from Figure 15.2, with equilibrium point *a* where the expenditure line $C + I + G + NX$ crosses the 45° line. Panel (b) shows the IS curve. On the vertical axis is the rate of interest and on the horizontal axis is output (national income). The equilibrium point *a* in panel (a) is associated with a rate of interest i_1. This is plotted as point *a** on panel (b). If interest rates fall then the expenditure line shifts upwards to the left and there will be a new equilibrium point *b* where the expenditure line $C + I + G + NX_1$ crosses the 45° line. This is plotted as *b** on panel (b) showing the equilibrium of the goods market at a lower interest rate associated with a higher level of national income. If we connect these two points we get the IS curve. The curve connects all possible points of equilibrium in the goods market associated with a particular interest rate and level of national income.

The IS curve shows an inverse relationship between the interest rate and output – a fall in interest rates leads to a rise in income and vice versa. The rise in income will be dependent on the size of the interest rate change and the size of the multiplier. The slope of the IS curve is determined by the responsiveness of consumption and investment $(C + I)$ to changes in interest rates. This is important because it leads to different outcomes; where economists tend to disagree is the *extent* to which $C + I$ are responsive to changes in interest rates rather than any disagreement about the fundamental relationship. The more responsive $C + I$ are, the flatter the IS curve.

FIGURE 15.3

The IS Curve

The IS curve is derived from the Keynesian cross diagram and shows all possible points of equilibrium in the goods market associated with a particular interest rate and level of income. In panel (a) initial equilibrium is where the C + I + G + NX line crosses the 45° line at point a. This point is plotted on the IS curve as point a*. An increase in C + I + G + NX to C + I + G + NX$_1$ shows a new equilibrium point in the goods market, b, which is plotted on the IS curve as b*. These two points are connected to form the IS curve.

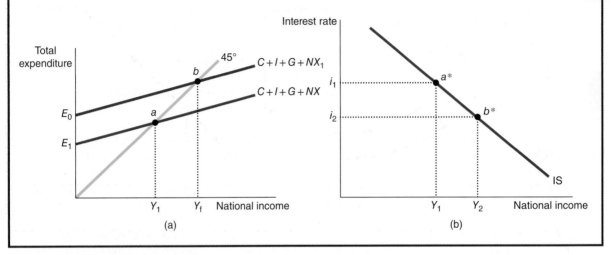

(a)   (b)

Shifts in the IS Curve Shifts in the IS curve come about as a result of changes in autonomous expenditure. If, for example, government spending rises this occurs independent of any change in interest rates. A rise in autonomous spending would be associated with a shift in the IS curve to the right – the prevailing interest rate would now be associated with a higher level of income. Equally, if autonomous spending fell then the IS curve would shift to the left showing a lower level of income at the prevailing interest rate.

The LM Curve

The LM curve shows all points where the money market is in equilibrium given a combination of the rate of interest and national income. In Figure 15.4, panel (a) shows the money market with the demand for money inversely related to the interest rate. The money supply is shown as a vertical line and it is assumed that the money supply is fixed by the central bank. Equilibrium in the money market is where the demand for money D_m intersects the money supply curve, M_s, at point a in panel (a) at interest rate i_1 and a quantity of real money balances (M). Panel (b) shows the LM curve with the interest rate on the vertical axis and national income on the horizontal axis. The equilibrium point a in the money market is plotted as point a* in panel (b). Increases in income will have an effect on the demand for money and assuming the money supply is fixed, will affect the equilibrium interest rate. Assume that national income rises; the demand for money curve in panel (a) would shift to the right to D_{m1} indicating that the public wish to hold higher money balances at all interest rates. At the prevailing interest rate the demand for money is now higher than the supply of money and so the interest rate would rise. The new equilibrium in the money market is given as point b and this is plotted on the LM diagram as point b*. If we connect the two points we get the LM curve. The LM curve plots all combinations of interest rates and national income where the money market is in equilibrium.

FIGURE 15.4

The LM Curve

The LM curve shows all points where the money market is in equilibrium given a combination of the rate of interest and national income. In panel (a), the money market is in equilibrium where the demand for money (D$_m$) equals the supply of money (MS) at point a. This point is plotted on the LM curve in panel (b) as point a*. An increase in the demand for money causes a shift of the curve to the right to D$_{m1}$ with a new equilibrium point of b. This is plotted on panel (b) as point b* and the points connected to form the LM curve.

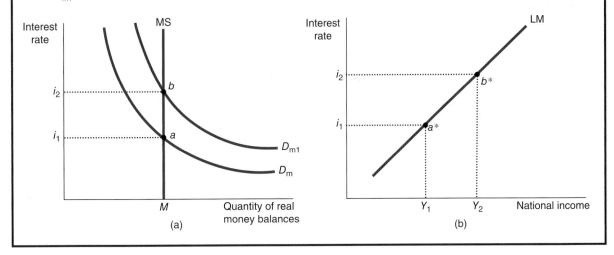

The LM curve has a positive slope showing that an increase in income is associated with an increase in the interest rate and vice versa. The slope of the LM curve will be dependent on the responsiveness of the demand for money to changes in interest rates. Again, the extent of this relationship is often a point of disagreement among economists.

Shifts in the LM Curve The LM curve can shift if the central bank expands or contracts the money supply (we will say more about how this might happen later in the chapter). Assuming income is held constant, a rise in the money supply (for example) will cause interest rates to fall and a new equilibrium will be reached at a given level of income. This would be associated with a shift of the LM curve downwards to the right showing a new combination of income and interest rate at which the money market is in equilibrium.

GENERAL EQUILIBRIUM USING THE IS-LM MODEL

Equilibrium is found where the IS curve intersects the LM curve. Remember that any point on either curve describes a point of equilibrium in the goods market and the money market at a rate of interest and level of national income. In Figure 15.5, the point where the IS curve intersects the LM curve gives a point where both markets are in equilibrium at an interest rate i_e and a level of national income Y_e. Hence, it follows that at this point planned expenditure equals actual expenditure ($E = Y$), and the demand for money equals the supply of money ($D_m = S_m$).

Having established this general equilibrium, we can use the model to analyse the impact of fiscal and monetary policy changes in an attempt to stabilize the economy and how these two policies are interrelated. Further analysis of both policies will be covered in the next chapter but this uses our model of IS-LM. The detail of IS-LM analysis is beyond the scope of this book, being found in most intermediate courses in macroeconomics. However, the remainder of this chapter will introduce some of the key implications of the model.

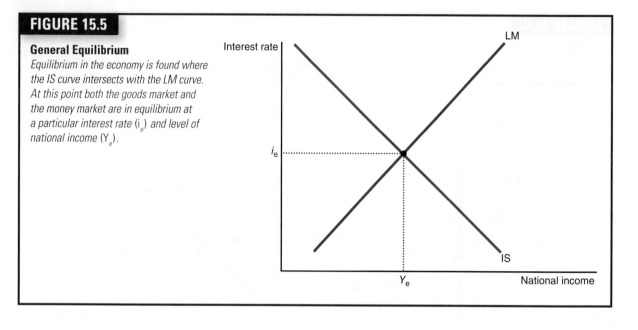

FIGURE 15.5

General Equilibrium
Equilibrium in the economy is found where the IS curve intersects with the LM curve. At this point both the goods market and the money market are in equilibrium at a particular interest rate (i_e) and level of national income (Y_e).

The Effect of a Change in Fiscal Policy

Assume that the government chooses to increase spending to boost economic activity. This increase in autonomous expenditure shifts the IS curve to the right as shown in panel (a) of Figure 15.6. The result is that national income will rise but there will also be an increase in interest rates. A similar outcome would occur if the government chose to cut taxes as the means of boosting the economy. The result of either policy would be dependent on the marginal propensity to withdraw and the size of the multiplier. The opposite would occur if the government chose to cut spending or increase taxes – national income and interest rates would both fall.

FIGURE 15.6

The Effects of Fiscal and Monetary Policy
In panel (a) a rise in government spending shifts the IS curve to the right resulting in a new equilibrium with a higher interest rate and level of national income. In panel (b) an increase in the money supply would shift the LM curve to the right and a new equilibrium would result in a lower interest rate and higher level of national income.

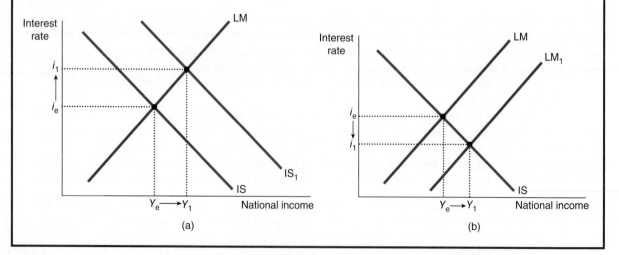

The Effect of a Change in Monetary Policy

If the central bank decided to expand the money supply the LM curve would shift to the right to LM_1 as shown in panel (b) of Figure 15.6. The new equilibrium would lead to a lower interest rate and a higher level of national income. The reverse outcome would occur if the central bank tightened monetary policy by reducing the money supply.

Fiscal and Monetary Policy Interactions In reality, central banks do not act totally in isolation of government even if they are independent. Central banks will be aware of what governments are doing as we will see when we look at the Case for an Active Stabilization Policy in Chapter 17. This presents a model to analyse the response of the central bank. The Bank of England, European Central Bank and the Federal Reserve have a responsibility to maintain price stability and this may be presented in the form of a target for inflation. Central banks will be monitoring the effect of fiscal policy changes on the economy and how these changes might affect inflationary pressures. These inflationary pressures can be influenced by the central bank's control over short-term interest rates through the rate at which it lends to the financial system. Governments may wish to implement fiscal policy with the aim of influencing unemployment, for example. Such a policy may have effects on inflationary pressures which the central bank wants to nullify.

Let us assume that the government reduces taxation to encourage more people to take jobs in the economy or to increase spending through consumers having more disposable income. The IS curve would shift to the right as shown in Figure 15.7 and national income and interest rates would rise. If the central bank wants to keep interest rates constant it must expand the money supply. By doing so the LM curve shifts to the right to LM_1, national income would rise further than if the central bank had not acted, to Y_2 and the interest rate will remain at its initial level. If the bank had not altered the money supply then the effects of the reduction in tax would have been partially offset by a rise in interest rates which would have curbed spending.

FIGURE 15.7

Maintaining Interest Rates Constant Following a Rise in the IS Curve
A shift in the IS curve to the right would, without central bank action, lead to a rise in the interest rate and in national income. If the central bank wants to maintain the interest rate it must increase the money supply and shift the LM curve to the right. The result would be to maintain the interest rate at i_e but the increase in national income would be greater than if the central bank had not acted.

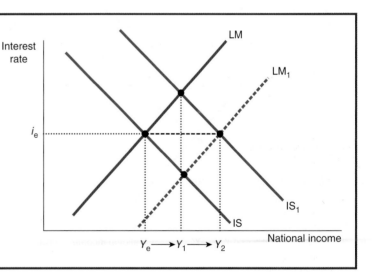

If government had increased taxes then the IS curve would shift to the left and both national income and interest rates would fall. If the central bank wants to keep interest rates constant it must reduce the money supply and the result would be that the fall in national income would be compounded. If the central bank wanted to avoid this outcome then it could expand the money supply and interest rates would fall. This would help to offset the shift in the IS curve and reduce the impact on national income.

FROM IS-LM TO AGGREGATE DEMAND

It is a short step from using this model to the aggregate demand and aggregate supply model that we will use to analyse changes in the economy later in the book. Remember that the supply of real money balances is what money can actually buy given by M, the money supply divided by P, the price level $\left(\dfrac{M}{P}\right)$.

Assume the average price of a unit of output in the economy is €10 and the money supply is €100 billion. The supply of real money balances is $\frac{100}{10} = 10$, that is at the current price level the supply of money in the economy can buy 10 units of output. If the average price of a unit of output in the economy rises to €20 and the money supply is constant, real money balances will fall to 5 units $\left(\frac{100}{20} = 5\right)$. This fall in the supply of real money balances shifts the LM curve to the left as shown in panel (a) of Figure 15.8. The result is that interest rates rise and national income falls. There is, therefore, an inverse relationship between the price level and national income. The aggregate demand curve is derived by plotting the relationship between national income and the price level as shown in panel (b) of Figure 15.8. The aggregate demand curve slopes downwards from left to right because of the inverse relationship between the price level and national income.

FIGURE 15.8

Deriving the Aggregate Demand Curve

In panel (a) a rise in the price level reduces real money balances and shifts the LM curve to the left to LM_1. This leads to a rise in the equilibrium interest rate to i_1 and a fall in national income from Y_0 to Y_1. The inverse relationship between the price level and national income is plotted in panel (b). A rise in the price level from P_1 to P_2 leads to a fall in national income from Y_0 to Y_1. The aggregate demand curve slopes downwards from left to right.

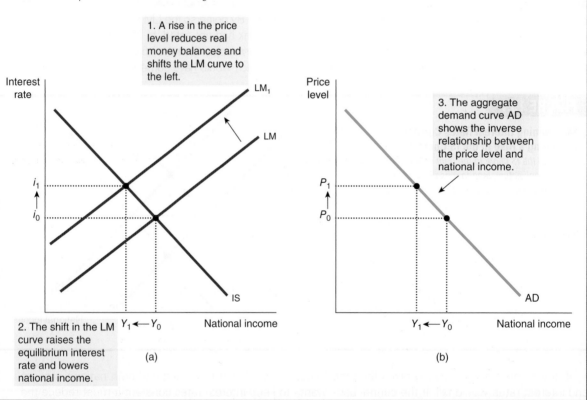

Shifts in the Aggregate Demand Curve If we assume the price level remains constant, a change in national income in the IS-LM model will result in a shift in the aggregate demand curve. Changes in both fiscal and monetary policy, assuming a given constant price level, will cause the aggregate demand curve to shift. If the government imposes an austerity package which seeks to cut government spending and raise taxes, at a given price level the IS curve will shift to the left and national income will fall. At the given price level, aggregate demand in the economy will now be less and the aggregate demand curve will shift to the left as shown in panel (a) of Figure 15.9.

If the central bank expands the money supply (possibly through a programme of asset purchasing or quantitative easing) the LM curve will shift to the right and national income will rise. At the given price level, the aggregate demand curve will shift to the right showing a higher level of national income at the given price level as shown in panel (b) of Figure 15.9.

A loosening of fiscal policy (increased government spending and/or lower taxes) and a reduction in the money supply (a tightening of monetary policy) will have the opposite effect to that described in Figure 15.9 respectively.

FIGURE 15.9

Shifts in the Aggregate Demand Curve as a Result of Monetary and Fiscal Policy

Panel (a) represents a situation where the government tighten fiscal policy which shifts the IS curve to the left and reduces national income. At a given price level the aggregate demand curve shifts to the left and a lower level of national income is associated with the given price level.

Panel (b) represents a situation where the central bank loosens monetary policy which causes the LM curve to shift to the right and lowers national income. At the given price level the aggregate demand curve shifts to the right with a higher level of national income.

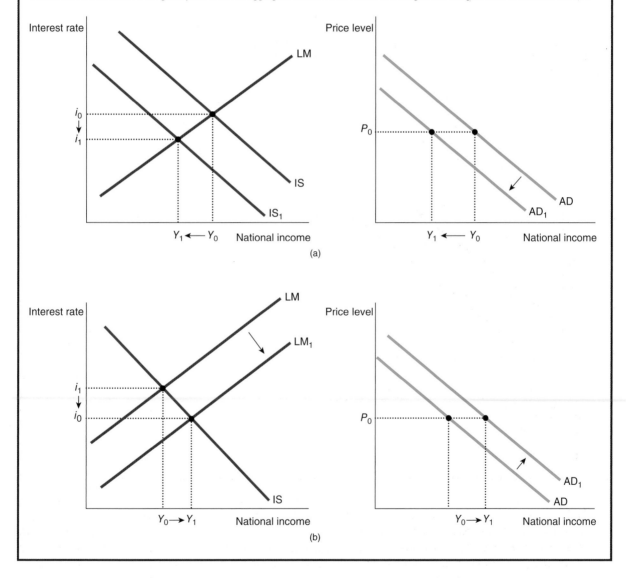

(a)

(b)

Criticisms of IS-LM and the Romer Model

This short introduction to IS-LM analysis and the effect of changes in fiscal and monetary policy helps to highlight a number of important issues that you may start to consider as your study of economics moves to the next level. The effects of changes in fiscal and monetary policy are dependent on a number of factors related to the slope of the IS and LM curves, their relative position and how far each shifts in response to changes in policy. It is entirely possible that a change in fiscal policy can be countered by a change in monetary policy that leaves national income unchanged. The potential outcomes are many and economists try to pinpoint more accurately what changes in policy will mean for the economy as a whole. This means conducting research to quantify such changes. The outcome of such research will be dependent on the value of variables that economists input into their models and, as has already been stated, most economists agree on the fundamentals of the model but disagree on the relative strength of factors affecting the variables in the model.

One example of how the model has developed is the role which microeconomic analysis plays in understanding the macroeconomy. Some economists argue that microeconomic principles cannot be divorced from the macroeconomy. We have seen in Chapter 14 how changing economic conditions may lead to wages and prices adjusting at different rates and slowly as a result. If national income falls, for example, then the assumption might be that prices and wages in the economy would also fall to help bring markets back into equilibrium. As we will see in the next chapter, these sticky wages and prices may lag behind the reduction in economic activity as firms may be forced into trying to maintain cash flow rather than seeking to expand market share. As prices are sticky, sales fall and firms cut back output which further impacts on economic activity. Price stickiness seemed to be counter to the prevailing assumption about rational behaviour.

Professor Mankiw was one of the economists who helped to reconcile the idea of sticky prices and menu costs with rational behaviour in his paper 'Small menu costs and large business cycles: A macroeconomic model of monopoly', published in The Quarterly Journal of Economics in 1985. The debate over IS-LM has continued and has generated large amounts of valuable and interesting research which has helped build our understanding of the economy as a whole. It still has its critics, however.

Indeed, one such disagreement focuses on a central assumption of the model itself. Some higher education institutions have questioned the value of teaching IS-LM at all because they argue that the world is now a very different place to the one Hicks knew back in the 1930s when he first developed Keynes' ideas. One of the major criticisms is that central banks no longer control the money supply but instead set interest rates. Setting interest rates is seen as leading to more stable economic conditions than policies targeting the money supply. Attempts to control the money supply have proved to be difficult and so targeting the interest rate is seen as being a more viable option to achieve policy objectives.

In Chapter 10 we looked at how central banks set interest rates through open market operations. If the central bank wishes to reduce interest rates, its traders will be instructed to buy bonds. Banks and financial institutions who sell these bonds will receive funds in return which will effectively expand the money supply. This in turn shifts the LM curve to the right and so interest rates fall. If the central bank increases interest rates the opposite occurs; traders will be instructed to sell bonds and thus take funds out of the banking system, reducing the money supply. The LM curve shifts to the left and interest rates rise.

One of Professor Mankiw's close colleagues, David Romer (indeed they are more than simply colleagues given that each was best man at the other's wedding), has suggested an approach termed the IS-MP model which attempts to build on the IS-LM model to reflect how central banks and the economy work today. The assumption in the model is that central banks adjust the money supply as outlined above to generate the interest rate that they want. The interest rate is adjusted in accordance with the inflation target that the central bank is working with or, as is the case with the Bank of England, has been set by the government. In the IS-LM model the money supply is assumed to be exogenous (determined by factors outside the model). In the IS-MP model, the monetary policy reaction function is exogenous. Romer assumes that when output rises, the central bank increases interest rates to dampen inflationary pressures and reduces interest rates when output falls to maintain the price level at its target. National income is a positive function of the interest rate, therefore. Romer plots this upward sloping relationship as the MP curve. The MP function is assumed to be exogenous but in reality both the money supply and the MP function can and do change in response to economic activity and events.

The MP function, therefore, takes into account the fact that central banks now target inflation and set interest rates to achieve this goal rather than simply assuming government (or a central bank) sets the money supply and that interest rates adjust to balance this supply of money with the demand for money. Crucially, Romer suggests that changes in inflation can cause a shift of the MP curve. If the central bank increases interest rates the money supply will fall which will affect the price level and expectations on inflation. Equally, if the central bank cuts interest rates the money supply will rise and expectations on inflation will also change as a result.

It is at this point where the microeconomic element of the analysis takes on some importance. Expectations of price changes may not match the reality because of the extent of price stickiness. If we assume that prices are completely sticky (i.e. the price level is fixed) it will not change when the money supply changes. Expectations on inflation will, therefore, be zero. If the money supply rises then the supply of real money balances, $\frac{M}{P}$, also rises and is greater than the demand for real money balances. As the money market is now out of equilibrium we might expect the interest rate to fall but it could also be that the level of income could rise or a combination of the two might occur. There will be a movement along the IS curve and a fall in interest rates will be accompanied by a rise in national income. This implies that the central bank can directly control the real interest rate by adjusting money supply appropriately to achieve the interest rate it desires.

If prices adjusted instantaneously then a change in the money supply would not affect the supply of real money balances because the ratio $\frac{M}{P}$ would hold as before at the rate of interest and level of income; in other words the money market would remain in equilibrium. There would be no movement along the IS curve and the central bank would not be able to affect the real interest rate.

In reality prices are not fixed, but the speed with which prices adjust to changes in economic conditions will vary – some will adjust relatively quickly, others will take much longer and will be sticky. These sticky prices will influence the ratio of the money supply to the price level (the supply of real money balances) and so there may be some expectations of inflation which will exist in the economy because M will rise by a greater proportion than P. An increase in the money supply will raise expected inflation and vice versa. If prices are sticky then an increase in the nominal money supply will cause the money market to move out of equilibrium but expected inflation will affect the real interest rate. The nominal interest rate may have to be higher as a result.

The extent to which prices are sticky, therefore, has an important influence on the way in which a central bank can influence the interest rate to achieve its inflation targets. Such an analysis raises interesting questions when interest rates are reduced as was the case in response to the financial crisis and the global recession in 2008–2009. The UK, Europe and the US saw their central banks reducing interest rates to historically low levels. To reduce interest rates the central bank instructs its traders to buy bonds and the money supply will rise. Increases in the money supply may be associated with an increase in the price level as noted in Principle 9 of the *Ten Principles of Economics*. Indeed, some economists have expressed alarm at the scale of quantitative easing conducted by central banks and have predicted hyperinflation. In times where economic activity is restrained, however, expectations of inflation may remain subdued and the money market may remain out of equilibrium as a result. The reason is that at these low interest rates people are willing to hold a greater amount of real money balances without any change in interest rate or output – after all, the interest rate cannot fall much further. This is the *liquidity trap* which is covered in the next chapter and which may imply that monetary policy can have little effect on stimulating economic growth.

SELF TEST Draw diagrams to show the effect on interest rates and the level of national income of: (a) a decision by the government to raise taxes to cut a public deficit; and (b) a decision by a central bank to increase interest rates.

A Return to Keynesianism?

The financial crisis of 2007–2009 led to a period of global recession. In many countries, economic growth has been slow to return to pre-crisis levels and levels of unemployment have been rising in many countries. The severity of the global recession led to calls for Keynesian style fiscal intervention to stimulate economic growth, particularly given the fact that central banks had largely exhausted traditional methods of monetary policy to stimulate growth. This reignited the debate about the value of Keynesian demand management policies and the news media and blogosphere has been alive with, what has sometimes been, bitter divisions between proponents of expansionary fiscal policy and those who focus more on the importance of governments reducing deficits. Indeed, in one instance, the website Wikipedia locked down a page to prevent editing following a series of edits and counter-edits between those in support of Nobel Prize-winning economist Paul Krugman, a supporter of Keynesian style intervention, and supporters of the Austrian school who tend to be sceptical of the benefits of government intervention and are more inclined to trust markets to sort out economic problems. Whether the 'editing war' was anything to do with Krugman himself is not clear but after a series of repeated cases where text was deleted and replaced by both sides, Wikipedia closed the page to further editing.

Regardless of the debate, a number of countries introduced fiscal stimulus packages in the wake of the financial crisis. This led to questions about the benefits of such packages and even whether they amount to a stimulus. In late 2008 the European Union (EU) announced a fiscal stimulus package of €200 billion; in the UK the Chancellor of the Exchequer had to admit that government borrowing might reach £175 billion and be 79 per cent of GDP in 2013–2014 (in the latter part of 2012 it stood at 73 per cent of GDP). In India public debt as a component of GDP is around 80 per cent; in the US the package was reported to be $800 billion. China was reported to be injecting $586 billion and Japan $275 billion. Critics were arguing that such packages were not enough to bridge the output gap that had widened in most economies. In the US, for example, the gap between potential and actual GDP was estimated by some economists at around $2 trillion. Other criticisms of fiscal stimulus packages suggested that they were not really what they seemed to be and if they were then they would not bring the benefits that were claimed for them because of crowding out.

For example, in a study of the EU stimulus package in February 2009, David Saha and Jakob von Weizsäcker said, 'It should be recognized that the likely real impact on aggregate demand in the near future may well be more limited than suggested by the headline figures' (http://aei.pitt.edu/10549/01/UPDATED-SIZE-OFSTIMULUS-FINAL.pdf accessed 6 October 2009). In their analysis of the fiscal stimulus in Italy, announced as €80 billion, Saha and Weizsäcker conclude that the stimulus was not a stimulus at all but a fiscal tightening amounting to €0.3 billion. In parts of Europe there were concerns that any major fiscal stimulus package would put pressure on the public debt and affect the stability of the euro around which so much of the future prosperity of the EU lies.

One of the concerns about any fiscal stimulus is the extent to which it creates 'real wealth'. Governments may spend more money but on what? If the money is spent on public works – the building of new schools, hospitals, roads and so on, then surely this would boost aggregate demand? To an extent it would but how is this additional spending to be financed? To raise the money governments will either have to tax their citizens more or increase borrowing. Additional spending on the construction of a new road may put money into the pockets of construction companies and its workers, but to fund this the government has to tax other wealth producers, thus offsetting some of the benefits of the stimulus. If the spending goes on additional benefits for those who become unemployed then critics argue that the government is not contributing to wealth creation; these individuals may be supported in times of hardship and may spend their benefits on food and other goods but they are not actually generating any wealth in return for the benefits they receive. Indeed. Keynes himself acknowledged that there limitations to stimulus packages. In an article in *The Times* newspaper in the UK in 1937, a year after the *General Theory* was published, he wrote:

> But I believe that we are approaching, or have reached, the point where there is not much advantage in applying a further general stimulus at the centre … It follows that the later stages of recovery require a different technique. To remedy the condition of the distressed areas ad hoc measures are necessary. The Jarrow marchers were, so to speak, theoretically correct … We are in more need today of a rightly distributed demand than of a greater aggregate demand.

Structural changes in the economy might require more long-term investment if improvements in unemployment prospects and growth are to be achieved.

If governments have to borrow more then crowding out may emerge. In this scenario the government is competing with the private sector for funds. Since the supply of loanable funds is finite, if governments take more of these funds it is argued that there will be less available for the private sector. If it is also assumed that the private sector uses such investment funds more efficiently than the public sector then not only do fiscal stimulus packages crowd out private investment they divert investment funds to less productive uses.

Whilst this view is widely accepted, there are those that suggest that extraordinary times call for extraordinary action. One such proponent of this view is Paul Krugman. Krugman has consistently argued that the depth of the financial crisis and global recession was such that a fiscal stimulus was necessary to get out of a liquidity trap and far from crowding out, fiscal stimuli would lead to 'crowding in'. A liquidity trap occurs when monetary policy is insufficient to generate the economic stimulus necessary to get out of recession. In the US and UK, for example, interest rates were lowered by the Fed and the Bank of England to near zero, the Bank of Japan's key interest rate stood at 0.1 per cent in August 2009 whilst the ECB had rates at 1 per cent.

Krugman argues that private investment is a function of the state of the economy and, given the depth of the global recession, investment has plummeted. Investment, therefore, in this situation is more responsive to product demand than to the rate of interest. If governments applied appropriate fiscal stimuli then this would improve the state of the economy and thus encourage private sector investment. As private sector investment increases then this improves the productive potential and helps bring economies out of recession. Far from crowding out, Krugman argues, the fiscal stimulus would lead to crowding in.

Critics of this view suggest that increased government spending will crowd out private investment to an extent and so any fiscal stimulus has to take into account the loss of the benefits of that private investment in assessing the success of such a policy. The success of a stimulus package in putting economies on a sounder footing and bringing benefits to future generations would be highly dependent on the type of spending carried out by governments worldwide. Spending on new schools and transport infrastructure may improve the future productive potential of the economy and tackle the structural problems that exist in some economies as referred to above. However, the issues of rent seeking and log rolling have to be taken into consideration. Remember that rent seeking occurs where decisions are made leading to resource allocation that maximizes the benefit to the decision-maker at the expense of another party or parties, and log rolling is where decisions may be made on resource allocation to projects that have less importance, in return for the support of the interested party in other decision-making areas. In both cases, it is argued that resource allocation is not as efficient as that carried out by the private sector and this has to be taken into consideration in assessing the benefits of public sector spending as a result of any stimulus package.

CONCLUSION

There is still much debate on whether Keynesian style interventions in the economy to manage demand represent an appropriate and viable response to the economic conditions currently facing many countries in the aftermath of the financial crisis. There is also some debate on the value and relevance of the IS-LM model. What is not in much doubt is that an understanding of the relationship between the goods market and the money market is a useful way of developing a broader understanding of analysing the economy as a whole. This short introduction to such analysis provides some pointers to the IS-LM model and to some of the issues that economists are debating. Depending on the university that you attend, a greater or lesser emphasis may be placed on the IS-LM model. Having some awareness of the model does help to develop a focus on the important connections between the money supply, interest rates and economic activity.

IN THE NEWS

Austerity and Growth

The aftermath of the financial crisis has presented economists with new challenges as many countries try and face problems of high levels of borrowing and debt which they wish to reduce, and faltering economies with weak growth, high unemployment and, in some cases, inflation, stubbornly persisting at levels above target.

Expansionary Austerity or Keynesian Intervention?

One of the legacies of the financial crisis was the wider public realization that governments around the world had been borrowing heavily to finance spending and this spending had helped to boost strong growth throughout much of the latter part of the 1990s and into the noughties. When the crisis hit, consumption spending, a key driver of growth, fell and the recession that followed was deep and long lasting.

Central banks responded to the crisis by cutting interest rates and in many countries historically low interest rates have persisted to the extent that it is not really possible for central banks to try and boost economic growth by traditional monetary policy tools any further. For governments, it is clear that debt levels have to be reduced if the risk of default and the ability of governments to borrow in the future is to be maintained. What is the way to reduce borrowing and debt? Cut government spending and increase taxes is the obvious policy choice and some finance ministers and political leaders are arguing that there is simply no alternative to such fiscal contraction.

Some economists have cited the experience in Ireland as justification for austerity. Ireland had to implement savage fiscal cuts to get financial assistance from the European Union and International Monetary Fund (IMF). The economy shrank alarmingly but forecasts put growth at 1.6 per cent in 2013 and 2.8 per cent in 2014. The head of the IMF, Christine Lagarde, was keen to praise the Irish government – and the people – for the progress the country has made in dealing with the deficit and the banking system. In a meeting with Irish government ministers in March 2013, Ms Lagarde said:

> 'What has been done is huge by any standard. The amount by which the deficit has been reduced, the determination shown in actually implementing a programme has been extraordinary … It doesn't mean to say that all has been done but I would say that more than two-thirds of the work has been done in terms of fiscal policies and there is still more work to do on the banking sector to make sure it is safe, solid.'

Such praise might be welcome for some in Ireland but the cost of austerity in terms of the sacrifices made by the people has been considerable – in March 2013, unemployment was over 14 per cent and was not forecast to fall much below 13.5 per cent by the end of 2014.

The experience of Ireland was not a surprise. Keynes argued in the 1930s that such policies would lead to depression. The economic conditions in many other countries across Europe look rather like those expected in a depression. When government spending is cut, public sector employment falls, government spending on benefits rises and tax revenue falls. The private sector might be able to expand to pick up the unemployed from the public sector (an approach which has been referred to as 'expansionary austerity') but in such gloomy economic times, many large corporates are hoarding cash and postponing investment. The size of public sector cuts and the resulting unemployment plus the gloomy news which dampens confidence and leads to negative expectations causes a further slowdown in spending – the cycle reinforces itself. With consumption spending falling, tax revenues from income and corporate taxes fall even further and governments are forced to borrow so the deficit and borrowing does not fall as far as finance ministers forecast. The markets get nervous and push up borrowing rates for sovereign debt which makes it more likely they will default on existing debt. In 1937, Keynes observed: 'The boom, not the slump, is the right time for austerity at the Treasury.'

What is needed, say some, is actually more borrowing not less. Policies are needed to get consumers spending again and firms investing, and governments can trigger this process by spending more on capital investment on key infrastructure projects which will improve the future productive capacity of the economy and address structural problems. Some economists argue that it is time to embrace once again the wisdom shown by Keynes and that the severity of the global downturn calls for coordinated global efforts to boost consumer spending and investment. Those economists who have called for a return to Keynesian intervention have used the data on countries like Ireland to point to the failures of austerity.

Robert Skidelsky, Emeritus Professor of political economy at Warwick University in the UK, a biographer of Keynes, noted the difference in the more expansionary approach taken by the Obama administration in the US up to 2013 and the austerity approach adopted by the UK government:

> Since May 2010, when US and British fiscal policy diverged, the US economy has grown – albeit slowly. The British economy is currently contracting. Unemployment in the United States has gone down by 1.4 percentage points; in Britain, it has

Robert Skidelsky, Emeritus Professor of political economy at Warwick University in the UK and famed biographer of Keynes, pointed out differences in the more expansionary approach taken by the Obama administration in the US up to 2013 and the austerity approach adopted by the UK government.

> gone up by 0.2 percentage points. And despite keeping up stimulus measures, the Obama administration has been more successful in reducing the government deficit – by 2.5 percentage points compared with Osborne's 1.9 percentage points. (http://www.newrepublic.com/article/politics/magazine/104220/austerity-keynes-uk-us-skidelsky).

Skidelsky's conclusion is that the poor performance of the UK economy and of those in other countries where austerity has been the dominant factor, it is not surprising to those who believe Keynesian

policies have a part to play in dealing with the economic problems of the post-crisis world. What he and other Keynesians are noting, however, is that whilst opinion is gradually changing against expansionary austerity, it may be too late.

Questions

1 How would central banks have brought about the considerable cuts in interest rates in the immediate aftermath of the financial crisis? Show the effect of such a policy on aggregate demand using the IS-LM model.

2 Use the concept of the multiplier to explain how cuts in government spending and higher taxes are likely to lead to a fall in national income.

3 Do you think that the benefits of implementing austerity measures in Ireland are justified? Explain your reasoning.

4 Outline why governments such as that in the UK, believe that there is no viable alternative to austerity if longer term sustainable growth is to be achieved.

5 To what extent do you agree with the view that 'expansionary austerity' has not worked and that the time has come for Keynesian fiscal expansion?

SUMMARY

- Keynes developed *The General Theory* as a response to the mass unemployment which existed in the 1930s.

- He advocated governments intervene to boost demand through influencing aggregate demand.

- The Keynesian cross diagram shows how the economy can be in equilibrium when $E = Y$.

- This equilibrium may not be sufficient to deliver full employment output and so the government can attempt to boost demand to help achieve full employment.

- John Hicks developed Keynes' ideas in the form of the IS-LM model which shows general equilibrium in the economy.

- The IS (investment–saving) curve shows all points of equilibrium in the goods market at a particular interest rate and level of national income.

- The LM (liquidity–money supply) curve shows points where the money market is in equilibrium at particular rates of interest and level of national income.

- General equilibrium occurs where the IS curve intersects the LM curve. At this interest rate and level of national income both the goods market and money market are in equilibrium.

- Fiscal policy and monetary policy can cause shifts in the IS and LM curves bringing about new equilibrium positions. The outcome will depend on a variety of factors including the response of consumption and investment to changes in interest rates and the public's response to holding monetary balances as a result of a change in interest rates.

- There have been criticisms that the IS-LM model does not represent the way monetary policy is conducted in modern economies.

- Economists have developed new models to incorporate the changes in policy.

QUESTIONS FOR REVIEW

1 Distinguish between planned expenditure and actual expenditure.

2 Draw a Keynesian cross diagram to show the effects of a rise in autonomous expenditure on an economy operating below full employment output.

3 What is meant by the terms: *inflationary gap* and *deflationary gap*?

4 What is the marginal propensity to consume?

5 Why does the $MPC + MPS = 1$?

6 What is the multiplier? Can the multiplier be negative as well as positive? Explain.

7 Explain how the marginal propensity to withdraw affects the outcome of a rise in autonomous expenditure.

8 Use diagrams to describe how the IS and LM curves are derived.

9 Using the IS-LM model, explain the effect on the economy of a reduction in autonomous expenditure resulting from a cut in public spending by the government.

10 A central bank wishes to reduce inflationary expectations by increasing interest rates. Use the IS-MP model to analyse the effect on the economy of such a move.

PROBLEMS AND APPLICATIONS

1 What, according to Keynes, was the main reason why recessions and depressions occurred? As a result of identifying this key reason, what did Keynes suggest was an appropriate policy repose?

2 Explain, using an appropriate diagram, how a deflationary gap can occur and how this gap can be eliminated.

3 Suppose economists observe that an increase in government spending of €10 billion raises the total demand for goods and services by €30 billion.

  a. If these economists ignore the possibility of crowding out, what would they estimate the marginal propensity to consume (*MPC*) to be?

  b. Now suppose the economists allow for crowding out. Would their new estimate of the *MPC* be larger or smaller than their initial one? Explain your answer.

4 Suppose the government reduces taxes by €2 billion, that there is no crowding out and that the marginal propensity to consume is 0.75.

  a. What is the initial effect of the tax reduction on aggregate demand?

  b. What additional effects follow this initial effect? What is the total effect of the tax cut on aggregate demand?

  c. How does the total effect of this €2 billion tax cut compare to the total effect of a €2 billion increase in government purchases? Why?

5 Assume the economy is in equilibrium. Analyse the effect of a cut in autonomous expenditure on economic activity and the level of unemployment. You should use a diagram to help illustrate your answer.

6 What does the IS curve show? What does the LM curve show?

7 What determines the slope of the IS curve? What determines the slope of the LM curve? In relation to your answer to these questions, explain why these determinants can be a source of disagreement amongst economists?

8 Use IS-LM analysis to explain the following:

  a. The government institutes significant cuts in public expenditure.

  b. The central bank institutes an asset purchasing facility which expands the money supply by €300 billion.

  c. The central bank fears that inflationary pressures are rising and increases interest rates.

  d. The government increases taxation to try and reduce a large budget deficit.

9 Assume that a period of deflation leads to a rise in the supply of real money balances. Explain the effect of this change on the economy using the IS-LM model and then what effect it would have on aggregate demand and why.

10 Do you think that Keynes' ideas still have some relevance today? Explain.

16 AGGREGATE DEMAND AND AGGREGATE SUPPLY

We have seen how economic activity can fluctuate over different time periods. What causes short-run fluctuations in economic activity? What, if anything, can public policy do to prevent periods of falling incomes and rising unemployment? When recessions and depressions occur, how can policymakers reduce their length and severity? These are the questions that we take up now.

The variables that we study are largely those we have already seen in previous chapters. They include GDP, unemployment and the price level. Also familiar are the policy instruments of government spending, taxes, the money supply, and interest rates. The focus of our analysis is on the economy's short-run fluctuations around its long-run trend.

Although there remains some debate among economists about how to analyse short-run fluctuations, and in the preceding chapter we introduced the IS-LM model, in this chapter we will look at the *model of AD and AS*, which is widely used among economists. Learning how to use this model for analysing the short-run effects of various events and policies is the primary task ahead.

THREE KEY FACTS ABOUT ECONOMIC FLUCTUATIONS

Short-run fluctuations in economic activity occur in all countries and in all times throughout history. As a starting point for understanding these year-to-year fluctuations, let's remind ourselves of some of their most important properties.

Fact 1: Economic Fluctuations are Irregular and Unpredictable

Economic fluctuations correspond to changes in business conditions. When real GDP grows rapidly, business is good. During such periods of economic expansion, firms find that customers are plentiful and that profits are growing. On the other hand, when real GDP falls during recessions, businesses have trouble. During such periods of economic contraction, many firms experience declining sales and dwindling profits. We saw in Chapter 14 that economic fluctuations are not at all regular, and they are almost impossible to predict with much accuracy.

Fact 2: Most Macroeconomic Quantities Fluctuate Together

Real GDP is the variable that is most commonly used to monitor short-run changes in the economy because it is the most comprehensive measure of economic activity. Real GDP measures the value of all final goods and services produced within a given period of time. It also measures the total income (adjusted for inflation) of everyone in the economy.

It turns out, however, that for monitoring short-run fluctuations, it does not really matter which measure of economic activity one looks at. Most macroeconomic variables that measure some type of income, spending or production, fluctuate closely together. When real GDP falls in a recession, so do personal income, corporate profits, consumer spending, investment spending, industrial production, retail sales, home sales, auto sales and so on. Because recessions are economy-wide phenomena, they show up in many sources of macroeconomic data.

Although many macroeconomic variables fluctuate together, they fluctuate by different amounts. In particular, investment spending varies greatly over the business cycle. When economic conditions deteriorate, much of the decline is attributable to reductions in spending on new factories, housing and inventories. Investment in the UK, for example, fell by 5.1 per cent in 2008, by −11.4 per cent in 2009, and was just positive at 0.1 per cent in 2010 before another fall of 2.9 per cent in 2011.

Fact 3: As Output Falls, Unemployment Rises

Changes in the economy's output of goods and services are strongly correlated with changes in the economy's utilization of its labour force. In other words, when real GDP declines the rate of unemployment rises. The negative relationship between unemployment and real GDP is referred to as **Okun's law** after the Yale economist who published his observations in the 1960s. Okun noted that in order to keep the unemployment rate steady, real GDP needs to grow at or close to its potential. If the unemployment rate is to be reduced then real GDP must grow above potential. Being more specific, to reduce the unemployment rate by 1 per cent in a year, real GDP must rise by around 2 per cent more than potential GDP over the year.

> **Okun's law** a 'law' which is based on observations that in order to keep the unemployment rate steady, real GDP needs to grow at or close to its potential

Okun's findings are hardly surprising: when firms choose to produce a smaller quantity of goods and services, they lay off workers, expanding the pool of unemployed. However, there is generally a time-lag between any downturn in economic activity and a rise in unemployment and vice versa. Even when positive growth resumes, therefore, unemployment is likely to continue to rise for some time afterwards. As we noted in Chapter 14, unemployment is referred to as a 'lagged indicator'.

EXPLAINING SHORT-RUN ECONOMIC FLUCTUATIONS

Describing the patterns that economies experience as they fluctuate over time is easy. Explaining what causes these fluctuations is more difficult. Indeed, compared to the topics we have studied in previous chapters, the theory of economic fluctuations remains controversial. In this chapter and the next two chapters, we develop the model that most economists use to explain short-run fluctuations in economic activity.

How the Short Run Differs from the Long Run

In previous chapters we developed theories to explain what determines most important macroeconomic variables in the long run. We have looked at the level and growth of productivity and real GDP; explained how the financial system works and how the real interest rate adjusts to balance saving and investment; why there is always some unemployment in the economy; explained the monetary system and how changes in the money supply affect the price level, the inflation rate and the nominal interest rate; and then extended this analysis to open economies in order to explain the trade balance and the exchange rate.

All of this previous analysis was based on two related ideas – the classical dichotomy and monetary neutrality. Recall that the classical dichotomy is the separation of variables into real variables (those that measure quantities or relative prices) and nominal variables (those measured in terms of money). According to classical macroeconomic theory, changes in the money supply affect nominal variables but not real variables. As a result of this monetary neutrality, we were able to examine the determinants of real variables (real GDP, the real interest rate and unemployment) without introducing nominal variables (the money supply and the price level).

Do these assumptions of classical macroeconomic theory apply to the world in which we live? The answer to this question is of central importance to understanding how the economy works: most economists believe that classical theory describes the world in the long run but not in the short run. Beyond a period of several years, changes in the money supply affect prices and other nominal variables but do not affect real GDP, unemployment or other real variables. When studying year-to-year changes in the economy, however, the assumption of monetary neutrality is no longer appropriate. Most economists believe that, in the short run, real and nominal variables are highly intertwined. In particular, changes in the money supply can temporarily push output away from its long-run trend.

To understand the economy in the short run, therefore, we need a new model. To build this new model, we rely on many of the tools we have developed in previous chapters, but we have to abandon the classical dichotomy and the neutrality of money.

The Basic Model of Economic Fluctuations

Our model of short-run economic fluctuations focuses on the behaviour of two variables. The first variable is the economy's output of goods and services, as measured by real GDP. The second variable is the overall **price level**, an average of prices of all goods and services in an economy as measured by the CPI or the GDP deflator. Notice that output is a real variable, whereas the price level is a nominal variable. Hence, by focusing on the relationship between these two variables, we are highlighting the breakdown of the classical dichotomy.

> **price level** an average of prices of all goods and services in an economy as measured by the CPI or the GDP deflator

We analyse fluctuations in the economy as a whole with the **model of aggregate demand** (AD) **and aggregate supply** (AS), which is illustrated in Figure 16.1. On the vertical axis is the overall price level in the economy. On the horizontal axis is the overall quantity of goods and services. The **aggregate demand curve**

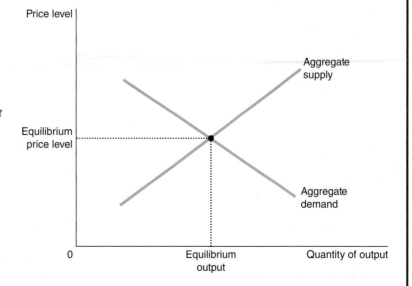

FIGURE 16.1

Aggregate Demand and Aggregate Supply
Economists use the model of AD and AS to analyse economic fluctuations. On the vertical axis is the overall level of prices. On the horizontal axis is the economy's total output of goods and services. Output and the price level adjust to the point at which the AS and AD curves intersect.

shows the quantity of goods and services that households, firms and the government want to buy at each price level. The **aggregate supply curve** shows the quantity of goods and services that firms produce and sell at each price level. According to this model, the price level and the quantity of output adjust to bring AD and AS into balance.

> **model of aggregate demand and aggregate supply** the model that most economists use to explain short-run fluctuations in economic activity around its long-run trend
> **aggregate demand curve** a curve that shows the quantity of goods and services that households, firms and the government want to buy at each price level
> **aggregate supply curve** a curve that shows the quantity of goods and services that firms choose to produce and sell at each price level

It may be tempting to view the model of AD and AS as nothing more than a large version of the model of market demand and market supply, which we introduced in Chapter 3. Yet in fact this model is quite different. When we consider demand and supply in a particular market for a good such as tablet computers, the behaviour of buyers and sellers depends on the ability of resources to move from one market to another. When the price of tablet computers rises, the quantity demanded falls because buyers will use their incomes to buy products other than tablets. Similarly, a higher price of tablets raises the quantity supplied because firms that produce these gadgets can increase production by hiring workers away from other parts of the economy. This *microeconomic* substitution from one market to another is impossible when we are analysing the economy as a whole. After all, the quantity that our model is trying to explain – real GDP – measures the total quantity produced in all of the economy's markets. To understand why the AD curve is downwards sloping and why the AS curve is upwards sloping, we need a *macroeconomic* theory. Developing such a theory is our next task.

> **SELF TEST** How does the economy's behaviour in the short run differ from its behaviour in the long run? ● Draw the model of AD and AS. What variables are on the two axes?

THE AGGREGATE DEMAND CURVE

The AD curve tells us the quantity of all goods and services demanded in the economy at any given price level. As Figure 16.2 illustrates, the AD curve is downwards sloping reflecting the inverse relationship between the price level and national income we outlined in Chapter 15. This means that, other things equal, a fall in the economy's overall level of prices (from, say, P_1 to P_2) tends to raise the quantity of goods and services demanded (from Y_1 to Y_2).

Why the Aggregate Demand Curve Slopes Downwards

Why does a fall in the price level raise the quantity of goods and services demanded? To answer this question it is useful to recall that GDP (which we denote as Y) is the sum of consumption (C), investment (I), government purchases (G) and net exports (NX):

$$Y = C + I + G + NX$$

Each of these four components contributes to the AD for goods and services. For now, we assume that government spending is fixed by policy. The other three components of spending – consumption, investment and net exports – depend on economic conditions and, in particular, on the price level. To understand the downwards slope of the AD curve, therefore, we must examine how the price level affects the quantity of goods and services demanded for consumption, investment and net exports.

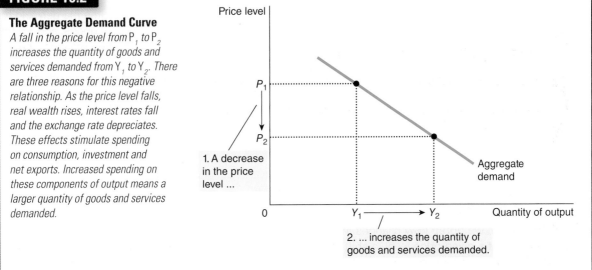

FIGURE 16.2

The Aggregate Demand Curve
A fall in the price level from P_1 to P_2 increases the quantity of goods and services demanded from Y_1 to Y_2. There are three reasons for this negative relationship. As the price level falls, real wealth rises, interest rates fall and the exchange rate depreciates. These effects stimulate spending on consumption, investment and net exports. Increased spending on these components of output means a larger quantity of goods and services demanded.

Price level

P_1

P_2

1. A decrease in the price level ...

Aggregate demand

0   Y_1 Y_2 Quantity of output

2. ... increases the quantity of goods and services demanded.

The Price Level and Consumption: The Wealth Effect Consider the money that you hold in your pocket and your bank account. The nominal value of this money is fixed, but its real value is not. When prices fall, this money is more valuable because then it can be used to buy more goods and services. Thus, a decrease in the price level makes consumers wealthier, which in turn encourages them to spend more. The increase in consumer spending means a larger quantity of goods and services demanded.

The Price Level and Investment: The Interest Rate Effect As we discussed in Chapter 11, the price level is one determinant of the quantity of money demanded. The lower the price level, the less money households need to hold to buy the goods and services they want. When the price level falls, therefore, households try to reduce their holdings of money by lending some of it out which in turn increases the supply of real money balances. For instance, a household might use its excess money to buy interest-bearing bonds. Or it might deposit its excess money in an interest-bearing savings account, and the bank would use these funds to make more loans. In either case, as households try to convert some of their money into interest-bearing assets, they drive down interest rates. Lower interest rates, in turn, encourage borrowing by firms that want to invest in new factories and equipment and by households who want to invest in new housing. Thus, a lower price level reduces the interest rate, encourages greater spending on investment goods, and thereby increases the quantity of goods and services demanded.

The Price Level and Net Exports: The Exchange Rate Effect As we have just discussed, a lower price level lowers the interest rate. In response, some investors will seek higher returns by investing abroad. For instance, as the interest rate on European government bonds falls, an investment fund might sell European government bonds in order to buy US government bonds. As the investment fund tries to convert its euros into dollars in order to buy the US bonds, it increases the supply of euros in the market for foreign currency exchange. The increased supply of euros causes the euro to depreciate relative to other currencies. Because each euro buys fewer units of foreign currencies, non-European goods (i.e. imports) become more expensive to European residents but exporters find that foreign buyers get more euros for each unit of their currency. This change in the real exchange rate (the relative price of domestic and foreign goods) increases European exports of goods and services and decreases European imports of goods and services. Net exports, which equal exports minus imports, also increase. Thus, when a fall in the European price level causes European interest rates to fall, the real value of the euro falls, and this depreciation stimulates European net exports and thereby increases the quantity of goods and services demanded in the European economy.

Summary There are, therefore, three distinct but related reasons why a fall in the price level increases the quantity of goods and services demanded: (1) consumers are wealthier, which stimulates the demand for consumption goods; (2) interest rates fall, which stimulates the demand for investment goods; and (3) the exchange rate depreciates, which stimulates the demand for net exports. For all three reasons, the AD curve slopes downwards.

It is important to keep in mind that the AD curve (like all demand curves) is drawn holding 'other things equal'. In particular, our three explanations of the downwards sloping AD curve assume that the money supply is fixed. That is, we have been considering how a change in the price level affects the demand for goods and services, holding the amount of money in the economy constant. As we will see, a change in the quantity of money shifts the AD curve. At this point, just keep in mind that the AD curve is drawn for a given quantity of money.

Why the Aggregate Demand Curve Might Shift

In Chapter 15, we noted how changes in monetary and fiscal policy can cause a shift in the LM and IS curves and, at a given price level, a shift in AD. We are going to explore shifts in the AD curve in more detail here. The downwards slope of the AD curve shows that a fall in the price level raises the overall quantity of goods and services demanded. Many other factors, however, affect the quantity of goods and services demanded at a given price level. When one of these other factors changes, the AD curve shifts.

Let's consider some examples of events that shift AD. We can categorize them according to which component of spending is most directly affected.

Shifts Arising from Consumption Suppose people suddenly become more concerned about saving for retirement and, as a result, reduce their current consumption. Because the quantity of goods and services demanded at any price level is lower, the AD curve shifts to the left. Conversely, imagine that a stock market boom makes people wealthier and less concerned about saving. The resulting increase in consumer spending means a greater quantity of goods and services demanded at any given price level, so the AD curve shifts to the right.

Thus, any event that changes how much people want to consume at a given price level shifts the AD curve. One policy variable that has this effect is the level of taxation. When the government cuts taxes, it encourages people to spend more, so the AD curve shifts to the right. When the government raises taxes, people cut back on their spending and the AD curve shifts to the left.

Shifts Arising from Investment Any event that changes how much firms want to invest at a given price level also shifts the AD curve. For instance, imagine that the computer industry introduces a faster line of computers, and many firms decide to invest in new computer systems. Because the quantity of goods and services demanded at any price level is higher, the AD curve shifts to the right. Conversely, if firms become pessimistic about future business conditions, they may cut back on investment spending, shifting the AD curve to the left.

Tax policy can also influence AD through investment. An investment tax credit (a tax rebate tied to a firm's investment spending) increases the quantity of investment goods that firms demand at any given interest rate. It therefore shifts the AD curve to the right. The repeal of an investment tax credit reduces investment and shifts the AD curve to the left.

Another policy variable that can influence investment and AD is the money supply. As we discuss more fully in the next chapter, an increase in the money supply lowers the interest rate in the short run (the LM curve shifts to the right). This makes borrowing less costly, which stimulates investment spending and thereby shifts the AD curve to the right at a given price level. Conversely, a decrease in the money supply shifts the LM curve to the left and raises the interest rate, discourages investment spending, and thereby shifts the AD curve to the left at the given price level. Many economists believe that changes in monetary policy have been an important source of shifts in AD in most developed economies at some points in their history.

Shifts Arising from Government Purchases The most direct way that policymakers shift the AD curve is through government purchases. For example, suppose the government decides to reduce purchases of new weapons systems. Because the quantity of goods and services demanded at any price level is lower, the AD curve shifts to the left. Conversely, if the government starts building more motorways, the result is a greater quantity of goods and services demanded at any price level, so the AD curve shifts to the right.

Shifts Arising from Net Exports Any event that changes net exports for a given price level also shifts AD. For instance, when the US experiences a recession, it buys fewer goods from Europe. This reduces European net exports and shifts the AD curve for the European economy to the left. When the US recovers from its recession, it starts buying European goods again, shifting the AD curve to the right.

Net exports sometimes change because of movements in the exchange rate. Suppose, for instance, that international speculators bid up the value of the euro in the market for foreign currency exchange. This appreciation of the euro would make goods produced in the euro area more expensive compared to foreign goods, which would depress net exports and shift the AD curve to the left. Conversely, a depreciation of the euro stimulates net exports and shifts the euro area AD curve to the right.

Summary In the next chapter we analyse the AD curve in more detail in relation to the tools of monetary and fiscal policy which can shift AD and whether policymakers should use these tools for that purpose. At this point, however, you should have some idea about why the AD curve slopes downwards and what kinds of events and policies can shift this curve. Table 16.1 summarizes what we have learned so far.

TABLE 16.1 **The AD Curve: Summary**

Why does the AD curve slope downward?

1 *The wealth effect*: A lower price level increases real wealth, which encourages spending on consumption.
2 *The interest-rate effect*: A lower price level reduces the interest rate, which encourages spending on investment.
3 *The exchange-rate effect*: A lower price level causes the real exchange rate to depreciate, which encourages spending on net exports.

Why might the AD curve shift?

1 *Shifts arising from consumption*: An event that makes consumers spend more at a given price level (a tax cut, a stock market boom) shifts the AD curve to the right. An event that makes consumers spend less at a given price level (a tax hike, a stock market decline) shifts the AD curve to the left.
2 *Shifts arising from investment*: An event that makes firms invest more at a given price level (optimism about the future, a fall in interest rates due to an increase in the money supply) shifts the AD curve to the right. An event that makes firms invest less at a given price level (pessimism about the future, a rise in interest rates due to a decrease in the money supply) shifts the AD curve to the left.
3 *Shifts arising from government purchases*: An increase in government purchases of goods and services (greater spending on defence or motorway construction) shifts the AD curve to the right. A decrease in government purchases on goods and services (a cutback in defence or motorway spending) shifts the AD curve to the left.
4 *Shifts arising from net exports*: An event that raises spending on net exports at a given price level (a boom overseas, an exchange rate depreciation) shifts the AD curve to the right. An event that reduces spending on net exports at a given price level (a recession overseas, an exchange rate appreciation) shifts the AD curve to the left.

SELF TEST Explain the three reasons why the AD curve slopes downwards. ● Give an example of an event that would shift the AD curve. Which way would this event shift the curve?

THE AGGREGATE SUPPLY CURVE

The AS curve tells us the total quantity of goods and services that firms produce and sell at any given price level. Unlike the AD curve, which is always downwards sloping, the AS curve shows a relationship that depends crucially on the time horizon being examined. In the long run, the AS curve is vertical, whereas in the short run the AS curve is upwards sloping. To understand short-run economic fluctuations, and how the short-run behaviour of the economy deviates from its long-run behaviour, we need to examine both the long-run AS curve and the short-run AS curve.

Why the Aggregate Supply Curve is Vertical in the Long Run

What determines the quantity of goods and services supplied in the long run? We implicitly answered this question earlier in the book when we analysed the process of economic growth. In the long run, an economy's production of goods and services (its real GDP) depends on its supplies of labour, capital and natural resources, and on the available technology used to turn these factors of production into goods and services. Because the price level does not affect these long-run determinants of real GDP, the long-run AS curve is vertical, as in Figure 16.3. In other words, in the long run, the economy's labour, capital, natural resources and technology determine the total quantity of goods and services supplied, and this quantity supplied is the same regardless of what the price level happens to be.

The vertical long-run AS curve is, in essence, just an application of the classical dichotomy and monetary neutrality. As we have already discussed, classical macroeconomic theory is based on the assumption that real variables do not depend on nominal variables. The long-run AS curve is consistent with this idea because it implies that the quantity of output (a real variable) does not depend on the level of prices (a nominal variable). As noted earlier, most economists believe that this principle works well when studying the economy over a period of many years, but not when studying year-to-year changes. Thus, the AS curve is vertical only in the long run.

One might wonder why supply curves for specific goods and services can be upwards sloping if the long-run AS curve is vertical. The reason is that the supply of specific goods and services depends on *relative prices* – the prices of those goods and services compared to other prices in the economy. For example, when the price of tablet computers rises, holding other prices in the economy constant, there is an incentive for suppliers of tablets to increase their production by taking labour, silicon, plastic and other inputs away from the production of other goods, such as mobile phones or laptop computers. By contrast, the economy's overall production of goods and services is limited by its labour, capital, natural resources and technology. Thus, when all prices in the economy rise together, there is no change in the overall quantity of goods and services supplied because relative prices and thus incentives have not changed.

Why the Long-Run AS Curve Might Shift

The position of the long-run AS curve shows the quantity of goods and services predicted by classical macroeconomic theory. This level of production is sometimes called *potential output* or *full-employment output*. To be more accurate, we call it the **natural rate of output** because it shows what the economy produces when unemployment is at its natural, or normal, rate. The natural rate of output is the level of production towards which the economy gravitates in the long run.

natural rate of output the output level in an economy when all existing factors of production (land, labour, capital and technology resources) are fully utilized and where unemployment is at its natural rate

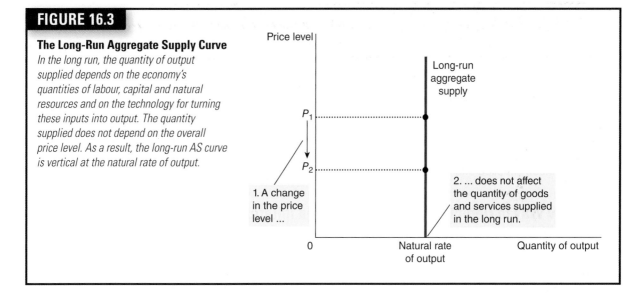

FIGURE 16.3

The Long-Run Aggregate Supply Curve
In the long run, the quantity of output supplied depends on the economy's quantities of labour, capital and natural resources and on the technology for turning these inputs into output. The quantity supplied does not depend on the overall price level. As a result, the long-run AS curve is vertical at the natural rate of output.

Any change in the economy that alters the natural rate of output shifts the long-run AS curve. Because output in the classical model depends on labour, capital, natural resources and technological knowledge, we can categorize shifts in the long-run AS curve as arising from these sources.

Shifts Arising from Labour Imagine that an economy experiences an increase in immigration from abroad. Because there would be a greater number of workers, the quantity of goods and services supplied would increase. As a result, the long-run AS curve would shift to the right. Conversely, if many workers left the economy to go abroad, the long-run AS curve would shift to the left.

The position of the long-run AS curve also depends on the natural rate of unemployment, so any change in the natural rate of unemployment shifts the long-run AS curve. For example, if the government were to raise the minimum wage substantially, the natural rate of unemployment would rise, and the economy would produce a smaller quantity of goods and services. As a result, the long-run AS curve would shift to the left. Conversely, if a reform of the unemployment insurance system were to encourage unemployed workers to search harder for new jobs, the natural rate of unemployment would fall and the long-run AS curve would shift to the right.

Shifts Arising from Capital An increase in the economy's capital stock increases productivity and, thereby, the quantity of goods and services supplied. As a result, the long-run AS curve shifts to the right. Conversely, a decrease in the economy's capital stock decreases productivity and the quantity of goods and services supplied, shifting the long-run AS curve to the left.

Notice that the same logic applies regardless of whether we are discussing physical capital or human capital. An increase either in the number of machines or in the number of university degrees will raise the economy's ability to produce goods and services. Thus, either would shift the long-run AS curve to the right.

Shifts Arising from Natural Resources An economy's production depends on its natural resources, including its land, minerals and weather. A discovery of a new mineral deposit shifts the long-run AS curve to the right. A change in weather patterns that makes farming more difficult shifts the long-run AS curve to the left.

In many countries, important natural resources are imported from abroad. A change in the availability of these resources can also shift the AS curve. Events occurring in the world oil market, in particular, have historically been an important source of shifts in AS.

Shifts Arising from Technological Knowledge Perhaps the most important reason that the economy today produces more than it did a generation ago is that our technological knowledge has advanced. The invention of the computer, for instance, has allowed us to produce more goods and services from any given amounts of labour, capital and natural resources. As a result, it has shifted the long-run AS curve to the right.

Although not literally technological, there are many other events that act like changes in technology. The opening up of international trade has effects similar to inventing new production processes, so it also shifts the long-run AS curve to the right. Conversely, if the government passed new regulations preventing firms from using some production methods, perhaps because they were too dangerous for workers, the result would be a leftwards shift in the long-run AS curve.

Summary The long-run AS curve reflects the classical model of the economy we developed in previous chapters. Any policy or event that raised real GDP in previous chapters can now be viewed as increasing the quantity of goods and services supplied and shifting the long-run AS curve to the right. Any policy or event that lowered real GDP in previous chapters can now be viewed as decreasing the quantity of goods and services supplied and shifting the long-run AS curve to the left.

A New Way to Depict Long-Run Growth and Inflation

Having introduced the economy's AD curve and the long-run AS curve, we now have a new way to describe the economy's long-run trends. Figure 16.4 illustrates the changes that occur in the economy from decade to decade. Notice that both curves are shifting. Although there are many forces that govern the economy in the long run and can in principle cause such shifts, the two most important in practice are technology and monetary policy. Technological progress enhances the economy's ability to produce goods and services, and this continually shifts the long-run AS curve to the right. At the same time, because the central bank increases the money supply over time, the AD curve also shifts to the right. As the figure illustrates, the result is trend growth in output (as shown by increasing Y) and continuing inflation (as shown by increasing P). This is just another way of representing the classical analysis of growth and inflation we conducted earlier in the book.

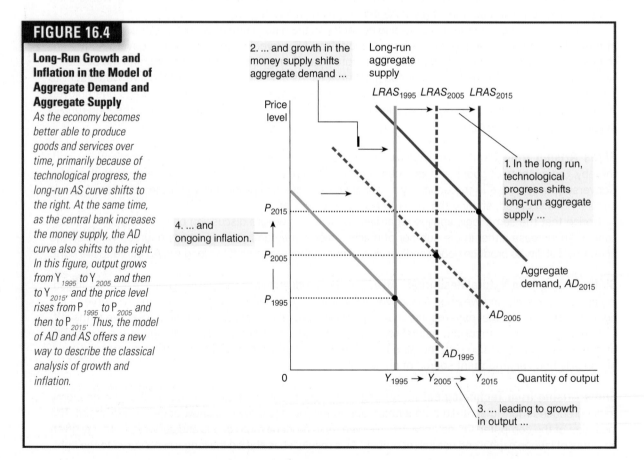

FIGURE 16.4

Long-Run Growth and Inflation in the Model of Aggregate Demand and Aggregate Supply

As the economy becomes better able to produce goods and services over time, primarily because of technological progress, the long-run AS curve shifts to the right. At the same time, as the central bank increases the money supply, the AD curve also shifts to the right. In this figure, output grows from Y_{1995} to Y_{2005} and then to Y_{2015}, and the price level rises from P_{1995} to P_{2005} and then to P_{2015}. Thus, the model of AD and AS offers a new way to describe the classical analysis of growth and inflation.

2. ... and growth in the money supply shifts aggregate demand ...

Long-run aggregate supply

$LRAS_{1995}$ $LRAS_{2005}$ $LRAS_{2015}$

Price level

1. In the long run, technological progress shifts long-run aggregate supply ...

4. ... and ongoing inflation.

P_{2015}

P_{2005}

P_{1995}

Aggregate demand, AD_{2015}

AD_{2005}

AD_{1995}

0 Y_{1995} → Y_{2005} → Y_{2015} Quantity of output

3. ... leading to growth in output ...

The purpose of developing the model of AD and AS, however, is not to dress our long-run conclusions in new clothing. Instead, it is to provide a framework for short-run analysis, as we will see in a moment. As we develop the short-run model, we keep the analysis simple by not showing the continuing growth and inflation depicted in Figure 16.4. But always remember that long-run trends provide the background for short-run fluctuations. Short-run fluctuations in output and the price level should be viewed as deviations from the continuing long-run trends.

Why the AS Curve Slopes Upward in the Short Run

We now come to the key difference between the economy in the short run and in the long run: the behaviour of AS. As we have already discussed, the long-run AS curve is vertical. By contrast, in the short run, the AS curve is upwards sloping, as shown in Figure 16.5. That is, over a period of a year or two, an increase in the overall level of prices in the economy tends to raise the quantity of goods and services supplied, and a decrease in the level of prices tends to reduce the quantity of goods and services supplied.

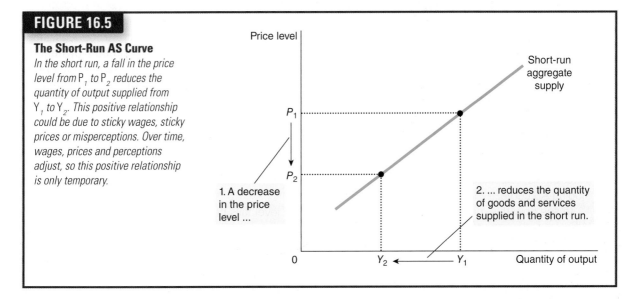

FIGURE 16.5

The Short-Run AS Curve
In the short run, a fall in the price level from P_1 to P_2 reduces the quantity of output supplied from Y_1 to Y_2. This positive relationship could be due to sticky wages, sticky prices or misperceptions. Over time, wages, prices and perceptions adjust, so this positive relationship is only temporary.

1. A decrease in the price level ...

2. ... reduces the quantity of goods and services supplied in the short run.

What causes this positive relationship between the price level and output? Macroeconomists have proposed three theories for the upward slope of the short-run AS curve. In each theory, a specific market imperfection causes the supply side of the economy to behave differently in the short run than it does in the long run. Although each of the following theories will differ in detail, they share a common theme: the quantity of output supplied deviates from its long-run or 'natural' level when the price level deviates from the price level that people *expected* to prevail. When the price level rises above the expected level, output rises above its natural rate, and when the price level falls below the expected level, output falls below its natural rate.

The Sticky Wage Theory The first and simplest explanation of the upwards slope of the short-run AS curve is the sticky wage theory which we initially encountered in Chapter 14. According to this theory, the short-run AS curve slopes upwards because nominal wages are slow to adjust, or are 'sticky', in the short run. To some extent, the slow adjustment of nominal wages is attributable to long-term contracts between workers and firms that fix nominal wages, sometimes for as long as three years. In addition, this slow adjustment may be attributable to social norms and notions of fairness that influence wage setting and that change only slowly over time.

To see what sticky nominal wages mean for AS, imagine that a firm has agreed in advance to pay its workers a certain nominal wage based on what it expected the price level to be. If the price level P falls below the level that was expected and the nominal wage remains stuck at W, then the real wage $\frac{W}{P}$ rises above the level the firm planned to pay. Because wages are a large part of a firm's production costs, a higher real wage means that the firm's real costs have risen. The firm responds to these higher costs by hiring less labour and producing a smaller quantity of goods and services. In other words, because wages do not adjust immediately to the price level, a lower price level makes employment and production less profitable, so firms reduce the quantity of goods and services they supply.

The Sticky Price Theory As we just discussed, the sticky wage theory emphasizes that nominal wages adjust slowly over time. The sticky price theory emphasizes that the prices of some goods and services also adjust sluggishly in response to changing economic conditions. This slow adjustment of prices occurs in part because of the *menu costs* to adjusting prices. These menu costs include the cost of printing and distributing price lists or mail-order catalogues and the time required to change price tags. As a result of these costs, prices as well as wages may be sticky in the short run.

To see the implications of sticky prices for AS, suppose that each firm in the economy announces its prices in advance based on the economic conditions it expects to prevail. Then, after prices are announced, the economy experiences an unexpected contraction in the money supply, which (as we have learned) will reduce the overall price level in the long run. Although some firms reduce their prices immediately in response to changing economic conditions, other firms may not want to incur additional menu costs and, therefore, may temporarily lag behind. Because these lagging firms have prices that are too high, their sales decline. Declining sales, in turn, cause these firms to cut back on production and employment. In other words, because not all prices adjust instantly to changing conditions, an unexpected fall in the price level leaves some firms with higher-than-desired prices, and these higher-than-desired prices depress sales and induce firms to reduce the quantity of goods and services they produce.

The Misperceptions Theory A third approach to the short-run AS curve is the misperceptions theory. According to this theory, changes in the overall price level can temporarily mislead suppliers about what is happening in the individual markets in which they sell their output. As a result of these short-run misperceptions, suppliers respond to changes in the level of prices, and this response leads to an upwards sloping AS curve.

To see how this might work, suppose the overall price level falls below the level that people expected. When suppliers see the prices of their products fall, they may mistakenly believe that their *relative* prices have fallen. For example, wheat farmers may notice a fall in the price of wheat before they notice a fall in the prices of the many items they buy as consumers. They may infer from this observation that the reward to producing wheat is temporarily low, and they may respond by reducing the quantity of wheat they supply. Similarly, workers may notice a fall in their nominal wages before they notice a fall in the prices of the goods they buy. They may infer that the reward to working is temporarily low and respond by reducing the quantity of labour they supply. In both cases, a lower price level causes misperceptions about relative prices, and these misperceptions induce suppliers to respond to the lower price level by decreasing the quantity of goods and services supplied.

Summary There are three alternative explanations for the upwards slope of the short-run AS curve: (1) sticky wages; (2) sticky prices; and (3) misperceptions. Economists debate which of these theories is correct, and it is very possible each contains an element of truth. For our purposes in this book, the similarities of the theories are more important than the differences. All three theories suggest that output deviates from its natural rate when the price level deviates from the price level that people expected. We can express this mathematically as follows:

$$
\begin{pmatrix} \text{Quantity} \\ \text{of output} \\ \text{supplied} \end{pmatrix} = \begin{pmatrix} \text{Natural} \\ \text{rate of} \\ \text{output} \end{pmatrix} + a \begin{pmatrix} \text{Actual} \\ \text{price} \\ \text{level} \end{pmatrix} - \begin{pmatrix} \text{Expected} \\ \text{price} \\ \text{level} \end{pmatrix}
$$

where *a* is a number that determines how much output responds to unexpected changes in the price level.

Notice that each of the three theories of short-run AS emphasizes a problem that is likely to be only temporary. Whether the upwards slope of the AS curve is attributable to sticky wages, sticky prices or misperceptions, these conditions will not persist forever. Eventually, as people adjust their expectations, nominal wages adjust, prices become unstuck and misperceptions are corrected. In other words, the expected and actual price levels are equal in the long run, and the AS curve is vertical rather than upwards sloping.

Why the Short-Run AS Curve Might Shift

The short-run AS curve tells us the quantity of goods and services supplied in the short run for any given level of prices. We can think of this curve as similar to the long-run AS curve but made upwards sloping by the presence of sticky wages, sticky prices and misperceptions. Thus, when thinking about what shifts the short-run AS curve, we have to consider all those variables that shift the long-run AS curve plus a new variable – the expected price level – that influences sticky wages, sticky prices and misperceptions.

Let's start with what we know about the long-run AS curve. As we discussed earlier, shifts in the long-run AS curve normally arise from changes in labour, capital, natural resources or technological knowledge. These same variables shift the short-run AS curve. For example, when an increase in the economy's capital stock increases productivity, both the long-run and short-run AS curves shift to the right. When an increase in the minimum wage raises the natural rate of unemployment, both the long-run and short-run AS curves shift to the left.

The important new variable that affects the position of the short-run AS curve is people's expectation of the price level. As we have discussed, the quantity of goods and services supplied depends, in the short run, on sticky wages, sticky prices and misperceptions. Yet wages, prices and perceptions are set on the basis of expectations of the price level. So when expectations change, the short-run AS curve shifts.

To make this idea more concrete, let's consider a specific theory of AS – the sticky wage theory. According to this theory, when workers and firms expect the price level to be high, they are more likely to negotiate high nominal wages. High wages raise firms' costs and, for any given actual price level, reduce the quantity of goods and services that firms supply. Thus, when the expected price level rises, wages are higher, costs increase, and firms supply a smaller quantity of goods and services at any given actual price level. Thus, the short-run AS curve shifts to the left. Conversely, when the expected price level falls, wages are lower, costs decline, firms increase production at any given price level, and the short-run AS curve shifts to the right.

A similar logic applies in each theory of AS. The general lesson is the following:

● An increase in the expected price level reduces the quantity of goods and services supplied and shifts the short-run AS curve to the left.
● A decrease in the expected price level raises the quantity of goods and services supplied and shifts the short-run AS curve to the right.

As we will see in the next section, this influence of expectations on the position of the short-run AS curve plays a key role in reconciling the economy's behaviour in the short run with its behaviour in the long run. In the short run, expectations are fixed, and the economy finds itself at the intersection of the AD curve and the short-run AS curve. In the long run, expectations adjust, and the short-run AS curve shifts. This shift ensures that the economy eventually finds itself at the intersection of the AD curve and the long-run AS curve.

You should now have some understanding about why the short-run AS curve slopes upward and what events and policies can cause this curve to shift. Table 16.2 summarizes our discussion.

SELF TEST Explain why the long-run AS curve is vertical. ● Explain three theories for why the short-run AS curve is upwards sloping.

TWO CAUSES OF ECONOMIC FLUCTUATIONS

Now that we have introduced the model of AD and AS, we have the basic tools we need to analyse fluctuations in economic activity. In particular, we can use what we have learned about AD and AS to examine the two basic causes of short-run fluctuations.

To keep things simple, we assume the economy begins in long-run equilibrium, as shown in Figure 16.6. Equilibrium output and the price level are determined by the intersection of the AD curve and the long-run

AS curve, shown as point A in the figure. At this point, output is at its natural rate. The short-run AS curve passes through this point as well, indicating that wages, prices and perceptions have fully adjusted to this long-run equilibrium. That is, when an economy is in its long-run equilibrium, wages, prices and perceptions must have adjusted so that the intersection of AD with short-run AS is the same as the intersection of AD with long-run AS.

TABLE 16.2

The Short-Run Aggregate Supply Curve: Summary

Why does the short-run aggregate supply curve slope upward?

1 *The sticky wage theory:* An unexpectedly low price level raises the real wage, which causes firms to hire fewer workers and produce a smaller quantity of goods and services.

2 *The sticky price theory:* An unexpectedly low price level leaves some firms with higher-than-desired prices, which depresses their sales and leads them to cut back production.

3 *The misperceptions theory:* An unexpectedly low price level leads some suppliers to think their relative prices have fallen, which induces a fall in production.

Why might the short-run aggregate supply curve shift?

1 *Shifts arising from labour:* An increase in the quantity of labour available (perhaps due to a fall in the natural rate of unemployment) shifts the AS curve to the right. A decrease in the quantity of labour available (perhaps due to a rise in the natural rate of unemployment) shifts the AS curve to the left.

2. *Shifts arising from capital:* An increase in physical or human capital shifts the AS curve to the right. A decrease in physical or human capital shifts the AS curve to the left.

3 *Shifts arising from natural resources:* An increase in the availability of natural resources shifts the AS curve to the right. A decrease in the availability of natural resources shifts the AS curve to the left.

4 *Shifts arising from technology:* An advance in technological knowledge shifts the AS curve to the right. A decrease in the available technology (perhaps due to government regulation) shifts the AS curve to the left.

5 *Shifts arising from the expected price level:* A decrease in the expected price level shifts the short-run AS curve to the right. An increase in the expected price level shifts the short-run AS curve to the left.

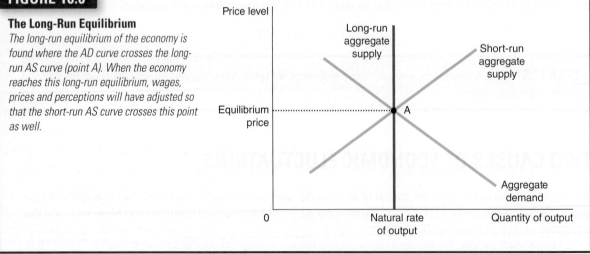

FIGURE 16.6

The Long-Run Equilibrium
The long-run equilibrium of the economy is found where the AD curve crosses the long-run AS curve (point A). When the economy reaches this long-run equilibrium, wages, prices and perceptions will have adjusted so that the short-run AS curve crosses this point as well.

The Effects of a Shift in Aggregate Demand

Suppose that for some reason a wave of pessimism suddenly overtakes the economy. The cause might be a government scandal, a crash on the stock market or the outbreak of war overseas. Because of this event, many people lose confidence in the future and alter their plans. Households cut back on their spending and delay major purchases, and firms put off buying new equipment.

What is the impact of such a wave of pessimism on the economy? Such an event reduces the AD for goods and services. That is, for any given price level, households and firms now want to buy a smaller quantity of goods and services. As Figure 16.7 shows, the AD curve shifts to the left from AD_1 to AD_2.

In this figure we can examine the effects of the fall in AD. In the short run, the economy moves along the initial short-run AS curve AS_1, going from point A to point B. As the economy moves from point A to point B, output falls from Y_1 to Y_2, and the price level falls from P_1 to P_2. The falling level of output indicates that the economy is in a recession. Although not shown in the figure, firms respond to lower sales and production by reducing employment. Thus, the pessimism that caused the shift in AD is, to some extent, self-fulfilling: pessimism about the future leads to falling incomes and rising unemployment.

FIGURE 16.7

A Contraction in Aggregate Demand

A fall in AD, which might be due to a wave of pessimism in the economy, is represented with a leftward shift in the AD curve from AD_1 to AD_2. The economy moves from point A to point B. Output falls from Y_1 to Y_2, and the price level falls from P_1 to P_2. Over time, as wages, prices and perceptions adjust, the short-run AS curve shifts to the right from AS_1 to AS_2, and the economy reaches point C, where the new AD curve crosses the long-run AS curve. The price level falls to P_3, and output returns to its natural rate, Y_1.

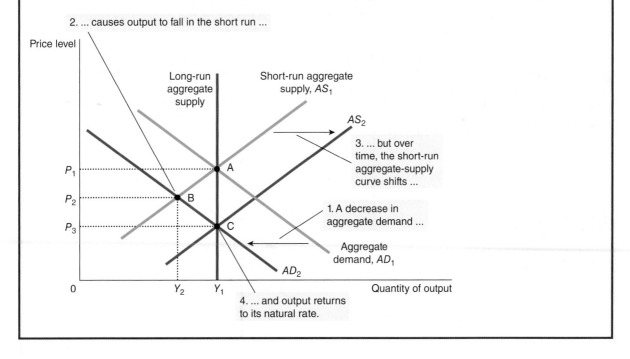

What should policymakers do when faced with such a recession? One possibility is to take action to increase AD. As we noted earlier, an increase in government spending or an increase in the money supply would increase the quantity of goods and services demanded at any price and, therefore, would shift the AD curve to the right. If policymakers can act with sufficient speed and precision, they can offset the initial shift in AD, return the AD curve back to AD_1 and bring the economy back to point A. (The next chapter discusses in more detail the ways in which monetary and fiscal policy influence AD, as well as some of the practical difficulties in using these policy instruments.)

Even without action by policymakers, the recession will remedy itself over a period of time. Because of the reduction in AD, the price level falls. Eventually, expectations catch up with this new reality, and the expected price level falls as well. Because the fall in the expected price level alters wages, prices and perceptions, it shifts the short-run AS curve to the right from AS_1 to AS_2 in Figure 16.7. This adjustment of expectations allows the economy over time to approach point C, where the new AD curve (AD_2) crosses the long-run AS curve.

In the new long-run equilibrium, point C, output is back to its natural rate. Even though the wave of pessimism has reduced AD, the price level has fallen sufficiently (to P_3) to offset the shift in the AD curve. Thus, in the long run, the shift in AD is reflected fully in the price level and not at all in the level of output. In other words, the long-run effect of a shift in AD is a nominal change (the price level is lower) but not a real change (output is the same).

To sum up, this story about shifts in AD has two important lessons:

● In the short run, shifts in AD cause fluctuations in the economy's output of goods and services.
● In the long run, shifts in AD affect the overall price level but do not affect output.

The Effects of a Shift in Aggregate Supply

Imagine once again an economy in its long-run equilibrium. Now suppose that suddenly some firms experience an increase in their costs of production. For example, bad weather might destroy some agricultural crops, driving up the cost of producing food products. Or political or military conflict might interrupt the shipping of crude oil, driving up the cost of producing oil products.

What is the macroeconomic impact of such an increase in production costs? For any given price level, firms now want to supply a smaller quantity of goods and services. Thus, as Figure 16.8 shows, the short-run AS curve shifts to the left from AS_1 to AS_2. (Depending on the event, the long-run AS curve might also shift. To keep things simple, however, we will assume that it does not.)

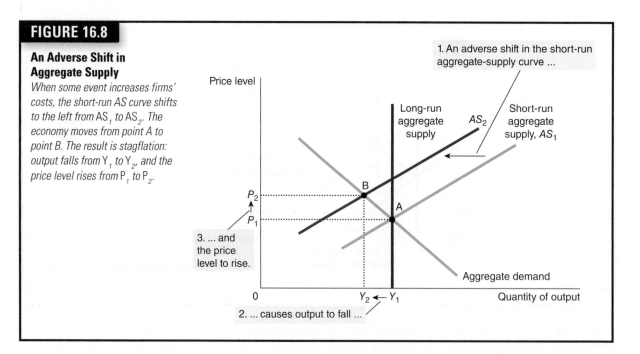

FIGURE 16.8

An Adverse Shift in Aggregate Supply
When some event increases firms' costs, the short-run AS curve shifts to the left from AS_1 to AS_2. The economy moves from point A to point B. The result is stagflation: output falls from Y_1 to Y_2, and the price level rises from P_1 to P_2.

1. An adverse shift in the short-run aggregate-supply curve ...

Price level

Long-run aggregate supply

Short-run aggregate supply, AS_1

AS_2

B

A

P_2

P_1

3. ... and the price level to rise.

Aggregate demand

0

$Y_2 \leftarrow Y_1$

Quantity of output

2. ... causes output to fall ...

In this figure we can trace the effects of the leftward shift in AS. In the short run, the economy moves along the existing AD curve, going from point A to point B. The output of the economy falls from Y_1 to Y_2 and the price level rises from P_1 to P_2. Because the economy is experiencing both *stagnation* (falling output) and *inflation* (rising prices), such an event is sometimes called **stagflation**.

> **stagflation** a period of falling output and rising prices

What should policymakers do when faced with stagflation? There are no easy choices. One possibility is to do nothing. In this case, the output of goods and services remains depressed at Y_2 for a while. Eventually, however, the recession will remedy itself as wages, prices and perceptions adjust to raise production costs. A period of low output and high unemployment, for instance, puts downwards pressure on workers' wages. Lower wages, in turn, increase the quantity of output supplied. Over time, as the short-run AS curve shifts back towards AS_1, the price level falls, and the quantity of output approaches its natural rate. In the long run, the economy returns to point A, where the AD curve crosses the long-run AS curve. This is the view that believers of free markets might adopt.

Alternatively, policymakers who control monetary and fiscal policy might attempt to offset some of the effects of the shift in the short-run AS curve by shifting the AD curve. This possibility is shown in Figure 16.9. In this case, changes in policy shift the AD curve to the right from AD_1 to AD_2 – exactly enough to prevent the shift in AS from affecting output. The economy moves directly from point A to point C. Output remains at its natural rate, and the price level rises from P_1 to P_3. In this case, policymakers are said to *accommodate* the shift in AS because they allow the increase in costs to permanently affect the level of prices. This intervention by policymakers would be seen as being desirable by supporters of Keynes.

FIGURE 16.9

Accommodating an Adverse Shift in Aggregate Supply
Faced with an adverse shift in AS from AS_1 to AS_2, policymakers who can influence AD might try to shift the AD curve to the right from AD_1 to AD_2. The economy would move from point A to point C. This policy would prevent the supply shift from reducing output in the short run, but the price level would permanently rise from P_1 to P_3.

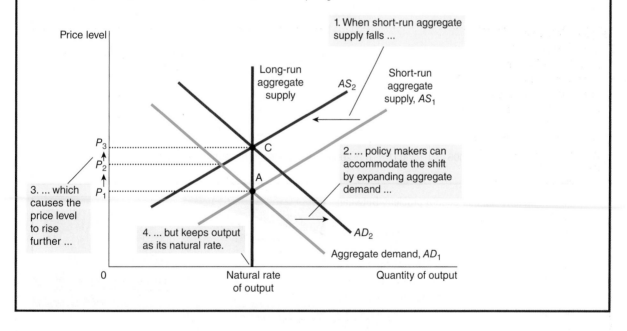

These different views on policy action form a key aspect of the debate between economists about action in the face of short-run fluctuations in economic activity.

To sum up, this story about shifts in AS has two important lessons:

● Shifts in AS can cause stagflation – a combination of recession (falling output) and inflation (rising prices).
● Policymakers who can influence AD cannot offset both of these adverse effects simultaneously.

Stagflation in Iceland?

The economy of Iceland was badly affected by the financial crisis with three of its main banks, Kaupthing, Landsbanki and Glitnir, all failing. The collapse of these banks led to the Icelandic economy slumping. Figure 16.10 shows how significant and rapid the decline in the economy was between mid-2007 and mid-2009. The annual change in GDP was reported as −18.2 per cent in 2008 and −9.1 per cent in 2009. The economy began to improve slowly and returned to growth in early 2010 and growing at a rate of 3 – 4 per cent between the middle of 2011 to November 2012 when the economy contracted once again.

FIGURE 16.10

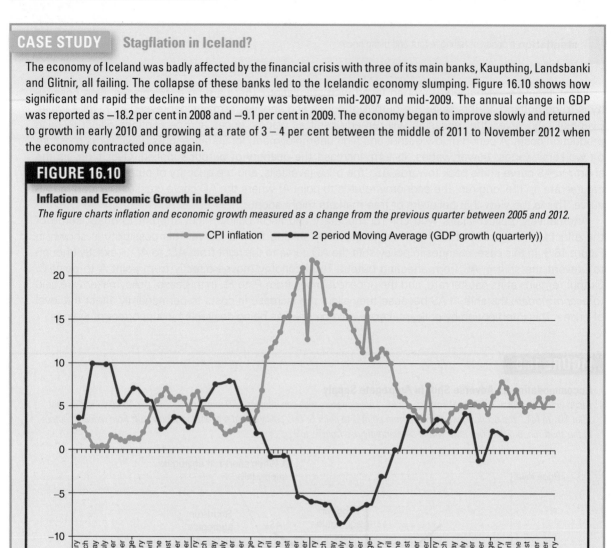

Inflation and Economic Growth in Iceland

The figure charts inflation and economic growth measured as a change from the previous quarter between 2005 and 2012.

Inflation, meanwhile, has been a problem. Between 2005 and March 2006, inflation was under 2.0 per cent but began to accelerate after that time before easing in the latter part of 2007. Once the full effects of the financial crisis took hold, inflation accelerated, quickly reaching a high of 21.9 per cent in January 2009. Inflation has eased since then but the trend since November 2010 is upwards.

The aftermath of the financial crisis left Iceland facing the twin problems of accelerating inflation and shrinking economic activity. It can be argued that the particular

The collapse of the banking system in Iceland not only affected the people of Iceland but across many other parts of Europe too.

circumstances of the banking collapse in Iceland led to the stagflation but what of the future for Iceland? There are fears that Iceland could again be heading for a period of stagflation. The rate of growth of inflation seems to be accelerating and some analysts expect inflation to be over 5 per cent in the coming years but at the same time growth seems to be slowing. Statistics Iceland reported that preliminary GDP figures for 2012 would show growth of 1.6 per cent – not a contraction in the economy but a growth rate below that forecast. There was a 50 per cent chance that these figures could be revised downwards.

> **SELF TEST** Suppose that the election of a popular prime minister suddenly increases people's confidence in the future. Use the model of AD and AS to analyse the effect on the economy.

NEW KEYNESIAN ECONOMICS

We introduced Keynesian economics and the IS-LM model in Chapter 15. Recall that Keynesian economics developed in response to the depression of the 1930s, when it appeared that the assumptions of classical economics that markets would clear, were failing. Keynesian ideas were the mainstay for economic policy across the developed world in the post-war era and there was something of a consensus amongst economists that our understanding of the macroeconomy was considerable. The latter part of the 1960s began to reveal some flaws in that assumption as global conditions changed. The breakdown of fixed exchange rates in the late 1960s and the oil crisis in the early 1970s presented macroeconomists with significant challenges in explaining the economic conditions that existed in some countries – stagflation in particular.

Economics came to be classified as a debate between Keynesians on the one hand, who pointed to markets not clearing quickly, and the neo or new classicists on the other hand, who re-emphasized the efficiency of markets and argued that microeconomics provided a foundation for understanding macroeconomics.

Out of this debate emerged a group who were referred to as the New Keynesians. New Keynesian economics placed an emphasis on providing sound microeconomic principles to underpin Keynesian macroeconomics. Specifically, the New Keynesians sought to explain how price and wage stickiness had its foundation in the microeconomic analysis of labour markets and price setting by firms.

Features of New Keynesian Economics

New Keynesians would argue that short-run fluctuations in economic output violate the classical dichotomy, as outlined earlier in this chapter. Changes in nominal variables like the money supply do have an influence on output and employment – real variables. In addition, they would argue that to develop an understanding of changes in economic activity, an understanding of the imperfections in the economy is necessary – that firms operate under imperfect competition, that consumers and firms are subject to imperfect information and that there are built-in rigidities in the economy which hinder the movement of prices and wages as we have noted.

So, can we conclude from this that the economists classed as New Keynesians are supporters of demand management but with some reservations? The answer to this is 'no'. The splitting of economics into different schools of thought has been convenient for the mass media to present disagreements between economists in relatively simple terms. The reality is that there is probably more agreement in economics that most members of the public would imagine. A difference in some base assumptions and a difference in the relative size of parameters in models is largely the reason why economists disagree. Many economists would subscribe to the view that changes in the money supply affect aggregate demand (a so-called 'monetarist' view) but also agree that price rigidities in the macroeconomy exist because of imperfections in the microeconomy. Some New Keynesian economists would, equally, not be in support of policy intervention to correct short-term fluctuations in the economy by attempting to manipulate aggregate demand. The main reason being that they would argue that the effects of such policy interventions take time to work through the economy by which time economic conditions have changed and so the policy will not be as effective as anticipated. Changes in interest rates, for example, are estimated to take around 18 months to work through the economy; tax changes might be received in different ways by different people and it is never certain enough to predict how people will react to a tax cut or a tax increase in any precise quantifiable way to make such a policy option a clear-cut choice. Equally, policies to increase government spending, on infrastructure projects for example, often take many years to have any effect even if such projects are 'shovel ready' – able to be put in operation quickly.

The response to the financial crisis has reinvigorated the debate between whether active intervention by central banks and governments to boost the economy in the face of persistent sluggish growth and rising unemployment is the best policy response, or whether a 'do nothing' option is preferable to allow markets to adjust to changed conditions. It is always easy to seize on one headline statement by any economist and immediately seek to pigeon-hole that view. New Keynesian economics reminds us that the complexities of the economy perhaps deserve a more discerning look at the detail behind what economists are actually saying and how much they agree and why they agree, as much as why they might disagree and the extent of such disagreements.

CONCLUSION

This chapter has achieved two goals. First, we have discussed some of the important facts about short-run fluctuations in economic activity. Second, we have introduced a basic model to explain those fluctuations, called the model of AD and AS. We continue our study of this model in the next chapter in order to understand more fully what causes fluctuations in the economy and how policymakers might respond to these fluctuations.

IN THE NEWS

Expectations

One of the key tasks of policymakers is to set the tone for expectations in the economy – such expectations have to be realistic and also believed by the population if the policy is to have any credence.

Moderating Inflationary Expectations in China

The Governor of the central bank of China, the People's Bank of China (PBoC), Zhou Xiaochuan, re-emphasized the commitment of the PBoC to keeping inflation under control in a speech made in March 2013. The comments followed the release of inflation data which showed the CPI accelerating to 3.2 per cent in February 2013, a ten-month high. Zhou noted that this was higher than forecast and that this emphasized the need to ensure the PBoC acted to moderate inflationary expectations in the economy.

To reinforce the message that inflation would be kept under control, Zhou announced that the growth in the money supply, as measured by M2, would be tightened with a target of 13

per cent growth in M2 for 2013. Zhou noted that this target was lower than the actual growth in M2 in 2012, which was over 14 per cent and reflected the desire by the PBoC to help boost economic growth in China. Part of the pro-growth policy that was a focus of 2012 included government spending on infrastructure and the looser monetary policy also allowed more people to be able to borrow money to buy property. However, the PBoC noted that house prices increased over 12 per cent in Beijing and had risen in 53 of 70 major cities across the country and house price inflation was something that it wanted to control.

Whilst China intends to tighten monetary policy, the PBoC also noted that it was monitoring the potential effect on China's economy of looser monetary policy being adopted

elsewhere in the world. Quantitative easing in the US and UK should lead to a higher money supply and was likely to lead to a weakening of the pound and dollar against the yuan. A stronger yuan would affect China's exporters and also raise the cost of imports which would put pressure on inflation.

Questions

1 **Using your understanding of the model of AD and AS, what factors might be causing an increase in inflation in China?**

2 **Why might the increase in the rate of inflation in March 2013 to a ten-month high, trigger expectations of higher inflation in the future and what effect might this have on the Chinese economy in the absence of policy changes by the Chinese authorities?**

3 **Why would the PBoC's announcement that monetary policy be tightened influence expectations and what would you think the results of such a policy announcement, assuming it was enforced, would be?**

4 **Assuming the growth of M2 is tightened, use the AD and AS model to analyse the likely effect on inflation and national income in China.**

5 **Why would a loose monetary policy in countries like the US and UK lead to a strengthening of the Chinese currency and what would you expect the effect on AD in China to be as a result?**

New housing development in China is partly in response to rising wage levels fuelling increased demand which in turn is leading to rising house prices.

SUMMARY

- All societies experience short-run economic fluctuations around long-run trends. These fluctuations are irregular and largely unpredictable. When recessions do occur, real GDP and other measures of income, spending and production fall, and unemployment rises.

- Economists analyse short-run economic fluctuations using the model of AD and AS. According to this model, the output of goods and services and the overall level of prices adjust to balance AD and AS.

- The AD curve slopes downwards for three reasons. First, a lower price level raises the real value of households' money holdings, which stimulates consumer spending. Second, a lower price level reduces the quantity of money households' demand; as households try to convert money into interest-bearing assets, interest rates fall, which stimulates investment spending. Third, as a lower price level reduces interest rates, the local currency depreciates in the market for foreign currency exchange, which stimulates net exports.

- Any event or policy that raises consumption, investment, government purchases or net exports at a given price level increases AD. Any event or policy that reduces consumption, investment, government purchases or net exports at a given price level decreases AD.

- The long-run AS curve is vertical. In the long run, the quantity of goods and services supplied depends on the economy's labour, capital, natural resources and technology, but not on the overall level of prices.

- Three theories have been proposed to explain the upwards slope of the short-run AS curve. According to the sticky wage theory, an unexpected fall in the price level temporarily raises real wages, which induces firms to reduce employment and production. According to the sticky price theory, an unexpected fall in the price level leaves some firms with prices that are temporarily too high, which reduces their sales and causes them to cut back production. According to the misperceptions theory, an unexpected fall in the price level leads suppliers to mistakenly believe that their relative prices have fallen, which induces them to reduce production. All three theories imply that output deviates from its natural rate when the price level deviates from the price level that people expected.

- Events that alter the economy's ability to produce output, such as changes in labour, capital, natural resources or technology, shift the short-run AS curve (and may shift the long-run AS curve as well). In addition, the position of the short-run AS curve depends on the expected price level.

- One possible cause of economic fluctuations is a shift in AD. When the AD curve shifts to the left, for instance, output and prices fall in the short run. Over time, as a change in the expected price level causes wages, prices and perceptions to adjust, the short-run AS curve shifts to the right, and the economy returns to its natural rate of output at a new, lower price level.

- A second possible cause of economic fluctuations is a shift in AS. When the AS curve shifts to the left, the short-run effect is falling output and rising prices – a combination called stagflation. Over time, as wages, prices and perceptions adjust, the price level falls back to its original level, and output recovers.

- New Keynesian economics represents a research tradition that questions the classical dichotomy and recognizes imperfections in the economy as key elements in explaining short run deviations from trend.

QUESTIONS FOR REVIEW

1 What do you understand by the term 'economic activity'?

2 What is the official definition of a recession?

3 Name two macroeconomic variables that decline when the economy goes into a recession. Name one macroeconomic variable that rises during a recession.

4 Draw a diagram with aggregate demand, short-run aggregate supply and long-run aggregate supply. Be careful to label the axes correctly.

5 List and explain the three reasons why the aggregate demand curve is downwards sloping.

6 Explain why the long-run aggregate supply curve is vertical.

7 List and explain the three theories for why the short-run aggregate supply curve is upwards sloping.

8 What might shift the aggregate demand curve to the left? Use the model of aggregate demand and aggregate supply to trace through the effects of such a shift.

9 What might shift the aggregate supply curve to the left? Use the model of aggregate demand and aggregate supply to trace through the effects of such a shift.

10 What outcomes are possible if both aggregate demand and aggregate supply are both shifting? Use the model of aggregate demand and aggregate supply to outline some of these possible outcomes.

PROBLEMS AND APPLICATIONS

1 Why do you think that investment is more variable over the business cycle than consumer spending? Which category of consumer spending do you think would be most volatile: durable goods (such as furniture and car purchases), non-durable goods (such as food and clothing) or services (such as haircuts and medical care)? Why?

2 Suppose that the economy is in a long-run equilibrium.

   a. Use a diagram to illustrate the state of the economy. Be sure to show AD, short-run AS and long-run AS.

   b. Now suppose that a financial crisis causes AD to fall. Use your diagram to show what happens to output and the price level in the short run. What happens to the unemployment rate?

   c. Use the sticky wage theory of AS to explain what will happen to output and the price level in the long run (assuming there is no change in policy). What role does the expected price level play in this adjustment? Be sure to illustrate your analysis with a graph.

3 Explain whether each of the following events will increase, decrease or have no effect on long-run AS.

   a. The country experiences a wave of immigration.

   b. The government raises the minimum wage above the national average wage level.

   c. A war leads to the destruction of a large number of factories.

4 In Figure 16.7, how does the unemployment rate at points B and C compare to the unemployment rate at point A? Under the sticky wage explanation of the short-run AS curve, how does the real wage at points B and C compare to the real wage at point A?

5 Explain why the following statements are false.

   a. 'The AD curve slopes downwards because it is the horizontal sum of the demand curves for individual goods.'

   b. 'The long-run AS curve is vertical because economic forces do not affect long-run AS.'

   c. 'If firms adjusted their prices every day, then the short run AS curve would be horizontal.'

   d. 'Whenever the economy enters a recession, its long-run AS curve shifts to the left.'

6 For each of the three theories for the upwards slope of the short-run AS curve, carefully explain the following.

   a. How the economy recovers from a recession and returns to its long-run equilibrium without any policy intervention.

   b. What determines the speed of that recovery?

7 Suppose the central bank expands the money supply, but because the public expects this action, it simultaneously raises its expectation of the price level. What will happen to output and the price level in the short run? Compare this result to the outcome if the central bank expanded the money supply but the public didn't change its expectation of the price level.

8 Suppose workers and firms suddenly believe that inflation will be quite high over the coming year. Suppose also that the economy begins in long-run equilibrium, and the AD curve does not shift.

   a. What happens to nominal wages? What happens to real wages?

   b. Using an AD/AS diagram, show the effect of the change in expectations on both the short-run and long-run levels of prices and output.

   c. Were the expectations of high inflation accurate? Explain.

9 Explain whether each of the following events shifts the short-run AS curve, the AD curve, both, or neither. For each event that does shift a curve, use a diagram to illustrate the effect on the economy.

   a. Households decide to save a larger share of their income.

   b. Cattle farmers suffer a prolonged period of foot-and-mouth disease which cuts average cattle herd sizes by 80 per cent.

   c. Increased job opportunities overseas cause many people to leave the country.

10 Suppose that firms become very optimistic about future business conditions and invest heavily in new capital equipment.

   a. Use an AD/AS diagram to show the short-run effect of this optimism on the economy. Label the new levels of prices and real output. Explain, in words, why the aggregate quantity of output supplied changes.

   b. Now use the diagram from part (a) to show the new long-run equilibrium of the economy. (For now, assume there is no change in the long-run AS curve.) Explain, in words, why the aggregate quantity of output demanded changes between the short run and the long run.

   c. How might the investment boom affect the long-run AS curve? Explain.

17 THE INFLUENCE OF MONETARY AND FISCAL POLICY ON AGGREGATE DEMAND

Imagine that you are a member of a central bank's monetary policy committee (MPC), which sets a country's monetary policy. You observe that the Finance Minister has announced in his budget speech that he is going to cut government spending. How should the MPC respond to this change in fiscal policy? Should it reduce interest rates (and so allow the money supply to expand faster), raise interest rates or leave interest rates the same?

To answer this question, you need to consider the impact of monetary and fiscal policy on the economy. In the preceding chapter we saw how to explain short-run economic fluctuations using the model of aggregate demand and aggregate supply. When the aggregate demand curve or the aggregate supply curve shifts, the result is fluctuations in the economy's overall output of goods and services and in its overall level of prices. As we noted in the previous chapter, monetary and fiscal policy can each influence aggregate demand. Thus, a change in one of these policies can lead to short-run fluctuations in output and prices. Policymakers will want to anticipate this effect and, perhaps, adjust the other policy in response.

In this chapter we examine in more detail how the tools of monetary and fiscal policy influence the position of the aggregate demand curve. We have previously discussed the long-run effects of these policies. In Chapters 6 and 7 we saw how fiscal policy affects saving, investment and long-run economic growth. In Chapters 10 and 11 we saw how the central bank controls the money supply and how the money supply affects the price level in the long run. We now see how these policy tools can shift the aggregate demand curve and, in doing so, affect short-run economic fluctuations.

As we have already learned, many factors influence aggregate demand besides monetary and fiscal policy. In particular, desired spending by households and firms determines the overall demand for goods and services. When desired spending changes, aggregate demand shifts. If policymakers do not respond, such shifts in aggregate demand cause short-run fluctuations in output and employment. As a result, monetary and fiscal policymakers sometimes use the policy levers at their disposal to try to offset these shifts in aggregate demand and thereby stabilize the economy. Here we discuss the theory behind these policy actions and some of the difficulties that arise in using this theory in practice.

HOW MONETARY POLICY INFLUENCES AGGREGATE DEMAND

The aggregate demand curve shows the total quantity of goods and services demanded in the economy for any price level. As you may recall from the preceding chapter, the aggregate demand curve slopes downwards for three reasons:

● *The wealth effect.* A lower price level raises the real value of households' money holdings, and higher real wealth stimulates consumer spending.
● *The interest rate effect.* A lower price level lowers the interest rate as people try to lend out their excess money holdings, and the lower interest rate stimulates investment spending.
● *The exchange rate effect.* When a lower price level lowers the interest rate, investors move some of their funds overseas and cause the domestic currency to depreciate relative to foreign currencies. This depreciation makes domestic goods cheaper compared to foreign goods and, therefore, stimulates spending on net exports.

These three effects should not be viewed as alternative theories. Instead, they occur simultaneously to increase the quantity of goods and services demanded when the price level falls and to decrease it when the price level rises.

Although all three effects work together in explaining the downwards slope of the aggregate demand curve, they are not of equal importance. Because money holdings are a small part of household wealth, the wealth effect is the least important of the three. Whether or not the exchange rate effect is important depends upon the degree of openness of the economy. For a relatively closed economy like the USA, for example, because exports and imports represent only a small fraction of US GDP, the exchange rate effect is not very large. In the UK and most other European economies, however, the economy is much more open in the sense that imports and exports represent a much larger fraction of total GDP, so that the exchange rate effect will be more important. However, the exchange rate effect is probably secondary to the interest rate effect even in relatively open economies, for two reasons. First, the interest rate effect impacts immediately upon the whole economy, affecting consumers, homebuyers and firms across the board, while the loss of competitiveness that is part of the exchange rate effect impacts only upon traded goods, and affects mainly firms producing tradable goods and consumers buying tradable goods. Secondly, many of the countries of Europe have a common currency – the euro – which they share with many of their major trading partners, so that the exchange rate effect is muted.

To understand how policy influences aggregate demand, therefore, we shall examine the interest rate effect in more detail. Here we develop a theory of how the interest rate is determined, called the **theory of liquidity preference**, which was originally developed by John Maynard Keynes in the 1930s. After we develop this theory, we use it to understand the downward slope of the aggregate demand curve and how monetary policy shifts this curve. By shedding new light on the aggregate demand curve, the theory of liquidity preference expands our understanding of short-run economic fluctuations.

> **theory of liquidity preference** Keynes' theory that the interest rate adjusts to bring money supply and money demand into balance

The Theory of Liquidity Preference

In his classic book, *The General Theory of Employment, Interest and Money*, John Maynard Keynes proposed the theory of liquidity preference to explain what factors determine the economy's interest rate. The theory is, in essence, just an application of supply and demand. According to Keynes, the interest rate adjusts to balance the supply and demand for money. We introduced some elements of the theories covered here in Chapter 15 as part of the IS-LM model.

You may recall that economists distinguish between two interest rates: the *nominal interest rate* is the interest rate as usually reported, and the *real interest rate* is the interest rate corrected for the effects of inflation. Which interest rate are we now trying to explain? The answer is both. In the analysis that follows, we hold constant the expected rate of inflation. (This assumption is reasonable for studying the economy in the short run, as we are now doing.) Thus, when the nominal interest rate rises or falls, the real interest rate that people expect to earn rises or falls as well. For the rest of this chapter, when we refer to changes in the interest rate, you should envision the real and nominal interest rates moving in the same direction.

Let's now develop the theory of liquidity preference by considering the supply and demand for money and how each depends on the interest rate.

Money Supply The first element of the theory of liquidity preference is the supply of money. As we have previously noted, the money supply is controlled by the central bank, such as the Bank of England, the European Central Bank or the US Federal Reserve. The central bank can alter the money supply by changing the quantity of reserves in the banking system through the purchase and sale of government bonds in outright open-market operations. When the central bank buys government bonds, the money it pays for the bonds is typically deposited in banks, and this money is added to bank reserves. When the central bank sells government bonds, the money it receives for the bonds is withdrawn from the banking system, and bank reserves fall. These changes in bank reserves, in turn, lead to changes in banks' ability to make loans and create money. In addition to these open-market operations, the central bank can alter the money supply by changing reserve requirements (the amount of reserves banks must hold against deposits) or the refinancing rate (the interest rate at which banks can borrow reserves from the central bank).

These details of monetary control are important for the implementation of central bank policy, and we discussed them in detail in Chapter 10, but they are not crucial in this chapter. Our goal here is to examine how changes in the money supply affect the aggregate demand for goods and services. For this purpose, we can ignore the details of how central bank policy is implemented and simply assume that the central bank controls the money supply directly. In other words, the quantity of money supplied in the economy is fixed at whatever level the central bank decides to set it.

Because the quantity of money supplied is fixed by central bank policy, it does not depend on other economic variables. In particular, it does not depend on the interest rate. Once the central bank has made its policy decision, the quantity of money supplied is the same, regardless of the prevailing interest rate. We represent a fixed money supply with a vertical supply curve in Figure 17.1.

FIGURE 17.1

Equilibrium in the Money Market

According to the theory of liquidity preference, the interest rate adjusts to bring the quantity of money supplied and the quantity of money demanded into balance. If the interest rate is above the equilibrium level (such as at r_1), the quantity of money people want to hold (M_1^d) is less than the quantity the central bank has created, and this surplus of money puts downward pressure on the interest rate. Conversely, if the interest rate is below the equilibrium level (such as at r_2), the quantity of money people want to hold (M_2^d) is greater than the quantity the central bank has created, and this shortage of money puts upward pressure on the interest rate. Thus, the forces of supply and demand in the market for money push the interest rate towards the equilibrium interest rate, at which people are content holding the quantity of money the central bank has created.

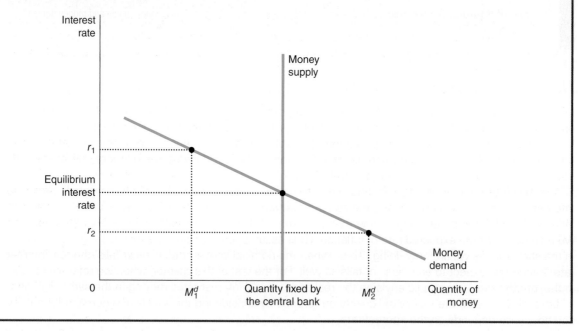

Money Demand The second element of the theory of liquidity preference is the demand for money. As a starting point for understanding money demand, recall that any asset's *liquidity* refers to the ease with which that asset is converted into the economy's medium of exchange. Money is the economy's medium of exchange, so it is by definition the most liquid asset available. The liquidity of money explains the demand for it: people choose to hold money instead of other assets that offer higher rates of return because money can be used to buy goods and services.

Although many factors determine the quantity of money demanded, the one emphasized by the theory of liquidity preference is the interest rate. The reason is that the interest rate is the opportunity cost of holding money. That is, when you hold wealth as cash in your pocket, instead of as an interest-bearing bond or bank account, you forgo the benefits of the interest you could have earned (the opportunity cost). An increase in the interest rate raises the opportunity cost of holding money. There is an incentive, therefore, for people to exchange cash holdings for interest-bearing deposits and this, as a result, reduces the quantity of money demanded. A decrease in the interest rate reduces the opportunity cost of holding money. The cost of the benefits forgone are not as high so there is more incentive to hold money as cash and as a result the quantity demanded increases. Thus, as shown in Figure 17.1, the money demand curve slopes downwards.

Equilibrium in the Money Market According to the theory of liquidity preference, the interest rate adjusts to balance the supply and demand for money. There is one interest rate, called the *equilibrium interest rate*, at which the quantity of money demanded exactly balances the quantity of money supplied. If the interest rate is at any other level, people will try to adjust their portfolios of assets and, as a result, drive the interest rate towards the equilibrium.

For example, suppose that the interest rate is above the equilibrium level, such as r_1 in Figure 17.1. In this case, the quantity of money that people want to hold, (M_1^d), is less than the quantity of money that the central bank has supplied. Those people who are holding the surplus of money will try to get rid of it by buying interest-bearing bonds or by depositing it in an interest-bearing bank account. Because bond issuers and banks prefer to pay lower interest rates, they respond to this surplus of money by lowering the interest rates they offer. As the interest rate falls, people become more willing to hold money until, at the equilibrium interest rate, people are happy to hold exactly the amount of money the central bank has supplied.

Conversely, at interest rates below the equilibrium level, such as r_2 in Figure 17.1, the quantity of money that people want to hold, (M_2^d), is greater than the quantity of money that the central bank has supplied. As a result, people try to increase their holdings of money by reducing their holdings of bonds and other interest-bearing assets. As people cut back on their holdings of bonds, bond issuers find that they have to offer higher interest rates to attract buyers. Thus, the interest rate rises and approaches the equilibrium level.

The Downwards Slope of the Aggregate Demand Curve

Having seen how the theory of liquidity preference explains the economy's equilibrium interest rate, we now consider its implications for the aggregate demand for goods and services. As a warm-up exercise, let's begin by using the theory to re-examine a topic we already understand – the interest rate effect and the downwards slope of the aggregate demand curve. In particular, suppose that the overall level of prices in the economy rises. What happens to the interest rate that balances the supply and demand for money, and how does that change affect the quantity of goods and services demanded?

As we discussed in Chapter 11, the price level is one determinant of the quantity of money demanded. At higher prices, more money is exchanged every time a good or service is sold. As a result, people will choose to hold a larger quantity of money. That is, a higher price level increases the quantity of money demanded for any given interest rate. Thus, an increase in the price level from P_1 to P_2 shifts the money demand curve to the right from MD_1 to MD_2, as shown in panel (a) of Figure 17.2.

Notice how this shift in money demand affects the equilibrium in the money market. For a fixed money supply, the interest rate must rise to balance money supply and money demand. The higher price level has increased the amount of money people want to hold and has shifted the money demand curve to the right. Yet the quantity of money supplied is unchanged, so the interest rate must rise from r_1 to r_2 to discourage the additional demand.

This increase in the interest rate has ramifications not only for the money market but also for the quantity of goods and services demanded, as shown in panel (b). At a higher interest rate, the cost of borrowing and the return to saving are greater. Fewer households choose to borrow to buy a

FYI

Interest Rates in the Long Run and the Short Run

At this point, we should pause and reflect on a seemingly awkward embarrassment of riches. It might appear as if we now have two theories for how interest rates are determined. Chapter 7 states that the interest rate adjusts to balance the supply of and demand for loanable funds (that is, national saving and desired investment). By contrast, we just established here that the interest rate adjusts to balance the supply and demand for money. How can we reconcile these two theories?

To answer this question we must again consider the differences between the long-run and short-run behaviour of the economy. Three macroeconomic variables are of central importance: the economy's output of goods and services; the interest rate; and the price level. According to the classical macroeconomic theory we developed in Chapters 6, 7 and 8, these variables are determined as follows:

1. *Output* is determined by the supplies of capital and labour and the available production technology for turning capital and labour into output. (We call this the natural rate of output.)
2. For any given level of output, the *interest* rate adjusts to

balance the supply and demand for loanable funds.
3. The *price* level adjusts to balance the supply and demand for money. Changes in the supply of money lead to proportionate changes in the price level.

These are three of the essential propositions of classical economic theory. Most economists believe that these propositions do a good job of describing how the economy works *in the long run*.

Yet these propositions do not hold in the short run. As we discussed in the preceding chapter, many prices are slow to adjust to changes in the money supply; this is reflected in a short-run aggregate supply curve that is upwards sloping rather than vertical. As a result, the overall price level cannot, by itself, balance the supply and demand for money in the short run. This stickiness of the price level forces the interest rate to move in order to bring the money market into equilibrium. These changes in the interest rate, in turn, affect the aggregate demand for goods and services. As aggregate demand fluctuates, the economy's output of goods and services moves away from the level determined by factor supplies and technology.

For issues concerning the short run, then, it is best to think about the economy as follows:

1. The *price level* is stuck at some level (based on previously formed expectations) and, in the short run, is relatively unresponsive to changing economic conditions.
2. For any given price level, the *interest rate* adjusts to balance the supply and demand for money.
3. The level of *output* responds to the aggregate demand for goods and services, which is in part determined by the interest rate that balances the money market.

Notice that this precisely reverses the order of analysis used to study the economy in the long run.

Thus, the different theories of the interest rate are useful for different purposes. When thinking about the long-run determinants of interest rates, it is best to keep in mind the loanable funds theory. This approach highlights the importance of an economy's saving propensities and investment opportunities. By contrast, when thinking about the short-run determinants of interest rates, it is best to keep in mind the liquidity preference theory. This theory highlights the importance of monetary policy.

new house, and those who do buy smaller houses, so the demand for residential investment falls. Fewer firms choose to borrow to build new factories and buy new equipment, so business investment falls. Thus, when the price level rises from P_1 to P_2, increasing money demand from MD_1 to MD_2 and raising the interest rate from r_1 to r_2, the quantity of goods and services demanded falls from Y_1 to Y_2.

FIGURE 17.2

The Money Market and the Slope of the Aggregate Demand Curve

An increase in the price level from P_1 to P_2 shifts the money demand curve to the right, as in panel (a). This increase in money demand causes the interest rate to rise from r_1 to r_2. Because the interest rate is the cost of borrowing, the increase in the interest rate reduces the quantity of goods and services demanded from Y_1 to Y_2. This negative relationship between the price level and quantity demanded is represented with a downwards sloping aggregate demand curve, as in panel (b).

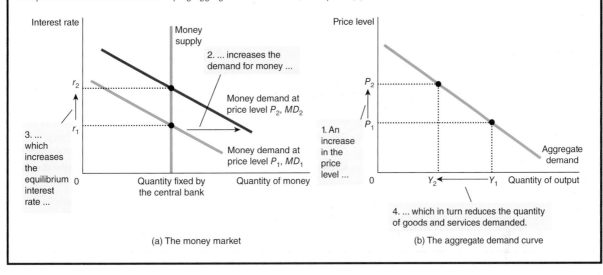

(a) The money market

(b) The aggregate demand curve

Hence, this analysis of the interest rate effect can be summarized in three steps:

1. A higher price level raises money demand.
2. Higher money demand leads to a higher interest rate.
3. A higher interest rate reduces the quantity of goods and services demanded.

Of course, the same logic works in reverse as well: a lower price level reduces money demand, which leads to a lower interest rate, and this in turn increases the quantity of goods and services demanded. The end result of this analysis is a negative relationship between the price level and the quantity of goods and services demanded, which is illustrated with a downwards sloping aggregate demand curve. This is the same conclusion we reached when looking at the effect of a shift in the LM curve in Chapter 15.

Changes in the Money Supply

So far we have used the theory of liquidity preference to explain more fully how the total quantity demanded of goods and services in the economy changes as the price level changes. That is, we have examined movements along the downwards sloping aggregate demand curve. The theory also sheds light, however, on some of the other events that alter the quantity of goods and services demanded. Whenever the quantity of goods and services demanded changes *for a given price level*, the aggregate demand curve shifts.

One important variable that shifts the aggregate demand curve is monetary policy. To see how monetary policy affects the economy in the short run, suppose that the central bank increases the money supply by buying government bonds in open-market operations. (Why the central bank might do this will become clear later after we understand the effects of such a move.) Let's consider how this monetary injection influences the equilibrium interest rate for a given price level. This will tell us what the injection does to the position of the aggregate demand curve.

As panel (a) of Figure 17.3 shows, an increase in the money supply shifts the money-supply curve to the right from MS_1 to MS_2. Because the money demand curve has not changed, the interest rate falls from r_1 to r_2 to balance money supply and money demand. That is, the interest rate must fall to induce people to hold the additional money that the central bank has created.

FIGURE 17.3

A Monetary Injection

In panel (a), an increase in the money supply from MS₁ to MS₂ reduces the equilibrium interest rate from r₁ to r₂. Because the interest rate is the cost of borrowing, the fall in the interest rate raises the quantity of goods and services demanded at a given price level from Y₁ to Y₂. Thus, in panel (b), the aggregate demand curve shifts to the right from AD₁ to AD₂.

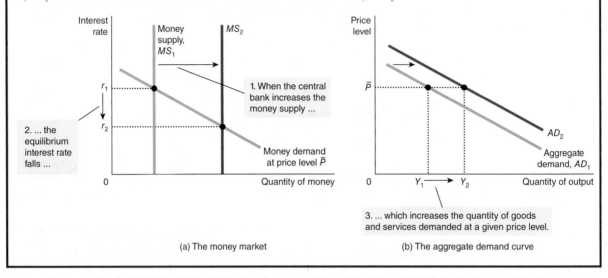

(a) The money market

(b) The aggregate demand curve

Once again, the interest rate influences the quantity of goods and services demanded, as shown in panel (b) of Figure 17.3. The lower interest rate reduces the cost of borrowing and the return to saving. Households buy more and larger houses, stimulating the demand for residential investment. Firms spend more on new factories and new equipment, stimulating business investment. As a result, the quantity of goods and services demanded at a given price level $\overline{P}$ rises from Y_1 to Y_2. Of course, there is nothing special about $\overline{P}$: the monetary injection raises the quantity of goods and services demanded at every price level. Thus, the entire aggregate demand curve shifts to the right.

To sum up: when the central bank increases the money supply, it leads to a fall in the interest rate and increases the quantity of goods and services demanded for any given price level, shifting the aggregate demand curve to the right. Conversely, when the central bank contracts the money supply, the interest rate rises to bring the money market into equilibrium and reduces the quantity of goods and services demanded for any given price level, shifting the aggregate demand curve to the left.

We explored the same principle in Chapter 15 as part of the introduction to the IS-LM model. In that case a loosening of monetary policy causes the LM curve to shift to the right and at the given price level the aggregate demand curve shifts to the right (and vice versa).

The Role of Interest Rates

Our discussion so far in this chapter has treated the money supply as the central bank's policy instrument. When the central bank buys government bonds in open-market operations, it increases the money supply and expands aggregate demand. When the central bank sells government bonds in open-market operations, it decreases the money supply and contracts aggregate demand.

Often, however, discussions of central bank policy treat the interest rate, rather than the money supply, as the central bank's policy instrument. Indeed, in recent years many of the major central banks, including the Bank of England, the European Central Bank and the US Federal Reserve, have conducted policy by setting the interest rate at which they will lend to the banking sector – the refinancing rate for the European Central Bank, the repurchase or 'repo' rate for the Bank of England, and the discount rate for the Federal Reserve.

The central bank's decision to set interest rates rather than target a certain level (or rate of growth) of the money supply does not fundamentally alter our analysis of monetary policy. The theory of liquidity preference illustrates an important principle: monetary policy can be described either in terms of the money supply or in terms of the interest rate. When the central bank sets a target for the refinancing rate of, say, *x* per cent, the central bank's bond traders are told: 'Conduct whatever open-market operations are necessary to ensure that the equilibrium interest rate equals *x* per cent.' In other words, when the central bank sets a target for the interest rate, it commits itself to adjusting the money supply in order to make the equilibrium in the money market hit that target.

As a result, changes in monetary policy can be viewed either in terms of a changing target for the interest rate or in terms of a change in the money supply. As noted in Chapter 10, when you read in the newspaper that the central bank has lowered interest rates, you should understand that this occurs only because the central bank's bond traders are doing what it takes to make it happen. If interest rates have been lowered, then the central bank's bond traders will have bought government bonds, and this purchase increases the money supply and lowers the equilibrium interest rate (just as in Figure 17.3).

The lessons from all this are quite simple: changes in monetary policy that aim to expand aggregate demand can be described either as increasing the money supply or as lowering the interest rate. Changes in monetary policy that aim to contract aggregate demand can be described either as decreasing the money supply or as raising the interest rate.

SELF TEST Use the theory of liquidity preference to explain how a decrease in the money supply affects the equilibrium interest rate. How does this change in monetary policy affect the demand curve?

HOW FISCAL POLICY INFLUENCES AGGREGATE DEMAND

The government can influence the behaviour of the economy not only with monetary policy but also with fiscal policy. Fiscal policy refers to the government's choices regarding the overall level of government purchases or taxes. Earlier in the book we examined how fiscal policy influences saving, investment and growth in the long run. In the short run, however, the primary effect of fiscal policy is on the aggregate demand for goods and services.

Changes in Government Purchases

We saw in Chapter 15 that changes in autonomous spending can have an effect on the level of spending in the economy which is greater than the initial injection. The multiplier effect means that aggregate demand will shift by a larger amount than the increase in government spending. However, the crowding-out effect, which we introduced in Chapter 8, suggests that the shift in aggregate demand could be *smaller* than the initial injection.

The Crowding-Out Effect

While an increase in government purchases stimulates the aggregate demand for goods and services, it also causes the interest rate to rise, and a higher interest rate reduces investment spending and chokes off aggregate demand. The reduction in aggregate demand that results when a fiscal expansion raises the interest rate is called the **crowding-out effect**.

crowding-out effect the offset in aggregate demand that results when expansionary fiscal policy raises the interest rate and thereby reduces investment spending

CASE STUDY — Negative Interest Rates and 'Crank' Ideas

Look around most developed countries in early 2013 and central bank interest rates are at historically low levels and have been so for some years following the financial crisis. Some central banks have also tried quantitative easing and other methods to try and get cash into the economy and trigger consumption and investment. There is some evidence to suggest that in many countries monetary policy is proving impotent in countering the fiscal austerity programmes governments have adopted and as a result economic growth remains sluggish. The Bank of England's QE programme, it is argued, has simply led to banks building up their balance sheets but not extending their lending to businesses and consumers to the extent that the Bank of England and the government would like.

If the traditional levers of monetary policy are not working might more creative ways to achieve desired policy objectives be used instead? In 2009, Professor Mankiw wrote an article in the *New York Times* suggesting negative interest rates. Borrow €1,000 today and pay back a smaller amount at some point in the future. If the interest rate was −4 per cent and you had borrowed the €1,000 for a period of a year, you would pay back €960 in a year's time. In that same article, Professor Mankiw recounted a discussion with one of his graduate students at Harvard about a scheme, put forward by the student, whereby the central bank announces that in one year's time it would pick a digit from one to nine out of a hat and any currency ending in that number would cease to be legal tender. People would thus know that in one year's time 10 per cent of the cash would cease to be legal tender, so what would they do? The logic is to spend it. The additional spending would increase aggregate demand and act as a boost to the economy. Such a policy might enable central banks to set negative interest rates provided the rate was less than 10 per cent because there would then be an incentive to lend at (say) −4 per cent rather than potentially losing 10 per cent.

Mankiw noted that the basic idea of a negative interest rate was not new – a late 19th-century economist, Silvio Gesell, had mooted such an idea and Gesell's idea was picked up by Keynes. Keynes noted that initially he saw Gesell's ideas as being those of a 'crank' but changed his opinion and even referred to Gesell as an 'unduly neglected prophet'.

In 2013, the idea of negative interest rates again surfaced when the Bank of England deputy governor outlined the possibility, albeit in very cautious terms, when giving evidence to the Treasury Select Committee. If the Bank of England reduced its lending rate to the banking system to negative rates then banks would be penalized for holding cash and would be incentivized to lend it out to avoid the penalty.

Economists expressed some surprise at the suggestion by Mr Tucker and many noted that it may have considerable unintended consequences and indeed Mr Tucker himself noted that it 'would be an extraordinary thing to do and it needs to be thought through very carefully'.

Former Bank of England deputy governor, Paul Tucker, mooted the idea of negative interest rates and whilst it has some appeal, there may be some unintended consequences as a result of one of the Ten Principles of Economics – people respond to incentives.

To see why the crowding-out effect occurs, let's consider what happens in the money market using an example we used in Chapter 15 when the government invests in nuclear power stations from Nucelec. As we discussed in Chapter 15, this increase in demand raises the incomes of the workers and owners of this firm (and, because of the multiplier effect, of other firms as well). As incomes rise, households plan to buy more goods and services and, as a result, choose to hold more of their wealth in liquid form. That is, the increase in income caused by the fiscal expansion raises the demand for money.

The effect of the increase in money demand is shown in panel (a) of Figure 17.4. Because the central bank has not changed the money supply, the vertical supply curve remains the same. When the higher level of income shifts the money demand curve to the right from MD_1 to MD_2, the interest rate must rise from r_1 to r_2 to keep supply and demand in balance.

FIGURE 17.4

The Crowding-Out Effect

Panel (a) shows the money market. When the government increases its purchases of goods and services, the resulting increase in income raises the demand for money from MD_1 to MD_2, and this causes the equilibrium interest rate to rise from r_1 to r_2. Panel (b) shows the effects on aggregate demand. The initial impact of the increase in government purchases shifts the aggregate demand curve from AD_1 to AD_2. Yet, because the interest rate is the cost of borrowing, the increase in the interest rate tends to reduce the quantity of goods and services demanded, particularly for investment goods. This crowding out of investment partially offsets the impact of the fiscal expansion on aggregate demand. In the end, the aggregate demand curve shifts only to AD_3.

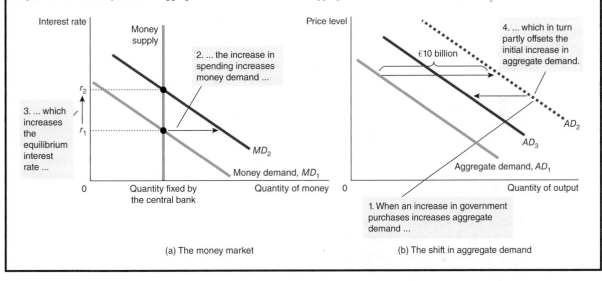

(a) The money market

(b) The shift in aggregate demand

The increase in the interest rate, in turn, reduces the quantity of goods and services demanded. In particular, because borrowing is more expensive, the demand for residential and business investment goods declines. That is, as the increase in government purchases increases the demand for goods and services, it may also crowd out investment. This crowding-out effect partially offsets the impact of government purchases on aggregate demand, as illustrated in panel (b) of Figure 17.4. The initial impact of the increase in government purchases is to shift the aggregate demand curve from AD_1 to AD_2, but once crowding out takes place, the aggregate demand curve drops back to AD_3.

To sum up: when the government increases its purchases by €10 billion, the aggregate demand for goods and services could rise by more or less than €10 billion, depending on whether the multiplier effect or the crowding-out effect is larger.

Changes in Taxes

The other important instrument of fiscal policy, besides the level of government purchases, is the level of taxation. When the government cuts personal income taxes, for instance, it increases households' take-home pay. Households will save some of this additional income, but they will also spend some of it on consumer goods. Because it increases consumer spending, the tax cut shifts the aggregate demand curve to the right. Similarly, a tax increase depresses consumer spending and shifts the aggregate demand curve to the left.

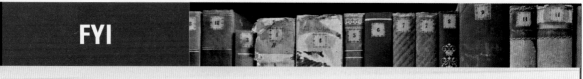

FYI

The Taylor Rule

In 1993 John Taylor, an economist at Stanford University in the United States, spent some time observing the behaviour of the Federal Reserve's Federal Open Market Committee (FOMC). Taylor's observations led him to put forward what has become known as the *Taylor rule* which has been an influential idea since it was published. For many economists, interest has centred on the extent to which the rule is followed in interest rate decision-making around the world, if at all. John Taylor was observing the US economy and the work of the FOMC. Inflation in the US had come under a far greater degree of control in the 1980s when the FOMC was headed by Paul Volcker. Part of Taylor's conclusion was that the FOMC had reacted more aggressively to inflation than had occurred before 1979. His observations led to the notion of the interest rate-setting body 'leaning into the wind' when it comes to inflation. By this he meant being willing to raise rates more significantly in response to an inflation threat than had been the case prior to 1979.

Taylor suggested that the pattern of FOMC behaviour with regard to interest rates during the period 1979–1992 could be expressed as a formula – the 'rule'. This formula, given below, has been simplified but in essence captures the main flavour of his original work.

$$r = p + 0.5y + 0.5(p - 2) + 2$$

In this formula, the following variables are expressed:

r = the short-term interest rate in percentage terms per annum
p = the rate of inflation over the previous four quarters measured as the GDP deflator
y = the difference between real GDP from potential output (the 'output gap').

Taylor made a number of assumptions about the US economy in this formula. He assumed that there was a target level of inflation, which he put at 2 per cent. He also made an assumption that the equilibrium real interest rate was also 2 per cent. The formula offers a rule or guide to policymakers about what the level of interest rates should be if there is a target for inflation of 2 per cent. In effect, interest rates can be set in response to the deviation of inflation from the target and the deviation of real output from potential output. It suggests that the response to inflation or output being off-target should be met with a more aggressive response to monetary policy – this is the so-called 'leaning into the wind'.

Suppose, for example, that the output gap was zero – that actual GDP was at its potential level – but that inflation was currently 5 per cent, 3 per cent above the assumed target level of 2 per cent. Then the *Taylor rule* would suggest that the central bank should aim to set the short-term interest rate at 8.5 per cent, corresponding to a real rate of interest of 8.5 − 5 = 3.5 per cent. If, however, GDP was, say, 2 per cent below its potential level, so that there was a an output gap of −2 per cent, then the *Taylor rule* would suggest setting the nominal interest rate a little lower, at 7.5 per cent.

How accurate is the *Taylor rule*? Studies have shown that a number of countries seem to have patterns of interest rates that follow the *Taylor rule* relatively closely. In reality, Taylor and other researchers appreciated that decision makers could not stick rigidly to such a rule because sometimes circumstances might dictate the need to apply discretion. Such circumstances might be, for example, when the World Trade Center was attacked in 2001, the intervention in Iraq or the financial crisis of 2007–2009. Taylor argued that whilst a rule gave a guideline to policymakers, it also implied that any deviation from the rule had to be explained through a coherent and well-argued case and that such a discipline was helpful to overall monetary policy decisions. The *Taylor rule* has provided researchers with a great deal of impetus to look at the whole way in which monetary policy decisions are arrived at. It also gives the financial markets the opportunity to be able to second guess the decision making of central banks and factor this into their thinking. In times of financial crisis, however, the rule may be jettisoned in favour of a more pragmatic approach to policy.

The size of the shift in aggregate demand resulting from a tax change is also affected by the multiplier and crowding-out effects. When the government cuts taxes and stimulates consumer spending, earnings and profits rise, which further stimulates consumer spending. This is the multiplier effect. At the same time, higher income leads to higher money demand, which tends to raise interest rates. Higher interest rates make borrowing more costly, which reduces investment spending. This is the crowding-out effect. Depending on the size of the multiplier and crowding-out effects, the shift in aggregate demand could be larger or smaller than the tax change that causes it.

In addition to the multiplier and crowding-out effects, there is another important determinant of the size of the shift in aggregate demand that results from a tax change: households' perceptions about whether the tax change is permanent or temporary. For example, suppose that the government announces a tax cut of €1,000 per household. In deciding how much of this €1,000 to spend, households must ask themselves how long this extra income will last. If households expect the tax cut to be permanent, they will view it as adding substantially to their financial resources and, therefore, increase their spending by a large amount. In this case, the tax cut will have a large impact on aggregate demand. By contrast, if households expect the tax change to be temporary, they will view it as adding only slightly to their financial resources and, therefore, will increase their spending by only a small amount. In this case, the tax cut will have a small impact on aggregate demand.

It should be noted that fiscal policy can also affect the aggregate supply curve and we will look at this in more detail in Chapter 19.

SELF TEST Suppose that the government reduces spending on motorway construction by €1 billion. Which way does the aggregate demand curve shift? Explain why the shift might be larger than €1 billion. Explain why the shift might be smaller than €1 billion.

USING POLICY TO STABILIZE THE ECONOMY

We have seen how monetary and fiscal policy can affect the economy's aggregate demand for goods and services. These theoretical insights raise some important policy questions: should policymakers use these instruments to control aggregate demand and stabilize the economy? If so, when? If not, why not?

The Case for an Active Stabilization Policy

Let's return to the question that began this chapter: when the government reduces its spending, how should the central bank respond? As we have seen, government spending is one determinant of the position of the aggregate demand curve. When the government cuts spending, aggregate demand will fall, this will depress production and employment in the short run. If the central bank wants to prevent this adverse effect of the fiscal policy, it can act to expand aggregate demand by increasing the money supply. A monetary expansion would reduce interest rates, stimulate investment spending and expand aggregate demand. If monetary policy responds appropriately, the combined changes in monetary and fiscal policy could leave the aggregate demand for goods and services unaffected.

This analysis is exactly the sort followed by the members of the policy-setting committees of central banks like the Bank of England, the European Central Bank and the Federal Reserve. They know that monetary policy is an important determinant of aggregate demand. They also know that there are other important determinants as well, including fiscal policy set by the government, and so they will watch debates over fiscal policy with a keen eye.

This response of monetary policy to the change in fiscal policy is an example of a more general phenomenon: the use of policy instruments to stabilize aggregate demand and, as a result, production and employment. We have seen in Chapter 15 how the Great Depression in the 1930s spawned a belief that governments should act to manage aggregate demand in the wake of the research which followed Keynes' *General Theory*. As a result, economic stabilization has been seen as an explicit or implicit goal of government macroeconomic policy in European and North American economies following World War II. In the UK, for example, this view was embodied in a government White Paper, published in 1944, which explicitly stated: 'The Government accepts as one of their primary aims and responsibilities the maintenance of a high and stable level of employment after the War.' In the USA, similar sentiments were embodied in the Employment Act of 1946. This explicit recognition by governments of a responsibility to stabilize the economy has two implications. The first, more modest, implication is that the government should avoid being a cause of economic fluctuations itself. Thus, most economists advise against large and sudden changes in monetary and fiscal policy, for such changes are likely to cause fluctuations in aggregate demand. Moreover, when large changes do occur, it is important that monetary and fiscal policymakers be aware of and respond to the other's actions.

The second, more ambitious, implication of this explicit admission of responsibility – and one that was especially dominant in the first 30 years after the end of World War II – was that the government should respond to changes in the private economy in order to stabilize aggregate demand. To put the reasons for the pursuit of active stabilization policies into context, it is important to note that politicians remembered the misery of the Great Depression before the war, and were keen to avoid a recurrence, not only because of the misery involved for millions of people, but also because of the political effects of economic depression which were associated with a rise in extremism. Poverty was directly linked with the rise of extremism and political instability. As the war ended, therefore, they wanted to look forward to a better world in which governments could help avoid major recessions and the associated political instability. The adoption of Keynesian demand management policies seemed to offer some promise that full employment could be achieved.

Keynes (and his many followers) argued that aggregate demand fluctuates because of largely irrational waves of pessimism and optimism. He used the term 'animal spirits' to refer to these arbitrary changes in attitude. When pessimism reigns, households reduce consumption spending, and firms reduce investment spending. The result is reduced aggregate demand, lower production and higher unemployment. Conversely, when optimism reigns, households and firms increase spending. The result is higher aggregate demand, higher production and inflationary pressure. Notice that these changes in attitude are, to some extent, self-fulfilling.

In principle, the government can adjust its monetary and fiscal policy in response to these waves of optimism and pessimism and, thereby, stabilize the economy. For example, when people are excessively pessimistic, the central bank can expand the money supply to lower interest rates and expand aggregate demand. When they are excessively optimistic, it can contract the money supply to raise interest rates and dampen aggregate demand.

The Case Against an Active Stabilization Policy

Some economists argue that the government should avoid active use of monetary and fiscal policy to try to stabilize the economy. They claim that these policy instruments should be set to achieve long-run goals, such as rapid economic growth and low inflation, and that the economy should be left to deal with short-run fluctuations on its own. Although these economists may admit that monetary and fiscal policy can stabilize the economy in theory, they doubt whether it can do so in practice.

The primary argument against active monetary and fiscal policy is that the effects of these policies may be to a large extent uncertain both in terms of magnitude and timing. As we have seen, monetary policy works by changing interest rates. This can have strong and rapid effects on consumer spending if (as in the United Kingdom) a large number of people are buying their house with a mortgage loan on which the interest rate can vary according to market interest rates: quite simply, if interest rates go up, then mortgage payments go up and people have less money to spend. Yet, if people have mortgages on which the interest rate is fixed for one or more years ahead, then the interest rate change will only affect mortgage payments with a very long lag. And if most people live in rented accommodation (as is the case in most of the countries of continental Europe) then a rise in interest rates will have no strong effects through this channel at all. In all cases, however, the interest rate rise will still clearly affect consumer spending because buying goods on credit (e.g. with a credit card) will be more expensive. The net effect on consumer spending may, therefore, be hard to predict, especially in terms of its timing.

Monetary policy can also affect aggregate demand through its influence on investment spending. But many firms make investment plans far in advance. Thus, most economists believe that it takes at least six months for changes in monetary policy to have much effect on output and employment. Most central banks readily admit that changes in interest rates can take up to 18 months to work their way through the economy. Moreover, once these effects occur, they can last for several years.

Critics of stabilization policy argue that because of these uncertain lags, the central bank should not try to fine-tune the economy. They claim that the central bank often reacts too late to changing economic conditions and, as a result, ends up being a cause of, rather than a cure for, economic fluctuations. These critics advocate a passive monetary policy, such as slow and steady growth in the money supply.

Fiscal policy may also work with a lag. Of course, the impact of a change in government spending is felt as soon as the change takes place and cuts in direct and indirect taxation can feed through into the economy quickly. However, considerable time may pass between the decision to adopt a government spending programme and its implementation. In the UK, for example, the government has often tended to undershoot on its planned spending, partly because of problems in attracting sufficient extra staff into key public services such as transport, education and health. At the same time, announcements about changes to income taxes (both personal and corporate) tend to occur months (and sometimes years) before implementation. In the intervening time period, households and businesses factor in the impending changes into their behaviour and so the effects are uncertain.

These lags in monetary and fiscal policy are a problem in part because economic forecasting is so imprecise. If forecasters could accurately predict the condition of the economy a year in advance, then monetary and fiscal policymakers could look ahead when making policy decisions. In this case, policymakers could stabilize the economy despite the lags they face. Decisions are made, in part, on the basis of existing statistical data which are fed into models. That data can be inaccurate and subject to revision as we have seen. Without accurate and up-to-date information, the outcome from modelling can vary considerably. In practice, however, major recessions and depressions arrive without much advance warning. The best policymakers can do at any time is to respond to economic changes as they occur.

Automatic Stabilizers

All economists – both advocates and critics of stabilization policy – agree that the lags in implementation render policy less useful as a tool for short-run stabilization. The economy would be more stable, therefore, if policymakers could find a way to avoid some of these lags. In fact, they have. **Automatic stabilizers** are changes in fiscal policy that stimulate aggregate demand when the economy goes into a recession without policymakers having to take any deliberate action.

> **automatic stabilizers** changes in fiscal policy that stimulate aggregate demand when the economy goes into a recession, without policymakers having to take any deliberate action

The most important automatic stabilizer is the tax system. When the economy goes into a recession, the amount of taxes collected by the government falls automatically because almost all taxes are closely tied to economic activity and because in many countries income taxes are progressive. This means that as economic activity increases an increasing proportion of income is paid in tax and vice versa. Income tax depends on households' incomes and corporation tax depends on firms' profits. Because incomes and profits both fall in a recession, the government's tax revenue falls as well. Taxes are a withdrawal from the circular flow which has the effect of dampening the level of aggregate demand. If tax revenues are lower it means that consumers have more disposable income to spend on consumption and businesses on investment. If economic activity increases then tax revenues will rise. These automatic tax changes either stimulate or dampen aggregate demand and, thereby, reduce the magnitude of economic fluctuations.

Government spending also acts as an automatic stabilizer. In particular, when the economy goes into a recession and workers are laid off, more people apply for state unemployment benefits, welfare benefits and other forms of income support. Extra spending on benefits and the welfare system helps to provide a cushion against too large a fall in economic activity. This increase in government spending stimulates aggregate demand at exactly the time when aggregate demand is insufficient to maintain full employment. However, it must be taken into consideration that in order to finance this additional spending (at a time when tax revenue is falling) governments may have to borrow. This additional borrowing can put upward pressure on interest rates and dampen the overall effect.

Automatic stabilizers are generally not sufficiently strong to prevent recessions completely. Nevertheless, without these automatic stabilizers, output and employment would probably be more volatile than they are. For this reason, most economists would not favour a policy of always running a balanced budget, as some politicians have proposed. When the economy goes into a recession, taxes fall, government spending rises, and the government's budget moves toward deficit. If the government faced a strict balanced-budget rule, it would be forced to look for ways to raise taxes or cut spending in a recession. In other words, a strict **balanced budget** rule would eliminate the automatic stabilizers inherent in our current system of taxes and government spending and would, in effect, be an 'automatic destabilizer'.

balanced budget where the total sum of money received by a government in tax revenue and interest is equal to the amount it spends, including on any debt interest owing

SELF TEST Suppose a wave of negative 'animal spirits' overruns the economy, and people become pessimistic about the future. What happens to aggregate demand? If the central bank wants to stabilize aggregate demand, how should it alter the money supply? If it does this, what happens to the interest rate? Why might the central bank choose not to respond in this way?

CONCLUSION

Before policymakers make any change in policy, they need to consider all the effects of their decisions. Earlier in the book we examined classical models of the economy, which describe the long-run effects of monetary and fiscal policy. There we saw how fiscal policy influences saving, investment and long-run growth, and how monetary policy influences the price level and the inflation rate.

In this chapter we examined the short-run effects of monetary and fiscal policy. We saw how these policy instruments can change the aggregate demand for goods and services and, thereby, alter the economy's production and employment in the short run. When the government reduces spending in order to balance the budget, it needs to consider both the long-run effects on saving and growth and the short-run effects on aggregate demand and employment. When the central bank reduces the growth rate of the money supply, it must take into account the long-run effect on inflation as well as the short-run effect on production. In the next chapter we discuss the transition between the short run and the long run more fully, and we see that policymakers often face a trade-off between long-run and short-run goals.

IN THE NEWS

The Multiplier and Fiscal Policy

In Chapter 15 and in this chapter we have spoken of fiscal policy being used as a tool to boost the economy. Part of the justification for using government spending and taxation in this way is the role of the multiplier.

Fiscal Multipliers

The theory seems intuitive enough – if government spends money on a major infrastructure project it is logical that the income received will be spent and feed through to other parts of the economy and as a result lead to a rise in national income that is a multiple of the initial injection. Most economists would not disagree with this base analysis but where they do disagree is on the size of the multiplier effect and therefore whether this is the best way to smooth out short-term fluctuations in economic activity. There has been a considerable amount of research into the size of fiscal or government expenditure multipliers – the change in output that arises as a result of a change in government expenditure. In part this research has arisen because of the stimulus packages that governments put in place, the fact that monetary policy options have been reduced and the continued sluggishness of economies across Europe and North America (perhaps to a lesser extent) has led to calls for further fiscal stimulus at a time when many countries are struggling to manage government borrowing.

Does the size of the fiscal multiplier matter? Well, take the difference in the estimates of the size of the fiscal multiplier according to two leading macroeconomists. Robert Barro, a Harvard professor, wrote in 2009 that the size of the fiscal multiplier in peacetime was close to zero; Christine Romer, a professor of economics at the University of California, Berkeley and a former Chair of Economic Advisors to President Obama, suggested that the multiplier was nearer to 1.6. When the US government passed a stimulus package of $787 billion (€604 billion) in 2009, the difference in the number of jobs created of these two estimates of the multiplier effects would be around 3.75 million according to three economists, Mendoza, Vegh and Ilzetzki, in an article published on Vox, a policy portal of the Centre for Economic Policy Research.

What the research does seem to show is that the size of the fiscal multiplier is dependent on a wide range of factors. The fiscal multiplier might be different in developed and less-developed countries, whether the government spending 'shock' is anticipated or unanticipated, how open the economy is, the exchange rate regime used by the country (whether exchange rates are fixed against other currencies, managed or allowed to float freely in response to market conditions), whether the economy is experiencing a financial or debt crisis and the time preferences of the population of a country. Time preferences refer to how people react to the fiscal stimulus; if a government cut taxes or increased spending, what proportion of the increase in income would be spent and what proportion saved and to what extent would people build into their decision-making the expectation that a 'windfall' now will 'inevitably' lead to tax rises in the future. The idea that people will save most of any increase in government spending because they expect to have to pay higher taxes in the future is called *Ricardian Equivalence* and was initially developed by David Ricardo in the 19th century but has been refined somewhat by Robert Barro. The size of the fiscal multiplier will depend in part, therefore, on the extent to which consumers are Ricardian in their response.

A discussion paper written by Gilberto Marcheggiano and David Miles (Bank of England External MPC Discussion Paper no. 39, January 2013) noted that 'Empirical studies ... face great challenges in measuring multipliers because of the difficulties of identifying exogenous fiscal shocks and controlling

(*Continued*)

for other factors that might affect output responses'. They further note that studies on the size of fiscal multipliers include estimates between 1.2 and 1.8 and in other cases, 0.8 to 1.5.

Large-scale investment in infrastructure projects like this construction of a high-speed rail line between Turin in Italy and Lyon in France helps to create jobs and generates a multiplier effect.

Questions

1 How do you think the size of the fiscal multiplier would vary when a government announced an increase in spending of €50 billion to be spent on infrastructure projects compared to a cut in income taxes which would put an equivalent amount into people's pockets?

2 Why do you think that Barro and Romer have such a different view of the size of the fiscal multiplier?

3 Why might the size of the fiscal multiplier depend on whether it is anticipated or unanticipated?

4 The size of the fiscal multiplier will depend on Ricardian Equivalence. To what extent do you think people adjust their spending decisions in response to expectations of future tax changes?

5 If it is difficult to empirically arrive at a reliable and accurate measure of the size of fiscal multipliers, does this mean that policymakers should avoid resorting to the use of fiscal policy as a means of stimulating an economy? Justify your answer.

SUMMARY

● In developing a theory of short-run economic fluctuations, Keynes proposed the theory of liquidity preference to explain the determinants of the interest rate. According to this theory, the interest rate adjusts to balance the supply and demand for money.

● An increase in the price level raises money demand and increases the interest rate that brings the money market into equilibrium. Because the interest rate represents the cost of borrowing, a higher interest rate reduces investment and, thereby, the quantity of goods and services demanded. The downwards sloping aggregate demand curve expresses this negative relationship between the price level and the quantity demanded.

● Policymakers can influence aggregate demand with monetary policy. An increase in the money supply reduces the equilibrium interest rate for any given price level. Because a lower interest rate stimulates investment spending, the aggregate demand curve shifts to the right. Conversely, a decrease in the money supply raises the

equilibrium interest rate for any given price level and shifts the aggregate demand curve to the left.

● Policymakers can also influence aggregate demand with fiscal policy. An increase in government purchases or a cut in taxes shifts the aggregate demand curve to the right. A decrease in government purchases or an increase in taxes shifts the aggregate demand curve to the left.

● When the government alters spending or taxes, the resulting shift in aggregate demand can be larger or smaller than the fiscal change. The multiplier effect tends to amplify the effects of fiscal policy on aggregate demand. The crowding-out effect tends to dampen the effects of fiscal policy on aggregate demand.

● Because monetary and fiscal policy can influence aggregate demand, the government sometimes uses these policy instruments in an attempt to stabilize the economy. Economists disagree about how active the government should be in this effort. According to advocates of active stabilization policy, changes in attitudes by households and firms shift aggregate demand; if the government does not respond, the result is undesirable and unnecessary fluctuations in output and employment. According to critics of an active stabilization policy, monetary and fiscal policy work with such long lags that attempts at stabilizing the economy often end up being destabilizing.

QUESTIONS FOR REVIEW

1 What are the three ways in which monetary policy affects aggregate demand?

2 What is the theory of liquidity preference?

3 How does the theory of liquidity preference help explain the downwards slope of the aggregate demand curve?

4 Use the theory of liquidity preference to explain how a decrease in the money supply affects the aggregate demand curve.

5 The government spends €500 million to buy police cars. Explain why aggregate demand might increase by more than €500 million. Explain why aggregate demand might increase by less than €500 million.

6 What is the crowding-out effect?

7 Suppose that survey measures of consumer confidence indicate a wave of pessimism is sweeping the country. If policymakers do nothing, what will happen to aggregate demand? What should the government do if it wants to stabilize aggregate demand? If the government does nothing, should the central bank stabilize aggregate demand? If so, how?

8 How might a government use taxation as a tool in expansionary fiscal policy?

9 Outline the arguments for and against an active stabilization policy.

10 Give an example of a government policy that acts as an automatic stabilizer. Explain why this policy has this effect.

PROBLEMS AND APPLICATIONS

1 Explain how each of the following developments would affect the supply of money, the demand for money and the interest rate. Illustrate your answers with diagrams.

  a. The central bank's bond traders buy bonds in open market operations.

  b. An increase in credit card availability reduces the cash people hold.

  c. The central bank reduces banks' reserve requirements.

  d. Households decide to hold more money to use for holiday shopping.

  e. A wave of optimism boosts business investment and expands aggregate demand.

  f. An increase in oil prices shifts the short-run aggregate supply curve to the left.

2 Suppose banks install automatic teller machines on every street corner and, by making cash readily available, reduce the amount of money people want to hold.

  a. Assume the central bank does not change the money supply. According to the theory of liquidity preference, what happens to the interest rate? What happens to aggregate demand?

  b. If the central bank wants to stabilize aggregate demand, how should it respond?

3 The economy is in a recession with high unemployment and low output.

  a. Use a graph of aggregate demand and aggregate supply to illustrate the current situation. Be sure to include the aggregate demand curve, the short-run aggregate supply curve, and the long-run aggregate supply curve.

  b. Identify an open-market operation that would restore the economy to its natural rate.

  c. Use a graph of the money market to illustrate the effect of this open-market operation. Show the resulting change in the interest rate.

  d. Use a graph similar to the one in part (a) to show the effect of the open-market operation on output and the price level. Explain in words why the policy has the effect that you have shown in the graph.

4 This chapter explains that expansionary monetary policy reduces the interest rate and thus stimulates demand for investment goods. Explain how such a policy also stimulates the demand for net exports.

5 Suppose government spending increases. Would the effect on aggregate demand be larger if the central bank took no action in response, or if the central bank were committed to maintaining a fixed interest rate? Explain.

6 In which of the following circumstances is expansionary fiscal policy more likely to lead to a short-run increase in investment? Explain.

a. When the investment accelerator is large, or when it is small?

b. When the interest sensitivity of investment is large, or when it is small?

7 Assume the economy is in a recession. Explain how each of the following policies would affect consumption and investment. In each case, indicate any direct effects, any effects resulting from changes in total output, any effects resulting from changes in the interest rate and the overall effect. If there are conflicting effects making the answer ambiguous, say so.

a. An increase in government spending.

b. A reduction in taxes.

c. An expansion of the money supply.

8 For various reasons, fiscal policy changes automatically when output and employment fluctuate.

a. Explain why tax revenue changes when the economy goes into a recession.

b. Explain why government spending changes when the economy goes into a recession.

c. If the government was to operate under a strict balanced-budget rule, what would it have to do in a recession? Would this make the recession more or less severe?

9 Recently, some members of the legislature have proposed a law that would make price stability the sole goal of monetary policy. Suppose such a law were passed.

a. How would the central bank respond to an event that contracted aggregate demand?

b. How would the central bank respond to an event that caused an adverse shift in short-run aggregate supply?

c. In each case, is there another monetary policy that would lead to greater stability in output?

10 Some economists have proposed that central banks should use the following rule for choosing their target interest rate (r):

$r = 2\% + p + \frac{1}{2}\frac{(y - y^*)}{y^*} + \frac{1}{2}(p - p^*)$, where p is the average of the inflation rate over the past year, y is real GDP as recently measured, y^* is an estimate of the natural rate of output and p^* is the central bank's target rate of inflation.

a. Explain the logic that might lie behind this rule for setting interest rates. Would you support the use of this rule?

b. Some economists advocate such a rule for monetary policy but believe p and y should be the forecasts of future values of inflation and output. What are the advantages of using forecasts instead of actual values? What are the disadvantages?

18 THE SHORT-RUN TRADE-OFF BETWEEN INFLATION AND UNEMPLOYMENT

Two closely watched indicators of economic performance in any advanced economy are inflation and unemployment. When the government agency responsible for producing national statistics releases data on these variables, policymakers are eager to hear the news. Sometimes commentators add together the inflation rate and the unemployment rate to produce a *misery index,* which purports to measure the health of the economy.

How are these two measures of economic performance related to each other? Earlier in the book we discussed the long-run determinants of unemployment and the long-run determinants of inflation. We saw that the natural rate of unemployment depends on various features of the labour market, such as minimum wage laws, the market power of unions, the role of efficiency wages and the effectiveness of job search. By contrast, the inflation rate depends primarily on growth in the money supply, which a nation's central bank controls. In the long run, therefore, inflation and unemployment are largely unrelated problems.

In the short run, just the opposite is true. One of the *Ten Principles of Economics* is that society faces a short-run trade-off between inflation and unemployment. If monetary and fiscal policymakers expand aggregate demand and move the economy up along the short-run aggregate supply curve, they can lower unemployment for a while, but only at the cost of higher inflation. If policymakers contract aggregate demand and move the economy down the short-run aggregate supply curve, they can lower inflation, but only at the cost of temporarily higher unemployment.

In this chapter we examine this trade-off more closely. The relationship between inflation and unemployment is a topic that has attracted the attention of some of the most important economists of the last half century. The best way to understand this relationship is to see how thinking about it has evolved over time.

THE PHILLIPS CURVE

'Probably the single most important macroeconomic relationship is the Phillips curve.' These are the words of economist George Akerlof from the lecture he gave when he received the Nobel Prize for Economics in 2001. The *Phillips curve* is the short-run relationship between inflation and unemployment.

Origins of the Phillips Curve

In 1958, a New Zealand economist working at the London School of Economics, A.W. Phillips, published an article in the British journal *Economica* that would make him famous. The article was entitled 'The Relationship Between Unemployment and the Rate of Change of Money Wages in the United Kingdom, 1861–1957'. In it, Phillips showed a negative correlation between the rate of unemployment and the rate of inflation. That is, Phillips showed that years with low unemployment tend to have high inflation, and years with high unemployment tend to have low inflation. (It should be noted that Phillips examined inflation in nominal wages rather than inflation in prices, but for our purposes that distinction is not important. These two measures of inflation usually move together because of the relationship between wage inflation and the excess demand for labour.) Phillips concluded that two important macroeconomic variables – inflation and unemployment – were linked in a way that economists had not previously appreciated.

Although Phillips's discovery was based on data for the United Kingdom, researchers quickly extended his finding to other countries. Two years after Phillips published his article, economists Paul Samuelson and Robert Solow published an article in the *American Economic Review* called 'Analytics of Anti-inflation Policy' in which they showed a similar negative correlation between inflation and unemployment in data for the United States. They reasoned that this correlation arose because low unemployment was associated with high aggregate demand, which in turn puts upwards pressure on wages and prices throughout the economy. Samuelson and Solow dubbed the negative association between inflation and unemployment the **Phillips curve**. Figure 18.1 shows an example of a Phillips curve like the one found by Samuelson and Solow.

Phillips curve a curve that shows the short-run trade-off between inflation and unemployment

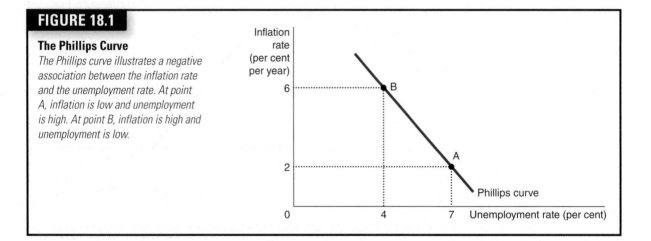

FIGURE 18.1

The Phillips Curve
The Phillips curve illustrates a negative association between the inflation rate and the unemployment rate. At point A, inflation is low and unemployment is high. At point B, inflation is high and unemployment is low.

As the title of their paper suggests, Samuelson and Solow were interested in the Phillips curve because they believed that it held important lessons for policymakers. In particular, they suggested that the Phillips curve offers policymakers a menu of possible economic outcomes. By altering monetary and fiscal policy to influence aggregate demand, policymakers could choose any point on this curve. Point A offers high unemployment and low inflation. Point B offers low unemployment and high inflation. Policymakers might prefer both low inflation and low unemployment, but the historical data as summarized by the Phillips curve indicate that this combination is impossible. According to Samuelson and Solow, policymakers face a trade-off between inflation and unemployment, and the Phillips curve illustrates that trade-off.

Aggregate Demand, Aggregate Supply and the Phillips Curve

The model of aggregate demand and aggregate supply provides an easy explanation for the menu of possible outcomes described by the Phillips curve. The Phillips curve simply shows the combinations of inflation and unemployment that arise in the short run as shifts in the aggregate demand curve move the economy along the short-run aggregate supply curve. As we saw in Chapter 16, an increase in the aggregate demand for goods and services leads, in the short run, to a larger output of goods and services and a higher price level. Larger output means greater employment and, thus, a lower rate of unemployment. In addition, whatever the previous year's price level happens to be, the higher the price level in the current year, the higher the rate of inflation. Thus, shifts in aggregate demand push inflation and unemployment in opposite directions in the short run – a relationship illustrated by the Phillips curve.

To see more fully how this works, let's consider an example. To keep the numbers simple, imagine that the price level (as measured, for instance, by the consumer prices index) equals 100 in the year 2014. Figure 18.2 shows two possible outcomes that might occur in year 2015. Panel (a) shows the two outcomes using the model of aggregate demand and aggregate supply. Panel (b) illustrates the same two outcomes using the Phillips curve.

FIGURE 18.2

How the Phillips Curve is Related to the Model of Aggregate Demand and Aggregate Supply

This figure assumes a price level of 100 for the year 2014 and charts possible outcomes for the year 2015. Panel (a) shows the model of aggregate demand and aggregate supply. If aggregate demand is low, the economy is at point A; output is low (7,500), and the price level is low (102). If aggregate demand is high, the economy is at point B; output is high (8,000), and the price level is high (106). Panel (b) shows the implications for the Phillips curve. Point A, which arises when aggregate demand is low, has high unemployment (7 per cent) and low inflation (2 per cent). Point B, which arises when aggregate demand is high, has low unemployment (4 per cent) and high inflation (6 per cent).

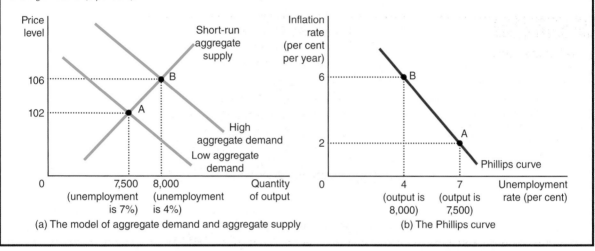

In panel (a) of the figure, we can see the implications for output and the price level in the year 2015. If the aggregate demand for goods and services is relatively low, the economy experiences outcome A. The economy produces output of 7,500, and the price level is 102. By contrast, if aggregate demand is relatively high, the economy experiences outcome B. Output is 8,000, and the price level is 106. Thus, higher aggregate demand moves the economy to an equilibrium with higher output and a higher price level.

In panel (b) of the figure, we can see what these two possible outcomes mean for unemployment and inflation. Because firms need more workers when they produce a greater output of goods and services, unemployment is lower in outcome B than in outcome A. In this example, when output rises from 7,500 to 8,000, unemployment falls from 7 per cent to 4 per cent. Moreover, because the price level is higher at outcome B than at outcome A, the inflation rate (the percentage change in the price level from the previous year) is also higher. In particular, since the price level was 100 in year 2014, outcome A has an inflation rate of 2 per cent, and outcome B has an inflation rate of 6 per cent. Thus, we can compare the two possible outcomes for the economy either in terms of output and the price level (using the model of aggregate demand and aggregate supply) or in terms of unemployment and inflation (using the Phillips curve).

As we saw in the preceding chapter, monetary and fiscal policy can shift the aggregate demand curve. Therefore, monetary and fiscal policy can move the economy along the Phillips curve. Increases in the money supply, increases in government spending, or cuts in taxes expand aggregate demand and move the economy to a point on the Phillips curve with lower unemployment and higher inflation.

Decreases in the money supply, cuts in government spending, or increases in taxes contract aggregate demand and move the economy to a point on the Phillips curve with lower inflation and higher unemployment. In this sense, the Phillips curve offers policymakers a menu of combinations of inflation and unemployment.

SELF TEST Draw the Phillips curve. Use the model of aggregate demand and aggregate supply to show how policy can move the economy from a point on this curve with high inflation to a point with low inflation.

SHIFTS IN THE PHILLIPS CURVE: THE ROLE OF EXPECTATIONS

The Phillips curve seems to offer policymakers a menu of possible inflation–unemployment outcomes. But does this menu remain stable over time? Is the Phillips curve a relationship on which policymakers can rely? Economists took up these questions in the late 1960s, shortly after Samuelson and Solow had introduced the Phillips curve into the macroeconomic policy debate.

The Long-Run Phillips Curve

In 1968 economist Milton Friedman published a paper in the *American Economic Review,* based on an address he had recently given as president of the American Economic Association. The paper, entitled 'The Role of Monetary Policy', contained sections on 'What Monetary Policy Can Do' and 'What Monetary Policy Cannot Do'. Friedman argued that one thing monetary policy cannot do, other than for only a short time, is pick a combination of inflation and unemployment on the Phillips curve. At about the same time, another economist, Edmund Phelps, also published a paper denying the existence of a long-run trade-off between inflation and unemployment.

Friedman and Phelps based their conclusions on classical principles of macroeconomics, which we discussed in Chapters 6 to 13. Recall that classical theory points to growth in the money supply as the primary determinant of inflation. But classical theory also states that monetary growth does not have real effects – it merely alters all prices and nominal incomes proportionately. In particular, monetary growth does not influence those factors that determine the economy's unemployment rate, such as the market power of unions, the role of efficiency wages, or the process of job search. Friedman and Phelps concluded that there is no reason to think the rate of inflation would, *in the long run*, be related to the rate of unemployment.

Here, in his own words, is Friedman's view about what the central bank can hope to accomplish in the long run:

> *The monetary authority controls nominal quantities – directly, the quantity of its own liabilities [currency plus bank reserves]. In principle, it can use this control to peg a nominal quantity – an exchange rate, the price level, the nominal level of national income, the quantity of money by one definition or another – or to peg the change in a nominal quantity – the rate of inflation or deflation, the rate of growth or decline in nominal national income, the rate of growth of the quantity of money. It cannot use its control over nominal quantities to peg a real quantity – the real rate of interest, the rate of unemployment, the level of real national income, the real quantity of money, the rate of growth of real national income, or the rate of growth of the real quantity of money.*

These views have important implications for the Phillips curve. In particular, they imply that monetary policymakers face a long-run Phillips curve that is vertical, as in Figure 18.3. If the central bank increases the money supply slowly, the inflation rate is low, and the economy finds itself at point A. If the central bank increases the money supply quickly, the inflation rate is high, and the economy finds itself at point B. In either case, the unemployment rate tends towards its normal level, called the *natural rate of unemployment*. The vertical long-run Phillips curve illustrates the conclusion that unemployment does not depend on money growth and inflation in the long run.

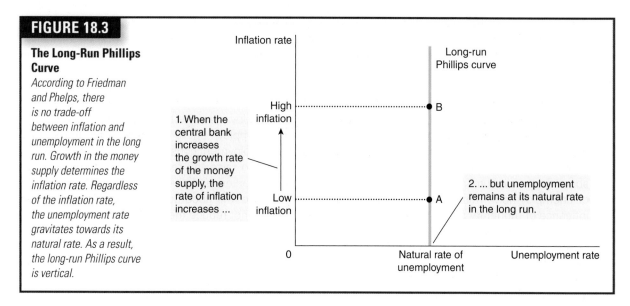

FIGURE 18.3

The Long-Run Phillips Curve

According to Friedman and Phelps, there is no trade-off between inflation and unemployment in the long run. Growth in the money supply determines the inflation rate. Regardless of the inflation rate, the unemployment rate gravitates towards its natural rate. As a result, the long-run Phillips curve is vertical.

The vertical long-run Phillips curve is, in essence, one expression of the classical idea of monetary neutrality. As you may recall, we expressed this idea in Chapter 16 with a vertical long-run aggregate supply curve. Indeed, as Figure 18.4 illustrates, the vertical long-run Phillips curve and the vertical long-run aggregate supply curve are two sides of the same coin. In panel (a) of this figure, an increase in the money supply shifts the aggregate demand curve to the right from AD_1 to AD_2. As a result of this shift, the long-run equilibrium moves from point A to point B.

FIGURE 18.4

How the Long-Run Phillips Curve Is Related to the Model of Aggregate Demand and Aggregate Supply

Panel (a) shows the model of aggregate demand and aggregate supply with a vertical aggregate supply curve. When expansionary monetary policy shifts the aggregate demand curve to the right from AD_1 to AD_2, the equilibrium moves from point A to point B. The price level rises from P_1 to P_2, while output remains the same. Panel (b) shows the long-run Phillips curve, which is vertical at the natural rate of unemployment. Expansionary monetary policy moves the economy from lower inflation (point A) to higher inflation (point B) without changing the rate of unemployment.

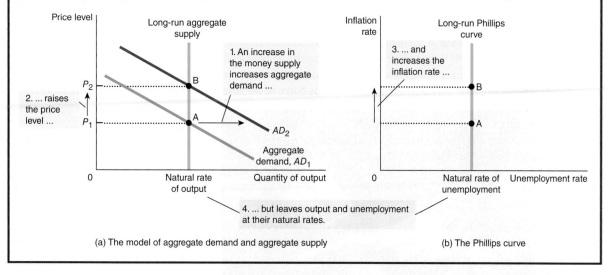

(a) The model of aggregate demand and aggregate supply

(b) The Phillips curve

The price level rises from P_1 to P_2, but because the aggregate supply curve is vertical, output remains the same. In panel (b), more rapid growth in the money supply raises the inflation rate by moving the economy from point A to point B. But, because the Phillips curve is vertical, the rate of unemployment is the same at these two points. Thus, the vertical long-run aggregate supply curve and the vertical long-run Phillips curve both imply that monetary policy influences nominal variables (the price level and the inflation rate) but not real variables (output and unemployment). Regardless of the monetary policy pursued by the central bank, output and unemployment are, in the long run, at their natural rates.

The Natural Rate of Unemployment What is so 'natural' about the natural rate of unemployment? Friedman and Phelps used this adjective to describe the unemployment rate towards which the economy tends to gravitate in the long run. Yet the natural rate of unemployment is not necessarily the socially desirable rate of unemployment. Nor is the natural rate of unemployment constant over time. For example, suppose that a newly formed union uses its market power to raise the real wages of some workers above the equilibrium level. The result is an excess supply of workers and, therefore, a higher natural rate of unemployment. This unemployment is 'natural' not because it is good but because it is beyond the influence of monetary policy. More rapid money growth would not reduce the market power of the union or the level of unemployment; it would lead only to more inflation.

Although monetary policy cannot influence the natural rate of unemployment, other types of policy can. To reduce the natural rate of unemployment, policymakers should look to policies that improve the functioning of the labour market. Earlier in the book we discussed how various labour market policies, such as minimum wage laws, collective bargaining laws, unemployment insurance and job-training schemes, affect the natural rate of unemployment. A policy change that reduced the natural rate of unemployment would shift the long-run Phillips curve to the left. In addition, because lower unemployment means more workers are producing goods and services, the quantity of goods and services supplied would be larger at any given price level, and the long-run aggregate supply curve would shift to the right. The economy could then enjoy lower unemployment and higher output for any given rate of money growth and inflation. We will look at some of these policies designed to affect the supply side of the economy in the next chapter.

CASE STUDY **A Fear of Inflation**

A key debate which continues following the financial crisis is whether weak growth being experienced in many countries needs to be countered by expansionary fiscal and monetary policy, and if so what danger there is to inflation in the coming years. There is a body of opinion that the sort of expansion necessary would lead to severe inflationary consequences and that expectations on managing inflation at stable levels need to be maintained. Such an argument would embrace the basic premise of the Phillips curve.

Some economists argue that monetary and fiscal expansion at this time would not lead to higher inflation because the economies of many countries are so depressed that there is no evidence to suggest that inflationary pressures exist outside of the increase in fuel prices that have been a major cause of higher than target inflation in countries like the UK. This would suggest that the size of the output or deflationary gap is sufficiently large to accommodate expansion without leading to inflationary pressures. This, in turn, suggests that shape of the Phillips curve would be such that the reduction in unemployment would be larger in comparison to the rise in inflation (the Phillips curve as we have drawn it in Figure 18.1 would be shallow).

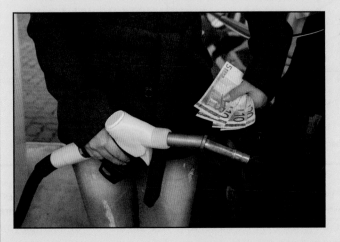

Rising fuel prices have meant inflation has stayed stubbornly high during the economic slowdown in some countries but would monetary expansion lead to the release of inflationary pressure across the economy as a whole?

Reconciling Theory and Evidence

At first, the conclusion of Friedman and Phelps of a long-run trade-off between inflation and unemployment might not seem persuasive. Their argument was based on an appeal to *theory*. In contrast, the negative correlation between inflation and unemployment documented by Phillips, Samuelson and Solow was based on *data*. Why should anyone believe that policymakers faced a vertical Phillips curve when the world seemed to offer a downwards sloping one? Shouldn't the findings of Phillips, Samuelson and Solow lead us to reject the classical conclusion of monetary neutrality?

Friedman and Phelps were well aware of these questions, and they offered a way to reconcile classical macroeconomic theory with the finding of a downwards sloping Phillips curve in data from the United Kingdom and the United States. They claimed that a negative relationship between inflation and unemployment holds in the short run but that it cannot be used by policymakers in the long run. In other words, policymakers can pursue expansionary monetary policy to achieve lower unemployment for a while, but eventually unemployment returns to its natural rate, and more expansionary monetary policy leads only to higher inflation.

Friedman and Phelps reasoned as we did in Chapter 16 when we explained the difference between the short-run and long-run aggregate supply curves. (In fact, the discussion in that chapter drew heavily on the legacy of Friedman and Phelps.) As you may recall, the short-run aggregate supply curve is upwards sloping, indicating that an increase in the price level raises the quantity of goods and services that firms supply. In contrast, the long-run aggregate supply curve is vertical, indicating that the price level does not influence quantity supplied in the long run. Chapter 16 presented three theories to explain the upwards slope of the short-run aggregate supply curve: sticky wages, sticky prices and misperceptions about relative prices. Because wages, prices and perceptions adjust to changing economic conditions over time, the positive relationship between the price level and quantity supplied applies in the short run but not in the long run. Friedman and Phelps applied this same logic to the Phillips curve. Just as the aggregate supply curve slopes upwards only in the short run, the trade-off between inflation and unemployment holds only in the short run. And just as the long-run aggregate supply curve is vertical, the long-run Phillips curve is also vertical.

To help explain the short-run and long-run relationship between inflation and unemployment, Friedman and Phelps introduced a new variable into the analysis: *expected inflation.* Expected inflation measures how much people expect the overall price level to change. As we discussed in Chapter 16, the expected price level affects the wages and prices that people set and the perceptions of relative prices that they form. As a result, expected inflation is one factor that determines the position of the short-run aggregate supply curve. In the short run, the central bank can take expected inflation (and thus the short-run aggregate supply curve) as already determined. When the money supply changes, the aggregate demand curve shifts and the economy moves along a given short-run aggregate supply curve. In the short run, therefore, monetary changes lead to unexpected fluctuations in output, prices, unemployment and inflation. In this way, Friedman and Phelps explained the Phillips curve that Phillips, Samuelson and Solow had documented.

Yet the central bank's ability to create unexpected inflation by increasing the money supply exists only in the short run. In the long run, people come to expect whatever inflation rate the central bank chooses to produce. Because wages, prices and perceptions will eventually adjust to the inflation rate, the long-run aggregate supply curve is vertical. In this case, changes in aggregate demand, such as those due to changes in the money supply, do not affect the economy's output of goods and services. Thus, Friedman and Phelps concluded that unemployment returns to its natural rate in the long run.

The Short-Run Phillips Curve

The analysis of Friedman and Phelps can be summarized in the following equation (which is, in essence, another expression of the aggregate supply equation we saw in Chapter 16):

$$\text{Unemployment rate} = \text{Natural rate of unemployment} - a(\text{Actual Inflation} - \text{Expected inflation})$$

This equation relates the unemployment rate to the natural rate of unemployment, actual inflation and expected inflation. In the short run, expected inflation is given. As a result, higher actual inflation is associated with lower unemployment. (How much unemployment responds to unexpected inflation is determined by the size of *a*, a number that in turn depends on the slope of the short-run aggregate supply curve.) In the long run, however, people come to expect whatever inflation the central bank produces. Thus, actual inflation equals expected inflation, and unemployment is at its natural rate.

This equation implies there is no stable short-run Phillips curve. Each short-run Phillips curve reflects a particular expected rate of inflation. (To be precise, if you graph the equation, you'll find that the short-run Phillips curve intersects the long-run Phillips curve at the expected rate of inflation.) Whenever expected inflation changes, the short-run Phillips curve shifts.

According to Friedman and Phelps, it is dangerous to view the Phillips curve as a menu of options available to policymakers. To see why, imagine an economy at its natural rate of unemployment with low inflation and low expected inflation, shown in Figure 18.5 as point A. Now suppose that policymakers try to take advantage of the trade-off between inflation and unemployment by using monetary or fiscal policy to expand aggregate demand. In the short run when expected inflation is given, the economy goes from point A to point B. Unemployment falls below its natural rate, and inflation rises above expected inflation. Over time, people get used to this higher inflation rate, and they raise their expectations of inflation. When expected inflation rises, firms and workers start taking higher inflation into account when setting wages and prices. The short-run Phillips curve then shifts to the right, as shown in the figure. The economy ends up at point C, with higher inflation than at point A but with the same level of unemployment.

Thus, Friedman and Phelps concluded that policymakers do face a trade-off between inflation and unemployment, but only a temporary one. If policymakers use this trade-off, they lose it.

FIGURE 18.5

How Expected Inflation Shifts the Short-Run Phillips Curve
The higher the expected rate of inflation, the higher the short-run trade-off between inflation and unemployment. At point A, expected inflation and actual inflation are both low, and unemployment is at its natural rate. If the central bank pursues an expansionary monetary policy, the economy moves from point A to point B in the short run. At point B, expected inflation is still low, but actual inflation is high. Unemployment is below its natural rate. In the long run, expected inflation rises, and the economy moves to point C. At point C, expected inflation and actual inflation are both high, and unemployment is back to its natural rate.

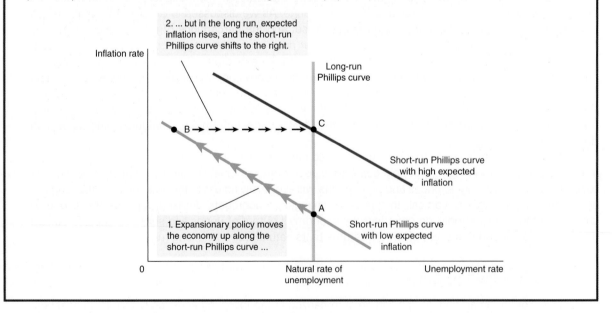

The Unemployment–Inflation Trade-Off

Friedman and Phelps had made a bold prediction in 1968: if policymakers try to take advantage of the Phillips curve by choosing higher inflation in order to reduce unemployment, they will succeed at reducing unemployment only temporarily. This view – that unemployment eventually returns to its natural rate, regardless of the rate of inflation – is called the **natural-rate hypothesis**.

> **natural-rate hypothesis** the claim that unemployment eventually returns to its normal, or natural, rate, regardless of the rate of inflation

To some economists at the time, it seemed ridiculous to claim that the Phillips curve would break down once policymakers tried to use it. But, in fact, that is exactly what happened in both the UK and the United States. Beginning in the late 1960s, the UK government, for example, followed policies that expanded the aggregate demand for goods and services. On top of this, the UK and many other developed economies in the late 1960s and early 1970s experienced an increase in aggregate demand due to American involvement in the Vietnam War, which increased US government spending (on the military), boosted US aggregate demand and so boosted net exports from other countries to the USA. In addition, in 1971, as a result of the relaxation of certain controls on bank lending, the UK experienced a major expansion in the money supply. In the following year, the government announced an extraordinarily expansionary fiscal policy, in terms of extra spending and tax reduction, and the economy began seriously to overheat and inflation started to rise (refer to Figure 14.2 to see the extent to which the economy of the UK grew at this time). But, as Friedman and Phelps had predicted, unemployment did not stay low.

From the end of World War II through to the late 1970s, many governments in the Western world adopted Keynesian policies as the basis for managing the economy. There was an emphasis on attempting to keep unemployment low. The experience of mass unemployment and the rise in extremism in many parts of Europe and the misery caused by the Great Depression in the United States in the 1930s had persuaded policymakers that a focus on unemployment was vital to stable economic and political life. In the 20 years after the war, fiscal policy was dominant; in times of rising unemployment fiscal policy was loosened and tightened when inflation began to speed up. The government could pull its fiscal levers of tax and public spending to 'fine tune' the economy. The unusual circumstances of post-war reconstruction across Europe and the US meant that inflation did not seem to present a major problem.

Some economists argued that the focus on fiscal policy meant that not only did households form expectations about inflation but also about government policy. In the UK, many large industries were in public ownership including the railways, coal, electricity, airports and airlines, telecommunications and steel. In addition, trade unions enjoyed considerable power in many industries. Workers came to expect, it was argued, increases in real wages each year and that this would be accommodated by monetary expansion. In addition, the government would respond by loosening fiscal policy if the economy slowed down. This, it was argued, led to a fall in productivity and increased inflationary pressures as the government and industry accommodated wage increases. In the aggregate, UK industry became sluggish, lacked flexibility and lost competitiveness.

These conditions led to rising inflation and an inability of the government to reduce unemployment below the natural rate. After the oil crisis and miners' strike of the early 1970s and the fiscal boom produced by the government, stagflation took hold and the UK seemed to lurch from 'boom to bust'. Eventually the government was forced to borrow money from the International Monetary Fund (IMF) in 1976. In a famous speech to the Labour Party Conference in the same year, the then Prime Minister, James Callaghan, echoed Friedman and Phelps' theory to the nation when he said:

We used to think that you could spend your way out of a recession and increase employment by cutting taxes and boosting government spending. I tell you in all candour that that option no longer exists, and in so far as it ever did exist, it only worked on each occasion since the war by injecting a bigger dose of inflation into the economy. And each time that happened, the average level of unemployment has risen. Higher inflation followed by higher unemployment. That is the history of the last 20 years.

This effectively saw a move away from Keynesian policies and a shift to monetary policy in the UK, while the US began to take greater steps to focus on the money supply. The focus of policy on the use of monetary and supply-side policies was seen as the way of keeping inflation under control and lowering the natural rate of unemployment. Throughout the 1980s, the UK and US governments trumpeted the benefits of supply-side policies. These looked at ways of expanding the productive capacity of the economy to shift the aggregate supply curve to the right (we will look at these policies in the next chapter). Such policies stressed the importance of enterprise, reducing business regulation, improving incentives through cutting taxes and benefits, reducing trade union power and investing in education and training to improve the workings and flexibility of the labour market in the long run.

Supply-side policies take some time to have an effect but structural economic reforms by the UK government throughout the 1990s led to a leftward shift in the Phillips curve. What caused this favourable shift in the short-run Phillips curve? Part of the answer lies in a low level of expected inflation. The policy of inflation targeting since 1992, combined with the independence of the Bank of England in 1997 created a credible policy framework in which workers and firms knew that interest rates would be raised if the economy began to overheat, and they tended to moderate their wage claims and price setting accordingly. Since the Bank of England now sets interest rates independently, people also know that there is no way in which politicians can use expansionary monetary policy for political reasons, such as to gain popularity before an election. This led to a period of relatively stable economic conditions in the UK with economic growth, low inflation and relatively low levels of unemployment right up until around 2008 when the financial crisis began to unravel.

In contrast, many European countries suffered relatively high levels of unemployment despite the European Central Bank having independence in the setting of monetary policy. Why was this? One argument that has been put forward to explain high European unemployment in the 21st century, and which seems to have some credibility, centres on the level of labour market regulation. As we pointed out above, the 1980s in the UK were characterized both by a weakening of the power of the trades unions and by a reduction in business regulation in general and in labour market regulation in particular. Whilst, for example, this had the effect of reducing job security for many people by making it easier for employers to terminate contracts, it also had the effect of making labour markets much more flexible. Thus, somewhat paradoxically perhaps, if it is harder to fire someone, firms will think hard before taking on new labour and unemployment may actually rise. Similarly, the minimum wage is typically set at a much higher level (relative to the average wage) in European countries like France and Germany, which again is a reason why the natural rate of unemployment might be higher in those countries.

Data on the history of UK inflation and unemployment from the early 1970s shows very little evidence of the simple negative relationship between these two variables that Phillips had originally observed. In particular, as inflation remained high in the early 1970s, people's expectations of inflation caught up with reality, and the unemployment rate rose along with inflation. By the mid-1970s, policymakers had learned that Friedman and Phelps were right: There is no trade-off between inflation and unemployment in the long run.

SELF TEST Draw the short-run Phillips curve and the long-run Phillips curve. Explain why they are different.

THE LONG-RUN VERTICAL PHILLIPS CURVE AS AN ARGUMENT FOR CENTRAL BANK INDEPENDENCE

Who would you rather was in charge of monetary policy – an elected government or an unelected central banker? Would it not be better to have the government in charge of the money supply and interest rates? After all, if they screw up, we can vote them out of office at the next election, while, on the other hand, the electorate has no such sanction over central bankers.

In fact, most economists – at least the majority of those who believe in a long-run vertical Phillips curve – would rather hand control of monetary policy to the central banker, particularly if the central banker in question had a reputation for being tough on inflation, and especially if he or she had a clear and publicly known target for the level of inflation to be achieved.

To see why, take another look back at Figure 18.5. Suppose we're at point A, with the natural rate of unemployment and a low level of inflation, and that the government is in charge of monetary policy in the sense that they can just tell the central bank to change interest rates or the money supply and it is done. Now imagine that we're just coming up to a general election in a few months' time: what do you suppose the government will do? Since unemployment is never a vote winner, it is perhaps likely that they will be tempted to reduce interest rates and expand the money supply so that the economy moves from point A to point B and unemployment falls. (In reality, because of the uncertain lags in monetary policy that we discussed earlier, the government won't be able to guarantee that the economy will get to precisely point B just before the election, but it will certainly move along the short-run Phillips curve from point A towards point B, with actual inflation above expected inflation.) Of course, once people's expectations of inflation catch up with actual inflation, the short-run Phillips curve will shift up and the economy will move to point C. At point C there is the same rate of unemployment as in the first place (the natural rate) and a higher level of inflation, so in the long run the economy is in a worse state than if monetary policy had remained neutral and the economy had stayed at A. If the election takes place before inflationary expectations catch up, however, the government has a higher chance of being re-elected because, so long as the economy remains on the initial short-run Phillips curve at some point between A and B, inflationary expectations are low while unemployment is falling. Not only is this likely to lead to extra votes from people who were previously unemployed and now grateful to be in a job, economic activity in general will rise in the economy and people in general will experience an economic 'feel-good factor' and be grateful to the government for running the economy so well. Once inflationary expectations have finally caught up and we move to point C on the long-run Phillips curve with the same old level of unemployment and higher inflation, the feel-good factor will evaporate, but it's too late – the election is over and the same government is back in power.

Of course, the story we have just told implies a pretty cynical view of politics, and most governments would strenuously deny that they would carry out such tricks just to get re-elected. More importantly, however, the story also implies that people (workers and managers of firms) are pretty stupid. Why? Because everyone will know that the government has a strong incentive to pursue an expansionary monetary policy just before an election. In fact, firms and workers may begin raising prices and wages before the election in anticipation of the expansionary monetary policy, so we could end up jumping straight from point A to point C without any intervening fall in unemployment! This is an interesting result, and one worth stressing: if people believe that the government is about to pursue an expansionary monetary policy, then inflationary expectations will increase and inflation will rise but unemployment will not fall. In essence, the economy jumps immediately to the new long-run equilibrium.

But suppose that whoever is in charge of monetary policy issues a statement saying that she has no intention of pursuing an expansionary monetary policy. Should firms and workers believe her? Probably not. In fact, firms and workers might reason that if they really believed that no monetary expansion would take place, then that is when the politician would be most tempted to bring about an expansion of the money supply, since then they really would be taken by surprise by the monetary expansion and it would take a while for their inflationary expectations to catch up with actual inflation. In the meantime, the economy would move along the short-run Phillips curve to point B, unemployment would fall and the government would become more popular. So the more credible the politician's promise seems to be, the less you should believe her! Hence, it seems that if monetary policy is left to the politicians, we shall always end up with higher inflation but with no reduction in unemployment, even in the short run.

What if, instead, the government gave the governor of the central bank full control over monetary policy and told him that he would be fired unless he achieved a certain low level of inflation over a reasonable period of time, regardless of what happened to unemployment? Say, in fact, that this target level of inflation was the one at point A in Figure 18.5. Because the central banker has no incentive to reduce unemployment, the problem goes away: firms and workers believe that the economy will stay at point A and so it does, because inflationary expectations are exactly the same as actual inflation. Hence, by passing control over monetary policy to the central bank, the economy ends up with unemployment no different from when the government was in control of monetary policy, but with a lower level of inflation.

So what's in it for the government? Well, for a start we should not perhaps think that all politicians are necessarily as cynical as we have portrayed them. Perhaps they have the longer-run well-being of the economy at heart rather than just wanting to be re-elected at any cost. Or perhaps they are cynical, but just more sophisticated. A cynical government would clearly prefer point B (or somewhere near it) to point A at election time, since unemployment is lower than the natural rate and people still expect low inflation – a sure vote-winning combination. However, the government knows that firms and workers will factor the government's temptation into their price and wage setting, so that in fact the economy will jump to point C just before the election.

In fact, this situation is an example of a *Nash equilibrium*. Remember that a Nash equilibrium is a situation in which economic actors interacting with one another each choose their best strategy given the strategies that all the other actors have chosen. Here, firms and workers know that if they don't raise inflationary expectations before an election, the government will most likely pursue an expansionary monetary policy and they will lose out because their prices and wages will be lower in real terms, and so they do raise inflationary expectations and the short-run Phillips curve shifts up and we move to point C in Figure 18.5. But doesn't the government still have the same temptation to inflate at point C? Well, possibly, but there will certainly be some point on the vertical, long-run Phillips curve where inflation is already so high that the government will not want to risk pushing it higher, even if it means a short-run reduction in unemployment. If firms and workers can guess roughly what this level of inflation is, they will set their wages and prices so that the economy will jump straight to that point – let's imagine that this is indeed point C. If, at point C, the government has no temptation to inflate the economy in order to gain popularity, and if firms and workers know this so that they have no incentive to change their price and wage setting behaviour, then we will have reached the Nash equilibrium.

Another way of thinking about this is to say that the Nash equilibrium (which we have assumed is at point C in Figure 18.5) represents the *time-consistent policy*. A time-consistent policy is simply one which a government does not have a temptation to renege on at some point in time and will usually represent a Nash equilibrium.

But take a look at point C: it may represent time-consistency in economic policy, but it is actually worse than point A for the government's electoral chances, since inflation is higher and unemployment is still at the natural rate. Hence, the best thing to do in order to maximize the chances of re-election is for the government to make the central bank independent in the sense of handing over control of monetary policy – providing of course that the central bank sees its role as the guardian of price stability; in other words, providing that the central bank is 'conservative' with respect to price stability. That way, the economy can just stay at A.

It is a testimony to the power of macroeconomic theory that this argument has persuaded many governments around the world to grant independence to their central bank in the conduct of monetary policy. The European Central Bank, for example, has been independent since its inception in 1998, and the Bank of England was granted independence in 1997. The ECB both designs its monetary policy (e.g. decides what level of inflation in the Euro Area to aim for) and implements it. The Bank of England, on the other hand, has independence in the implementation of monetary policy but does not decide on the design of monetary policy – in particular, its inflation target is set by the UK Chancellor of the Exchequer. The US Federal Reserve is also independent in both the design and implementation of monetary policy. Although, unlike the ECB and the Bank of England, the Fed does not formally pursue an inflation target, it has a strong reputation for 'conservatism' with respect to inflation, so the overall effect is similar. A long-run vertical Phillips curve is a compelling case for taking control over monetary policy out of the hands of politicians and handing it over to a 'conservative central banker'.

SHIFTS IN THE PHILLIPS CURVE: THE ROLE OF SUPPLY SHOCKS

Friedman and Phelps had suggested in 1968 that changes in expected inflation shift the short-run Phillips curve, and the experience of the early 1970s convinced most economists that Friedman and Phelps were right. Within a few years, however, the economics profession would turn its attention to a different source of shifts in the short-run Phillips curve: shocks to aggregate supply.

This time, the shift in focus came not from two economics professors but from a group of Arab sheikhs. Conflict between Israel and its Arab neighbours triggered a series of oil price shocks as Arab oil producers used their market power to exert political pressure on Western governments who supported Israel. In 1974, the Organization of Petroleum Exporting Countries (OPEC) also began to exert its power as a cartel in order to increase its members' profits. The countries of OPEC, such as Saudi Arabia, Kuwait and Iraq, restricted the amount of crude oil they pumped and sold on world markets. This reduction in supply caused the price of oil to almost double over a few years in the 1970s.

A large increase in the world price of oil is an example of a supply shock. A **supply shock** is an event that directly affects firms' costs of production and thus the prices they charge; it shifts the economy's aggregate supply curve and, as a result, the Phillips curve. Oil is a constituent part of so many production processes that increases in its price have far-reaching effects. For example, when an oil price increase raises the cost of producing petrol, heating oil, tyres, plastic products, distribution and many other products, it reduces the quantity of goods and services supplied at any given price level. As panel (a) of Figure 18.6 shows, this reduction in supply is represented by the leftward shift in the aggregate supply curve from AS_1 to AS_2. The price level rises from P_1 to P_2, and output falls from Y_1 to Y_2 and the economy experiences stagflation.

> **supply shock** an event that directly alters firms' costs and prices, shifting the economy's aggregate supply curve and thus the Phillips curve

This shift in aggregate supply is associated with a similar shift in the short-run Phillips curve, shown in panel (b). Because firms need fewer workers to produce the smaller output, employment falls and unemployment rises. Because the price level is higher, the inflation rate – the percentage change in the price level from the previous year – is also higher. Thus, the shift in aggregate supply leads to higher unemployment and higher inflation. The short-run trade-off between inflation and unemployment shifts to the right from PC_1 to PC_2.

Confronted with an adverse shift in aggregate supply, policymakers face a difficult choice between fighting inflation and fighting unemployment. If they contract aggregate demand to fight inflation, they will raise unemployment further. If they expand aggregate demand to fight unemployment, they will raise inflation further. In other words, policymakers face a less favourable trade-off between inflation and unemployment than they did before the shift in aggregate supply: they have to live with a higher rate of inflation for a given rate of unemployment, a higher rate of unemployment for a given rate of inflation, or some combination of higher unemployment and higher inflation.

FIGURE 18.6

An Adverse Shock to Aggregate Supply

Panel (a) shows the model of aggregate demand and aggregate supply. When the aggregate supply curve shifts to the left from AS_1 to AS_2, the equilibrium moves from point A to point B. Output falls from Y_1 to Y_2, and the price level rises from P_1 to P_2. Panel (b) shows the short-run trade-off between inflation and unemployment. The adverse shift in aggregate supply moves the economy from a point with lower unemployment and lower inflation (point A) to a point with higher unemployment and higher inflation (point B). The short-run Phillips curve shifts to the right from PC_1 to PC_2. Policymakers now face a worse trade-off between inflation and unemployment.

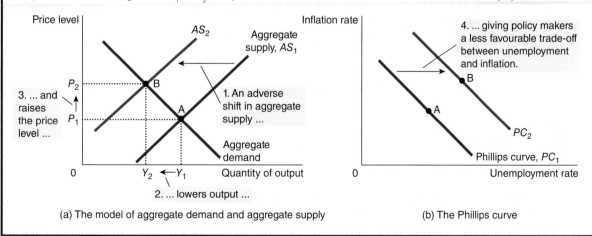

(a) The model of aggregate demand and aggregate supply

(b) The Phillips curve

An important question is whether this adverse shift in the Phillips curve is temporary or permanent. The answer depends on how people adjust their expectations of inflation. If people view the rise in inflation due to the supply shock as a temporary aberration, expected inflation does not change, and the Phillips curve will soon revert to its former position. But if people believe the shock will lead to a new era of higher inflation, then expected inflation rises, and the Phillips curve remains at its new, less desirable position.

SELF TEST Give an example of a favourable shock to aggregate supply. Use the model of aggregate demand and aggregate supply to explain the effects of such a shock. How does it affect the Phillips curve?

THE COST OF REDUCING INFLATION

In 1979, the UK electorate voted in Margaret Thatcher as Prime Minister. The Conservative government she headed pursued policies that were focused on the tenets of monetarism and on the supply side – policies which were effectively rooted in the idea of a vertical long-run supply curve or vertical long-run Phillips curve. With inflation running at over 20 per cent and unemployment rising, Mrs Thatcher's government focused their attention on a policy of *disinflation* – a reduction in the rate of inflation. Economic theory suggested how this could be done through controlling the money supply. But what would be the short-run cost of disinflation? The answer to this question was much less certain.

The Sacrifice Ratio

To reduce the inflation rate, the central bank has to pursue contractionary monetary policy. Figure 18.7 shows some of the effects of such a decision. When the central bank slows the rate at which the money supply is growing, it contracts aggregate demand. The fall in aggregate demand, in turn, reduces the quantity of goods and services that firms produce, and this fall in production leads to a fall in employment. The economy begins at point A in the figure and moves along the short-run Phillips curve to point B, which has lower inflation and higher unemployment. Over time, as people come to understand that prices are rising more slowly, expected inflation falls, and the short-run Phillips curve shifts downward. The economy moves from point B to point C. Inflation is lower, and unemployment is back at its natural rate.

Thus, if a nation wants to reduce inflation, it must endure a period of high unemployment and low output. In Figure 18.7, this cost is represented by the movement of the economy through point B as it travels from point A to point C. The size of this cost depends on the slope of the Phillips curve and how quickly expectations of inflation adjust to the new monetary policy.

Many studies have examined the data on inflation and unemployment in order to estimate the cost of reducing inflation. The findings of these studies are often summarized in a statistic called the **sacrifice ratio**. The sacrifice ratio is the number of percentage points of annual output lost in the process of reducing inflation by 1 percentage point. A typical estimate of the sacrifice ratio is around 3 to 5. That is, for each percentage point that inflation is reduced, 3 to 5 per cent of annual output must be sacrificed in the transition.

sacrifice ratio the number of percentage points of annual output lost in the process of reducing inflation by 1 percentage point

According to studies of the Phillips curve and the cost of disinflation, this sacrifice could be paid in various ways. Assume that inflation was running at 10 per cent and a government wanted to reduce it to 5 per cent. If each percentage point reduction in inflation would cost 3 per cent of annual output then the cost would be 15 per cent of annual output lost in a year. Such an outcome would be extremely harsh even for the most hard-line inflation hawks. Another option would be to spread out the cost over several years. If the reduction in inflation took place over five years, for instance, then output would have to average only 3 per cent below trend during that period to add up to a sacrifice of 15 per cent. An even more gradual approach would be to reduce inflation slowly over a decade. Whatever path was chosen, however, reducing inflation would not be easy.

FIGURE 18.7

Disinflationary Monetary Policy in the Short Run and Long Run

When the central bank pursues contractionary monetary policy to reduce inflation, the economy moves along a short-run Phillips curve from point A to point B. Over time, expected inflation falls, and the short-run Phillips curve shifts downwards. When the economy reaches point C, unemployment is back at its natural rate.

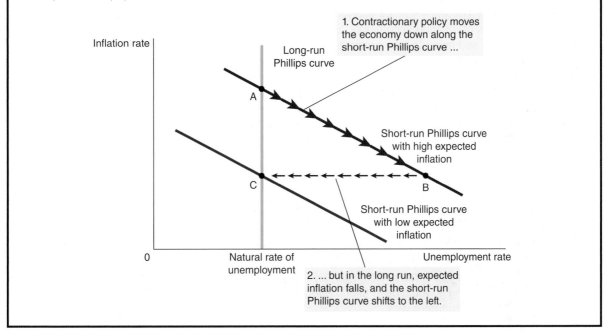

Rational Expectations and the Possibility of Costless Disinflation

As policymakers in the early 1980s were pondering how costly reducing inflation might be, a group of economics professors were leading an intellectual revolution that would challenge the conventional wisdom on the sacrifice ratio. This group included such prominent economists as Robert Lucas, Thomas Sargent and Robert Barro. Their revolution was based on a new approach to economic theory and policy called **rational expectations**.

> **rational expectations** the theory according to which people optimally use all the information they have, including information about government policies, when forecasting the future

The rational expectations model came to supplant the **adaptive expectations** model which was the idea that individuals and organizations base their expectations of inflation in the future on past actual inflation rates. Critics of the model argued that individuals take into account more information when forming their judgement than simply past inflation rates. The rational expectations model took into account this available information. According to the theory of rational expectations, therefore, people optimally use all the information they have, including information about government policies, when forecasting the future.

> **adaptive expectations** a model which states that individuals and organizations base their expectations of inflation in the future on past actual inflation rates

This new approach has had profound implications for many areas of macroeconomics, but none is more important than its application to the trade-off between inflation and unemployment. As Friedman and Phelps had first emphasized, expected inflation is an important variable that explains why there is a trade-off between inflation and unemployment in the short run but not in the long run. How quickly the short-run trade-off disappears depends on how quickly expectations adjust. Proponents of rational expectations built on the Friedman–Phelps analysis argue that when economic policies change, people adjust their expectations of inflation accordingly. Studies of inflation and unemployment that tried to estimate the sacrifice ratio had failed to take account of the direct effect of the policy regime on expectations. As a result, estimates of the sacrifice ratio were, according to the rational expectations theorists, unreliable guides for policy.

In a 1982 paper entitled 'The End of Four Big Inflations' (one of which was the UK inflation of the late 1970s and early 1980s), Thomas Sargent described this new view as follows:

> *An alternative 'rational expectations' view denies that there is any inherent momentum to the present process of inflation. This view maintains that firms and workers have now come to expect high rates of inflation in the future and that they strike inflationary bargains in light of these expectations. However, it is held that people expect high rates of inflation in the future precisely because the government's current and prospective monetary and fiscal policies warrant those expectations. … An implication of this view is that inflation can be stopped much more quickly than advocates of the 'momentum' view have indicated and that their estimates of the length of time and the costs of stopping inflation in terms of forgone output are erroneous. This is not to say that it would be easy to eradicate inflation. On the contrary, it would require more than a few temporary restrictive fiscal and monetary actions. It would require a change in the policy regime. … How costly such a move would be in terms of forgone output and how long it would be in taking effect would depend partly on how resolute and evident the government's commitment was.*

According to Sargent, the sacrifice ratio could be much smaller than suggested by previous estimates. Indeed, in the most extreme case, it could be zero. If the government made a credible commitment to a policy of low inflation, people would be rational enough to lower their expectations of inflation immediately. The short-run Phillips curve would shift downward, and the economy would reach low inflation quickly without the cost of temporarily high unemployment and low output. The credibility of government policy is thus of prime importance.

The Thatcher Disinflation

In the UK, Prime Minister Margaret Thatcher did succeed at reducing inflation. Inflation came down from almost 20 per cent in 1980 to about 5 per cent in 1983 and 1984. The Thatcher disinflation did, however, come at the cost of high unemployment. In 1982 and 1983, the unemployment rate was about 11 per cent – about double its level when the Thatcher government came to power. At the same time, the production of goods and services as measured by real GDP was well below its trend level.

Does this experience refute the possibility of costless disinflation as suggested by the rational expectations theorists? Some economists have argued that the answer to this question is a resounding yes. To make the transition from high inflation (point A in Figure 18.7) to low inflation (point C), the economy had to experience a painful period of high unemployment (point B).

Yet perhaps there is good reason not to reject the conclusions of the rational expectations theorists so quickly. Even though the Thatcher disinflation did impose a cost of temporarily high unemployment, the cost was not as large as many economists had predicted. Most estimates of the sacrifice ratio based on the Thatcher disinflation are smaller than estimates that had been obtained from previous data. It seems that Prime Minister Thatcher's tough stand on inflation did have some direct effect on expectations, as the rational expectations theorists claimed.

SELF TEST What is the sacrifice ratio? How might the credibility of the government's commitment to reduce inflation affect the sacrifice ratio?

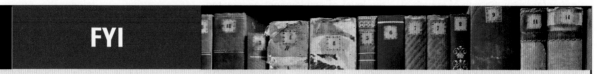

FYI

Wage Curve Theory

We have said that Phillips's research looked at the relationship between the rate of growth of wages and unemployment. The relationship of the wage rate to unemployment takes us a small step towards linking the level of inflation with unemployment. The rate of growth in wages is a factor that influences the overall level of prices in the economy. Wages represent a cost to employers; other things being equal, if they rise then employers might well seek to raise prices to cover the increased cost. If this happens throughout the economy on an aggregate level, wage growth leads to inflation. If the rate of growth of wages slows down, we might expect the labour market to be looser; in other words, the demand for labour in relation to the supply of labour is falling. Under normal market conditions, we would expect the wage rate to start to fall. In reality, this translates to the slowing down in the rate of growth of wages.

We then saw how further research into the Phillips curve led to the development of the so-called expectations augmented Phillips curve, captured in the following formula:

$$\Delta p_t = E_t \Delta p_t + 1 + (NR_t - RU_t)$$

This simply says that the change in the inflation rate in a time period (Δp_t) is equal to expected inflation in a time period ($E_t \Delta p_t + 1$) and the natural rate of unemployment minus the national unemployment rate. This helped to explain what seemed to be happening in many Western economies in the 1970s. Households were *anticipating* inflation in the future and basing their behaviour and decision making on those expectations: therefore, the Phillips curve was shifting. This helped to explain how higher inflation might also be experienced at the same time as higher unemployment – so-called 'stagflation'.

There have, however, been a number of economists who have questioned the existence of the Phillips curve. One economist did pose that very question. David Blanchflower has worked at a number of institutions, including the University of Surrey and Warwick University, in the UK. He is a former member of the Bank of England's Monetary Policy Committee and works at Dartmouth College in New Hampshire in the United States.

Remember that the assumption of the Phillips curve is that there is a relationship between the rate of growth of wages and unemployment. When unemployment rises, the *rate of growth of wages* falls and vice versa. This makes intuitive sense since if there is a large pool of unemployed workers, employed workers will be hesitant to push for higher wage claims for fear of joining the rank of unemployed.

Blanchflower has been quoted as suggesting that as a result of his work, 'the Phillips curve is wrong, it's as fundamental as that'. The following is a summary of his analysis in support of this view. The traditional Phillips curve relates the rate of growth of wages with the level of unemployment. Within this relationship, a higher level of unemployment is associated with a lower level of the rate of growth of wages. Conversely, if unemployment rates were low, the rate of growth of wages would be higher. Such a relationship is given as a macroeconomic one rather than microeconomic, i.e. it holds for the economy as a whole. If the level of unemployment increases, therefore, it suggests there will be excess supply in the labour market. In such cases, the labour market will adjust and the rate of growth of wages will fall to eliminate the excess supply.

(Continued)

Blanchflower and his colleague, Andrew Oswald, spent time researching links between unemployment and wage rates at a *microeconomic level* and found that the relationship between unemployment and wages might be different depending on the region that was being investigated. Their research looked at the *level of pay rather* than the rate of growth of wages. They argued that the *level* of pay was negatively related to the level of unemployment rather than the rate of growth in pay.

According to this argument, a worker in region A, which has a high level of unemployment, would earn lower wages than an equivalent worker in region B with lower levels of unemployment. Blanchard and Oswald's research casts doubt upon the standard explanation, in both regional economics and labour economics, that the wage rate in an area is positively linked to the level of unemployment in an area. In other words, the higher the level of unemployment, the higher the wage level needed to persuade someone to work in that area and vice versa.

Their work would tend to call into question some of the basic 'laws' of economics, particularly those related to something like the minimum wage. The conventional wisdom might be that if the minimum wage was introduced into an economy, the higher wage levels would be associated with a rise in unemployment. Blanchflower and Oswald's analysis suggests that this may not be the case and that in some areas there might even be a rise in the level of employment associated with a rise in wage levels.

Figure 18.8 highlights the traditional view of the effect of the imposition of a minimum wage set above the market wage level (W_1) on the level of unemployment. The minimum wage causes a fall in the quantity of labour demanded and an increase in the quantity supplied of labour (a movement along the D and S curves for labour). The result is an increase in the amount of unemployment, shown by the distance $Q3 - Q2$.

To understand this, it is important to refer back to the basic model of the labour market shown in Figure 18.9. If the demand for labour, for example, rose as indicated by a shift in the demand for labour curve to the right ($D_L - D_{L1}$), then there would be an excess demand for labour shown by the distance $Q2 - Q1$. Wage rates would rise in response to this shortage of labour and as the shortage is competed away, more people would end up being employed ($Q3$) at higher wage rates (W_2). A rise in wage rates, therefore, is positively correlated with a fall in unemployment and vice versa.

Blanchflower and Oswald's research was based around millions of observations. They identified the existence of wage curves in 16 countries and since the publication of their research in 1994, a number of other researchers have confirmed their findings. Blanchflower and Oswald suggested that their wage curve would have an elasticity of −0.1. What this refers to is the responsiveness of rates of pay to changes in unemployment. An elasticity of −0.1, therefore, would suggest that if we took two regions within an economy, region A and region B, and if unemployment was 2 per cent in region B but 4 per cent in region A, we would expect wages to be around 10 per cent lower in region A than B. This suggests some sort of causal relationship stemming from the level of unemployment in an area feeding through to the level of wages in that area, rather than the other way round.

The suggestion that there is a relationship between the rate of growth of wages (and by implication, inflation)

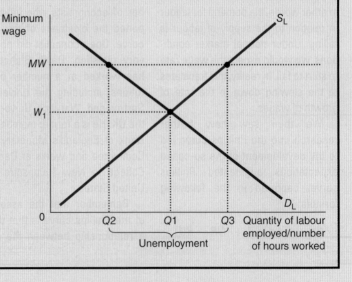

FIGURE 18.8

The Traditional Explanation of the Effect of a Minimum Wage Set Above the Equilibrium Wage Level

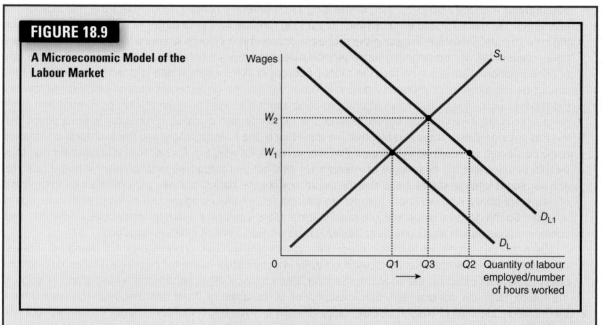

FIGURE 18.9

A Microeconomic Model of the Labour Market

and unemployment, as we saw in the early part of this chapter, has implications for policymakers. This is based in part on the idea that controlling the rate of growth in wages (and hence inflation) is an important step in controlling unemployment. If, however, Blanchflower and Oswald's research on wage curves is correct, it changes the emphasis of policy making both at a macro and at a micro level. Let us assume that the government are looking at an unemployment rate that they consider too high, and so want to reduce that rate. If they refer to

traditional macroeconomic models of the labour market, they might look at wages as being one way of reducing unemployment in that area – in other words, a fall in wages would help to bring about a reduction in unemployment.

If a wage curve does exist, then attempts to reduce unemployment in this way could backfire, since falling wages would be associated with higher unemployment! In addition, it might be believed that high unemployment in an area might be affected most dramatically by

focusing on high unemployment groups in that area – those with low levels of education, for example. It might be expected that these groups of people will be most likely to take on jobs that are created at lower wages and as such, policies to reduce unemployment could be achieved without a major impact on inflation. Again, the existence of a wage curve would tend to provide an argument against doing this. This is partly because it is the *level* of wages that are important rather than the rate of growth of wages.

INFLATION TARGETING

In many countries of the world today, including the UK and the Euro Area, the framework of monetary policy involves setting targets for inflation to be achieved over the medium run of two years or so, and then adjusting interest rates in order to achieve this objective. As we have pointed out in earlier chapters, setting interest rates is tantamount to setting the money supply if there is a stable and known relationship between the money supply and interest rates. However, the explicit focus on interest rates as the instrument of monetary policy, and medium-run inflation as the target of monetary policy, appears to have worked well for many economies. In the UK the move to the framework of inflation targeting arose as much out of the lessons of experience as out of the logic of economic reasoning.

Targeting

The level of the money supply and the exchange rate can be thought of as intermediate targets of monetary policy. That is to say, they may be targeted in order to achieve certain other, policy targets, such as real GDP growth, employment and inflation. Now, an important principle that we have learnt in our study of monetary policy is that, in the long run, monetary policy cannot affect the real side of the economy – i.e. real GDP and employment. In the long run, the only final target of monetary policy can be the inflation rate. Therefore, targeting the money supply or the exchange rate as a framework for monetary policy means that we are targeting those variables because it is felt that they will ultimately affect the rate of price inflation. Also, since neither the money supply nor the exchange rate is directly controllable, they cannot be instruments of monetary policy. In other words, the government cannot just set the level of the money supply it wants, it must attempt to bring about that level by open market operations and other means; similarly, it cannot just set the level of the exchange rate it wants, it must try to bring about that level by setting interest rates and by other means. Hence, the money supply and the exchange rate should really be viewed as intermediate targets that the government may aim for because it is believed that they will ultimately affect the final target of inflation. So why not just target the inflation rate? Interest rates (or at least some interest rates) are under the control of central banks, so they are definitely an instrument of monetary policy. And we know that raising interest rates reduces aggregate demand and so dampens inflation. So the government could just raise interest rates whenever inflation rose above a level that was considered desirable – say 2 per cent. This would be a crude form of inflation targeting.

There are two problems with this crude inflation targeting. First, changing (or not changing) interest rates today will not affect inflation today, it will only affect inflation in the future, since it takes time for the policy to have an effect on the economy. Second, there may be other factors that would affect inflation in the future. Suppose, for example, that inflation was at its target of 2 per cent per year. The central bank therefore decides not to change interest rates, since it is achieving its inflation target. However, suppose there was at the same time a wave of very high wage settlements in the economy, above any increases in labour productivity. Over the next six months to a year, this is expected to lead to a rise in price inflation in the economy as workers spend more and as firms pass on some of the wage increases in the form of higher prices. Should the central bank wait for the inflation to arrive, or should it act now by raising interest rates in anticipation of the inflationary pressures coming from higher wages? Clearly, the better policy is to target not today's inflation, which it is already too late to have any effect on, but future inflation. Of course, no one knows with certainty what future inflation is going to be, therefore a policy of inflation targeting generally involves targeting the forecast rate of inflation.

The inflation target in the UK at the time of writing is 2 per cent per year, as measured by the CPI, and to some extent, success in achieving the target is measured by whether the Bank of England's own inflation forecast up to two years ahead falls within 1 per cent of the target, above or below. Of course, it might be argued that the Bank of England is having it easy in the sense that it can judge itself whether or not it has achieved the target. However, an important element of successful inflation targeting is transparency: the Bank of England publishes detailed analyses of its forecasts and these are closely scrutinized. Second, if actual inflation does ever fall outside the range of plus or minus 1 per cent of the target, the Governor of the Bank of England is required to write a formal letter to the Chancellor of the Exchequer, explaining why inflation is out of the target range, what measures are being taken to get it back on course, and when it is expected to be back on target.

As we discussed in Chapter 10, both the Bank of England and the European Central Bank now pursue a policy of inflation targeting, and both target a level of inflation of 2 per cent. The country that pioneered inflation targeting was New Zealand, which adopted this policy in 1990. It was followed in 1991 by Canada, and in 1992 by the UK and Sweden. Like the UK, Sweden also adopted a policy of inflation targeting after it was forced to abandon its exchange rate peg in 1992. Other countries that have adopted inflation targeting in recent years include Norway and Switzerland.

CONCLUSION

This chapter has examined how economists' thinking about inflation and unemployment has evolved over time. We have discussed the ideas of many of the best economists of the 20th century: from the Phillips curve of Phillips, Samuelson and Solow, to the natural-rate hypothesis of Friedman and Phelps, to the rational expectations theory of Lucas, Sargent and Barro. Five of this group have already won Nobel prizes for their work in economics, and more are likely to be so honoured in the years to come. Our discussion has been based around the UK economy but the principles apply across other economies too – the UK is a convenient case study in the changing interpretation and application of economic theory.

Although the trade-off between inflation and unemployment has generated much intellectual turmoil over the past 40 years, certain principles have developed that today command consensus. Here is how Milton Friedman expressed the relationship between inflation and unemployment in 1968 (in an *American Economic Review* paper entitled 'The Role of Monetary Policy'):

> *There is always a temporary trade-off between inflation and unemployment; there is no permanent trade-off. The temporary trade-off comes not from inflation per se, but from unanticipated inflation, which generally means, from a rising rate of inflation. The widespread belief that there is a permanent trade-off is a sophisticated version of the confusion between 'high' and 'rising' that we all recognize in simpler forms. A rising rate of inflation may reduce unemployment, a high rate will not.*
>
> *But how long, you will say, is 'temporary'? … We can at most venture a personal judgment, based on some examination of the historical evidence that the initial effects of a higher and unanticipated rate of inflation last for something like two to five years.*

Today, nearly 40 years later, this statement still summarizes the view of most macroeconomists.

IN THE NEWS

Inflation Targeting

Having a target for inflation has been a mainstay of central bank policy over the last 20 years in many countries. However, the protracted economic difficulties following the financial crisis have raised questions about whether such targets ought to be abandoned.

Should Central Banks Abandon Inflation Targeting?

Ever since the Bank of England was granted independence in 1997, its main policy task has been to maintain inflation at a target level set by the government. Inflation targeting was first introduced in 1992 in the UK. Initially the target rate for inflation was 2.5 per cent but since 2003 has been 2.0 per cent. The average UK inflation rate from 1993–2013 has been 2.1 per cent but in the period from 2008, the average has been 3.2 per cent – well above the 2.0 per cent target. Having a target is meant to send out a signal to everyone that the central bank will act to bring inflation to as close to the target as possible. If inflation persists

above target interest rates may have to be raised to help achieve that target. But, in recent years the idea of raising interest rates has not been top of the Monetary Policy Committee (MPC) agenda; in a period where the economy of the UK has struggled, the idea of raising interest rates would be seen as potentially damaging to the economy.

This has raised the question of whether it is now time to abandon inflation targeting. In July 2013, the Bank of England got a new governor, Mark Carney. In the six months prior to him taking up his position he sparked a debate about whether his tenure would see him follow the inflation targeting which his predecessor, Mervyn King, believed in so strongly. Indeed, Mr Carney, giving

evidence before a Treasury Select Committee in February 2013 noted that under his watch, the Bank of England would follow in the footsteps for the US Federal Reserve in keeping interest rates low to ensure economic recovery was firmly underway and if that meant higher inflation in the process then that would be a price worth paying.

There were also suggestions that the UK Chancellor of the Exchequer would change the targets in the March 2013 budget and ask the Bank of England to focus on the twin targets of employment and inflation. This would allow the Bank of England to set interest rates with the aim of achieving set numerical targets for unemployment regardless of what happens to inflation. There has also

(*Continued*)

been talk that the Bank of England should adopt a policy of targeting nominal GDP (which effectively has the effect of reducing unemployment). The consequences, however, would be higher inflation (most economists agree with this) which in a time of weak economic growth might be seen as a reasonable trade-off. Question is, would the higher inflation be seen as temporary and once

Mervyn King was the governor of the Bank of England until July 2013.

recovery was well under way and strong, how would people react to the central bank tightening policy once again to bring inflation back under control? Would the credibility of the central bank be destroyed?

Some economists have already put forward the argument that the Bank of England abandoned inflation targeting around 2009 as the consequences for the economy of the financial crisis became more obvious, and it was clear that a period of continued sluggish growth and periodic recessions was in prospect. The fact that inflation has averaged well above the 2.0 per cent target is testament to this, they argue, and note that the explanatory letters from the Governor to the Chancellor of the Exchequer have been 'unconvincing'.

Mervyn King expressed some concern at the idea of abandoning inflation targeting and cited the experience of the 1960s when the UK targeted increasing economic growth which King said was unrealistic and unsustainable in that the price was higher inflation.

Questions

1 **Explain how monetary policy can be used to target inflation.**

2 **The average inflation rate in the UK has been just over the current target of 2.0 per cent over the 20-year period from 1993–2013. Should the success of inflation targeting be judged over such a period of time or is the fact that inflation has been much higher than target in the five years from 2009 to 2013 been more indicative of the success of monetary policy?**

3 **How would a central bank go about setting policies designed to target nominal GDP at a growth rate of (say) 5 per cent?**

4 **Why would central bank action to boost economic growth be likely to lead to more rapidly accelerating inflation?**

5 **Given the difficult economic conditions in many countries following the financial crisis, should central banks abandon inflation targeting and pursue a policy of growth?**

SUMMARY

- The Phillips curve describes a negative relationship between inflation and unemployment. By expanding aggregate demand, policymakers can choose a point on the Phillips curve with higher inflation and lower unemployment. By contracting aggregate demand, policymakers can choose a point on the Phillips curve with lower inflation and higher unemployment.

- The trade-off between inflation and unemployment described by the Phillips curve holds only in the short run. In the long run, expected inflation adjusts to changes in actual inflation, and the short-run Phillips curve shifts. As a result, the long-run Phillips curve is vertical at the natural rate of unemployment.

- The short-run Phillips curve also shifts because of shocks to aggregate supply. An adverse supply shock, such as the increase in world oil prices during the 1970s, gives policymakers a less favourable trade-off between inflation and unemployment. That is, after an adverse supply shock, policymakers have to accept a higher rate of inflation for any given rate of unemployment, or a higher rate of unemployment for any given rate of inflation.

- When the central bank contracts growth in the money supply to reduce inflation, it moves the economy along the short-run Phillips curve, which results in temporarily high unemployment. The cost of disinflation depends on how quickly expectations of inflation fall. Some economists argue that a credible commitment to low inflation can reduce the cost of disinflation by inducing a quick adjustment of expectations.

QUESTIONS FOR REVIEW

1 Phillips originally looked at the rate of change in money wages rather than inflation but the Phillips curve has come to be associated with the trade-off between inflation and unemployment. What is the relationship between the rate of change of money wages and inflation?

2 Explain why, in the short run, there might be a trade-off between inflation and unemployment.

3 Draw the short-run trade-off between inflation and unemployment. How might the central bank move the economy from one point on this curve to another?

4 Draw the long-run trade-off between inflation and unemployment. Explain how the short-run and long-run trade-offs are related.

5 Why do economists place such importance on the role of expectations in macroeconomic policy?

6 What's so natural about the natural rate of unemployment? Why might the natural rate of unemployment differ across countries?

7 Explain how expected inflation might cause a shift in the short-run Phillips curve.

8 Suppose a drought destroys farm crops and drives up the price of food. What is the effect on the short-run trade-off between inflation and unemployment?

9 What reasons are put forward for keeping central banks independent in setting monetary policy?

10 The central bank decides to reduce inflation. Use the Phillips curve to show the short-run and long-run effects of this policy. How might the short-run costs be reduced?

PROBLEMS AND APPLICATIONS

1 Suppose the natural rate of unemployment is 6 per cent. On one graph, draw two Phillips curves that can be used to describe the four situations listed here. Label the point that shows the position of the economy in each case.

   a. Actual inflation is 5 per cent and expected inflation is 3 per cent.

   b. Actual inflation is 3 per cent and expected inflation is 5 per cent.

   c. Actual inflation is 5 per cent and expected inflation is 5 per cent.

   d. Actual inflation is 3 per cent and expected inflation is 3 per cent.

2 Illustrate the effects of the following developments on both the short-run and long-run Phillips curves. Give the economic reasoning underlying your answers:

   a. a rise in the natural rate of unemployment
   b. a decline in the price of imported oil
   c. a rise in government spending
   d. a decline in expected inflation.

3 Suppose that a fall in consumer spending causes a recession.

   a. Illustrate the changes in the economy using both an aggregate supply/aggregate demand diagram and a Phillips curve diagram. What happens to inflation and unemployment in the short run?

   b. Now suppose that over time expected inflation changes in the same direction that actual inflation changes. What happens to the position of the short run Phillips curve? After the recession is over, does the economy face a better or worse set of inflation–unemployment combinations?

4 Suppose the economy is in a long-run equilibrium.

   a. Draw the economy's short-run and long-run Phillips curves.

   b. Suppose a wave of business pessimism reduces aggregate demand. Show the effect of this shock on your diagram from part (a). If the central bank undertakes expansionary monetary policy, can it return the economy to its original inflation rate and original unemployment rate?

   c. Now suppose the economy is back in long-run equilibrium, and then the price of imported oil rises. Show the effect of this shock with a new diagram like that in part (a). If the central bank undertakes expansionary monetary policy, can it return the economy to its original inflation rate and original unemployment rate? If the central bank undertakes contractionary monetary policy, can it return the economy to its original inflation rate and original unemployment rate? Explain why this situation differs from that in part (b).

5 Suppose the central bank believed that the natural rate of unemployment was 6 per cent when the actual natural rate was 5.5 per cent. If the central bank based its policy decisions on its belief, what would happen to the economy?

6 Suppose the central bank announced that it would pursue contractionary monetary policy in order to

reduce the inflation rate. Would the following conditions make the ensuing recession more or less severe? Explain.

a. Wage contracts have short durations.

b. There is little confidence in the central bank's determination to reduce inflation.

c. Expectations of inflation adjust quickly to actual inflation.

7 Some economists believe that the short-run Phillips curve is relatively steep and shifts quickly in response to changes in the economy. Would these economists be more or less likely to favour contractionary policy in order to reduce inflation than economists who had the opposite views?

8 Imagine an economy in which all wages are set in three-year contracts. In this world, the central bank announces a disinflationary change in monetary policy to begin immediately. Everyone in the economy believes the central bank's announcement. Would this disinflation be costless? Why or why not? What might the central bank do to reduce the cost of disinflation?

9 Given the unpopularity of inflation, why don't elected leaders always support efforts to reduce inflation? Economists believe that countries can reduce the cost of disinflation by letting their central banks make decisions about monetary policy without interference from politicians. Why might this be so?

10 Suppose policymakers accept the theory of the short run Phillips curve and the natural-rate hypothesis and want to keep unemployment close to its natural rate. Unfortunately, because the natural rate of unemployment can change over time, they aren't certain about the value of the natural rate. What macroeconomic variables do you think they should look at when conducting monetary policy?

19 SUPPLY-SIDE POLICIES

The focus of policy in the post-war era was firmly on managing aggregate demand. In the late 1960s and into the 1970s demand management came to be questioned and some economists began looking at the capacity of the economy – aggregate supply. In particular, economists began looking at the effects of (often) frequent changes in taxes which was a feature of demand management on the supply-side of the economy.

We have seen that in the long run, the aggregate supply curve is vertical but in the short run it slopes upwards from left to right. Shifting the AS curve to the right would increase the capacity of the economy and increase national income (and thus lower unemployment) but reduce pressure on prices. A focus on the supply-side of the economy could, therefore, help to bring about sustainable economic growth; higher growth, lower unemployment and stable or even lower inflation. Supply-side policies, therefore, focused on ways of influencing the factors which affect aggregate supply. If aggregate supply represents the quantity of goods and services that firms choose to produce at different price levels then looking at what influences firms' behaviour is an important starting point.

SHIFTS IN THE AGGREGATE SUPPLY CURVE

There is a range of factors which can cause the aggregate supply curve to shift as we saw in Chapter 16. We summarized these as changes in labour, physical or human capital, the availability of natural resources, changes in technology and expectations of the price level. This summary provides us with the bare bones on which to explore in more detail how shifts in the aggregate supply curve might arise.

So far we have looked at the AS curve in the short run as being upwards sloping and in the long run as vertical. The vertical long-run AS curve makes intuitive sense if you think about AS in terms of the capacity of the economy. Imagine that every individual in an economy who wanted to work at the going wage rate could find work (i.e. there was full employment), that every firm was producing at its maximum capacity and there were no machines lying idle then the economy would be producing at its maximum capacity which we will refer to as full employment output (Y_f).

We know that in the short run the AS curve can shift causing temporary deviations from this full employment output but eventually, once changes in prices, wages and misperceptions work through the economy, output returns to its long-run equilibrium. Changes in AD can cause fluctuations in economic activity and governments can use fiscal and monetary policy to manage demand to try and stabilize the fluctuations. However, if policies are put in place to boost AD, for example, the effects might depend on the extent of the output gap that exists and the flexibility of the economy to respond to the increase in AD. The extent to which unemployment is reduced and how far the price level changes will be affected by the flexibility of the economy.

Figure 19.1 shows a different shaped AS curve to those we have looked at so far. At the full employment level of output, the AS curve is vertical but between Y_1 and Y_f, the AS curve becomes increasingly steep, whereas between Y_2 and Y_1, the AS curve is almost horizontal. This is referred to as the new Keynesian aggregate supply curve.

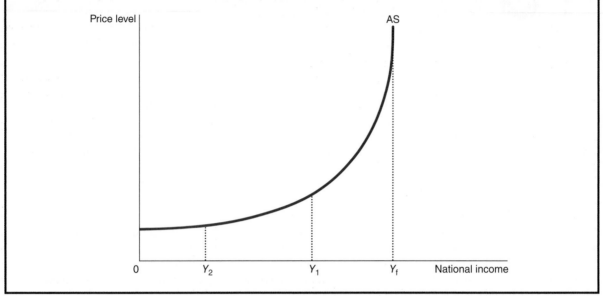

FIGURE 19.1

The New Keynesian Aggregate Supply Curve

The new Keynesian aggregate supply curve is vertical at full employment output Y_f. At low levels of national income, the AS curve is virtually horizontal reflecting the fact that there is considerable spare capacity in the economy but, as national income rises, the ability of firms to expand output becomes more difficult and so the AS curve becomes gradually steeper until it becomes vertical at full employment output.

Between the origin and Y_2, there is a considerable amount of spare capacity in the economy but that spare capacity begins to diminish the closer to full employment output at Y_f. This has implications for the effect on national income and the price level if aggregate demand shifts as shown in Figure 19.2. If the economy starts out at Y_1 with the price level P_1, there is considerable spare capacity in the economy and the output gap is large. If fiscal and/or monetary policy shifts the AD curve to the right, the increase in national income rises by a relatively large amount from Y_1 to Y_2. The increase in the price level is only small, suggesting that the Phillips curve is relatively shallow and the trade-off between the reduction in unemployment and the rise in the price level is favourable. If policy continues to push AD to the right, the trade-off changes and the increase in national income begins to get smaller the nearer to full employment output whilst the rise in the price level increase at a faster rate.

Why does the trade-off become less favourable over time? The reason is that as aggregate demand increases, the pressure on society's scarce resources becomes greater. If AD increased from AD_3 to AD_4, for example, firms would be looking to expand output to meet the increased demand and so would look to buy more factor inputs. As the demand for these factor inputs rises, the price of them increases. Certain types of labour might become scarce more quickly than others and wage rates in these industries might rise sharply as a result. The demand for skilled labour in the construction industry, for example, might rise but the supply of people with these skills tends to be inelastic in the short run. It takes time to train skilled bricklayers, plumbers, plasterers and electricians. Those who have these skills will find them in demand and they can sell their labour for higher wages as a result. Firms that pay the higher wages see their costs increase but with demand rising they feel they can pass on these higher costs to the consumer in the form of higher prices and so inflation begins to accelerate. The closer the economy comes to full employment output the greater will be the production bottlenecks that arise as resources become scarcer so the effect on prices will be greater but the ability of the economy to grow further will decline.

The supply-side focus arises because of the difficulty of policymakers knowing what the size of the output gap is at any particular moment in time; that is, where the economy is on the AS curve. The output gap can be calculated in two ways. The first is to subtract actual output from potential output where potential output is based on the assumption that markets are perfectly competitive. The second is to subtract actual output from natural output where natural output assumes imperfect competition and rigidities in prices and wages. We have seen how monetary and fiscal policy operate side-by-side and even if governments are not deliberately trying to influence aggregate demand, changes in tax rates, allowances and government spending decisions will have effects on the level of aggregate demand, whilst changes in monetary policy affect investment decisions and the exchange rate, and, as a result, net exports. If the net effect of monetary and fiscal policy is to boost aggregate demand, the size of the output gap will have an effect on the resulting changes in the price level and national income.

FIGURE 19.2

The Aggregate Supply Curve and Production Bottlenecks

Increases in AD when there is considerable spare capacity in the economy can lead to relatively large increases in national income with only relatively small rises in the price level. If AD keeps increasing resource constraints will eventually mean that national income will only rise by relatively small amounts but the pressure on resources will cause the price level to rise more quickly.

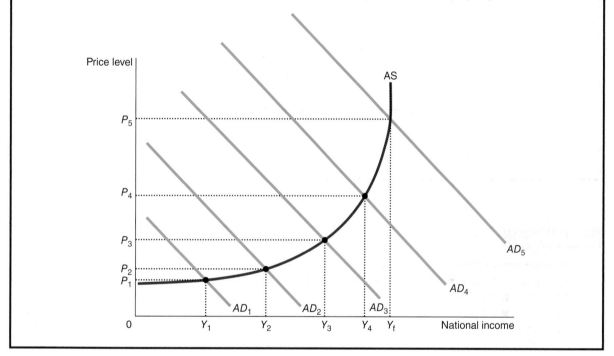

This is illustrated in Figure 19.3. Assume the economy in panel (a) is in equilibrium at Y_1. The output gap is given by the distance between full employment output and actual output $Y_f - Y_1$. An increase in AD to AD_2 would lead to a rise in national income to Y_2 and a rise in the price level to P_2. The output gap narrows but the economy is beginning to experience some bottlenecks in production and as a result the increase in national income has come at a price of accelerating inflation. Any further increases in AD would mean the economy is in danger of overheating – where supply-side constraints mean that the pressure on prices increases.

In panel (b), the initial equilibrium is given by Y_1 but the output gap, again given by $Y_f - Y_1$, is much smaller. The economy is already nearing the vertical section of the AS curve and an increase in AD means that the increase in national income is very small but the effect on the price level is much stronger. The economy is overheating and does not have the capacity to be able to cope with the rise in AD and so the main effect feeds through to prices.

The size of the output gap is simple in practice but much more difficult in reality to estimate. The models used vary and the size of the various parameters that modellers input into the equations can lead to widely differing results. If policymakers base decisions on an estimated output gap that is incorrect the effects of policy can be different to those anticipated. It is for this reason that supply-siders argue that a focus on increasing the productive capacity of the economy needs to be an important element of the policy mix.

FIGURE 19.3

The Effect of the Size of the Output Gap
Panel (a) shows the effect on national income and the price level of a rise in aggregate demand where the output gap is relatively large. In contrast, if the economy is in an initial equilibrium when the output gap is small as in panel (b), then a rise in AD will have a much larger effect on the price level.

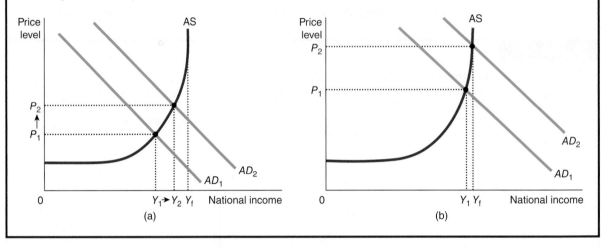

Supply-side economists suggest that if policy is focused on increasing the capacity of the economy then in the long run it is possible to increase national income but keep the price level more stable. This is illustrated in Figure 19.4. Assume society faces an initial AS curve, AS_1, and AD curve, AD_1. The initial equilibrium is at point A with a price level of P_1 and national income at Y_1. An increase in AD to AD_2 would, given the initial AS curve, see the economy begin to experience more significant production bottlenecks

FIGURE 19.4

Sustained Economic Growth
If supply-side policies are successful in shifting the AS curve from AS_1 to AS_2, an increase in aggregate demand from AD_1 to AD_2 results in a relatively large increase in national income from Y_1 to Y_2 but with only a modest increase in the price level from P_1 to P_2. The new AS curve is associated with an increased capacity of the economy shown by the increase in full employment output from Y_{f1} to Y_{f2}.

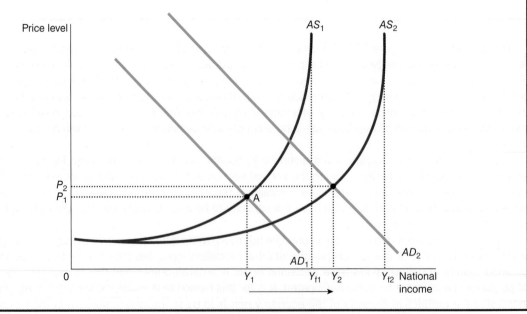

and as a result the price level would start to accelerate. If supply-side policies succeeded in shifting the AS curve to the right to AS_2, this would give a new full employment output capacity at Y_{f2} compared to Y_{f1}. The increase in aggregate demand to AD_2 would now result in a rise in national income to Y_2 from Y_1 but the increase in the price level would be relatively small rising from P_1 to P_2. Many economists would argue that a little inflation in an economy is a good thing as it acts as an incentive to firms to produce and expand. By shifting AS to the right, the economy could increase standards of living and reduce unemployment but keep prices stable (where price stability is defined as having an inflation rate which was deemed acceptable – i.e. the target inflation rate). This would represent sustained economic growth.

SELF TEST What are the factors which can cause a shift in the AS curve to the right? What is meant by 'production bottlenecks'?

TYPES OF SUPPLY-SIDE POLICIES

Supply-side economists have a fundamental belief in the power of markets and the private sector to allocate resources efficiently – at least more efficiently than might be the case with public sector provision. Policies, therefore, focus on the extent to which the working of markets can be improved to ensure more efficient allocation of resources. These policies are classed as **market-orientated supply-side policies**. If governments are going to intervene in the economy then supply-siders believe that the focus should be on investing in resources that improve the working of the economy such as developing infrastructure, improving research and development and investing in education. These policies are referred to as **interventionist policies**. We will now look at the policies which come under these broad classifications in more detail.

> **market-orientated supply-side policies** policies designed to free up markets to improve resource allocation through more effective price signals
> **interventionist supply-side policies** policies focused on improving the working of markets through investing in infrastructure, education and research and development

Market Orientated Supply-Side Policies

The intention of market orientated supply-side policies is to help markets work more effectively by improving the effectiveness of price signals so that resources are allocated more efficiently. Underpinning these policies is a philosophical belief that markets are the most effective way of allocating resources. The use of Keynesian demand management policies had led to government becoming more and more involved in the economy, with a number of industries or firms run by the state on behalf of the people as a whole. Many governments increasingly built up the welfare state to support those in need and, of course, all this government spending meant taxes had to be raised to pay for the increase in the services provided by the state.

Supply-side policies came to the fore in the 1980s when governments in the developed world were trying to cope with stagflation. This section is not intended to be a history lesson but there will be references to policies put in place by the governments in the United States and the UK to highlight key issues arising in supply-side policies. A core focus of what was referred to as the 'supply-side revolution' was on rolling back the influence of the state in the economy, cutting government spending, reforming the tax and benefit system to improve incentives, freeing up the labour market to make it more flexible and encouraging a more entrepreneurial culture in society. Many of the policies implemented were designed to improve incentives, which, as we know, is one of the *Ten Principles of Economics*.

Reform of Tax and Welfare Policy We have seen that taxes have an effect on incentives and can lead to distortions in market outcomes. Welfare payments can be viewed as negative taxes giving people support when they fall on hard times. Few would disagree with the necessity of taxing firms, products and individuals to generate tax revenue for government and also to influence behaviour in desired directions such as reducing smoking or encouraging reductions in waste. If we acknowledge the fact that taxes – positive and negative – distort market outcomes, then the debate shifts to the level of taxation.

In many countries in Europe and in the US, income and corporate taxes have been relatively high in the 1970s and 1980s. In the UK, for example, the basic rate of income tax was 33 per cent in 1978, there were also other higher rates associated with higher levels of income, with the top tax rate being 98 per cent on unearned income and 83 per cent on earned income. Corporation tax in the UK in 1978 was 53 per cent for larger companies and 42 per cent for small companies. In the US, income tax rates ranged from 14 per cent to 70 per cent and corporate tax rates were near 50 per cent. Corporate taxes in Germany in 1981 were around 56 per cent, in Norway just over 50 per cent, 48 per cent in the Netherlands and in Sweden almost 58 per cent. Table 19.1 shows the top rates of income tax in a selection of nine European countries for 1979, 1995 and 2012.

TABLE 19.1	Top Rates of Income Tax in Nine European Counties, 1979–2012		
Country	Top Income tax rate 1979 (%)	Top Income tax rate 1995 (%)	Top Income tax rate 2012 (%)
Belgium	76.3	55.0	50.0
Denmark	66.0	63.5	55.0
Germany	56.0	53.0	45.0
Ireland	60.0	48.0	48.0
Netherlands	72.0	60.0	52.0
Norway	75.4	13.7	47.8
Portugal	80.0	40.0	46.5
Sweden	86.5	30.0	56.6
UK	83.0	40.0	50.0

Supply-siders argued that high rates of income and corporate taxes were acting as a disincentive to individuals and to businesses. We need here to remind ourselves of the distinction between average and marginal tax rates. Remember that marginal tax rates refer to the amount of tax taken on every extra euro of earnings. In the UK, some people faced a marginal tax rate of 83 per cent – the government would leave the individual with just 17 pence from every extra pound earned. Supply-siders argued that such high rates of tax acted as a significant disincentive to work and to be entrepreneurial if the rewards from hard work were subject to such rates.

Cutting both income and corporate taxes, therefore, could lead to the incentive for people to take work and work harder (more hours) if the rewards were greater. Income tax rates, it was argued, altered the trade-off between work and leisure. Higher tax rates reduce the opportunity cost of leisure and so people will opt to reduce work and take more leisure. If tax rates are lowered and people get to keep more of the income they earn, the effect is like an increase in wages. The substitution effect is reinforced by the income effect and labour supply increases.

High corporate and income taxes also act as an incentive for firms and individuals to engage in tax avoidance (which is legal) or tax evasion (which is illegal). Higher tax rates, it is argued, do encourage firms and individuals to find ways in which their tax liability can be reduced, which may include putting money into offshore 'tax havens', firms spending money on tax-deductible assets which may not have any major impact on productivity (like investing in plusher office suites, buying luxury company cars, locating conferences at more luxurious venues and so on), or on channelling income into offshore companies which then return the money in the form of 'loans' on which there is no income tax. Such schemes are not illegal but some would claim that they are morally wrong. Tax evasion is illegal and refers to attempts by firms and individuals to avoid declaring income which is subject to taxation. This might be in the form of traders accepting cash for work carried out which is then not declared as income, through to more sophisticated money laundering schemes. Estimates in the UK, for example, put the cost of tax evasion at around £14 billion a year and some research by the Tax Justice Network in 2011 put the cost of tax avoidance across 145 countries at $3.1 trillion (€2.39 trillion or £2.03 trillion).

Reducing tax rates can change incentives to work and also incentives to avoid or evade paying taxes. Cutting tax rates can, therefore, mean that tax revenues actually increase. An example serves to illustrate. Assume that the top rate of income tax in a country is 80 per cent and that this rate applies to the whole of an individual's income (in reality most income tax regimes in country's are progressive and stepped so that those on lower incomes pay a lower rate compared to those on higher rates). An individual earning €500,000 would have to pay €400,000 in tax and gets to keep the remaining €100,000. If the government reduced the tax rate to 60 per cent, the individual faces the incentive that they get to keep more of every €1 of earnings which acts as a powerful incentive to work harder. The individual works harder in the next year and earns €750,000, on which her pay tax of €450,000 and gets to keep €300,000. The individual has more of an incentive to work harder because she gets to keep more of her earnings and the government generates more in overall tax revenue.

Income and corporate tax rates fell in many countries across Europe in the 1980s and into the 1990s. In addition to reducing actual tax rates, governments can also change tax allowances which relate to the amount of income which can be earned before having to pay tax. In the UK, for example, the Coalition Government, which took office in 2010, changed tax allowances so that workers will not pay tax on the first £10,000 of income compared to an allowance of around £6,500 which was in existence when it took office. Changing tax rates not only acts as an incentive to work harder and be more entrepreneurial, it is argued, it also has an effect on those who are looking for work. If tax rates are high or tax allowances are low, it can be the case that the incentive for people to go into work and come off benefits is also low. Assume, for example, an individual was receiving €10,000 a year in various benefits but pays no income tax. A job becomes available which pays €12,000. If the worker takes the job but then becomes liable for tax at a rate of (say) 25 per cent on all his earnings, then he will receive an after-tax income of €9,000. There is no incentive for the person to take the job, to come off benefits and pay income tax. If the tax rate were reduced to (say) 10 per cent, the person would receive an after tax income €10,800 and so there would be more of an incentive to take the job and come off benefits. Not only would the government be better off by not having to pay this individual benefits, it would be receiving €1,200 in tax revenue – a net benefit to the government of €11,200. In addition, by getting a job the individual is now not subject to the same issues and problems we out-lined as the costs of unemployment to individuals in Chapter 7, which reduces the social externalities associated with unemployment.

This approach is also linked with reform of the welfare system to provide incentives to individuals to get off benefits and into work. By making access to benefits subject to more rigorous tests and/or reducing welfare payments, individuals are forced to reassess their position, not become so reliant on the welfare state and look to find ways to support themselves. This means they might have to be more flexible in taking jobs which they may otherwise have shunned because they did not match to their expectations, wage demands or qualifications.

The combined effects of these policies mean that the labour market is more efficient with fewer people being voluntarily unemployed, with those in work prepared to work harder and be more productive and for enterprise and initiative to be rewarded.

The analysis so far is fairly intuitive but the reality depends on a number of factors not least the elasticity of supply of labour. If the elasticity of supply of labour is relatively low then any increase in wages through tax cuts or changes in allowances will only have a limited effect on the increase in the supply of labour (often measured in labour hours). If the elasticity of supply of labour was 0.1, for example, a rise in the wage rate of 5 per cent would only lead to an increase in labour supply of 0.5 per cent. The long run elasticity of supply of labour, however, might be larger than those in the short run because workers have time to adjust their behaviour. Research by Nobel Prize-winning economist, Edward Prescott, in 2002 suggested that there was a considerable difference between the elasticities of labour supply in France and the US which were largely due to differences in tax systems between the two countries.

CASE STUDY   The Laffer Curve and Supply-Side Economics

One day in 1974, rumour has it that the American economist, Arthur Laffer, sat in a Washington restaurant with some prominent journalists and politicians. He took out a napkin and drew a figure on it to show how tax rates affect tax revenue. The illustration looked like that shown in Figure 19.5. Laffer then suggested that the United States was on the downwards sloping side of this curve. Tax rates were so high, he argued, that reducing them would actually raise tax revenue.

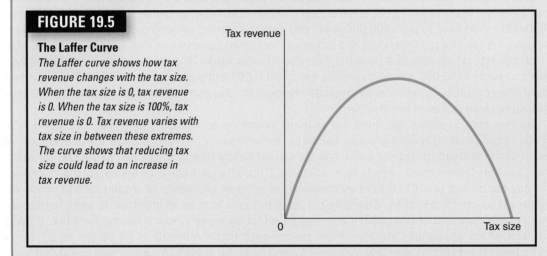

FIGURE 19.5

The Laffer Curve
The Laffer curve shows how tax revenue changes with the tax size. When the tax size is 0, tax revenue is 0. When the tax size is 100%, tax revenue is 0. Tax revenue varies with tax size in between these extremes. The curve shows that reducing tax size could lead to an increase in tax revenue.

Tax revenue

0   Tax size

Most economists were sceptical of Laffer's suggestion. The idea that a cut in tax rates could raise tax revenue was correct as a matter of economic theory, but there was more doubt about whether it would do so in practice. There was little evidence for Laffer's view that tax rates – in the United States or elsewhere – had in fact reached such extreme levels.

Nevertheless, the thinking underlying the **Laffer curve** (as it became known) became very influential in policy circles during the 1980s, particularly in the USA during the years of President Ronald Reagan's administration and in the UK during Prime Minister Margaret Thatcher's government. Tax rates – particularly income tax rates – were cut aggressively in both countries during the 1980s.

> **Laffer curve** the relationship between tax rates and tax revenue

In the UK, for example, under Prime Minister Thatcher the top marginal rate of income tax was cut from 83 per cent to 60 per cent in 1980 and then again to 40 per cent in 1988. Economists have, however, found it hard to trace any strong incentive effects of these tax cuts leading to increases in total tax revenue as the Laffer curve would suggest. A study by the UK Institute for Fiscal Studies (IFS), for example, concluded that at most about 3 per cent of the increase in tax revenue between 1980 and 1986 could be attributed to the 1980 income tax cut.

In the USA, President Reagan also cut taxes aggressively, but the result was less tax revenue, not more. Revenue from personal income taxes in the United States (per person, adjusted for inflation) fell by 9 per cent from 1980 to 1984, even though average income (per person, adjusted for inflation) grew by 4 per cent over this period. The tax cut, together with policymakers' unwillingness to restrain spending, began a long period during which the US government spent more than it collected in taxes. Throughout Reagan's two terms in office, and for many years thereafter, the US government ran large budget deficits.

Yet Laffer's argument is not completely without merit. Although an overall cut in tax rates normally reduces revenue, some taxpayers at some times may be on the wrong side of the Laffer curve. The idea that cutting taxes can raise revenue may be correct if applied to those taxpayers facing the highest tax rates, but most people face lower marginal rates. Where the *typical* worker is on the top end of the Laffer curve, it may be more appropriate. In Sweden in the early 1980s, for instance, the typical worker faced a

Arthur Laffer – the man behind the Laffer curve.

marginal tax rate of about 80 per cent. Such a high tax rate provides a substantial disincentive to work. Studies have suggested that Sweden would indeed have raised more tax revenue if it had lowered its tax rates.

Policymakers disagree about these issues in part because they disagree about the size of the relevant elasticities. The more elastic that supply and demand are in any market, the more taxes in that market distort behaviour, and the more likely it is that a tax cut will raise tax revenue. There is no debate, however, about the general lesson: how much revenue the government gains or loses from a tax change cannot be computed just by looking at tax rates. It also depends on how the tax change affects people's behaviour.

SELF TEST Consider the respective size of the income and substitution effects on the supply of labour curve as a result of a cut in higher rate taxes. ● Under what circumstances would a cut in tax rates actually lead to a backwards bending supply curve of labour?

Flexible Labour Markets In addition to changing the tax and benefits system, supply-siders argue for more flexibility in labour markets. There are different aspects to this policy which include reducing the power of trade unions and improving market signals to both employers and workers. Trade unions can raise wages above market rates. The more powerful are trades unions the higher they can push wages above market rates. In the 1970s and into the 1980s, the power of trade unions in the UK was substantial; days lost to strikes averaged 12.8 million per year in the 1970s. The UK government argued that trade unions exercised too much power and passed a series of new laws which reduced their power considerably. The result has been that trade unions had to adapt and evolve and the number of people belonging to trade unions and the number of days lost to strikes fell sharply in the latter part of the 1980s and beyond. Many more people now negotiate pay levels with employers individually or at local level rather than through unions and supply-siders would argue that wage rates more accurately reflect market conditions.

More flexible labour markets also relate to the ease with which employers can respond to market conditions by adjusting the labour force. This is sometimes referred to as the ability to 'hire and fire'. The more flexible the labour market, the fewer rigidities that would exist.

Flexible labour markets might include the use of short-term contracts with workers, having more flexible working arrangement so that workers with the right skills are attracted to work, and being able to shed workers more easily when the economy is contracting. Critics argue that flexible labour markets can put the interests of employers before those of workers and a balance does have to be struck between the rights of both parties.

Labour markets can also be made more flexible by improving market information for both employers and employees such that those people looking for work can be matched with those seeking employment. Many governments provide so-called 'job centres' through which employers can advertise jobs and those looking for work can attend to get advice, be put in touch with prospective employers and given help with improving their CVs, interview skills, job application techniques and so on.

Reducing Government Spending The more money government spends the more it has to raise in tax revenue and also to borrow. We have seen in Chapter 17 how any fiscal expansion can be moderated by the crowding out effect. It follows that if governments were able to reduce spending and borrow less the opposite effect would occur – sometimes referred to as 'crowding-in'. Cutting back the amount that governments borrow has been a feature of the post-financial crisis austerity programmes which many countries have had to implement. If borrowing can be scaled back, interest rates will fall and this has an effect on firms' decisions to invest.

In addition to the crowding-in argument, there is a fundamental belief among supply-siders that government spending is not likely to be as efficient as the equivalent spending by the private sector. If government, therefore, steps back from its involvement in the economy and leaves resource allocation more to the private sector, the funds will be used more productively and more efficiently which will improve the productive capacity of the economy.

In practice, many governments find it extremely difficult to cut back spending. The effects on government services and those who use it can be considerable and the sort of people who are most affected are often the poor and the most vulnerable in society such as the elderly, the mentally ill, children and those who require social and/or health care. The political decisions which have to be made when government spending is cut back are extremely difficult – few governments can be so sure of the mandate they receive from the electorate to make the sorts of decisions which would lead to a substantial fall in government spending when so many people are likely to be affected in an adverse way. Closing hospitals, schools, social care programmes, homes for the elderly and mentally ill might save considerable sums of money but represent electoral suicide.

Privatization and Deregulation One of the major changes in the economy of the UK in the last 30 years has been **privatization**, the move to transfer public ownership of assets to the private sector and the increase in the role of private sector firms in providing government services. Privatization has also been a feature of other European countries including Austria, Denmark, Finland, France, Germany, Ireland, Italy, the Netherlands and Spain.

> **privatization** the transfer of public ownership of assets to the private sector

In the post-war era in the UK, many industries were state owned – coal, the railways, the utilities (water, gas and electricity), steel, and telecommunications being key examples and in addition a number of firms were taken into state ownership including some in the motor, aviation and engineering industries. During the 1980s and 1990s, many of these industries and firms were sold and became private sector entities. In addition other services such as refuse collection, cleaning and catering services were opened up to provision by private sector organizations.

Once again, the philosophical underpinning of privatization in all its forms is the belief that the private sector, driven by providing high quality services and the profit motive, are more likely to provide the services required by the public at lower cost, at higher productivity levels and more efficiently than if provision was in the public sector. It was also argued that transferring assets to the private sector would help increase competition with the resulting benefits of lower prices and increased choice.

It is the subject of much debate as to the extent to which the benefits which were at the heart of the justification for privatization have been realized. The privatization of natural monopolies such as water, gas and electricity has created a complex system which many consumers find difficulty in understanding and despite regulatory bodies being set up to monitor the activities of these now private monopolies, there is some suspicion that the existence of monopoly power has reduced consumer surplus and led to deadweight losses. There are some studies that have suggested that privatization has delivered better services, improved products, lower prices and more choice, more efficiently for the public.

In addition to privatization programmes, many governments looked to pass legislation which cut back on the regulations that were argued to impede the efficient working of financial and goods markets. Deregulation has succeeded in removing some of these imperfections in the market. For example, in transport, local bus routes have been deregulated to prevent local monopolies which have resulted in more choice and lower prices for consumers. In financial markets, there has been an explosion of new products and much greater freedom for individuals and firms to be able to access credit. Whilst this did have some impact on the global economy in the 1990s and into the 2000s, many have argued that deregulation went too far and that appropriate checks and balances were not in place to prevent the financial crisis in 2007–2008.

SELF TEST Why do policies to improve the flexibility of labour markets have to balance the rights of employers and employees?

Interventionist Supply-Side Policies

The creation of knowledge is a public good and that firms free ride on knowledge created by others and as a result devote too few resources to creating new knowledge. In addition, the investment in infrastructure such as communications networks, roads, rail, ports and airports is vital to the effectiveness of an economy but the sort of sums needed to invest in this sort of infrastructure and the risk involved is often extremely high and the exploitation of the assets for profit by private firms not always easy, obvious or in some cases desirable. For example, the development of new motorway systems raises concerns among local people who are affected by the negative externalities and of environmentalists. The planning process can often take many years and be extremely expensive in addition to the actual cost of construction. The result is that governments often take the lead in the provision of such infrastructure, albeit using private firms as noted above. Interventionist supply-side policies refer to the ways in which governments seek to encourage investment in education, training, research and development and infrastructure and location of firms in order to help the economy work more effectively and efficiently.

Infrastructure Investment Governments will often take the lead in providing funds for infrastructure projects which have been identified as having long-term beneficial effects on the economy and will help to improve capacity. The sort of projects that governments support are invariably identified as being important in helping businesses to be more efficient, cutting costs and waste and improving supply chains. Improvements to roads, rail, ports and airports help firms to distribute goods more efficiently; improvements to communications networks help to make service industries more efficient and developments to energy and water supplies through the development of new power stations or improvements to supply networks can also help firms secure their energy needs and can help reduce cost if these networks operate more efficiently.

Investment in Education and Training The school and higher education system in an economy is a source of improvements in the quality of future human capital. Whilst many would not see education as purely a means of producing future workers, the sort of skills which school and university leavers have influence their ability to secure work and their productivity levels. As we have seen, productivity is a key factor in improving economic growth and standards of living.

The sort of education system that a country has will, therefore, be important and a number of countries have invested in trying to improve standards. The difficulty comes in defining what appropriate standards are for the individuals and for wider society. Some countries place a heavy emphasis on improving maths and science skills because these are crucial in helping to create new knowledge and innovation in industry.

Governments might provide grants or allowances to help boost interest in maths, science and engineering degrees; maths and physics graduates may be given incentives to put their skills to use in teaching in schools where there tends to be a paucity of highly qualified individuals in these subject areas.

Governments may also help to support training; firms may be reluctant to invest too many resources into training workers because of the lack of control they have over what workers do with the training they receive. On the one hand, a better trained workforce is beneficial to a firm because it makes workers more productive. It also makes workers more marketable and there is a risk that the worker moves on to a better job and another firm will benefit from the investment in training made by the initial firm. By providing help and support for training, governments may help to overcome this free-rider problem.

Research and Development R&D is essential to the long-term improvement of knowledge creation, the development of new products and new processes. R&D is, however, expensive and, as noted, unless the results can be protected in some way, the knowledge created becomes a public good. This is one of the reasons why many governments invest in supporting and funding research and development. Research bodies can be set up which receive requests for funding from firms and from higher education institutions, sometimes in partnership, who then decide on the allocation of funds based on the perceived value and importance of the research being proposed. Governments may also provide tax credits, tax relief or grants to help support R&D in smaller firms.

Regional or Industrial Policies In a number of European countries, the economy is now evenly balanced – there are regions which are poorer than others. Firms will often gravitate to locate where the markets are biggest or where there are natural advantages such as ports, good infrastructure links and so on. Some regions are poor because they used to be the centre of industries that have declined. The decline of industries such as shipbuilding, iron and steel, the motor industry and the coal industry, for example, has not been matched by new industries springing up to absorb the jobs lost and as a result a negative multiplier process can take hold which means the region may stay economically undeveloped for long periods. Governments may seek to reverse such economic imbalance by locating some of its own activities in these regions, providing investment grants, premises at reduced rents, employment subsidies and other measures to encourage firms to locate in these areas and develop jobs. The intention is that in encouraging investment in these areas a regional multiplier effect will take hold.

SELF TEST Why is investing in the right sort of education and training considered important to the success of interventionist policies?

CONCLUSION

Supply-side policies have an intuitive feel to them; one of the main problems, however, is that shifting the aggregate supply curve to the right is a long-term process. Investing in education, training and research and development, for example, can boost the quality of human capital but the benefits to the economy may not be felt for many years. Market-orientated policies may sound impressive and laudable but the evidence to support the effectiveness of such policies is not overwhelming. It is perhaps safe to say that policies to improve the efficiency of markets and the capacity of the economy have to be carried out hand-in-hand with other policies and not be seen as being an either/or policy option to fiscal and monetary policy. Indeed, the differences between fiscal, monetary and supply-side policies are sometimes difficult to disentangle. If a government announces it is investing billions in a high-speed rail network does this represent a fiscal boost or is it purely focused on improving the supply-side of the economy?

IN THE NEWS

Supply-Side Policies in an Economic Slowdown

The economic problems facing many countries in the wake of the financial crisis have presented new challenges to policymakers. After several years of attempting to reverse economic decline through fiscal and monetary policy, attention is once again turning to the supply-side option.

Time to Look at the Supply-side Again?

Consider the scenario facing governments in a number of European countries in 2013. Economic growth is barely above zero, inflation remains at levels above target, unemployment in some countries is extremely high but in others, whilst having risen, has not reached the sort of levels predicted or implied by the sluggish GDP growth rates. Interest rates are at historically low levels but concerns over the size of government debt mean that austerity measures have to be pursued if confidence in the financial markets in the government and its policies is to be maintained. This means that the fiscal options open to governments are very limited; if anything, taxes have to be increased and government spending cut back further if targets to reduce debt are to be realized. With the further options for monetary and fiscal policy looking exhausted do supply-side options offer any hope? Why would supply-side policies fare any better? One suggestion is that the problems facing the UK government in 2013 is that there are major structural deficiencies in the economy. The fact that inflation in the UK had been way above target (an average of 3.2 per cent for the five-year period prior to 2013 compared to a target level of 2.0 per cent) would suggest that demand deficiency is not the problem. The fact that unemployment had not risen to the sort of levels predicted after the financial crisis, accompanied by increases in employment rates, further hint at

the problems facing the UK not being with a lack of demand.

The stagnant economic growth in the UK and a number of other European countries would suggest that solutions lie with further monetary policy options such as more quantitative easing and/or, as had been advocated by the UK Labour party in opposition, that it was pertinent to borrow in the short-term to stimulate growth by spending on projects to kick-start the economy. In an interview with the *Asahi Shimbun*, a Japanese news service in March 2013, the outgoing Governor of the Bank of England, Mervyn King, said: 'I think governments in the industrialized world do need to understand the importance of supply-side policies, such as deregulation, in order to ensure that demand will recover, not just in order to make the economy more efficient, but as a mechanism for supporting current demand.' Around the same time, the *New Statesman* magazine published a list of 20 recommendations for the Spring 2013 Budget for the UK Chancellor. Part of the recommendations included some supply-side reforms such as a Small Business Incentive Scheme which included exemptions from regulations for small businesses, such as not having to pay the minimum wage for those under 21, abolishing national pay bargaining in the public sector, simplifying planning legislation and encouraging local councils to cooperate in identifying sites for new Garden Cities. Such calls for a renewed focus on supply-side policies might suggest that the fiscal and monetary options are indeed

exhausted and that the solution to the problems of sluggish growth in many European countries and in the UK, lie in the longer-term restructuring of the economy to improve capacity.

Questions

1 **Why have some governments had to adopt austerity policies to cut back borrowing and shrink the size of the deficit even though their economies have been either in recession or barely growing?**

2 **What is meant by 'structural deficiencies' in an economy?**

3 **In the UK in 2012–2013, employment rates were rising and inflation remained above target. Using an AS/AD diagram which utilizes the new Keynesian AS curve, explain what you think might be happening to the economy as aggregate demand rises.**

4 **Given your answer to Question 3 above, how would supply-side policies remedy the situation?**

5 **Look at the supply-side reforms suggested by the *New Statesman*. Explain how these reforms, if implemented, would help boost the supply-side of the economy?**

Reform of planning laws would make it easier to redevelop derelict land and would be one example of a supply-side policy which might help to stimulate the economy.

SUMMARY

- Supply-side policies became a focus of many governments in the 1980s and into the 1990s.
- The focus is on policies designed to shift the AS curve to the right.
- Shifting the AS curve to the right can lead to sustained economic growth which increases national income but keeps prices stable countering the production bottlenecks that can occur if the focus is on increasing aggregate demand through fiscal or monetary policy.

- Supply-side policies can take two main forms – market-orientated policies or interventionist policies.
- Market-orientated policies are designed to free up markets so that they allocate resources more effectively and efficiently.
- Interventionist policies are designed to improve the working of the market and which require government intervention to overcome the public good element of the investment in infrastructure education, training and research and development.

QUESTIONS FOR REVIEW

1 What is meant by 'sustainable economic growth'?

2 Explain the shape of the new Keynesian AS curve.

3 What are the two ways in which the output gap can be calculated and what is the difference between them?

4 What is the relevance of the size of the output gap in policy making?

5 Using an AS/AD diagram, show how a rise in AD could lead to a rise in national income but with no change in the price level.

6 What are the two main types of supply-side policy and what is the difference between them?

7 Why do supply-siders emphasize the importance of marginal tax rates in relation to incentives?

8 What is the Laffer curve?

9 Why do flexible labour markets improve the efficiency and capacity of the economy?

10 Why is it necessary for governments to invest in education, training and research and development?

PROBLEMS AND APPLICATIONS

1 Using the new Keynesian AS curve, explain why when the output gap is very large the AS curve has an almost horizontal slope.

2 Why might governments find it difficult to accurately measure the size of the output gap?

3 Assume that a government is successful in shifting the AS curve to the right. Show what happens to the Phillips curve in such a situation.

4 What sort of trade-offs do governments face if a decision was being considered to reduce the level of welfare benefits as part of a market-orientated supply-side policy?

5 Governments who have implemented major cuts in higher rates of income tax have been accused of giving more money to the rich at the expense of the poor. Construct an argument to counter such an accusation.

6 What sort of assumptions underlie the policy that cuts in income taxes would increase the supply of labour hours offered in an economy?

7 What are the potential costs and benefits of policies designed to improve the flexibility of labour markets?

8 Why do governments find it difficult to reduce spending?

9 A government announces a decision to increase investment in spending on higher education with the intention of increasing the participation rate in higher education by young people to 45 per cent (i.e. that 45 per cent of school leavers choose to go to university).

a. Does it matter what sort of degrees these young people do at university?

b. To what extent is the proportion of young people going on to university an important factor in improving the quality of human capital?

c. What else might the government need to put in place to ensure that the policy was a longer-term success (hint: will there be appropriate jobs for young people when they graduate)?

10 How would a government be able to tell whether a policy of increasing private sector involvement in public sector services provision actually lead to a more efficient outcome compared to having those same services provided by the public sector?

PART 8
INTERNATIONAL MACROECONOMICS

20 COMMON CURRENCY AREAS AND EUROPEAN MONETARY UNION

During the 1990s, a number of European nations decided to give up their national currencies and use a new, common currency called the *euro* by joining European Economic and Monetary Union (EMU). Why did these countries decide to do this? What are the costs and advantages of adopting a common currency among a group of countries? Is it optimal for Europe to have a single currency? In this chapter we'll look at some of these issues, drawing on our macroeconomics tool box that we've been developing over the past several chapters.

First, a definition: a **common currency area** is a geographical area throughout which a single currency circulates as the medium of exchange. Another term for a common currency area is a *currency union*, and a closely related phenomenon is a *monetary union*: a monetary union is, strictly speaking, a group of countries that have adopted permanently and irrevocably fixed exchange rates among their various currencies. Nevertheless, the terms common currency area, currency union and monetary union are often used more or less interchangeably, and in this chapter we'll follow this practice.

common currency area a geographical area throughout which a single currency circulates as the medium of exchange

Usually we speak of common currency areas when the people of a number of economies, generally corresponding to different nation states, have taken a decision to adopt a common currency as their medium of exchange, as was the case with the European monetary union. Let's start by taking a closer look at EMU and its currency, the euro.

THE EURO

There are currently 18 countries that have joined **European Economic and Monetary Union**, or EMU. (Note that 'EMU' stands for 'Economic and Monetary Union', not European Monetary Union, as is often supposed.) The countries that currently form the euro area are Austria, Belgium, Cyprus, Estonia, Finland, France, Germany, Greece, Ireland, Italy, Latvia, Luxembourg, Malta, the Netherlands, Portugal, Slovakia, Slovenia and Spain (informally known as 'euroland' but more correctly as the euro area). The move towards a single European currency has a very long history. The main landmarks in its formation, started in 1992 with the Maastricht Treaty (formally known as the Treaty on European Union), which laid down (among other things) various criteria for being eligible to join the proposed currency union. In order to participate in the new currency, member states had to meet strict criteria such as a government budget deficit of less than 3 per cent of GDP, a government debt-to-GDP ratio of less than 60 per cent, combined with low inflation and interest rates close to the EU average. The Maastricht Treaty also laid down a timetable for the introduction of the new single currency and rules concerning the setting up of a European Central Bank (ECB). The ECB actually came into existence in June 1998 and forms, together with the national central banks of the countries making up the common currency area, the European System of Central Banks (ESCB), which is given responsibility for ensuring price stability and implementing the single European monetary policy.

> **European Economic and Monetary Union** the European currency union that has adopted the euro as its common currency

The single European currency – the euro – officially came into existence on 1 January 1999 when 12 countries adopted it (although Greece did not join the EMU until 1 January 2001). On this date, exchange rates between the old national currencies of euro area countries were irrevocably locked and a few days later the financial markets began to trade the euro against other currencies such as the US dollar, as well as to trade securities denominated in euros.

The period from the beginning of 1999 until the beginning of 2002 was a transitional phase, with national currencies still circulating within the euro area countries and prices in shops displayed in both euros and local currency. On 1 January 2002 the first euro notes and coins came into circulation and, within a few months, the switch to the euro as the single medium of exchange was complete throughout the euro area.

The formation of EMU was an enormously bold step for the 12 countries initially involved. Most of the national currencies that have been replaced by the euro had been in circulation for hundreds if not thousands of years. Why did these countries deem it so important to abandon these currencies and adopt a single, common currency? Undoubtedly, part of the answer to this question lies in the realm of politics as much as in the realm of economics. However, there was also a belief that having a common European currency would help 'complete the market' for European goods, services and factors of production that had been an on-going project for much of the post-war period. More generally, the costs and benefits of adopting a common currency can be analysed within the framework of macroeconomic theory. Let's start by taking a look at the euro and its relationship to the Single European Market.

THE SINGLE EUROPEAN MARKET AND THE EURO

Following the devastation of two World Wars in the first half of the 20th century, each of which had initially centred on European conflicts, some of the major European countries (in particular France and Germany) expressed a desire to make further wars impossible between them through a process of strong economic integration that, it was hoped, would lead to greater social and political harmony. This led to the development of the European Economic Community (EEC) – now referred to as the **European Union**, or EU. Initially the EU consisted of just six countries: Belgium, Germany, France, Italy, Luxembourg and the Netherlands. In 1973, Denmark, Ireland and the United Kingdom joined. Greece joined in 1981, Spain and Portugal in 1986, and Austria, Finland and Sweden in 1995. In 2004 the biggest ever enlargement took place with ten new countries joining. Croatia became a member state in July 2013 and at the time of writing there are five 'candidate countries' seeking membership. These are Turkey, the Former Yugoslav Republic of Macedonia, Iceland, Serbia and Montenegro. Albania, Bosnia and Herzegovina and Kosovo are potential candidates. The official website of the European Union defines the EU as 'a family of democratic European countries, committed to working together for peace and prosperity'.

> **European Union** a family of democratic European countries committed to working together for peace and prosperity

The EU has certainly been successful in its original central aim of ensuring European peace: countries such as France, England, Germany, Italy and Spain who have been at war with each other on and off for centuries now work together for mutual benefit. This has led to greater emphasis being given to the EU's second objective – namely prosperity – and, to this end, a desire to create a **Single European Market** (SEM) throughout which labour, capital, goods and services can move freely. As member states got rid of obstacles to trade between themselves, it was argued, companies would start to enjoy economies of scale as they expanded their market across Europe, just as US companies enjoy economies of scale as they expand across American states. At the same time, inefficient firms would be exposed to more cross-border competition, either forcing them out of business or forcing them to improve their efficiency. The aim was to provide businesses with an environment of fair competition in which economies of scale could be reaped and a strong consumer base developed from which they could expand into global markets. Households, on the other hand, would benefit from lower prices, greater choice of goods and services, and work opportunities across a wide area, while the economy in general would benefit from the enhanced economic growth that would result.

> **Single European Market** a (still not complete) EU-wide market throughout which labour, capital, goods and services can move freely

Early steps towards the creation of the SEM included the abolition of internal EU tariff and quota barriers in 1968 and a movement towards greater harmonization in areas such as indirect taxation, industrial regulation, and in common EU-wide policies towards agriculture and fisheries.

Nevertheless, it proved difficult to make progress on the more intangible barriers to free movement of goods, services, capital and labour. For example, even though internal tariffs and quotas had been abolished in the EU, local tax systems and technical regulations on goods and services still differed from country to country so that it was in practice often difficult to export from one country to another. Thus, a car produced in the UK might have to satisfy a certain set of emission and safety requirements in one European country and another set of requirements in another EU country. Or a qualified engineer might find that her qualifications, obtained in Italy, were not recognized in Germany. The result was that during the 1970s and early 1980s, growth in the EU member states began to lag seriously behind that of international competitors – especially the United States and Japan. Therefore, in 1985 a discussion document (in the jargon, a 'White Paper') was produced by the European Commission that subsequently led to a European Act of Parliament – the 1986 Single European Act. This identified some 300 measures that would have to be addressed in order to complete the Single European Market and set 31st December 1992 as the deadline for completion. The creation of the SEM was to be brought about by EU Directives telling the governments of member states what changes needed to be put into effect in order to achieve four goals:

- The free movement of goods, services, labour and capital between EU member states.
- The approximation of relevant laws, regulations and administrative provisions between member states.
- A common, EU-wide competition policy, administered by the European Commission.
- A system of common external tariffs implemented against countries who are not members of the EU.

Over 20 years on from the Single European Act, the SEM is still far from complete. In particular, there still exist between EU members strong differences in national fiscal systems, while academic and professional qualifications are not easily transferable and labour mobility across EU countries is generally low. Some of the reasons for this are hard to overcome: language barriers and relative levels of economic development hamper the movement of factors and member states continue to compete with one another economically, at times seeking their own national interest rather than the greater good of the EU.

Nevertheless, the years between 1985 and 1992 did see some important steps in the development of the SEM and the resulting achievements of the SEM project were not negligible: the European Commission estimates that the SEM helped create 2.5 million new jobs and generated €800 billion in additional wealth in the ten years or so following 1993.

In the context of the Single European Market project, therefore, the creation of a single European currency was seen as a final step towards 'completing the market', by which was meant two things: (a) getting rid of the transaction costs from intra-EU trade that result from different national currencies (and which act much as a tariff) and (b) removing the uncertainty and swings in national competitiveness among members that result from exchange rate movements. Before EMU, most EU countries participated in the Exchange Rate Mechanism (ERM), which was a system designed to limit the variability of exchange rates between members' currencies. However, the ERM turned out not to be a viable way of reducing volatility in the exchange rate and, in any case, had no effect on the transaction costs arising from bank charges associated with changing currencies when engaging in intra-EU trade.

It is clearly important, therefore, to see EMU within a broader European framework and, in particular, the Single European Market project. Nevertheless, the benefits of adopting a single currency across a geographical area can be analysed more generally using macroeconomic theory. Moreover, these benefits must be weighed against the costs of joining a common currency area.

THE BENEFITS AND COSTS OF A COMMON CURRENCY

Benefits of a Single Currency

Elimination of Transaction Costs One obvious and direct benefit of a common currency is that it makes trade easier between members and, in particular, there is a reduction in the transaction costs involved in trade between members of the common currency area. When a German company imports French wine, it no longer has to pay a charge to a bank for converting German marks into French francs with which to pay the wine producer, it can just pay in euros. Of course, the banking sector loses out on the commission it used to charge for converting currencies, but this does not affect the fact that the reduction in transaction costs is a net gain. This is because paying a cost to convert currencies is in fact a deadweight loss in the sense that companies pay the transaction cost but get nothing tangible in return. OK, so the banks were getting commission before and this was used to employ people who worked on currency transactions, but these people can now be used more productively in the economy, making everyone better off.

Reduction in Price Discrimination It is sometimes argued that a second albeit indirect gain to the members of a common currency area results from the reduction in price discrimination that should ensue when there is a single currency. If goods are priced in a single currency it should be much harder to disguise price differences across countries. As we have discussed, price discrimination involves a deadweight loss to society, so this is a further gain from a single currency. This argument assumes that the transparency in prices that results from a common currency will lead to arbitrage in goods across the common currency area: people will buy goods where they are cheaper (tending to raise their price in that location) and reduce their demand for goods where they are more expensive (tending to reduce the price in that location).

Overall, however, EMU seems unlikely to bring an end to price discrimination across euro area countries. For items like groceries, having a single currency is unlikely to be much of an impetus to price convergence across the common currency area because of the large transaction costs (mainly related to travelling) involved in arbitraging, relative to the prices of the goods themselves. Would you travel to another country to do your grocery shopping if you knew the prices there were lower? Perhaps you might – when it is easy to travel this does happen. Doing so across the whole of the EU means that the effects are necessarily more limited. On the other hand, big ticket items like household appliances and electronic goods, where the transaction costs may be lower as a percentage of the price of the good in question, are also unlikely to be arbitraged heavily across national borders by consumers because of their durable nature and the need for confidence in after-sales service. Would you want to buy a fridge-freezer in a foreign country and run the risk of having to take it back or get someone from there to fix it for you if it goes wrong? In addition, the fact that different countries in the EU still have different plugs and power systems, which are difficult to harmonize, might also reduce the overall impact.

Reduction in Foreign Exchange Rate Variability A third argument relates to the reduction in exchange rate variability and the consequent reduction in uncertainty that results from having a single currency. Exchange rates can fluctuate substantially on a day-to-day basis. Before EMU, when a German supermarket imported wine from France to be delivered, say, three months later, it had to worry about how much a French franc would be worth in terms of German marks in three months' time and therefore what the total cost of the wine would be in marks. This uncertainty might deter the supermarket company from importing wine at all, and instead lead it to concentrate on selling German wines, thereby foregoing the gains from trade and reducing economic welfare. The supermarket could have eliminated the uncertainty by getting a bank to agree to sell the francs at an agreed rate against marks to be delivered three months later (an example of a forward foreign exchange contract). But the bank would charge for this service, and this charge would be equivalent to a tariff on the imported wine and so this again would represent a deadweight loss to society.

The reduction in uncertainty arising from the removal of exchange rate fluctuations may also affect investment in the economy. This would clearly be the case for companies that export a large amount of their output to other euro area countries, since less uncertainty concerning the receipts from its exports means that it is able to plan for the future with less risk, so that investment projects such as building new factories appear less risky. An increase in investment will benefit the whole economy because it is likely to lead to higher economic growth.

Costs of a Single Currency

The major cost to an economy in joining a common currency area relates to the fact that it gives up its national currency and thereby gives up its freedom to set its own monetary policy and the possibility of macroeconomic adjustment coming about through movements in the external value of its currency. Clearly, if the nations of the euro area have only one money, they can have only one monetary policy, which is set and implemented by the ECB. This must be the case because, since there is only one currency, it's not possible to have a different set of interest rates in different countries. Why is this a potential problem?

Suppose, for example, that there is a shift in consumer preferences across the common currency area away from goods and services produced in one country (Germany, say) and towards goods and services produced in another country (France, say). This situation is depicted in Figure 20.1, which shows a leftwards shift in the German short-run aggregate demand curve and a rightwards shift in the French short-run aggregate demand curve. What should policymakers in France and Germany do about this? One answer to this is, nothing: in the long run, each economy will return to its natural rate of output. In Germany, this will occur as the price level falls and wages, prices and perceptions adjust. In particular, as unemployment rises in Germany, wages eventually begin to fall. Lower wages reduce firms' costs and so, for any given price level, the amount supplied will be higher. In other words, the German short-run aggregate supply curve will shift to the right, until eventually it intersects with the new short-run aggregate demand curve at the natural rate of output. The opposite happens in France, with the short-run aggregate supply curve shifting to the left. The adjustment to the new equilibrium levels of output is also shown in Figure 20.1.

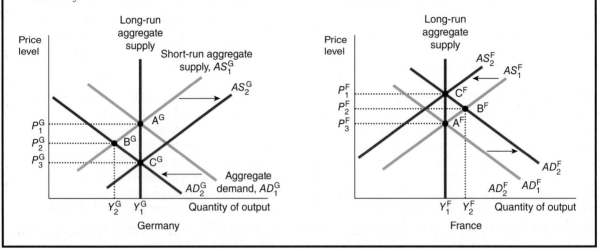

FIGURE 20.1

A Shift in Consumer Preferences Away from German Goods Towards French Goods
The German fall in aggregate demand leads to a fall in output from Y_1^G to Y_2^G, and a fall in the price level from P_1^G to P_2^G. The increase in French aggregate demand raises output from Y_1^F to Y_2^F. Over time, however, wages and prices will adjust, so that German and French output return to their natural levels, Y_1^G and Y_1^F, with lower prices in Germany, at P_3^G, and higher prices in France, at P_3^F.

Note that, if Germany and France had maintained their own currencies and a flexible foreign exchange rate, then the short-term fluctuations in aggregate demand would be alleviated by a movement in the exchange rate: as the demand for French goods rises and for German goods falls, this would increase the demand for French francs and depress the demand for German marks, making the value of francs rise in terms of marks in the foreign currency exchange market. This would make French goods more expensive to German residents since they now have to pay more marks for a given number of French francs. Similarly, German goods become less expensive to French residents. Therefore, French net exports would fall, leading to a fall in aggregate demand. This is shown in Figure 20.2, where the French aggregate demand schedule shifts back to the left until equilibrium is again established at the natural rate of output. Conversely – and also shown in Figure 20.2 – German net exports rise and the German aggregate demand schedule shifts to the right until equilibrium is again achieved in Germany.

In a currency union, however, this automatic adjustment mechanism is not available, since, of course, France and Germany have the same currency (the euro). The best that can be done is to wait for wages and prices to adjust in France and Germany so that the aggregate supply shifts in each country, as in Figure 20.1. The resulting fluctuations in output and unemployment in each country will tend to create tensions within the monetary union, as unemployment rises in Germany and inflation rises in France. German policymakers, dismayed at the rise in unemployment, will favour a cut in interest rates in order to boost aggregate demand in their country, while their French counterparts, worried about rising inflation, will be calling for an increase in interest rates in order to curtail French aggregate demand. The ECB will not be able to keep both countries happy. Most likely, it will set interest rates higher than the German desired level and lower than the French desired level. The ECB pursues an inflation targeting strategy, and the inflation rate it targets is based upon a consumer prices index constructed as an average across the euro area. If a country's inflation rate (or expected inflation rate) is below the euro area average, the ECB's monetary policy will be too tight for that country; if it is above the average, the ECB's monetary policy will be too loose for it. All that is possible is a 'one size fits all' monetary policy. It is for this reason that entry to the eurozone is restricted to those countries that can meet the criteria outlined above where inflation and interest rates are close to the EU average.

FIGURE 20.2

A Shift in Consumer Preferences with Flexible Exchange Rates

The fall in German aggregate demand leads, before prices have had time to adjust, to a fall in output from Y_1^G to Y_3^G. However, because this is due to a fall in net foreign demand, the value of the German currency falls, making German goods cheaper abroad. This raises net exports and restores aggregate demand. The converse happens in France: the increase in net foreign demand raises the external value of the French currency, making French goods more expensive abroad and choking off aggregate demand to its former level.

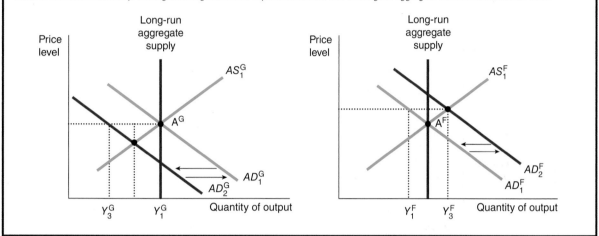

SELF TEST List and discuss the key costs and benefits of joining a currency union.

THE THEORY OF OPTIMUM CURRENCY AREAS

Optimum currency area (OCA) theory attempts to set down a set of criteria for a group of countries such that, if the criteria were satisfied, then it would in some sense be 'optimal' for the countries to adopt a common currency. The qualifier 'optimal' here refers to the ability of each of the countries to limit the costs of monetary union and enhance the benefits. It is generally used loosely, since there is no way for certain of ensuring whether it is indeed optimal for a group of countries to form a currency union and, more often than not, countries will fulfil some but not all of the OCA criteria.

> **optimum currency area** a group of countries for which it is optimal to adopt a common currency and form a currency union

Characteristics that Reduce the Costs of a Single Currency

Consider first the characteristics of a group of countries that would reduce the costs of adopting a common currency. As we have discussed, the main cost to participating in a monetary union is the loss of monetary policy autonomy for the individual countries concerned, as well as ruling out the possibility of macroeconomic adjustment through exchange rate movements. One way in which the economic (and political) tensions arising from the loss of the exchange rate instrument and the imposition of a 'one-size-fits-all' monetary policy will be alleviated is if the economies in question move rapidly to long-run equilibrium following a macroeconomic shock: since we know there is only a short-run trade-off between inflation and unemployment, the faster the economies concerned can get to the long run – in other words, return to their natural rates of output and unemployment – the better. This speed of adjustment to long-run equilibrium will be high if there is a high degree of wage flexibility in the common currency area, and/or if there is a high degree of labour mobility.

Another way in which tensions across the common currency area would be alleviated would be if all countries in the currency union were prone to the same kind of demand shocks (e.g. if aggregate demand fell in all countries simultaneously), since then each would favour similar macroeconomic policy decisions (e.g. a reduction in interest rates).

We consider each of these types of characteristics in turn.

Real Wage Flexibility Suppose there is a high degree of wage flexibility in each of the member countries, so that wages respond strongly to rises and falls in unemployment. This means that the adjustment to long-run equilibrium, as shown in Figure 20.1, occurs very quickly. In our example, the shift in aggregate demand in Germany leads to falling wages, so that firms make more profit for any given level of prices and the aggregate supply curve shifts to the right and Germany returns to the natural rate of output. If wages are very flexible, this adjustment may be very rapid, so that the short run is very short indeed. Similar for France: the rightwards shift in aggregate demand leads to rapidly rising wages and firms find it less profitable to produce any given level of output, so that the supply curve shifts leftwards and a new long-run equilibrium is established at the natural rate of output. Hence, by compressing the short run, tensions across the monetary union are ironed out very quickly.

Note that it is the real wage that is of importance here: it is real wages that must adjust in order to affect the aggregate supply curve by making it more (or less) profitable for firms to produce a given level of output at any given level of prices.

Labour Mobility Alternatively, suppose that labour is highly mobile between the member countries of the currency union: unemployed workers in Germany simply migrate to France and find a job. Again, the macroeconomic imbalance is alleviated, since unemployment in Germany will fall as many of the unemployed have left the country, and inflationary wage pressures in France decline as the labour force expands with the migrants from France. Therefore, it is clear that labour mobility may in some measure cushion a currency union from **asymmetric shocks**, a situation where changes in aggregate demand and/or supply differ from one country to another.

> **asymmetric shocks** a situation where changes in aggregate demand and/or supply differ from one country to another

Capital Mobility Sometimes economists argue that capital mobility can also compensate for the loss of monetary autonomy and the absence of exchange rate adjustment among the members of a common currency area. A distinction should be made here between physical capital (plant and machinery) and financial capital (bonds, company shares and bank loans). In terms of cushioning a currency union from asymmetric shocks, movements in physical capital can help by expanding productive capacity in countries experiencing a boom, as firms in other member countries build factories there. However, given the long lags involved in the installation of plant and equipment, physical capital mobility is likely to be helpful mainly for narrowing persistent regional disparities rather than offsetting short-term shocks.

The mobility of *financial* capital may be more useful in cushioning economies from short-term output shocks. For example, residents of a country experiencing a recession may wish to borrow money from the residents of a country experiencing a boom in order to overcome their short-term difficulties. In our two-country example, German residents would effectively borrow money from French residents in order to make up for their temporary fall in income. Clearly, this would require that German residents can easily borrow from French residents through the capital markets, so that financial capital mobility will be highest between countries whose capital markets are highly integrated with one another. For example, if a bank has branches in more than one country of a currency union, then borrowing and lending between growth and recession countries will be more or less automatic, as residents in the growth country increase the money they are holding in the bank as their income goes up and residents of the country in recession increase their overdrafts (or reduce their money holdings) as their income goes down.

We can relate this discussion back to the notion of permanent income, and to the market for loanable funds. Recall that a family's ability to buy goods and services depends largely on its permanent income, which is its normal, or average income, since people tend to borrow and lend to smooth out transitory variations in income. Now, when an aggregate demand shock adversely affects the German economy, a large amount of German households will see their transitory income fall and will want to borrow in order to increase income back up to the permanent or normal level. But since many German households are now doing this at the same time, if borrowing is restricted to German financial markets, this will tend to raise interest rates and generally make borrowing more difficult. If the market for loanable funds is restricted to the domestic market, then we might expect the supply of loanable funds to decrease in a recession and the demand to increase, raising interest rates. The resulting rise in interest rates may even make the recession worse by reducing investment.

On the other hand, in France, the economic boom means that many households are experiencing income levels above their permanent or average level, and so will tend to increase their saving. Now, if the German households can borrow from the French households – if the market for loanable funds covers both France and Germany – they can both consume at a level consistent with their normal or average levels of income with less of an effect on interest rates. There will be an increase in the supply of loanable funds because French residents are saving more and this will partly or even wholly offset the increase in the demand for loanable funds arising from German residents who want to borrow more. When the German economy comes out of recession and goes into recovery, German households can then repay the loans.

Of course, although we have discussed only bank loans, there are other forms of financial capital, such as bonds and company shares, but the principle of the recessionary economy being able to obtain funds from the booming economy remains the same. In effect, therefore, financial capital market integration across countries allows households to insure one another against asymmetric shocks so that the variability of consumption over the economic cycle can be reduced.

Symmetric Macroeconomic Shocks Note that, in describing the costs of belonging to a monetary union, we have used the example of a positive demand shock in one country and a simultaneous negative demand shock in another. A similar analysis would have followed if we had simply allowed either a positive or a negative demand shock in one country and no shock at all in the other country. The central point was that the demand shock was asymmetric in the sense that it impacted differently on different members of the currency union, requiring different short-run policy responses. Clearly, if the shock were symmetric there would be no problem. If, for example, aggregate demand rose simultaneously in all member countries, increasing expected future inflation, then a policy of raising interest rates would be welcomed by all members of the monetary union. This would be the case if the economic cycles of each of the countries making up the currency were synchronized in the sense that the various economies tended to enter recession at the same time and enter the recovery phase of the cycle at the same time, so that disagreements about the best interest rate policy are less likely to occur.

Characteristics that Increase the Benefits of a Single Currency

High Degree of Trade Integration The greater the amount of trade that takes place between a group of countries – i.e. the greater the degree of trade integration – the more they will benefit from adopting a common currency. One of the principal benefits of a currency union, and the most direct benefit, is the reduction in transaction costs that are incurred in trade transactions between the various countries when there is a constant need to switch one national currency into another on the foreign currency exchange market. Clearly, therefore, the greater the amount of international trade that is carried out between member countries – and therefore the greater the amount of foreign currency transactions – the greater the reduction in transaction costs that having a common currency entails.

The reduction in exchange rate volatility – another benefit of a currency union – will also clearly be greater, the greater is the degree of intra-union trade, since more firms will benefit from knowing with certainty exactly the revenue generated from their sales to other currency union members, rather than having to bear the uncertainty associated with exchange rate fluctuations.

> **SELF TEST** What is meant by an optimum currency area? • List and discuss the key characteristics of an optimum currency area.

IS EUROPE AN OPTIMUM CURRENCY AREA?

Having determined what characteristics of a group of countries would make the benefits of a single currency stronger and the costs weaker, we can take a closer look to see whether Europe – and in particular the group of 18 countries that comprise the euro area – forms an optimum currency area.

Trade Integration

The degree of trade integration can be assessed by looking at imports from and exports to other EU countries expressed as a percentage of GDP. The degree of trade integration across Europe is quite variable, but nevertheless on average quite high – with the notable exception of Greece. The degree of European trade integration has been rising over time, in nearly every country in the EU but the integration has been more marked in some countries such as Austria than others such as the UK and Italy.

This has led some economists to argue that some of the criteria for an optimum currency area – such as a high degree of trade integration – may actually be endogenous: actually being a member of a currency union may enhance the degree of trade done between members of the union, precisely because of the decline in transaction costs in carrying out such trade.

Overall many – if not all – European countries have gained a great deal from the reduction in transaction costs in international trade as a result of the single currency. Indeed, these gains have been estimated at about one quarter to one half of one per cent of euro area GDP. This may not sound massive, but remember that transaction costs are a deadweight loss. Moreover, the gains are not one-off: they accrue continuously as long as the single currency persists, since they would have to be paid in the absence of the currency union. They therefore become cumulative. In addition, if the degree of euro area trade integration tends to rise over time as a result of the single currency, as some economists have suggested, then the implicit gain from not having to pay transaction costs also rises over time.

The other, indirect benefit of a single currency when there is a high degree of trade integration, follows from the reduction in uncertainty associated with doing away with the volatility in the exchange rates between members' national currencies (since those currencies are replaced with a common currency). These gains are hard to quantify, but it is not incorrect to suggest that they are not negligible for the euro area.

Real Wage Flexibility

A great deal of research has been done on real wage flexibility in Europe and virtually all of it concludes that continental European labour markets are among the most rigid in the world, while the UK labour market, at least since the 1980s, has become one of the most flexible. One reason for this is the fact that all European Union countries have minimum wage laws, although this is not the whole story since the UK also has a minimum wage. Perhaps a more important reason is the high degree of collective wage bargaining that is common in continental Europe – i.e. wage agreements that cover a large number of workers. Figures on the degree of unionization of the labour force are quite deceptive in this sense: for example, in the early 2000s, in the UK, Italy and Germany about 30 per cent of the workforce belonged to a trade union, while in France the figure was around 10 per cent. Continental European unions, however, often have collective bargaining and other workplace rights that UK trade unionists can only envy. The power of unions and the inflexibility of the labour market is something that has been a concern in France for some time and in 2013, an agreement was reached between the government and unions on reforms to the country's complex and strict labour laws. The agreement was greeted with mixed responses with some saying it did not go far enough and others suggesting the agreement marked the end of workers' rights in France.

The introduction of the single European currency may also have had a negative effect on European wage flexibility, since many European collective wage agreements between workers and a firm in one country will also often extend to the firm's workforce in other European countries, and a single currency brings transparency in wage differences across countries, as well as price transparency. To return again to our example of a negative demand shock in Germany and a positive shock in France, a company with employees in both countries would find it hard to reduce real wages in Germany while raising them in France.

Furthermore, European labour law is generally very much more restrictive in many continental European countries than it is in the UK or the USA, as is the level of payroll taxes, so that a firm's costs of either reducing the workforce or increasing it can be very high. This means that, even if there were movements in the real wage, firms would be slow to expand or contract their output in response, so that shifts in aggregate supply will be slow to come about.

On the whole, therefore, adjustment to asymmetric shocks through real wage movements is unlikely to be significant in the euro area.

Labour Mobility

Labour is notoriously immobile across European countries, at least if one rules out migration from the newer eastern European members of the EU such as Poland, Romania and Bulgaria, and considers just the 18 euro area countries or these plus Denmark, Sweden and the UK. In part this may perhaps be attributed to differences in language, culture and other social institutions across Europe that make it difficult for workers to migrate. However, it seems that European workers are also very loath to move location even within their own countries. Indeed, the degree of labour mobility as measured by the percentage of the workforce that moves geographical location over any given period, is much lower within any particular European country than it is within the United States, and is even lower between the euro area countries. Europe therefore scores very low on this optimum currency area criterion.

Financial Capital Mobility

In discussing financial capital mobility, a distinction must be made between the wholesale and the retail capital markets. The wholesale financial markets are the capital markets in which only financial institutions such as banks and investment funds operate, as well as very large corporations, while the retail financial markets (such as high street banks) are those open to individual households and to small and medium-sized corporations. Prior to the introduction of the euro, financial integration among euro area countries was probably quite low, in both the wholesale and retail sectors. However, following the introduction of the euro, integration of the wholesale financial markets has increased dramatically. In particular, a liquid euro money market with single interbank market interest rates was established so that a bank in, say, Luxembourg can now borrow euros just as easily and at the same rate of interest from another bank in Frankfurt as it can from a bank located in the same street in Luxembourg. In the government bond market, the degree of market integration is also high, and this is shown by the fact that the interest rates on government bonds of the different euro area countries are very close to one another and tend to move very closely together. On the other hand, the integration of retail market products, such as loans to households and small and medium-sized enterprises, is lagging behind compared with the wholesale market products. This becomes evident from persistent cross-country differences in bank lending rates and the rather limited cross-border retail banking activity. Indeed, national banking sectors have remained largely segregated with only marginal cross-border penetration.

Symmetric Demand Shocks

The economic cycle across the countries of the euro area does appear to be positively correlated, in the sense that the timing of strong growth and downturns appear to be very close. In Figure 20.3 we have graphed data on annual growth rates in real GDP for France, Germany and the euro area as a whole for every year from 2005 to 2014. Clearly, the movements in growth rates over this period for France and Germany and for the whole euro area are very close. There is no clear example of asymmetric demand shocks impacting upon these countries as in the example we have used to illustrate the potential problems of a monetary union.

FIGURE 20.3

Growth Rates in Germany, France and the Whole Euro Area
The figure shows annual growth rates in real GDP for France, Germany and the euro area as a whole for every year from 2005 to 2014. French, German and euro area (17) growth rates (Latvia only joined the euro area in January 2014) tend to move closely together and there is no clear example of asymmetric demand shocks.

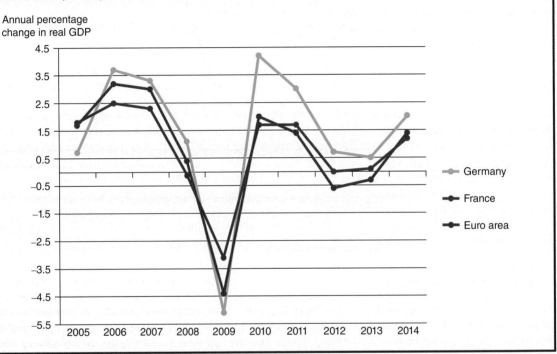

In Figure 20.4, however, we have plotted real GDP growth rates for the euro area, Greece and Ireland over the same period. The problem that is evident from this graph is not so much that the turning points do not coincide, but that Ireland and Greece's growth rate outstripped the performance of the euro area as a whole between 2005 and 2007 but then both saw considerable problems as a result of the financial crisis. Whilst Ireland has seen a recovery and is performing at a rate higher than the euro area as a whole, Greece has seen its growth shrinking throughout the period 2008–2013. Whilst the euro area as a whole saw some weak recovery in that period, Greece did not share in that recovery. Monetary policy for the euro area as a whole has not been matched to the needs of the Greek and Irish economies over the period noted.

Overall, therefore, the evidence is a little mixed, although on the whole it suggests that the problem of asymmetric demand shocks is not a great one for the current member countries of EMU. The fact that there is not strong evidence of asymmetric demand shocks at the aggregate level, however, does not rule out the possibility that there may be asymmetric shocks at other levels in the economy.

FIGURE 20.4

Growth Rates in Ireland, Greece and the Whole Euro Area

The figure shows annual growth rates in real GDP for Ireland, Greece and for the euro area as a whole for every year from 2005 to 2014 (note, 2014 is an estimate). The growth rates do not move closely together; Ireland and Greece's growth rate was higher than that of the euro area as a whole up to 2007, but Ireland slipped into recession first and the depth of Greece's recession has been much worse than that of the euro area

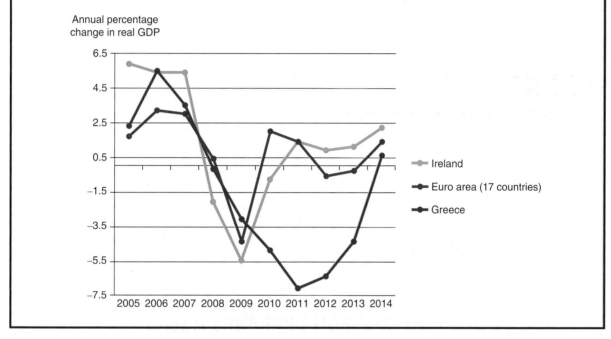

In fact, researchers have found that many of the shocks that impact upon European countries asymmetrically tend to be specific to a region or to an industry rather than to a country as a whole. This is not a problem made worse by joining a monetary union, however, since a country that experienced, say, a negative shock to one of its industries or regions would not in any case be able to deal with this using monetary or exchange rate policy without generating imbalances in its other regions or industries. The idea of a two-speed EU with the countries that have experienced debt crisis problems since the financial crisis, Portugal, Ireland, Italy, Greece and Spain (the so called 'PIIGS' countries) has highlighted that there are some countries that seem better able to weather economic storms than others. Germany, France, the Netherlands, Denmark and Sweden have all recovered from the financial crisis more quickly than have the PIIGS, albeit that the strength of the recovery has been muted. Economists have noted that the degree of integration of the euro area and the EU as a whole does impact on the ability of countries to recover from economic shocks. If EU countries rely on each other for export-led growth, then if a group of these countries face considerable fiscal difficulties and have to implement austerity measures, then the level of demand in these economies falls and this affects demand in the other economies, thus dragging down growth in all the euro area countries and the EU as a whole.

Summary: So is Europe an Optimum Currency Area?

As in many policy debates in economics, there is no clear-cut answer to this question. Certainly, many European countries have a high degree of intra-union trade and have economic cycles that are more or less synchronized. However, labour mobility and wage flexibility (and labour market flexibility in general) are low in Europe, and while the euro has increased financial market integration in the euro area's wholesale financial markets, the retail markets remain highly segregated at the national level.

Overall, therefore, if very strong differences in the economic cycle were to emerge across the euro area, the lack of independent monetary and exchange rate policy would be acutely felt. This could be a case argued in relation to the situations in Ireland and Greece as highlighted in Figure 20.4. For that reason, many economists argue that Europe – meaning the current euro area – is not an optimum currency area. Nevertheless, as we have noted in our discussion, it is possible that some of the optimum currency area criteria may be endogenous. In particular, the single currency is likely to generate even greater trade among EMU members. Given this, it is likely that the economic cycles of member currencies will become even more closely synchronized as aggregate demand shifts in one country have stronger and stronger spillover effects in other euro area countries; this may, however, take some time to synchronize and the problems the EU has faced since the financial crisis have exposed the differences in the relative strength of the economies of the countries, in the euro area in particular, which has pushed EMU to its limits.

Over time, the single currency, if it survives, may also raise labour mobility across Europe in the long run, since being paid in the same currency as in one's home country is one less issue to come to terms with when moving location to find a job. Also, with time, one would expect financial market integration to spread to the retail capital markets (indeed there is already strong pressure being exerted on the European banking industry by the European Central Bank and the European Commission for the introduction of new payment schemes for electronic credit transfers and direct debits between euro area banks, as well as for a unified framework for debit and credit cards).

Perhaps the only true test of whether the euro area is an optimum currency area (or can become one) is to see whether EMU survives in the long run. The challenges faced by the euro area since the financial crisis have put the long-term survival of the whole euro project in doubt. Significant changes to the structure of the euro, in particular financial regulation and fiscal reform, are the subject of on-going discussion and fiscal policy is the subject of our next section.

FISCAL POLICY AND COMMON CURRENCY AREAS

Our discussion so far has tended to centre on the loss of autonomy in monetary policy that is entailed in adopting a single currency among a group of countries. However, it is obvious that there is nothing in the adoption of a common currency that implies that members of the currency union should not still retain independence in fiscal policy. For instance, in our example of an asymmetric demand shock that expands demand in France and contracts aggregate demand in Germany, the French government could reduce government spending in order to offset the demand shock, while the German government could expand government spending. In fact, even if France and Germany did not make up an optimal currency because wages were sticky and labour mobility was low between the countries, national fiscal policy could, in principle, still be used to ameliorate the loss of monetary policy autonomy. Let's discuss further the issue of fiscal policy and currency unions.

Fiscal Federalism

Suppose that a currency union had a common fiscal policy in the sense of having a single, common fiscal budget covering tax and spending decisions across the common currency area. This means that fiscal policy in the currency union would work much as fiscal policy in a single national economy works, with a surplus of government tax revenue over government spending in one region used to pay for a budget deficit in another region. Return again to our example of an asymmetric demand shock that expands aggregate demand in France and contracts aggregate demand in Germany, as in Figure 20.1. Remember that there are automatic stabilizers built into the fiscal policy of an economy that automatically stimulate aggregate demand when the economy goes into recession without policymakers having to take any deliberate action. In particular, since almost all taxes are closely related to the level of economic activity in the economy, tax revenue will automatically decline in Germany as a result of the aggregate demand shock that shifts it into recession. At the same time, transfer payments in the form of unemployment benefit and other social security benefits will also rise in Germany. The opposite will be true in France, where the automatic stabilizers will be operating in reverse as transfer payments fall and tax receipts rise with the level of economic activity. These changes will tend to expand aggregate demand in Germany and contract it in France, to some extent offsetting the asymmetric demand shock.

Now, if the governments of France and Germany have a common budget, then the increased net government revenue in France can be used to offset the reduction in net government revenue in Germany. If the resulting movements in aggregate are not enough to offset the demand shock, then the French and German governments may even go further and decide to increase government expenditure further in Germany and pay for it by reducing spending and perhaps raising taxes in France.

This kind of arrangement – a fiscal system for a group of countries involving a common fiscal budget and a system of taxes and fiscal transfers across countries – is known as **fiscal federalism**. The problem with it is that the taxpayers of one country (here France) may not be happy in paying for government spending and transfer payments in another country (in this example, Germany).

> **fiscal federalism** a fiscal system for a group of countries involving a common fiscal budget and a system of taxes and fiscal transfers across countries

National Fiscal Policies in a Currency Union: The Free Rider Problem

Assuming that, for political reasons, fiscal federalism is not an option open to the currency union, we still need to explore the possibility of individual members of the union using fiscal policy in order to offset asymmetric macroeconomic shocks that cannot be dealt with by the common monetary policy. In particular, in our example, what is wrong with Germany running a big government budget deficit in order to counteract the fall in aggregate demand and borrowing heavily in order to finance the deficit? One answer may lie in the effect on other members of the currency union of a rise in the debt of a member country.

Whenever a government raises its levels of debt to very high levels, there is always the possibility that the government may default on the debt. In general, this can be done in one of two ways. Where a country is not a member of a currency union and controls its own monetary policy, it can engineer a surprise inflation by a sudden increase in the money supply, so that the real value of the debt shrinks. In addition, when there is a sharp rise in the price level, this will usually be accompanied by a sharp fall in the foreign currency value of the domestic currency. This means that, valued in foreign currency, the stock of government debt will now be worth far less. Thus, the government has in effect defaulted on a large portion of its debt by reducing its value both internally and externally.

If this is not possible – for example because, as in a currency union, the country no longer enjoys monetary policy autonomy and is not able to devalue the external value of its currency (since it uses the common currency) – then the only other way of reneging on the debt is through an outright default (e.g. stopping interest payments or failing to honour capital repayments when they fall due). Generally, the financial markets are good at disciplining governments that run up large debts, by charging them high rates of interest on the debt that the government issues – after all, if you thought there was even a slight possibility that you might not get your money back if you lent it, you would want to be paid a higher rate of interest in order to compensate for that risk. Figure 20.5 shows the interest rate on ten-year government debt in a selection of EU countries in March 2013 compared to March 2012. The overall cost to governments of borrowing was lower in March 2013 reflecting the slightly more calm economic conditions that prevailed at the time compared to a year previously. The differences in the cost of borrowing is stark, however. The PIIG countries all face much higher interest rates on borrowing compared to the stronger economies of Germany, France, the Netherlands, Sweden, Denmark, the UK and Switzerland. The interest rate on Greek debt is extreme reflecting the parlous state of that country's economy. It is rarely impossible for a country to borrow money on international markets but if interest rates are higher than about 7 per cent then the cost of servicing the debt becomes unsustainable in the longer term, particularly if economic growth is weak as it has been in the PIIG countries. If the cost of borrowing is consistently above 7 per cent then it is likely that governments will be in even more trouble and become more likely to default.

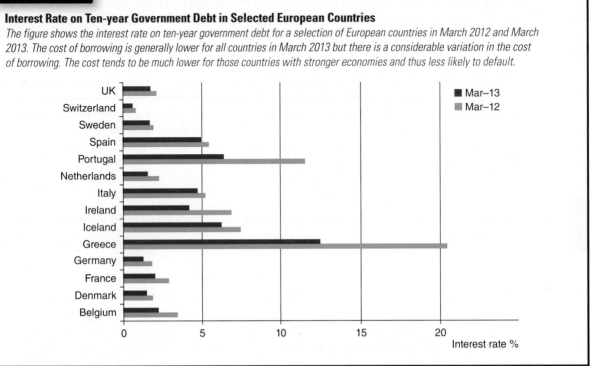

FIGURE 20.5

Interest Rate on Ten-year Government Debt in Selected European Countries

The figure shows the interest rate on ten-year government debt for a selection of European countries in March 2012 and March 2013. The cost of borrowing is generally lower for all countries in March 2013 but there is a considerable variation in the cost of borrowing. The cost tends to be much lower for those countries with stronger economies and thus less likely to default.

In the case of a monetary union, therefore, this means that excessive debt issuance by one member country will tend to force up interest rates throughout the whole of the common currency area. Although the ECB controls very short-term interest rates in the euro area through its refinancing operations, it does not control longer-term interest rates such as those paid on 10- or 20-year government bonds. Hence, fiscal profligacy by a government in the euro area will tend to push up the cost of borrowing for all members of the currency union.

However interest rates may not be raised enough to discipline properly the high-borrowing government. This is because the markets feel that the other members of the monetary union would not allow the country concerned actually to default, and that if it threatened to do so the other members would probably rush in and buy up its government debt and 'bail out' the country concerned. If the markets believe in this possibility then the debt will not be seen as risky as it otherwise would be and so the interest rates charged to the debtor country on its debt will not be as high as they otherwise might be. The intervention by the ECB, EU finance ministers and the International Monetary Fund (IMF) to bail out the economies of Ireland, Greece and other countries since the financial crisis has been a case in point as ministers struggled to keep EMU together.

The net effect is for that government to pay interest rates on its large stock of debt that are lower because of the implicit belief that it will be bailed out if it has problems servicing the debt, and for all other members of the currency union to pay higher interest rates on their government debt because the government has flooded the financial markets with euro-denominated government bonds. In essence, this is an example of the free rider problem: the government is enjoying the benefits of a fiscal expansion without paying the full costs.

In addition, if that government is using the proceeds of its borrowing to fund a strong fiscal expansion, this may undo or work against the anti-inflationary monetary policy of the ECB by stoking up aggregate demand throughout the whole of the euro area.

In order to circumvent some of these problems, the currency union members can enter into a 'no bail-out' agreement that states that member countries cannot expect other members to come to their rescue if their debt levels become unsustainable, as an attempt to convince the markets to charge

CASE STUDY The Stability and Growth Pact: A Ferocious Dog with No Teeth

The Stability and Growth Pact (SGP) was a set of formal rules by which members of EMU were supposed to be bound in their conduct of national fiscal policy. Its main components were as follows:

- Members should aim to achieve balanced budgets.
- Members with a budget deficit of more than 3 per cent of GDP will be subject to fines that may reach as high as 0.5 per cent of GDP unless the country experiences exceptional circumstances (such as a natural disaster) or a very sharp recession in which GDP declines by 2 per cent or more in a single year.

Clearly, however, if EMU members adhered to the SGP, then it would rule out any free rider problems associated with excessive spending and borrowing in any one member country by forcing members to put a limit on the national government budget. The choice of a maximum budget deficit of no more than 3 per cent of GDP was related to a clause in the 1992 Maastricht Treaty that suggested that a 'prudent' debt-to-GDP ratio should be no more than 60 per cent. This itself was perhaps somewhat arbitrary – although it was very close to the actual debt-to-GDP ratio of Germany in 1992. To see, however, that a 60 per cent ratio of debt to GDP could entail 'prudent' budget deficits of no more than 3 per cent a year, let's do some simple budgetary arithmetic. Suppose a country is enjoying real GDP growth of 3 per cent a year and inflation of 2 per cent a year, so that nominal GDP is growing at the rate of 5 per cent a year. This means that the nominal value of its government debt can grow at a rate of 5 per cent a year and still be sustainable. But if the debt-to-GDP ratio is 60 per cent, this means that debt can increase by 5 per cent of 60 per cent, or 3 per cent of GDP a year while keeping the debt-to-GDP ratio constant. In other, words, it can run a budget deficit of 3 per cent of GDP a year.

While, however, there was some logic in setting a maximum budget deficit of 3 per cent a year (given a maximum prudent debt-to-GDP ratio of 60 per cent), it is not clear why the SGP suggested that members should aim for a balanced budget. It should be clear from the budgetary arithmetic just discussed that it is not imprudent for countries to run small budget deficits as long as they are enjoying sustained long-term growth in GDP. The effective straitjacketing of national fiscal policy that the SGP implied may have reflected a desire among the architects of EMU for the ECB to maintain an effective monopoly on demand management, so that its polices could not be countered by national fiscal policies.

The crucial question for the SGP, however, was whether or not the maximum allowable budget deficit would be enough for a country to let its automatic fiscal stabilizers come into play when it goes into recession. This is crucial in a monetary union because member countries will have already given up their right to pursue an independent monetary policy and they cannot use the exchange rate as an instrument of policy.

In practice, the SGP proved to be something of a toothless watchdog. As the euro area experienced sluggish growth in the early years of EMU, several member countries – and in particular France and Germany, two of the largest member countries – found themselves in breach of the SGP excessive deficit criteria. However, both France and Germany managed to persuade other EMU members not to impose fines and, in 2004, the European Commission drew up guidelines for softening the SGP. These guidelines included considering more widely the sustainability of countries' public finances on an individual basis, paying more attention to overall debt burdens and to long-term liabilities such as pensions, rather than to a single year's deficit. The consequences of the financial crisis have made the limitation of the SGP even more clear.

Critics of the SGP suggested that when it came to the test it failed to impose discipline.

profligate spend-and-borrow countries higher interest rates on their debt. In fact, exactly such a no bail-out agreement exists among members of EMU. Unfortunately, however, it seems clear that the no bail-out clause is not credible: the attempts by members to support profligate countries throughout the sovereign debt crisis have confirmed this. If an EMU member were to default on its debt, this would have strong repercussions throughout the euro area as it would lead to the financial markets losing confidence in debt issued by other members and to strong selling of the euro in the foreign currency exchange market. In order to avoid this, EMU members have acted to bail out member countries threatening to default on their debt.

For these reasons, the members of the currency union may wish to impose rules on one another concerning the conduct of national fiscal policies in order to avoid fiscal profligacy by any one member. At the outset of EMU, a set of fiscal rules was indeed drawn up and agreed to by EMU members. This set of rules was known as the Stability and Growth Pact (SGP). The SGP not only laid down strict rules on the maximum permissible budget deficit and debt-to-GDP ratio for EMU members, it also stipulated harsh punishments – fines amounting to as much as 0.5 per cent of GDP – for offenders. In the event, several countries, including France and Germany, breached the SGP but managed to persuade other members not to impose fines.

> **SELF TEST** What is fiscal federalism? ● How may it aid in the functioning of a common currency area?

The Fiscal Compact

The problems with the debt crisis faced by a number of European countries in the wake of the financial crisis and the attempts to keep the euro area together led to the negotiation of a treaty which came in to force on 1 January 2013. This has become known as the fiscal compact but its full title is the *Treaty on Stability, Coordination and Governance in the Economic and Monetary Union.* The intention of the fiscal compact is to:

> strengthen the economic pillar of the Economic and Monetary Union by adopting a set of rules intended to foster budgetary discipline through a fiscal compact, to strengthen the coordination of economic policies and to improve the governance of the euro area, thereby supporting the achievement of the European Union's objectives for sustainable growth, employment, competitiveness and social cohesion.

The treaty echoes some of the features of the SGP in that it requires the budgets of participating member states to be in balance or in surplus and that the structural deficit does not exceed 0.5 per cent of the country's nominal GDP. A **structural deficit** refers to a situation where the deficit is not dependent on movements in the economic cycle but indicate that a government is 'living beyond its means' – spending what it has not got and contrasts with a **cyclical deficit** where government spending and income is disrupted by deviations in the 'normal' economic cycle.

> **structural deficit** a situation where a government's deficit is not dependent on movements in the economic cycle
> **cyclical deficit** a situation when government spending and income is disrupted by the deviations in the 'normal' economic cycle

Each member country will have a minimum benchmark figure for long-term sustainability which will be reviewed annually. Deviation from the balanced budget rule will be allowed in exceptional circumstances, such as a severe economic downturn but if the member state deviates from the rule, an automatic correction mechanism which has to be built into the country's legal system, will be triggered. Participant countries will have been expected to have this legal mechanism enshrined in law by 1 January 2014. Member states will be subject to a budgetary and economic partnership programme which will outline detailed structural reforms that will have to be put into place if the deficit rules are breached which will detail how the country intends to remedy its deficit problems. The rules apply to all 25 countries which signed the agreement apart from the Czech Republic and the UK who both opted out of the agreement.

At the time of writing it is by no means certain that these new rules will be any more successful than the SGP. Only months into the new treaty there are concerns that France will breach the rules and a number of economists have noted that the rules do not make sense. Imposing greater fiscal discipline might sound sensible to prevent governments from profligacy and reducing the free rider problem but the consequences are essentially simple – if debt is too high the government concerned must cut spending and raise taxes. If governments are seeking to balance budgets, account must be taken of the effect on the other aspects of the economy.

Recall that savings of households and firms is denoted as S and that in equilibrium, savings equals investment ($S = I$) in a closed economy. If governments have a balanced budgets then tax receipts (T) equal government spending (G): $T = G$. The external current account is given by net exports, $X - M$. If there is an imbalance in private savings and/or government budgets, this shows up in net capital outflow as we saw in Chapter 12. In Chapter 13, we noted the link between the market for loanable funds and the market for foreign currency exchange as $S = I + NX$. This can be rearranged to give $S - I = NX$ and rearranging the national accounting formula gives us $(S - I) + (T - G) = NX$ where $T - G$ is the government deficit. If the government is to balance its budget then the sum of the other elements of the economy must also balance. Bringing these other aspects into balance is not easy.

If the government is forced to cut spending and increase taxes to bring the budget into balance, national income will fall, *ceteris paribus.* An increase in taxes will have the effect of reducing private saving; if saving falls then interest rates rise, investment may decline and the net result is a rise in unemployment. In addition, the reduced investment leads over time to a lower stock of capital. A lower capital stock reduces labour productivity, real wages, and the economy's production of goods and services. The political ramifications of bringing the budget into balance could be severe for governments and lead to political instability which further undermines market confidence.

CONCLUSION

This chapter has developed some of the main issues around common currency areas, focusing in particular on European monetary union. Where there is a high degree of trade among a group of countries, there are benefits to be had from forming a currency union, largely arising from the reduction of transaction costs in international trade and reductions in exchange rate uncertainty. However, there are also costs associated with joining a monetary union, largely associated with the loss of monetary autonomy (member countries are no longer free to set their own interest rates) and the loss of exchange rate movements as a means of achieving macroeconomic adjustment. Any decision to form a currency union must weigh these costs and benefits against one another to see if there is an overall net benefit. Although, in the long run, the loss of exchange rate adjustment and monetary autonomy may have little effect on the equilibrium levels of output and unemployment in the economies involved, there may be substantial short-term economic fluctuations in these macroeconomic variables as a result of joining the currency union. This is particularly the case if there are asymmetric demand shocks impacting on the currency union so that it is impossible to design a 'one-size-fits-all' monetary policy to suit every country. Short-run adjustment will also be long and painful when wages do not adjust very quickly, although this problem may be overcome by labour mobility across the member countries.

A group of countries for which the benefits of monetary union are high and the costs are relatively low is termed an optimum currency area. Even though there is quite a high degree of trade integration among the member countries of the current European monetary union and their economic cycles do seem more or less synchronized and of a similar amplitude (with some exceptions), labour mobility and wage flexibility in Europe are both notoriously low, and integration of euro area financial markets, although high in the wholesale sector, has so far been disappointing in the retail financial markets. Overall, therefore, the euro area is probably not an optimum currency area. Nevertheless, it is possible that some of these criteria may be endogenous: EMU may lead to increasing economic integration in the euro area that will in turn significantly raise the benefits and reduce the costs to each country of remaining in the monetary union.

IN THE NEWS

A Euro-Budget

The effects of the financial crisis have led to a reassessment of some of the assumptions of the way in which the euro area has been operating. Some economists suggest that each member state ought to contribute funds to create a euro-budget that could be used to help offset asymmetric shocks.

Does the Eurozone Need a Budget?

The Maastricht Treaty created a restrictive European monetary union by keeping fiscal policy national, subject only to a stability pact. Was this a wise choice? Many observers now argue that the Achilles' heel of the euro is that it has no mechanism to ease shocks to individual member states. The euro area, they argue, needs its own budget to provide some automatic insurance to individual countries when they are hit by these asymmetric shocks.

Even proponents of a sizeable 'federal' euro budget admit that permanent shocks (for example the collapse of a major export market) require permanent adjustment in wages and expenditure. But what is lacking is allegedly a mechanism to redistribute funds from countries experiencing temporary booms to those in recession. This, they say, would dampen the normal ups and downs of an economy and make short term shocks easier to absorb. They usually hold up the United States and its redistributive federal system as an example of how this can work.

But a closer look reveals that this doesn't work as well as is widely assumed. It is true that in the US, as in most federal states, the federal budget redistributes income across regions and thus offsets at least part of the inter-regional differences in income. But the inference that redistribution is equivalent to a shock absorber is wrong.

For example, in the US, the federal budget offsets a substantial part of the differences in the level of income per capita across states – generally believed to be between 30 per cent and 40 per cent – because poorer states contribute on average lower income tax and receive higher social security payments. However, this does not imply that these mechanisms also provide an insurance against temporary shocks to individual states. Many of the transfers from the federal government, especially basic social support such as food stamps, etc. change little with the local business cycle. For example, retirees in Florida receive their pensions whether or not the local economy is doing well (as during the real estate boom up to 2007). These pensions do not increase when the local economy enters a

bust, as it did after 2008. This type of transfer payments from the federal government thus does not provide any buffer against local shocks.

On the revenue side the degree to which federal taxes absorb shocks at the state level cannot be very large for the simple reason that the main federal sources of revenues that react to the business cycle, such as federal income tax, accounts for less than 10 per cent of GDP.

This low sensitivity of both federal expenditure and revenues to local business cycle conditions explains why on average only a small fraction – estimated about between 10 and 15 per cent – of any shock to the GDP of any individual state is absorbed via automatic transfers to and from the US federal budget.

A related idea which has come up repeatedly in the European context is to create some European, or euro area, unemployment insurance fund. This idea is very attractive at first sight. But here again the reference to the US experience is misleading: in the US, unemployment insurance is actually organized at the state level. The federal government intervenes only in the case of major nationwide recessions and provides some supplementary benefits for the long-term unemployed. But this support is given to all states and thus does not provide those most affected with much more support than the others.

Moreover, unemployment benefits are not as important as often assumed. In most countries they amount to only about between 2 and 3 per cent of GDP, even during a major recession. In the US, the supplementary federal expenditure amounted to only about 1 per cent of GDP in recent years. It is thus clear that a euro area unemployment insurance system would never be able to offset major shocks, such as the ones hitting Ireland or Greece where GDP has fallen by more than 10 per cent.

All in all, it is difficult to rest the case for some euro area fiscal shock absorber on the US experience.

If business-cycle shocks were really the key problem, individual member states could first of all 'self-insure' by running a prudent fiscal policy and lower their debt level so that they have the freedom to run temporary deficits in case they face temporary shocks. The 'Fiscal Compact' with its target of approximate balance in cyclically adjusted terms is implicitly based on this idea.

Moreover, those member states that feel most exposed to business cycle shocks could very well agree among themselves to some mutual insurance scheme. There would be no need to make this scheme compulsory for all member states if the aim is only to pool limited risks on an actuarially fair basis. It is of course true that the risk pooling becomes more efficient the more member countries participate (and the less their business cycles are correlated). This implies that if a subgroup of member states starts such a system (in the spirit of what is called in EU legal terms a 'reinforced cooperation') the other member states should be attracted as well. The force of attraction of such a scheme would provide a litmus test of its usefulness.

Proponents of the idea that the euro area needs a fiscal shock-absorbing mechanism might thus do better proposing a concrete mechanism that could be implemented among a subgroup of member states instead of jumping to the conclusion that all member states be forced to pay a large part of their tax revenues into a euro area budget.

Questions

1 What do you think is meant by the statement: 'The Maastricht Treaty created a restrictive European monetary union by keeping fiscal policy national, subject only to a stability pact'?

2 Why do you think that the lack of a 'mechanism to ease shocks to individual member states' is described as the 'Achilles' heel of the euro?

3 Explain how a 'federal euro budget' would help to reduce the impact of short-term shocks to member economies?

4 Why is the argument for a euro-budget based on a comparison with the United States likely to be weak, according to the author of this article?

5 Why might a voluntary risk-pooling scheme among interested member states be more likely to succeed, according to the author, than an enforced EU-wide scheme?

There are stark contrasts in economic welfare across Europe. In parts of Italy there are regions suffering very weak economic growth, whereas in parts of Germany the population benefits from the strong German economy, as exemplified by the snow-covered mansions in Heidelberg.

SUMMARY

- A common currency area (a.k.a. currency union or monetary union) is a geographical area through which one currency circulates and is accepted as the medium of exchange.

- The formation of a common currency area can bring significant benefits to the members of the currency union, particularly if there is already a high degree of international trade among them (i.e. a high level of trade integration). This is primarily because of the reductions in transaction costs in trade and the reduction in exchange rate uncertainty.

- There are, however, costs of joining a currency union, namely the loss of independent monetary policy and also of the exchange rate as a means of macroeconomic adjustment. Given a long-run vertical supply curve, the loss of monetary policy and the lack of exchange rate adjustment affect mainly short-run macroeconomic adjustment, however.

- These adjustment costs will be lower the greater is the degree of real wage flexibility, labour mobility and capital market integration across the currency union, and also the less the members of the currency union suffer from asymmetric demand shocks.

- A group of countries with a high level of trade integration, high labour mobility and real wage flexibility, a high level of capital market integration that does not suffer asymmetric demand shocks across the different members of the group, is termed an optimum currency area (OCA). An OCA is most likely to benefit from currency union.

- It is possible that a group of countries may become an OCA after forming a currency union, as having a common currency may enhance further trade integration, thereby helping to synchronize members' economic cycles, and having a single currency may also help foster increased labour mobility and capital market integration.

- While the current euro area displays, overall, a high degree of trade integration and does not appear to be plagued by asymmetric demand shocks, real wage flexibility and labour mobility both appear to be low. And while the introduction of the euro has led to a high degree of euro area financial market integration at the wholesale level, retail financial markets remain nationally segregated. Overall, therefore, the euro area is probably not at present an optimum currency area, although it may eventually become one.

- The problems of adjustment within a currency union that is not an OCA may be alleviated by fiscal federalism – a common fiscal budget and a system of taxes and fiscal transfers across member countries. In practice, however, fiscal federalism may be difficult to implement for political reasons.

- The national fiscal policies of the countries making up a currency union may be subject to a free rider problem, whereby one country issues a large amount of government debt and pays a lower interest rate on it than it might otherwise have paid, but also leads to other member countries having to pay higher interest rates. It is for this reason that a currency union may wish to impose rules on the national fiscal policies of its members.

QUESTIONS FOR REVIEW

1 What are the main advantages of forming a currency union? What are the main disadvantages?

2 Are the advantages and disadvantages you have listed in answer to question 1 long run or short run in nature?

3 Is a reduction in price discrimination across countries likely to be an important benefit of forming a currency union? Explain.

4 What are the main characteristics that reduce the costs of a common currency?

5 How would an asymmetric supply-side shock to a country that was a member of a currency union affect the country and the other members of the currency union?

6 What is an optimum currency area (OCA)? List the criteria that an OCA must satisfy.

7 Is EMU an optimum currency area?

8 What is fiscal federalism? How might the problems of macroeconomic adjustment in a currency union be alleviated by fiscal federalism?

9 Why might the members of a currency union wish to impose rules on the conduct of national fiscal policies?

10 What are the main features of the fiscal pact?

PROBLEMS AND APPLICATIONS

1 Consider two countries that trade heavily with one another – Cornsylvania and Techoland. The national currency of Cornsylvania is the cob, while the Techoland national currency is the byte. The output of Cornsylvania is mainly agricultural, while the output of Techoland is mainly high-technology electronic goods. Suppose that each economy is in a long-run macroeconomic equilibrium.

  a. Use diagrams to illustrate the state of each economy. Be sure to show aggregate demand, short-run aggregate supply and long-run aggregate supply.

  b. Now suppose that there is an increase in demand for electronic goods in both countries, and a simultaneous decline in demand for agricultural goods. Use your diagrams to show what happens to output and the price level in the short run in each country. What happens to the unemployment rate in each country?

  c. Show, using your diagrams, how each country could use monetary policy to reduce the short-run fluctuation in output.

  d. Show, using your diagrams, how movements in the cob–byte exchange rate could reduce short-run fluctuations in output in each country.

2 Suppose Techoland and Cornsylvania form a currency union and adopt the electrocarrot as their common currency. Now suppose again that there is an increase in demand for electronic goods in both countries, and a simultaneous decline in demand for agricultural goods. As president of the central bank for the currency union, would you raise or lower the electrocarrot interest rate, or keep it the same? Explain. (Hint: you are charged with maintaining low and stable inflation across the electrocarrot area.)

3 Suppose that Techoland and Cornsylvania decide to engage in fiscal federalism and adopt a common fiscal budget.

  a. Show, again using aggregate demand/aggregate supply diagrams, how fiscal policy can be used to alleviate the short-run fluctuations generated by the asymmetric demand shock.

  b. Given the typical lags in the implementation of fiscal policy, would you advise the use of federal fiscal policy to alleviate short-run macroeconomic fluctuations? (Hint: distinguish between automatic stabilizers and discretionary fiscal policy.)

4 The United States can be thought of as a non-trivial currency union since, although it is a single country, it encompasses many states that have economies comparable in size to those of some European countries. Given that the USA has had a single currency for 200 years, it may be thought of as a successful currency union. Yet many of the American states produce very different products and services, so that they are likely to be impacted by different kinds of macroeconomic shocks (expansionary and recessionary) over time. For example, Texas produces oil, while Kansas produces agricultural goods. How do you explain the long-term success of the US currency union given this diversity? Are there any lessons or predictions for Europe that can be drawn from the US experience?

5 Explain, giving reasons, whether the following statements are true or false.

  a. 'A high degree of trade among a group of countries implies that there would be benefits from them adopting a common currency and forming a currency union.'

  b. 'A high degree of trade among a group of countries implies that they should definitely adopt a common currency and form a currency union.'

6 Do you think that the free rider problem associated with national fiscal policies in a currency union, as we discussed in the text, is likely to be a problem in actual practice? Justify your answer.

7 What is the function of the European Commission? What are the other five main institutions of the European Union and what are their respective roles? What are the other important EU bodies and what are their respective roles? (Hint: go to the European Union website: www.europa.eu.int.)

8 If the interest rate on Spanish government debt is rising whilst that of Germany is falling:

  a. What does this tell you about the view of the markets on the two countries?

  b. If the interest rate is rising, what is happening to the price of bonds for the two countries? Explain.

9 In order for a common currency area to work effectively it is argued that on joining, member states need to be at a similar stage in the economic cycle. Why do you think this is the case?

10 The fiscal pact would be fine if all countries in the euro area were at the same stage in the economic cycle and it was designed to act as a deterrent for profligacy in the future. As a means of solving the debt crisis in Europe it is doomed to fail. To what extent would you agree with this statement?

21 THE FINANCIAL CRISIS AND SOVEREIGN DEBT

One of the things that makes economics fascinating is the speed with which things can change. In 2005 few people were predicting the calamitous events which would take place over the next three years. Some commentators had warned that the rise in house prices both in the UK and the US would at some point have to suffer a correction but arguments differed about the relative size of that correction and the effects on the economy as a consequence. In a speech in 2004 (http://www.federalreserve .gov/newsevents/speech/bernanke20070517a.htm) Ben Bernanke, an acknowledged scholar of the Great Depression, said: 'One of the most striking features of the economic landscape over the past 20 years or so has been a substantial decline in macroeconomic volatility.' He coined this 'The Great Moderation'. Bernanke put down the reduction in volatility to structural change, improved macroeconomic policies, in particular the focus on achieving stable and low inflation rates, and good luck!

The government in the UK was typical of many in the West who were confident of continued macroeconomic stability. In what was his last Budget speech on 21 March 2007, the Chancellor and soon-to-be Prime Minister, Gordon Brown, said:

> In this, my eleventh Budget, my report to the country is of rising employment and rising investment; continuing low inflation, and low interest and mortgage rates; and this is a Budget ... built on the foundation of the longest period of economic stability and sustained growth in our country's history ... Our forecast and the consensus of independent forecasts agree that looking ahead to 2008 and 2009 inflation will also be on target... And by holding firm to our commitment to maintain discipline in public sector pay, we will not only secure our 2 per cent inflation target but create the conditions for maintaining the low interest and mortgage rates that since 1997 have been half the 11 per cent average of the previous 20 years. And we will never return to the old boom and bust.
>
> So Mr Deputy Speaker, with consumption forecast to rise in each of the next two years by 2¼ to 22¾ per cent, investment and exports by more than 3 per cent, we expect that next year, in 2008, alongside North America, our growth will again be the highest in the G7 – between 2½ and 3 per cent – with the same rate of growth also in 2009 – under this Government, with stability in this as in every other Budget the foundation, sustained growth year on year.

Within a few months of that speech, the global economy experienced a crisis that has led to one of the deepest and longest-lasting periods of economic downturn and weak growth in history. Given the confidence of the UK Chancellor in early 2007, one might ask questions about whether there were signs of the problems to come and why did such a change in fortunes for so many countries around the world happen so quickly?

BUBBLES AND SPECULATION

One of the areas of disagreement amongst economists was the extent to which the pre-crisis financial landscape was subject to a 'bubble'. An **economic bubble** occurs when prices of assets and securities rise way above their true or fundamental value. Once a bubble bursts, asset and security prices collapse.

The collapse in asset and security prices was a feature of the financial crisis but the origins of the bubble (and some would argue the word is meaningless) lie in the way in which economies changed in the 30 years prior to the crisis.

> **economic bubble** when prices of assets and securities rise way above their true or fundamental value

Deregulation

During the 1980s, the move towards supply-side policies led to a period of deregulation. In particular, rules and deregulation surrounding the activities of financial institutions were abolished or relaxed. In the UK and US in particular, successive governments gradually picked away at regulation during the 1980s and 1990s allowing financial institutions to trade globally and with more freedom to innovate than ever before. Deregulation went hand-in-hand with developments in technology and led to further innovation.

Deregulation meant that the average person in the street had access to credit which was much easier than it had ever been. In the US and UK, this was further enhanced by the rise in house prices which gave many people positive equity in their homes which they could use as security to access credit. What these funds could be used for was also relaxed and so more homeowners were in a position to borrow money to buy cars, holidays, finance weddings and other luxuries as well as carry out home improvements and extensions.

In the US, shocks to the system in the form of the dot.com collapse and the terrorist attacks of 9/11 led to dips in economic activity. In each case the Fed responded by cutting interest rates and flooding the markets with cash. In addition, preparations for a predicted IT disaster at the turn of the millennium (the Y2K threat) had meant that many large financial organizations had invested heavily in technology which meant that they possessed advantages that enabled them to improve productivity – possibly ahead of time if that investment into the Y2K threat had not occurred. Even in the face of concerns about the fragility of consumer spending, profitability in banks rose.

As the search for returns intensified, banks looked to widen the market segments that they were prepared to do business with in the search for new markets and opportunities to improve returns. In addition, the prevalence of relatively low rates of interest meant the prospect of high yield returns became even more attractive, especially given the fact that such returns could be linked to bonuses for staff. Deregulation and global trading meant that capital movements across national boundaries were much easier. Funds could be borrowed from countries with low interest rates (particularly Japan which experienced negative interest rates at times in the early 2000s) and invested in assets in countries with higher yielding currencies.

The Rise in House Prices

The thirst for credit on both sides of the Atlantic, particularly in the form of mortgage lending, has been cited as being a cause of the bubble in house prices. Panel (a) in Figure 21.1 shows UK house prices from 1983–2008. It can be clearly seen that the average house price rose dramatically from the late 1990s to 2007. Panel (b) of Figure 21.1 shows the index of house prices in the US. Between 2000 and 2008, house prices in the US had risen by around 80 per cent.

As house prices rise, the difference between the principal borrowed and the value of the house increases – positive equity. An individual may have a mortgage for £250,000 but a property worth £375,000 and thus have positive equity of £125,000. Lenders were not shy in allowing borrowers to exploit positive equity and with the security of a valuable asset (and the expectation that prices would continue to rise) the ease with which homeowners were able to add to their debt increased.

The effects of deregulation, the existence of relatively low interest rates, apparently stable economic conditions and the increase in risk seeking activity amongst financial institutions, all came together to create a rise in house prices fuelled by rising demand and easier access to credit. In the UK, the increase in the number of people being able to access mortgages was the direct result of the willingness of banks and building societies to develop new products to allow those who would previously not have been able to

FIGURE 21.1

The Rise in House Prices

Panel (a) shows the rise in the average house price in the UK between 1983 and 2008. The average house price in 1983 was around £30,000 but by 2007 had peaked at around £190,000. Panel (b) shows the Standard & Poors (S&P)/Case–Schiller US National Home Price Index between 2000 and 2009 indicating the sharp increase in house prices in the first years of the noughties.

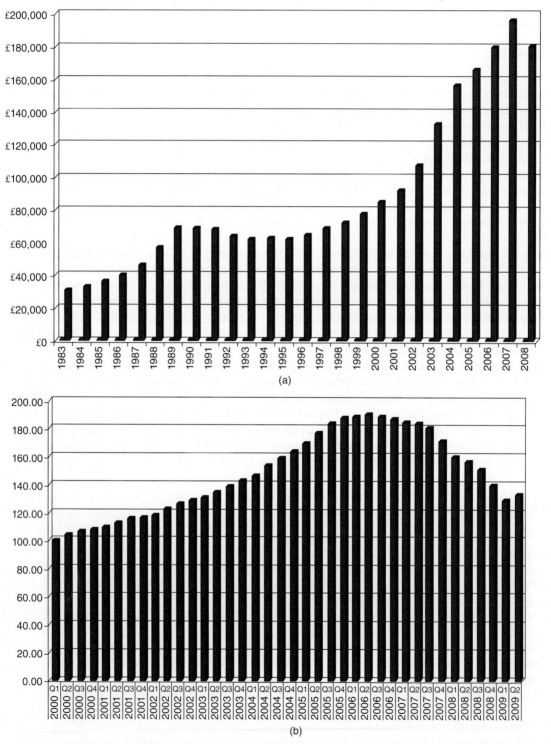

have access to a mortgage, to do so. In the US it was those whose credit histories were very weak who were targeted. As market prices rose the desire to get on the housing ladder further fuelled demand. For those who had managed to access the market in the early 1980s, the amount of positive equity in their properties was such that it allowed some to borrow to fund home extensions, holidays, new cars, home improvements and for a growing number, a second property. This second property might be a retreat near the coast or in the countryside, an apartment in one of the many new developments in Spain or a property bought with the intention of letting it out and using the rent to help pay for the second mortgage.

The Sub-Prime Market

In the United States, extending mortgage opportunities to those not traditionally seen as being part of the market was also part of the way in which banks and other lenders sought to increase their lending. Individuals seen as being an acceptable risk for mortgage lending were known as the prime market; the term is said to have derived from analogy with the best cuts of meat from an animal. It followed that there was a 'sub-prime' group for whom access to mortgages was altogether more difficult. Some of these people had credit histories that were very poor, some did not have jobs, but in an atmosphere of risk seeking and changed priorities this group provided lenders with a market opportunity.

Individuals may have been contacted in the first instance by a broker who outlined the possibilities for the borrower often referred to as 'affordability products'. These products sometimes included so-called 'teaser rates' which offered low interest rates for an initial period, often two years, and in some cases zero interest rates for the first two years. Interest rates after the first two years could rise significantly but the attraction for many prospective house buyers was that the chance to access mortgage funds was being made available to them for the first time. Typical of these types of loan were 2/28 or 3/27 loans. The 2 and 3 indicated the number of years of the teaser rate and the remainder the period over which a variable rate would apply.

Brokers would then look to sell the mortgage to a bank or other mortgage provider and received a commission for doing so. Under 'normal' circumstances the bank would not only have acquired a liability but also an asset (the payments received by the borrower on the mortgage). The mortgage would generate a stream of cash flows in the form of the payment of the mortgage principal and interest over a period of years. Such an asset could be valuable in the new deregulated banking environment and led to the securitization of these assets which we covered in Chapter 10.

The growth of sub-prime mortgages began to take an increasing share of the total mortgage market in the US and the risk involved in terms of the loan to value of property also rose from around 50 per cent to over 80 per cent by 2005–2006. Sub-prime loans accounted for around 35 per cent or all mortgages issued in 2004. It was not only the poor who were taking advantage of the sub-prime market, however. Existing homeowners took advantage of the positive equity in their properties to re-mortgage or buy second homes. Speculation in the housing market was not confined to just those in the financial markets that could benefit from new financial instruments that could be traded for profit. Some saw opportunities to enter the housing market, borrow funds to buy property and almost immediately put it back onto the market – a phenomenon known as 'flipping'. The hope was that rapidly rising house prices would mean that the property could be sold quickly and a profit realized.

The macroeconomic background to this was a sharp cut in interest rates by the Fed in response to the collapse of the dot.com boom and also in response to 9/11. A low interest rate environment seemed to insulate sub-prime mortgage holders from the extent of the debt which they had taken on. From 2003 onwards, interest rates stayed at 1 per cent and for 31 consecutive months the inflation-adjusted interest rate was effectively negative. Meanwhile the rise in house prices further contributed to economic growth as employment in housing related business expanded to meet the growth in activity. The housing market was responsible for creating over 788,000 jobs in the US between 2001 and 2005 – some 40 per cent of the total increase in employment.

With the benefit of hindsight it might seem rather foolish for anyone, let alone a bank, to have contemplated lending money to people with bad credit histories and low incomes. Surely banks knew the risk they were taking? Part of the answer is that they *thought* they did and whilst risk seeking might have been a more dominant behavioural trait than risk aversion, strategies had been put in place to limit the risks of the banks and other lenders to the exposure of lending to the sub-prime market. As we have seen in

CASE STUDY   The South Sea Bubble

In 1720, Isaac Newton is quoted as saying 'I can calculate the motions of the heavenly bodies but not the madness of people'. Newton had made a profit of £7,000 (about £800,000 or €937,500 in today's values) selling shares of the South Sea Company in April of that year. Along with many other people, however, Newton believed that the value of the company would continue to rise and he purchased more shares as the price of the company continued to rise. Newton ended up losing £20,000 (about £2.3 million or €2.7 million).

The South Sea Company was formed in 1711. It entered into an agreement to assume part of the debt of the government, which at the time was financing the War of Spanish Succession, in return for a monopoly on the trade to Spanish colonies in South America. The Treaty of Utrecht was signed in 1713 to end the war. Its terms were not favourable to the South Sea Company as it limited trade opportunities to the Spanish colonies. A further debt conversion was announced in 1719 where the South Sea Company became just one of three corporations, including the Bank of England, which owned around 36 per cent of the total national debt. Despite the fact that the company had no real evidence of trading success, the directors of the company continued to make claims to shareholders of the wealth and riches that trade promised, not least large quantities of gold and silver just waiting to be brought back to Europe.

In January 1720, the South Sea Company's share price was £128. The claims by the Company pushed up the share price and more dabbling in debt conversion with Parliament saw its price rise to £330 by the end of March. Newton sold his shares in April; by May the price had risen further to £550. In June Parliament passed the Bubble Act which was introduced by the South Sea Company and required all joint-stock companies to acquire a royal charter. Part of the reason for the legislation was to help control the explosion of companies entering the market all making claims for their ventures which were sending prices rising causing mini-bubbles. Cynics would argue that the South Sea Company also used the legislation to manage the growing threat of competition it faced. Having received its royal charter, shareholders took this as being a sign that the company's claims were sound and demand for its shares continued to rise. By the end of June the share price had risen to £1,050.

For some reason (and this perhaps is where Newton's lament over the madness of people is most pertinent), some people began to sell their shares and the share price began to fall in July. For those that had come in near the top of the market (like Newton's second purchase) the imperative to sell became more urgent. The price continued to fall quickly and by September stood at around £175. The collapse affected thousands of people and a number of institutions. Subsequent investigations into the collapse revealed bribery and corruption practices and prosecutions of company officials and members of the government.

The South Sea Bubble was an example of how asset prices can rise way above their true market value. It seems that history can repeat itself and in many ways, the issues that existed then (a lack of knowledge by participants in the market) is similar to today. The complexities of how markets operate may be far greater and the technologies far more sophisticated, but the success of markets relies to a large extent on participants having good information on which to base their decisions. No matter how intelligent an individual is, it seems, if they do not have access to all available information then poor decisions can be made as Newton found out to his cost.

The South Sea Scheme *a caricature by William Hogarth, an 18th-century sociocritical English painter and graphic artist.*

earlier chapters, new products which securitized the loans that were being made along with the development of credit default swaps (see Chapter 8) to help insure against the risk of default, changed the nature of banking as we outlined in Chapter 10.

In the case of sub-prime loans the individual taking out the mortgage clearly has some credit risk by definition. Individually such a loan has a credit risk which is likely to be much higher compared to a loan made to a corporation. It would be unlikely that the risk for such a debt could be passed on to someone else. However, bundling up a collection of such debts makes the proposition somewhat different. Putting together a collection of loans and assessing the risk of default was subject to statistical analysis. A proportion of the collection is likely to be subject to default; a mathematician or statistician can provide detailed analysis of the extent of the risk involved (which is why such skills are highly valued in financial markets). Collectively, therefore, these loans can be offered as a far more attractive proposition to a potential group of investors looking to increase their earnings.

The incentives for those involved in banks and other financial institutions were to assume a risk-seeking approach, therefore. The demand by shareholders for better returns, the existence of a bonus culture which could provide some individuals with millions each year, the desire by individuals to get on the property ladder and, some argue, the lack of rigour in regulation and oversight by the central banks combined to provide a situation where the bubble could feed on itself and generate ever greater lending and the search for ever more attractive investments.

SELF TEST Why did financial institutions increase lending to the sub-prime market? Was such lending always doomed to failure?

The Bubble Bursts

The use of credit default swaps (CDS) represent sound business principles when the risk of default is very low which was the case when these were first developed in the late 1990s and when the bonds being insured were corporate bonds with a low risk attached to them. The expansion of CDS presented a different challenge to the financial markets when the collapse came. It must be remembered that not only were these contracts taken out in relation to bonds linked to sub-prime loans but the trade of these contracts might mean that banks and other financial institutions might be buying the contract whilst not possessing the asset (the bond). Contracts could also be bought and sold as part of speculative deals which means the web of financial interdependence grows – all based, remember, on a collection of sub-prime mortgages. Traders might, therefore, deliberately buy CDS on the expectation that the bond associated with it would fail. If it did then the trader stands to gain a return in the form of the bond value which has been insured or the collateral which has been set aside. The market progressed from being one which insured bond holders against risk to one where accurate speculation could generate large returns for dealers. Those buying these derivatives (so called because their value is based on something else) may have little if any idea of the strength of the underlying assets associated with their trade.

The CDS market was also not subject to any form of regulation. It is referred to as an 'over-the-counter' market, a private financial transaction between two parties. There is no official record, therefore, of who has made a trade and whether the seller can actually meet the obligations it is entering into. The precise value of the CDS market by 2007 is difficult to pinpoint for this reason but it has been estimated at between $45 and $60 trillion. To put this into some sort of perspective, $60 trillion is more than global GDP which is estimated at around $55 trillion! The number of CDS trades, the number of derivative trades and precisely who owns all these trades are not easy to identify. A number of major banks had exposure to CDS including Lehman Bros, Icelandic banks, Barclays and RBS, and in addition insurance companies like AIG were also heavily committed.

In 2006–2007 the prevailing concern among central banks was over the development of inflationary pressure. In the UK, for example, inflation as measured by the Consumer Prices Index rose to a high of 5.2 per cent by September 2008 but the Bank of England had started to increase interest rates in June 2006 and a series of quarter-point rises saw Base Rate increase to 5.75 per cent by July 2007. In the US, the Fed raised interest rates for 16 consecutive months to June 2006 and the Federal Funds Rate reached 5.25 per cent by the autumn of 2006. As interest rates rose, borrowers, especially those on sub-prime mortgages, began to feel the pressure and reports of the number of defaults on sub-prime loans began to rise.

Once mortgage defaults began to rise to alarming numbers the number of financial institutions affected and their exposure became clearer. The whole edifice was based on the expectation that the underlying assets would continue to generate the income stream over time – in other words, the mortgage holders would continue to pay their monthly mortgage repayments. How did these mortgage defaults begin to happen? We have already seen how teaser rates tempted many to take on the burden of a mortgage but this was not necessarily accompanied by a full understanding of the financial commitments being undertaken. After the teaser rate period finished the mortgages had to be restructured based on a new rate of interest. The new rate of interest not only reflected the need to claw back some of the interest not paid in the initial teaser rate period but also the fact that these borrowers were higher risk.

As mortgage rates rose, borrowers found it increasingly difficult to meet their monthly payments. In some cases the difference between initial monthly payments and restructured payments based on new interest rates was significant; many homeowners found their payments more than doubling. The sub-prime market contained a large number of people who were least able to cope with significant changes in monthly payments but in addition those that had taken out sub-prime mortgages for second homes and the buy-to-let market also found themselves stretched.

Faced with payments they could not afford, borrowers looked to either sell their property or face the prospect of foreclosure – the point where the mortgage lender seizes the property. As the number of foreclosures increased, house prices fell. As house prices fell, more and more people were caught in negative equity. The option of selling the house to get out of the debt was not an option for many; they would still be left with a large debt which they had no hope of paying off. The situation was particularly bad in certain areas of the US. The house price bubble had been focused on particular areas in Las Vegas, Los Angeles and Miami. These were areas that were hit worse by the rise in foreclosures. As the number of foreclosures rose the supply of housing increased and, true to basic economic principles of supply and demand, the price of houses fell further.

Note that foreclosure means seizing the property – to get to this stage a number of other routes and methods to help recover the debt will have been taken so this really represents the last straw in the process. Once foreclosure has occurred then the bank or mortgage lender acquires the property as an asset against the loan but then has to incur the cost of managing the property – maintaining it, paying property taxes and insurance, for example, as well as the cost of trying to sell it to realize the cash. In times of falling house prices the cash realized on the sale may be far less than the original value of the asset. As a result banks have to write down the value of their assets.

As the sub-prime market collapsed, the exposure to bad debt started to become more obvious and a number of banks reported significant write-downs and losses. Confidence in the banking system, so important to its functioning, began to fall. Banks were not sure of their own exposure to these bad debts (referred to as toxic debt) and so were also unsure about the extent of other banks exposure. Interbank lending began to become much tighter as banks were unwilling to lend to each other and also faced the task of trying to shore up their own balance sheets. Interbank lending effectively ground to a halt. (See Chapter 10 for an outline of how the process unwound.)

The seizing up of credit markets had an effect around the world. Banks in Iceland failed; in eastern Europe the Ukraine applied for a $16.5 billion loan from the IMF whilst Hungary looked for $10 billion, this after receiving a €5 billion loan from the European Central Bank and raising interest rates by 3 per cent to 11.5 per cent. Turkey, Belarus and Serbia also sought financial assistance as credit dried up and banks around the world found they had increasing difficulties in meeting their liabilities. Belarus looked for a $2 billion loan from the IMF and Hungary. In the Ukraine, the currency, the hryvnia, fell by 20 per cent and around 80 per cent was wiped off stock market values. The Ukraine central bank was forced to use reserves to try to buy hryvnia in an effort to support the currency. The Russian stock market fell by around 66 per cent between May and October 2008. Put simply, most of these banks had lent too much money, had been exposed to the debts related to purchases of CDS and could not meet payments which were falling due. Without financial assistance these institutions could have collapsed and financial systems in these and associated countries were grinding to a halt.

The Collapse of Lehman Lehman Bros had been a bank at the forefront of the sub-prime and CDS market. It had built its business on leveraging – borrowing heavily to finance its activities. Over the weekend of 13 and 14 September 2008, last-ditch talks were convened to try and find a way of rescuing Lehman Bros. The debts at Lehman and the extent of their exposure to sub-prime and CDS were too great, however, and Lehman Bros filed for Chapter 11 bankruptcy protection on 15 September. When Lehman collapsed it led to billions of dollars of claims on Lehman CDS – payments which had to be made by those who sold the protection. As a means of settling these claims, Lehman's bonds were sold via auction in early October 2008. The value of the bonds was set by the auction at around 8 cents to the dollar. So a $10 million bond would only be worth $800,000 meaning that protection sellers would have to make up the remaining $9,200,000 to meet the CDS obligation. With claims estimated at anything between $400 and $600 billion this put a massive strain on the financial system and many banks who had sold CDS on Lehman were now exposed and in danger of failing themselves, which put further pressure on the system. Basically, banks found that they had to meet payment obligations and did not have the funds available in reserves to do so. Banks who were struggling to meet their obligations may have looked to the interbank market to raise funds which we have already seen, was almost at a standstill. Banks around the world found themselves in this difficult position as the extent of the web of securitization began to become clearer. As the problems surrounding securitization unwound, banks had to take some of the assets back onto their balance sheet. This then meant that they had to reinstate sufficient reserves to support these liabilities and this further reduced their willingness to lend. Instead the focus shifted to trying to restore balance sheets by taking in deposits but not lending.

The drip feed of news from banks, large and small, regarding the perilous position they were in sparked a drop in confidence in the whole system. If Lehman could fail what about other banks? Banks that had to make payments would either have to deplete their capital and thus become seriously overstretched and thus at greater risk, or take on the liabilities of the special purpose vehicles (see Chapter 10) and take them onto their balance sheet further depleting their positions. As their positions worsened their credit ratings would fall; if this happened and they held CDS seller positions this would further increase the collateral calls on them and put them under further pressure.

The collapse of Lehman was seen as a spectacular event because it showed that central banks were not prepared to step in to help any bank that got into trouble. Bear Stearns and Merrill Lynch had survived by being bought by J.P. Morgan and Bank of America and the US government had stepped in to bail out the mortgage lenders, Fannie Mae and Freddie Mac. The collapse of Lehman Bros was closely followed by it becoming clear that insurance group AIG was in trouble. AIG had been an active seller of CDS and the collapse of Lehman had left it seriously exposed. The US government stepped in to support this company because so much of the rest of the economy and financial institutions were implicated if AIG had been allowed to go to the wall. In the UK, Northern Rock, RBS and HBOS were all subject to support of various kinds including the speeding up of permission for Lloyds TSB to take over HBOS before it collapsed. Some have suggested, however, that Lehman may have been a sacrificial lamb at the altar of moral hazard.

The Path to Global Recession

The problems in financial markets began to translate themselves to the real economy fairly quickly. As the housing market slumped, many people involved in real estate were affected. The number of jobs created in the US that were linked to the house price boom began to be reversed. As confidence fell, economic activity declined across many parts of the world. The effect of the tight credit market helped exacerbate the depth of recession in many countries. Businesses, especially small businesses, rely on cash flow for their survival. Many need flexibility and understanding from their banks when faced with shocks to their cash flow and the tight credit markets meant that many businesses found banks unwilling to lend to them and to extend overdrafts. If the bank was prepared to lend, the interest rate attached to the loan was often prohibitive. Faced with cash flow problems and an inability to get the finance to support them many smaller businesses began to close. Larger businesses were not immune from the problems. The motor vehicle industry, in particular, suffered significant falls in sales. In January 2008, monthly production of vehicles in the US was 817,767; by February 2009 this had fallen to 388,267 – a fall of 52.2 per cent in just over a year. The fall in production affected component suppliers and the negative multiplier effect worked its way through the economy.

As demand fell, businesses closed and unemployment rose. In the US, the unemployment rate rose from 6.2 per cent in August 2008 to 9.7 per cent a year later (US Bureau of Labor Statistics), the unemployment rate in the UK rose by 2.4 per cent over the same period and unemployment across the EU reached 9.7 per cent in 2010–2011. The increase in unemployment impacts on business confidence. High street sales in many countries slowed, spending on goods and services with a relatively high income elasticity of demand also fell and as this happened business saw revenues falling with the resulting pressure on cash flow. Many businesses cut back on stocks and this further affected businesses along the supply chain. The Boston Consulting Group (BCG) produced its *Global Wealth Report* in September 2009 which looked at the asset management industry and estimated that global wealth had fallen by 11.7 per cent in 2008 to around $92 trillion (about €72 trillion or £60.5 trillion).

The Role of Central Banks

As the financial crisis unravelled, focus centred on the response of central banks around the world. The role of monetary policy in helping to alleviate the worst effects of the financial crisis and the resulting recession is seen as important and has since come under scrutiny with regard to the effectiveness of the action of key policy makers. The markets were looking for three key aspects of policy response from central banks: speed of intervention, innovation and coordination. There were aspects of each of these that have occurred since the crisis developed but there are also important differences in the degree to which each of the main central banks responded, partly because of the different levels of flexibility that each enjoyed.

The early signs of crisis emerged in 2007 when rumours of rising levels of default from sub-prime mortgages began to increase. In July, Standard & Poors and Moody's downgraded ratings on bonds backed by sub-prime mortgages. In late July a German bank, IKB, said that it was in financial trouble as a result of its exposure to sub-prime and was swiftly taken over by German government-owned bank, KfW (Kreditanstalt für Wiederaufbau). By early August the ramifications of the downgrading of funds related to sub-prime were starting to unravel and, on 3 August, Bear Stearns had to contact its shareholders following the collapse of two hedge funds that it managed and the subsequent fall in its share price. On 9 August, French bank BNP Paribas announced that it was ceasing trading three of its funds and with that credit markets effectively froze. Interbank lending ground to a halt as banks began to recognize that their exposure to sub-prime could be extensive.

The freezing of credit markets effectively marked the start of intervention by central banks around the world. The ECB was one of the first to react on 9 August with the then President, Jean-Claude Trichet, authorizing an injection of €95 billion into the financial markets to help ease overnight liquidity problems. On the following day a further €61 billion was authorized. Soon after the ECB move the Fed announced that it would inject $38 billion to help ease liquidity; the Bank of England, however, did not follow suit. On 10 August, the Bank was involved in the growing problems at Northern Rock which had expanded rapidly in previous years but now found its expansion based on leverage unsustainable and, as credit markets froze, it was struggling to continue. In the coming weeks the extent of the problems at Northern Rock became public and a run on the bank ensued. Queues formed outside Northern Rock branches as worried account holders looked to withdraw their money. Moves to calm the situation did not seem to have too much effect and on 17 September the government, in consultation with the Bank, agreed to guarantee all existing Northern Rock deposits.

As banks around the world began to falter over the coming months; the question of which bank should be rescued and which left to fail had to be considered by central bank leaders. The Bank of England had issued warnings that it was concerned investors were not pricing risk appropriately. In the US, Ben Bernanke had made a number of statements attempting to calm the fears over the extent to which sub-prime would affect the real economy. In May 2007 he had given a speech at a conference in Chicago and said:

We believe the effect of the troubles in the subprime sector on the broader housing market will likely be limited, and we do not expect significant spillovers from the subprime market to the rest of the economy or to the financial system. (http://www.federalreserve.gov/newsevents/speech/bernanke20070517a .htm accessed 27 October 2009)

He reiterated this view a month later when he said:

At this point, the troubles in the subprime sector seem unlikely to seriously spill over to the broader economy or the financial system. (http://www.federalreserve.gov/newsevents/speech /Bernanke20070605a.htm accessed 27 October 2009)

Whether this was an attempt to exert some psychological influence over decision-makers or a lack of information or understanding of the situation is open to debate. In hindsight, it is easy to isolate quotes and point fingers at central banks. The reluctance of the Bank of England to inject funds into the markets was partly seen as the concern with moral hazard but also the subjugating of financial stability to a lesser role. However, the Bank of England, at that time, had limited tools available to it to deal with the events that were unfolding in comparison to other central banks. It was not until the passing of the Banking Act in 2009 that the Bank of England was given additional powers and responsibilities that enabled it to improve its control of financial stability.

In the event, the Bank of England eventually announced that it would provide financial help to institutions that needed overnight funds but that any such borrowing would incur a penalty rate. By April 2008 it had gained the authority to lend to banks against mortgage debt – something that the ECB could do which the Bank could not. The Bank was given authority to issue short-dated UK government bonds in exchange for mortgage securities. However, at the end of August 2007 it emerged that Barclays had asked the Bank for a loan of £1.6 billion and the news, which would not normally have made front page headlines, was interpreted as being another sign that a major bank was in trouble. Barclays needed the funds because of a malfunction in computer systems related to clearing and had tried borrowing from the wholesale markets. The Bank then removed the penalty rate, since it seemed that far from calming nerves it merely served to increase the sense of panic.

As the crisis began to gather momentum, monetary policy around the world was eased. The Fed cut the repo rate by 0.75 per cent in January 2008; the ECB held its rate at 4.0 per cent. The Bank had cut rates by a quarter-point in February and April 2008 but by May that year the Fed had cut rates seven times in eight months with the Fed Funds Rate standing at 2.0 per cent. As 2008 progressed the financial situation did show clear signs that it was 'spilling over' to the economy and output levels began to contract in economies across the globe. The problems were such that, in October, seven major economies, the UK, US, China, the EU, Canada, United Arab Emirates (UAE) and Sweden, announced a coordinated 0.5 per cent cut in interest rates. By then end of October the Fed cut again to 1 per cent.

In the US, discussions were taking place to set up the Troubled Asset Relief Plan (TARP), a $700 billion plan to support the banking system. In November the Fed announced a further $800 billion support fund. In that same month the Bank reduced rates by 1.5 per cent – the largest single change in rates since it was given independence in 1997. By March 2009 the MPC had cut interest rates in the UK to 0.5 per cent, the lowest since the Bank of England was established in 1694. The Fed cut its rates to a target of between 0 and 0.25 per cent and the ECB had cut rates to 1 per cent.

The scale of the intervention by central banks and the various fiscal stimulus programmes announced by governments made it clear that the crisis was serious. The 'contagion' from the sub-prime fall-out and the collapse of banks around the world accompanied by the alarming declines in output meant that global recession was now the real threat and not the prospects for inflation, which remained stubbornly high in countries like the UK.

There are those who believe that, given the circumstances, central banks acted according to the three key aspects of policy response outlined above. The speed with which central banks intervened and the extent of these interventions did differ, largely because of technical as well as ideological differences, but many see their role as having been decisive in exceptional circumstances. When inflationary pressures eased then central banks did relax monetary policy and acted in a coordinated way in October 2008 to bring down interest rates. Central banks have had to be flexible and innovative in dealing with the issues that were highly unusual. As with the Bank of England, central banks have expanded their roles and assumed new powers and responsibilities and introduced new tools and instruments. Two such examples have been the growth of bilateral swap agreements between central banks of different countries where local currencies can be swapped against the US dollar to enable trade to be financed and liquidity to be eased and the use of quantitative easing.

SELF TEST Use the concept of the reverse multiplier to explain how the financial crisis led to a global economic downturn.

Lessons Learned?

The Organization for Economic Cooperation and Development (OECD) trace the development of the financial crisis through a series of four main stages.

1. A drive on the part of politicians to widen access to home ownership to the poor. Changes to regulations to facilitate this drive led to a growth in lending that was not prudent. This political impetus was evident through successive US Presidents from Clinton onwards and in the UK via New Labour. As a result the expansion of sub-prime lending in the US and cases of banks in the UK lending at 125 per cent of the value of homes, wider access to credit cards and the build-up of debt and limited background checks for credit worthiness were not acted upon by regulators with sufficient vigour.
2. Changes in regulatory structures, particularly in the US, which allowed entry of new businesses into the mortgage market.
3. Basel II regulations which created incentives and the conditions for banks to develop off-balance sheet entities. (Basel II refers to a framework of regulations developed through discussions at the Bank for International Settlements (BIS).)
4. Changes in policy by national regulatory authorities such as the SEC in the US and the FSA in the UK which allowed banks to change leverage ratios from around 15:1 to 40:1. (Leverage ratios, such as debt-to-equity ratios, measure the proportion of debt to equity.)

The OECD has been critical of national regulatory bodies suggesting that there were weaknesses in the way banks were regulated and that regulatory frameworks had not only failed to prevent the financial crisis but had been culpable in contributing to it. It identified a number of key causes which include:

● the bonus culture
● credit ratings agencies
● failures in corporate governance
● poor risk management strategies and understanding.

The International Monetary Fund (IMF) has broadly concurred with the OECD in its analysis of the key issues. It suggests that financial institutions and investors were both too bullish on asset prices and risk. The low interest rate environment and the extent of financial innovation (encouraged by changes in regulation) allowed excessive leverage to be carried out which increased the web of interconnectedness of financial products but at the same time rendered the inherent risks more opaque. It highlighted the lack of coordination between regulatory bodies and the legal constraints which prevented information sharing to be more widespread thus helping authorities to be able to understand what was going on.

This fragmented approach mean that there were differences in the way in which national regulatory bodies dealt with bank failures and insolvency when in many cases these banks had a global presence not reflected by a global coordinated response by the regulators. The actions that were taken have been described as being 'piecemeal' and 'uncoordinated' which not only led to a weakening of the impact of the policy response but also to market distortion. It also pointed to the lack of appropriate tools available to some central banks to provide the necessary liquidity support in times of crisis, as outlined above.

Other criticisms of the regulatory regimes in place throughout the world highlight the fact that the rules that are in place may not be appropriate to deal with the pace of change in financial markets, that regulators spend too much time 'ticking boxes' rather than identifying poor practice and intervening. There have been accusations that the existence of rules means that regulators are able to hide behind them and shift blame. For example, there were a number of subsidiaries of the three Icelandic banks which failed (Kaupthing, Glitnir and Landsbanki) operating in the UK but the FSA argued that these were, technically, outside its jurisdiction. In the US it has been estimated that the total assets of entities which were outside the banking system and the scope of regulation, but which act like banks, is as big as the 'official' banking system itself – a value of around $10 trillion in late 2007.

Part of the reason for these problems stems from internal problems of the regulators themselves. To have a high level of understanding of the financial system to be able to regulate it effectively, employees of the regulators have to be highly experienced and knowledgeable about the system itself. Over-regulation, it has been argued, was partly responsible for creating the incentives for financial innovation to generate improved returns. These new products were complex and highly interconnected to the extent that regulators and government financial departments had insufficient understanding of them. It has been argued that a number of senior executives in the banks themselves did not fully understand the complexity of securitization models, lacked the skills in asset valuation techniques and risk models and were unaware of the extent to which 'tail losses' (the extremes of the normal distribution) could impact on their operations. One reason for this was that such models were based on statistics from the 'good times' and had not been 'tested' by a downturn. If those at the forefront of such operations did not understand what they were dealing with is it possible to expect those working at the FSA, for example, to do so?

Recruitment of the expertise and skills necessary to staff regulatory bodies effectively is a further issue. Why work for the FSA, for example, for a salary of £116,000 when the skills possessed by individuals of the calibre to work in the FSA could be sold to other sectors of the industry for many millions? Without the resources to do the job properly therefore, regulators will always be hampered.

THE SOVEREIGN DEBT CRISIS

One of the consequences of the financial crisis has been the focus on the problems faced by a number of countries in Europe in managing debt. Budget deficits are the difference between the amount of tax revenue and government spending. Deficits are financed by government borrowing and as borrowing increases the overall debt increases. Governments have to manage this debt by ensuring that they have enough funds to be able to pay back government bonds when they reach maturity and also to pay the interest on the bonds which are outstanding. Lending to governments has invariably been seen as being relatively risk-free; in the wake of the financial crisis it became clear that for some governments, this was not the case.

The macroeconomic shock created by the financial crisis led to a global slowdown in economic activity. When countries experience a prolonged period of economic slowdown, tax revenues decline but spending on welfare systems increases. Whilst automatic stabilizers moderate the effects as we have seen, in a severe recessionary period these automatic stabilizers can be diluted. In this environment, governments need to increase borrowing but the confidence of markets in the ability of some governments to be able to pay back their borrowing means that some countries can be brought to the verge of bankruptcy. In other words, they cannot raise enough funds to be able to meet debt and everyday public spending obligations.

The Greek Debt Crisis

The country which has come to epitomize the sovereign debt crisis is Greece. The problems faced in Greece have been replicated to some extent in Ireland, Spain, Italy and Portugal. In 2009, Greece announced that its deficit would reach almost 13 per cent of GDP, double the amount it had forecast a year previously. In early 2010 the country's debt was reported as €300 billion; more than the value of its gross domestic product (GDP). In fact its debt was 115.1 per cent of its GDP (remember that the original Stability and Growth Pact rules laid down that debt should not exceed 60 per cent of GDP). The budget deficit rose to nearly 14 per cent – well beyond the 3 per cent required as the terms of membership of the European

Monetary Union. Other members of the EU, notably Germany, accused Greece of being 'profligate' and living beyond its means on the back of its membership of the euro area.

Greece had to raise around €50 billion in 2010 to meet its debt obligations. On 19 May 2010 it needed to pay €8.5 billion to bondholders. On 25 January 2010 the Greek government went to the markets to borrow money in the form of its first bond issue of the year. In the event, the issue was oversubscribed as investors sought to pick up the bonds. Why? A simple reason, the interest on the bonds had to be high to persuade investors to take the risk. It was reported that the issue was valued at around €5 billion with a coupon of 6.12 per cent. Given that interest rates around the world at that time were at record low levels this was high. The spread between the interest Greece had to pay to borrow compared with the Germans was almost 4.0 per cent. The wider the spread on different financial instruments (the difference in the coupon of similar bonds in this instance), the more the market is factoring in the risk of default on the bonds considered more risky – the Greek bonds in this case.

In February and March of 2010, the Greek government had tried to take a stance on public spending, proposing major cuts in jobs, pensions, wages and services. Greek workers took to the streets in protest. It seemed as though the government would find it difficult to implement the sort of fiscal cuts necessary to build confidence with the markets and on the back of the announcements about the increasing size of its debt and the deficit, by April it seemed likely that it would find it difficult to raise further money to meet its obligations. Ratings agencies steadily cut the country's ratings until by late April, Greek debt was officially classed as 'junk'.

The spread between Greek and German bonds continued to rise into April reaching 19 per cent on two-year bonds and 11.3 per cent on ten-year bonds. The nervousness on the financial markets over Greece's debt problems began to spread to other European countries. It became a real possibility that Greece would default and be forced to leave the euro. This fear led to a sharp drop in the value of the euro – if there is an expectation that the price of something is going to fall then there is a possibility of making some money and that is exactly what happened in February 2010. Data from the Chicago Mercantile Exchange (CME) showed that short positions against the euro from hedge funds and traders rose sharply. Traders took positions on the expectation that the euro would fall in value. Traders taking out contracts that the price of the euro would fall could exercise these contracts and make a profit if and when the euro fell in value. Data from the CME showed that over 40,000 contracts had been taken out against the euro with a total value of around $8 billion.

The crisis began to gather momentum and the markets looked to other EU governments to organize a bail-out. On 10 April 2010, the finance ministers of the euro area announced an agreement on a package of loans to Greece totalling €30 billion. Greece said that it did not intend to use the loans and instead rely on its 'austerity measures'. The extent to which Greece could deliver on these austerity measures was something the financial markets were not convinced about.

A week later the Greek Prime Minister, George Papandreou, finally bowed to what many thought was the inevitable and announced that Greece would take advantage of the emergency loans. Negotiations took place with the EU and the IMF on the structure of these loans, which were predicted to rise to €100 billion.

Whilst it was generally accepted that Greece needed the financial support there were questions raised about the terms under which the loans were to be given. The German government was financing a proportion of the loans with €8.4 billion being spoken of as a possible figure. In order to appease German taxpayers who were not supportive of bailing out the 'profligate Greeks', Chancellor Angela Merkel, under pressure from German taxpayers to take a strong line, insisted on very strict terms and a condition that the Greek government make significant cuts to public spending. The argument that Greece has exploited the free rider problem within a common currency area as we outlined in the previous chapter seemed to be strong. For many Greeks, there was a feeling that their future was being dictated by outsiders, most notably the Germans. The Germans argued that it was unfair that its taxpayers should have to suffer to bail out a country which had clearly not played by the euro rules. On May Day, traditional worker protests had a new focus and the extent and severity of the violence which broke out shocked many. Austerity was clearly not going to be easy to implement and the strength of feeling against the Germans was clear. The Greek government was being squeezed from all sides. The financial markets were nervous that the problems in Greece would spread to other high debt countries (so-called 'contagion effect') and there were fears that the crisis could tip Europe back into recession.

The Development of the Crisis

Greece and Italy had never achieved the 60 per cent debt to GDP ratio required of membership for the euro – both countries had persistently run ratios over 90 per cent since the 1990s. Other PIIG countries, Ireland, Spain and Portugal, had managed to reduce their debt ratios just below the 60 per cent mark by 2007. At this time, the spread of interest rates across euro area sovereign debt was relatively small suggesting that markets did not anticipate the sort of problems that beset some governments post-crisis. Underlying this apparently benign macroeconomic environment, however, was a sharp rise in borrowing from the private sector in Portugal, Spain, Ireland and Greece. In Greece, domestic credit as a proportion of GDP rose from around 32 per cent in 1998 to 84 per cent in 2007; in Ireland the increase was from around 81 per cent to 184 per cent, in Portugal, from 92 per cent to almost 160 per cent and in Spain from almost 81 per cent to 168.5 per cent. One of the reasons given for this domestic credit boom was that banks could borrow euros on international markets. Prior to the euro, these banks would have had to borrow in other currencies and fluctuations in exchange rates would have made the borrowing more risky. Borrowing was made much easier by the low interest rates which existed throughout much of the early years of the noughties.

This borrowing was used to help finance the boom in housing and construction which took place in each of these countries and helped to drive economic growth. When the financial crisis hit, credit dried up, the housing market collapsed and construction was badly hit. The banking systems across Europe were trying to identify the extent of the exposure that they faced, the potential size of the losses they were likely to make and the possibility of having to borrow to overcome short-term financing problems. Any such borrowing would be difficult or expensive because of the credit-crunch. The reliance of countries like Greece, Ireland, Spain and Portugal on the ability to borrow internationally meant that they were hit hard by the credit crunch. As banks in these countries teetered on the brink of collapse, they looked to national governments for support. If governments allowed these banks to fail then the effect on the population as a whole was likely to be significant, not to mention the wider banking sector in Europe. In order to help support their banking systems, governments had to borrow money – few of these governments had the fiscal flexibility to do so without increasing borrowing.

In addition, the extent of the post-crisis recession had started to affect tax revenues and government spending. In countries like Spain and Ireland, tax revenues decreased as a result of the contraction in the construction industry which had been fuelling pre-crisis growth. This in turn increased the size of budget deficits and with GDP shrinking the size of the deficit to GDP ratio grew. As it became clearer that these governments were likely to breach EU fiscal rules, and with the need to support banking systems growing in intensity, the financial markets' confidence fell and interest rate on the sovereign debt of these countries rose. The gap between the interest rates of the PIIG countries and other EU members widened. Europe had always had countries which were economically sound such as Germany, the Netherlands, Sweden and France and a group of weaker countries. Increasingly, Portugal, Spain, Ireland and Greece came to be referred to as 'the periphery'.

The first part of the Greek bailout was negotiation in late April into May of 2010. In November of 2010, Ireland's government also had to seek support and in May 2011, Portugal followed suit. In June 2011, Greece needed a second bailout which was eventually agreed in March 2012. As part of the agreement, private sector creditors had to accept a 'haircut', losing 50 per cent of the value of their investments. The background of an increasing number of countries being dragged into the crisis and the somewhat chaotic response of the EU to the situation, merely increased nervousness on the financial markets and spreads widened further between the periphery and the core EU countries. The accusation that the response to the crisis had been chaotic led to self-fulfilling speculative attacks from financial markets. High risk countries are more likely to default so investors require higher yields to take on the debt of these countries. If countries have to borrow at higher rates of interest, this in itself increases the risk of default.

Why was the response so chaotic? One reason was the clear divide between those countries that had maintained some degree of fiscal restraint and the periphery which had been seen to free ride on their membership of the EU. Another reason was the realization that political pressures on domestic governments were huge. To satisfy domestic political pressure, the stronger countries such as Germany had to show that it was being firm with these profligate countries. The terms of the bailout packages required the implementation of significant cuts in public spending and tax rises. Some element of fiscal consolidation was vital to show financial markets that some discipline would be exerted and that the countries seeking support were serious in their willingness to abide by the fiscal rules of the euro.

At the same time, governments knew that implementing austerity packages would be extremely unpopular and impose considerable hardship on the people. Politically, this represented suicide; few governments could be confident of re-election under such circumstances. Opposition parties might promise to stand up to the 'bullies' in the EU who were imposing these policies and to abandon austerity. Such a manifesto might be alluring to people suffering cuts in wages, loss of jobs, cuts to public services, cuts in pension and increases in taxes, but the reality was that even if these opposition groups did find themselves in power, the reality of the situation was not going to go away. If countries did become bankrupt the potential damage to people could have been even worse than the effects of the austerity packages.

In June 2012, Spain had to seek help and in March 2013, the banking system in Cyprus was on the verge of collapse. With banks closed for almost two weeks whilst the Cypriot government negotiated with the EU and IMF, the debate over the extent to which depositors in Cypriot banks should have to accept losses was a key focus. An initial bailout deal imposed a tax on all depositors in an attempt to raise €5.8 billion as part of a bailout deal. The tax was rejected and subsequent negotiations led to an agreement where those with deposits of over €100,000 would be taxed to raise the €5.8 billion contribution to the overall €10 billion bailout. It might seem that those who have such large deposits ought to be the ones shouldering the biggest burden and the amount of deposits from so-called Russian oligarchs in the Cypriot banking system was a feature of the news reporting at the time. However, it will not be just wealthy Russians who, for whatever reason, deposited money in Cypriot banks who will be likely to suffer a 'haircut' – businesses will also be hit. One news report noted that a school deposited fees into its bank which took its total deposits to over the €100,000 threshold. The 'haircut' would mean that it would struggle to pay its bills including wages. Cypriot banks would also be subject to considerable restructuring and whilst banks re-opened there were significant limitations on the amount of money that could be withdrawn and capital controls on money leaving Cyprus were also imposed. At the time of writing it is not clear what the outcome of the Cyprus crisis will be but whilst it is taking place, analysts have begun to look at Slovenia as being the next possible crisis.

The European Financial Stability Fund (EFSF) and the European Stability Mechanism (ESM) The discussions over the Greek bailout and the expectation that more would be needed led European finance ministers to establish the European Financial Stability Fund (EFSF) in May 2010 to provide support for countries that faced default. The EFSF raised funds by issuing bonds and other financial instruments through capital markets. The money raised is lent to countries seeking assistance on the understanding that reforms are put in place. The sum of €750 billion was initially identified as needing to be raised. The initial bailout of Greece accounted for €110 billion of these funds; Ireland's €85 billion and Portugal around €80 billion. The establishment of the EFSF may have resolved some of the more immediate problems that existed in 2010 but merely led to the markets turning their attention to other states deemed to be in danger of default, notably Spain and Italy.

The situation in Italy was of significance because it accounted for a much larger proportion of total EU GDP than Greece. If Italy were to default the consequences for the euro area and the global economy would be dire. This is because Italy is the third largest economy in Europe but has a public debt reported at €1.9 trillion (about five times that of Greece). Between 2011 and 2014, Italy had obligations to redeem around €656 billion in debt. With interest rates on Italian debt at around 6.75 per cent, the cost of servicing this size of debt in a period of economic slump places huge pressure on the government. If interest rates rose by a further 1 per cent, it has been estimated that it would cost Italy a further €38 billion over three years, €78 billion over five years and €313 billion over the life of the debt it has. It might be forced to borrow even more to help service its debt.

In October 2012, the inauguration of the ESM meant that it assumed the tasks of the European Financial Stability Facility (EFSF) and the European Financial Stabilization Mechanism (EFSM). Although the Treaty was signed by the then 17 euro area countries, the ESM will also be open to non-euro area EU countries for ad hoc participation in financial assistance operations. Based in Luxembourg, the ESM is meant to provide a 'permanent crisis resolution mechanism'. The ESM is classed as an intergovernmental organization with a subscribed capital of €700 billion. The 18 members of the euro area are the shareholders and its lending capacity is around €500 billion. Like the EFSF, the ESM will raise funds on the capital markets and will work with the IMF in dealing with member states who request assistance. The ESM is expected to be part of the solution to member states' problems and will operate in conjunction with the fiscal compact in addressing the fiscal and structural problems facing member states. The ESM will only provide support if the member state seeking help agrees to implement fiscal adjustment and structural reform. Structural reform refers to changes in the labour and capital markets which are designed to help improve the efficiency of the economy. One of the elements of ESM support is a consideration of the situation of the member country and the overall stability of the euro area. If it is considered that the financial stability of the euro area is under threat then the ESM can provide support.

Bailout funds have been used, in part, to help support the banking sectors in each country and help banks recapitalize. Domestic banks, however, typically hold relatively high levels of sovereign debt, if the country is in danger of default then this further weakens the banks' position. Because these countries are part of the single currency and as we have seen, wholesale financial markets are more integrated, the risk of any single country defaulting leading to contagion in other European countries has been a key element of the sovereign debt crisis.

AUSTERITY POLICIES – TOO FAR TOO QUICKLY?

A feature of the sovereign debt crisis has been the adoption by a number of countries of austerity programmes – significant cuts in public spending, tax rises and structural reforms. In principle, it is easy to say that if a country is borrowing too much and has debt problems that it must cut its spending and raise more revenue. The practical implications of this policy are more complex. Not only are the people of the country where austerity programmes are implemented likely to be severely affected, if such policies are adopted during a period of weak economic activity the effects are likely to be that national income will decline and unemployment rise. A deep and lasting recession in Greece, for example, means that the prospects for any growth-led recovery looked bleak; if a country like Greece is experiencing GDP growth rates of −7 per cent then the chances of generating tax revenue to pay off debt and invest in improving the economy are slim. Firms are more likely to fail in such an environment and so corporate borrowing comes under pressure as the risk of default is higher. If corporate bond rates rise then firms will not be able to afford to borrow which further hampers the productive capacity of the economy. The periphery countries find themselves in a very difficult situation.

The UK is also experiencing similar problems. The Coalition Government pledged to cut the deficit and borrowing when it came into office in 2010. Cuts in public spending and tax increases have led to weak economic growth and the economy going back into recession. With the economy performing so badly, the government has found it difficult to see short-term improvements in public finances and re-emphasized the need to stick with its policies for the long-term good of the country. There are many economists who agree that sorting out the UK's debt and deficit problem is important but there are also those that argue that the extent of the austerity measures in a time of weak global economic growth is too much too quickly and have argued that policies focusing on growth are necessary.

Structural and Cyclical Deficits

The focus on public sector deficits raises questions about the difference between cyclical and structural deficits. As we have seen, a cyclical deficit occurs when government spending and income is disrupted by the 'normal' economic cycle. In times of strong economic growth government revenue from taxes will rise and spending on welfare and benefits will fall and so public finances will move into surplus (or the deficit shrinks appreciably). In times of economic slowdown the opposite occurs and the size of the budget deficit will rise (or the surplus shrinks). A structural deficit refers to a situation where the deficit is not dependent on movements in the economic cycle but indicate that a government is 'living beyond its means' – spending what it has not got.

Economists are divided in their views about the nature and importance of structural deficits. What follows is a summary of the arguments on both sides.

Argument 1: Policymakers Need to Eradicate Structural Deficits The existence of a structural deficit implies that the public finances will be even worse when entering a recession, necessitating increasing levels of borrowing which is unsustainable in the long term. Cyclical effects will merely serve to make the deficit worse. This was seen in examples of European government deficits in 2010 – some of the largest deficits in peacetime history and created in part by governments committing to spending too much in the 'good times'.

As a result of the size of these deficits, the risk of default by governments on their debt is greater; increasingly they will find it difficult to service their debt and the cost of so doing will rise. This also creates uncertainty in financial markets and threatens the survival of the euro. As a result fiscal consolidation is essential to reduce long-term interest rates and currency instability and help to promote economic growth. This fiscal consolidation should primarily be in the form of cuts in public spending rather than increases in taxes which may damage employment and investment.

Argument 2: The Idea of a Structural Deficit is a Myth The idea that government deficits are structural is unhelpful. The assumption is that governments have to borrow more because of the gap between income and expenditure but how certain can we be that the only reason governments are borrowing money is simply due to the changes to public finances wrought by the recession? The whole notion of a structural deficit assumes that it is the amount governments borrow when the economy is operating at its trend level. This implies that to measure it we need to know how far the economy is operating below trend – the output gap.

The problem is that there is considerable disagreement on the size of the output gap. It is accepted that the recession will have destroyed some potential output but how much is open to some interpretation. There have been a number of studies attempting to quantify the impact of economic downturns on the output gap and the outcomes vary significantly. In the UK the Institute for Fiscal Studies (IFS) has estimated that the output loss of the economic downturn from 2008 could be as much as 7.5 per cent whereas the Treasury estimates 5 per cent and other estimates put the gap as low as 2 per cent.

The size of the output gap is important because it has a direct effect on the cyclical component of the deficit – the larger the output gap the larger will be the cyclical component and the smaller the structural. This in turn affects any estimates of the size of borrowing when the economy does return to trend – in other words, the size of the structural deficit. Any calculations on the deficit would also be subject to assumptions about the sensitivity of taxes and spending to changes in GDP. How does tax revenue rise in relation to changes in GDP? This will depend in part on assumptions about the number of people who are able to find work as the economy expands but also on the extent to which potential output has been destroyed. How do changes in government spending vary in relation to changes in GDP? How many people will get off benefits and what effect will short-term fiscal stimulus measures have on spending?

As an increasing number of assumptions are made, calculations of the size of the structural deficit could be very different; which one should be used as the basis for policy decisions? In the light of this analysis is it useful to think of the idea of a structural deficit at all?

SELF TEST Explain why inaccurate information might affect forecasts of economic growth and thus the size of government budget deficits.

Fiscal Consolidation

The extent to which budget deficits should be a cause for concern is a persistent macroeconomic debate. Austerity measures imply that governments should consolidate fiscal policy to reduce deficits and 'balance the books'. In the UK, for example, the Chancellor of the Exchequer of the Coalition government has regularly referred to 'balancing the budget'. Whether a government should seek to balance budgets is a source of debate amongst economists. Our study of financial markets showed how budget deficits affect saving, investment and interest rates. But how big a problem are budget deficits?

Argument 1: The Government Should Balance its Budget When a government fails to balance its budget, it has to borrow money by issuing bonds in order to make up the shortfall. The most direct effect of high and rising government debt is to place a burden on future generations of taxpayers. When these debts and accumulated interest come due, future taxpayers will face a difficult choice. They can pay higher taxes, enjoy less government spending, or both, in order to make resources available to pay off the debt and accumulated interest. Or they can delay the day of reckoning and put the government into even deeper debt by borrowing once again to pay off the old debt and interest. In essence, when the government runs a budget deficit and issues government debt, it allows current taxpayers to pass the bill for some of their government spending on to future taxpayers. Inheriting such a large debt may lower the living standard of future generations.

In addition to this direct effect, budget deficits also have various macroeconomic effects. Because budget deficits represent *negative* public saving, they lower national saving (the sum of private and public saving). Reduced national saving causes real interest rates to rise and investment to fall. Reduced investment leads over time to a smaller stock of capital. A lower capital stock reduces labour productivity, real wages, and the economy's production of goods and services. Thus, when the government increases its debt, future generations are born into an economy with lower incomes as well as higher taxes.

There are, nevertheless, situations in which running a budget deficit is justifiable. Throughout history, the most common cause of increased government debt is war. When a military conflict raises government spending temporarily, it is reasonable to finance this extra spending by borrowing. Otherwise, taxes during wartime would have to rise precipitously. Such high tax rates would greatly distort the incentives faced by those who are taxed, leading to large deadweight losses. In addition, such high tax rates would be unfair to current generations of taxpayers, who already have to make the sacrifice of fighting the war.

Similarly, it is reasonable to allow a budget deficit during a temporary downturn in economic activity. When the economy goes into a recession, tax revenue falls automatically, because income tax and payroll taxes are levied on measures of income, and transfer payments such as unemployment benefit increase. People also spend less so that government income from indirect taxes also falls. If the government tried to balance its budget during a recession, it would have to raise taxes or cut spending at a time of high unemployment. Such a policy would tend to depress aggregate demand at precisely the time it needed to be stimulated and, therefore, would tend to increase the magnitude of economic fluctuations. When the economy goes into recovery, however, the opposite is true: tax receipts rise as the level of economic activity rises and transfer payments tend to fall. The government should therefore be able to run a budget surplus and use the money to pay off the debt incurred by the budget deficit it ran during the recession.

Wars aside, therefore, over the course of the business cycle, there is no excuse for not balancing the budget. If the government runs a deficit when the economy is in a recession, it should run a comparable surplus when the economy recovers, so that on average the budget balances. Compared to the alternative of on-going budget deficits, a balanced budget – or, at least, a budget that is balanced over the business cycle – means greater national saving, investment and economic growth. It means that future university graduates will enter a more prosperous economy.

Argument 2: The Government Should Not Balance its Budget The problem of government debt is often exaggerated. Although government debt does represent a tax burden on younger generations, it is often not large compared with the average person's lifetime income. Often, the case for balancing the government budget is made by confusing the economics of a single person or household with that of a whole economy. Most of us would want to leave some kind of bequest to friends or relatives or a favourite charity when we die – or at least not leave behind large debts. But economies, unlike people, do not have finite lives – in some sense, they live forever, so there is never any reason to clear the debt completely.

Critics of budget deficits sometimes assert that the government debt cannot continue to rise forever, but in fact it can. Just as a bank evaluating a loan application would compare a person's debts to his income, we should judge the burden of the government debt relative to the size of the nation's income. Population growth and technological progress cause the total income of the economy to grow over time. As a result, the nation's ability to pay the interest on the government debt grows over time as well. Really, we should not be looking at the total amount of debt but at the ratio of debt to income. As long as this is not increasing, then the level of debt is sustainable. In other words, as long as the level of government debt grows more slowly than the nation's income, there is nothing to prevent government debt from growing forever. Some numbers can put this into perspective. Suppose the output of the economy grows on average about 3 per cent per year. If the inflation rate averages around 2 per cent per year, then nominal income grows at a rate of 5 per cent per year. Government debt, therefore, can rise by 5 per cent per year without increasing the ratio of debt to income.

Moreover, it is misleading to view the effects of budget deficits in isolation. The budget deficit is just one piece of a large picture of how the government chooses to raise and spend money. In making these decisions over fiscal policy, policymakers affect different generations of taxpayers in many ways. The government's budget deficit or surplus should be considered together with these other policies. For example, suppose the government reduces the budget deficit by cutting spending on public investments, such as education. Does this policy make young generations better off? The government debt will be smaller when they enter the labour force, which means a smaller tax burden. Yet if they are less well educated than they could be, their productivity and incomes will be lower. Many estimates of the return to schooling (the increase in a worker's wage that results from an additional year in school) find that it is quite large. Reducing the budget deficit rather than funding more education spending could, all things considered, make future generations worse off. A distinction has to be made between borrowing to finance investment, which helps boost the future productive capacity of the economy and borrowing to finance current government expenditure (on things such as wages for public sector workers).

The qualification that the government budget on current expenditure will be balanced on average over the business cycle allows for the effect of automatic stabilizers, such as the increase in welfare expenditure and reduction in tax revenue that automatically occur in a recession (the opposite in a boom) and so helps flatten out economic fluctuations. Allowing a budget deficit on investment expenditure is sensible because, although it leads to rising public debt, it also leads to further growth opportunities through spending on education, roads and so on. Just asserting that the government should balance its budget, irrespective of the economic cycle and irrespective of what kind of expenditures it is making, is overly simplistic.

SELF TEST Why might we wish to distinguish between government current expenditure and government investment expenditure and take account of the economic cycle when judging whether the government should balance its budget?

Austerity or Growth?

The arguments outlined above crystallize the debate over the importance of austerity policies. Whilst there might be general agreement that countries do need to get more control over debt and their deficits, the current policies being adopted are, some argue, counter-productive.

In the UK, the Chancellor has had to announce further cuts in public spending and observed that austerity would have to last much longer than he originally thought. Opposition politicians have argued that the government went too far too quickly with its austerity measures and that the continued weakness in the economy was testament to the fact that austerity was not working to reduce the deficit and debt. Why the difference?

One reason is the assumptions that underpin the models that are used in calculating the effects of austerity. In the UK, the independent Office for Budget Responsibility (OBR) based its calculations on the assumption of a fiscal multiplier of 0.5. In other words, every £1 of cuts in public spending would reduce economic output in the economy by 50p. The IMF have estimated the size of these fiscal multipliers to be much higher, atsomewhere between 0.9–1.7. At the upper end of the estimates of the fiscal multiplier the effect on the economy is considerable. Estimates have put the effect of the government's cuts at around 8 per cent of GDP over five years if the fiscal multiplier is assumed to be 1.3, about the middle of the IMF's range. The government of the UK would argue that even if the size of the fiscal multiplier was at this level, some of the effects would be offset by the level of quantitative easing by the Bank of England.

The Argument for Austerity Countries must take steps to get public finances under control. If attempts are made to increase borrowing to spend their way out of recession the effect will be increased inflation, higher borrowing costs across the whole of the EU and further uncertainty which threatens the whole of the euro area. There is also a moral dimension to the necessity for austerity – it is not fair to expect the taxpayers of countries which have maintained a sound fiscal stance and abided by the rules of the euro area to pay for the lax behaviour of governments in other countries.

In the short to medium term the effects of austerity are considerable but the long-term benefits of sounder finances, improved structural reforms and a stronger banking sector will mean that all countries in Europe will be more competitive and in a position to benefit from stronger and more sustained economic growth in the future.

The Argument for Growth   The main cause of the problems facing Europe stem from the financial system not from government debt. Austerity at a time of economic slowdown will affect economies considerably and will be further exacerbated by the lack of credit in economies caused by banks seeking to recapitalize and rebuild their balance sheets. Without an adequate supply of credit, consumer spending and business investment will decline and lead to a prolonged and damaging period of economic depression. If output declines, tax revenues will fall and government spending on benefits will rise and far from alleviating the debt crisis will merely mean governments are forced to borrow more. The only way to solve the debt crisis is to get economies growing again. Governments need to adopt Keynesian style stimulus spending; stronger economic growth will lead to increased tax revenues and if unemployment falls, government spending on welfare support drops reducing the need to borrow.

A Resolution?

At the time of writing the outcome of the debate over austerity and growth is far from resolved and indeed it is probably unfair to suggest that the argument is a simple split between those pushing to maintain austerity at all costs and those who want to abandon austerity and go for growth. The EU Commission issued a statement in the Spring of 2013 refuting suggestions that austerity policies lacked flexibility and that the necessity for growth was being ignored.

The Commission argues that the extent of the spreads on sovereign debt did indicate that there were legitimate concerns over the threat of default by some countries but acknowledge that there were also some speculative reasons for the extent of the spreads. It also points to the policy adopted by the ECB of outright monetary transactions (OMT) where the ECB buys the bonds of Europe's indebted countries to help push up the price and lower yields. This will not only help reduce the cost of servicing the debt but also signals to the markets that the euro will be protected. To make such a policy credible, structural reforms and fiscal consolidation is necessary. Structural reforms, such as improving the flexibility of labour and product markets will help to reduce wage and price rigidities, will take time to yield benefits but are essential if Europe is to be competitive in a global economy. The lowering of yields and spreads on sovereign debt in the latter part of 2012 and into 2013 was testament, it argued, that the policy was starting to have some impact.

IN THE NEWS

Sovereign Debt

Three years after the height of the sovereign debt crisis, are the sacrifices made by the countries who asked for a bailout and the EU showing any signs of bearing fruit?

The PIIGS – Three Years On

The first quarter of 2013 saw some optimism returning to financial markets around the world. The stock market in the US rose as did the London Stock Exchange. Bullish sentiment on stock prices was driven in part by more optimistic economic news coming out of the US and by the feeling that the worst of the sovereign debt crisis had been weathered. The banking crisis in Cyprus did set back sentiment but the relatively speedy agreement to organize a bailout seemed to calm nerves once again. What of the rest of the euro area? Is the cause for optimism backed up by what is happening in sovereign debt markets?

In the latter part of March 2013, Italy sold €3.9 billion in five-year debt but the yield rose from 3.59 per cent to 3.65 per cent, the highest since October 2012 and analysts noted that the demand for the debt was 'soft'. Italy also sold €3.0 billion of ten-year debt and the yield here fell from

One of the major fears of the problems which originated in Greece was contagion – the potential for the euro crisis to spread to the weaker economies of the euro area and cause the collapse of the euro.

4.83 per cent to 4.66 per cent. In the same month, Spain sold €5.83 billion of three- and six-month treasury bills amidst stronger demand and a lower yield (0.79 per cent compared to 0.85 per cent).

At the same time, Greek banks announced losses, after a €100 billion write-down in sovereign debt. The National Bank reported losses of €2.14 billion for the year in March 2013, Alpha Bank reported losses of €1.09 billion. Both banks are part of the recapitalization process that is a term of the continued funding arrangements from the EU. Both banks need to ensure that at least 10 per cent of any new capital they secure comes from private investors. Ireland, meanwhile, managed to sell debt on the markets for the first time since 2010 and the Irish Taoiseach, Enda Kenny, noted that the country had made considerable progress in its plans to leave the bailout programme it agreed to in 2010. Part of the Irish government's plans include ensuring that promises made by the EU to help Ireland develop initiatives such as guaranteeing young people the right to receive training are acted upon. The Taoiseach said that '… it's absolutely critical for governments to be able to bring people with them and to explain both the nature of the problem, the scale of that problem, the plan and the strategy to deal with it'.

The ratio of public debt to GDP in Portugal rose between the second and third quarters of 2012 and reached 120.3 per cent, up from 117.4 per cent. Yields on Portuguese

debt are falling, however; ten-year government bonds attracted a yield of 12.5 per cent in mid-April 2012 but a year later yields were hovering nearer the 6 per cent mark. Ratings agencies, however, confirmed that they retained a negative outlook on Portuguese debt with Moody's rating it at Ba3 (the equivalent of BB- or non-investment grade, speculative).

Questions

1 **If optimism leads to increases in average stock prices, does this mean that there is also optimism that the sovereign debt crisis is over the worst? Explain.**

2 **What does the movement in the yield of Italian five- and ten-year debt tell you about the price and the view of the markets of Italian debt?**

3 **Why do you think that the Irish Taoiseach placed an emphasis on it being '… absolutely critical for governments to be able to bring people with them and to explain both the nature of the problem, the scale of that problem, the plan and the strategy to deal with it' in managing an orderly exit from an EU bailout?**

4 **Can any conclusions be drawn on the movement of the size of the debt in Portugal, its yields and the ratings on the state of the Portuguese economy?**

5 **To what extent do you think that the terms of the bailouts of countries like Greece, Ireland and Portugal have been justified?**

SUMMARY

- Deregulation of financial markets encouraged new ways of lending and made it easier for lenders to access funds and the relatively benign economic climate of the early 2000s encouraged banks to become more risk seeking.

- Banks around the world increased lending rapidly and this helped to fuel a rise in property prices. New financial products meant that risk was perceived to be lower but many involved did not have a complete understanding of the complexity of the products or the models on which they were based.

- When central banks began to start raising interest rates to control accelerating inflation, the number of defaults on sub-prime mortgages began to increase and as the web on interconnectivity between financial institutions began to unravel, credit became tight.

- The banking crisis led to a sharp reduction in interbank lending as credit dried up which fed through the housing market causing a collapse in house prices and quickly fed through to the real economy leading to rising unemployment, shrinking economic activity.

- When the crisis hit, central banks responded by reducing interest rates and developing new techniques to complement fiscal stimuli such as quantitative easing.

- Both central banks and regulators have come in for criticism about their role in the crisis and their response after and reforms to banking systems and regulation continue to be discussed.

- The sovereign debt crisis developed as a result of the financial crisis. Countries experiencing economic slowdown were forced to borrow more and the extent of their debt created nervousness of the prospect of default.

- The spreads on sovereign debt widened into 2010 and 2011 and a number of countries had to seek financial assistance from the EU and IMF. The ESM represents a permanent mechanism to help support countries in financial difficulties.

- Part of the conditions for receiving assistance has been the implementation of austerity programmes which have further impacted on economic growth across the EU.

- A debate between the benefits of austerity and the need to promote growth has developed which is on-going.

QUESTIONS FOR REVIEW

1 What is meant by 'deregulation of the financial markets'?

2 How do 'bubbles' in asset prices occur?

3 What were the main causes of the rise in asset prices in the run up to the financial crisis?

4 What were the main causes of the financial crisis?

5 Why did the financial crisis have such an impact on global economic activity?

6 How did central banks respond to the financial crisis?

7 Why did governments such as those in Greece, Spain, Ireland, Portugal and Italy experience such a rise in deficits and debt in the wake of the financial crisis?

8 What is meant by the term 'contagion' in the context of the sovereign debt crisis?

9 What are the main arguments for the continuation of austerity programmes in countries which have experienced sovereign debt problems?

10 What are the main arguments against austerity programmes as a solution to the sovereign debt crisis?

PROBLEMS AND APPLICATIONS

1 Explain how deregulation of the financial system may have affected the following:

   a. a newly married couple aged 24 who have just secured their first jobs and want to buy a house

   b. joint homeowners with a house valued at €350,000 with a mortgage of €200,000 who want to celebrate their 25th wedding anniversary with a world cruise and who are looking to borrow money to do so

   c. the market for newly constructed properties.

2 In the face of a financial crisis such as that created by the dot.com collapse and the 9/11 terrorist attacks in the United States, why would a central bank have

responded by lowering interest rates and flooding the markets with liquidity?

3 Eugene Fama, a key figure in the development of the theory of the efficient markets hypothesis, commented in an interview with the *New Yorker* (13 January 2010):

'If a bubble means an extended period during which asset prices depart quite significantly from economic fundamentals that means that somebody must have made a lot of money betting on that, if you could identify it. It's easy to say prices went down, it must have been a bubble, after the fact. I think most bubbles are twenty-twenty hindsight. Now after the fact you always find people who said before the fact that prices are too high. People are always saying that prices are too high. When they turn out to be right, we anoint them. When they turn out to be wrong, we ignore them. They are typically right and wrong about half the time.'

To what extent do you think that the rise in asset prices leading up to the financial crisis was a 'bubble' or that in the aftermath of the crisis reference to a bubble was just twenty-twenty hindsight?

4 To what extent do you think that the response by central banks to the financial crisis was 'fragmented'?

5 Why have some critics argued that the cause of the sovereign debt crisis lies in the poor design of the euro system and the ability of countries within the euro area to free ride?

6 What is the role of the European Stability Mechanism in managing sovereign debt problems of member countries?

7 Is there any meaningful difference between a cyclical deficit and a structural deficit? Explain your answer.

8 Governments across Europe have instituted austerity measures in an attempt to cut budget deficits which ballooned after the financial crisis. Are they right to do this at a time when the European economic recovery is acknowledged as being fragile?

9 Suppose the government cuts taxes and increases spending, raising the budget deficit to 12 per cent of GDP. If nominal GDP is rising 7 per cent per year, are such budget deficits sustainable forever? Explain. If budget deficits of this size are maintained for 20 years, what is likely to happen to your taxes and your children's taxes in the future? Can you do something today to offset this future effect?

10 The chapter says that budget deficits reduce the income of future generations, but can boost output and income during a recession. Explain how both of these statements can be true.

GLOSSARY

actual spending, saving or investment the realized or *ex post* outcome resulting from actions of households and firms

adaptive expectations a model which states that individuals and organizations base their expectations of inflation in the future on past actual inflation rates

aggregate demand curve a curve that shows the quantity of goods and services that households, firms and the government want to buy at each price level

aggregate risk risk that affects all economic actors at once

aggregate supply curve a curve that shows the quantity of goods and services that firms choose to produce and sell at each price level

amplitude the difference between peak and trough and trend output

appreciation an increase in the value of a currency as measured by the amount of foreign currency it can buy

arbitrage a trade which seeks to exploit price differences in order to make profit

asymmetric shocks a situation where changes in aggregate demand and/or supply differ from one country to another

automatic stabilizers changes in fiscal policy that stimulate aggregate demand when the economy goes into a recession, without policymakers having to take any deliberate action

autonomous spending or autonomous expenditure spending which is not dependent on income/output

balanced budget where the total sum of money received by a government in tax revenue and interest is equal to the amount it spends, including on any debt interest owing

balanced trade a situation in which exports equal imports

Bank of England the central bank of the United Kingdom

barter the exchange of one good or service for another

bond a certificate of indebtedness

brain drain the emigration of many of the most highly educated workers to rich countries

business cycle the fluctuations in economic growth around trend growth

business cycle fluctuations in economic activity such as employment and production

capital the equipment and structures used to produce goods and services

capital flight a large and sudden reduction in the demand for assets located in a country

catch-up effect the property whereby countries that start off poor tend to grow more rapidly than countries that start off rich

central bank an institution designed to regulate the quantity of money in the economy

circular-flow diagram a visual model of the economy that shows how money and production inputs and outputs flow through markets among households and firms

classical dichotomy the theoretical separation of nominal and real variables

coincident indicator an indicator which occurs at the same time as changes in economic activity

collective bargaining the process by which unions and firms agree on the terms of employment

commodity money money that takes the form of a commodity with intrinsic value

common currency area a geographical area throughout which a single currency circulates as the medium of exchange

common currency area a geographical area, possibly covering several countries, in which a common currency is used

comovement the movement of pairs of variables over time

competitive market a market in which there are many buyers and sellers so that each has a negligible impact on the market price

complements two goods for which an increase in the price of one leads to a decrease in the demand for the other

compounding the accumulation of a sum of money in, say, a bank account, where the interest earned remains in the account to earn additional interest in the future

consumer prices index a measure of the overall prices of the goods and services bought by a typical consumer

consumption spending by households on goods and services, with the exception of purchases of new housing

contraction when real output is lower than the previous time period

countercyclical a variable that is below trend when GDP is above trend

credit default swap (CDS) a means by which a bondholder can insure against the risk of default

crowding out a decrease in investment that results from government borrowing

crowding-out effect the offset in aggregate demand that results when expansionary fiscal policy raises the interest rate and thereby reduces investment spending

currency the paper banknotes and coins in the hands of the public

cyclical deficit a situation when government spending and income is disrupted by the deviations in the 'normal' economic cycle

cyclical unemployment the deviation of unemployment from its natural rate

deflationary gap or output gap the difference between full employment output and expenditure when expenditure is less than full employment output

demand curve a graph of the relationship between the price of a good and the quantity demanded

demand deposits balances in bank accounts that depositors can access on demand by using a debit card or writing a cheque

demand schedule a table that shows the relationship between the price of a good and the quantity demanded

depreciation a decrease in the value of a currency as measured by the amount of foreign currency it can buy

depression a severe recession

deterministic trends trends that are constant, positive or negative independent of time for the series being analysed

discount rate the interest rate at which the Federal Reserve lends on a short-term basis to the US banking sector

diversification the reduction of risk achieved by replacing a single risk with a large number of smaller unrelated risks

double coincidence of wants a situation in exchange where two people each have a good or service that the other wants and can thus enter into an exchange

economic activity how much buying and selling goes on in the economy over a period of time

economic bubble when prices of assets and securities rise way above their true or fundamental value

economic growth the increase in the amount of goods and services in an economy over a period of time

economics the study of how society manages its scarce resources

efficient markets hypothesis the theory that asset prices reflect all publicly available information about the value of an asset

endogenous variable a variable whose value is determined within the model

equilibrium or market price the price where the quantity demanded is the same as the quantity supplied

equilibrium quantity the quantity bought and sold at the equilibrium price

equity – the property of distributing economic prosperity fairly among the members of society

European Central Bank (ECB) the overall central bank of the 18 countries comprising the European Monetary Union

European Economic and Monetary Union the European currency union that has adopted the euro as its common currency

European Union a family of democratic European countries committed to working together for peace and prosperity

Eurosystem the system made up of the ECB plus the national central banks of each of the 18 countries comprising the European Monetary Union

exogenous variable a variable whose value is determined outside the model

externality the cost or benefit of one person's decision on the well-being of a bystander (a third party) which the decision maker does not take into account in making the decision

fiat money money without intrinsic value that is used as money because of government decree

finance the field of economics that studies how people make decisions regarding the allocation of resources over time and the handling of risk

financial intermediaries financial institutions through which savers can indirectly provide funds to borrowers

financial markets financial institutions through which savers can directly provide funds to borrowers

financial system the group of institutions in the economy that help to match one person's saving with another person's investment

fiscal federalism a fiscal system for a group of countries involving a common fiscal budget and a system of taxes and fiscal transfers across countries

Fisher effect the one-for-one adjustment of the nominal interest rate to the inflation rate

foreign direct investment capital investment that is owned and operated by a foreign entity

foreign portfolio investment investment that is financed with foreign money but operated by domestic residents

fractional-reserve banking a banking system in which banks hold only a fraction of deposits as reserves

frictional unemployment unemployment that results because it takes time for workers to search for the jobs that best suit their tastes and skills

full employment a point where those people who want to work at the going market wage level are able to find a job

fundamental analysis the study of a company's accounting statements and future prospects to determine its value

future value the amount of money in the future that an amount of money today will yield, given prevailing interest rates

GDP at constant prices gross domestic product calculated using prices that existed at a particular base year which takes into account changes in inflation over time

GDP at current or market prices gross domestic product calculated by multiplying the output of goods and services by the price of those goods and services in the reporting year

GDP deflator a measure of the price level calculated as the ratio of nominal GDP to real GDP times 100

GDP per capita gross domestic product divided by the population of a country to give a measure of national income per head

government purchases spending on goods and services by local, state and national governments

gross domestic product (GDP) the market value of all final goods and services produced within a country in a given period of time

gross domestic product per capita (head) the market value of all goods and services produced within a country in a given period of time divided by the population of a country to give a per capita figure

gross investment the total spending on capital stock per period of time in an economy

hysteresis the lagging effects of past economic events on future ones

idiosyncratic risk risk that affects only a single economic actor

indexed the automatic correction of a money amount for the effects of inflation by law or contract

inferior good a good for which, *ceteris paribus*, an increase in income leads to a decrease in demand (and vice versa)

inflation an increase in the overall level of prices in the economy

inflation rate the percentage change in the price index from the preceding period

inflation tax the revenue the government raises by creating money

inflationary gap the difference between full employment output and actual expenditure when actual expenditure is greater than full employment output

informationally efficient reflecting all available information in a rational way

interventionist supply-side policies policies focused on improving the working of markets through investing in infrastructure, education and research and development

investment spending on capital equipment, inventories and structures, including household purchases of new housing

investment fund an institution that sells shares to the public and uses the proceeds to buy a portfolio of stocks and bonds

job search the process by which workers find appropriate jobs given their tastes and skills

labour the human effort both mental and physical that goes in to production

labour force the total number of workers, including both the employed and the unemployed

labour force participation rate (or economic activity rate) the percentage of the adult population that is in the labour force

Laffer curve the relationship between tax rates and tax revenue

lagging indicator an indicator which occurs after changes in economic activity have occurred

land all the natural resources of the earth

law of demand the claim that, other things equal (*ceteris paribus*) the quantity demanded of a good falls when the price of the good rises

law of supply the claim that, *ceteris paribus*, the quantity supplied of a good rises when the price of a good rises

law of supply and demand the claim that the price of any good adjusts to bring the quantity supplied and the quantity demanded for that good into balance

leading indicator an indicator which can be used to foretell future changes in economic activity

liquidity the ease with which an asset can be converted into the economy's medium of exchange

macroeconomics the study of economy-wide phenomena, including inflation, unemployment and economic growth

marginal changes small incremental adjustments to a plan of action

marginal propensity to consume (*MPC*) the fraction of extra income that a household consumes rather than saves

marginal propensity to save the fraction of extra income that a household saves rather than consumes

market a group of buyers and sellers of a particular good or service

market economy an economy that addresses the three key questions of the economic problem through allocating resources through the decentralized decisions of many firms and households as they interact in markets for goods and services

market failure a situation where scarce resources are not allocated to their most efficient use

market for loanable funds the market in which those who want to save supply funds and those who want to borrow to invest demand funds

market-orientated supply-side policies policies designed to free up markets to improve resource allocation through more effective price signals

market power the ability of a single economic agent (or small group of agents) to have a substantial influence on market prices

medium of exchange an item that buyers give to sellers when they want to purchase goods and services

menu costs the costs of changing prices

microeconomics the study of how households and firms make decisions and how they interact in markets

model of aggregate demand and aggregate supply the model that most economists use to explain short-run fluctuations in economic activity around its long-run trend

monetary neutrality the proposition that changes in the money supply do not affect real variables

monetary policy the set of actions taken by the central bank in order to affect the money supply

money the set of assets in an economy that people regularly use to buy goods and services from other people

money market the market in which the commercial banks lend money to one another on a short-term basis

money multiplier the amount of money the banking system generates with each unit of reserves

money stock the quantity of money circulating in the economy

money supply the quantity of money available in the economy

multiplier effect the additional shifts in aggregate demand that result when expansionary fiscal policy increases income and thereby increases consumer spending

national saving (saving) the total income in the economy that remains after paying for consumption and government purchases

natural rate of output the output level in an economy when all existing factors of production (land, labour, capital and technology resources) are fully utilized and where unemployment is at its natural rate

natural rate of unemployment the normal rate of unemployment around which the unemployment rate fluctuates

natural resources the inputs into the production of goods and services that are provided by nature, such as land, rivers and mineral deposits

natural-rate hypothesis the claim that unemployment eventually returns to its normal, or natural, rate, regardless of the rate of inflation

net capital outflow the purchase of foreign assets by domestic residents minus the purchase of domestic assets by foreigners

net exports spending on domestically produced goods by foreigners (exports) minus spending on foreign goods by domestic residents (imports)

net investment spending on the capital stock taking into account spending on depreciation of the existing capital stock

nominal exchange rate the rate at which a person can trade the currency of one country for the currency of another

nominal GDP the production of goods and services valued at current prices

nominal interest rate the interest rate as usually reported without a correction for the effects of inflation

nominal variables variables measured in monetary units

nonstationary data time series data where the mean value can either rise or fall over time

normal good a good for which, *ceteris paribus*, an increase in income leads to an increase in demand (and vice versa)

normative statements claims that attempt to prescribe how the world should be

Okun's law a 'law' which is based on observations that in order to keep the unemployment rate steady, real GDP needs to grow at or close to its potential

open-market operations the purchase and sale of non-monetary assets from and to the banking sector by the central bank

opportunity cost – whatever must be given up to obtain some item; the value of the benefits foregone (sacrificed)

optimum currency area a group of countries for which it is optimal to adopt a common currency and form a currency union

outright open-market operations the outright sale or purchase of non-monetary assets to or from the banking sector by the central bank without a corresponding agreement to reverse the transaction at a later date

peak where economic activity reaches a high and real output begins to decline

Phillips curve a curve that shows the short-run trade-off between inflation and unemployment

physical capital the stock of equipment and structures that are used to produce goods and services

planned spending, saving or investment the desired or intended actions of households and firms

positive statements claims that attempt to describe the world as it is

present value the amount of money today that would be needed to produce, using prevailing interest rates, a given future amount of money

price level an average of prices of all goods and services in an economy as measured by the CPI or the GDP deflator

private saving the income that households have left after paying for taxes and consumption

privatization the transfer of public ownership of assets to the private sector

procyclical a variable that is above trend when GDP is above trend

producer prices index a measure of the change in prices of a basket of goods and services bought by firms

productivity the quantity of goods and services produced from each hour of a worker or factor of production's time

public saving the tax revenue that the government has left after paying for its spending

purchasing power parity a theory of exchange rates whereby a unit of any given currency should be able to buy the same quantity of goods in all countries

quantity demanded the amount of a good that buyers are willing and able to purchase at different prices

quantity equation the equation $M \times V = P \times Y$, which relates the quantity of money, the velocity of money, and the currency value of the economy's output of goods and services

quantity supplied the amount of a good that sellers are willing and able to sell at different prices

quantity theory of money a theory asserting that the quantity of money available determines the price level and that the growth rate in the quantity of money available determines the inflation rate

random walk the path of a variable whose changes are impossible to predict

rational expectations the theory according to which people optimally use all the information they have, including information about government policies, when forecasting the future

real exchange rate the rate at which a person can trade the goods and services of one country for the goods and services of another

real GDP the measure of the value of output in the economy which takes into account changes in prices over time

real interest rate the interest rate corrected for the effects of inflation

real money balances what money can actually buy given the ratio of the money supply to the price level $\frac{M}{P}$

real variables variables measured in physical units

real wages the money wage adjusted for inflation measured by the ratio of the wage rate to price $\frac{W}{P}$

recession a period of declining real incomes and rising unemployment. The technical definition gives recession occurring after two successive quarters of negative economic growth

refinancing rate the interest rate at which the European Central Bank lends on a short-term basis to the euro area banking sector

repo rate the interest rate at which the Bank of England lends on a short-term basis to the UK banking sector

repurchase agreement the sale of a non-monetary asset together with an agreement to repurchase it at a set price at a specified future date

reserve ratio the fraction of deposits that banks hold as reserves

reserve requirements regulations on the minimum amount of reserves that banks must hold against deposits

reserves deposits that banks have received but have not loaned out

risk the probability of something happening which results in a loss or some degree of hazard or damage

risk averse exhibiting a dislike of uncertainty

sacrifice ratio the number of percentage points of annual output lost in the process of reducing inflation by 1 percentage point

scarcity the limited nature of society's resources

shoeleather cost the resources wasted when inflation encourages people to reduce their money holdings

shortage a situation in which quantity demanded is greater than quantity supplied at the going market price

Single European Market a (still not complete) EU-wide market throughout which labour, capital, goods and services can move freely

stagflation a period of falling output and rising prices

standard of living refers to the amount of goods and services that can be purchased by the population of a country. Usually measured by the inflation-adjusted (real) income per head of the population

stationary data time series data that have a constant mean value over time

stochastic trend where trend variables change by some random amount in each time period

stock (or share or equity) a claim to partial ownership in a firm

store of value an item that people can use to transfer purchasing power from the present to the future

structural deficit a situation where a government's deficit is not dependent on movements in the economic cycle

structural unemployment unemployment that results because the number of jobs available in some labour markets is insufficient to provide a job for everyone who wants one

sub-prime market individuals not traditionally seen as being part of the financial markets because of their high credit risk

substitutes two goods for which an increase in the price of one leads to an increase in the demand for the other

supply curve a graph of the relationship between the price of a good and the quantity supplied

supply schedule a table that shows the relationship between the price of a good and the quantity supplied

supply shock an event that directly alters firms' costs and prices, shifting the economy's aggregate supply curve and thus the Phillips curve

surplus a situation in which the quantity supplied is greater than the quantity demanded at the going market price

technological knowledge society's understanding of the best ways to produce goods and services

the economy all the production and exchange activities that take place every day

theory of liquidity preference Keynes' theory that the interest rate adjusts to bring money supply and money demand into balance

time series data observations on a variable over a time-period and which are ordered over time

toxic debt mortgage-backed securities and other debt (such as bonds) that are not able to be repaid in many cases because the value of the assets against which they are secured have fallen significantly

trade balance the value of a nation's exports minus the value of its imports; also called net exports

trade deficit an excess of imports over exports

trade policy a government policy that directly influences the quantity of goods and services that a country imports or exports

trade surplus an excess of exports over imports

transaction cost the opportunity cost of carrying out a transaction in any market

transfer payment a payment for which no good or service is exchanged

trend the underlying long term movement in a data series

trough where economic activity reaches a low and the decline ends

unemployment insurance a government programme that partially protects workers' incomes when they become unemployed

unemployment rate the percentage of the labour force that is unemployed

union density a measure of the proportion of the workforce that is unionized

unit of account the yardstick people use to post prices and record debts

velocity of money the rate at which money changes hands

wealth the total of all stores of value, including both money and non-monetary assets

INDEX

CREDITS

All Figures, Tables and artwork *not* listed on this credit page are the authors' own work and so do not require any credit lines, permissions acknowledgements or referencing citations.

IMAGES

The following Images have been reproduced with the kind permission of the copyright holders:

Image 1.1 A typical supermarket shelf … p. 4.
Source: © Kumar Sriskandan/Alamy

Image 1.2 Adam Smith, p. 7. *Source*: © Classic Image/Alamy

Image 1.3 Providing a monetary incentive … p. 13.
Source: © Shutterstock

Image 2.1 Models are used in many different disciplines … p. 21. *Source*: © Shutterstock

Image 3.1 The fracking process is controversial … p. 55.
Source: © Shutterstock

Image 3.2 Changes in the price of cotton … p. 69.
Source: © Andrew Ashwin

Image 4.1 The complexity of capturing data … p. 80.
Source: © Shutterstock

Image 4.2 Observe the similarities between this 1930s Depression … p. 89. *Sources*: © Everett Collection Historical/Alamy (left) and © Geoffrey Robinson/Alamy (right)

Image 5.1 The number one film of all time … p. 102.
Source: © Robert Harding Picture Library Ltd/Alamy

Image 5.2 Technology changes over time … p. 106.
Source: © Shutterstock

Image 6.1 Copper prices fluctuate over short periods of time … p. 118. *Source*: © Shutterstock

Image 6.2 Professor Justin Yifu Lin … p. 130.
Source: © Justin Yifu Lin

Image 6.3 Thomas Robert Malthus, p.127. *Source*: © The Print Collection/Alamy

Image 7.1 The rise in youth unemployment across Europe … p. 138. *Source*: © Shutterstock

Image 7.2 In reality the labour market is not perfect … p. 151. *Source*: © Shutterstock

Image 8.1 Austerity policies have affected a lot of people in Ireland … p. 161. *Source*: © Shutterstock

Image 8.2 An offshore oil rig in the Campos Basin … p. 172. *Source*: © Shutterstock

Image 9.1 David Li was referred to by some … p. 184.
Source: © Ken Tam/Alamy

Image 9.2 Eugene Fama was acknowledged for his work … p. 191. *Source*: © Eugene Fama, 2012

Image 10.1 Ludwig von Mises … p. 200. *Source*:
© Ludwig von Mises

Image 10.2 The People's Bank of China … p. 216.
Source: © TAO Images Limited/Alamy

Image 11.1 Some question whether quantitative easing … p. 237. *Source*: © Copyright 2007-2013 Truth Alliance inc.

Image 12.1 Wherever you go in the world the Big Mac … p. 253. *Source*: © incamerastock/Alamy

Image 12.2 The Bank of England … p. 255. *Source*: © Biz/ed

Image 13.1 Money from criminal gangs … p. 270.
Source: © Shutterstock

Image 14.1 Finn E. Kydland (left) and Edward C. Prescott (right) … p. 286. *Source*: © WOLFGANG RATTAY/Reuters/Corbis

Image 14.2 Productivity is a measure of output … p. 288.
Source: © Shutterstock

Image 15.1 To produce goods, a firm needs equipment … p. 296. *Source*: © MOHAMED ABD EL GHANY/Reuters/Corbis

Image 15.2 Robert Skidelsky … p. 313. *Source*: © Robert Skidelsky

Image 16.1 The collapse of the banking system in Iceland … p. 332. *Sources*: © Shutterstock (left) and © Ecojoe/Alamy (right)

Image 16.2 New housing development in China … p. 335.
Source: © Shutterstock

Image 17.1 Former Bank of England deputy governor, Paul Tucker … p. 346. *Source*: © epa european pressphoto agency b.v./Alamy

Image 17.2 Large-scale investment in infrastructure projects … p. 354. *Source*: © epa european pressphoto agency b.v./Alamy

Image 18.1 Rising fuel prices … p. 362. *Source*:
© Shutterstock

Image 18.2 Mervyn King … p. 378. *Source*: © epa european pressphoto agency b.v./Alamy

Image 19.1 Arthur Laffer … p. 389. *Source*: © Bob Daemmrich/Cross/Alamy

Image 19.2 Reform of planning laws … p. 393.
Source: © Shutterstock

Image 20.1 Critics of the SGP … p. 411.
Source: © Cengage Learning EMEA

Image 20.2 There are stark contrasts in economic welfare across Europe … p. 415. *Source*: © Shutterstock

Image 21.1 *The South Sea Scheme* … p. 422.
Source: © Falkensteinfoto/Alamy

Image 21.2 One of the major fears of the problems which originated in Greece … p. 438. *Source*: © Shutterstock

FIGURES

The following Figures have been reproduced with the kind permission of the copyright holders:

Figure 5.1 *Two Measures of Inflation*, p. 100.
Source: ONS and HM Treasury, Crown Copyright and public domain.

Figure 5.2 *GDP Deflator (EU 27)*, p. 100. *Source*: Eurostat. Reproduction of Eurostat data/documents for both commercial and non-commercial dissemination are automatically authorised provided appropriate acknowledgement is given to Eurostat as the source.

Figure 5.3 *Real and Nominal Interest Rates*, p. 104. *Source*: Bank of England and UK Office for National Statistics.

Figure 6.1 *EU 27 GDP at Market Prices, Purchasing Power Standard Per Capita, 2003–2011 (€)*, p. 110. *Source*: Eurostat. Reproduction of Eurostat data/documents for both commercial and non-commercial dissemination are automatically authorised provided appropriate acknowledgement is given to Eurostat as the source.

Figure 6.2 *Growth and Investment*, p. 120. *Source*: Fair use as author calculations and some World Bank data.

Figure 6.4 *Corruption Perceptions Index 2012*, p. 125. *Source*: CPI Transparency

Figure 7.1 *UK Unemployment Rate Since 1971*, p. 137. *Source*: UK Office for National Statistics and HM Treasury. Crown Copyright and public domain.

Figure 10.1 *Three Measures of the Money Stock for the Euro Area*, p. 199. *Source*: ECB

Figure 11.3 *The Velocity of Circulation, 1959–2013*, p. 227. *Source*: Economagic.org

Figure 11.4 *The UK Nominal Interest Rate and the Inflation Rate*, p. 230. *Source*: Bank of England and UK Office for National Statistics. © Bank of England and public domain.

Figure 14.1 *GDP in the UK and Europe, 1960–2011*, p. 275. *Source*: World Bank

Figure 14.2 *UK GDP Growth Rate, 1960–2011 (%)*, p. 276. *Source*: World Bank

Figure 14.3 *OECD Area Composite Leading Indicators (CLI) Index, 2003–2013*, p. 280. *Source*: OECD

Figure 20.3 *Growth Rates in Germany, France and the Whole Euro area*, p. 406. *Source*: Eurostat. Reproduction of Eurostat data/documents for both commercial and non-commercial dissemination are automatically authorised provided appropriate acknowledgement is given to Eurostat as the source.

Figure 20.4 *Growth Rates in Ireland, Greece and the Whole Euro area*, p. 407. *Source*: Eurostat. Reproduction of Eurostat data/documents for both commercial and non-commercial dissemination are automatically authorised provided appropriate acknowledgement is given to Eurostat as the source.

Figure 21.1 *The Rise in House Prices*, p. 420. *Source*: Halifax House Price Index and Standard & Poors © Lloyds Banking Group and © 2013 Standard & Poor's Financial Services LLC, a part of McGraw Hill Financial. All rights reserved.

TABLES

The following Tables have been reproduced with the kind permission of the copyright holders:

Table 1.1, p. 10. *Source*: Fair use, data compiled from a variety of sources including http://stats.oecd.org/index and http://data.worldbank.org/indicator

Table 1.2, p. 12. *Source*: This is a blog which has been confirmed to be in the public domain: *http://signsofchaos.blogspot.com/2005/11/price-elasticity-of-supply-and-web.html*

Table 2.1, p. 26. *Source*: Adapted from Richard M. Alston, J.R. Kearl and Michael B. Vaughn, 'Is There Consensus among Economists in the 1990s?' *American Economic Review* (May 1992): 203–209. Used by permission.

Table 5.2, p. 96. *Source*: Office of National Statistics, public domain.

Table 5.3, p. 98. *Source*: Eurostat. Reproduction of Eurostat data/documents for both commercial and non-commercial dissemination are automatically authorised provided appropriate acknowledgement is given to Eurostat as the source.

Table 5.4, p. 102. *Source*: The Movie Times (www.the-movie-times.com)

Table 6.1, p. 111. *Source*: World Bank

Table 7.1, p. 136. *Source*: Office of National Statistics, public domain.

Table 19.1, p. 386. *Source*: OECD

CASE STUDIES

No Case Studies text required permission.

IN THE NEWS

The following In The News items have been reproduced with the kind permission of the copyright holders:

Ch 1 In The News *Latest Thinking in Economics: Incentives*, p. 12. *Source*: Adapted from Gneezy, U. Meier, S & Ray-Biel, p. (2011). 'When and why incentives (don't) work to modify behaviour'. In Journal of Economic Perspectives. 25:4, pp. 191–210.

Ch 20 In The News *Does The Eurozone Need a Budget?* p. 414. *Source*: www.euractiv.com 22nd March 2013, *Daniel Gros* © EurActiv.com PLC, 2013.

FYIS

No FYI text required permission.